W9-AXX-898

ELEMENTS OF WRITING

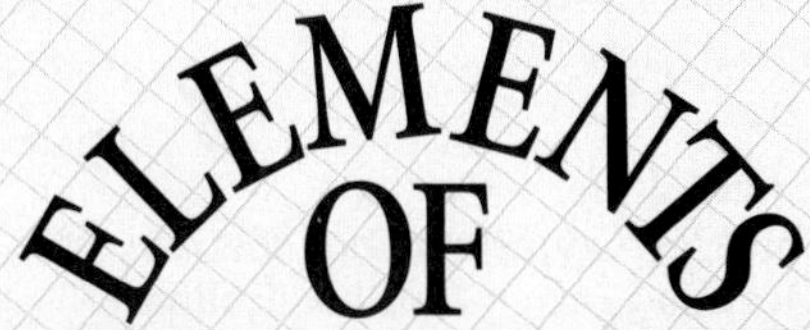

James L. Kinneavy
John E. Warriner

Complete Course

Holt, Rinehart and Winston
Harcourt Brace Jovanovich

Austin • Orlando • San Diego • Chicago • Dallas • Toronto

Critical Readers

Grateful acknowledgment is made to the following critical readers who reviewed pre-publication materials for this book:

Anthony Buckley
East Texas State University
Commerce, Texas

Elaine A. Espindle
Peabody Veterans Memorial High School
Peabody, Massachusetts

Barbara Freiberg
Louisiana State University
Laboratory School
Baton Rouge, Louisiana

Martha Morrow
Clements High School
Athens, Alabama

Vincenza Pentick
Kingston City School District
Kingston, New York

Carol Piper
Eldorado High School
Albuquerque, New Mexico

Linda E. Sanders
Jenks High School
Tulsa, Oklahoma

Janet Sanner
Berkeley County School District
Moncks Corner, South Carolina

Robert Sinclair
Brooklyn Technical High School
Brooklyn, New York

Virginia Tincher
Chardon High School
Chardon, Ohio

Brena Walker
Anderson College
Anderson, South Carolina

Acknowledgments: See pages 1146–1154, which are an extension of the copyright page.

Printed in the United States of America

ISBN 0–03–047149–4

4 5 6 7 8 9 045 97 96 95 94

Authors

James L. Kinneavy, the Jane and Roland Blumberg Centennial Professor of English at The University of Texas at Austin, directed the development and writing of the composition strand in the program. He is the author of *A Theory of Discourse* and coauthor of *Writing in the Liberal Arts Tradition*. Professor Kinneavy is a leader in the field of rhetoric and composition and a respected educator whose teaching experience spans all levels—elementary, secondary, and college. He has continually been concerned with teaching writing to high school students.

John E. Warriner developed the organizational structure for the Handbook of Grammar, Usage, and Mechanics in the book. He coauthored the *English Workshop* series, was general editor of the *Composition: Models and Exercises* series, and editor of *Short Stories: Characters in Conflict*. He taught English for thirty-two years in junior and senior high school and college.

Writers and Editors

John Algeo is Professor of English at the University of Georgia. He is coauthor with Thomas Pyles of *The Origins and Development of the English Language*.

Ellen Ashdown has a Ph.D. in English from the University of Florida. She has taught composition and literature at the college level. She is a professional writer of educational materials and has published articles and reviews on education and art.

Norbert Elliot has a Ph.D. in English from the University of Tennessee. A director of the writing program at New Jersey Institute of Technology, he is a specialist in test development and writing assessment.

Phyllis Goldenberg has an A.B. in English from the University of Chicago. She has been a writer and editor of educational materials in literature, grammar, composition, and critical thinking for over thirty years.

Alice M. Sohn has a Ph.D. in English Education from Florida State University. She has taught English in middle school, secondary school, and college. She has been a writer and editor of educational materials in language arts for twelve years.

Glenda A. Zumwalt has an Ed.D. in Teaching Composition and Rhetoric from East Texas State University. She teaches composition at Southeastern Oklahoma State University. She is a writer of educational materials in composition and literature.

Acknowledgments

We wish to thank the following teachers who participated in field testing of pre-publication materials for this series:

Susan Almand-Myers
Meadow Park Intermediate School
Beaverton, Oregon

Theresa L. Bagwell
Naylor Middle School
Tucson, Arizona

Ruth Bird
Freeport High School
Sarver, Pennsylvania

Joan M. Brooks
Central Junior High School
Guymon, Oklahoma

Candice C. Bush
J. D. Smith Junior High School
N. Las Vegas, Nevada

Mary Jane Childs
Moore West Junior High School
Oklahoma City, Oklahoma

Brian Christensen
Valley High School
West Des Moines, Iowa

Lenise Christopher
Western High School
Las Vegas, Nevada

Mary Ann Crawford
Ruskin Senior High School
Kansas City, Missouri

Linda Dancy
Greenwood Lakes Middle School
Lake Mary, Florida

Elaine A. Espindle
Peabody Veterans Memorial High School
Peabody, Massachusetts

Joan Justice
North Middle School
O'Fallon, Missouri

Beverly Kahwaty
Pueblo High School
Tucson, Arizona

Lamont Leon
Van Buren Junior High School
Tampa, Florida

Susan Lusch
Fort Zumwalt South High School
St. Peters, Missouri

Michele K. Lyall
Rhodes Junior High School
Mesa, Arizona

Belinda Manard
McKinley Senior High School
Canton, Ohio

Nathan Masterson
Peabody Veterans Memorial High School
Peabody, Massachusetts

Marianne Mayer
Swope Middle School
Reno, Nevada

Penne Parker
Greenwood Lakes Middle School
Lake Mary, Florida

Amy Ribble
Gretna Junior-Senior High School
Gretna, Nebraska

Kathleen R. St. Clair
Western High School
Las Vegas, Nevada

Carla Sankovich
Billinghurst Middle School
Reno, Nevada

Sheila Shaffer
Cholla Middle School
Phoenix, Arizona

Joann Smith
Lehman Junior High School
Canton, Ohio

Margie Stevens
Raytown Middle School
Raytown, Missouri

Mary Webster
Central Junior High School
Guymon, Oklahoma

Susan M. Yentz
Oviedo High School
Oviedo, Florida

Contents in Brief

Table of Contents

PART ONE WRITING

The Movers and the Shapers

CHAPTER 2 UNDERSTANDING PARAGRAPH STRUCTURE 56

London

Paris

CHAPTER 8 WRITING TO PERSUADE 290

CHAPTER 9 WRITING TO EXPLORE 344

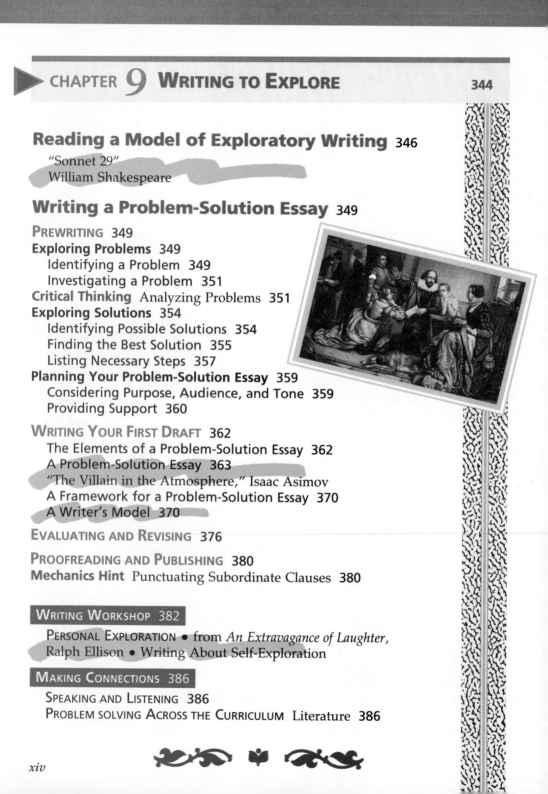

SHORT STORIES

CHAPTER 12 ENGLISH: HISTORY AND DEVELOPMENT 494

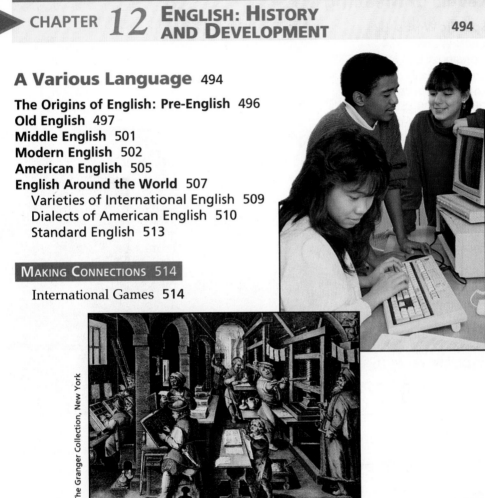

The Granger Collection, New York

CHAPTER 13 STYLE IN WRITING 515

BULLS
23

PART TWO HANDBOOK

CHAPTER 18 THE PARTS OF A SENTENCE 629

Subject, Predicate, Complement

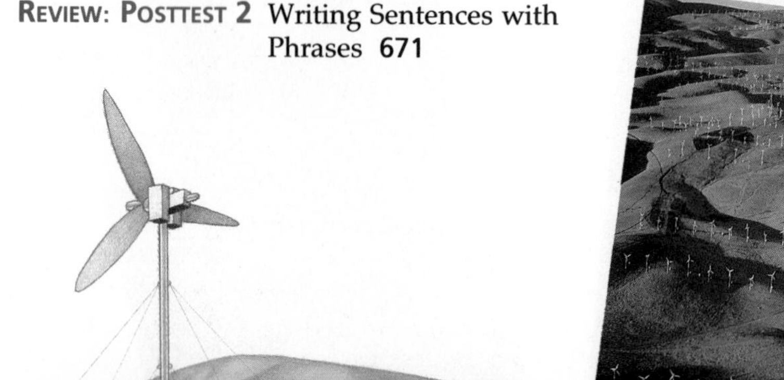

CHAPTER 22 CORRECT PRONOUN USAGE 726

Case Forms of Pronouns; Special Problems

MEXICO

CHAPTER 24 CORRECT FORM AND USE OF VERBS 764

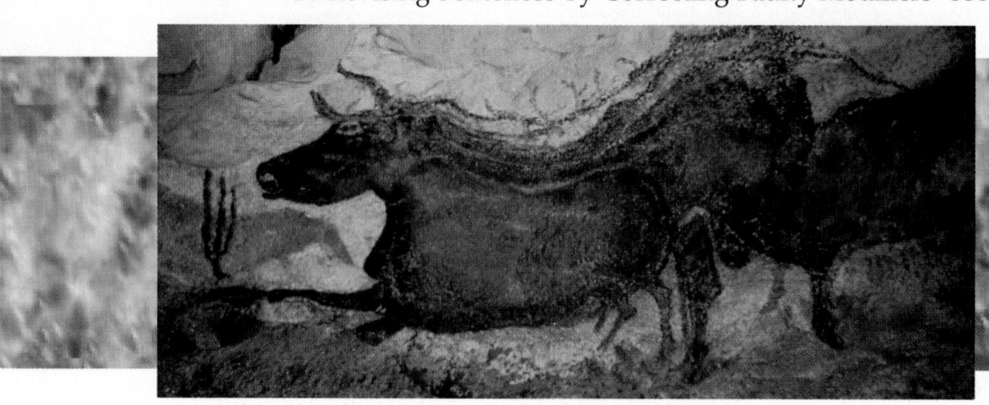

Other Marks of Punctuation

Georgia O'Keeffe, 3¼ × 4¼ saf. neg., January 15, 1953. Laura Gilpin, Photographer. Laura Gilpin Collection, Amon Carter Museum, Ft. Worth, TX.

PART THREE **RESOURCES**

CHAPTER 32 FORMAL SPEAKING AND DEBATE 992

CHAPTER 33 COMMUNICATION SKILLS 1008

Types and Techniques

CHAPTER 34 THE LIBRARY/MEDIA CENTER 1019

Finding and Using Information

CHAPTER 38 LETTERS AND FORMS 1056

Models

Fiction

Elizabeth Bowen, "The Demon Lover," *The Collected Stories of Elizabeth Bowen*
Truman Capote, "A Christmas Memory," *Breakfast at Tiffany's*
Lewis Carroll, *Through the Looking-Glass*
Eugenia Collier, "Marigolds," *Negro Digest*
Manuela Williams Crosno, "The Precious Stones of Axolotyl," *Sudden Twists*
Charles Dickens, *Great Expectations, A Tale of Two Cities*
Richard Erdoes and Alfonso Ortiz, "Why the Owl Has Big Eyes," *American Indian Myths and Legends*
William Faulkner, "Spotted Horses," *Uncollected Stories of William Faulkner*
F. Scott Fitzgerald, *The Great Gatsby*
Ernesto Galarza, *Barrio Boy*
Nadine Gordimer, "The Soft Voice of the Serpent," *Selected Stories*
Egyirba High, "The Lion Sleeps Tonight," *Tight Spaces*
Langston Hughes, "Thank You, M'am," *The Langston Hughes Reader*
Gus Lee, *China Boy*
Beryl Markham, *West with the Night*
N. Scott Momaday, "It Will Not Be Seen Again," *The Names*
Flannery O'Connor, "Revelation," *Everything That Rises Must Converge*
Paul Theroux, "Dengue Fever," *The Consul's File*
Maurice Walsh, "The Quiet Man"
Jessamyn West, "Then He Goes Free," *Cress Delahanty*
Hisaye Yamamoto, "Reading and Writing," *Seventeen Syllables*

Nonfiction

Maya Angelou, *Singin' and Swingin' and Gettin' Merry Like Christmas;* "Why Blacks Are Returning to Their Southern Roots," *Ebony*
Woody Allen, "The Colorization of Films Insults Artists and Society," *The New York Times*
Isaac Asimov, "The Villain in the Atmosphere," *Past, Present, and Future*
Margaret Atwood, "An End to Audience?," *Second Words*
Ted Baer, *How To Teach Your Old Dog New Tricks*
Melinda Beck, "The Lost Worlds of Ancient America," *Newsweek*
Jane Brody, "Heat Disorders: When the Body Gets Too Hot," *Jane Brody's The New York Times Guide to Personal Health*
Art Buchwald, "The Killers," *I Think I Don't Remember*
Rachel Carson, *The Sea Around Us, Silent Spring*
Judith Ortiz Cofer, *Silent Dancing*
"Dog Tales," *Country*
Ralph Ellison, "An Extravagance of Laughter," *Going to the Territory*
Linda Flower, *Problem-Solving Strategies for Writing*
Hugh Gallagher, "The Wonder Years," *Literary Cavalcade*
Frederic Golden, "Clever Kanzi," *Discover*
Susan Shown Harjo, "I Won't Be Celebrating Columbus Day," *Newsweek*
August Heckscher, "Doing Chores," *Short Essays*
Jamake Highwater, *Native Land: Sagas of the Indian Americas*
Jeanne Wakatsuki Houston and James D. Houston, *Farewell to Manzanar*
Zora Neale Hurston, "How It Feels to Be Colored Me"
"I wish I could give my son a wild raccoon.", ed. Eliot Wigginton
Bruce E. Johansen, *Forgotten Founders*
LeRoi Jones, *Blues People: Negro Music in White America*
Alvin M. Josephy, *The Indian Heritage of America*
Richard A. Kerr, "Dinosaurs and Friends Snuffed Out?," *Science*
Martin Luther King, Jr., "I Have a Dream," "Letter from Birmingham Jail," *Why We Can't Wait*
Stephen King, "Now You Take 'Bambi' and 'Snow White'—*That's* Scary!," *TV Guide*
Harold Krents, "Darkness at Noon," *Short Essays: Models for Composition*
William Langewiesche, "The World in Its Extreme," *The Atlantic*
"Large Pizza, Hold the Microchips," *Discover*
William Least Heat-Moon, *Blue Highways*
Connie Leslie, et al., "Classrooms of Babel," *Newsweek*
Abraham Lincoln, "The Gettysburg Address"
Barry Lopez, *Arctic Dreams*
Meg Lukens, "Skiing a Formidable Course," *Sports Illustrated*

Jay Mathews, *Escalante: The Best Teacher in America*
Steve Nadis, "Road Show," *Omni*
V. S. Naipaul, *India: A Wounded Civilization*
Madeleine Nash, "A Bumper Crop of Biotech," *Time*
Katherine Payne, "Elephant Talk," *National Geographic*
Alexander Petrunkevitch, "The Spider and the Wasp," *Scientific American*
David Roberts, "The Decipherment of Ancient Maya," *The Atlantic*
Paul Robeson, *The Whole World in His Hands*
Skip Rozin, "People of the Ruined Hills"
Carl Sagan, "Nuclear War and Climatic Catastrophe: A Nuclear Winter," *Reading Critically, Writing Well* by Rise B. Axelrod and Charles R. Cooper
Steve H. Scheuer, review of "Back to the Future," *The Complete Guide to Videocassette Movies*
"Scourge of the South May Be Heading North," *National Geographic*
Vilhjalmur Stefanson, "Clothes Make the Eskimo," *Natural History*
Joanna L. Stratton, "Days of Valor," *Pioneer Women: Voices from the Kansas Frontier*
Amy Taubin, "He Did It," *The Village Voice*
Paul Theroux, *Riding the Iron Rooster: By Train Through China*
Dylan Thomas, *A Child's Christmas in Wales*
Susan Trausch, "Out, out, telltale spot!" *The Boston Globe*
Abigail van Buren, "Dear Abby"
Joyce L. Vedral, "Life Is Not a Television Show," *My Teacher Is Driving Me Crazy*
Booker T. Washington, "Up from Slavery," *African American Literature*
E. B. White, "Dog Training," *One Man's Meat*
Lindsey Williams, "Our Fascinating Past," *Charlotte Sun Herald*
Zheng Zhensen and Alice Low, *A Young Painter*
Carl Zimmer, "Bicycle in Dataspace," *Discover*

Poetry

Jimmy Santiago Baca, *Martín and Meditations on the South Valley*
Elizabeth Bishop, "One Art," *The Complete Poems*
Nina Cassian, "The Bear," *Lady of Miracles: Poems by Nina Cassian*
Henry Wadsworth Longfellow, *The Song of Hiawatha*
William Shakespeare, "Sonnet 29," "Sonnet 33"
Percy Bysshe Shelley, "Ozymandias"
George A. Strong, "The Modern Hiawatha," *Parodies: An Anthology from Chaucer to Beerbohm—and After*
Alfred, Lord Tennyson, "The Eagle"
Nguyen Thi Vinh, "Thoughts of Hanoi"

Drama

Bernard Shaw, *Pygmalion*

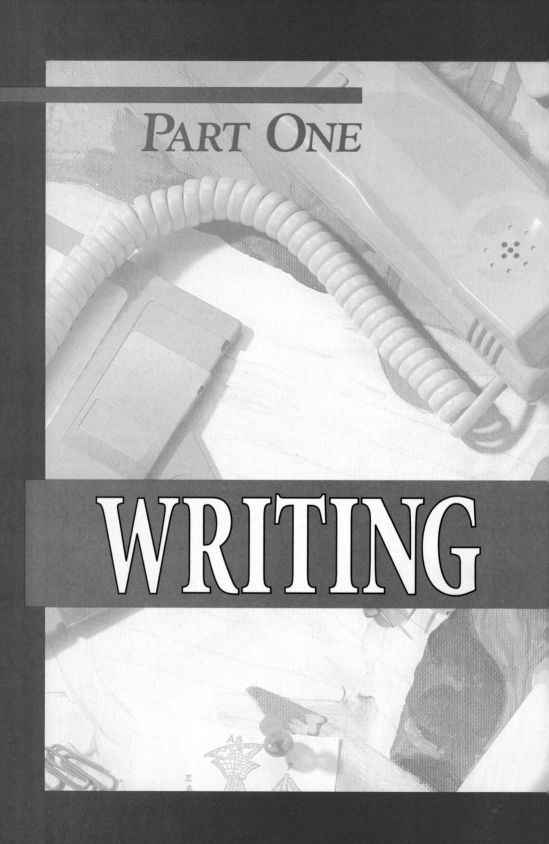

PART ONE

WRITING

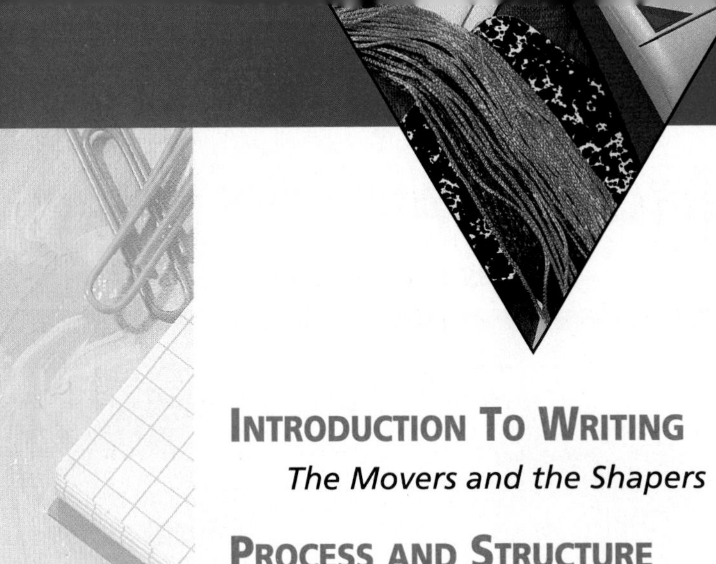

INTRODUCTION TO WRITING

THE MOVERS AND THE SHAPERS

James L. Kinneavy

Take any area of life, and it's not hard to put your finger on people who **move** the world's wheels and **shape** its future.

Government: Abraham Lincoln, whose courageous decisions helped unite our divided country.

Work and business: Lee Iacocca, who boldly rejuvenated an American car company that everyone assumed was dying.

Entertainment and art: Bill Cosby, whose comic genius tickles funny bones but also moves minds toward harmony and fairness.

Humanitarianism: Jane Addams, winner of the Nobel Prize for peace, who championed—against all odds—the causes of the poor and burdened.

But now try to put your finger on what these movers and shapers have in common.

Lincoln, Iacocca, Cosby, Addams: their spheres of life are so different. Is it possible that success in Washington, in a corporate board room, on a television sound stage, and in a Chicago settlement house are related in any way? Do all movers and shapers share a crucial skill? Yes. And they share it with you.

Clockwise from top left: Roberto Clemente, Connie Chung, Gloria Steinem, Theodor Seuss Geisel, Sequoyah, Martin Luther King, Jr., and Maya Angelou.

What's Common to All Uncommon Leaders?

Leaders, no matter what their fields, actually share many qualities and abilities. You can probably suggest several: drive, intelligence, vision. But there's something else absolutely essential to any leader who influences followers: communication. After all, if word doesn't get out, heartfelt beliefs, hard work, innovative ideas, and creative talent have no effect. Leaders have to let people know.

Using words well is common to people who get things done. Abraham Lincoln, Lee Iacocca, Bill Cosby, and Jane Addams have had a tremendous impact on America. And they couldn't have done it without their abilities to speak their minds, prepare speeches, entertain through words, and write proposals, contracts, and books.

But famous figures aren't the only ones who use words to move people and shape ideas. Think of your city's mayor, the manager of your favorite restaurant, a popular local singer, the head of a homeless shelter. Would they be where they are if they couldn't communicate? Think of any important goal you have for your life. What role could words play in making you a standout?

It doesn't matter where your interests lie. In the worlds of politics, business, art, and social service, communication is crucial. Movers and shapers put words to work.

The Power of Communication

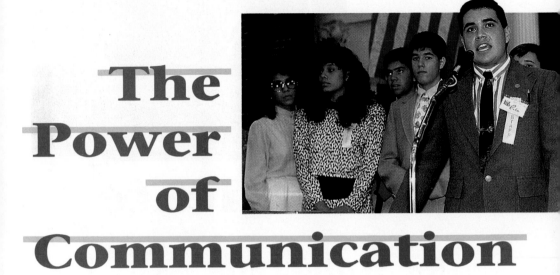

Making an impact with words is a special, liberating power, but it's one that is accessible to all of us. All communication requires is someone who wants to communicate (a ***writer***) about something (a ***subject***), someone to say it to (an ***audience***), and a way to say it (a ***language***). Visualize these elements as a communications triangle. Language—both written and spoken—is at the center.

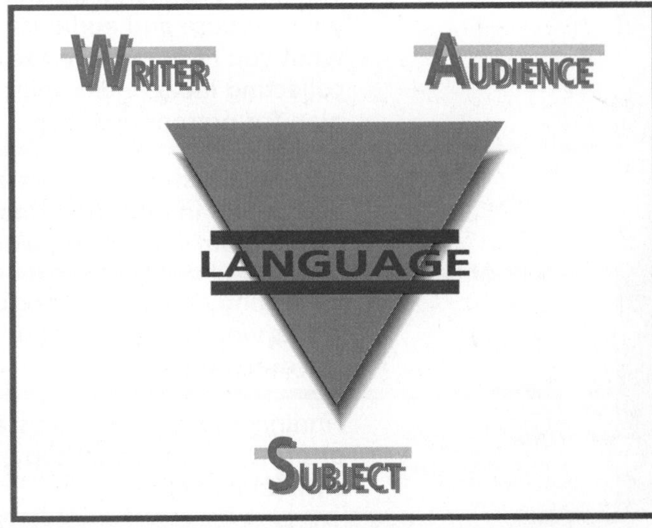

How Do They Communicate?

The Writing Process

Besides effective communication, all movers and shapers have something else in common: the way they go about that communication. They, like all writers, use the stages of the ***writing process*** to go from first idea to final realization in words. As you would expect, each writer can use the process differently. Thought, language, and *people* will never be confined in rigid steps, but the stages below are basic elements in leading yourself from rough thought to clear expression.

Prewriting	Thinking and planning: thinking about your purpose and audience; determining what you're going to write about; collecting ideas and details; creating a plan for presenting ideas
Writing	Writing a first draft: expressing ideas and details in sentences and paragraphs; carrying out the writing plan
Evaluating and Revising	Reviewing the draft to decide what works well and what doesn't; changing the draft to improve it
Proofreading and Publishing	Finding and correcting mistakes; writing or printing out a final copy; sharing it with an audience

Why Do They Communicate?

The Aims of Writing

Consider Lee Iacocca and Bill Cosby, and you might conclude that writers write for limitless reasons. While it's true that each piece of writing has its own individual purpose, the aims of writing as a whole aren't infinite. Writers actually have four basic ***aims,*** or reasons, for writing.

Expository	**Informative:** Writers sometimes want to give facts or other kinds of information. **Explanatory:** Writers may want to explain something in detail. **Exploratory:** Writers may also investigate in depth a complex idea or seek an answer to a question.
Persuasive	Writers often want to convince others to accept an idea or take a specific action.
Self-Expressive	Sometimes writers simply want to express personal feelings or thoughts.
Literary	Writers also create imaginative works—novels, short stories, poems, plays, songs.

The models that follow all relate to the same topic, but each is written by a different writer and illustrates a different basic aim. As you read, think about each writer's purpose.

EXPOSITORY WRITING

Local College Students Uncover Archaeological Find

Seven Westhaven College students may have uncovered a more than 3,000-year-old Egyptian statue. The students, under the direction of Professor Ramón Arcaro, made the discovery Tuesday while digging on the east bank of the Nile River, between Karnak and Luxor in Egypt.

The students were completing the final week of a six-week exploratory dig when Li Kwan and Ivan McAfee uncovered what appears to be the foot of a sandstone statue. "We were about four feet down in the sand when we hit it," said Kwan. "The excitement was indescribable."

Arcaro says there is every reason to believe they have uncovered one of the hundreds of statues constructed by Ramses II, an Egyptian pharaoh of the 19th dynasty (1304–1237 B.C.). If so, the statue could be 30 to 50 feet in height and is considered a major archaeological find.

The college has filed a declaration of the find with the Egyptian government. The students continue logging data and photographing the site, but will return home later this week to await approval from Cairo to continue the dig. In the meantime, the college will begin fund-raising for the statue's excavation.

Reader's Response

1. What are you most curious about after reading this report? What one question would you like to ask Li Kwan or Professor Arcaro?
2. Does the writer of this article stick to the facts about the incident, or include personal opinions and feelings? Explain.

PERSUASIVE WRITING

Dear Westhaven College Alumni:

Westhaven College has a once-in-a-lifetime opportunity to contribute to the world's understanding of the past and to enhance its academic reputation. On December 3 Professor Ramón Arcaro of the Westhaven Archaeology Department and his students uncovered a portion of a statue on the east bank of the Nile River. They believe the statue may have been constructed by the Egyptian pharaoh, Ramses II, over three thousand years ago.

Unfortunately, Professor Arcaro and his students made the discovery during the final two days of their six-week dig. About $500,000 is needed to complete the excavation and authenticate the find. The Archaeology Department does not have this money, and all the hard work and the credit for it are in danger of being lost.

But that's where you can help. By making a contribution to the final excavation, you can give Westhaven students a unique educational experience. Your gift will also keep giving back to the college, as Westhaven's discovery attracts international attention.

Time is short; Professor Arcaro must make a commitment to the Egyptian government by January 31. Please write your check and use the enclosed envelope to mail it today. Your gift will truly make a difference.

Sincerely,

Annette Kaufman

Annette Kaufman, Director of Alumni Giving

Reader's Response

1. What do you think of the role of history and archaeology? Has a knowledge of history ever been significant for you?
2. Would this letter convince you to make a contribution? What did the writer say that was most convincing? least convincing?

EXPRESSIVE WRITING

Today I think I hit the high point and the low point of my life. Around three P.M. I was working with two students who were removing sand from around a piece of sandstone. Think it's the foot of a huge statue, probably one of the statues Ramses II built to honor himself. What a find! My first thought was that it could make my career and the careers of my students. Could do a lot for Westhaven, too. But now that I've had time for a second thought, I'm panicked. How will I ever get the money to go on with the excavation?

To give up now—when we're so close. Let someone else, some other university, take the credit for the find because they had the money and we didn't? Don't think I could stand it. What can I do? Get a corporate sponsor? Call the college president? Would she support a fund-raising campaign for this? Call tomorrow, soon as she's in her office.

Later. Had to go out and take one more look at the foot we uncovered. The moon was bright, so I could see. I had a thought—Ramses II looked at the same moon. I wonder what he was really like. All that ego, dozens of statues. Where did they get him?

READER'S RESPONSE

1. From this journal, what can you tell about Professor Arcaro? How would you describe his personality?
2. How would you feel if you found a 3,000-year-old statue?

The "antique land" in this poem is Egypt, where over three thousand years ago, the Pharaoh Ramses II built hundreds of palaces, temples, and monuments commemorating his own greatness. Ramses II is referred to here as "Ozymandias," perhaps another version of "User-Maet-Re," the name used for Ramses at the temples at Abu Simbel.

OZYMANDIAS

BY PERCY BYSSHE SHELLEY

I met a traveller from an antique land
Who said: Two vast and trunkless legs of stone
Stand in the desert . . . Near them, on the sand,
Half sunk, a shattered visage lies, whose frown,
And wrinkled lip, and sneer of cold command,
Tell that its sculptor well those passions read
Which yet survive, stamped on these lifeless things,
The hand that mocked them, and the heart that fed:
And on the pedestal these words appear:
"My name is Ozymandias, king of kings:
Look on my works, ye Mighty, and despair!"
Nothing beside remains. Round the decay
Of that colossal wreck, boundless and bare
The lone and level sands stretch far away.

Reader's Response

1. The phrase "colossal wreck" sums up the irony many readers see in this poem: Ramses/Ozymandias is conquered by sand. But could you write a poem about this broken statue that would celebrate the king's power through the ages? How would you do it?
2. Besides "colossal wreck," what other words of Shelley's stand out vividly for you in this poem? Is there any place in the poem where meaning is not as clear to you as in the sentences of the other models? Where? How do you interpret the passage?

Writing and Thinking Activities

1. Get together with two or three other students to discuss the following questions.
   a. Which model persuades readers to do something? How?
   b. Which one provides facts and details to inform readers about an event?
   c. Which writer used words in a way that is different from ordinary speech? What's the effect of these differences?
   d. Which model is mostly about the writer's thoughts and feelings?
2. You are a constant communicator, and your own communication patterns may surprise you. How much of your communication is expository: informing, explaining, or exploring? How much is persuasive? How much is self-expressive? How much is literary? Research yourself. Jot down all your uses of language—writing, reading, speaking, listening—during a typical day. Then meet with two or three classmates to discuss what you've learned.

3. Bring a copy of a magazine or newspaper to class. Work with two or three other students to find examples of all four types of writing: expository, persuasive, self-expressive, literary. (Look at *all* the writing, not just articles.) Analyze the mix. Is one aim more common than the others? Do all the publications have the same mix of the four aims for writing?
4. Choose a radio or TV station to listen to or watch for a period of three hours—6 to 7 P.M. on a week night, 8 to 9 P.M. on a week night, and 3 to 4 P.M. on Saturday or Sunday. Categorize all programs, as well as short features and ads, according to the aim. Then get together with another student who studied a different station and compare the two.
5. Can you take the idea from a poem and convert it to a news story, a persuasive piece, or an expressive piece? Look for a poem in your literature book or the library and try to write another piece on the same topic, but with a different aim.

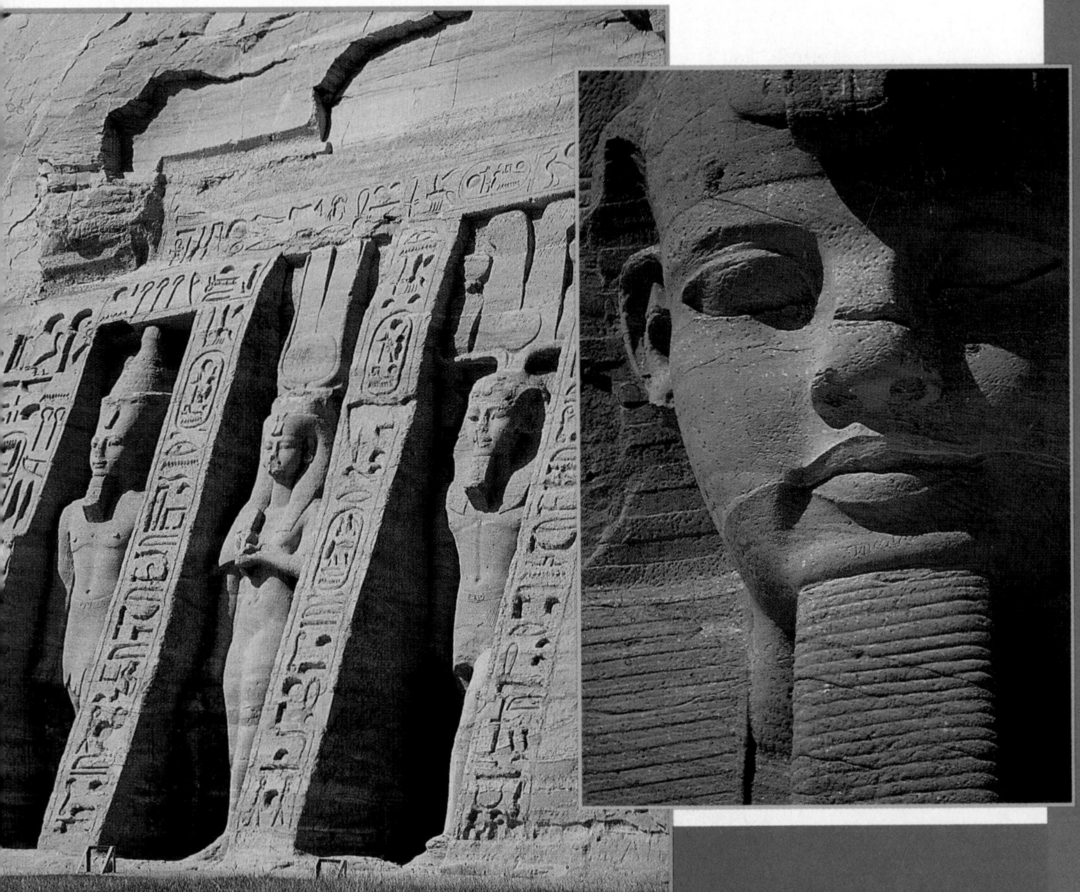

1 Writing and Thinking

Looking at the Process

Have you heard of "automatic writing"? It's a **process** of "ghost writing" in the truest sense: an unseen force supposedly pushes the pen while the "writer" merely watches. Unbelievable? Yes; but it's unbelievable for more reasons than our doubts about unseen forces.

Writing and You. When was your writing ever totally unconscious, with words filling the page while you remarked, "Why, look at that!"? Never! When you write, your brain is engaged before, during, and after putting words on paper. Planning, judging, and just mentally doodling are indispensable, because the writing process involves more than a moving hand; it takes a working brain, too. But that doesn't make writing *un*mysterious. Since writing is thinking, it is always a process of discovery; it often surprises the person holding the pen.

As You Read. Writer Margaret Atwood believes writing is about as automatic a process as brain surgery. Her comparison is a joke, but she's serious, too. Why does she say many people misunderstand writing?

Pablo Picasso. *Interior with a Girl Drawing.* Paris, February 1935. Oil on canvas, 51 1/4" × 6' 4 5/8". Collection, The Museum of Modern Art, New York. Nelson A. Rockefeller Bequest. © 1993 ARS, NY/SPADEM, Paris.

from Second Words

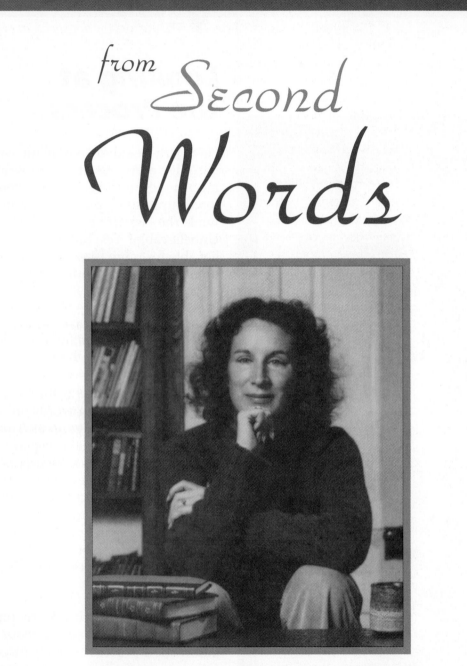

by Margaret Atwood

A friend of mine told me once that when she'd been in France a man, upon hearing she was a writer, commented, "It is an honorable profession." In Canada we don't—even now—think of writing as an honorable profession. We don't think of it as a profession at all. We think of it, still, as something called "expressing yourself." I'm sure you've all heard the one about the writer and the brain surgeon who met at a cocktail party. "So you write," said the brain surgeon. "Isn't that interesting. I've always wanted to write. When I retire and have the time I'm going to be a writer." "What a coincidence," said the writer, "because when I retire I'm going to be a brain surgeon."

Deep down inside, most people think that writing is something anyone can do, really, because after all it's only expressing yourself. Well, it's probably true that anyone can write. Anyone can play the piano too, but doing it well is another thing. If writing is merely and only self-expression, then all the philistine reactions to it I've been caricaturing above would be, in my opinion, quite justified.

Readers and critics both are still addicted to the concept of self-expression, the writer as a kind of spider, spinning out his entire work from within. This view depends on a solipsism, the idea that we are all self-enclosed monads, with an inside and an outside, and that nothing from the outside ever gets in. It goes hand in hand with that garland of clichés, the one with which women writers in particular are frequently decorated, the notion that everything you write *must* be based on personal experience. *Must,* because those making this assumption have no belief in the imagination, and are such literalists that they will not invest interest in anything they do not suppose to be "true." Of course all writing is based on personal experience, but personal experience is experience—wherever it comes from—that you identify with, *imagine* if you like, so that it becomes personal to you. If your mother dies and you don't feel a thing, is this death a personal experience? "If a clod be washed away by the sea, Europe is the less," said John Donne; or, to paraphrase him as Adrienne Rich does, "Every woman's death diminishes me."

> "I happen to believe that at its best writing is considerably more and other than mere self-expression."

We like to think of writing as merely personal, merely self-expression, and hopefully neurotic, because it lets us off the hook. If that's all it is, if it is not a true view of the world or, Heaven forefend, of a human nature of which we ourselves partake, we don't have to pay any serious attention to it. I happen to believe that at its best writing is considerably more and other than mere self-expression.

Reader's Response

1. Margaret Atwood usually writes fiction and poetry, and in this essay, she uses the term *writing* to mean creative writing. Do you agree with Atwood that most people think imaginative writing is "something anyone can do"? that it's always "based on personal experience"? or that it's something you "don't have to pay any serious attention to"? What is your own opinion about creative writing? Before you answer, have a group discussion, using specific examples of stories, songs, or movies. Then write your opinion in your journal.
2. Atwood says an experience becomes personal when you can imagine or identify with it, not necessarily live it. Look back at the last three or four pieces of writing you have done for school. What "experiences" played a part in the writing that became personal to you through reading, watching, listening, or imagining?
3. The last sentence says "at its best writing is considerably more and other than mere self-expression." Explain what you think Atwood means by the words *more* and *other* and whether you agree with her.

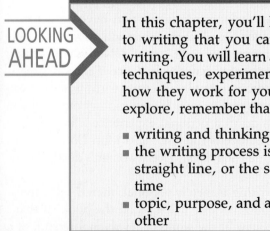

LOOKING AHEAD

In this chapter, you'll look at a general approach to writing that you can use with many types of writing. You will learn about some specific writing techniques, experiment with them, and decide how they work for you. As you read, write, and explore, remember that

- writing and thinking are inseparable
- the writing process isn't a set of rigid steps, a straight line, or the same for everyone every time
- topic, purpose, and audience always shape each other

Aim—The "Why" of Writing

Writing gets things done. It has purpose. This is true not only for instruction manuals, congressional bills, news bulletins, and articles explaining medical discoveries, but for *any* writing: a cereal ad, a cartoon script, a secret entry in your journal, a note to a friend.

A person who puts words on a page is communicating, even if only privately in a personal journal. This active, purposeful aspect of writing is one to keep in mind as you write, because it unites you with all other writers and readers. It may appear that the reasons for writing are limitless. Still, no matter what the specific intent for a particular piece of writing (and each is different), it will usually fall within four basic purposes.

WHY PEOPLE WRITE	
To express themselves	To understand themselves better; to find some kind of meaning in their own lives
To inform, to explain, or to explore	To provide knowledge, facts, or data to other people; to make something clear or understandable; to investigate an idea or problem
To persuade	To convince other people to do something or believe something
To create literary works	To be creative with language; to say something in a unique way

Of course, communicating is as multifaceted as people are—that is, any one piece of writing can have more than one side, or purpose. In fact, you are more likely to combine purposes than to have one simple, pure purpose—like writing "Danger! Keep out!" For example, you may want to write a suspenseful short story and also explore the idea of loyalty. You may want to explain organic pesticides and at the same time urge people to use them.

Process—The "How" of Writing

If you view the writing process as a general way of thinking and writing that is common to all writers and all writing, you are right. But you also need to think of the writing process as something that is tremendously flexible, a process that can be individualized to fit your working style and whatever you are trying to write at the moment. That's the beauty of the writing process; once you've learned the basic thinking skills, strategies, and techniques, you can manipulate them to suit your own needs.

The following diagram illustrates the flexibility of the writing and thinking process. At any point in the process, you can stop and spend more time, go back to an earlier stage, or retrace your steps.

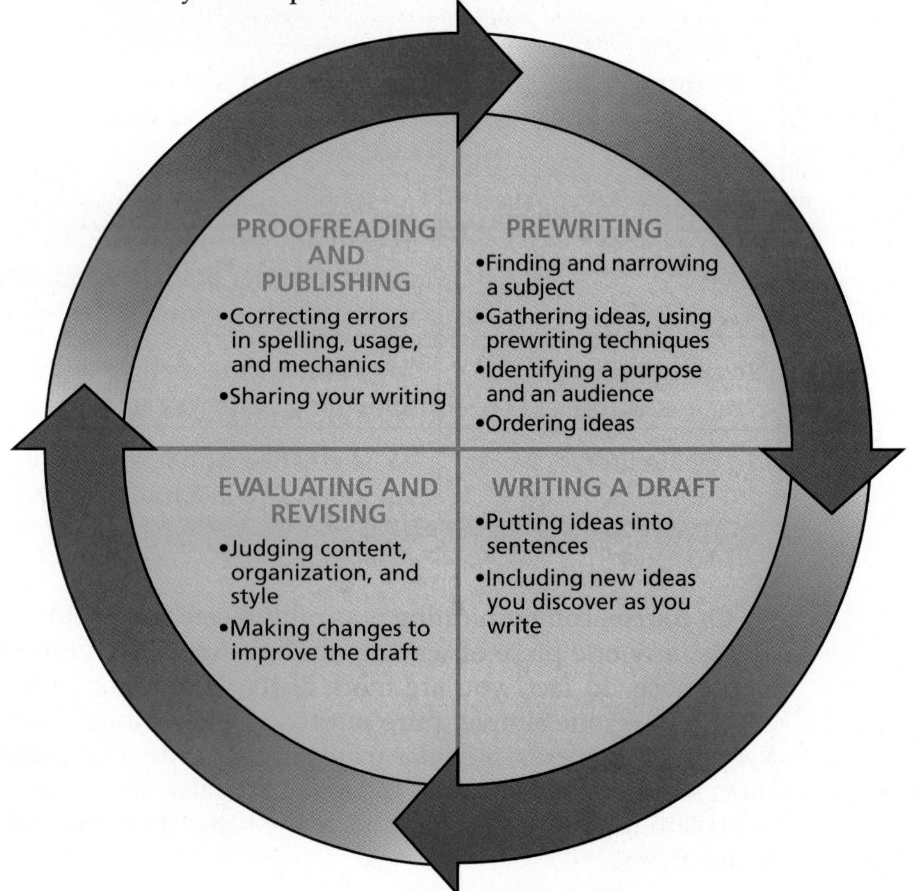

PROOFREADING AND PUBLISHING
•Correcting errors in spelling, usage, and mechanics
•Sharing your writing
PREWRITING
•Finding and narrowing a subject
•Gathering ideas, using prewriting techniques
•Identifying a purpose and an audience
•Ordering ideas
EVALUATING AND REVISING
•Judging content, organization, and style
•Making changes to improve the draft
WRITING A DRAFT
•Putting ideas into sentences
•Including new ideas you discover as you write

Finding Ideas for Writing

All writers face two beginning challenges: coming up with a good idea and gathering the information needed to put that idea across. Like any art, however, writing is a very individual matter. A prewriting technique that works well for another writer may not work for you.

Still, over the years, many writers have found the following techniques useful. In the following pages you have the opportunity to test them and determine which ones feel natural to you and which ones fit well with certain writing tasks.

PREWRITING TECHNIQUES		
Writer's Journal	Recording personal experiences and observations	Page 22
Freewriting	Writing for a few minutes about whatever comes to mind	Pages 22–23
Brainstorming	Listing ideas as quickly as they come to mind	Pages 23–24
Clustering	Using circles and lines to show connections between ideas	Page 24
Asking Questions	Using the reporter's *5W-How?* questions	Page 25
Observing	Observing details of sight, sound, smell, taste, touch	Page 26
Imagining	Probing your imagination for ideas, often using a "What if?" approach	Page 27
Reading with a Focus	Reading to find specific information	Page 28
Listening with a Focus	Listening to find specific information	Page 28

Keeping a Writer's Journal

A ***writer's journal*** can be kept in almost any form: a notebook, three-ring binder, scrapbook, file folder, or computer. You can use your journal to record your dreams and beliefs, your disappointments, your hopes, and your happy times. You can also include anything that catches your attention: newspaper and magazine clippings, quotations, song lyrics, poems, cartoons, or photos. Stocked with material that's important to you, your journal can become a great source for writing ideas. Here are some tips for keeping a writer's journal.

1. Find time each day to write a dated entry in your journal. You may set aside a specific time for writing, or you may carry your journal with you for spontaneous entries.
2. Concentrate on getting your thoughts down. Perfect grammar and punctuation aren't necessary for a journal entry.
3. Be imaginative. Create song lyrics and poetry; draw or sketch; recast an event in your life as a dramatic scene in a movie script. (Change the ending, if you wish!)
4. Jot down notes beside your entries, reacting to and reflecting on what you write and include. Why was this important? Why did you choose it?

Freewriting

To ***freewrite,*** quickly write down your first thoughts on any given subject.

1. Write for three to five minutes without stopping.
2. Start with any topic or word—such as *pollution* or *diets* or *Shakespeare* or *treason.*

3. Write down any ideas, images, details, or associations that come into your head without worrying about grammar or punctuation.
4. If you become "stuck," just copy your last word until a fresh idea strikes, or write questions to yourself about why you're temporarily out of ideas.
5. As a variation, try ***focused freewriting,*** or ***looping.*** Select one word or phrase from your freewriting and use it as a starting point to "loop" to more writing.

HERE'S HOW

Special Olympics. National finals televised. Celebrities, etc. Started by whom? A good way for these kids to build achievement and self-esteem. It really works! I know this from last summer—volunteering there was the best experience of my life. Everyone came away a winner. I remember Kathy didn't walk until she was 5 (she's 10 now) but was in a race. When they put the ribbon around her neck, her head was high!

EXERCISE 1 **Freewriting from a Journal Entry**

If you don't keep a journal yet, start by answering one of these questions: *What new thing did I learn yesterday? Which of yesterday's experiences would I like to undo or do over, and why?* After writing your journal entry, select one word or topic from it as your subject for freewriting. Freewrite for three or four minutes.

Brainstorming

Brainstorming, which helps you generate a free flow of ideas on any given subject, can be used either to find a topic or to gather information. Although you can brainstorm alone, the process works even better with a partner or in a group.

1. Write down one specific subject or topic on your paper or on the chalkboard.

2. Record every word or phrase that comes to mind. In a group, brainstorm out loud and ask one person to write down all responses.
3. Work quickly. Don't stop to evaluate your ideas; just continue until your ideas run out.

Clustering

Like brainstorming, ***clustering*** can help you make associations or break down a topic. But with clustering, you create a diagram that helps you discover relationships among ideas.

1. Write down a subject or topic on your paper and circle it.
2. Around the subject, quickly write down and circle all related ideas that come to mind. Draw lines connecting the new ideas either to your original subject or to one another.
3. Keep associating and connecting as long as you can.

Clustering is sometimes called *webbing* or *making connections*. Your finished cluster may not make perfect sense to someone else, but you'll understand your own connections.

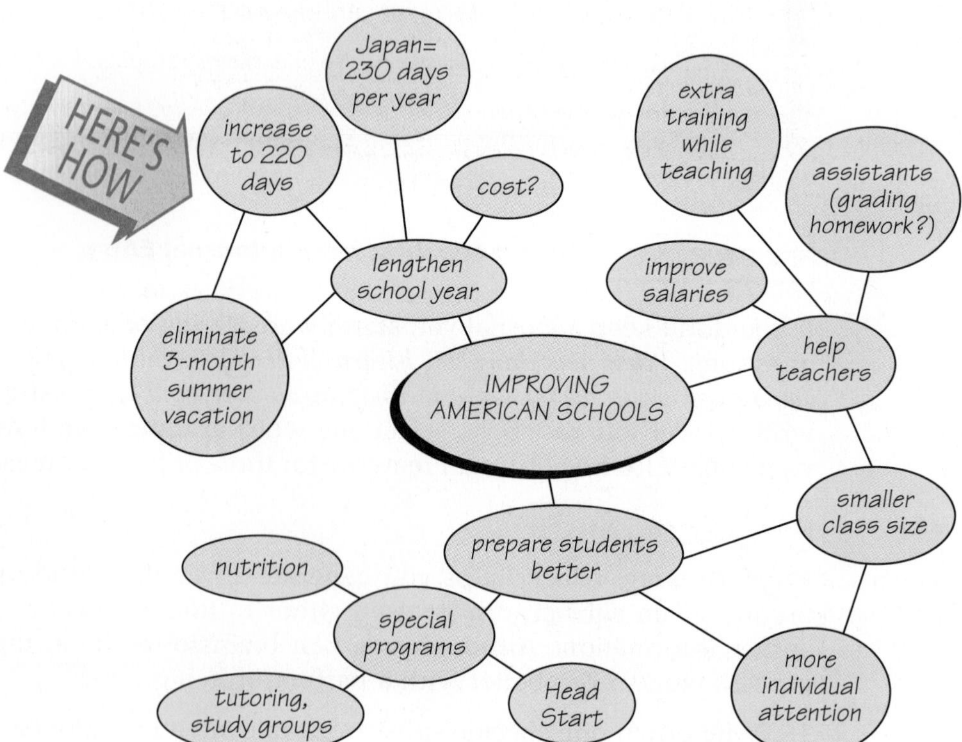

Using Brainstorming and Clustering

Test the theory that two heads are better than one. Working with a partner, list as many ideas as you can about one of the following topics, or choose your own.

computers	nuclear power
favorite vacation spots	television comedians
national monuments	women athletes

Next, work together to choose a second topic for clustering, but work individually to create your clusters. Compare the two webs when you finish. Where did your minds travel similar paths? Where did they diverge?

Asking Questions

One of the best ways to gather information is to ask questions. But what questions? The reporter's ***5W-How? questions*** (*Who? What? Where? When? Why?* and *How?*) are a good place to start. Like many other prewriting techniques, this one is flexible. You don't have to use a question word if it doesn't apply to your topic, and you can use the same question word many times. The following questions about the topic "the history of the Academy Awards" are just some of the questions that are possible.

WHO?	Who began the Academy Awards? Who won the first awards for best actor, actress, and director? Who has won the most Academy Awards?
WHAT?	What are the significant changes in the awards over the years? What were some famous, or amusing, acceptance speeches?
WHERE?	Where were the first and last year's ceremonies held?
WHEN?	When is the deadline for nominations? When was the ceremony first televised?
WHY?	Why are the awards important to a winner's career? Why is the little golden statuette called "Oscar"?
HOW?	How are winners chosen?

EXERCISE 3 **Asking the *5W-How?* Questions**

Where will you be at this time next year? Since finding the right school or job may depend on asking the right questions, identify a particular university, college, training program, apprenticeship, or job and ask as many good *5W-How?* questions as you can. Compare your list with those of others.

Observing

Think about the best meal you've ever had. Can you remember the smell and taste of the food? Can you almost hear the background sounds? Can you picture who you were with? If you were going to write about that special event, you would need to bring all your senses into play—touch, sound, smell, taste, and sight.

Using all five of your senses will increase your ability to observe and improve your writing. Here are details recorded from a first snow-skiing experience.

HERE'S HOW

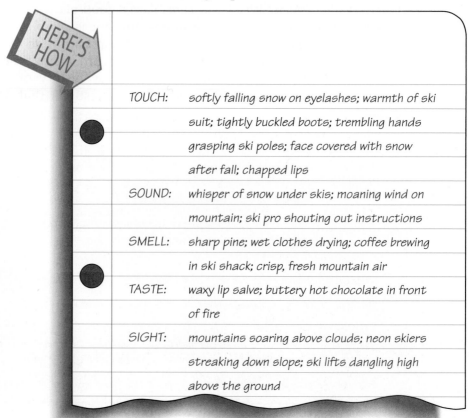

TOUCH: *softly falling snow on eyelashes; warmth of ski suit; tightly buckled boots; trembling hands grasping ski poles; face covered with snow after fall; chapped lips*

SOUND: *whisper of snow under skis; moaning wind on mountain; ski pro shouting out instructions*

SMELL: *sharp pine; wet clothes drying; coffee brewing in ski shack; crisp, fresh mountain air*

TASTE: *waxy lip salve; buttery hot chocolate in front of fire*

SIGHT: *mountains soaring above clouds; neon skiers streaking down slope; ski lifts dangling high above the ground*

Imagining

Who asks "What if?" questions? The scientist trying to develop a new cure asks, "What if we synthesized these compounds?" The scriptwriter asks, "What if a passenger falls off a cruise ship?" The store manager trying to attract more business asks, "What if we offered a preferred-customer bonus?"

Anyone trying to solve a problem or to create literary works needs to be imaginative. Asking ***"What if?" questions*** like the following ones can stimulate your imagination.

- *What if I could change the past?* (What if the Vietnam War hadn't happened? What if a woman had written all of Shakespeare's plays?)
- *What if something we take for granted were totally different?* (What if eating meat were against the law? What if all people could speak a common language?)

You can ask "What if?" questions about specific topics, too. Writing about the homeless, for example, you could ask, *What if the government paid people to house the homeless?*

EXERCISE 4 **Observing and Imagining**

Use careful observation along with your imagination to develop ideas about life among Native Americans a hundred years ago. Begin by looking at the following photograph of a Sioux camp in South Dakota around 1880.

1. Identify three things you can tell about life in this Native American camp by looking at this picture.
2. What if you were one of the people in this picture? List at least ten things you might see, hear, feel, smell, or taste.

Ed Bodein, circa 1879. From Collection of Lynda Abbott.

3. Imagine that the photograph on page 27 is the opening setting of a short story you're writing, and write three "What if?" questions about what might happen next.

Reading with a Focus

Since gathering information often involves reading, reading efficiently can save you both time and trouble. When you've found a possible source of information, keep the following tips in mind.

1. Preview the material by glancing through the table of contents, headings and subheadings, index, illustrations, and charts. Be alert for material related to your topic.
2. Skim until you find information about your topic; then read carefully. Take notes on main ideas and relevant details, and be sure to keep track of your sources.

Listening with a Focus

You take for granted reading before writing, but think of all the ways you can *listen* to learn: videotapes and audiotapes, radio and television programs, conversations with experts, and live speeches and performances. To collect the details you need from these sources, prepare yourself for concentrated listening.

1. Because familiarity with your topic will make understanding easier, do some background investigation first.
2. Create a list of the main information you need to gather or questions you want to ask, and keep the list.
3. Take notes even when you are also recording, and plan your note-taking method so you aren't trying to write every word. Use phrases and abbreviations, and try circling or underlining key points to make them stand out.

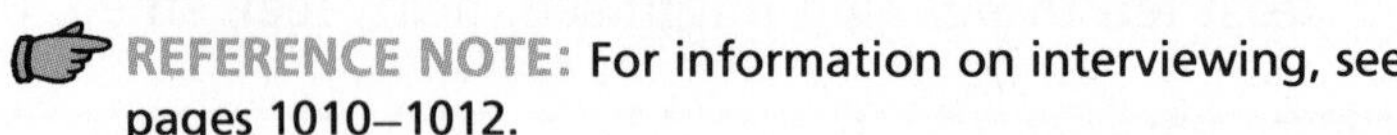

REFERENCE NOTE: For information on interviewing, see pages 1010–1012.

EXERCISE 5 **Reading and Listening for Specific Information**

"The yo-yo is enjoying a comeback," claims a 1991 newspaper article. When was it popular before? Do a little reading about amusement fads and see if you can find answers to the following questions.

1. What was an amusement fad from the 1950s? from the 1920s?
2. What are two dance fads from the past, and when were they popular?
3. What's something that began as a fad but became part of the mainstream culture?

After reading about past fads, use listening to discover what's popular today. For the next few days, listen to radio (perhaps call-in shows and National Public Radio), television (sitcoms, commercials, "entertainment news," and MTV), and the conversations of students at your school. What fads are people following today? What might they be doing tomorrow? Compare your answers with those of classmates.

CRITICAL THINKING

Analyzing a Subject

You're told, "Write about what interests you." But maybe the interests that first occur to you—perhaps *dance, history, windsurfing,* or *movies*—are likely to be too broad for any paper, even a full-blown research report.

In writing, your first step after deciding on a subject that interests you is usually ***analyzing:*** breaking the subject down into parts or aspects. This is necessary to develop a better understanding of the broad subject and to find a manageable topic for the length of the paper you plan. For example, if you were interested in the Supreme Court, you could analyze it to discover specific aspects of the Court you might write about.

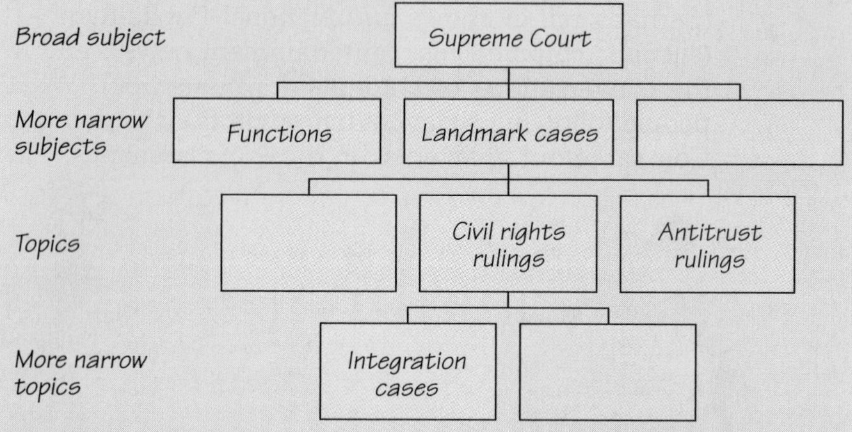

CRITICAL THINKING EXERCISE: Analyzing Subjects and Topics

Practice your analytical thinking skills by working with a partner to answer the following questions. If your knowledge of the Supreme Court is limited, you may have to do some research.

1. You will notice empty "boxes" in the diagram. At every level of the analysis, there could be additional or different subdivisions. Under *civil rights rulings,* what topics could you add to *integration*? Under *landmark cases,* can you identify topics other than *civil rights* and *antitrust*?
2. What narrower aspect of the final topic, *landmark integration cases,* could you focus on?
3. Perform an entirely different analysis. Instead of *landmark cases,* analyze *functions* through all the levels shown, or think of another first-level subdivision and analyze it fully.

Considering Purpose, Audience, and Tone

Purpose. As you read earlier in this chapter, all writing generally has one of four *purposes* (page 19). But within those purposes, you have a broad range of writing forms to use, including the following possibilities.

MAIN PURPOSE	FORMS OF WRITING
Self-Expressive	Journal, letter, personal essay
Literary	Short story, poem, play
Expository: Informative, Explanatory, Exploratory	Science and social science writing, newspaper and magazine articles, biography, autobiography, travel essay
Persuasive	Persuasive essay, letter to the editor, advertisement, political speech

Audience. To understand the importance of ***audience,*** think about yourself. You *are* an audience, and writers who want your attention must write in a style that grabs your interest, make their subject appealing to you, and use language that doesn't lose you. When you write, you have the same goal; asking yourself these questions will help accomplish that goal.

- Who is my audience? (Am I writing for a teacher? a friend? classmates? younger students? newspaper readers?)
- What does my audience already know about the topic?
- What background or technical information do I need to provide? Do I need to define technical terms?
- What topic, details, or approach will interest my audience?
- What level of language should I use—formal or informal? Should I use simple or complex words and sentences?

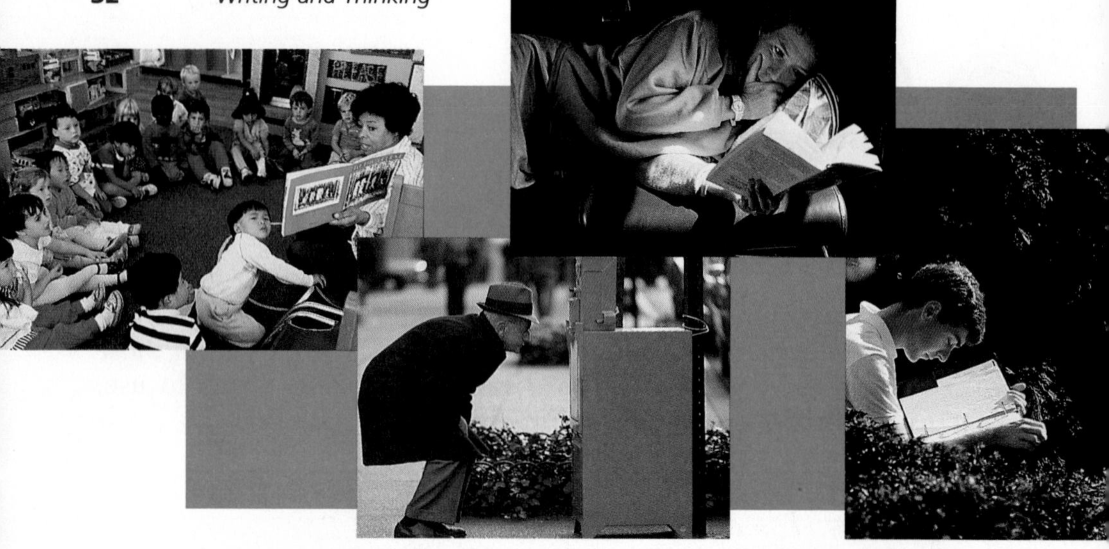

Tone. Words carry feeling as well as meaning. ***Tone,*** your attitude toward your topic and readers, comes through in the choice of words and details and even in the rhythm of your sentences. Many times you will want to have a knowledgeable, somewhat serious tone, especially if you are explaining something or trying to persuade. But tone is always tied to topic, purpose, and audience. There are many times when some other tone—funny, sympathetic, indignant—is called for.

CRITICAL THINKING

Analyzing Purpose, Audience, and Tone

The critical thinking skill of **analysis** is essential when you begin to plan any piece of writing. Unless you analyze your purpose, your audience, and your own attitude toward your topic, you will be unable to control the tone—and indirectly the effect—of what you are writing. To understand the difference tone can create, read the following examples, both of which are about the kudzu plant.

The first example is from an informative article in a national magazine with a general audience. Its tone is objective.

Kudzu, a vine with lush green leaves and beautiful purple flowers that originated in Japan, first appeared in the U.S. at the 1876 Centennial Exposition in Philadelphia. It became popular in the Southeast in the 1930s, when soil conservationists urged farmers to plant it to halt erosion.

They succeeded—too well. Kudzu is now a common weed from East Texas to Florida and as far north as southeastern Pennsylvania. It can grow a foot a day and covers roadsides, trees, utility poles, and anything else in its path. Kudzu is tough, too: It takes repeated doses of strong and expensive herbicides to eradicate it.

"Scourge of the South May Be Heading North,"
National Geographic

The second example is a letter to the editor of a newspaper.

To the Editor:

Our city is being taken over by kudzu! Known to grow a foot a day, this jungle-like eyesore has become a real hazard. In many locations, it has taken over utility poles, threatening cables and electrical wires. In some cases, it shorts out or corrodes electrical utility boxes and transformers, disrupting power supplies and communications. It is also strangling trees that have grown in our city and surrounding farms and woods for decades.

As concerned citizens, we must find a way to stop the growth of this dangerous plant. Right now our only defense against this dangerous pest is repeated blasts of killer chemicals. Money should be given to our state university immediately so that researchers there can find a way to get rid of the kudzu safely and inexpensively before it takes over the entire city!

Albert Morelli

Here the writer is addressing a local audience and urging them to take action. The tone is more informal and decidedly anti-kudzu. Much of the same information is conveyed in the article and in the letter, but the differences in tone help to achieve very different effects.

CRITICAL THINKING EXERCISE: Analyzing Purpose and Audience

You are a summer camp counselor entertaining your seventh-grade charges with a short before-bedtime campfire story, "The Attack of the Killer Kudzu." Analyze your purpose and audience, as well as your attitude toward the topic. Then write a passage from the story, controlling the tone to achieve the effect you want. Will you go for goose bumps?

Arranging Ideas

After collecting information for a paper, a moment of confusion isn't unusual. *Where will I begin? And besides that, where will I stop?* Deciding on the flow of your ideas is an important part of planning, and with practice it is a manageable one. The following chart shows four common methods of ordering information.

TYPE OF ORDER	DEFINITION	EXAMPLES
Chronological	Narration: Order that presents events as they happen in time	Story; narrative poem; explanation of a process; history; biography; drama
Spatial	Description: Order that describes objects according to location	Descriptions (near to far; left to right; top to bottom; etc.)
Importance	Evaluation: Order that gives details from least to most important or the reverse	Persuasive writing; description; explanations (main idea and supporting details); evaluative writing
Logical	Classification: Order that relates items and groups	Definitions; classifications; comparisons and contrasts

The specific order you use in a paper can depend on your subject as well as on earlier decisions you've made. For example, in the following paragraph, Jay Mathews is introducing his subject, math teacher Jaime Escalante, who was depicted in the film *Stand and Deliver*. He's writing for a general audience of readers, and he wants both to describe Escalante and to convey his charisma and style. Mathews uses order of importance.

I noticed his hands first. His thick brown fingers swept the air when he lectured and ground chalk into the blackboard with an audible crack. He had a stocky build, a large square head with prominent jaw, and a widening bald spot covered with a few stray hairs, like a threadbare victory wreath on a Bolivian Caesar. He looked oddly like the school mascot, a gruff bulldog, and exuded a sense of mischief that made me and, I discovered later, many others want to keep a close eye on him.

Jay Mathews, *Escalante: The Best Teacher in America*

However, if Mathews were describing his subject for an audience who had to pick Escalante out in a crowd, he might have chosen spatial order (top to bottom) for his details and begun with the "widening bald spot covered with a few stray hairs." And if he wanted to relate how Escalante's students changed from hating math to liking it and winning scholarships, a natural order would have been chronological.

Often your material suggests a natural order, but you have choices, too. Decide what you want your writing to *do*, and create a sensible order to guide your readers smoothly through your ideas.

EXERCISE 6 Arranging the Order of Details

Like most people, you probably spend about one third of your time in your bedroom. First, brainstorm and list details of this familiar place. Next, arrange these details for a paragraph describing your room to someone who has never seen it. What order best does that job? Then, reorder your details for a paragraph telling how you clean up your room (or how you *would* if you did). What order did you use? Last, write both paragraphs.

Using Charts

Charts offer a visual way to group and arrange information and ideas, allowing you to display several pieces of information at once and map their relationships. Here's a chart one writer developed for a paper on the creative accomplishments of the Harlem Renaissance, a period of great artistic activity in America during the 1920s and 1930s. Notice that the chart has both horizontal and vertical headings.

HERE'S HOW

ART FORMS	REPRESENTATIVE ARTISTS	EXAMPLES OF WORK
Music	W. C. Handy	"St. Louis Blues" "Beale Street Blues"
	Fats Waller	"Honeysuckle Rose" "Ain't Misbehavin' "
Literature	Claude McKay	<u>Harlem Shadows</u> (poems) <u>Home to Harlem</u> (novel)
	Jean Toomer	<u>Cane</u> (poetic novel)
	Countee Cullen	<u>Color</u> (poems) <u>Copper Sun</u> (poems)
	Langston Hughes	<u>The Weary Blues</u> (poems) <u>Not Without Laughter</u> (novel)
Theater	Nobel Sissle and Eubie Blake	<u>Shuffle Along</u>
	Paul Robeson	roles in <u>Shuffle Along</u>, <u>All God's Chillun Got Wings</u>, and <u>The Emperor Jones</u>

l Robeson

Countee Cullen

Langston Hughes

Fats Waller

A paper answering the question "What factors helped to nurture the Harlem Renaissance?" might have used a fishbone chart showing causes and results.

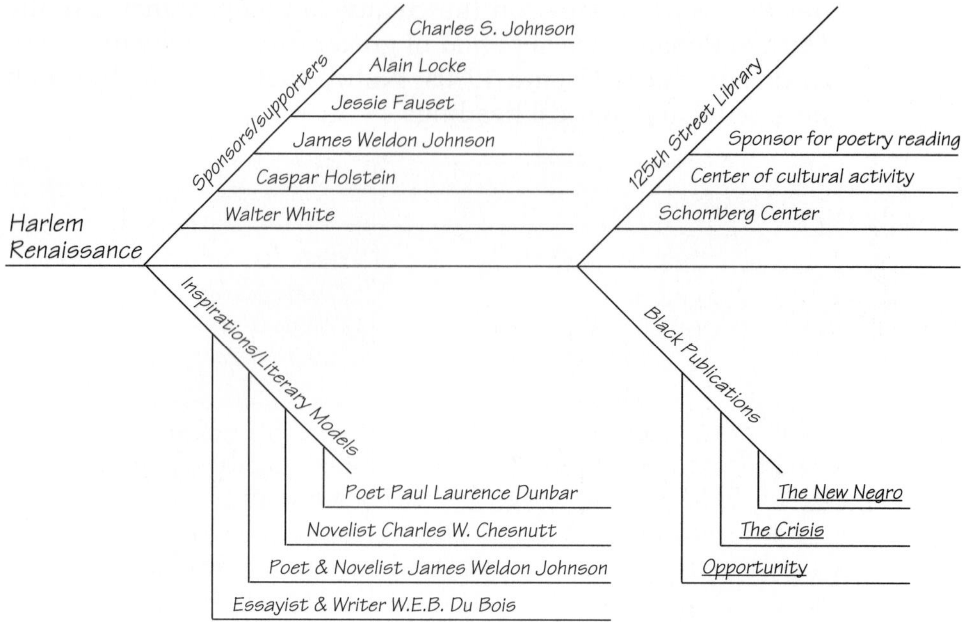

CRITICAL THINKING

Classifying Information

For many types of charts, you group together ideas or details that are similar in some way: you ***classify*** your information. The following questions are useful when you attempt to classify material.

- Which items have something in common? What heading describes this common trait?
- Are any items subdivisions of other items? Which ones?
- Are any items left over? Should a new heading be created for them? Should they be discarded?

CRITICAL THINKING EXERCISE: **Classifying Information**

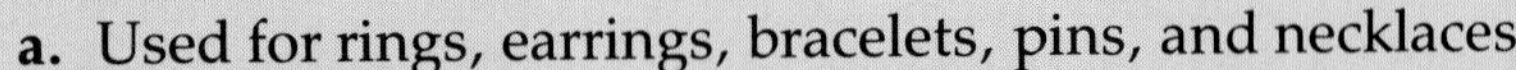

Read these notes for a paper on diamonds, looking for similarities among the items. Then answer the questions that follow.

- **a.** Used for rings, earrings, bracelets, pins, and necklaces
- **b.** Hardest material found in the natural world
- **c.** Most diamonds sold at monthly "sights"
- **d.** Koh-i-noor diamond once possessed by Indian and Persian rulers; now one of England's crown jewels
- **e.** Top mining nations: Australia, Botswana, the former Soviet Union, Zaire
- **f.** Doctors use diamond-edged knives during surgery
- **g.** Found in meteorites from space
- **h.** Minerals formed from carbon within igneous rock
- **i.** Found in subsurface rock formations called "pipes"
- **j.** Hope Diamond: world's largest blue diamond on view in Washington, D.C., at Smithsonian Institution
- **k.** Jewelers use diamonds to cut other gem stones
- **l.** Uncut stones used in automobile and airplane manufacturing and electronics
- **m.** Found in river gravel and coastal sand dunes
- **n.** Most form about 100 miles beneath the earth's surface
- **o.** Cullinan Diamond largest single rough diamond ever found: 1905, in South Africa; weighed 3,106 carats
- **p.** Diamond-studded rotary bits used to drill oil wells and bore tunnels in solid rock

1. One obvious heading for items in the list is *Uses.* Which items fall under this heading?
2. Decide on at least two other classifications for items in the list, and create a simple three-column chart that includes your headings as well as *Uses.*
3. *Uses* can include other classifications, or subheadings. What are they? Rearrange, or rechart, the *Uses* column to show the new subgroupings and their items visually.
4. Compare your charting with other students' work. Did you use the same classifications? Are your charts visually alike or different? What, if any, items did not fit into your classifications?

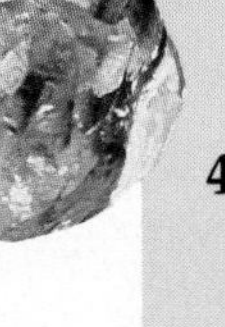

Writing a First Draft

A first draft is simply a way to get your thoughts down on paper. Professional writers usually write several drafts; they add new ideas, delete weak details, rearrange information, and improve wording until they are satisfied with their work.

As you write your first draft, keep these thoughts in mind.

- Follow your prewriting plan, but don't hesitate to include additional thoughts or details that occur to you.
- Write freely, but try to present your ideas clearly.
- Don't overedit. You can evaluate, revise, and proofread later.

Here is a draft of a short paper about genealogy.

The British royal family can trace its ancestors back through fifty generations and nearly twelve hundred years. Genealogists warn that it is almost impossible for most people to track down their family histories very far. They also say that each generation's number of direct ancestors--parents, grandparents, great-grandparents, and so on--doubles. And think about when relatives have remarried and started a second set of kids. Over a time span of thirty generations, everyone has more than one billion ancestors. [check number] It can get complicated!

If you are going to take on the job of tracing your inheritance [right word?], genealogists suggest~~s~~ that you begin with public records. ~~This~~ These can be birth, death, and marriage registrations. You can also obtain what you need to know from census returns, wills, and parish registers. [something else?] A great deal of family history can usually be uncovered just by talking with older people.

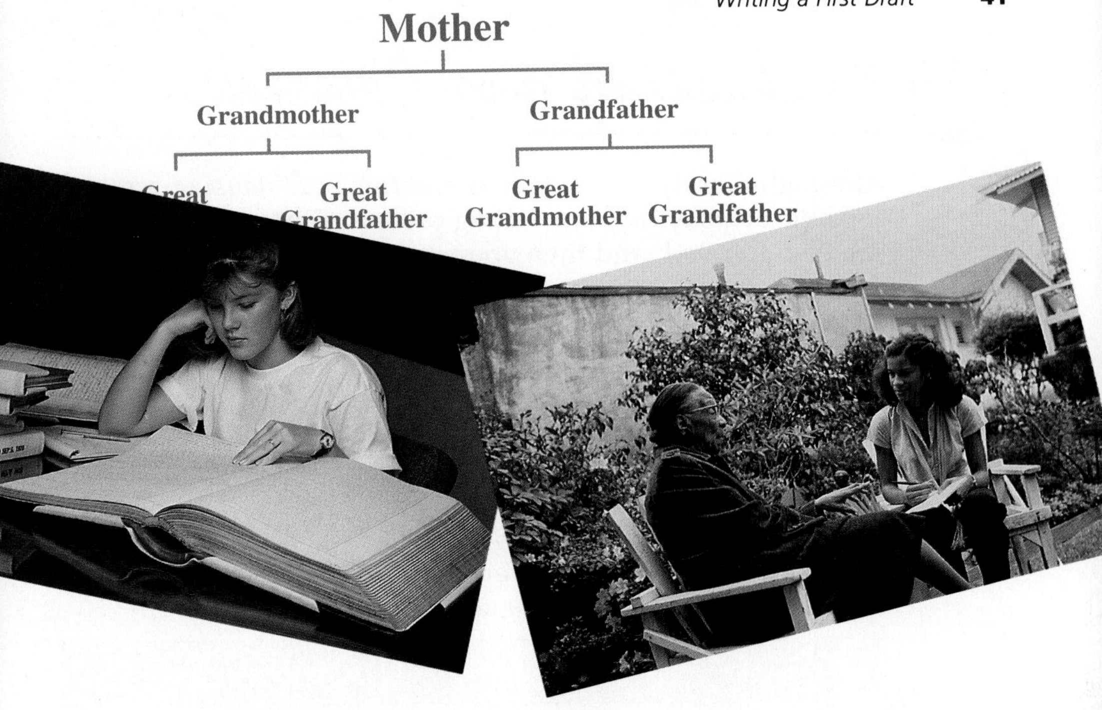

EXERCISE 7 **Writing a First Draft**

Using the following prewriting notes, write another paragraph concerning genealogy, adding or dropping details as needed. Arrange the information and then start drafting.

Before written records many peoples kept track of ancestry through oral history

In Africa some Gambian tribes have *griots*—old men who memorize centuries of clan histories

Oral family histories fostered family pride, established inheritance claims

Longest oral history known (seventy generations) told by Indonesian living on an island off coast of Sumatra

Ancient Scandinavians, Irish, Scots, and Welsh kept oral histories (bards or storytellers)

Some African, Indonesian, and Pacific Island tribes still use oral history

Late 1960s, Alex Haley (*Roots*) traced his African ancestry to 1700s—used *griot*

Recently a Polynesian chieftain recited 34-generation history, proving claim to a piece of territory—took three days!

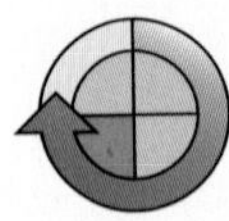

Evaluating and Revising

Although closely connected, ***evaluating*** and ***revising*** are two separate steps within the writing process. First you judge what can be improved, and then you execute needed changes.

Evaluating

Since evaluating your writing is one of the most important steps in the writing process, don't allow yourself to cut corners. To evaluate, you must look critically at what you have written. Are you saying what you mean to say? Will your audience understand it? Will it accomplish your purpose?

Self-Evaluation. It's never easy to evaluate your own work objectively, but the following techniques will help.

TIPS FOR SELF-EVALUATION

1. **Reading Carefully.** Read your draft several times, with a different purpose in mind each time. Read first for ***content*** (what is said), then for ***organization*** (arrangement of ideas), and finally for ***style*** (the way you use words and sentences).
2. **Listening Carefully.** Read your paper aloud, listening for confusing statements and awkward wording. Besides forcing you to slow down and pay attention to each word, reading aloud gives you a good sense of your paper's flow, its movement from sentence to sentence and idea to idea.
3. **Taking Time.** Gain some distance from your writing by setting it aside for awhile and going back to it later. This will help you see it fresh, and you will be more objective.

Peer Evaluation. It's often helpful to have a classmate or a group of peers read your draft and comment on it; others may see strengths and weaknesses in your writing that you miss. In peer evaluation, you benefit both from receiving evaluations of your work and from evaluating the work of others. The following guidelines will help you in both roles.

PEER-EVALUATION GUIDELINES

Guidelines for the Writer

1. Tell your evaluator your concerns. Where do you think you need the most help?
2. Accept the evaluator's comments gracefully, without becoming defensive or argumentative.

Guidelines for the Evaluator

1. Point out strengths as well as weaknesses.
2. Offer specific, positive solutions to the problems you identify. A criticism without a suggestion for a remedy may leave a writer feeling lost.
3. Be sensitive to the writer's feelings. It's true that it's not *what* you say as much as *how* you say it.
4. Focus your comments on content, organization, and style. Because proofreading comes later, ignore mechanical errors, such as spelling and punctuation, unless they interfere with your understanding.

LUANN reprinted with special permission of North America Syndicate, Inc.

Revising

Every problem you have uncovered in the evaluation stage can be corrected by applying one or more of four basic revising techniques: **add, cut, replace,** and **reorder.** This simplicity is good to keep in mind, because revision—let's be honest—is a tough part of writing for many people.

The following chart gives you some overall guidelines for evaluating and revising your writing using the four revision techniques. Other chapters will supply charts for particular types of writing.

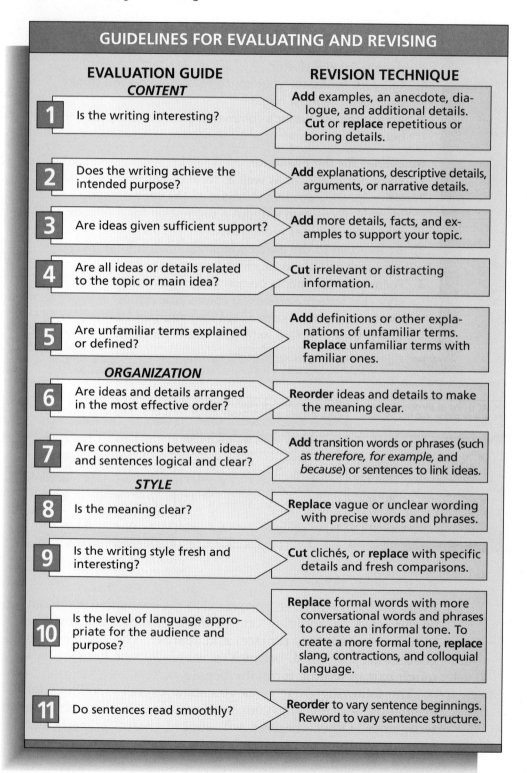

GUIDELINES FOR EVALUATING AND REVISING

	EVALUATION GUIDE	REVISION TECHNIQUE
	CONTENT	
1	Is the writing interesting?	**Add** examples, an anecdote, dialogue, and additional details. **Cut** or **replace** repetitious or boring details.
2	Does the writing achieve the intended purpose?	**Add** explanations, descriptive details, arguments, or narrative details.
3	Are ideas given sufficient support?	**Add** more details, facts, and examples to support your topic.
4	Are all ideas or details related to the topic or main idea?	**Cut** irrelevant or distracting information.
5	Are unfamiliar terms explained or defined?	**Add** definitions or other explanations of unfamiliar terms. **Replace** unfamiliar terms with familiar ones.
	ORGANIZATION	
6	Are ideas and details arranged in the most effective order?	**Reorder** ideas and details to make the meaning clear.
7	Are connections between ideas and sentences logical and clear?	**Add** transition words or phrases (such as *therefore, for example,* and *because*) or sentences to link ideas.
	STYLE	
8	Is the meaning clear?	**Replace** vague or unclear wording with precise words and phrases.
9	Is the writing style fresh and interesting?	**Cut** clichés, or **replace** with specific details and fresh comparisons.
10	Is the level of language appropriate for the audience and purpose?	**Replace** formal words with more conversational words and phrases to create an informal tone. To create a more formal tone, **replace** slang, contractions, and colloquial language.
11	Do sentences read smoothly?	**Reorder** to vary sentence beginnings. Reword to vary sentence structure.

The following paragraphs on genealogy illustrate the use of all four revision techniques. You may want to check the chart of Symbols for Revising and Proofreading on page 52 to understand the changes. Notice that the questions noted in the first draft (page 40) are answered here.

Draft	Technique
Although The British royal family can trace its	**add**
ancestors back through fifty-three	
generations and fifteen hundred years, ;	**replace**
Genealogists warn that it is almost im-	
possible for most people to track down their	
family histories ~~very far~~ much past three or four generations. They also say that	**replace**
each generation's number of direct	
ancestors--parents, grandparents, great-	
grandparents, and so on--doubles. ~~And~~	**cut**
~~think about~~ This is especially true when relatives have remarried	**replace/reorder**
and started a second set of ~~kids~~ children. Over a ~~time~~	**replace/cut**
span of thirty generations, everyone has	
more than ~~one~~ two billion ancestors. ~~[check~~	**replace/cut**
~~number] It can get complicated!~~	
If you are ~~going to take on the job of~~ planning to	**replace**
~~tracing~~ trace your ~~inheritance [right word?]~~ ancestry,	**replace**
genealogists ~~suggests~~ suggest that you begin with	
public records. ~~This~~ These can be birth, death,	
and marriage registrations. You can also	
obtain what you need to know from census	
returns, wills, parish registers, and military records.	**reorder/add**
~~[something else?]~~ A great deal of family	**cut**
history can usually be uncovered just by	
talking with older ~~people~~ members of your family.	**replace**

CRITICAL THINKING

Evaluating Writing

Evaluating is one stage in the writing process, and it is also an extremely important critical thinking skill. When you **evaluate,** you assess, appraise, or make a judgment about the value of something by applying a set of criteria or standards. You use this skill whether you are buying a car (criteria might include cost and condition) or deciding what to read (criteria would include readability, clarity, and interest).

How does evaluating apply to your own writing process? If what you write doesn't meet readers' criteria, you won't have readers. To keep from losing your audience, you have to apply readers' criteria to your own writing and make any changes necessary to meet them. You can find criteria in the chart on page 44 or in the individual chapters in this book.

CRITICAL THINKING EXERCISE:

Evaluating and Revising a Paragraph

Evaluate the following paragraph to see if it meets readers' criteria for interest and clarity. With a partner or small group, apply the specific criteria in the chart on page 44. After evaluating, try revising the paragraph and then compare your revision with that of another team.

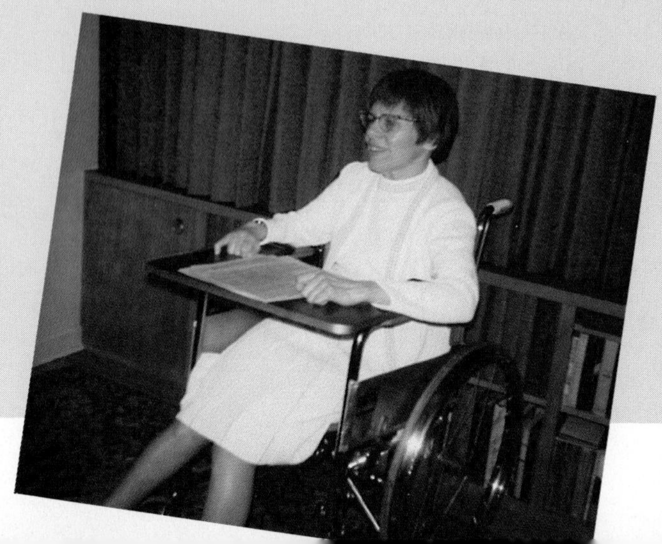

Where there's a will, there's a way is the motto for Phyllis Stearner's life. Phyllis wanted to play in her high school band even though she did not have full use of her right hand. She was born with cerebral palsy in 1919. She talked to the band leader. She soon was happily playing the trombone. It doesn't need right finger movement. Another time, she learned that state money was available to her for training after high school. But not for college. She talked to state officials and changed their minds. Ultimately she earned a Ph.D. in zoology, her first step toward becoming an internationally known radiation biologist. Phyllis also used her problem-solving abilities in college. She asked her father, a Scandinavian immigrant who worked as a carpenter, for driving lessons. She made it to class on time by driving between buildings and using a special parking permit.

Proofreading and Publishing

Proofreading

A writer who is at the proofreading stage is like a skilled worker who has to make a final check for mistakes and surface blemishes—a scratch in the paint of a car, a nick in the wood of a desk. For your final writing check, you're looking for any errors in grammar, usage, and mechanics (spelling, capitalization, and punctuation). Again, putting your paper aside for a while is a help. When you come back to it, you'll be able to see your mistakes more clearly. Here are other useful techniques.

- To focus on one line at a time, use a sheet of paper to cover all the lines below the one you are proofreading. Also try beginning at the bottom line and working your way to the top.
- Because it's easier (and more pleasant!) to catch someone else's errors, exchange papers with a classmate.
- Don't take the easy way out: look up any words or information you are unsure of. Use a college dictionary for spelling and a handbook like the one on pages 596–989 for grammar, usage, capitalization, and punctuation.
- Mark changes by using the revising and proofreading symbols on page 52.

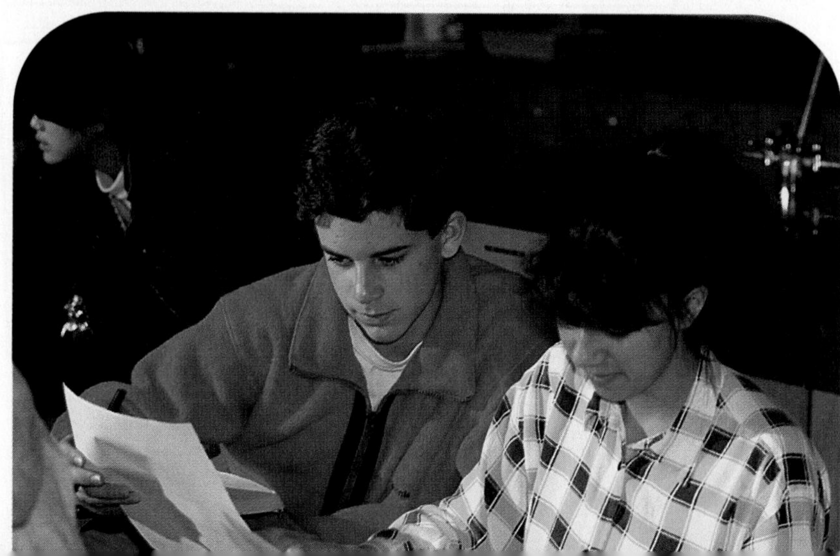

The following guidelines will refresh your memory about the types of errors you are trying to catch. You can use them as a guide to proofreading most types of school writing.

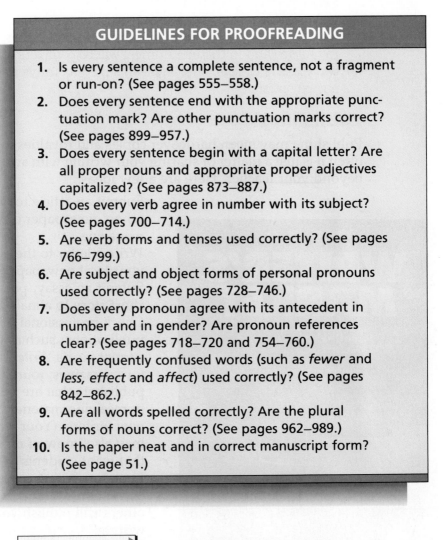

GUIDELINES FOR PROOFREADING

1. Is every sentence a complete sentence, not a fragment or run-on? (See pages 555–558.)
2. Does every sentence end with the appropriate punctuation mark? Are other punctuation marks correct? (See pages 899–957.)
3. Does every sentence begin with a capital letter? Are all proper nouns and appropriate proper adjectives capitalized? (See pages 873–887.)
4. Does every verb agree in number with its subject? (See pages 700–714.)
5. Are verb forms and tenses used correctly? (See pages 766–799.)
6. Are subject and object forms of personal pronouns used correctly? (See pages 728–746.)
7. Does every pronoun agree with its antecedent in number and in gender? Are pronoun references clear? (See pages 718–720 and 754–760.)
8. Are frequently confused words (such as *fewer* and *less, effect* and *affect*) used correctly? (See pages 842–862.)
9. Are all words spelled correctly? Are the plural forms of nouns correct? (See pages 962–989.)
10. Is the paper neat and in correct manuscript form? (See page 51.)

EXERCISE 8 Proofreading a Paragraph

Try to find all ten grammar, usage, spelling, and mechanics errors in the following paragraph. Use the handbook at the back of this book and a college dictionary to identify errors and make corrections.

Many high school students find it real hard to choose a college major. This problem should not have no affect on a student's decision to attend college, however. Tanya and her teacher, Mrs. Jackson, discussed her feelings about Junior College. Tanya said, "My parents and me agree that this would be a good way to save on tuition while I contemplate my future and in the meantime, I will be completing my first two years of college. Mrs. Jackson said that Tanya had chose a good option.

Publishing

Publishing may mean hardcover copies and royalties, but more often it is just a matter of sharing your writing with an audience beyond your teacher. Here are a few ideas.

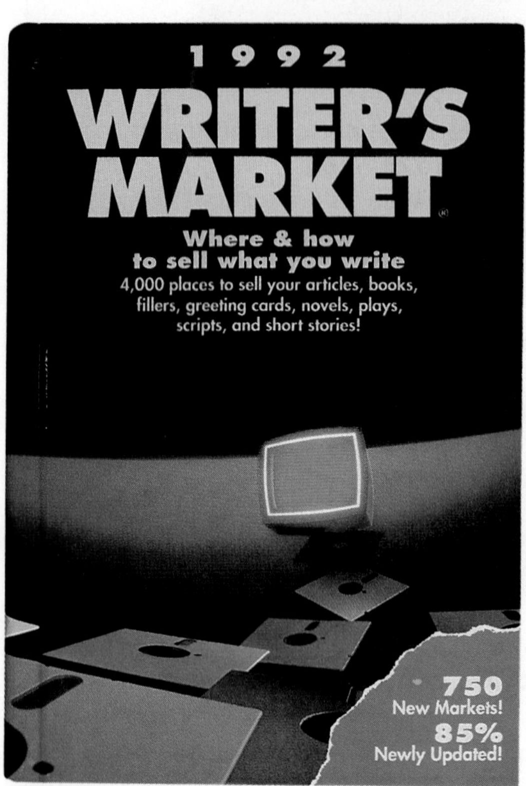

- Submit an article to your school newspaper or magazine.
- Write a letter to the editor of your local newspaper.
- Submit an essay, poem, or short story to a magazine. Check professional writers' publications, such as the current year's *Writer's Market*, for magazines, journals, and publishers that are interested in receiving material from new writers. (Your teacher may also know of magazines that want students' work.)
- Look for writing contests to enter. Some offer prizes; others will publish your writing.
- Mail an essay on a contemporary subject to local, state, or federal governmental representatives.
- Organize an issue forum, presenting class essays in the form of speeches.

As you make a final copy of your paper for publication, follow these guidelines for a clean, professional look.

GUIDELINES FOR MANUSCRIPT FORM

1. Use only one side of a sheet of paper.
2. Write in blue or black ink, or type.
3. If you write, do not skip lines. If you type, double-space the lines.
4. Leave margins of about one inch at the top, sides, and bottom of a page.
5. Indent the first line of each paragraph.
6. Number all pages (except the first page) in the upper right-hand corner, about one-half inch from the top.
7. All pages should be neat and legible. You may make a few corrections with correction fluid, but they should be barely noticeable.
8. Follow your teacher's instructions for placement of your name, the date, your class, and the title of your paper.

EXERCISE 9 Publishing Your Writing

With your classmates, brainstorm for other publishing ideas. Work in teams to follow up on each suggestion. For example, find and list names and addresses of potential publishers, types of materials accepted, manuscript requirements, deadlines, and payments or awards. As you compile information, work with a computer programming class or experienced programmers in your class to create a database for students seeking publishing information.

SYMBOLS FOR REVISING AND PROOFREADING

SYMBOL	EXAMPLE	MEANING OF SYMBOL
(cap) ≡	805 Linden avenue	Capitalize a lowercase letter.
(lc) /	the First of May	Lowercase a capital letter.
∧	one of my friends	Insert a missing word, letter, or punctuation mark.
∧	appear	Change a letter.
∧	in at the beginning	Replace a word.
	Give me a a number	Leave out a word, letter, or punctuation mark.
	a misstake	Leave out and close up.
	a touch down	Close up space.
	beleive	Change the order of letters.
(tr)	He walked slowly forward.	Transfer the circled words. (Write *(tr)* in nearby margin.)
¶	¶"Yes," she answered.	Begin a new paragraph.
⊙	Follow me⊙	Add a period.
∧ ,	Oh, not now!	Add a comma.
#	upper atmosphere	Add a space.
(:)	the following items(:)	Add a colon.
∧ ;	Columbus, Ohio; Orlando, Florida; and Seattle, Washington	Add a semicolon.
=	one=third portion	Add a hyphen.
∨ '	Juan's idea	Add an apostrophe.
(stet)	A faster method	Keep the crossed-out material. (Write *(stet)* in nearby margin.)

MAKING CONNECTIONS

EXPLORING THE WRITING PROCESS

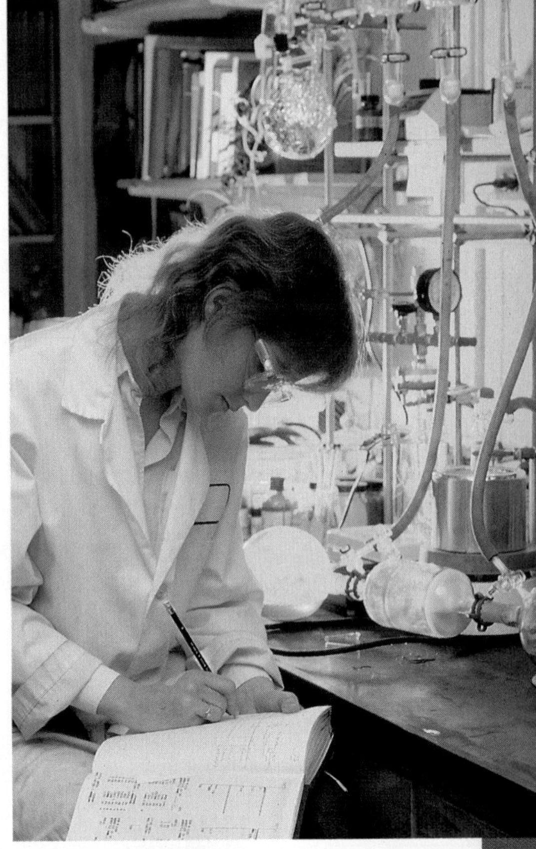

What would you like to be doing five or ten years from now? Will you be writing? You may be surprised at the answer! Professional writers and editors are not the only ones who spend the majority of their day composing. One research scientist estimates that he spends 30 percent of his time doing experiments and 70 percent writing letters, grant proposals, reports, and articles.

To explore the importance of writing, find someone working in a profession you're considering. Ask him or her the questions that follow. Take notes on the answers, and share your findings with classmates. Is there writing in your future?

What types of writing do you do?
Do you make lists? write memos?
Do you take notes in meetings? while you're on the telephone?
Do you write up proposals? estimates? bills? receipts? diagnoses? summaries? reports? messages?
What writing technique that you learned in school or have developed is most helpful to you now?

IMITATING A WRITING STYLE

Now used extensively by mystery, adventure, and soap opera writers for television, the cliffhanger has a long literary tradition. In the nineteenth century Charles Dickens's novels were originally serialized in weekly magazines. To make sure his readers bought the next installment, Dickens often ended with a cliffhanger, a scene that broke off in the middle of the action and left his readers wondering "What happens next?"

The following passage ends an original episode of *Great Expectations*. The story's young narrator, Pip, is sitting in fear and trembling at Christmas dinner. Earlier he had stolen a pork pie and delivered it to an escaped convict who threatened him direly. Pip is terrified of the convict, full of guilt over his theft, and sure he is "gone" as soon as his horribly strict older sister discovers she has no pie to serve her guests.

My sister went out to get it. I heard her steps proceed to the pantry. I saw Mr. Pumblechook balance his knife. I saw re-awakening appetite in the Roman nostrils of Mr. Wopsle. I heard Mr. Hubble remark that "a bit of savoury pork pie would lay atop of anything you could mention, and do no harm," and I heard Joe say, "You shall have some, Pip." I have never been absolutely certain whether I uttered a shrill yell of terror, merely in spirit, or in the bodily hearing of the company. I felt that I could bear no more, and that I must run away. I released the leg of the table, and ran for my life.

> But I ran no further than the house door, for there I ran head foremost into a party of soldiers with their muskets; one of whom held out a pair of handcuffs to me, saying, "Here you are, look sharp, come on!"
>
> Charles Dickens, from *Great Expectations*

You've held your breath during dozens, maybe hundreds, of books and movies, so you should be able to create your own cliffhanger. Here's the situation:

> Ignatius M. Goode—computer whiz, non-nerd, and nice guy—is standing at the corner, waiting for the annual Swine Time parade to pass. He must cross the street and get to the police station. Hidden in his cap is a letter with absolute proof that Daemon Fry—computer whiz, athlete, and sicko—infected Lowe High School's computers with the electronic virus that changed, in the school's official records, the gender, grades, and eye color of every graduating senior.
>
> To I. M.'s right: from a block away Daemon (who knows good-guy Goode has the letter) trotting toward him through the parade. At his back: parade watchers, ten bodies deep. To his left down the hill: the riverfront, where the parade ends and floats are piling up. Straight ahead of him: the King and Queen of Pork, waving from their float. Around the float: all of the town's first-graders, dressed as piglets, bacon slices, and corn dogs.

It's your turn. Write, with others if you want, an edge-of-your-seat cliffhanger for I. M. Goode. What does he do? What unpredictable event happens (predictable is forbidden)? What *don't* readers know when the scene ends?

2 UNDERSTANDING PARAGRAPH STRUCTURE

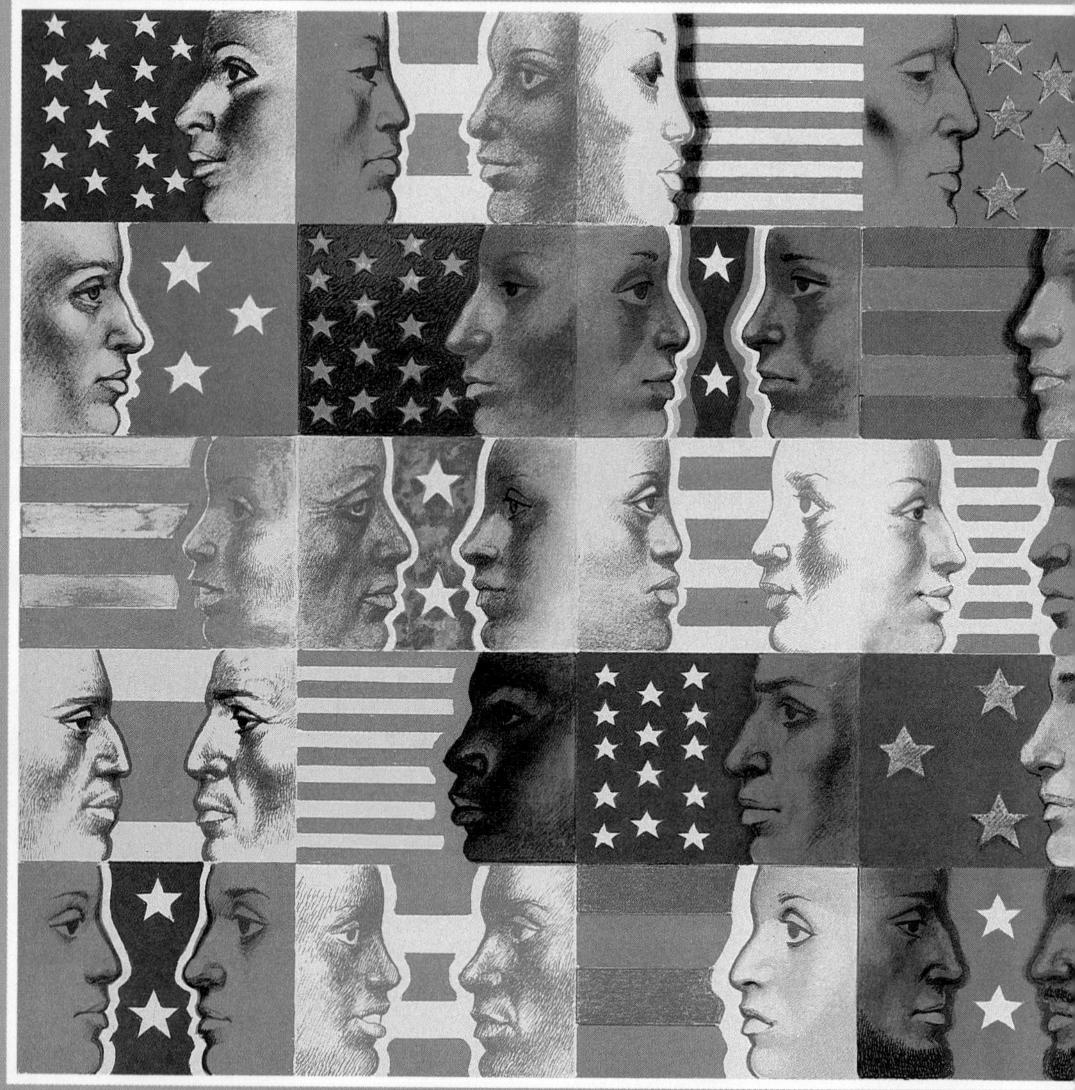

Looking at the Parts

You wouldn't look for paragraphs in most poems, plays, or song lyrics. However, you will find them in almost every other kind of writing—ads, articles, books, short stories, lab reports. They are the **parts** that make up the whole.

Writing and You. Paragraphs are difficult to define because they come in so many shapes and sizes. A paragraph may be as short as a single word or as long as many pages. It may be structured around a main idea, provide a transition from one idea to the next, or show emphasis. A paragraph may stand alone or may be part of a long, unified piece of writing that has been divided to make it easier to read. How do you use paragraphs?

As You Read. In the following selection, notice how the writer uses paragraphs to organize and relate her ideas about being an African American.

Colleen Browning, *Union Mixer* (1976). Lithograph, 20" × 33". Courtesy of ACA Galleries, NY.

from

how it feels to be colored me

by Zora Neale Hurston

But I am not tragically colored. There is no great sorrow dammed up in my soul, nor lurking behind my eyes. I do not mind at all. I do not belong to the sobbing school of Negrohood who hold that nature somehow has given them a low-down dirty deal and whose feelings are all hurt about it. Even in the helter-skelter skirmish that is my life, I have seen that the world is to the strong regardless of a little pigmentation more or less. No, I do not weep at the world—I am too busy sharpening my oyster knife.

Someone is always at my elbow reminding me that I am the granddaughter of slaves. It fails to register depression with me. Slavery is sixty years in the past. The operation was successful and the patient is doing well, thank you. The terrible struggle that made me an American out of a potential slave said "On the line!" The Reconstruction said "Get set!"; and the generation before said "Go!" I am off to a flying start and I must not halt in the stretch to look behind and weep. Slavery

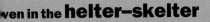

ven in the **helter–skelter** **skirmish** that is my life, have seen that the world is o the **strong** regardless of little **pigmentation. . . .**"

is the price I paid for civilization, and the choice was not with me. It is a bully adventure and worth all that I have paid through my ancestors for it. No one on earth ever had a greater chance for glory. The world to be won and nothing to be lost. It is thrilling to think—to know that for any act of mine, I shall get twice as much praise or twice as much blame. It is quite exciting to hold the center of the national stage, with the spectators not knowing whether to laugh or to weep.

The position of my white neighbor is much more difficult. No brown specter pulls up a chair beside me when I sit down to eat. No dark ghost thrusts its leg against mine in bed. The game of keeping what one has is never so exciting as the game of getting.

I do not always feel colored. Even now I often achieve the unconscious Zora of Eatonville before the Hegira. I feel most colored when I am thrown against a sharp white background.

For instance at Barnard. "Beside the waters of the Hudson" I feel my race. Among the thousand white persons, I am a dark rock surged upon, and overswept, but through it all, I remain myself. When covered by the waters, I am; and the ebb but reveals me again.

Sometimes it is the other way around. A white person is set down in our midst, but the contrast is just as sharp for me. For instance, when I sit in the drafty basement that is The New World Cabaret with a white person, my color comes. We enter chatting about any little nothing that we have in common and are seated by the jazz waiters. In the abrupt way that jazz orchestras have, this one plunges into a number. It loses no time in circumlocutions, but gets right down to business. It constricts the thorax and splits the heart with its tempo and narcotic harmonies. This orchestra grows rambunctious, rears on its hind legs and attacks the tonal veil with primitive fury, rending it, clawing it until it breaks through to the jungle beyond. I follow those heathen—follow them exultingly. I dance wildly inside myself; I yell within, I whoop; I shake my assegai [a light spear used by tribesmen in southern Africa] above my head, I hurl it true to the mark yeeeeooww! I am in the jungle and living in the jungle way. My face is painted red and yellow and my body is painted blue. My pulse is throbbing like a war drum. I want to slaughter something—give pain, give death to what, I do not know. But the piece ends. The men of the orchestra wipe their lips and rest their fingers. I creep back slowly to the veneer we call civilization with the last tone and find the white friend sitting motionless in his seat, smoking calmly.

"Good music they have here," he remarks, drumming the table with his fingertips.

Music. The great blobs of purple and red emotion have not touched him. He has only heard what I felt. He is far away and I see him but dimly across the ocean and the continent that have fallen between us. He is so pale with his whiteness then and I am *so* colored.

"The great blobs of purple and red emotion have not touched him. . . . He is so pale with his whiteness then and I am *so* colored."

Reader's Response

1. Hurston wrote this piece more than sixty years ago. Do you feel that music divides ethnic and racial groups today, or do you think it helps to unify them? Explain your answer in a short journal entry.
2. Hurston says that life since slavery "is a bully adventure and worth all that I have paid through my ancestors for it." How is this comment similar to or different from what you know or what you have heard about the black experience? Do you think that opportunities can grow out of hardships? How?

Writer's Craft

3. Paragraphs are often structured around a main idea. What is the main idea of Hurston's first paragraph? Does she state the main idea in a sentence, or does she just suggest it?
4. Hurston's paragraphs vary in length from one sentence to seventeen. Why does the length of her paragraphs vary so much? What does she accomplish in her longer paragraphs? in her shorter ones?

In this chapter, you will study some of the principles of form and structure in paragraphs. As you work through the chapter, keep in mind that

- an important use of paragraphs is to develop a main idea
- paragraphs have many uses
- the strategies of description, narration, classification, and evaluation are ways of developing paragraphs
- sensory details, facts and statistics, examples, and anecdotes are ways to support or prove the paragraph's main idea

The Uses of Paragraphs

A paragraph is usually defined as a group of sentences that develop a main idea. Sometimes, however, you will find brief paragraphs—perhaps just one sentence in length—that are used in a different way by sources such as newspapers, magazines, advertising copy, and instruction manuals. Here, for example, are eight short paragraphs that make up a magazine article. What do you think is the purpose of these paragraphs?

Dog Tales

What's good for the goose may be good for the gander . . . but it's not always good for an Australian shepherd.

"Ginger," owned by Bill and Helen Gerdes of Burlington, Iowa, spent a busy day roaming around the fields and meadows on the Gerdeses' farm.

To her surprise, when she returned to her doghouse at the end of the day, an uninvited tenant had moved in and claimed squatter's—err, setter's rights.

"A large African goose had moved in and made a nest out of the straw in the house," says Helen, "and she wasn't about to give in to the previous tenant.

"She not only made herself at home, she eventually laid eight eggs there.

"Ginger's been pretty cooperative and a little confused by all this. One day when the goose was out of the house, Ginger went in and laid on the eggs without disturbing them.

"Our other dog and our cat get curious enough to come close now and then, and the goose lets them know with no uncertainty that they're to stay away from her nest.

"But Ginger and the goose seem to have come to some sort of coexistent agreement that's working."

from *Country*

All but one of the paragraphs in "Dog Tales" have only one sentence each. These one-sentence paragraphs make the article attractive to readers; it looks easy to read. Short paragraphs can also call attention to an important point or provide a transition between the ideas in longer paragraphs. Reread the following paragraph from the opening selection.

> I do not always feel colored. Even now I often achieve the unconscious Zora of Eatonville before the Hegira. I feel most colored when I am thrown against a sharp white background.

This paragraph does not develop an idea: It provides a transition between the paragraphs that explain the advantages she sees in being colored and the paragraphs that explain how she is sometimes very conscious of her color.

EXERCISE 1 **Surveying the Uses of Paragraphs**

Work with a few classmates to survey the many different uses of paragraphs in the "real" world. Check ads, album or CD notes, letters, bulletins, and magazine articles. These might include popular "grocery store" magazines, as well as more thoughtful magazines such as *Smithsonian* and *Discover*. Make a list of the different uses, noting where you found each type. Share your results with other groups.

Paragraphs That Develop a Main Idea

Paragraphs in essays and other types of nonfiction often develop main ideas. Each of these paragraphs is a kind of "mini-composition": Each one usually—but not always—has a topic sentence and several supporting sentences.

It is important to remember that all of the paragraphs in this chapter were written as part of longer works. The paragraphs are taken out of context so that you can study their form and structure.

The Topic Sentence

A ***topic sentence,*** which specifically states the paragraph's main idea, is one of the many options writers have when they are creating paragraphs.

Location of a Topic Sentence. The topic sentence is often the first or second sentence of the paragraph, but you can find it in other parts of the paragraph as well. A topic sentence at the end of a paragraph may create surprise, or it may summarize or reinforce the main idea. In the following paragraph, the writer states her topic—that recognizing the "needs of the reader is often crucial to your success as a writer"—in the first sentence. She goes on to support that idea, the topic, with an extended example.

> The ability to adapt your knowledge to the needs of the reader is often crucial to your success as a writer. This is especially true in writing done on a job. For example, as producer of a public affairs program for a television station, eighty percent of your time may be taken up planning the details of new shows, contacting guests, and scheduling the taping sessions. But when you write a program proposal to the station director, your job is to show how the program will fit into the cost guidelines, the FCC requirements for relevance, and the overall programming plan for the station. When you write that report your role in the organization changes from producer to proposal writer. Why? Because your reader needs that information in order to make a decision. He may be *interested* in your scheduling problems and the specific content of the shows, but he *reads* your report because of his own needs as station director of that organization. He has to act.
>
> Linda Flower, *Problem-Solving Strategies for Writing*

Importance of a Topic Sentence. Many paragraphs don't have topic sentences at all. In some paragraphs, for example, the main idea is implied, or suggested, rather than directly stated. In still other paragraphs, a sequence of events or actions (rather than a topic sentence or implied main idea) keeps the paragraph focused.

Topic sentences are useful, however, even though they aren't required. Stating your main idea in a topic sentence can help you avoid straying from the topic when you are writing. A topic sentence also helps the reader; it focuses the main idea in the reader's mind.

EXERCISE 2 Identifying Main Ideas and Topic Sentences

Now, apply the explanation you have just read to three paragraphs. Each of the paragraphs has a main idea, but not all of them have a topic sentence. Using your own words, state the main idea of each paragraph. If the paragraph has a topic sentence, identify it. If it doesn't, write a sentence that states the topic. [Hint: You can state the main idea of a sequence of events or actions by giving a one-sentence summary of the events or actions.]

1. Sometimes a law is just on its face and unjust in its application. For instance, I have been arrested on a charge of parading without a permit. Now, there is nothing wrong in having an ordinance which requires a permit for a parade. But such an ordinance becomes unjust when it is used to maintain segregation and to deny citizens the First-Amendment privilege of peaceful assembly and protest.

   Martin Luther King, Jr., "Letter from Birmingham Jail"

Amendment 1
Congress shall make no law respecting an establishment of religion, or prohibiting the free exercise thereof; or abridging the freedom of speech, or of the press; or the right of the people peaceably to assemble, and to petition the government for a redress of grievances.

2. When she is touring, she is always surrounded by reporters, with all their questions. She says she prefers a quieter life, with more time for painting. She looks forward to having time to herself so that she can do things on her own, rather than having everything arranged for her. And, she says, she would like to see more of the countryside wherever she goes, to see animals, mountains, and fields.

Zheng Zhensun and Alice Low, *A Young Painter*

3. Tree stumps, floating debris, rocks, white water, swimmers, and other canoers can all be hazards on a river. You can't canoe responsibly without keeping a sharp eye out, but the feeling you get from moving silently through beauty is unequaled. The perspectives are new and always changing. And there's the feeling of being in the open air and sometimes sharing the adventure with like-minded friends. Canoeing requires vigilance, but the rewards far outweigh the effort it takes to do it safely.

Supporting Sentences

What is your reaction to these statements? Do you believe them?

> **Most of those huge ferocious dinosaurs weren't carnivores—they ate "veggies."**
> **American students' standardized test scores show that our educational system is on the decline.**
> **Americans are killing themselves with their forks.**

You probably want more details, in ***supporting sentences,*** before you decide whether or not the statements are responsible ones. Supporting sentences may consist of sensory details, facts and statistics, examples, or anecdotes. They are used to develop the main ideas found in topic sentences. You can develop a paragraph with one type of detail or with a combination of types.

Sensory Details

When you describe the sounds on a football field or the smell of hot popcorn, you are using ***sensory details.*** These are words that describe what you know through your five senses: sight, hearing, touch, taste, and smell. In the following paragraph, the writer uses the sense of hearing to describe singers preparing for a performance and the senses of sight and touch to describe her own preparations for a dance performance.

> They took no notice of me, but I couldn't do the same with them. I had never been so close to trained singers and the reverberations shook in my ears. I left the room and walked down the corridor to find my place in the wings. Sounds came out of each door I passed. One baritone roared like a wounded moose, another wailed like a freight train on a stormy night. The tenors yelped in high screeches. There were whines and growls and the siren of an engine on its way to a four-alarm fire. Grunts overlapped the high-pitched "ha ha ho ho's" and the total cacophony tickled me; I could have laughed outright. These exquisite singers who would soon stand on the stage delivering the most lovely and liquid tones had first to creak like rusty scissors and wail like banshees. I remembered that before I could lift my torso and allow my arms to wave as if suspended in water, I had to bend up and down, sticking my

> behind in the air, plié and relevé until my muscles ached, arch-roll and contract and release until my body begged for deliverance. The singers were not funny. They were working. Preparation is rarely easy and never beautiful. That was the first of many lessons *Porgy and Bess* taught me.
>
> Maya Angelou, *Singin' and swingin' and gettin' merry like Christmas*

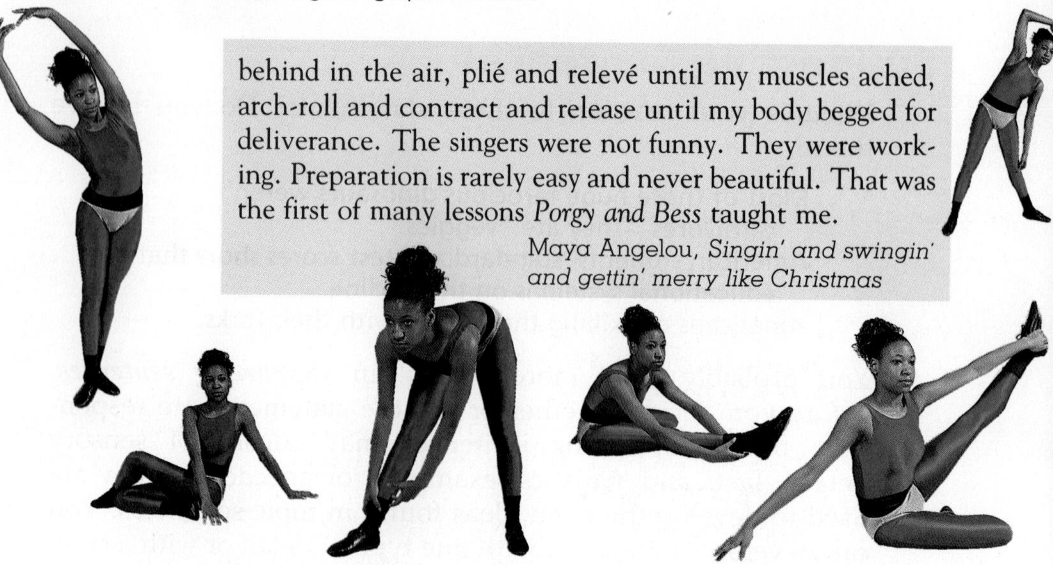

Facts and Statistics

The main idea of a paragraph can also be supported by *facts* and *statistics*. A ***fact*** is a statement that can be proved true by concrete information: *George Bush was president of the United States during the Persian Gulf Conflict*. A ***statistic*** is a fact based on numbers: *President Reagan received 54,455,075 votes in the 1984 presidential election*. You can check the accuracy of facts and statistics in reference sources. In the following paragraph, the author uses facts and statistics to describe the climate of the Sahara desert.

> The Sahara is hot because it is sunny. In Adrar out of some 4,400 hours of annual daylight there are 3,978 hours of direct sun, on average. (Paris, home of the great Saharan colonizers, gets 1,728 hours of sun.) Elsewhere in the desert the count is equally high. And this is steep-angle sunlight, powerful stuff. In the winter, air temperatures can drop to freezing at night and rise to 90 by noon; soil temperatures can fluctuate so brutally that rocks split, a process called insolation weathering. In the summer the Sahara is the hottest place on earth. The record, 136° Fahrenheit, is held by al Azizia, Libya. Airborne dust makes things worse. It traps heat radiated by the hot soil, and is why in Adrar the desert does not cool much on summer nights.
>
> William Langewiesche, "The World in Its Extreme"

Examples

Sometimes the best way to support a main idea is to give examples of it. ***Examples*** are specific instances or illustrations of a general idea. In the following paragraph, the writer gives examples of goal-oriented (but often boring) activities that face people.

> You probably have more experience in goal-oriented activity than you think. Didn't you read the boring driver's manual in order to pass the road test, or bring your grades up to qualify for a school team, or do that humdrum clerical work last summer to buy the stereo system you wanted? People sometimes put up with a lot in order to reach their goals. They memorize all sorts of facts for job advancement or a higher salary, they read complicated instruction booklets in order to find out how to operate certain machinery, and on and on. So when a teacher assigns a book to read, just think of it as good training for life and get on with the job.
>
> Joyce Vedral, *My Teacher Is Driving Me Crazy*

Anecdotes

When writers support a main idea by using an extended example or telling a little story, they are using ***anecdotes***. Notice how, in the following paragraph, the writer uses an anecdote to show that Mother was plucky and resolute.

> "Mother has always been the gamest one of us. I can remember her hanging on to the reins of a runaway mule team, her black hair tumbling out of its pins and over her shoulders, her face set and white, while one small girl clung with chattering teeth to the sides of the rocking wagon and a baby sister bounced about on the floor in paralyzed wonder. I remember, too, the things the men said about 'Leny's nerve.' But I think, as much courage as it took to hang on to the reins that day, it took more to live twenty-four hours at a time, month in and out, on the lonely and lovely prairie, without giving up to the loneliness."
>
> Joanna L. Stratton, *Pioneer Women: Voices from the Kansas Frontier*

EXERCISE 3 Identifying Supporting Details

Get together with two or three classmates and some magazines. Then have each person choose a different one of the following types of supporting details: sensory details, facts and statistics, examples, or anecdotes. Each of you should then look through the magazines to find at least two paragraphs that use the kind of supporting details you chose. When you have identified the paragraphs, share them within your group. Discuss what main idea was developed in each paragraph and why the writer selected a particular type of supporting detail.

The Clincher Sentence

A ***clincher sentence*** can be used at the end of a paragraph to wrap it up with a final thought, summarize supporting sentences, or draw a conclusion. In the following paragraph, Barry Lopez uses a clincher sentence to give a slightly different twist to the point he makes in his topic sentence, the first sentence of the paragraph.

> A Yup'ik hunter on Saint Lawrence Island once told me that what traditional Eskimos fear most about us is the extent of our power to alter the land, the scale of that power, and the fact that we can easily effect some of these changes electronically, from a distant city. Eskimos, who sometimes see themselves as still not quite separate from the animal world, regard us as a kind of people whose separation may have become too complete. They call us, with a mixture of incredulity and apprehension, "the people who change nature."
>
> Barry Lopez, "An Encounter on the Tundra"

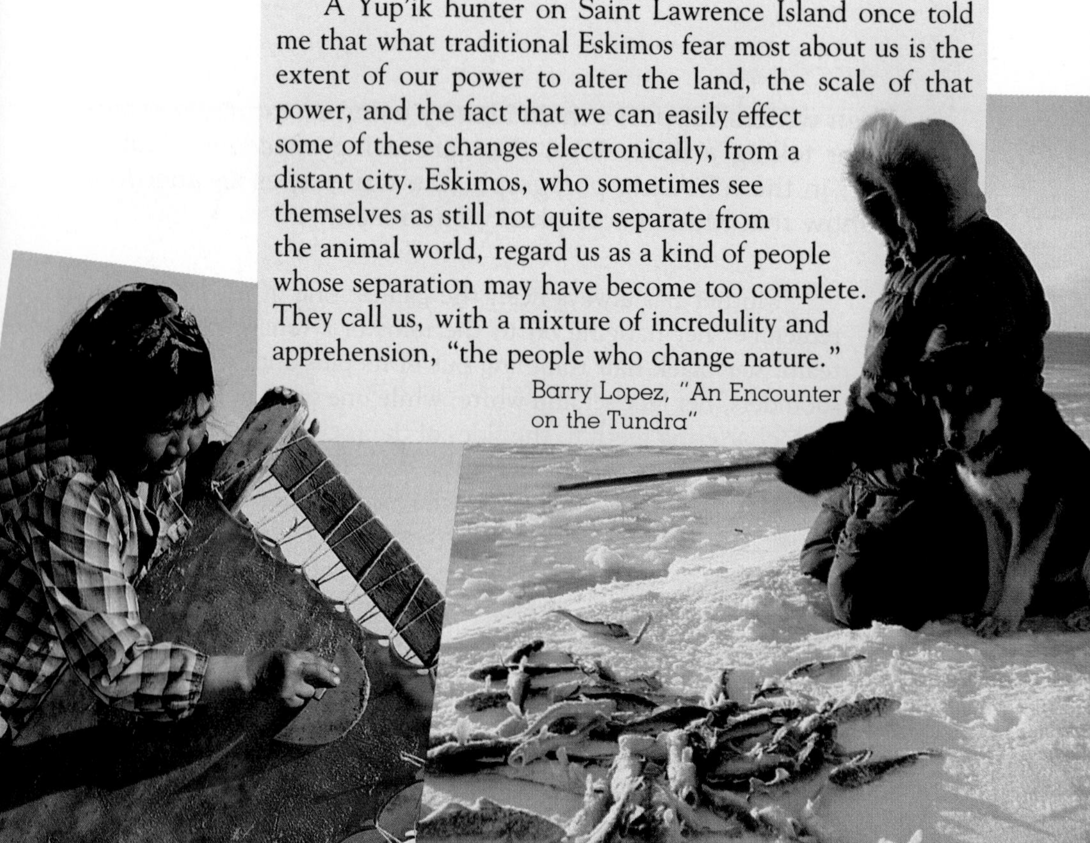

Unity

To be clear and effective, a paragraph must have ***unity:*** All of the sentences must relate to and develop one main idea. This need for unity exists whether the main idea is stated in a topic sentence, implied, or inherent in a sequence of events and actions.

All Sentences Relate to the Main Idea in the Topic Sentence. In the following paragraph, the first sentence states the main idea—that the silver wedding anniversary of the writer's parents was the high point of the years preceding World War II. Each of the remaining sentences provides details to show how grand the event was.

> If any single event climaxed those prewar years, it was, for me at least, the silver wedding anniversary we celebrated in 1940. Papa was elegant that day, in a brand-new double-breasted worsted suit, with vest and silk tie and stickpin. He was still the dude, always the dude, no matter what, spending more money on his clothes than on anything else. Mama wore a long, crocheted, rose-colored dress. And I see them standing by our round dining room table, this time heaped not with food but with silver gifts—flatware, tureens, platters, trays, gravy bowls, and brandy snifters. The food was spread along a much larger table, buffet style, in glistening abundance—chicken teriyaki, pickled vegetables, egg rolls, cucumber and abalone salad, the seaweed-wrapped rice balls called *sushi,* shrimp, prawns, fresh lobster, and finally, taking up what seemed like half the tablecloth, a great gleaming roast pig with a bright red apple in its mouth.
>
> Jeanne Wakatsuki Houston and
> James D. Houston, *Farewell to Manzanar*

All Sentences Relate to an Implied Main Idea. The following paragraph lacks a topic sentence, but all the sentences provide details about an implied main idea: overpopulation in Bombay, India.

> It is said that every day 1,500 more people, about 350 families, arrive in Bombay to live. They come mainly from the countryside and they have very little; and in Bombay

there isn't room for them. There is hardly room for the people already there. The older apartment blocks are full; the new skyscrapers are full; the small, low huts of the squatters' settlements on the airport road are packed tightly together. Bombay shows its overcrowding. It is built on an island, and its development has been haphazard. Outside the defense area at the southern tip of the island, open spaces are few; cramped living quarters and the heat drive people out into such public areas as exist, usually the streets; so that to be in Bombay is always to be in a crowd. By day the streets are clogged; at night the pavements are full of sleepers.

V. S. Naipaul, *India: A Wounded Civilization*

All Sentences Relate to a Sequence of Events. You won't find a topic sentence in the following paragraph, but you will find a main idea—the formation of the island of Bermuda. The paragraph has unity because all the sentences relate to the sequence of events involved in the formation of the island.

Millions of years ago, a volcano built a mountain on the floor of the Atlantic. In eruption after eruption, it pushed up a great pile of volcanic rock, until it had accumulated a mass a hundred miles across at its base, reaching upward toward the surface of the sea. Finally its cone emerged as an island with an area of about 200 square miles. Thousands of years passed, and thousands of thousands. Eventually the waves of the Atlantic cut down the cone and reduced it to a shoal—all of it, that is, but a small fragment which remained above water. This fragment we know as Bermuda.

Rachel L. Carson, *The Sea Around Us*

EXERCISE 4 Analyzing Notes for Unity

How much do you know about lightning? Here is a cluster diagram of notes for a paragraph with the topic sentence "Although all lightning has a common origin, it appears in many different forms." Get together with two or three classmates, and try to decide which of the notes in the diagram will work together to create a unified paragraph and which should be discarded.

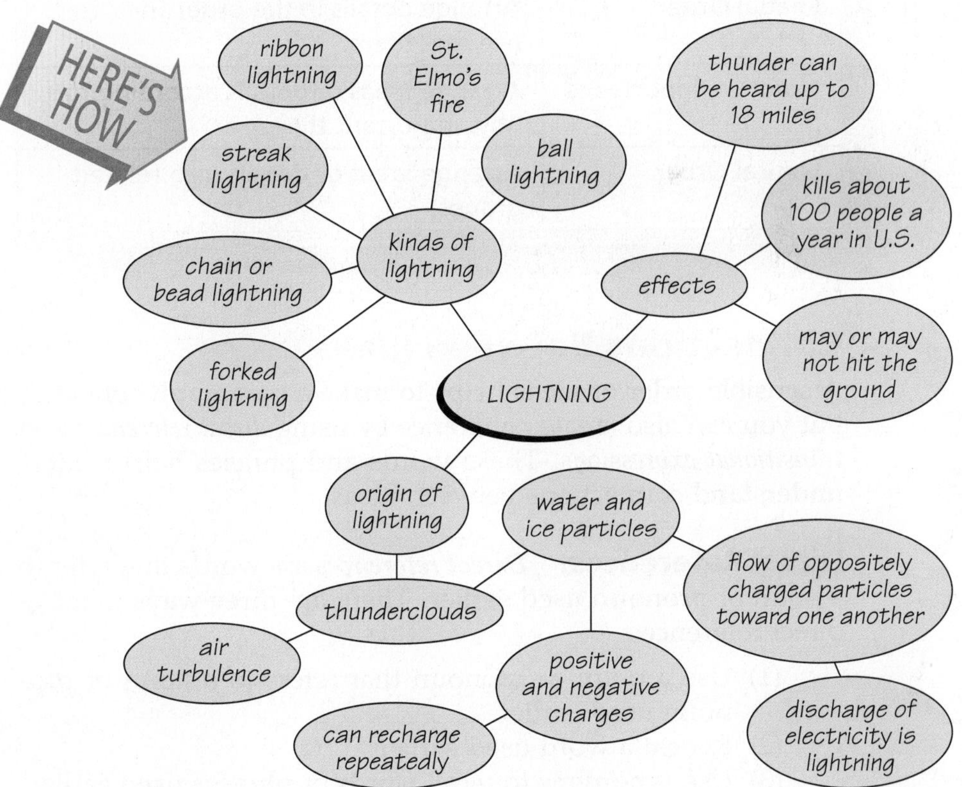

Coherence

Unity is one quality of a good paragraph; *coherence* is another. When a paragraph has ***coherence,*** the ideas are arranged in an order that makes sense, and the reader knows how the ideas are related to each other. Two things can help you to make paragraphs coherent: (1) the order you use to arrange ideas, and (2) the connections you make between ideas.

Order of Ideas

The chart below lists four basic ways of arranging ideas to make their relationships clear. You will learn more about how ideas can be organized in the section **Strategies of Development,** on pages 79–87.

WAYS OF ORDERING IDEAS	
Chronological Order	Arrange events in the order they happen.
Spatial Order	Arrange details in the order that the eye sees them.
Order of Importance	Arrange ideas or details according to how important they are.
Logical Order	Arrange ideas or details into related groups.

Connections Between Ideas

A sensible order of ideas helps to make a paragraph coherent, but you can also create coherence by using *direct references* and *transitional expressions.* These words and phrases help readers understand connections between ideas.

Direct References. ***Direct references*** are words that refer to a noun or pronoun used earlier. There are three ways to make direct references:

(1) Use a noun or pronoun that refers to a noun or pronoun used earlier.
(2) Repeat a word used earlier.
(3) Use synonyms to recall words or phrases used earlier.

The following paragraph has examples of the three types of direct references. Superscript numbers indicate which of the three types the writer is using.

> Juano Hernandez, born in Puerto Rico in 1896, was *one*[1] of the most highly regarded black *actors*[1] in the history of the movies. As a *young man*[1], *he*[1] worked in vaudeville and did other stage work that led to *acting*[1] on Broadway, where *he*[1] established a reputation as a fine *dramatic actor*[2]. *Hernandez*[2] was one of the first *black*[2] *thespians*[3] to be featured in *stage*[2] and *cinema*[3] roles. *His*[1] most famous *screen*[3] *portrayal*[3] is as the intended lynching victim in the 1949 *film*[3] *Intruder in the Dust. Hernandez*[2] read extensively, and spoke four languages fluently. *His*[1] aversion to the prejudice *he*[1] encountered in everyday life in the United States caused *him*[1] to keep his home in *Puerto Rico*[2] until his death in 1970.

Transitional Words and Phrases. Words and phrases that connect by showing transitions between ideas are called ***transitional expressions.*** They include prepositions that show chronological or spatial order and conjunctions that connect ideas and show relationships. The following chart lists some transitional expressions, grouped according to the relationships they usually indicate. The chart also shows the type of writing in which the expressions are likely to be used.

TRANSITIONAL WORDS AND PHRASES		
Comparing Ideas/Classification and Definition		
also	just	moreover
and	like	similarly
another	likewise	too
Contrasting Ideas/Classification and Definition		
although	in spite of	on the other hand
but	instead	still
however	nevertheless	yet
Showing Cause and Effect/Narration		
accordingly	consequently	so
as a result	for	so that
because	since	therefore
Showing Time/Narration		
after	finally	next
at last	first	then
at once	immediately	thereafter
before	lately	until
early	later	when
eventually	meanwhile	while
Showing Place/Description		
above	beside	inside
across	between	into
around	beyond	next
before	down	over
behind	here	there
below	in	under
Showing Importance/Evaluation		
first	mainly	then
last	more important	to begin with

Notice how the writer uses transitional words in the following paragraph to show how the ideas in his description are connected.

> Before 1980, when hearing-impaired people watched television, they missed out on the real enjoyment of it because they could not follow the dialogue. However, a technological advance in the late 1970s opened a way to transmit speech in subtitles to a television screen. Then, in 1980, the Federal Communications Commission required that thereafter, part of each television signal be reserved for the broadcast of closed captions. As a result, caption-decoding adapters for television sets immediately came on the market and made possible the viewing of written dialogue with any closed-captioned broadcast. Moreover, after July 1, 1993, closed-caption decoders will be built into all thirteen-inch or larger television sets made or sold in the United States. Although closed captioning was developed mainly to benefit the hearing impaired, those who are learning English as a new language find it similarly useful.

EXERCISE 5 Identifying Direct References and Transitional Expressions

Most paragraphs have coherence because writers use both direct references and transitional words and phrases. As you read through this paragraph, list as many of each as you can find.

Today Vincent van Gogh is one of the most appreciated artists who ever lived, but during his lifetime virtually no one even liked his art. When he was young, he didn't intend to be an artist, although between the ages of sixteen and twenty-three he worked in art galleries and studied art. Then, for the next four years, he studied for the ministry. At the end of the fourth year, van Gogh decided to devote his life to art. From then until his death ten years later, he produced more than fifteen hundred paintings and drawings. Unfortunately, he was able to sell only one during his lifetime. Eventually, people realized the importance of his art, and it has continued to increase in popularity and value.

Vincent van Gogh, "Self Portrait." Paris, Musée d'Orsay/Giraudon/Art Resource, New York.

Strategies of Development

Paragraphs are written for different purposes, and different purposes call for different strategies of development. There are four basic strategies writers use for developing paragraphs: description, narration, classification, and evaluation.

STRATEGIES OF DEVELOPMENT	
Description	Looking at individual features of a person, place, or thing
Narration	Looking at changes in a subject over a period of time
Classification	Looking at a subject in relation to other subjects
Evaluation	Looking at the subject's value

Description

What does your driver's license photo look like? How could you describe the place where you live so that someone else could recognize it?

When you describe someone or something, you use sensory details—details of hearing, sight, smell, taste, and touch—to create a verbal picture. Descriptions of places and objects are frequently organized by ***spatial order;*** in other words, the details are arranged by location in space. Descriptions of people are more likely to be organized in the ***order of importance,*** starting or ending with the detail the writer wants to emphasize.

> Miss Lottie's house was the most ramshackle of all our ramshackle homes. The sun and rain had long since faded its rickety frame siding from white to a sullen gray. The boards themselves seemed to remain upright not from being nailed together but rather from leaning together like a house that a child might have constructed from cards. A brisk wind might have blown it down, and the fact that it was still standing implied a kind of enchantment that was stronger than the elements. There it stood, and as far as I

> know is standing yet—a gray rotting thing with no porch, no shutters, no steps, set on a cramped lot with no grass, not even any weeds—a monument to decay.
>
> Eugenia W. Collier, "Marigolds"

EXERCISE 6 **Using Description as a Strategy**

Choose one of the following subjects and list at least five sensory details that you could use to describe it. Try to use as many different senses as possible. When you have finished your list, decide how you would arrange the details in a paragraph so that the description would be clear to a reader.

1. a summer night in your back yard
2. your school the minute you return after summer vacation
3. the last second of a tied championship basketball game
4. yourself—the first time you drove alone
5. a concert, dance, or jam session you attended

Narration

What happens when Romeo finds Juliet in the tomb? How does the water cycle work? What caused the United States to get involved in the Persian Gulf Conflict?

When you answer questions like these, you are using the strategy of ***narration*** to explain changes over time. Narration can take several forms. You can use it to tell a story (what happens to Romeo), explain a process (how the water cycle works), or explain causes and effects (U.S. involvement in the Persian Gulf Conflict). Writers often use ***chronological order,*** telling events or actions in the order they occur, to arrange the details in paragraphs that are developed through the strategy of narration.

Telling a Story. Whenever you tell a story—whether it's fiction or nonfiction—you use narration to tell about events and actions that occur over a period of time. In the following paragraph, the writer uses narration to tell the story of an encounter with a rattlesnake.

> When Bill was a teenager, he loved to read westerns. One of his favorites had a hero so tough, he'd even pick up a rattlesnake by the tail and snap its head off by cracking it like a whip. Bill was fascinated by the concept—he read the book over and over, and then went to find a rattlesnake. He found one sunning itself on a rock, grabbed it by the tail, and raised his arm in a whip-snapping gesture. The snake, much heavier and wilier than anticipated, had other plans. It twisted to face Bill, and began wrapping itself around his arm. The book hadn't mentioned this possibility. The furious struggle ended only when Bill was finally able to hold the snake's head under his boot while he, bent double, uncoiled the rest from his arm. After he staggered home, Bill burned the book and gave up reading westerns for a long time.

Explaining a Process. When you explain a process—how something works or how to do something—you are also using narration. The steps or events in the process change over time, just like the events or actions in a story. In the following paragraph, the writer uses the strategy of narration to explain how to teach a dog to crawl.

> A crawl is easily achieved by first giving your dog the command "*Down.*" Position yourself on the floor next to and slightly ahead of her. Use her name followed by the command, "*Come, crawl.*" The come command will help communicate to her that she should move toward you. Hold a piece of food in your hand and tempt her into stretching forward for it. Use your other hand to gently keep her in the *down* position if she attempts to get up. Allow her to succeed in reaching the food, but require her to reach a little farther each time. In the *crawl,* she needs to shift her front paws to move forward and scoot her hindquarters along. If necessary, you can help her by moving one paw at a time so that she gets the idea and also the food reward! She should be crawling on her first lesson.
>
> Ted Baer, *How To Teach Your Old Dog New Tricks*

Explaining Causes and Effects. Whenever you explain causes and effects, you also use the strategy of narration to look at the way things change over time. To make cause-and-effect connections clear, you often need to arrange them in chronological order, cause before effect. In the following paragraph, the writer explains how the Civil War helped to cause the development of the form of music known as the blues.

> Primitive blues-singing actually came into being because of the Civil War, in one sense. The emancipation of the slaves proposed for them a normal human existence, a humanity impossible under slavery. Of course, even after slavery the average Negro's life in America was, using the more ebullient standards of the average American white man, a shabby, barren existence. But still this was the black man's first experience of time when he could be alone. The leisure that could be extracted from even the most desolate sharecropper's shack in Mississippi was a novelty, and it served as an important catalyst for the next form blues took.
>
> LeRoi Jones, *Blues People*

EXERCISE 7 Using Narration as a Strategy

As you have seen, narration is a flexible strategy for developing paragraphs. It lets you tell a story, explain a process, or explain causes and effects. Now try it out on these subjects. Just follow the directions.

1. What Shakespearean play or Greek myth do you remember best? Briefly tell (in a talk or in writing) what happens in one of the plays or myths.
2. You are teaching a four-year-old how to ride a bike. Write out the basic steps and major points of bike riding.
3. Write down at least three causes that made you decide to go or not to go to college. Then list at least three effects your decision is likely to have.

Classification

Which states are doing the most to control pollution? What is a Shakespearean sonnet? What's the difference between jazz and blues?

If you answer any of these questions, you are using the strategy of ***classification.*** You are examining a subject and its relationship to other subjects. When you classify, you can divide a subject (the fifty states) into its parts, you can define it (Shakespearean sonnet), or you compare and contrast it (jazz and blues).

Writers usually use ***logical order*** to arrange ideas in paragraphs that classify. Logical order groups related ideas together.

Dividing. Often you need to discuss a subject by looking at the parts that make it up. For example, if you are writing about the National League pennant race, you will probably need to divide the league into its teams and discuss each one. In the following paragraph about the social system of the ancient American civilization of the Mayas, the writer divides the society into three groups and then discusses each group.

> Maya society displayed a rigid structure based on class distinction. The most dominant persons were *almehen*—nobles—a hereditary elite, with close association to the priesthood. But the Maya appear to have lived in a secular society despite the austerity and authority of their religion.

> The nobility possessed private lands and held the most important offices—ranking warriors, merchants, and clergy. Peasants were free workers. Slaves were mainly commoners taken in war (ranking prisoners of war were sacrificed). Slavery was hereditary, but menials could buy their freedom. Under the authority of the Maya nobility, the life of the peasant and slave was entirely devoted to cultivating the soil, to constructing and repairing public spaces, and to the strict observation of religious life: prayer, offerings, homage, and sacrifices.
>
> Jamake Highwater, *Native Land: Sagas of the Indian Americas*

Defining. When you define a new term or idea, you help the reader understand your meaning by first identifying the large group or class to which it belongs (A *democracy* is "a form of government . . ."). Then you identify features that make the term or idea different from all the others in that class (". . . under which the people rule directly or through elected representatives"). In the following paragraph, the writer defines *terracide* by relating it to a group of words (those ending in *–cide*), and then pointing out how it is different from other words in the group.

> The word is terracide. As in homicide, or genocide. Except it's terra. Land. It is not committed with guns and knives, but with great, relentless bulldozers and thundering dump trucks, with giant shovels like mythological creatures, their girdered necks lifting massive steel mouths high

> above the tallest trees. And with dynamite. They cut and blast and rip apart mountains to reach the minerals inside, and when they have finished there is nothing left but naked hills, ugly monuments to waste, stripped of everything that once held them in place, cut off from the top and sides and dug out from the inside and then left, restless, to slide down on houses and wash off into rivers and streams, rendering the land unlivable and the water for miles downstream undrinkable.
>
> Skip Rozin, "People of the Ruined Hills"

Comparing and Contrasting. A third way of classifying is by ***comparing***—telling how things are alike—and ***contrasting***—telling how things are different. In the following paragraph, the writer compares and contrasts dog ownership today with dog ownership at the turn of the century.

> The possession of a dog today is a different thing from the possession of a dog at the turn of the century, when one's dog was fed on mashed potato and brown gravy and lived in a doghouse with an arched portal. Today a dog is fed on scraped beef and Vitamin B_1 and lives in bed with you.
>
> E. B. White, "Dog Training"

EXERCISE 8 **Using Classification as a Strategy**

How can you divide it, define it, compare and contrast it? For practice, try classifying cars. Use the following directions.

1. Based on the advertising you have seen and the cars you are familiar with, what kinds of cars are available? Try to classify them into four or five categories (such as sports, luxury, and so on). Give examples of cars in each category, and then tell about their characteristics in each category.
2. What's your dream car? Define it by describing its individual features and telling how it is different from other cars.
3. How do you think the cars of today might be similar to the cars people will drive in fifty years? How might they be different? Compare and contrast cars of today with cars fifty years in the future.

Evaluation

Should everyone over eighteen be allowed to vote? What kind of Hamlet did Mel Gibson make?

These questions call for an ***evaluation,*** or judgment, of the value of some idea or thing. Writers use evaluation to inform readers or to persuade them to think or act differently. An effective evaluation is always backed up with reasons to support the writer's evaluation. Writers often use ***order of importance*** to arrange reasons and information when they are evaluating. With order of importance, you can emphasize something by listing it first or last in the paragraph.

In the following paragraph, the writer evaluates the 1985 movie *Back to the Future.* At the same time the reviewer gives his opinion of the film, he also gives reasons for his opinion.

> Director Robert Zemeckis's hip tale of time travel is a witty blend of comedy, manic characterizations, and special effects that pumps new life into the familiar time-travel genre. Every-teenager Marty McFly (Michael J. Fox) is transported back to 1955 and meets his nerdy father and lascivious mother as young adults. It's up to Marty to attract these two opposites to one another, or he will cease to exist before he can get "back to the future." Even though the

movie telegraphs its plot twists, Zemeckis vigorously works around his self-imposed barriers to create one of the wackiest, most original science-fiction films in recent years—a picture that mixes nuclear-powered DeLoreans, Libyan terrorists, sock hops, and malt shops. It's obvious that everyone loves the material they're working with—especially Christopher Lloyd as the maddest scientist since Dr. Frankenstein. *Back to the Future* is an irresistibly enthusiastic film made in the Spielberg tradition, and produced by the master himself.

Steven H. Scheuer, *The Complete Guide to Videocassette Movies*

EXERCISE 9 Using Evaluation as a Strategy

What is your opinion? Write a sentence giving your opinion of each of the following topics. Then write three reasons to support each of your opinions.

1. the value of a high school diploma
2. the importance of being popular in high school
3. the quality of public transportation in your city or state
4. the quality of the last movie you saw

MAKING CONNECTIONS

WRITING PARAGRAPHS FOR DIFFERENT PURPOSES

In this chapter, you have studied some principles of the form and structure of paragraphs. Now it's time to apply what you have learned by writing paragraphs for the four basic purposes of writing: self-expression, exposition, persuasion, and literature.

Writing a Self-Expressive Paragraph

You write to express yourself when you write about your thoughts and feelings—perhaps in a letter, a journal entry, or even song lyrics. Self-expressive writing is useful because it helps you to sort out confusing thoughts and feelings and, sometimes, to understand yourself better.

Self-expressive writing can be completely personal—your own thoughts in your own way—and doesn't have to be seen by any other person. Or, it can be directed toward an audience. Using one of the following sentences as a starting point, write a paragraph expressing your thoughts and feelings.

Starter Sentences for Expressive Writing

The thing I would like most to change in the world is ____.
What I like best about myself is ____.
It scares me to think that ____.
The one thing I'd most like to do in the next five years is ____.
____ is a real concern of mine because ____.

Prewriting. Getting started is often the hardest part of writing. To help you get started with your self-expressive paragraph, quickly jot down some words and phrases that immediately come to your mind when you think about your starter sentence. These can be used to jog your memory when you develop your ideas into a paragraph.

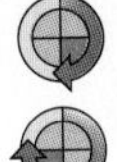

Writing, Evaluating, and Revising. If you are writing the paragraph for yourself, just say what you want and then stop. However, if you have struggled with a problem or developed a special insight that others in your situation might find useful, you might want to share your paragraph with others. If so, revise your paragraph for this wider audience.

Proofreading and Publishing. If you intend to share your self-expressive paragraph, proofread it and then correct any grammar, usage, or mechanics errors. You might want to include it in a scrapbook, along with photographs and other keepsakes. In later years, the paragraph will be a kind of verbal photograph, a reminder of "the inner you" of the past.

Writing an Expository Paragraph

Many of the paragraphs that you write, especially in school, have an expository aim. And one type of expository paragraph is informative—the writer shares information with the reader. When you write this type of exposition, your purpose is to present the information as accurately and as clearly as possible.

Here is some information about tourism in the United States. Use the information to write an expository paragraph about the pros and cons of tourism in this country. You might want to use the following topic sentence for your paragraph.

> **Topic Sentence:** Tourism is one of America's largest and fastest growing industries, but it is not without its problems.

TOURISM IN THE UNITED STATES

Tourism is America's third largest retail industry, amounting to more than $350 billion annually.

Tourism is America's second largest employer.

Jobs related to tourism are often low-paying. They usually demand long hours, rarely offer benefits (such as health insurance), and are subject to long layoffs during the off-season.

Tourism is among the top three industries in 46 states.

State spending on tourism increased from $120 million to $339 million between 1980 and 1993.

(continued)

TOURISM IN THE UNITED STATES *(continued)*

When states calculate the benefits of tourism, they do not include certain hidden costs, such as the expense of added police protection or of welfare programs to assist tourism workers who are laid off or without health insurance.

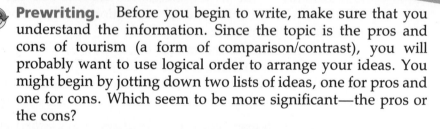

Prewriting. Before you begin to write, make sure that you understand the information. Since the topic is the pros and cons of tourism (a form of comparison/contrast), you will probably want to use logical order to arrange your ideas. You might begin by jotting down two lists of ideas, one for pros and one for cons. Which seem to be more significant—the pros or the cons?

Writing, Evaluating, and Revising. Use the information from the chart or from your own research to develop the main idea in the topic sentence. However, don't copy the information just as it appears here; put it into your own words. Once you have grouped pros and cons together in a logical order, you might use order of importance to arrange information within each group. Maintain this order by discussing the most important pro (or con) first, the next most important pro (or con) next, and so on. When you evaluate and revise, be certain that each supporting sentence develops the main idea in the topic sentence.

Proofreading and Publishing. Accuracy is very important in expository writing, so be certain that the facts and statistics you've taken from the chart have been copied accurately. If you have done some research on your own, double-check to be sure that your sources are trustworthy and that your information is accurate. Publish your paragraph by sharing it with a friend. Ask your friend to tell you whether the information is clear and logical.

Writing a Persuasive Paragraph

When you write to convince someone to think or act in a certain way, you are writing persuasion. The ability to write persuasively will be useful long after you leave school. You will use it to get a job or raise, to convince friends to go to the restaurant you prefer, or to convince people of ideas that you think are important.

To begin working on your ability to persuade, choose an issue that you think is important—one at school, on your part-time job, in your community, or for the nation as a whole. You might, for example, choose an issue like one of these:

- changing the school year from a nine-month to a twelve-month calendar
- raising the minimum wage
- regulating the cost of car insurance for teenagers
- increasing the amount of federally funded college loans

Write a paragraph that states your conviction about an issue and gives reasons to support it. Remember that you are trying to persuade readers to support your view.

Prewriting. Jot down notes about why you feel the way you do. If possible, do some research to find facts, examples, and other specific evidence that will support your viewpoint. Think about the biggest single objection that readers might have to your position, and be prepared to refute that objection.

Writing, Evaluating, and Revising. Begin your paragraph with a strong topic sentence that states your opinion. Then support your opinion with reasons, including specific facts and examples. Consider arranging your reasons in order of importance, ending with the most important one.

When you finish your first draft, evaluate the paragraph to decide how convincing you have been. Do your reasons make sense? Do your facts and examples support your position? Revise your paragraph to make it more persuasive by adding reasons, facts, and examples.

Proofreading and Publishing. Proofread your paragraph for errors in grammar, usage, and mechanics. Then consider publishing your paragraph by using it as the basis for a letter to the editor of your school or community newspaper or to another appropriate publication.

Writing a Literary Paragraph

Another purpose of writing is to create a work of art—a piece of literature. Just as a composer uses notes to create music, a writer can use language to create a poem, a story, a play, or even a simple paragraph.

Try out your knowledge of paragraphs and your artistic skills by writing a paragraph. Start by looking at the following piece of visual art—the painting *Nighthawks* by Edward Hopper.

Edward Hopper, American, 1882–1967, "Nighthawks," oil on canvas, 1942, 76.2 × 144 cm, Friends of American Art

The people in this painting seem to be caught in the midst of life, as though they had been somewhere, doing something, before Hopper painted them. Use your imagination to create a description of another person to be put into this painting, a person who isn't there now, but could be. The following questions should help trigger your imagination.

1. Who are the people in the painting? Did they know each other before this meeting in the diner?
2. What brings the people in the painting to this lonely diner in the middle of the night?
3. What other person might be in this diner? How would the new person you are creating be dressed? What kind of facial features and hairstyle would this person have?
4. What kind of expression would this new person have on his or her face—sad? grim? amused?

Prewriting. Examine the painting carefully, jotting down notes that help answer the questions. Think about the kind of person who might fit into the mood that you see in the painting. The person you create can be of either sex and any age. He or she can be based on a real person or a movie or TV character, or the person can be created wholly from your imagination.

Writing, Evaluating, and Revising. Begin your paragraph with a statement that introduces the person or that grabs your readers' attention. Then describe the features that make this person unique. Use specific details to show your readers what the person looks like, but also try to reveal your subject's personality. Describe the person's facial expression, his or her posture, the way the person wears his or her clothes. When you revise your paragraph, replace vague words with precise details that will help readers "see" the person and understand how he or she fits into the painting.

Proofreading and Publishing. Review your paragraph for errors in grammar, usage, and mechanics. Draw a sketch of the person you have created, or ask a classmate who takes art classes to draw a sketch based on your paragraph. Show the sketch to people who read your description and ask them how well the verbal description and the sketch match. Post the sketches on a bulletin board under the heading "Nighthawks."

3 Understanding Composition Structure

Looking at the Whole

What do you think of when someone says, "Picture your school in your mind"? Do you think of isolated parts—the science lab, the second floor hall, your locker, the principal's office? Or do you see the building as a whole—as if you were viewing it through a wide-angle lens? A composition is a little like your image of the school; you can look at its parts, or you can look at it as a **whole.**

Writing and You. In *Sports Illustrated* you find an interesting editorial on professional athletes and the Olympics. In *Time* magazine you read a review of the new movie you think you would like to see. And in English class, you write a persuasive essay on preserving our environment. Have you noticed that all these pieces of writing have something in common? They use a standard composition form.

As You Read. In the following article, Steve Nadis uses standard composition form. How do the parts come together to create a whole piece of writing?

Georgia O'Keeffe, American 1887–1986. *Oriental Poppies* (1928). Oil on canvas, 30" × 40 1/8". Collection University Art Museum, University of Minnesota, Minneapolis.

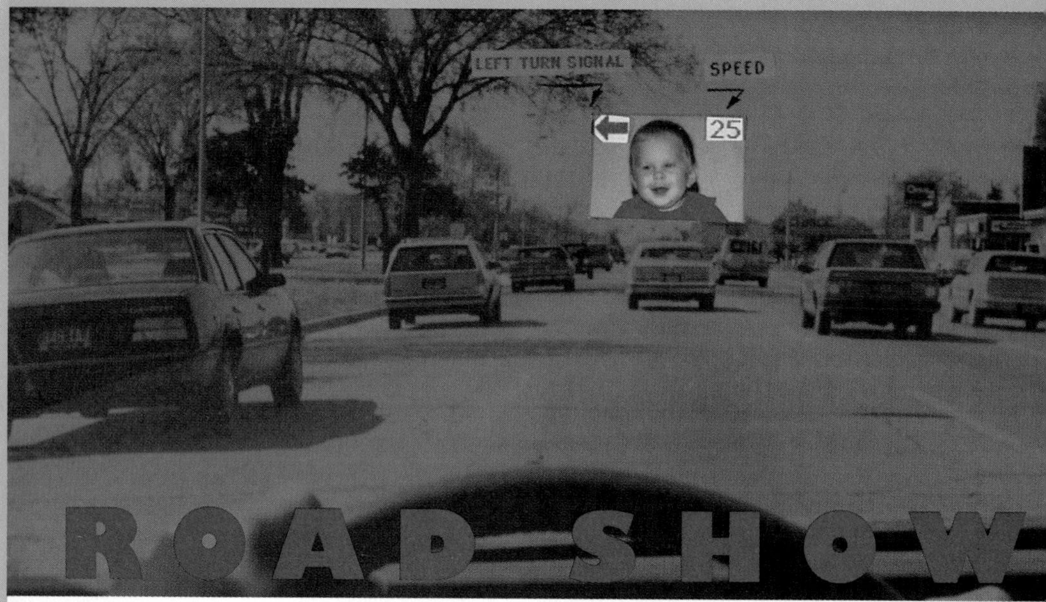

ROAD SHOW

BY STEVE NADIS

"... couch potatoes of the future won't be confined to the living room sofa—they'll be able to watch their favorite TV shows while driving their cars."

If Jay Schiffman has his way, couch potatoes of the future won't be confined to the living room sofa—they'll be able to watch their favorite TV shows while driving their cars.

Schiffman, an electrical engineer, got his idea 15 years ago while designing head-up display (HUD) systems for military aircraft. HUD systems project images into a space in front of the pilots, allowing them to check their instruments without taking their eyes off the sky. Schiffman realized that a similar projection scheme would enable drivers to watch a TV show without taking their eyes off the road.

His AutoVision device, recently patented by AutoVision Associates in Ferndale, Michigan, is a miniature projector located on the roof inside the car. It beams a picture through a small mirrorlike lens on the windshield, which reflects a "virtual image" that appears to float above the road, about 15 feet in front of the car. The device has been tested for six years, with some 300 drivers logging more than 200,000 miles "without so much as a scratched fender," according to Schiffman.

Paul Green, an associate research scientist at the University of Michigan's Transportation Research Institute, has driven a car fitted with the device and discovered that "it's not as outlandish as you might think. But that doesn't mean that it's safe." He says that independent experiments are now needed to determine the conditions, if any, under which AutoVision could be used.

Car radios, which were introduced 60 years ago, may serve as a precedent: The devices were outlawed in many areas of the country because lawmakers feared they would distract drivers. But recent tests by Green and his colleagues have shown that radios help keep drivers alert. Car TVs may serve the same function, Green says, "or you might be better off with just a radio."

". . . 'it's not as outlandish as you might think. But that doesn't mean that it's safe.' "

Reader's Response

1. What do you think of Jay Schiffman's invention? Do you think you could drive safely with AutoVision operating? What do you think the effect on traffic would be if everyone had it?
2. Do you believe that people tend to fear and resist new technology? Why or why not?

Writer's Craft

3. What is the thesis statement—the sentence that states the main idea—in this article?
4. In the conclusion of the article, what is the author demonstrating by pointing out the reaction of the public sixty years ago to the car radio? What does the author compare this to? How does this comparison relate to the main idea?

LOOKING AHEAD

In this chapter, you'll study the structure of a composition. You'll learn that

- most compositions have a thesis statement
- most have an introduction that catches the reader's attention
- the paragraphs of the body are unified and coherent
- most compositions have a conclusion that ties ideas together and brings the composition to a satisfying close

What Makes a Composition

You've already written a lot of compositions—you've probably called them *essays* or *reports*. And you'll continue to write compositions even after you're out of school. College and job applications usually involve writing short compositions, and many jobs require the ability to use the principles of composition form in memos, letters, and reports. In later chapters, you'll use what you learn in this chapter to write expository essays, persuasive essays, and problem-solution essays. You'll also use principles of composition form in writing about literature and in writing a research paper.

The Thesis Statement

When you write a composition, you usually have a *thesis,* or main idea, in mind. Your thesis is not your topic, but what you want to say about it. The expression of this thesis, or main idea, in one or two sentences is the ***thesis statement.***

The thesis statement often appears somewhere in the introduction, where it introduces and summarizes the main idea (or ideas) of the composition. However, some writers may put their thesis statements later in their compositions. Their thesis statements may even be implied, rather than directly stated.

Thesis statements vary according to your aim for writing. When your aim is to give information, the thesis statement may simply announce the topic: "Computers are widely used in elementary and high school classrooms." When your aim is to explain or to persuade, the thesis statement may tell what you intend to prove in the composition: "Unless there are drastic changes in public education, this country won't be able to compete in the world market of the future."

Your thesis statement can be long or short, one sentence or more than one. What's important is that it lets readers know about the main ideas of your composition.

HINTS FOR WRITING AND USING A THESIS STATEMENT

1. **Develop your thesis statement from your prewriting notes.** Look over the facts and details that you have gathered during prewriting. What's the most important idea?
2. **Identify both your limited topic and your main ideas about it.** A thesis statement should identify your topic and state the points you wish to make about it. For example, here's a thesis statement about classroom computers: "Computers have brought new dimensions to classrooms everywhere by opening up worlds of information and help for students and teachers, but they're not without problems." The limited topic is computers in the classrooms. The main idea is that computers help students and teachers, but may cause some problems.

(continued)

HINTS FOR WRITING AND USING A THESIS STATEMENT *(continued)*

3. **Make your thesis statement clear and specific.** Notice the difference between the thesis statement you've just read and this one that's too vague: "There are good and bad things about computers in the classrooms."
4. **Be guided by your thesis statement as you plan and write.** As you plan your composition, set aside ideas or details that don't support or develop your thesis statement. Later, you might decide to revise your thesis statement to include them. If not, discard them. Remember, your composition should support and develop the central ideas expressed in your thesis statement.

As you're planning your composition, you'll develop a preliminary thesis statement that will guide your first draft. Later, during revision, you can revise your thesis statement to make it more interesting. Here are examples of a preliminary and a revised thesis statement. Notice how much more interesting the revised statement is.

PRELIMINARY Many critics believe that the SAT doesn't measure critical thinking skills or students' true potential.

REVISED In a yearly ritual, millions of high school students suffer the anguish of the SAT; many critics, however, believe the exam fails to measure students' critical thinking skills or their true potential.

EXERCISE 1 Analyzing Thesis Statements

Now you'll have an opportunity to check out what you have learned about thesis statements. Four of the following five thesis statements have specific topics and clear main ideas. Find the one that doesn't. Then rewrite it to make it more effective.

1. Despite being confined to a wheelchair by the crippling effects of motor neuron disease, British physicist Stephen Hawking expands our understanding of the universe through his brilliant writing.
2. When you're ready to study subjects in both Spanish and English, two-way immersion may prove to be a beneficial alternative to bilingual education.
3. Rap music, which nobody knew very much about until it became popular a while ago, is a very entertaining form of music.
4. Robots don't perform experiments, but they do carry out many precision tasks in today's laboratories.
5. Would you like to interpret your dreams? Here are keys that will unlock the mysteries.

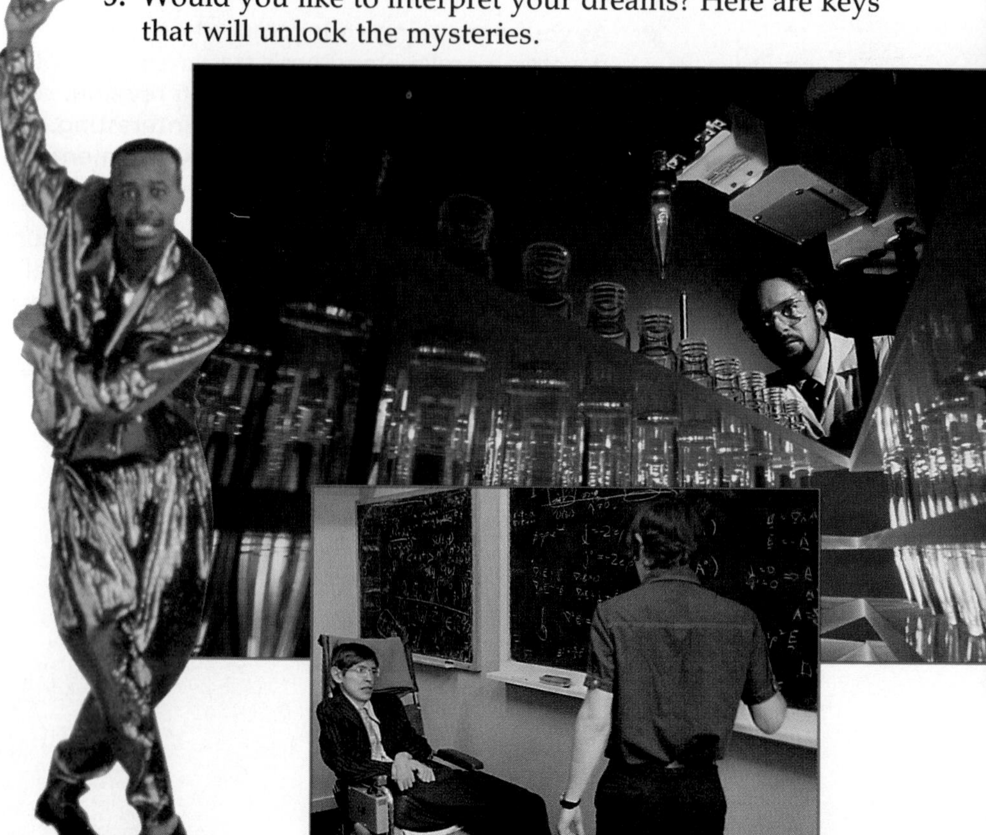

EXERCISE 2 Writing Thesis Statements

The ability to write clear and specific thesis statements comes with practice; here's your chance to get some of that practice. Following are two limited topics with ideas and details. Decide what main idea is central to each list of ideas and details. Then write a thesis statement for each limited topic that clearly expresses the topic and main idea.

1. Limited topic: effect of houseplants on indoor air pollution
Ideas and details:
- EPA reports health risks from indoor pollution greater than risks from outdoor pollution
- examples of indoor pollutants: formaldehyde from plywood, carpeting, some household cleaners; benzene from paints, tobacco smoke, detergents; trichloroethylene from paints, varnishes, dry cleaning
- reports that one houseplant per 100 square feet of floor space removes over 85 percent of indoor pollutants

2. Limited topic: coping with the rising costs of colleges
Ideas and details:
- college costs—average increase more than 6 percent annually
- parents and students—both need to plan ahead for college costs; save money
- many students eligible for financial aid—scholarships, low-interest loans, work-study programs
- information through Foundation Center about tuition assistance from foundations

Early Plans and Formal Outlines

In the prewriting stage (see pages 21–38), you gather information to support your thesis, the unifying idea of your composition. Sometimes, the information comes from your own knowledge or experience. Other times, you go "outside" for the information—to reference materials, to films or recordings, to experts on your topic. Organizing all this information is easier if you make an *early plan* or a *formal outline.* Either one helps you to identify major ideas and to group and order information under these major ideas.

The Early Plan

An ***early plan,*** or informal outline, is very simple—you don't need to worry about Roman numerals or letters of the alphabet. It just gives you a rough idea of how you want to group the information. It can also indicate gaps in information about one of your ideas.

Grouping. You group things all the time. Your tapes or CDs, for example, may be grouped together according to performer or type of music. The following steps can help you group ideas for your composition, so that you discuss similar ideas together.

- Put each piece of information on a separate note card or piece of paper.
- Sort through the cards, setting aside details that don't seem to support your thesis, or main idea. Save these details for now, in case you change your thesis later.
- Sort the cards into stacks, putting related details together.
- Give each stack of cards a label.

Here's how a writer grouped and labeled details in an early plan for a composition on classroom computers. (Remember that an early plan, like a rough draft, may change.)

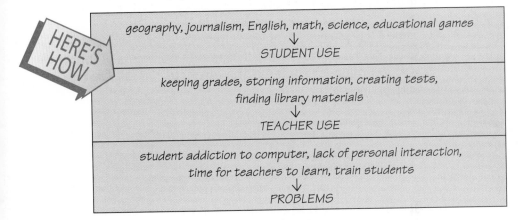

geography, journalism, English, math, science, educational games ↓ STUDENT USE
keeping grades, storing information, creating tests, finding library materials ↓ TEACHER USE
student addiction to computer, lack of personal interaction, time for teachers to learn, train students ↓ PROBLEMS

Ordering. *Ordering* makes your ideas easy to follow so that readers can understand them easily. In a composition, two kinds of order are important: the order of paragraphs and the order of details within each paragraph.

The topic for your composition may lend itself to a certain order. For example, ***chronological order*** is a natural way to describe a sequence of events, a cause and effect, or a step-by-step process. Writers often use ***spatial order*** to describe a place or an object in detail. To point out similarities and differences between two subjects, you'd use ***logical order*** to compare and contrast features. For a persuasive composition, you might use ***order of importance,*** arranging ideas from the least to the most important, or vice versa.

 **REFERENCE NOTE:** For more information on arranging details, see pages 74 and 79–87.

The Formal Outline

An early plan puts your notes roughly in order. A ***formal outline*** uses Roman numerals, letters, and numbers to organize your headings and subheadings. There are two types of formal outline: a ***topic outline,*** which has single words or short phrases, and a ***sentence outline,*** which has all complete sentences.

 **REFERENCE NOTE:** For more information on formal outlines, see pages 460–461.

Here's a formal topic outline for the composition on computers in the classroom, pages 108–110. (Notice that the introduction and conclusion aren't part of the outline.)

Title: Computers: The New Kids in Class
Thesis Statement: Computers have brought new dimensions to classrooms everywhere by opening up worlds of information and help for students and teachers, but they're not without problems.

I. Student use of computers
  A. Geography
    1. Maps
    2. Games
    3. Growth and weather patterns
  B. English and journalism
    1. Essays
    2. Lessons and games
    3. Desktop publishing
  C. Math
  D. Science
    1. Dry labs
    2. Physics labs
    3. Animal dissection

II. Teacher use of computers
  A. Grades
  B. Image production and projection
  C. Tests
  D. Professional growth

III. Problems
  A. Student addiction
  B. Noninteraction
  C. Teacher time

EXERCISE 3 Making an Early Plan and a Formal Outline

Here are some notes about jumping rope as aerobic exercise. Working with a partner, organize the notes into an early plan and then into a formal topic outline. [Hint: You will probably have three headings, or major ideas.] You may add to, delete, or combine any of the information. When you write the formal outline, you may need to rewrite phrases so that items are parallel.

Jumping Rope to Keep Fit

leather or beaded ropes
easier on body than running
equipment inexpensive
strengthens muscles
variety of surfaces
cross-training or aerobic shoes
improves coordination
rotate wrists and forearms, not shoulders
feet together or alternate feet
improves circulation
do 3–5 times a week for 20 minutes
burns calories
stand straight
keep elbows at sides
wood, carpet, or asphalt surface
improves heart and lung health

A WRITER'S MODEL

Here's the final draft of a composition that follows the outline on page 106. You'll see that the writer has added information since the early plan. Much of the information in the composition comes from the writer's own knowledge and experience, but some comes from outside sources—interviews with a student and a teacher. Notice what the parts of the paper are and how they are put together to create a *whole* piece of writing.

Computers: The New Kids in Class

INTRODUCTION

Seventeen-year-old Wyatt Pierce attends high school in a very small town in Oregon, but through classroom computers, he has access to a much wider world. He can see up-to-date maps, browse through the on-line catalog of the state library, even design shelves for the ranch where he lives. Computers have brought new dimensions to classrooms everywhere by opening up worlds of information and help for students and teachers, but they're not without problems.

BODY
Major idea: Student use of computers

Experts see computers as one way of remedying the poor geography skills of most high school and elementary school students. Geography students use computer software featuring world, country, and state maps that include physical features, population statistics, and economics of each area. Students also play geography games that require research in encyclopedias, atlases, travel guides, and almanacs. In addition, geography software is available that shows students the changing patterns of growth in population areas as well as weather patterns.

In English classes, computers make the dreaded essay a little easier to swallow. Students write papers using word-processing software with thesauruses, spelling checkers, dictionaries, and even grammar-and-style checkers. Other types of software feature vocabulary, spelling, and grammar lessons and games. Some schools even have desktop publishing systems that enable students to write and print the school newspaper or to produce professional versions of their essays.

Math and science classes have also benefited from classroom computers. Students in math classes use computers at every level from early arithmetic to the most advanced math. User interactive software "watches" students' attempts to solve math problems and gives them help when they need it. "Nice try. Why don't you try this?" is becoming a familiar computer refrain to many students.

In science classes, computers make possible "dry labs" where experiments and tests are carried out without physical contact with hazardous materials such as toxins or carcinogens. They simulate situations and act as precise stopwatches in physics labs, and allow animal dissection without animals in biology.

Major idea: Teacher use of computers

Teachers' lives have been affected by computers, too. Many teachers now keep grades on spreadsheets instead of in grade books and use the computers to calculate grades. With sophisticated computers, teachers can hook an overhead projector into a computer screen. Whatever image the teacher calls up on the screen is then projected to the students on the overhead screen. When enough classroom computers become available, teachers may finally be freed from the hassle of dusty chalkboards and messy duplicating masters.

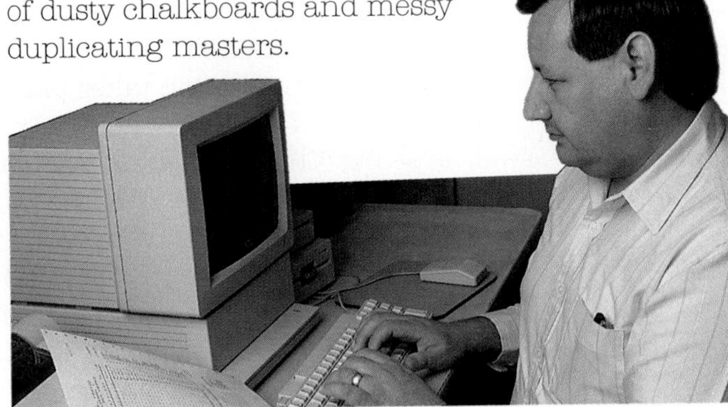

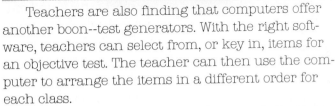

Teachers are also finding that computers offer another boon--test generators. With the right software, teachers can select from, or key in, items for an objective test. The teacher can then use the computer to arrange the items in a different order for each class.

Finally, computers help teachers in their professional growth. In most school districts, teachers are required to update their credentials continually with new courses. In smaller districts, it is often difficult for teachers to find the library materials they need. Computers can allow teachers to search through sources such as the Readers' Guide, newspaper indexes, and the on-line catalogs of

large libraries. Interlibrary loan programs, often through a modem, can help teachers get the materials they need.

Major idea: Problems with classroom computers

Classroom computers aren't without their problems, however. Students can sometimes become addicted to them, especially to the games. In addition, some students tune out all but computer teaching. In classrooms where each student has a computer and work is geared to the student's own pace, very little human interaction takes place. Why talk to a person when the computer knows it all?

Another problem is that although computers save teachers time in some ways, they require more time in others. Software takes hours to evaluate and order and then many more hours to train students to use it. Sometimes, teachers must write their own programs for obsolete systems. Then, too, teachers may find it a time-consuming challenge to stay ahead of students who have grown up using computers.

CONCLUSION

No one doubts that computers in the classroom are here to stay. They open doors into vast new worlds, and students and teachers can benefit from them enormously. Concerns about classroom computer use are real, but they are minor compared with the benefits computers offer. Robert Halfhill, who teaches both English and computers, sums up the advantages of computers this way: "Computers are the most valuable tool to be introduced into the classroom in the last two hundred years. They remove the walls and allow students and teachers to expand the learning experience far beyond the limits of the classroom."

Outside source—interview

The Introduction

An ***introduction*** can be as short as one sentence or as long as several paragraphs. But regardless of its length, an introduction should do these three things:

- get the readers' attention (so they'll read on)
- set the tone (humorous, friendly, critical, casual, and so on)
- state the thesis (usually at the end of the introduction)

Techniques for Writing Introductions

Experienced writers have many options they use in writing an interesting introduction. Following are eight techniques they sometimes use. Try one or more of them yourself—they can be combined—when you write an introduction.

1. **Start with a question.** An intriguing question or a question readers will apply to their own lives can be an effective "hook." Notice how this introduction begins with a question.

> Can an ape master anything like human language? Although primatologists have reported such abilities, the high priests of linguistics have scoffed. The animals, they said, displayed a gift for mimicry, reinforced by rewards of food and play, rather than true understanding.
>
> Frederic Golden, "Clever Kanzi"

2. **Open with an anecdote or example.** An ***anecdote,*** a brief story, or an extended example can also hook readers. This introduction relates an anecdote about an Eskimo woman caught in a storm. The composition goes on to explain how the woman used her clothing to survive the storm and what others can learn from Eskimos about sensible dress.

> During the winter of 1909, an elderly woman of Flaxman Island, northern Alaska, went out to gather driftwood half a mile from her house. She was wearing only one coat or shirt, hair side turned in. With a sudden onslaught rare in the Flaxman country, a gale descended. She could not find her way home; she had to wait the storm out.
>
> Vilhjalmur Stefansson, "Clothes Make the Eskimo"

3. **Open with a startling or unusual fact, idea, or opinion.** This technique makes people want to read on to learn more. In this introduction, for example, the author depicts some unusual possibilities.

> Imagine a cow that produces skim milk, a canola seed rich in sperm-whale oil or a naturally decaffeinated coffee bean. Such curios may sound like science fiction, but they are real possibilities in the brave new world being created by the marriage of biotechnology and agriculture. In scores of experiments, scientists are changing the genetic endowments of plants and animals, and the results could spawn a revolution in farm fields, feedlots and dairy barns.
>
> J. Madeleine Nash, "A Bumper Crop of Biotech"

4. **Address the reader directly.** By addressing the reader directly, the writer immediately involves the reader and sets a friendly, informal tone, as in this introduction to a writer's story about his travels through China.

> The bigness of China makes you wonder. It is more like a whole world than a mere country. "All beneath the sky" (*Tianxia*) was one Chinese expression for their empire, and another was "All between the four seas" (*Sihai*). These days

> people go there to shop, or because they have a free week and the price of a plane ticket. I decided to go because I had a free year. And the Chinese proverb *We can always fool a foreigner* I took to be a personal challenge. To get to China without leaving the ground was my first objective. And then I wanted to stay for a while—in China, on the ground, going all over the place.
>
> Paul Theroux, *Riding the Iron Rooster*

5. **Simply state your topic or thesis.** Often, a well-worded statement of the topic or thesis is interesting in itself. Here's an introduction that uses this technique. The writer goes on to describe the barrenness of a desert landscape.

> There's something about the desert that doesn't like man, something that mocks his nesting instinct and makes his constructions look feeble and temporary. Yet it's just that inhospitableness that endears the arid rockiness, the places pointy and poisonous, to men looking for its discipline.
>
> William Least Heat-Moon, *Blue Highways*

6. **Describe a person, object, or place.** If your composition involves a person, object, or place that's unusual or especially interesting, you can start with a description. In the following introduction, the author describes the labs where a new product is being developed. The product—a solar-powered bicycle—is the topic of the composition.

> The "labs" are really just a single room filled with equipment: computers, machine-shop tools, boxes full of ragged road maps, flutes, a wooden recorder. In the middle of it all sits what looks like the mutant spawn of a bicycle crossed with a computer. Roughly speaking, that's what it is—a fully self-sufficient, solar-powered bicycle incorporating the most advanced computer technology available—and it answers to the name Behemoth.
>
> Carl Zimmer, "Bicycle in Dataspace"

7. **Begin with interesting, specific details.** These may often be sensory details that help readers see, hear, taste, smell, and touch the subject. This introduction is to an article about the civilizations that existed in the "New World" long before Columbus.

> In his explorations of the New World, Columbus found only primitive inhabitants—"a very poor people . . . without weapons or laws." He didn't go far enough. In Mexico there were towering temples and a teeming city as big as any in Europe. In Peru stretched the vast Incan empire, resplendent in silver and gold. In the Guatemalan jungles—and in the great plains of America—lay the ruins of other civilizations that had thrived centuries before.
>
> Melinda Beck, "The Lost Worlds of Ancient America"

8. **Begin with your stand on an issue.** A direct statement of your stand on an issue can often be the most effective introduction for a persuasive essay. This introduction is from an article about the harmful effects of European explorations on Native Americans. It was written shortly before the five hundredth anniversary of Columbus's voyage to the "New World."

> Columbus Day, never on Native America's list of favorite holidays, became somewhat tolerable as its significance diminished to little more than a good shopping day. But this next long year of Columbus hoopla will be tough to take amid the spending sprees and horn blowing to tout a five-century feeding frenzy that has left Native people and this red quarter of Mother Earth in a state of emergency. For Native people, this half millennium of land grabs and one-cent treaty sales has been no bargain.
>
> Suzan Shown Harjo, "I Won't Be Celebrating Columbus Day"

EXERCISE 4 Analyzing Introductions

What makes a good introduction work? Analyze the following introductions to find out. Answer these questions about each introduction.

- What technique or combination of techniques does the writer use?
- Does the technique work well? Does it make you want to read the article?
- What's the tone of the writing? What's the topic?

1. Stamps, Arkansas, is a little larger than the page upon which its name is printed, yet it looms in my thoughts wider than the Steppes of Russia or Africa's Sahara Desert. Why does a small town, a whistle stop, a red dirt burg of 5,000 souls, a hamlet I left forever over 40 years ago, weigh so heavily on my present-day 1990, big-city, internationally wise, sophisticated mind? The answer to that multiphased question is because Stamps is located in the

American South and I am an African-American. The answer to the question "Why are so many young Black people moving South today?" is that the American South sings a siren song to all Black Americans. The melody may be ignored, despised or ridiculed, but we all hear it.

Maya Angelou, "Why Blacks Are Returning To Their Southern Roots"

2. If you walk into a pizzeria in Pittsburgh this spring, don't be surprised if the person running the place is a quadriplegic. And don't be surprised if he calls out your order to a robot, which then whips together your pizza. It's just the latest experiment in socially responsible robotics.

"Large Pizza, Hold the Microchips," *Discover*

Bill Redic/©1991 Discover Magazine

EXERCISE 5 Writing an Introduction

The introduction to "Road Show" (page 96) takes the reader right into the topic. Read that introduction again, and then write a new introduction for the "Road Show" composition, using one or more of the techniques you've just read about. Be sure you include the thesis statement and set the tone. When you finish your rewrite, compare your new introduction with the introductions of other students. What different techniques were used?

The Body

The ***body*** of a composition develops the major points that support the thesis. One or more paragraphs develop each point and support, or prove, it with details. Readers can follow these points clearly and easily if the body of the composition has these characteristics:

- unity—all paragraphs and details relate to the main idea set out in the thesis statement
- coherence—relationships between ideas are obvious
- emphasis—important ideas stand out more than ideas that are less important

 REFERENCE NOTE: For strategies of paragraph development, see pages 79–87.

Unity

Unity is the condition of being "one." For a composition to have unity, all the major points must relate to the main idea in the thesis statement. In addition, all the details in each paragraph must relate to the point expressed in the topic sentence of that paragraph.

Coherence

Coherence describes an orderly relationship. In a coherent composition, ideas are clearly connected. Readers get the sense that sentences and paragraphs flow smoothly and sensibly from one to the other. You can use three techniques to make a composition coherent: (1) transitional words and phrases, (2) direct references, and (3) in a longer composition, a short paragraph that acts as a transition between the paragraph before and the one after.

 REFERENCE NOTE: For more about the use of direct references and transitional words and phrases, see pages 74–77.

Emphasis

When you ***emphasize*** something, you stress it. In a composition, you can emphasize ideas by giving them extra space and attention. That is, you'll write more about one main point than another. If you want to give equal emphasis to two main points, you'll give each about the same amount of space.

EXERCISE 6 Analyzing Unity and Coherence

How do professional writers achieve unity and coherence in their compositions? Read the following paragraph from an article about Diana Golden, an accomplished athlete who skis on one leg. Then answer these questions about the paragraph.

- What's the main idea of the paragraph? Do all the details in the paragraph support that main idea?
- How is the paragraph organized? What order do most of the ideas follow? (See pages 74 and 79–87 for more about order of ideas.)
- What transitional words or phrases and what direct references does the writer use to connect ideas?

Golden's record as a disabled champion will not, however, stand as her greatest legacy to skiing. She will be most significantly remembered as the woman who, perhaps more than any other athlete, brought crossover credibility to the disabled-sports movement. Golden was among the first to persuade sponsors and the public to perceive disabled athletes as *athletes,* period. She was awarded numerous titles never before granted to a disabled person. In 1986, for instance, she won the U.S. Ski Association's (USSA) Beck Award, given to the best American racer in international skiing. *Ski Racing* magazine named her the 1988 U.S. Female Alpine Skier of the Year. And the U.S. Olympic Committee stunned the international sports community when it bypassed all of 1988's two-legged competitors and named Golden the Female Skier of the Year. Not disabled skier. No asterisk. Just Skier of the Year.

Meg Lukens, "Skiing a Formidable Course"

The Conclusion

Readers usually remember longest what they read last. The ***conclusion*** of your composition should leave readers with a final thought and a sense of closure—it should clearly say THE END. Note the following techniques.

Techniques for Writing Conclusions

1. **Restate your thesis.** To be sure your main idea hits home, say it again in a different way. The model composition on pages 108–110 has this kind of conclusion, combined with a final comment.
2. **Summarize your major points.** This type of conclusion helps to reinforce what you've said.
3. **Direct your readers' attention to consequences or future directions.** The following conclusion ends with a look at the possibilities for future research in Native American languages.

> Maya was long considered the only true writing system to have developed in the New World. Now we know that another written language, perhaps belonging to the Olmec people, developed more or less independently. Some 400 glyphs are discernible on the stela. Simply on the basis of their variety Grube speculates that the La Mojarra language may have fewer signs than Maya, and may thus represent an even more phonetic, less logographic system. But unless many more carved stones are found in Veracruz, the glyphs will probably never be read.
>
> David Roberts, "The Decipherment of Ancient Maya"

4. **Close with a call to action.** Writers often ask readers to take action in persuasive essays and articles, but a call to action also suits other types of compositions. The following conclusion is from a composition urging people to conserve fuel.

> Do you really need the vehicles you have? Why not take inventory? How often do you use that gas-guzzler, and when you do, would a smaller, more economical vehicle do the job as well? Every person who switches to a more envi-

> ronmentally sound vehicle becomes a part of the solution instead of contributing to the pollution. It's our earth and our air and our ozone layer. And it's the pollution from our vehicles that's destroying them. Let's change our ways now.

5. **End with an appropriate quotation.** A quotation that sums up your main point or that's particularly striking can make a strong ending. This technique concludes "Road Show," page 97, and is used in the following conclusion.

> Being a stranger in a strange land is never easy. "All the English-speaking kids should learn a foreign language. Then they'd know how hard it is for us sometimes," says 17-year-old Sufyan Kabba, a Maryland high-school junior, who left Sierra Leone last year. But here they are, part of the nation's future, young Yankees who in the end must rely on the special strength of children: adaptability.
>
> Connie Leslie, Daniel Glick, and Jeanne Gordon, "Classrooms of Babel"

6. **Refer to the introduction.** Bring your composition full circle by mentioning something in your introduction. Carl Zimmer begins "Bicycle in Dataspace" (page 114) by describing the laboratory setting where a solar-powered bicycle is being developed. He refers to the lab in his one-sentence conclusion.

> It's going to be another late night in the back of Building Four.
>
> Carl Zimmer, "Bicycle in Dataspace"

The title of your composition is your first chance to grab your reader's attention. And it can also act as a very short summary, pointing your reader toward your main ideas. Go for a title that's both catchy and pointed. Writers often give their compositions a tentative title as they're writing and then revise the title once they're finished. Even then, it usually takes several drafts before they're satisfied with the results. Here are some examples of titles for the composition on pages 108–110. What's your choice for the most effective title?

Computers in the Classroom
Computers: The New Kids in Class
Computers: The New Way to Teach

EXERCISE 7 Writing a Conclusion

Working with a small group, reread the conclusion to Steve Nadis's "Road Show" (page 97) or the conclusion to the Writer's Model (page 110). Then write a new conclusion for one of these compositions, using one or more of the techniques you've just read about. (Don't be afraid to experiment!)

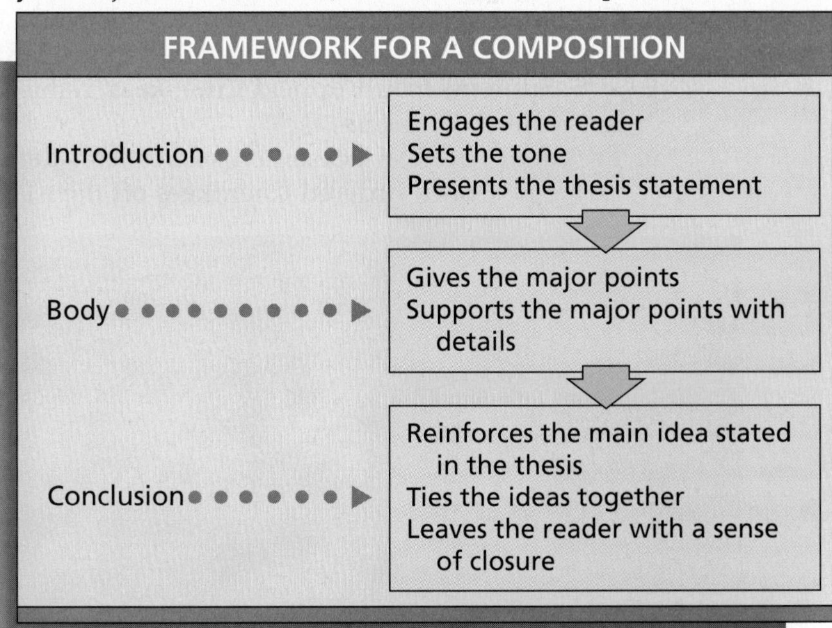

FRAMEWORK FOR A COMPOSITION
Introduction
Engages the reader
Sets the tone
Presents the thesis statement
Body
Gives the major points
Supports the major points with details
Conclusion
Reinforces the main idea stated in the thesis
Ties the ideas together
Leaves the reader with a sense of closure

MAKING CONNECTIONS

Writing an Informative Composition

You've learned that a composition includes an introduction, a body, and a conclusion. You can adapt this structure to many purposes—to inform or explain, to express yourself, to be creative, or to persuade. Now you can use what you've learned to write an informative composition about the Trail of Tears. The following facts have been gathered for you. Before you begin, you might want to review the basic parts of a composition.

Trail of Tears

1. Cherokees—lived in Georgia, most owned houses, some had plantations
2. Had a written language, published a newspaper, had their own government—written constitution, schools, legislative and judicial systems, and a militia
3. Rights protected by treaties with U.S. government
4. Gold discovered in Georgia, white settlers and land speculators wanted now valuable Cherokee lands
5. U.S. Supreme Court upheld Cherokees' rights to land and possessions
6. President Andrew Jackson broke treaties—defied the Supreme Court, ordered Cherokees off their lands

Jerome Tiger, "Untitled, Trail of Tears," 1966. Courtesy of Mr. & Mrs. J.T. Anderson.

7. Indian Removal Act of 1830—authorized forced removal of eastern Indians to west of Mississippi
8. 1838—14,000 Cherokees taken from their homes, allowed to take only clothes they had on, and forcibly marched to Indian Territory (Oklahoma) during the winter—denied adequate clothing, shelter, or decent food, and some kept chained day and night
9. More than 4,000 died during marches that took place over a period of time and covered four different routes between Georgia and Oklahoma—removal and marches called the Trail of Tears
10. U.S. highways following most northern of the four trails recently designated Trail of Tears route as memorial

Prewriting. You may add information you already know to the list of facts or do research on the Trail of Tears before you start writing. You don't need to use all of the information listed; just be sure you have enough to write a short composition. Then decide what you want to say about the Trail of Tears, express this main idea in a thesis statement, and make your early plan.

Writing, Evaluating, and Revising. Use your early plan to guide your thoughts and your writing. Do some areas seem thin? Do you need to return to prewriting to gather details? Use one or more of the introduction techniques on pages 111–115, and include your thesis statement in the introduction. In the body of your composition, make sure each paragraph and detail supports your thesis statement and places emphasis where you want it. Write a conclusion, using one or more of the techniques on pages 119–120, tying your ideas together and giving a satisfying ending to your composition. Set your essay aside for a while and then reread, evaluate, and revise it.

Proofreading and Publishing. After revising your paper, reread it, looking for errors in grammar, spelling, capitalization, and punctuation. You might trade papers with a classmate and proofread each other's work, using the guidelines on page 49. After making a clean, error-free copy of your composition, share it with your teacher and classmates and perhaps another person who is interested in the Trail of Tears.

4 EXPRESSIVE WRITING

Discovering Yourself

All your life you have been **discovering things about yourself**—that music brings you joy, that relationships can bring pain. Those discoveries help you understand yourself; but more than that, they help you understand being human.

Writing and You. In a published speech, Sandra Cisneros recalls her experience making tortillas and then reflects on her accomplishments as a woman and a writer. In an essay, E. B. White expresses his feelings about the death of his pet pig. When have you written to discover something about yourself?

As You Read. In the following speech, a man reflects on his dreams for the future. What are they?

Donald Crowley, *The Critics* (1990). Oil on canvas, 48″ × 60″. Courtesy of the artist.

from

I Have a Dream

by Martin Luther King, Jr.

I SAY TO YOU TODAY, my friends, that in spite of the difficulties and frustrations of the moment, I still have a dream. It is a dream deeply rooted in the American dream.

I have a dream that one day this nation will rise up and live out the true meaning of its creed: "We hold these truths to be self-evident: that all men are created equal."

I have a dream that one day on the red hills of Georgia the sons of former slaves and the sons of former slave owners will be able to sit down together at the table of brotherhood.

I have a dream that my four little children will one day live in a nation where they will not be judged by the color of their skin but the content of their character.

I have a dream today.

I have a dream that one day every valley shall be exalted, every hill and mountain shall be made low, the rough places will be made plains, and the crooked places will be made straight, and the glory of the Lord shall be revealed, and all flesh shall see it together.

This is our hope. This is the faith with which I return to the South. With this faith we will be able to hew out of the mountains of despair a stone of hope. With this faith we will be able to transform

the jangling discords of our nation into a beautiful symphony of brotherhood. With this faith we will be able to work together, to pray together, to struggle together, to go to jail together, to stand up for freedom together, knowing that we will be free one day.

This will be the day when all of God's children will be able to sing with new meaning, "My country, 'tis of thee, sweet land of liberty, of thee I sing. Land where my fathers died, land of the Pilgrim's pride, from every mountainside, let freedom ring."

And if America is to be a great nation, this must become true. So let freedom ring from the prodigious hilltops of New Hampshire. Let freedom ring from the mighty mountains of New York. Let freedom ring from the heightening Alleghenies of Pennsylvania. Let freedom ring from the curvaceous peaks of California!

Let freedom ring from Stone Mountain of Georgia!

Let freedom ring from every hill and molehill of Mississippi. From every mountainside, let freedom ring.

"... my four little children will one day live in a nation where they will not be judged by the color of their skin but the content of their character."

When we let freedom ring, when we let it ring from every village and every hamlet, from every state and every city, we will be able to speed up that day when all of God's children, black men and white men, Jews and Gentiles, Protestants and Catholics, will be able to join hands and sing in the words of that old Negro spiritual, "Free at last! Free at last! Thank God almighty, we are free at last!"

Reader's Response

1. Imagine that you are in Washington, D.C., on August 28, 1963, listening to King's speech. It is a glorious day of deep blue sky and sunshine glinting off the Washington Monument. What thoughts and feelings do you have as King speaks?
2. Think of who you are and the future ahead of you. What do you dream? In a journal entry, freewrite about your dreams, trying to envision specific images for the future as King does in his speech.

Writer's Craft

3. Reflective writing usually begins with a specific incident or idea that triggers broader reflections. Read over the first few paragraphs of King's speech (page 126). What experiences or ideas might have triggered the speech?
4. King uses many specific images to depict his dream, including "a beautiful symphony of brotherhood." Which images most appeal to you? Why?

Ways to Express Yourself

You don't have to search far to find examples of expressive writing. You find it in greeting card stores, where you search for a card that says exactly what you feel. You find it in the lyrics of the tapes and CDs that "speak" to you. And you read it in letters, journals, and articles or essays in magazines. The following examples illustrate how the four basic writing strategies can be used for self-expression.

Narration: telling a friend about a frightening experience; writing in your journal about the events at the senior prom.

Description: describing the old mementos, photos, and letters you discovered in the attic and the feelings they evoked; describing the pain of lost love in a song lyric.

Classification: in a letter, comparing your dreams and plans for yourself now with what they were two years ago; in a college application, explaining your three main goals for yourself.

Evaluation: in your journal, exploring your thoughts about the unfairness of a new curfew for teenagers; in a personal essay, expressing your hometown's significance to you.

LOOKING AHEAD

In the main assignment in this chapter, you will use the strategies of narration and evaluation to write a personal, reflective essay. As you work through the writing assignments, keep in mind that a personal, reflective essay

- begins with a concrete experience
- weaves in personal thoughts and feelings to convey a theme or main idea
- moves from a personal to a universal level
- gradually reveals the full significance of the experience

Writing a Reflective Essay

Prewriting

Choosing a Personal Experience

At first, you may notice that some people are always late for class or that they always park in front of "No Parking" signs. Then you take your thinking a step further and apply what you have noticed to your own life, wondering why you sometimes want to rebel against limits, like tardy bells and "No Parking" zones. Once again you look outward, observing that other people also feel rebellious at times. Just noticing the actions of a few people has led you to reflect about human nature in general.

That's an example of what you can do in a reflective essay—use a specific incident as a springboard to reflect about your feelings and behavior, then those of other people, then the human condition. You do not have to be involved in the "triggering" incident; you may be just an observer. Nor do you have to observe or participate in a single incident: There may be a series of incidents that inspire you to write.

You can begin your search for an experience for reflection by brainstorming for memories of incidents that have moved you to explore broader meanings. You might also do some brainstorming or freewriting to explore what those meanings are. Following is the freewriting one writer did while deciding on a topic for a reflective essay.

Watching Tamara, 7-year-old niece, get ready for party. She's wearing party dress—ruffles, bows, everything—but other kids wearing jeans. She doesn't care—willing to be different. But am I? Are any of us?

Communist coup, 1991—very dangerous. Seeing on TV Boris Yeltsin standing on top of tank to defy Communists. All my friends thought he was very brave. Would we be willing to do same? We complain about the way adults run the country, but what will we do when it's our time? Does younger generation always have the ideals, but then lose them?

Went snorkeling for the first time. Water was sort of a dirty gray and I expected underwater to be like on top. Didn't expect the bright colors—fish and coral. Like a different world underneath. I'd judged the ocean based on its surface. Do I do that with people—make judgments based on outward appearances? Is that what leads to bigotry and prejudice?

WRITING ASSIGNMENT

PART 1:

Choosing an Experience for a Reflective Essay

What has happened to you that's made you wonder about your own thoughts and actions, about those of other people, about what it means to be human? What has affected your view of yourself and of others? Choose one of these experiences as the "anchor" for your reflective essay. Remember that the experience may actually have been a series of experiences and that you may have been just an observer.

Planning Your Reflective Essay

When you write a reflective essay, you are taking readers on a guided tour through a personal experience and your reflections about it. To make certain the tour is a memorable one, you need to plan your essay carefully.

Thinking About Purpose, Audience, and Tone

Your main *purpose* in writing a reflective essay is to explore and discover the significance of an incident or experience. You'll want to show how and why the incident was significant for you.

When you start your essay, you might not know what "truths" you will discover. That's okay. Uncovering layers of meaning in personal experience is part of the process of writing a reflective essay. Your first *audience,* then, is yourself. But you'll also want to broaden the experience to show why others might find significance in it, so you will need to consider other readers, too. Think about the kinds of details they will need in order to understand the significance of the experience.

A reflective essay has an informal *tone,* almost as if the writer is thinking out loud. You can achieve this tone by using the first-person point of view and conversational language. A reflective essay is effective when your readers feel they can trust you, when they feel you are being honest with them.

Recalling Details

A reflective essay is based, first of all, on a personal experience. In some essays that experience is mentioned only briefly before the writer moves on to a reflection on it, but in other essays the experience may be more important. The following two examples show how writers might treat experiences differently.

- One writer briefly tells about the experience of seeing the first buds of spring on an apple tree. The writer then quickly moves into a reflection on how it is almost always possible to make a new start in life.

- Another writer relates the experience of an agonizing defeat in the last moments of a championship basketball game. Enough of the experience is described so that readers understand the pain of defeat for the writer. Then the writer reflects on the difficulty of learning to lose.

Whatever the experience, you need to recall details that will set the stage for your reflections. There are two types of details to think about: *narrative* and *descriptive*. ***Narrative details*** tell specifically about actions and events: "My seven-year-old niece flounced into the room. My sister glanced over at her and groaned." ***Descriptive details,*** both factual and sensory, describe important people, places, and objects: "Tamara's party dress was all over ruffles, lace, and bows. Lace stockings and shiny white patent leather shoes completed the outfit."

Other types of details you might use include these:

- *Your thoughts and feelings.* What are your thoughts and feelings about the events you're narrating? Do they help to trigger ideas that expand the meaning of the experience?
- *Examples.* What examples can you cite from other people or other experiences that might illustrate your own thoughts and reflections?
- *Anecdotes.* What anecdotes (brief, illustrative stories) about other people might show how the meaning of the experience expands to include them?

REFERENCE NOTE: For more information about narrative and descriptive details, see pages 67–68 and 179–180.

As you try to recall your experience, your memory may be a little vague, but keep digging for details and recording them until you can see the experience clearly. Select only those details that will focus the experience for readers. Don't, for example, take time to describe unimportant people, places, and objects. Since you will be sharing your reflections on the experience, not just telling about it, try to choose details that will sharpen its meaning for readers.

EXERCISE 1 **Speaking and Listening: Recalling Details**

Can you clearly remember the experience you'll be writing about? To test your recall, work with a partner and take turns relating the narrative and descriptive details of your experience. Prompt each other by asking for more details in areas that seem unfocused or vague. Keep talking until your partner is satisfied that he or she can "see" your experience clearly.

Exploring the Meaning of an Experience

Once you have recalled the details of your experience, you are ready to explore its meaning. Even though you may have some initial ideas, you should spend some time studying the experience to identify further levels of meaning.

CRITICAL THINKING

Analyzing an Experience for Meaning

Analysis is a thinking skill you use whenever you need to examine something in detail, to understand something fully. Analyzing an experience to find its meaning is like studying the impact of a stone tossed into a pond, watching as its impact makes a circle, then another and another until the ripple has exhausted itself. First, you consider the impact of the experience on yourself. Then, you look outward to see what other ripples of meaning the experience might have in the larger world. In other words, you move from the center outward—from yourself to the human condition, from the personal to the universal.

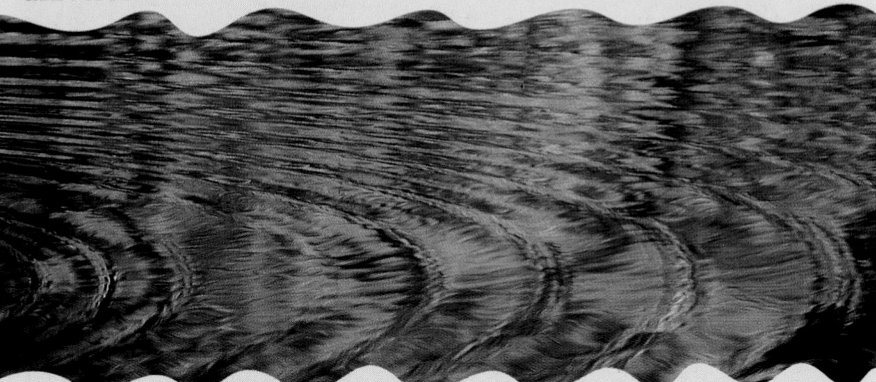

You can use the following types of questions to guide an analysis of the meaning of an experience.

1. What does the experience mean to me?
2. What does the experience show me about myself—about what I believe, the way I act, what I think is important?
3. What ideas about people in general can I form from my own reactions to the experience?
4. What are some related experiences that show the same ideas?

Experience: Watching my seven-year-old niece Tamara get dressed for a birthday party.

1. *The experience impressed me because Tamara didn't care if she dressed differently from all the other kids. I was a little surprised by her reaction.*
2. *I always worry about how I dress. Clothes are important to me—I like to feel accepted.*
3. *Here are some ideas about people: clothes can make a person fit in; people like to be part of groups; it's scary to be different; it's easy and safe to be part of a crowd.*
4. *Related experiences: being afraid to take shop because no other girls do; watching my dad mow the grass because neighbors do; hearing my mom worry about what to wear.*

Going through such a questioning process will give you some ideas to consider about the meaning of your experience. Later on, though, as you write and revise, you may discover different meanings.

CRITICAL THINKING EXERCISE:
Analyzing Experiences for Meaning

Now, you decide. Get together in a small group and practice analyzing the meanings of experiences. There are no "right" and "wrong" answers that your group must discover, just possible meanings about the human condition. Use the four questions you have just read to guide your discussion.

1. overhearing two students grumbling about a new coach's win/loss record
2. finding a half-starved animal by the side of the road
3. calling an office or a department store and getting recorded messages that direct you to push different buttons before you can speak to a human being
4. getting excited because you win a twenty-five-cent prize inside a cereal box
5. spending a Saturday with other volunteers who are cleaning up the side of a highway

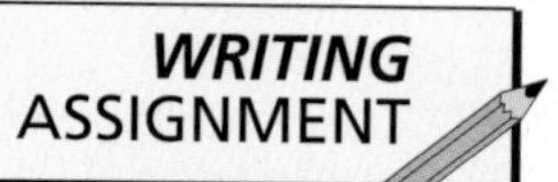

PART 2:
Recalling Details and Exploring Meanings

Now see what you can do with your own experience. To recall the details, brainstorm or talk to people who shared the experience. After you have listed a number of narrative and descriptive details, use the questions on page 135 to analyze the meanings of the experience. Don't censor yourself at this point; write down all your ideas.

Organizing Ideas and Details

Depending upon the type of expressive writing you do, you might use *chronological order, spatial order, order of importance,* or *logical order*. The following chart shows how different types of expressive writing might be organized.

ORGANIZATIONAL PATTERNS IN EXPRESSIVE WRITING	
Personal narrative or reflective essay on an event	Chronological order to relate series of events or series of actions within a single event, sometimes adding flashbacks to recall events that happened earlier in time or a flash-forward to look at what may happen in the future
Personal or reflective essay on a place or person	Spatial order to show details from left to right, near to far, and so forth; order of importance to show what characteristics of the person are most important to the writer; or chronological order to trace the history of the relationship between this person and the writer
Personal or reflective essay of definition	Logical order, such as general to specific or specific to general, to show how the definition has been developed
Personal or reflective essay of evaluation	Logical order, such as best to worst, or order of importance to show criteria used and judgment made

Often you may need to use a combination of two or more organizational patterns. For example, in a reflective essay about an event, you might use chronological order in the beginning, to discuss the event itself. Then you might use logical order or order of importance as you discuss your thoughts about the event's meaning, how it affects other people, and what it says about life in general. For more information on organizational patterns, see pages 74 and 79–87.

As with any other kind of writing, the most important thing is to make sure you don't jump around from point to point and confuse your readers. Following is one writer's organizational plan for a reflective essay about clothes and people.

The event itself, what Tamara did	*chronological order—Tamara comes into room; my sister groans about her dress; Tamara doesn't worry; she goes happily off to party*
My reflections about self and others	*logical order would be to start with me; give specific examples of others—Mom, Dad; go to discussion for what this says about all of us*
Return to event	*go back to time of Tamara's return from party; connect her actions to earlier reflections*

To plan a reflective essay

- think of a meaningful experience you had or witnessed
- explore the layers of meaning and significance—as they apply to you, to other people you know, and to life in general
- take notes on the details of the experience and your thoughts and feelings (reflections) about the experience
- look for a way, or a combination of ways, to organize the details and ideas so they will make sense to your readers

PART 3:
Organizing Details

Begin by looking over your notes from Writing Assignment, Part 2 (page 136) to decide how you might want to arrange them. Remember that you might use a combination of organizational patterns. Make a plan like the one at the top of this page and save it to use as a guide for your first draft.

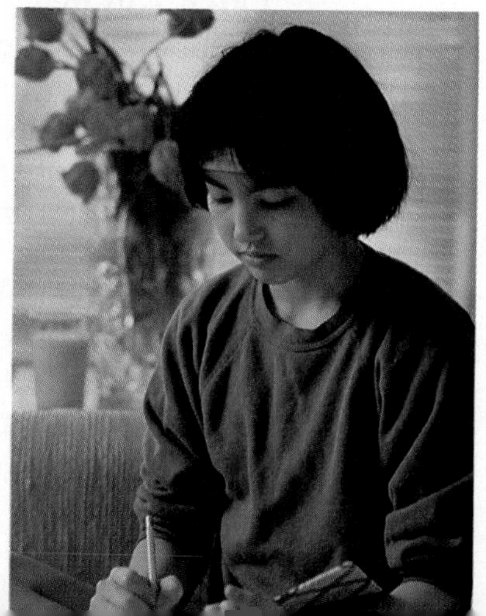

Writing Your First Draft

The Elements of a Reflective Essay

As you begin to draft your essay, you might still be fuzzy on the significance of the experience you have chosen. Don't worry. Writing a reflective essay is a discovery process, and you might find that writing a first draft unlocks the significance of the experience for you. As you draft, keep in mind the following tips:

- **Create an interesting beginning.** A reflective essay, like any other essay you might write, needs a strong beginning to grab the reader's interest. You could "set up" the experience by beginning with its most important moment and then giving a hint or two concerning the overall significance of the experience. Just remember not to announce your theme as you would in a thesis statement for an expository or persuasive essay.
- **Use dialogue and vivid, realistic details.** Your essay may use very little dialogue, but make sure any dialogue is effective. Capturing exact words isn't as important as creating dialogue that conveys the meaning and mood of the experience. Use vivid and realistic details in the same way—to show, not tell.
- **Interweave events and reactions.** As you relate your experience, mix your thoughts and comments in with the events. Relating all the events first and then concluding with your reflections may make your essay seem forced or artificial.
- **End well.** By the time readers get to the end of your essay, they should already understand the significance of your experience. Avoid a pat *And that's what my experience meant to me.* Try, instead, to end in a fresh way by referring to the beginning, relating one final example, or asking a question that sums up your reflections.

In the following reflective essay, the writer remembers her first day of school and then reflects on the strong feelings that day aroused. Notice how the passage exhibits the techniques you have just read about and also presents a ***flashback,*** a return to earlier events and thoughts.

A PASSAGE FROM AN AUTOBIOGRAPHY

from Silent Dancing: A Partial Remembrance of a Puerto Rican Childhood

by Judith Ortiz Cofer

INTRODUCTION

My mother walked me to my first day of school at La Escuela Segundo Ruiz Belvis, named after the Puerto Rican patriot born in our town. I remember yellow cement with green trim. All the classrooms had been painted these colors to identify them as government property. This was true all over the Island. Everything was color-coded, including the children, who wore uniforms from first through twelfth grade. We were a midget army in white and brown, led by the hand to our battleground. From practically every house in our barrio emerged a crisply ironed uniform inhabited by the wild creatures we had become over a summer of running wild in the sun.

Sensory details

Hint of meaning

BODY

At my grandmother's house where we were staying until my father returned to Brooklyn Yard in New York and sent for us, it had been complete chaos, with several children to get ready for school. My mother had pulled my hair harder than usual while braiding it, and I had dissolved into a pool of total self-pity. I wanted to stay home with her and Mamá, to continue listening to stories in

Event

Feelings

the late afternoon, to drink *café con leche* with them, and to play rough games with my many cousins. I wanted to continue living the dream of summer afternoons in Puerto Rico, and if I could not have that, then I wanted to [go] back to Paterson, New Jersey, back to where I imagined our apartment waited, peaceful and cool for the three of us to return to our former lives. Our gypsy lifestyle had convinced me, at age six, that one part of life stops and waits for you while you live another for a while—and if you don't like the present, you can always return to the past. Buttoning me into my stiff blouse while I tried to squirm away from her, my mother tried to explain to me that I was a big girl now and should try to understand that, like all the other children my age, I had to go to school.

Unfolding meaning

Narrative details

"What about him?" I yelled pointing at my brother who was lounging on the tile floor of our bedroom in his pajamas, playing quietly with a toy car.

Dialogue/ Descriptive and narrative details

"He's too young to go to school, you know that. Now stay still." My mother pinned me between her thighs to button my skirt, as she had learned to do from Mamá, from whose grip it was impossible to escape.

"It's not fair, it's not fair. I can't go to school here. I don't speak Spanish." It was my final argument, and it failed miserably because I was shouting my defiance in the language I claimed not to speak. Only I knew what I meant by saying in Spanish that I did not speak Spanish. I had spent my early childhood in the U.S. where I lived in a bubble created by my Puerto Rican parents in a home where two cultures and languages became one. I learned to listen to the English from the television with one ear while I heard my mother and father speaking in Spanish with the other. I thought I was an ordinary American kid—like the children on the shows I watched—and that everyone's parents spoke a secret second language at home. When we came to Puerto Rico right before I started first grade, I switched easily to Spanish.

Event

Feelings

Flashback

Narrative details

Unfolding meaning

It was the language of fun, of summertime games. But school—that was a different matter.

Event

I made one last desperate attempt to make my mother see reason: "Father will be very angry. You know that he wants us to speak good English." My mother, of course, ignored me as she dressed my little brother in his playclothes. I could not believe her indifference to my father's wishes. She was usually so careful about our safety and the many other areas that he was forever reminding her about in his letters. But I was right, and she knew it. Our father spoke to us in English as much as possible, and he corrected my pronunciation constantly—not "jes" but "y-es." Y-es, sir. How could she send me to school to learn Spanish when we would be returning to Paterson in just a few months?

Narrative details

Meaning expanded

But, of course, what I feared was not language, but loss of freedom. At school there would be no playing, no stories, only lessons. It would not matter if I did not understand a word, and I would not be allowed to make up my own definitions. I would have to learn silence. I would have to keep my wild imagination in check. Feeling locked into my stiffly starched uniform, I only sensed all this.

Movement from personal to universal

I guess most children can intuit their loss of childhood's freedom on that first day of school. It is separation anxiety too, but mother is just the guardian of the "playground" of our early childhood.

CONCLUSION
Narrative and descriptive details

The sight of my cousins in similar straits comforted me. We were marched down the hill of our barrio where Mamá's robin-egg-blue house stood at the top. I must have glanced back at it with yearning. Mamá's house—a place built for children—where anything that could be broken had already been broken by my grandmother's early batch of offspring (they ranged in age from my mother's oldest sisters to my uncle who was six months older than me). Her house had long since been made child-proof. It had been a perfect summer place. And now it was September—the cruelest month for a child.

Full meaning completed

EXERCISE 2 Analyzing a Reflective Essay

Do you remember your first day of school as vividly as Cofer does hers? After you have finished reading her reflections (pages 140–143), meet with two or three classmates to discuss these questions.

1. What memories of your first day of school did this essay evoke?
2. What technique does Cofer use in her introduction to get her reader's attention?
3. Although Cofer uses mostly chronological order to organize her essay, there are not many events that actually happen. What are the few events that do take place?
4. In between events, Cofer reflects on her feelings. What is the theme, or main idea, expressed in these reflections? Where is the main idea expressed most directly in the essay?
5. Cofer uses narrative and descriptive details to describe how her mother gets her ready for school. What are some of the details? How do they contribute to the overall feelings of loss that Cofer suggests?

A Basic Framework for a Reflective Essay

Judith Ortiz Cofer's reflections about the first day of school are organized as a narrative; she uses the events and conversations of that day to reflect on why she dreaded school. If you are writing about a milestone experience, you might want to follow a similar narrative structure in your essay. However, if your experience is merely the starting point, rather than the focal point, you might want to spend less time describing the experience and more time reflecting, as the writer in the following essay does. As you read, notice how the writer uses a brief, seemingly insignificant experience to reflect on the importance of fitting in.

A WRITER'S MODEL

Fitting In

INTRODUCTION
Descriptive details

My seven-year-old niece, Tamara, flounced into the room in her best dress, a dress covered with ruffles, lace, and bows. Lace stockings and shiny white patent leather shoes completed the outfit. "I'm ready," she announced.

Dialogue

My sister glanced over at her. "Tamara, you're not wearing that. This is an outdoor birthday party, sweetie. All the other kids will have on shorts and tennis shoes."

"But I won't," Tamara said.

After a few more tries to get Tamara to change, my sister gave up, and Tamara went off to the party.

Hint of meaning

I admired her spunk and her determination to be different. I wondered how long it would last.

BODY
Related example

I thought about the way I act. Before I go anywhere, I go through a mental checklist to make sure I've worn the "right" thing. Sometimes I don't trust my judgment, so I call my best friend, María, to see what she's wearing. She doesn't mind; usually she's just about to call me to ask the same thing. Like most other girls in our group, María and I spend hours thinking about our clothes.

Related example

Descriptive details

It isn't just the girls who are concerned about clothes. The guys at school have a dress code, too. Otherwise, athletic shoes that cost as much as $150 wouldn't be so popular, and there wouldn't be a certain way to tie the shoes. For a few months, you could walk down the hall and almost never see the laces tied at the top. The "proper" style was to leave them untied and dangling. And then there are the same clothing labels that you see on almost every teenage boy's clothes--on the outside of their shirts and jeans.

Related example

Dialogue

Descriptive details

Adults haven't outgrown this concern about clothes and fitting in, either. Just the other day I overheard my mother on the phone discussing a school meeting. "Do you think slacks will be all right?" she asked her friend. She sounded just like my friends and I do. And when my father leaves the house, he looks just like every other adult male in our neighborhood. Their "uniform" consists of jeans and a short-sleeved shirt for casual wear, slacks and a tie for dressier times.

Reflection on previous examples

What all this tells me is that fitting in is important, not just to me, not just to teenagers, not just to one sex or the other. But why? Maybe it is because we're all scared to be alone. I can understand why we feel scared, though. The truth is, it's risky to stand alone. It's risky to wear jeans when everyone else is

Focus on universal meanings

wearing something dressier. It's risky to take shop when everyone else is taking typing. It's risky to study and make good grades when everyone else is thinking of partying. You might get noticed. Then you might get laughed at. Worst of all, you might get excluded, banished forever by the unwritten code of "the group." Alone.

Thoughts and feelings

It's a scary thought. I know I need the security of a group. I want to feel loved, accepted, even approved of by someone. And I don't think I'm unusual. Let's face it. It takes courage to stand alone.

Extended meaning

Details

Some people do have that courage. They are trendsetters and innovators who aren't afraid to be different. Think of the Wright brothers, who clung to the dream of flight through years of disappointment until that day in Kitty Hawk that changed history. Think of Rosa Parks, who defied tradition and rules by refusing to give up her seat on a Montgomery bus. And think of the immigrants to the United States who often endured poverty and hard work to make better lives for themselves and a better country for us all.

CONCLUSION

Return to introduction

I was still thinking about these trendsetters when my niece Tamara returned from the party. "What were the other kids wearing?" my sister asked. Tamara looked puzzled. "I don't know," she shrugged. Spoken like a true trendsetter. Maybe one day I will sound like one, too.

The following framework for a reflective essay shows how the Writer's Model is developed. Notice how it includes the characteristics of a reflective essay—thoughts, feelings, dialogue, and so forth—that you studied earlier in the chapter. You might want to use this framework in your own essay.

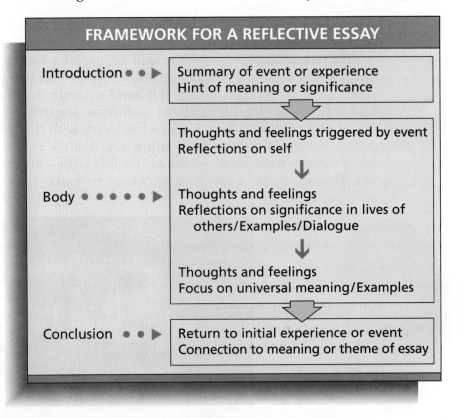

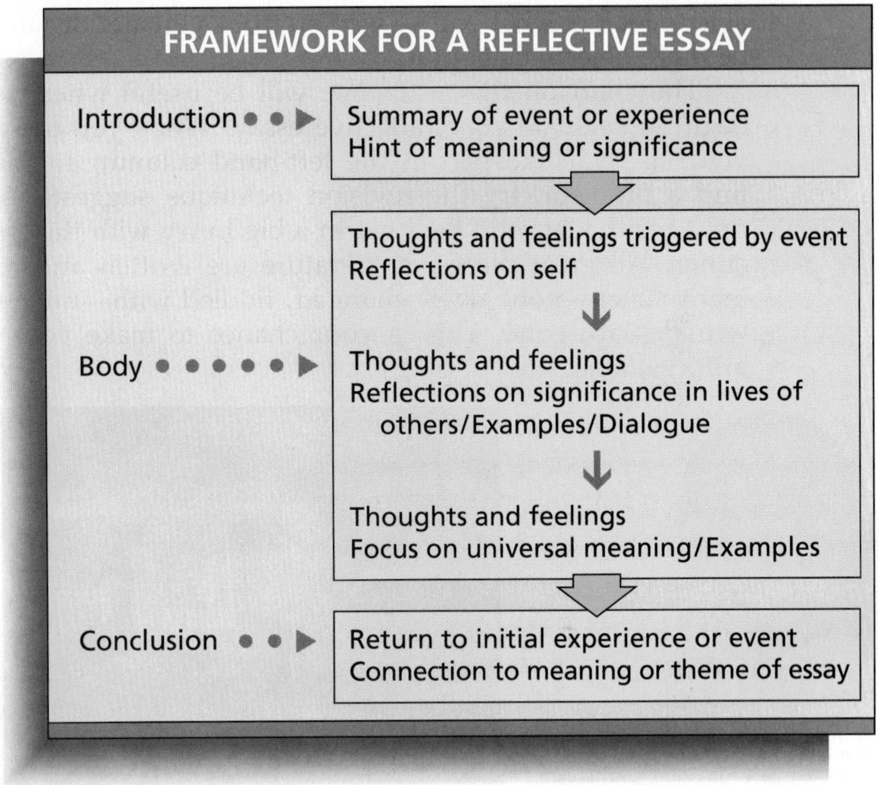

FRAMEWORK FOR A REFLECTIVE ESSAY

Introduction	Summary of event or experience Hint of meaning or significance
Body	Thoughts and feelings triggered by event Reflections on self ↓ Thoughts and feelings Reflections on significance in lives of others/Examples/Dialogue ↓ Thoughts and feelings Focus on universal meaning/Examples
Conclusion	Return to initial experience or event Connection to meaning or theme of essay

PART 4:
Writing a Draft of Your Reflective Essay

Your reflective essay is a journey, one that may be taking you to ideas that surprise you. Continue on the most exciting and demanding part of your journey by writing a first draft. Start with all the ideas and details you collected and organized in Part 2 and Part 3 of the Writing Assignment, and then let your reflections unfold as you write. Don't worry about creating the perfect essay now; you will evaluate and revise later.

Evaluating and Revising

After you have written a first draft, let it rest a while before you attempt to evaluate and revise it. As time passes, you will be able to look at what you've written from a greater distance and be more objective about it.

The chart on the next page will be useful when you do begin to evaluate your reflective essay. When you use it, ask yourself each question in the left-hand column; and, if you find a problem, try the revision technique suggested in the right-hand column. Don't get in a big hurry with this process either. All great pieces of literature are written and revised many times—gone over, changed, fiddled with—until all the wrinkles are gone. This is your chance to make your essay unforgettable.

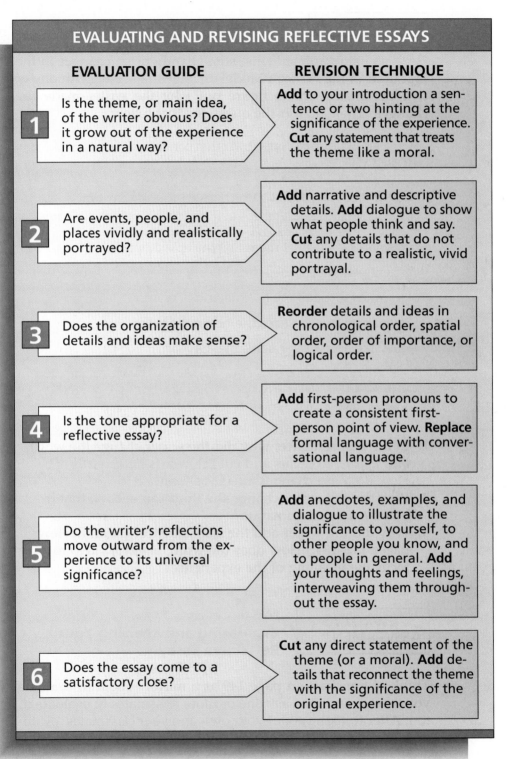

EVALUATING AND REVISING REFLECTIVE ESSAYS

	EVALUATION GUIDE	REVISION TECHNIQUE
1	Is the theme, or main idea, of the writer obvious? Does it grow out of the experience in a natural way?	**Add** to your introduction a sentence or two hinting at the significance of the experience. **Cut** any statement that treats the theme like a moral.
2	Are events, people, and places vividly and realistically portrayed?	**Add** narrative and descriptive details. **Add** dialogue to show what people think and say. **Cut** any details that do not contribute to a realistic, vivid portrayal.
3	Does the organization of details and ideas make sense?	**Reorder** details and ideas in chronological order, spatial order, order of importance, or logical order.
4	Is the tone appropriate for a reflective essay?	**Add** first-person pronouns to create a consistent first-person point of view. **Replace** formal language with conversational language.
5	Do the writer's reflections move outward from the experience to its universal significance?	**Add** anecdotes, examples, and dialogue to illustrate the significance to yourself, to other people you know, and to people in general. **Add** your thoughts and feelings, interweaving them throughout the essay.
6	Does the essay come to a satisfactory close?	**Cut** any direct statement of the theme (or a moral). **Add** details that reconnect the theme with the significance of the original experience.

EXERCISE 3 Analyzing a Writer's Revisions

Here's a paragraph showing some handwritten changes in the first draft of the Writer's Model on pages 144–146. With one or two classmates, try to figure out why the writer made the changes. Then answer the questions that follow.

Adults haven't outgrown this concern about ~~their apparel~~ clothes and ~~the necessity of~~ fitting in, either. Just the other day I overheard my mother on the phone discussing a school meeting. "Do you think slacks will be all right?" She asked her friend ~~whether slacks would be all right~~. She sounded just like my friends and I do. And when my father leaves the house, he looks just like every other adult male in our neighborhood. Their "uniform" consists of jeans and a short-sleeved shirt for casual wear, slacks and a tie for dressier times.

replace/cut

add

cut

add

1. In the first sentence, why did the writer change the words *their apparel* to *clothes* and cut the words *the necessity of*? How do these changes affect the tone?
2. Why did the writer change the third sentence so that it became a direct quotation?
3. Why did the writer add the last sentence? [Hint: Review pages 132–134.] How does the word *"uniform"* help to focus the meaning of the experience?

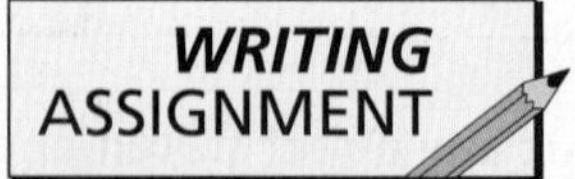

PART 5:
Evaluating and Revising Your Reflective Essay

Think of the chart on page 149 as a mirror. Use it to evaluate your essay, and then ask one or more classmates to evaluate it, too. After thinking about your own and your classmates' evaluations, make the changes you think will improve your essay.

Proofreading and Publishing

Once you have revised your essay, you need to look at it in a different way. Appearances are important to your readers, even in a personal essay, so you need to carefully proofread for mistakes in mechanics and usage. Then you might try one of the following suggestions for publishing your essay:

- If your essay is too private to share with a wider audience, consider starting a collection of private reflections. These would be similar to journal entries, but more finished and organized. Add to the collection as you write other reflective essays.
- With classmates who wish to share their thoughts, organize a booklet of essays. Title it "Reflections on ____ " and then make a table of contents page that lists the subject of each essay. See how many different ideas and topics are represented.

GRAMMAR HINT

Using Sentence Fragments Effectively

A personal essay has a more relaxed, informal tone than many other types of essays. That informality extends to the essay's sentence structure. Sentence fragments are usually considered a glaring error, but there are times in an informal essay when they can be used deliberately and effectively. Dialogue is one such place because people often talk in phrases, not complete sentences.

ORIGINAL: Jake couldn't believe what Gina had just said. "That's what you'd see in your dreams," he glared.

REVISED: Jake couldn't believe what Gina had just said. "In your dreams," he glared.

Fragments may also be used to emphasize a point or repeat a theme. Notice how the writer of the essay on fitting in, pages 144–146, uses a sentence fragment in the fourth paragraph from the end.

Alone.

This fragment helps to focus the writer's meaning—it emphasizes the most important reason for fitting in. The next-to-the-last sentence of the essay is also a fragment. "Spoken like a true trendsetter" calls attention to the writer's last point. It also reinforces the reflective nature of the essay by mimicking the writer's thoughts and reactions to the experience. Use sentence fragments cautiously in informal writing and not at all in formal essays with a more serious tone.

PART 6:

Proofreading and Publishing Your Essay

Put the finishing touches on your essay by proofreading it and correcting all mistakes. Make sure that any sentence fragments are confined to dialogue or used in another effective way. Then, using the second suggestion on page 151 or an idea of your own, share your work with others.

WRITING WORKSHOP

A Humorous Personal Essay

A reflective personal essay examines the meaning of an experience that was important to the writer, but with just a little twist, these same experiences might take a humorous turn. In the following essay, for example, Susan Trausch reflects on an experience most people have had—getting spots on clothing. To make her point, Trausch relies heavily on *exaggeration,* a form of humor that stretches reality.

As you read the essay, notice that the writer grabs your attention in the beginning with a humorous statement that also summarizes her main idea. Trausch also supports her main idea with a series of comic experiences and concludes with a humorous reflection. Where does the title of the essay come from? Why is it appropriate for the essay?

Out, out, telltale spot!

by Susan Trausch

It must be nice to be a slob.

There is a magnificence to people who can walk around all day with egg salad on a jacket and not care.

"Oh yeah," they say when people point, "that's my egg salad."

Most of us will never achieve such cool. We splotch up an outfit and want to go home. A spot becomes a billboard advertising our ineptitude, an all-points bulletin announcing that we are not the professionals we pretend to be.

"Some big-shot lawyer—can't even eat soup."

I remember lunching with a psychologist who, in the middle of an interview on societal stress, began screaming obscenities at his tie.

"Look at this," he shouted, whipping off the offending accessory and dunking it into his water glass. "Salad dressing! On silk!"

He gripped the tie in a stranglehold. The dirty little traitor! He'd have to buy a new one after lunch, drive back to his apartment and change, or try to do something creative with his tie clip.

He decided on a fourth option—wearing his jacket buttoned, even though the temperature was near 90.

Desperation transcends logic on such occasions. We wrap ourselves in sweaters, turn collars under, raise belts, or try to roll up the sleeves of a blazer. Sometimes we keep our hands over the spot and tell people we have heartburn.

I once wore a raincoat to hide the ink stain on a skirt. Then I spilled ice cream on the coat and covered it by holding a large brown envelope strategically over the chocolate. By the time I got home I needed an appointment with the psychologist.

There is probably a long name for this neurotic behavior, but I think of it as The Lady Macbeth Syndrome.

"Out, out!" we cry, working over our garments in the company washroom, usually making the problem worse. A tomato splatter on a white shirt becomes a smeared tomato splatter on a drenched white shirt.

And when we get back to our desks, the boss calls us in for a strategy session.

"Why are you carrying that magazine, Benson?"

"Interesting article in here . . . on spot metals."

The only thing worse than a stain front and center is one behind.

"You sat in something," says an observer, with that note of superiority clean people have when speaking to the soiled. "Looks like blueberries. You remember sitting in blueberries?"

One of the more inane questions of all time, but it is invariably asked. I always want to say, "Yes, I remember it well. It was 1:15 at the Ritz. I asked the waiter to bring over a big bowl of blueberries and dump them on my chair."

Who knows how half the stuff that we get on us gets there? Maybe it comes from God to keep us humble. It just appears, that's all, telling the world that here is a person who cannot control his fettuccine.

A fortune could be made with the invention of a solution guaranteed to remove stains instantly. We'd carry small vials of it with us everywhere, discreetly spritzing ourselves and eliminating spot shame forever.

I bet the president of the United States has it already. The Pentagon probably developed it years ago as a national security measure.

"If the prez stands there with beet juice on his suit, everybody will think we're a second-class power," said the generals. "Nuke that sucker."

Has the president or any other head of state ever been seen in public looking like the rest of us do after eating a submarine sandwich? Of course not. I rest my case.

But until the stuff is marketed to the public, we'll simply have to try harder to be slobs. With a little discipline and practice, we could learn to relax with our dirt.

On the other hand, maybe we should just wear more paisley.

The Boston Globe

Trausch's essay is an example of gentle humor. Instead of making biting, cruel fun of people, she is laughing at human nature, including herself in the crowd.

Writing a Humorous Personal Essay

Prewriting. Think of a human frailty you have noticed, perhaps one you have experienced yourself. It might be tripping over something when there's a crowd around, dropping things, saying the wrong thing at the wrong time. What is so embarrassing about the experience? What might the situation reveal about human nature? What's funny about it? Brainstorm examples or anecdotes of the experience happening to people. Jot down details that support your main point—what the experience says about human nature.

Writing, Evaluating, Revising. Relax while you write, but allow your imagination to work overtime. If you think of any way to add humor by exaggerating details and dialogue, do it. Before revising, share your draft with some classmates or friends. Find out what parts make your readers laugh, and go back to work on the parts they find dull.

Proofreading and Publishing. Check your revised essay for mistakes and then correct them. Consider reading your essay aloud to the class or sharing it with a person whose sense of humor is similar to yours. People really enjoy laughing. Your essay might make someone's day!

MAKING CONNECTIONS

Writing a Brief Autobiography

Like a reflective essay, an autobiography is also a form of self-expression. As a senior in high school, you may soon be asked to write a brief autobiographical statement on an application for a job or college. When you sit down to plan and draft it, use the skills you have learned in writing your reflective essay. Express what has occurred in your life and why it is significant. Interweave experience and thoughts. And most of all, relax: Don't let applications intimidate you.

On the next two pages is a humorous reply to a standard college application, written by an eighteen-year-old student named Hugh Gallagher. You might not want to take the light-hearted approach Gallagher took to a serious question, but the approach did work for him. His essay won first prize in the humor category of a writing contest.

"The writer of any work, and particularly any nonfiction work, must decide two crucial points: what to put in and what to leave out."

Annie Dillard

The Wonder Years

by Hugh Gallagher

QUESTION: ARE THERE ANY SIGNIFICANT EXPERIENCES YOU HAVE HAD, OR ACCOMPLISHMENTS YOU HAVE REALIZED, THAT HAVE HELPED TO DEFINE YOU AS A PERSON?

I am a dynamic figure, often seen scaling walls and crushing ice. I have been known to remodel train stations on my lunch breaks, making them more efficient in the area of heat retention. I translate ethnic slurs for Cuban refugees, I write award-winning operas, I manage time efficiently. Occasionally, I tread water for three days in a row.

I woo women with my sensuous and godlike trombone playing, I can pilot bicycles up severe inclines with unflagging speed, and I cook Thirty-Minute Brownies in twenty minutes. I am an expert in stucco, a veteran in love, and an outlaw in Peru.

Using only a hoe and a large glass of water, I once single-handedly defended a small village in the Amazon Basin from a horde of ferocious army ants. I play bluegrass cello, I was scouted by the Mets. I am the subject of numerous documentaries. When I'm bored, I build large suspension bridges in my yard. I enjoy urban hang gliding. On Wednesdays, after school, I repair electrical appliances free of charge.

I am an abstract artist, a concrete analyst, and a ruthless bookie. Critics worldwide swoon over my original line of corduroy evening wear. I don't perspire. I am a private citizen, yet I receive fan mail. I have been caller number nine and have won the weekend passes. Last summer I toured New Jersey with a traveling centrifugal-force demonstration. I bat .400. My deft floral arrangements have earned me fame in international botany circles. Children trust me.

I can hurl tennis rackets at small moving objects with deadly accuracy. I once read *Paradise Lost, Moby-Dick,* and *David Copperfield* in one day and still had time to refurbish an entire dining room that evening. I know the exact location of every food item in the supermarket. I have performed covert operations for the CIA. I sleep once a week; when I do sleep, I sleep in a chair. While on vacation in Canada, I successfully negotiated with a group of terrorists who had seized a small bakery. The laws of physics do not apply to me.

I balance, I weave, I dodge, I frolic, and my bills are all paid. On weekends, to let off steam, I participate in full-contact origami. Years ago I discovered the meaning of life but forgot to write it down. I have made extraordinary four-course meals using only a Mouli and a toaster oven. I breed prizewinning clams. I have won bullfights in San Juan, cliff-diving competitions in Sri Lanka, and spelling bees at the Kremlin. I have played Hamlet, I have performed open-heart surgery, and I have spoken with Elvis.

But I have not yet gone to college.

Harper's Magazine

You might try writing your own autobiographical sketch. It can be serious or humorous, depending on your purpose. Or you might try finding an example of an autobiographical sketch to share with your class. Just be sure it illustrates how a significant experience or accomplishment has affected someone.

Self-Expression and the Future: Setting Goals

Exploring the meaning of an experience in a reflective essay is just one way you might discover yourself. Another way is to think about how you might affect the future. What dreams do you have for yourself? for others? for the world around you? The dream Martin Luther King, Jr., spoke of began with his personal dreams for racial equality.

Although you may not plan to march on Washington, you still have a future to mold and shape, and one way to shape it is by creating a statement of goals. Look ahead to your life five years from now. What kind of person do you want to be? What kind of relationships do you want to have with others? And how do you want the world around you to be? Using these three questions, write a statement of goals for yourself, as in the following example. Notice that the writer also includes a list of ways to meet each goal.

1. Five years from now I want to be the kind of person who is *intellectually curious*. How will I get there?

I'll continue to read, not just required stuff, but newspapers, books, and magazines that broaden my knowledge.

I'll take a few risks with courses I'm not especially good at, like science and foreign languages.

I'll try not to be obsessed with grades and getting a job.

I'll take advantage of opportunities to broaden my horizons, like attending concerts and meeting international students.

2. Five years from now, I want people to see me as the kind of person who is *a leader*. How will I get there?

   I'll take a stand on issues I believe in, even if they're not popular.

   I'll look for ways to exercise leadership—in clubs, at work, at home.

   I'll follow through on commitments.

3. Five years from now, I want the physical, social, and political world to be *environmentally safer*. How will I get there?

   I'll make a serious effort to recycle as much as possible.

   I'll register and vote for candidates who support this issue.

   I'll join clubs that promote a cleaner, safer environment.

   I'll talk to people about doing their part.

You don't have to share your own goals with other people, but do so if you wish. Then save them, and read them again in six months or a year to see whether you need to make any adjustments.

"... I always try to write on the principle of the iceberg. There is seven-eighths of it under water for every part that shows."

Ernest Hemingway

5 CREATIVE WRITING

Imagining Other Worlds

It has been said that what distinguishes human beings from animals isn't reason at all, but imagination. The ability to **imagine other worlds** is a remarkable, rather mysterious gift, isn't it?

Writing and You. You use your imagination so often that you probably take it for granted. For example, a novelist lets you live among a fantastic race of trolls. A scriptwriter puts you on the streets of St. Louis or on a mountain in Colorado, no matter where you really live. The combination of language and imagination in stories, films, plays, and comic strips gives all of us opportunities to experience other lives, other times, other places. What imaginative world have you inhabited recently?

As You Read. Some characters in the following story fail to find what they're searching for. Is there a message here about imagination?

Doug Webb, *American Dream* (1986). Serigraph, 29″ × 35″.

The Precious Stones of Axolotyl

by Manuela Williams Crosno

Once long ago, there was an old woman who lived near the village of Agua Clara, which means "clear water." Although she was to live for many years more, she seemed older than anyone in the village. No one could remember where she came from or when.

She lived in a small lean-to built against a great rock. Among her few possessions were a herd of goats and an oddly shaped stick on which it was her custom to lean heavily as she went about her work.

She was so wrinkled one could not see her eyes to tell what color they were. Her skin was deep brown, like pine cones when they fall to the ground. And when she laughed she showed just two teeth. Because no one knew her name, and because she seemed to have lived in the mountains from their very beginning, she was called "La Vieja de las montañas"—the old woman of the mountains.

Now there resided in the village of Agua Clara three small boys whose names were Anselmo, Felipe, and Guillermo. They lived in separate houses built of adobe. The houses were almost as alike as the boys, who were the same age and were constant companions.

One time when they went toward the mountains, they came upon the goats of La Vieja, unwatched, and eating peacefully at the sparse gramma grass that grew about. Guillermo began to throw stones at the animals. Anselmo howled like a coyote. Felipe gave the weird cry of the mountain lion. The goats, in a panic, began to run in all directions.

Suddenly, the voice of La Vieja called to them. The goats stopped where they were and again ate grass in a peaceful manner. The boys turned homeward, but standing in their pathway and leaning on her stick was La Vieja.

Shaking her stick in his direction, she said to Anselmo, "You howled like a coyote to frighten my goats. You are unwise." And to Guillermo, "You threw stones to hurt my goats. You are unkind." Then to Felipe, "You cried like the lion of the mountains to make my goats run away. You have little understanding." To all three she said, "When you have learned wisdom, kindness, and understanding, then I will show you the precious stones of axolotyl."

Stepping aside, she disappeared behind a rock, leaving the boys somewhat frightened. For many days they thought about this meeting with La Vieja, and they *never forgot* the words of the old woman.

Many years passed and Guillermo, Anselmo, and Felipe grew to manhood. Anselmo was judge of all disputes in the village and was considered to be very wise. However, if anyone had a story to tell and needed a sympathetic ear, he went to Felipe who could always be counted upon for understanding. Guillermo was the one to call when a child was hurt, for he ministered to the ill and needy. It was well known in the village that no one was as kind and as gentle as Guillermo.

Now when Otero became governor, he sent his soldiers about the country to seize any possessions of value which they might discover. They had heard of the precious stones of axolotyl which were said to belong to La Vieja, and although the soldiers thought this talk was probably just a fable, they went to the old woman.

"We have come for your jewels!" they said.

She was silent for a long moment. Then she smiled—a smile they could not interpret. It showed her two teeth, but since they could not see her eyes, they did not know whether or not she was angry.

"They are the jewels of axolotyl, the water dog," she said, finally. "Come with me and I will show them to you."

The soldiers followed La Vieja past the place where the goats were corralled, and beyond her house into the wooded foothills. She walked slowly and leaned heavily on her stick. Finally, she came to a

pool beyond a waterfall where it seemed the waters, after their noisy dash over the rocks, had stopped to rest. There was no movement in the still depths of the pool. Glistening far below the surface were rocks of many colors.

"See the green one?" she asked, pointing to a green pebble near the bottom of the pool. "See the scarlet one," she said, selecting a red pebble still farther in the clear depths. "See the perfectly white one?" she asked, thrusting the stick toward the deepest part of the pool. The soldiers nodded and looked at one another.

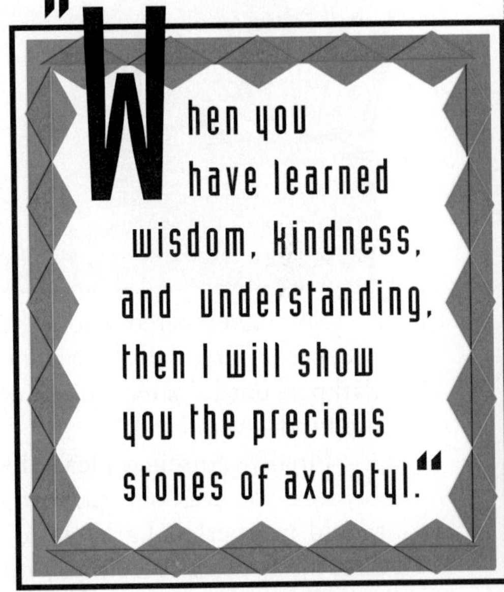
"When you have learned wisdom, kindness, and understanding, then I will show you the precious stones of axolotyl."

"Those," she cried, laughing triumphantly, "are the precious stones of axolotyl!"

Now axolotyl is a water dog and is reported to be poisonous. Long ago, it is said, he took the soul of one of the people. So the soldiers were afraid of him or the mention of his name. They looked at the rocks shining in the pool. They looked at La Vieja.

"She is a foolish old woman," they whispered together. "These are not precious stones, they are but rocks."

Since she had no jewels, and because they felt that she had attempted to deceive them, the soldiers took La Vieja to Agua Clara. There she was locked in a small room where she was to remain for many days. After some time, there was a knock at her door and Felipe stood outside. He had heard that she was ill and had come with food. She would accept nothing, however. Instead, she said these words which she repeated many times:

"You understand, amigo, you understand."

Still later, there was a voice at her window in the dark and Guillermo whispered, "La Viejita, I have cared for your goats and brought you your walking stick which I found near the corral."

She remembered where the soldiers had thrown her stick and she accepted it gratefully. For a long time she looked at Guillermo in the darkness until she recognized who he was. Then she said, "Amigo, you are kind—very kind."

Finally, Anselmo pleaded with the governor to let the woman go because she was old and owned no precious stones. The governor would not permit La Vieja to be freed until Anselmo had promised him many pesos to help pay for the soldiers.

The old woman of the mountains thanked Anselmo for her release, and said to him, "Amigo mio, I see that you are one who is very wise. Tomorrow, bring Felipe and Guillermo with you and come to see me."

Since he wished to please her, Anselmo called his friends the next day. Together they went to the place where La Vieja was tending her goats. She smiled when she saw the three friends and said, "You have indeed learned wisdom and kindness and understanding. Come with me."

Slowly she led them to the pool which was bathed in sunlight and shadow. It was the pool she had shown the soldiers. Pointing to the three stones shining within it, she said, "These are the precious stones of axolotyl."

Now she took the long stick on which she had always leaned so heavily, and turned the knob outward. They saw that it was a cup which swiveled, and that when the stick was turned about, it resembled a large dipper. Thus, she thrust the stick into the pool once and brought up the white stone, and gave it to Anselmo saying, "For wisdom." In the same manner she dipped the stick into the pool again, and gave the green stone to Guillermo, telling him only that he had become very kind. Again the stick went into the water, and this time the red stone was placed in the hand of Felipe, "For understanding."

Soon after this, La Vieja died, but she was never forgotten. Felipe, Guillermo, and Anselmo carried the stones in their pockets for some time before they learned that one was a diamond, another an emerald, and the third one, a ruby. Yet they never considered them as priceless as the real jewels of axolotyl.

READER'S RESPONSE

1. Did you believe the stones were jewels when La Vieja showed them to the soldiers? Why or why not?
2. Why do you think a very old, mysterious person—whether wise or sinister—figures in so many stories, from ancient times to today? What examples can you think of besides La Vieja?
3. What reward have you received that you didn't expect or that came from a surprising source? Why was it unexpected, and what did you learn from it? Write about the experience in your journal.

WRITER'S CRAFT

4. A story without tension isn't a story. There's always a conflict or problem that someone faces and must resolve. What conflicts do you find in "The Precious Stones of Axolotyl"?
5. From the very first, we have a sense of La Vieja's mystery and power. Through what specific details does the writer convey these qualities?
6. Crosno used her imagination to create a story with a message, or theme. If you removed the imaginary world and simply stated the theme, what would you say?

Strategies for Writing Creatively

Writers whose purpose is to be creative, to use language in an original, imaginative way, may write stories, poems, novels, movie and TV scripts—even comic strips and song lyrics. Whatever form their creative expression takes, however, they make use of the four basic strategies of writing. These examples show how the four strategies can be used when your purpose is to write creatively.

Narration: in a movie script, telling about a team of scientists shrunk to the size of molecules for a journey inside a human body; in a short story, telling about a man who wakes up one day to find himself turned into a giant cockroach.

Description: in a poem, describing a strange palace, caverns, woods, and a sacred river; in a drama, a character describing the teacher who taught her to read.

Classification: in a story, contrasting an older woman sitting on a park bench with a young couple sitting next to her; in a poem, naming many different kinds of "dappled things."

Evaluation: in a play, showing how ambition and pride can lead to evil deeds; in a long poem, telling the consequences of the thoughtless killing of an albatross.

LOOKING AHEAD

In this chapter, you will use the strategies of narration and description to create a short story, a scene, and a poem. As you work through the chapter's main assignment, which is to write a story, keep in mind that a good short story

- holds the reader's attention with believable characters and an interesting plot
- involves the main character in a problem or conflict that must be resolved
- may communicate some insight about life

Writing a Short Story

Exploring Story Ideas

You can start small when looking for a story idea. Just a glimpse of some person, place, or situation may be the seed your imagination can water.

- A computer that runs a spaceship decides to take control from the human crew.
- An old fisherman, alone in his small boat, hooks an enormous fish.
- An ambitious general hears a mysterious prophecy that he will be crowned king.

Do these seeds sound familiar? Even the fascinating, full-blown stories of *2001: A Space Odyssey, The Old Man and the Sea,* and *The Tragedy of Macbeth* sprang from something particular—and not yet complete. To begin your search for a story idea, be alert to anything and everything that captures your attention, sticks in your memory, or turns your imagination on high.

Observing and Reading. Keep your antennae out. Watching television, reading a magazine, or even sitting on a bench may bring something into your vision that could grow into a story—a fire in a high-rise, a man who keeps twenty dogs in his house, a young girl who is training for a marathon.

Remembering. Brainstorming or freewriting can help you pluck kernels of story ideas from memories of people you have known or from situations you have experienced. Do you have a recurring dream of coming to school in pajamas? Does your eight-year-old cousin do fantastic things with computers?

Imagining. Because some of your best ideas come from letting your imagination go, try asking yourself "What if?" questions. What if the President of the United States were a teenager? What if a tornado hit your neighborhood?

WRITING ASSIGNMENT

PART 1:
Finding a Story Idea

You have looked at several methods—observing and reading, remembering, and imagining—that you can use to identify a story idea. Try one or more of these methods now; and when you have your story idea, write it in a few sentences.

Planning Your Story

Where is your story idea leading you? Who will be in your story? What will happen? It is some distance (and discovery) from first idea to finished story, but the rest of this chapter will help you find your way. And it will be *your* way: You'll use basic short-story elements to tell your unique tale.

Developing Conflict and Plot

The ***plot,*** or events, of your story offers you much freedom but has one indispensable part: a ***conflict,*** or problem, that the main character (or characters) faces. The character can cause a crisis or be confronted with one, can hunger for something or fear a terrible decision. The possibilities are endless, but the reader must wonder, "How will this turn out?"

TYPES OF CONFLICT	
A character struggles against another character, a group, or society's rules.	Josh and his best friend are competing for the same scholarship.
A character struggles against a force of nature.	The car carrying the wrestling team stalls in a blinding blizzard.
A character struggles with personal feelings, values, or needs.	Suzette regrets leaving home but feels she can't go back.

With a conflict established, your job is to decide (1) how to solve that conflict and (2) how to keep the story moving forward and readers interested until the solution is reached.

Most story writers use a basic shape to drive their plots and draw in readers. After the conflict sets events in motion, ***complications*** may arise. These setbacks or additional conflicts make the outcome less sure. What you're always leading to, though, is a ***climax:*** a scene of keen interest when the conflict will be settled. The climax may be a small gesture (sharing a plate of food), or it may be action-packed excitement (roping a runaway horse). (Another name for climax is ***high point,*** and that's the image to keep in mind.)

After the climax, or high point, of the action, you need to "resolve" the problem or conflict for your readers. This ending of a story is the ***resolution,*** the final details that show how everything works out and that bring the story to a satisfying close.

Here's one writer's plan for the plot of her story.

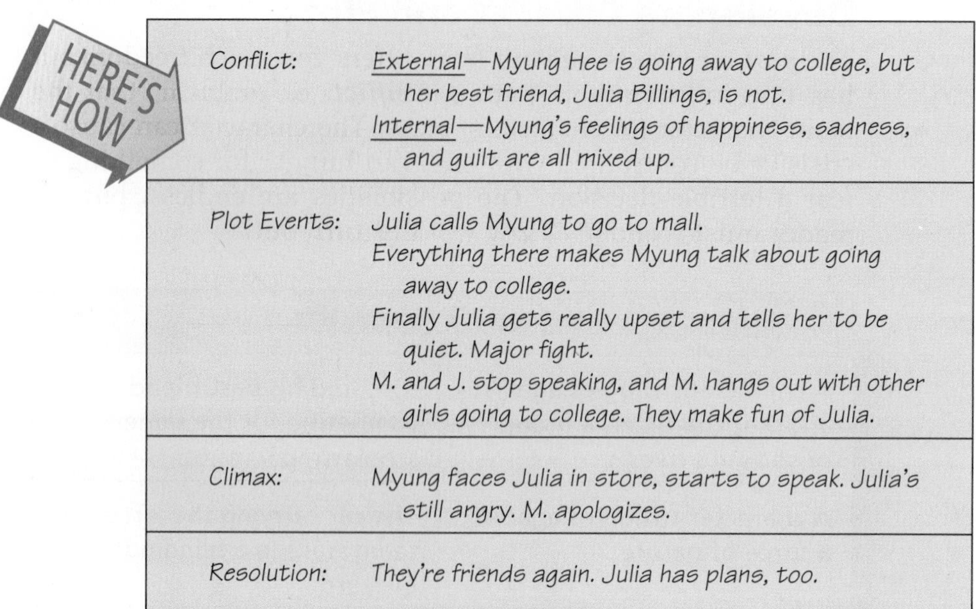

Conflict:	*External—Myung Hee is going away to college, but her best friend, Julia Billings, is not.* *Internal—Myung's feelings of happiness, sadness, and guilt are all mixed up.*
Plot Events:	*Julia calls Myung to go to mall.* *Everything there makes Myung talk about going away to college.* *Finally Julia gets really upset and tells her to be quiet. Major fight.* *M. and J. stop speaking, and M. hangs out with other girls going to college. They make fun of Julia.*
Climax:	*Myung faces Julia in store, starts to speak. Julia's still angry. M. apologizes.*
Resolution:	*They're friends again. Julia has plans, too.*

PART 2:

Developing Your Conflict and Plot

You may have already identified a conflict when you chose a story idea for Writing Assignment, Part 1. Now check that idea and expand it if necessary to make sure your main character has a struggle against someone or something else, or a struggle within himself or herself. Then brainstorm for complications and decide how the conflict will be resolved. Pull it all together in a plot plan like the one shown above.

Exploring Characters and Setting

Characters. Like Frankenstein's monster, your *characters* are entirely your own creation; but if you make them real enough, they may eventually start acting on their own. Plan to give each one a distinct personality, appearance, and history. You may create characters that are totally imaginary, or you may combine traits from real-life people. For example, you could create a main character with the humor of Eddie Murphy, the strength of Arnold Schwarzenegger, and the looks of your Uncle John. Collect enough details to develop a full sense of who your characters are—even though you may not use all the details you invent. Here are some questions to use.

- How old are the characters? What do they look like (height, weight, eye color, skin color, hair color and style, clothing)?
- How do they move (clumsily, gracefully, sneakily) and speak (tone of voice, accent, expressions)?
- What are some important personality traits (bossy, angry, arrogant, timid, kind, confident, sneaky)?
- What do they think about (wishes, hopes, worries)?
- How do they get along with other characters?

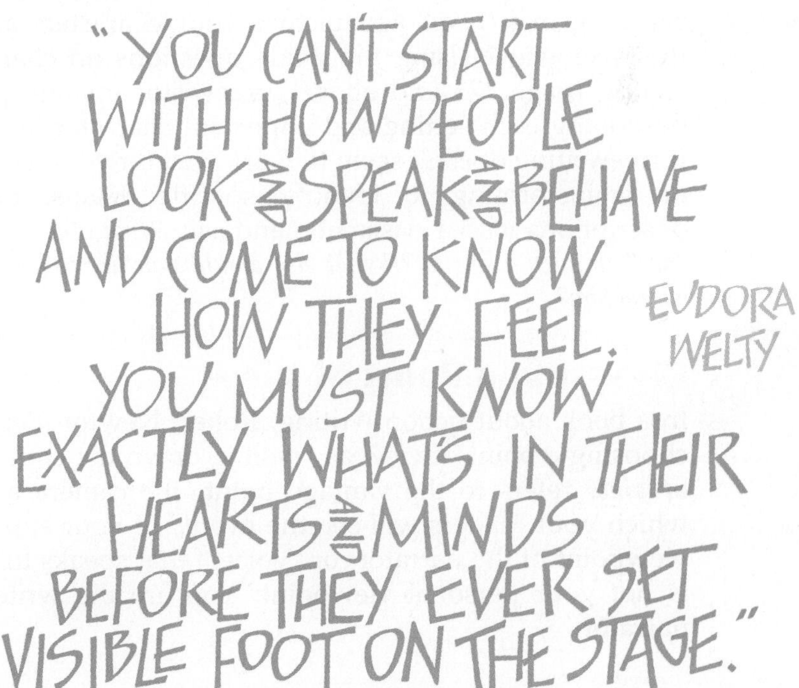

"YOU CAN'T START WITH HOW PEOPLE LOOK AND SPEAK AND BEHAVE AND COME TO KNOW HOW THEY FEEL. YOU MUST KNOW EXACTLY WHAT'S IN THEIR HEARTS AND MINDS BEFORE THEY EVER SET VISIBLE FOOT ON THE STAGE."
EUDORA WELTY

Setting. A story's setting can be as ordinary as Saturday morning in a kitchen or as strange as a space colony a thousand years from now; it can be extremely important to the development of the story or only a minor element. ***Setting*** includes the time and place, weather and season—even the objects in a room.

Sensory details of place and time often help create a story's ***mood,*** or general feeling. The testing room at a shampoo factory, for instance, can be scary or funny, depending on the sounds, smells, and sights the writer describes. As you think about your setting, ask yourself these questions:

- Where and when will my story take place?
- What sensory details about time, place, or weather could contribute to the story's mood?
- What details of setting could reveal information about the characters or plot?

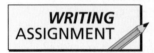

PART 3:
Exploring Your Setting and Characters

Can you imagine your setting so clearly that you feel you're standing in it? Can you picture your characters and predict their behavior? Using the guide questions on characters and setting (page 173 and above), freewrite separate paragraphs describing each setting and important character in your story. If freewriting doesn't seem to work well for you, use clustering or brainstorming to identify specific details. Share your descriptions with a classmate, and ask: *What other details do you "see" in such a setting? What else would you like to know about the characters?*

Choosing a Point of View

In a book about fiction writing, Robert Newton Peck refers to choosing a point of view as "nailing down the corners." ***Point of view*** refers to the vantage point, the camera angle, from which your readers will see the events of your story. It is the viewpoint of the narrator, or "voice," that speaks to readers. It is not your personal viewpoint: You are the writer, *not* the narrator.

A basic choice in point of view is whether to use a first-person or third-person narrator. A first-person narrator communicates immediacy and a distinct personality, while a third-person narrator (either limited or omniscient) is a more distant and faceless reporter. Each point of view has some advantages and disadvantages, but whichever you choose, be consistent. You'll confuse readers if you switch the point of view from a first-person narrator to a third-person narrator.

POINT OF VIEW	
First-person: This point of view can make a story personal and build strong response to a character, but the reader can be told only what the character sees, hears, knows, and believes.	"It was partly her own fault, of course. How was I to know? She was pretty clever about it. And she never once came out and admitted she was illiterate. It took me years to catch on, and by then it was much too late." Hisaye Yamamoto, *Reading and Writing*
Third-person limited: This outside point of view focuses on one character's perspective. The narrator can enter that character's mind without being restricted to the character's actions or location.	"She felt so much the change in her own face that she went to the mirror, polished a clear patch in it and looked at once urgently and stealthily in." Elizabeth Bowen, "The Demon Lover"
Third-person omniscient: *Omniscient* means "all-knowing." This outside narration, the most flexible, can enter the mind of *any* character. It gives a wider view, presenting any detail or viewpoint—even revealing the future.	"She had a white nape to her neck and short red hair above it, and Shawn liked the color and wave of that flame. . . . Ellen, her heart desolate, lay on her side, staring into the dark, grieving for what she had said and unable to unsay it." Maurice Walsh, *The Quiet Man*

EXERCISE 1 Speaking and Listening: Experimenting with Point of View

Read the following passage, which is told by a first-person narrator. Then rewrite the passage from another point of view—as a different first-person narrator (one of the Tulls), as a third-person limited narrator, or as an omniscient narrator. After you have finished writing, read what you've written aloud to the members of your class and ask them to identify the point of view you are using. If you have done a good job, they will be able to identify it correctly.

> That horse. It ain't never missed a lick. It was going about forty miles a hour when it come to the bridge over the creek. It would have had a clear road, but it so happened that Vernon Tull was already using the bridge when it got there. He was coming back from town; he hadn't heard about the auction; him and his wife and three daughters and Mrs. Tull's aunt, all setting in chairs in the wagon bed, and all asleep, including the mules. They waked up when the horse hit the bridge one time, but Tull said the first he knew was when the mules tried to turn the wagon around in the middle of the bridge and he seen that spotted varmint run right twixt the mules and run up the wagon tongue like a squirrel. He said he just had time to hit it across the face with his whip-stock, because about that time the mules turned the wagon around on that ere one-way bridge and that horse clumb across one of the mules and jumped down onto the bridge again and went on, with Vernon standing up in the wagon and kicking at it.
>
> William Faulkner, "Spotted Horses"

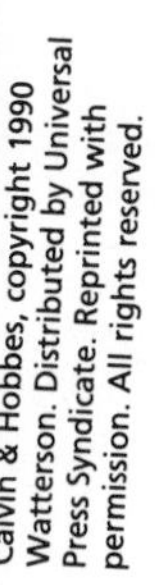

Thinking About Purpose, Audience, and Tone

Purpose and Audience. When you write a story, your main *purpose* is to be creative, to exercise your imagination through words. That purpose includes entertaining your *audience,* but "entertaining" doesn't necessarily mean amusing them or making them happy. It means keeping them interested, compelling them to turn the page, and creating *any* effect you want to achieve. Depending on how you tell it, a story about a seventy-year-old woman who collars a robber in a bodega (grocery store) can move your readers to tears, white knuckles, or tender smiles.

Part of your purpose may also be to communicate an idea, or *theme.* Perhaps your story about the bodega has a message about elderly people or desperately poor people or city barrios (districts). Usually you don't state the theme directly, as you might state an idea in an essay (*we often underestimate old people*), but you can show it through characters and events.

Tone. *Tone* plays a part in the effect you create because it expresses your attitude toward characters, plot, and readers. You can create a serious, silly, romantic, or ironic tone with your choice of events, details, and language. Point of view, the narrator who "speaks," affects tone, too. Notice how the tone changes in these two descriptions of the same scene. The first tone is matter-of-fact, clear and simple, and informal. The second is poetic and dramatic.

> I bought six cartons of umbrellas and got stampeded the day I set up on Eighty-fifth Street. It poured so hard the $3.98 specials were gone by noon.

Like a tide of ants attacking a chocolate bar, buyers swarmed around the umbrella seller. Crimson, black, and polka-dot umbrellas billowed into the wind-whipped rain, with their new owners struggling beneath them.

To plan your story

- put a main character into a conflict and decide how the conflict will end
- map plot events that move steadily, with possible complications, to a climax and resolution
- sketch details of main characters and setting
- decide on point of view
- think ahead about what you want readers to feel and whether you want them to reflect on an idea or theme

PART 4:
Completing a Plan for Your Story

To complete the planning for your story, take time to think about your audience, purpose, and tone. Do you want your audience to laugh, cry, reflect on some idea about life? This is also the time to decide on your point of view. Remember that your choice of point of view will determine how close your readers feel to the characters, as well as how much flexibility you'll have as a writer. When you have finished your plan, save it for later use.

Writing Your First Draft

Combining the Basic Elements of Stories

A good story suspends reality. No matter how fantastic—a smooth crystal planet with stick-fast, rubber inhabitants—we believe in it as a living world. How do writers do it? They combine the basic elements of stories—characters, plot, setting—with specific techniques that bring both the characters and the story to life.

Creating Living, Breathing Characters. Telling readers about a character is fine; it's a direct, to-the-point technique of defining character: *Eddie really cared about other people, at least when he took the time to think about them.* But if you overuse this direct-statement approach, you will lose all the life in your characters. Instead, develop characters by showing their

- **appearance, actions, and thoughts:** *Eddie bounced his way down the street, glancing in every store window to check out his new black jeans. He was definitely looking good—in fact, he was looking better every day.*
- **effects on other characters:** *This time Sara had had it with Eddie. She wasn't going to forgive being stood up for the third time in a week.*
- **speech (dialogue):** *"Aw, Sara," Eddie wheedled, "what you want? I'm supposed to stop going to practice? Coach ran us so hard I slept all afternoon. I didn't forget—I just wasn't awake."*

Creating Vivid Descriptions. You can also create a world that seems real by using vivid, concrete details. This means using words that are as precise as possible (*kayak,* not *boat; slithered,* not *moved*) and ***images,*** details that create sights, sounds, smells, tastes, and textures for readers. ***Figures of speech*** (unusual comparisons) such as ***metaphors*** and ***similes*** are another way your language can be vivid and surprising—for example, comparing steam shovels to yellow dinosaurs or garden hoses to green snakes.

In the following passage, look for all three of these descriptive strategies. The narrator is describing his martial-arts instructor practicing on the YMCA roof.

Then he did *katas,* attacking the head, stabbed, and punctured the dummy with kicks, then with punches, and then with combinations. He was unbelievably quick, his hands, feet blurs in the high roof wind. He had a turn kick, rotating his body like a 78 rpm record, his back horizontal to the ground as his free leg punched into the dummy, making it bend on its stake and crack back. He cried, "Keee-YAT!" as he did his work. It was like watching Victor Mature kill the lion, or Big Willie do Kai Ting. This was *wu-shu,* the combat of my ancestry. Uncle Han knew how to do this, in China.

Gus Lee, *China Boy*

Did Gus Lee's descriptive techniques make this scene seem real to you? Can you see the blur of the man's hands and feet? Does the comparison between the man's turn kick and a rotating record create a vivid image in your mind? If you can see the man's actions in your mind, the writer made these techniques work.

REFERENCE NOTE: For more about figurative language, see page 534.

Make your descriptions work for you, not overwhelm readers. An avalanche of descriptions, no matter how vivid, will clutter the story path for readers. Give them sensory experiences that make a difference in a story, as the description of the *wu-shu* practice helps to reveal character, build mood, and prepare for later action.

Building a Tight Plot. There is one way in which your story can't be *too* much like real life: It can't be as messy—as full of random, accidental, inconsequential events. To keep your readers interested, the plot can't wander or change direction on whim. Keep your story in line and your readers involved with the following techniques:

- **Arouse interest immediately.** Open with sharp dialogue, a mood-setting description, a puzzle, or fast action.
- **Establish conflict quickly, and never forget it.** Get to the main problem as soon as possible, and make sure all events and details are important to it. This doesn't mean you can't provide background and colorful details—just make them *count* in the plot.
- **Keep current action clear but the future uncertain.** Create suspense or curiosity about what may happen, but don't pull tricks (like old boyfriends or erupting volcanoes) out of a hat. Even a surprise ending should be believable. Keep events in chronological order (see pages 74 and 80–82) unless you must give a ***flashback,*** a memory or a scene of important past events.
- **Resolve the conflict in a satisfying, original way.** After the climax of the conflict, the reader needs to see that the loose ends are tied up—and that's all. This is not the time to drag things out; and unless you are writing a fable, it isn't the time to announce a moral or theme. Instead, try showing the main character in a final moment of action, thought, or dialogue.

CRITICAL THINKING

Evaluating Dialogue

Evaluating means judging the quality or effectiveness of something. How do you judge the dialogue in a story? Isn't it the writer's decision what characters say? Yes, the writer decides what to say, but *readers* decide whether the speech sounds forced, fake, or forgettable. Here are some important qualities of effective dialogue in stories.

1. **Dialogue is speech: spoken language, not written language.** You should try to write the way people talk, using contractions, slang, and fragments when necessary. (Think of your own conversations or those you overhear in public places.)
2. **Dialogue fits the character.** Teenagers and grandparents don't usually talk the same way; neither do Russian immigrants and midwestern farmers. Choose a character's words and sentence structure carefully. In some cases, you might want to change spellings to show ***dialect,*** special speech characteristics.
3. **Dialogue serves a purpose.** Make your dialogue contribute to the story. Does it reveal character, move the plot forward, add background information?

CRITICAL THINKING EXERCISE:
Evaluating and Revising Dialogue

Work with one or two of your classmates to evaluate the dialogue in the following passage. It's definitely ineffective, but *why*? Keep in mind the three important qualities of effective dialogue: It should sound like spoken language; it should fit the character; and it should serve a purpose. Then rewrite the passage to create more effective dialogue for each character. Your group might enjoy comparing your revisions with another group's work.

Kate was so mad she was talking to herself. "Fiddlesticks and rats," she said. She'd been waiting for Burton for two hours. He was supposed to bring her homework and visit for a while. Didn't he know she was sick of being at home with two broken legs, one broken arm, and the mysterious ear rash? "Some compatriot you have shown yourself to be," she muttered. "Slime bag bozo."

When Burton arrived, he came in apologizing. "Whew, a tad late. Are you especially irritated? Forgive me, dear heart. Where do the hours fly? I dunno, I dunno. I believe I'll park it in this chair today." He continued with a grin, "But then, where was ya gonna go? Out dancing?"

Kate said that she would like to hit him with her crutch if she could reach it.

Looking at a Short Story

Now you will see how one writer combines the basic story elements into a unique short story. As you read, notice especially how Egyirba High immediately focuses your attention on an unforgettable character who always stirs things up.

A SHORT STORY

The Lion Sleeps Tonight

by Egyirba High

Attention grabber/Song

In the jungle
the mighty jungle
the lion sleeps tonight . . . .

First-person point of view

Eloise Carter wasn't my blood relative. She was just Aunt Eloise.

In the jungle
the mighty jungle
the lion sleeps
tonight.

She was the odd one.

A weema way, a weema way
A weema way, a weema way
A weema way, a weema way
A weema way, a weema way

Conflict

At least that's what the folks wanted us to believe—that Aunt Eloise was crazy or something.

Character developed/ Appearance and responses of others

Bright orange or yellow caftans flowing, purple and brown and green turbans sitting stately upon her head. She was regal. Her face was not extraordinary, but bathed and dressed in Africa, she was exquisite. She was all Africa. She was out of step. She embarrassed them.

Setting/Sensory images

Flashbacks

Sometimes, after church on Sundays, we'd go to her home. I remember once smelling something good in the kitchen and then jumping back ten feet when I peeked in and saw a large cow tongue in the pot. I grabbed my throat and wondered how painful it must be not to be able to talk.

Then there was the time when she cooked hogshead cheese. I looked at the finished product and tried to figure out what the head of the hog must have looked like.

Characters developed/ Dialogue

"Go on and taste it."

"It looks ugh, Aunt Eloise."

"Come on, take this little, bitty cracker and put some cheese on it, just a little itsy-bitsy."

I looked at her intently to see if she was serious. Her face bore a deadpan expression.

Sensory detail

"Okay, just a little." My mouth turned up, imagining the worst, as I bit into the jelly-like substance.

"It's still ugh."

Characters developed/Actions and dialogue

And peals of laughter came bellowing out of her mouth.

"Well, good, then. More for me."

"You can have it."

***End of Flashback*/ Background details**

"You know, Michelle, that's how Negroes had to survive in slavery times – with what they had."

Characters developed/ Actions, dialogue, others' responses

Those conversations happened on her more subdued days. She was a teacher and always teaching me and my sisters when we came to visit. But the most curious, exciting times had to do with African dancing.

Aunt Eloise would sit and chat for a while and then, as if by cue, she would glide over to the record player. This was the signal that there was about to be a show. Stef or Lisa would giggle, “Uh oh, she’s getting ready to start,” and I’d turn towards the grownups to catch their reactions. Mama and Daddy would sigh a big here-we-go-again sigh, and the voice of Miriam Makeba filled the room.

Sensory detail

She danced. My sisters, Stefanie and Lisa, stood by and watched her with great curiosity. None of us had ever seen dancing like it before, and nobody did it except Aunt Eloise.

All the time the music played, Aunt Eloise danced. And danced. And then as she danced, she remembered us.

“Come dance, girls.”

Conflict building

Timidly, Stef and I would get behind her and try to copy her steps. Lisa hid in the corner.

The grownups, Mama and Daddy, her husband, Uncle John, and their daughter, Brenda, were always ashamed.

Dialogue/Feelings and plot details

“Woman, sit down. Don’t nobody wanna see all that spook stuff.”

No response.

“Eloise, come on over here and talk to your company. You can’t leave these people just sitting here.”

Sensory images

Still no response. Only the beat of drums growing louder in the room as the silence of discomfort grew, and Uncle John quit trying to reason with his wife. He’d look back at Mama and Daddy, and then they’d play the eye game, which was also known as the what-can-I-say-you-know-how-she-is look.

Mama would pick up his cue, glance back at Uncle John with “I-know-but-you-have-to-let-her-be,” while my daddy just grunted, to no one in particular, his feelings of disgust. Brenda, who had no patience with her mother’s shenanigans, would sigh loudly, turn on her heels, and walk quickly out of the room.

Dialogue/ Character development and background

“Ahwoo! Ahwoo! Ah! Ah! Uhn! Ah! You have to feel it, Michelle. Feel the beat. See the drummer playing there. Feel it. You can see the blood spilled across centuries. Feel and know all things."

Description/ Images

Character developed/ Thoughts and actions ***Complication*** **Suspense**

Dancing. Bending and stretching to the earth, her right foot touched down, and she'd swoon in place. Then her left foot, her body yielding to African gods. Somewhere inside I knew it wasn't really funny. I felt awkward trying to dance. Something stirred in me, though it would not be named. I would dance with her until I became conscious of the stares again, and the silent reprobations would stop me cold.

Climax

Confused, I'd look back at Aunt Eloise, who never stopped dancing. She had greeted 'Legba and was now possessed by Yemaya. Or caught up in Oshun. I wasn't sure. I wanted to know . . . to dance . . . but they were looking. Their stares would reach into my awkwardness. And I'd freeze, aching to go where she was. Then suddenly, the drumming ended.

Setting/Character development

Even when the music stopped, the feeling didn't. Aunt Eloise, with new gusto, would go on talking about Africa, the beauty of Black people, how Cleopatra was Black and Elizabeth Taylor could only wish she was. She immortalized our heroes in the poems she wrote, and her stories left me curious and hungry for more. The walls were covered with pictures of Benjamin Banneker, Joe Louis, Phillis Wheatley, Mary McLeod Bethune,

Jesse Owens. On every spare shelf were African carvings of animals, goddesses and gods.

"Michelle, did you know that Charles Drew invented blood plasma?"

"No, Aunt Eloise."

"He did. And guess what?" she'd say, pointing to his picture on the wall. "He died needing blood, because he was turned away from a white hospital."

"Ohhhh." I'd nod my head, not because I knew this but as a sign for her to go on. I was young and overwhelmed by the essence of her. She was ambrosia to my spirit, ever sustaining her image by the charms and magic she brought to my life. She whirled endlessly in her dreams. I drank of her. I tasted her. I savored it.

Direct explanation, narrator

Aunt Eloise wasn't crazy. She was a sleeping lion ready to spring on cue to the moment. She was life and she was music. We only had to wonder. She knew and hoped we'd care. It was years later, after her death, that I realized I had received her legacy of love. She gave me Africa, and I love it passionately. When I hear her notes now, I sing her praises loudly, skin oiled in red earth, body dressed in the blackness of my people, soul moving to the rhythms of talking drums. She smiles, my ancestor, placated by my gifts, and returns to her throne, content, awaiting her invitation to the next celebration of life.

Resolution

Theme expressed

Sensory images

EXERCISE 2 **Analyzing the Elements of a Short Story**

With a partner or small group, discuss the following questions.

1. As the preceding story shows, a first-person narrator is not always the main character. What is the effect of telling the story from Michelle's, not Aunt Eloise's, point of view?
2. The main conflict in this story—the one that starts the plot—is an external one. What is it? This external conflict causes an internal conflict in Michelle. What is it, and how does it come to a climax in the story?
3. The narrator says that Aunt Eloise was "always teaching me and my sisters." Find examples of dialogue, events, and details of setting that *show,* not *tell,* what Aunt Eloise taught. Michelle is an important character, too. How does the writer let you know what she is like?
4. One theme of the story is labeled on page 187. Do you find other messages or ideas? Explain.
5. Do some elements of the story—plot, characters, setting, description—seem stronger to you than others? What has the writer done to make these elements stand out?

Using a Framework for a Short Story

"The Lion Sleeps Tonight" (pages 183–187) gives a vivid portrait of a strong character, but the plot is actually subdued. The pattern of a whole life, not a few specific events, is the writer's concern. In the following story, "The Rest of Her Life," the writer takes a more usual approach to plot—the two main characters definitely have important events to deal with. You may want to use this story's framework as a model. Notice especially how the writer uses dialogue to develop conflict and plot.

A WRITER'S MODEL

The Rest of Her Life

Main character
Third-person, Myung's thoughts

Every night Myung thought about what college would be like. She couldn't wait. She'd be away from her nosy little brother and nagging parents. She'd make cool new friends, meet boys, go to parties. And, of course, she'd study. She didn't intend to blow away her hard work in high school and have to come home.

Characters developed/ Dialogue and setting

The phone next to Myung's bed squealed. Without even a hello, her best friend's voice rushed out, "I feel like I've been let out of prison!"

"Julia," Myung laughed, "what's going on?"

"Dad says he can handle the store and I can leave. Want to go to the mall? Please!"

"Have I ever said no to hanging out? I am ready to get out of here immediately. Meet you at the bus stop in fifteen minutes."

Flashback

Julia, Myung thought, was one of a kind--and not because of frantic mall calls. As she hung up, Myung's mind was going back to another phone call from Julia, one she'd actually cried over. "I'm

Conflict

not going to the university," Julia had pronounced flatly.

It still seemed unreal. Unfair. Julia came out on top in every test, every essay contest. "You won a scholarship!" Myung protested. But Julia said it

Dialogue/Plot details

wasn't enough, not now. "Mother's too sick," she explained, "and Dad needs me in the store. I can't go."

Internal conflict

And that was it. Julia just dropped it. For a while Myung was afraid to talk about college at all with Julia, but now she'd relaxed. Julia acted fine, as if nothing had changed. She was something else.

End of flashback

Characters developed/ Actions, appearance, and setting details

At the mall, the two friends started their usual stroll around the food court, Julia leading with her typical long stride and tiny Myung chattering and constantly pushing her dark bangs out of her eyes. Julia finished her frozen yogurt and sighed, "Free-dom. Sometimes I'm so sick of that hardware store I feel like throwing the hammers. It's--"

Description

"Yeah, I baby-sat my brother every day last week, and it was worse than prison." Myung spun around. "The record store! Let's go there."

Julia was right behind her. "Look," she pointed. "That tape I've been wanting is on sale!"

Myung kept going. "Uh, in a minute. I want to look at the posters. You know, for my dorm room.

Conflict built/ Actions and dialogue

Annella got the coolest one last week."

Julia was sitting on a bench outside the store when Myung got finished. "Tired?" Myung asked.

"No, just waiting. Let's go to Lane's. I need a lipstick."

"Sure," Myung agreed, but then she ran to another window. "Look at those bulletin boards! I didn't even think of that. I can't take my old beat-up one. It'll just take a minute."

"I don't want to," Julia said, too loudly.

"What?" Myung stood still.

Characters and conflict developed/ Dialogue

"I don't want to. I don't want to go there. I don't want to follow you. Can't you talk about anything but college, college, college?"

"What's that supposed to mean?"

"What does it sound like?" Julia snapped. Myung had never heard this voice. "Don't you ever think about my feelings?"

Sensory image

Myung felt her temper rising, too. Her black eyes burned. "Sure. Of course. But that doesn't mean you have to take them out on me. I'm not keeping you from college. Am I supposed to pretend I'm not going so you'll feel better? You're jealous!"

It was said before she thought.

Descriptive detail

"Jealous!" Julia stepped so close Myung could see her shaking. "Well, you're selfish, and that's worse." Julia paused. "And you're not much of a friend." She walked away without looking back.

Character and plot developed/ Thoughts and actions

Myung's phone didn't ring that night, and she couldn't call either. Had she done something so terrible? Did she deserve to be yelled at? The days at school were bad at first. She and Julia had most of the same classes, and it wasn't easy always looking the other way. Or she'd see Julia ahead of her in the hall, long brown hair streaming down her blue jacket, and slow down so they wouldn't meet.

Description

Complication

It was weird not sitting together in the cafeteria, but Myung started meeting Annella and Patty. She didn't have to worry about what she said to them. They <u>liked</u> to talk about college. Why have friends if you can't share things?

One day Myung, Annella, and Patty walked after school to the post office. As usual, they were talking about college--freedom, fun, fraternities--when Myung saw they were going right by Billings Hardware. Patty nodded at Julia behind the counter. "Look. How would you like to do that for the rest of your life? She always thought she was so smart."

Complication **Dialogue/ Reactions to character**

Annella barely turned her head. "Well, brains don't do everything," she said. "She'll get over it. Lots of people don't go to college."

Preparation for climax/Thoughts and feelings

Myung stared at them. Did they have to put Julia down? Did they think they were better than Julia? They didn't know what she was like! Myung saw Julia hand a customer change and then turn to the next one. The rest of her life? Myung turned back to her friends. She couldn't think of anything to say. She felt disoriented, as if she were waking up in a strange place.

Dialogue/Action

Now they were staring at her. "Why are you stopping?" Annella and Patty waited nervously.

Myung realized she was standing frozen. Her mind churned. "Look, I don't feel so hot. I'd better go back." Before they could ask questions, she turned.

Setting details

All the customers in the hardware store were gone, but it still seemed crowded and cramped. Julia turned around as Myung walked in. She looked surprised for only a moment and then her face hardened.

Complication **(anger)**

Myung searched for words. She really did feel sick now. "Julia, I know it's been a long time--"

"Well, what a surprise! We just got in new bulletin boards. You must have heard."

Sensory detail, figurative language, suspense

Julia's icy voice knotted Myung's stomach more. What was she doing here? She stepped back toward the door.

Climax

Conflict outcome/ Dialogue and action

"I just saw you through the window," Myung began again, faintly. Julia glared. "I thought . . ." Julia's hands fidgeted over the counter display. "Look, Julia," Myung blurted out. "I'm sorry. I don't blame you for hating me. I was really stupid and blind, but I thought you were okay! It's," she fought for words, "hard to admit you think only your life counts." Myung looked very small as she turned back to the door.

Julia exhaled as if she were letting something go. "I was jealous." She came out from behind the counter. "Myung, I'm sorry too. And I was just as blind! I didn't know how disappointed I was. Really, I know you didn't mean to hurt me." She raised her eyes to Myung's. "But--the terrible things I said!"

Neither moved or spoke, but both knew something had ended. Julia touched Myung's arm. "Come to the back. I can put the Closed sign up for a minute."

Setting details/ Mood

They sat together on a torn plaid sofa where Julia's mother used to rest. Myung had never noticed how much it sagged. "Julia," she whispered, "right now I don't even want to go to college."

Resolution

"Of course you do!" Julia almost sounded angry. "I do, too. And I'm not giving up. Our fight woke me up in some ways. So what if my plans didn't work out? Can't I make new ones? I found out they'll hold my scholarship for one year, and Dad is trying to get his cousin to buy into the store." She seemed to run down. "Things can happen."

Characters deepened/Actions, dialogue, and thoughts

Myung brightened. "It might work out. It might be the same as we planned."

Julia looked at her. She plucked at a tear in the couch. "Maybe. Maybe not quite the same. But we're friends. That's the same."

Myung smiled. She'd never felt so close to Julia. She liked sitting on the lumpy couch and wanted to stay there forever. She closed her eyes and was still for once.

"So," Julia broke the silence, "about those bulletin boards!" She was already rising.

When Myung looked up, Julia's face seemed miles away. She laughed, "Okay, I see it's back to business." Then she said with no laughter, "I'll remember today, Julia, no matter where I am."

Julia turned the sign to Open and stood staring out into the street.

"Yes, we do have some memories, don't we?"

A basic framework for a short story, similar to the pattern of the Writer's Model, follows. You may want to use it for your own story.

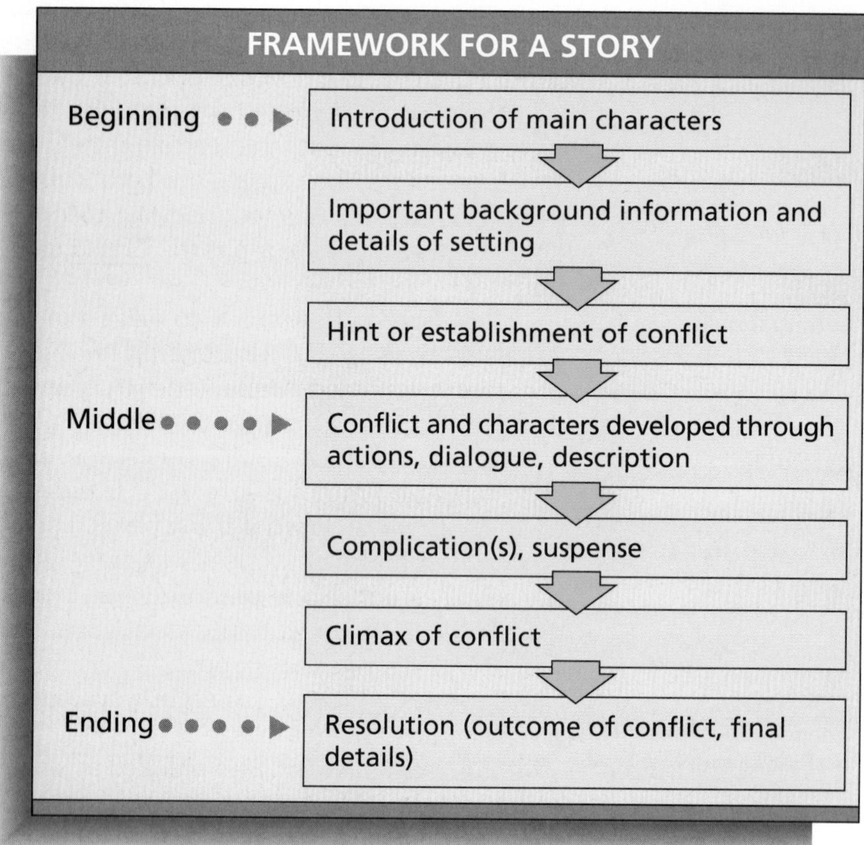

FRAMEWORK FOR A STORY
Beginning
Introduction of main characters
Important background information and details of setting
Hint or establishment of conflict
Middle
Conflict and characters developed through actions, dialogue, description
Complication(s), suspense
Climax of conflict
Ending
Resolution (outcome of conflict, final details)

USAGE HINT

Using Verbs and Adverbs in Dialogue Tags

Most dialogue has a *tag* that identifies the speaker: "Get your feet off the couch," **Dad said.** *Said* is a perfectly functional verb in dialogue tags, and sometimes its plainness is best. But also consider using precise verbs. They can vividly show a speaker's mood, tone of voice, or intention.

"Get your feet off the couch," Dad (*yelled, pleaded, murmured, repeated, whined, coaxed, sighed, threatened*).

You can also combine a verb and an adverb in dialogue tags to sharpen description. While this technique can be effective, too many verb-adverb tags can make your dialogue seem overdone and monotonous.

"Get your feet off the couch," Dad said (*firmly, pleadingly, impatiently*).
"I didn't mean it," Joshua whispered *piteously*.

EXERCISE 3 Writing Tom Swifties

Tom Swift was the hero in a series of adventure novels begun in the 1910s. In those novels, the writer used so many verb-adverb dialogue tags that readers created a form of *puns*—wordplay—called Tom Swifties. In Tom Swifties, the adverb in the dialogue tag creates a humorous pun on the action, as in the following examples:

"We're stuck in this glacier," Monica intoned icily.
"So you can't stand a little pain?" challenged the surgeon cuttingly.
"I wasn't sleeping on the job!" the guard said uprightly.

With a partner or small group, make up five Tom Swifties to share with the class.

PART 5: Writing a Draft of Your Story

The professional short story and the Writer's Model give you examples of ways to begin a story, develop its characters and conflict, and bring the plot to an end. They may even have given you ideas for *changing* your story plan. Don't hesitate to try out new ideas whenever you have them. As you write your first draft, use your prewriting notes, but don't lock your imagination in a closet.

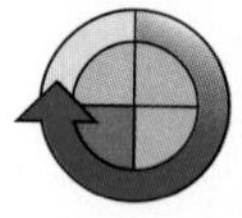

Evaluating and Revising

Like many writers, you may have a tendency to fall in love with what you have written. When you first read it over, you can't find anything that should be changed. But if you allow some time to pass before rereading your draft, you'll find you are more objective.

It's also a good idea to test your story on other readers: What part do they think is really good? What parts seem to need a jolt of life? Both you and your readers can use the chart on page 198 to pinpoint strengths and weaknesses. Then you can use the suggested revision techniques to solve the problems you have identified.

EXERCISE 4 Analyzing a Writer's Revision

Here's how the writer of "The Rest of Her Life" (pages 188–193) revised two paragraphs of her story. After studying the changes she made, answer the questions that follow.

One day Myung, Annella, and Patty
walked after school to the post office. ~~They~~
~~were now spending almost every afternoon~~ **cut**
~~together.~~ As usual, they were talking about
college, — freedom, fun, fraternities — when Myung saw they were going **add**
right by Billings Hardware. Patty ~~said,~~ nodded at Julia behind the counter. "Look. **replace**
How would you like to do that for the rest of
your life? ~~I'm sure I wouldn't want to."~~ She always thought she was so smart." **replace**

Annella barely turned her head. ~~It was~~ "Well, brains don't do everything," she said. "She'll get over it. **replace**
~~obvious that she had no feelings for Julia~~
~~and didn't even care what happened to her.~~
~~She knew that~~ Lots of people don't go to
college."

1. Why is the entire second sentence cut?
2. What details and information does the writer add to the third sentence? How does that change improve the paragraph?
3. What is the replacement for *said* in the fourth sentence? Why is it an improvement?
4. What is the effect of the replacement sentence at the end of the first paragraph? What does it contribute to character development?
5. The writer changed the last two sentences to dialogue. What other changes were necessary to do this? How does this change make the story more effective?

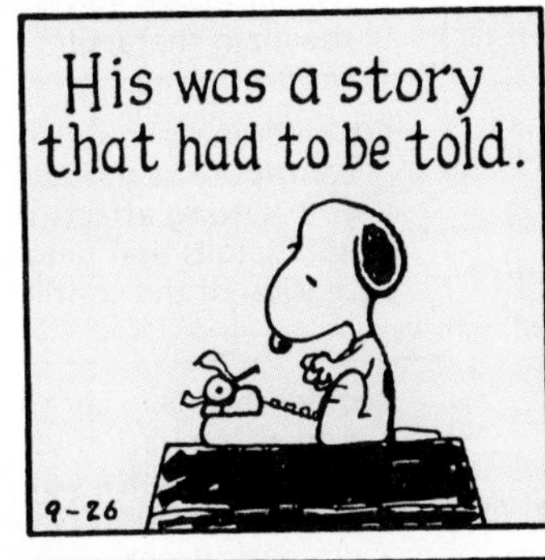

PART 6:

Evaluating and Revising Your Story

Use the chart on page 198 and your classmates' suggestions to evaluate and revise the first draft of your story. Remember that a story is a *streamlined* and *heightened* version of life. Cut wordy parts that go nowhere, jazz up characters, and increase the tension in your plot. Aim to rivet your readers.

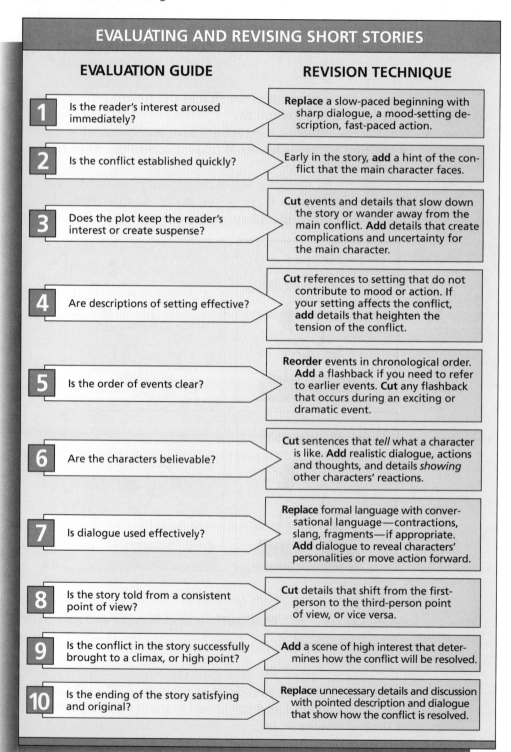

EVALUATING AND REVISING SHORT STORIES

	EVALUATION GUIDE	REVISION TECHNIQUE
1	Is the reader's interest aroused immediately?	**Replace** a slow-paced beginning with sharp dialogue, a mood-setting description, fast-paced action.
2	Is the conflict established quickly?	Early in the story, **add** a hint of the conflict that the main character faces.
3	Does the plot keep the reader's interest or create suspense?	**Cut** events and details that slow down the story or wander away from the main conflict. **Add** details that create complications and uncertainty for the main character.
4	Are descriptions of setting effective?	**Cut** references to setting that do not contribute to mood or action. If your setting affects the conflict, **add** details that heighten the tension of the conflict.
5	Is the order of events clear?	**Reorder** events in chronological order. **Add** a flashback if you need to refer to earlier events. **Cut** any flashback that occurs during an exciting or dramatic event.
6	Are the characters believable?	**Cut** sentences that *tell* what a character is like. **Add** realistic dialogue, actions and thoughts, and details *showing* other characters' reactions.
7	Is dialogue used effectively?	**Replace** formal language with conversational language—contractions, slang, fragments—if appropriate. **Add** dialogue to reveal characters' personalities or move action forward.
8	Is the story told from a consistent point of view?	**Cut** details that shift from the first-person to the third-person point of view, or vice versa.
9	Is the conflict in the story successfully brought to a climax, or high point?	**Add** a scene of high interest that determines how the conflict will be resolved.
10	Is the ending of the story satisfying and original?	**Replace** unnecessary details and discussion with pointed description and dialogue that show how the conflict is resolved.

Proofreading and Publishing

Before proofreading, you may want to review the rules for punctuating, capitalizing, and paragraphing dialogue (see pages 935–938). The rules can be tricky, and they are important because they prevent confusion about who is speaking and when she or he stops. You might want to proofread your paper in your usual way and then do a separate check for dialogue.

Once you have corrected each error, your story will be ready to bring pleasure to an audience. Your creativity will be the reader's gain. Here are some ideas for publishing:

- Adapt your story into a comic book. If you don't like to draw, find someone who does and collaborate.
- Along with your classmates, choose five or six stories from your class that would appeal to junior high or middle school students. Create a booklet of these stories and distribute it in the junior high or middle school. If you have access to a computer with desktop publishing capabilities, make the booklet as inviting and professional-looking as you can.
- Present your stories in a reader's theater. You and a few classmates can take turns reading your stories. You might even play different parts, with someone acting as narrator and others reading each character's dialogue. You might also use this approach to present your stories as radio plays.

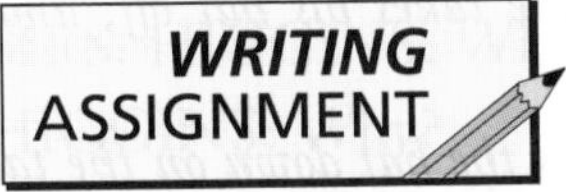

PART 7:
Proofreading and Publishing Your Story

Apply what you've learned about proofreading and publishing to your own story. Proofread it first; then decide how you can publish it. Do you have an idea of your own, or do you want to try the comic book or collaborative booklet described above?

MRS. HIGGINS: Do you know what you would do if you really loved me, Henry?

HIGGINS: Oh bother! What? Marry, I suppose.

MRS. HIGGINS: No. Stop fidgeting and take your hands out of your pockets. [*With a gesture of despair, he obeys and sits down again.*] That's a good boy. Now tell me about the girl.

HIGGINS: She's coming to see you.

MRS. HIGGINS: I don't remember asking her.

HIGGINS: You didn't. *I* asked her. If you'd known her you wouldn't have asked her.

MRS. HIGGINS: Indeed! Why?

HIGGINS: Well, it's like this. She's a common flower girl. I picked her off the kerbstone.

MRS. HIGGINS: And invited her to my at-home!

HIGGINS: [*Rising and coming to her to coax her*] Oh, that'll be all right. I've taught her to speak properly; and she has strict orders as to her behavior. She's to keep to two subjects: the weather and everybody's health – Fine day and How do you do, you know – and not to let herself go on things in general. That will be safe.

MRS. HIGGINS: Safe! To talk about our health! about our insides! perhaps about our outsides! How could you be so silly, Henry?

HIGGINS: [*Impatiently*] Well, she must talk about something. [*He controls himself and sits down again.*] Oh, she'll be all right: don't you fuss. Pickering is in it with me. I've a sort of bet on that I'll pass her off as a duchess in six months. I started on her some months ago; and she's getting on like a house on fire. I shall win my bet. She has a quick ear; and she's easier to teach than my middle-class pupils because she's had to learn a complete new language. She talks English almost as you talk French.

MRS. HIGGINS: That's satisfactory, at all events.

HIGGINS: Well, it is and it isn't.

MRS. HIGGINS: What does that mean?

HIGGINS: You see, I've got her pronunciation all right; but you have to consider not only how a girl pronounces, but what she pronounces . . .

1. What is the basic conflict in this scene? How does the dialogue reveal it?
2. What is the time and place of this scene?
3. Choose any stage direction and explain why you think Shaw wanted to specify it. Why is it important?
4. How would you describe Higgins's personality? What details in the script created this impression?

Writing a Scene

Prewriting. Since you are going to be writing a single scene, you'll need to think of a conflict that can take place in a single place and time. Brainstorm, scan the news headlines, ask "What if?" questions. You'll need at least two characters, but more than three or four will be unmanageable. Flesh out your characters and setting by answering the questions on pages 173 and 174. Finally, make a brief plan of what will happen at the beginning, middle, and end of your scene.

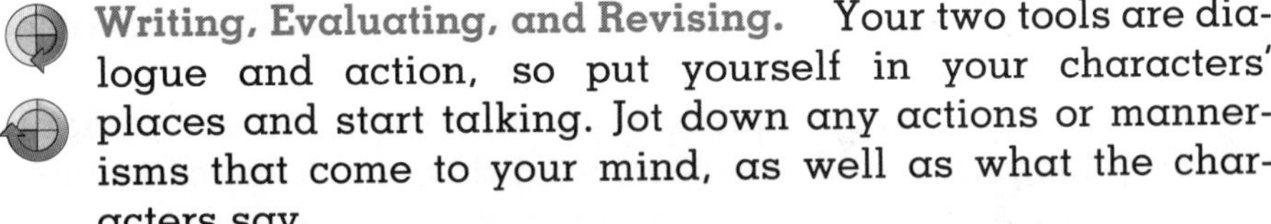

Writing, Evaluating, and Revising. Your two tools are dialogue and action, so put yourself in your characters' places and start talking. Jot down any actions or mannerisms that come to your mind, as well as what the characters say.

The best way to evaluate your script is to ask friends to read it aloud and act it out. Do they need more stage directions? dialogue more in keeping with the characters? a clearer conflict? Make any changes you feel are needed.

Proofreading and Publishing. Follow the format for dialogue and stage directions used in the scene from *Pygmalion*. Then cast the parts, rehearse the actors, and schedule a performance for your class.

WRITING WORKSHOP

A Poem

Poetry, like fiction (stories, drama, novels), is a form of literary writing; your purpose in writing is to use language imaginatively to create a work of art. But when you write poetry, you are more concerned with emotions, with the musical sounds of language, and with the images you create in your readers' minds.

Poetry can be divided into two basic types—narrative and lyric. Narrative poems, such as Samuel Taylor Coleridge's "The Rime of the Ancient Mariner," tell whole stories. Characters are involved in conflicts, and we as readers look forward to seeing how the conflicts are finally resolved. Lyric poems, on the other hand, may suggest glimpses of stories, but they don't tell a whole story. Rather, they capture the essence of an important moment, a feeling, an object, or a person.

Often, what makes a poem work is the use of figurative language and special sound devices. The following chart has examples of the various kinds of figurative language and sound devices you can use when you write poetry.

FIGURATIVE LANGUAGE AND SOUND DEVICES	
Imagery: Concrete details that appeal to the senses of sight, hearing, smell, taste, or touch	Listen! you hear the grating roar Of pebbles which the waves draw back, and fling, At their return, up the high strand Matthew Arnold, "Dover Beach"
Simile: Comparison of two unlike things using *like, as, than, resembles,* etc.	My heart is like a singing bird Christina Rossetti, "A Birthday"

(continued)

FIGURATIVE LANGUAGE AND SOUND DEVICES *(continued)*	
Metaphor: Comparison that equates two unlike things	The crowds upon the pavement Were fields of harvest wheat. W. H. Auden, "Song: As I Walked Out One Evening"
Personification: Human qualities given to something nonhuman	The sullen wind was soon awake, It tore the elm-tops down for spite, And did its worst to vex the lake Robert Browning, "Porphyria's Lover"
Rhyme: Repetition of an accented vowel and end sound in words that are close together	So long as men can breathe, or eyes can see, So long lives this, and this gives life to thee. William Shakespeare, "Sonnet 18"
Alliteration: Repetition of initial consonant sounds	O **w**ild **W**est **W**ind Percy Bysshe Shelley, "Ode to the West Wind"
Assonance: Repetition of vowel sounds	Old **a**ge should burn and r**a**ve at close of d**a**y Dylan Thomas, "Do Not Go Gentle into That Good Night"
Onomatopoeia: A word's sound that imitates its meaning	And full-grown lambs loud **bleat** from hilly bourn John Keats, "To Autumn"
Rhythm: Beat made by accented and unaccented syllables. ***Metrical verse*** has ***meter,*** regular pattern of beats. **Free verse** does not have meter (for example, see "The Bear").	Ĭ wándĕred lónely ás ă clóud Thăt floáts ŏn hígh o'ĕr váles ănd hílls William Wordsworth, "I Wandered Lonely as a Cloud"

The following poem about a captive bear is written in *free verse*, a verse form that uses repetition, pauses, and the natural beats of speech to create rhythm. Read the poem once silently and then aloud if you can. What "music" do you hear? What images strike your senses?

The Bear

by Nina Cassian, translated by Laura Schiff

The bear paces the cage for hours
the four bars in the four corners
drip with his saliva and sniffs
the bear's snout up and down on
the four bars, only the four bars
a frenzy for four sides.
If the cage were completely round
he'd stand in the center for hours
feeling all points narrowing tight
to a prison and at last he'd lose
the tragic illusion of a road along
one side and from there again along
another side and from there again along
another side and from there, again . . .

1. How would you describe the mood or feeling of this poem? What words and sounds create this effect?
2. What sound devices can you find in this poem? What meaning or emotion do they suggest?
3. What single image from the poem do you remember when you close your eyes? Why?
4. A symbol is an object, place, person, or event that represents something beyond itself. Could the bear in this poem be meant as a symbol? Why?

Writing a Poem

Prewriting. You are going to be writing a lyric poem describing an object or a moment in time, and the first thing you need to do is free your imagination. Brainstorm or look for ideas in your writer's journal. Think of an intense moment in your life—one of fright, total gloom, pure excitement, blissful peace. Or picture an object that fascinates you, frightens you, reminds you of something pleasant or something unpleasant. Once you capture the basic idea, you can begin to flesh it out. Make notes of words, phrases, even figures of speech that you might use.

Writing, Evaluating, Revising. Before you start, review the chart of techniques on pages 204–205. Experiment with a few lines to decide whether you'll use rhyme and meter or free verse. Choose whichever feels more comfortable. In a poem, each word counts, so use specific nouns, lively verbs, and many sensory details. Try to include at least one metaphor or simile. If you're writing free verse, line and stanza breaks can occur where they seem natural. After you write your draft, read your poem aloud, listening for the precision of descriptions and rhythms of the language. Let your ear guide you to changes.

Proofreading and Publishing. Before you write your final copy, check your spelling and punctuation, making sure that you have stops and pauses where you want them. Practice reading your poem aloud, and plan a poetry-reading session with the class. Use a tape recorder to record all the readings.

MAKING CONNECTIONS

CREATING A STORYBOARD

When you write a script for a stage play, you have to think about the requirements of the medium. You have to close the curtain or darken the stage to change scenes; you have to have a way to get actors on and off the stage; your audience is always the same distance from the stage. But when you write a script for film or video, you have to consider the possibilities of an entirely different medium. It's not as intimate, but you can change scenes with ease and you can focus on a close-up of a pebble or an eagle-eye view of a whole valley. You're probably familiar with several visual techniques used in videos and films: fade in and out; close-ups and long shots; panning (moving) shots and zooms; cuts or dissolves.

A television or movie script includes written directions for the visual and sound effects, just like stage directions, but sometimes a storyboard is created as well. As you can see from the following example, a storyboard is a visual plan of what will be filmed.

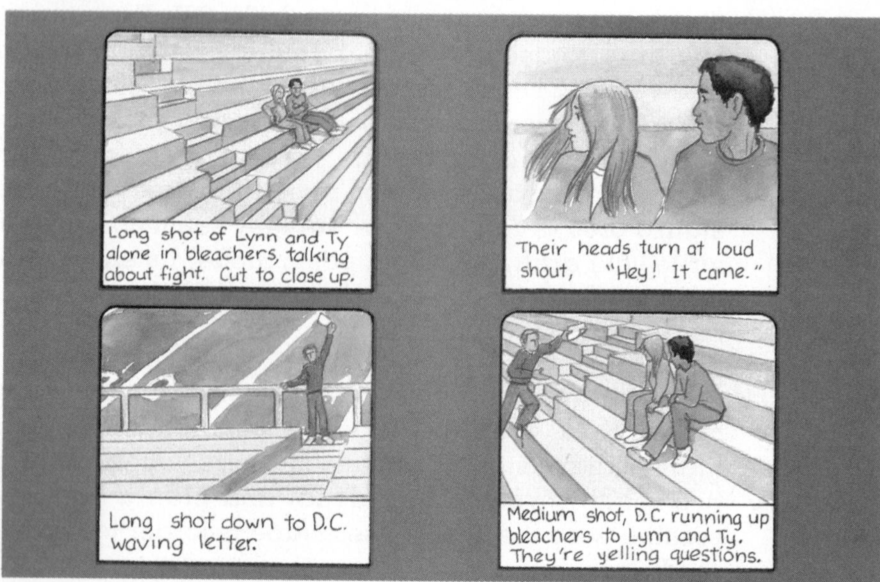

Long shot of Lynn and Ty alone in bleachers, talking about fight. Cut to close up.
Their heads turn at loud shout, "Hey! It came."
Long shot down to D.C. waving letter.
Medium shot, D.C. running up bleachers to Lynn and Ty. They're yelling questions.

Now try creating a storyboard for the scene you wrote in the scenewriting workshop (pages 200–203), or for a scene from any play you've read and enjoyed. Remember to visualize the scene on the screen, not on a stage, and to write directions for action, camera work, special effects, music, props, and so forth. Sketch a storyboard of at least six panels, beginning a new panel whenever there's a significant visual shift in the scene.

DESCRIPTION IN CREATIVE WRITING

The strategy of description is very important in creative writing, for it is description that allows a writer to create pictures and images that will live on in readers' minds. Fiction writers as well as poets make use of sharp and vivid sensory details and, sometimes, figurative language to create effective descriptions. Earlier in this chapter you read vivid descriptions of Aunt Eloise in her flowing caftans (page 183) and a bear pacing in his cage (page 206); and you find similarly memorable descriptions in most of the stories, novels, and poetry that you read. Here's another vivid description, one of a character's view of her home as she returns after a great shock.

> As their pick-up truck turned into their own dirt road and made the crest of the hill, Mrs. Turpin gripped the window ledge and looked out suspiciously.
>
> The land sloped gracefully down through a field dotted with lavender weeds and at the start of the rise their small yellow frame house, with its little flower beds spread out around it like a fancy apron, sat primly in its accustomed place between two giant hickory trees. She would not have been startled to see a burnt wound between two blackened chimneys.
>
> Flannery O'Connor, "Revelation"

Can you create a memorable description of a place that is important to you? Here's a chance to try. Picture the place in your mind—perhaps it's your house, the beach, your favorite street. Then write a brief description using specific, sharp sensory details and at least one example of figurative language. Create a memory for your readers.

6 WRITING TO INFORM

Seeing Patterns and Relationships

What do African myths and Native American myths have in common? Which foods are most dangerous to your health? What is the definition of the word *courage*? When we ask questions like these, we're seeking information; and when we answer them, we are informing. One way to gain and share information is to look at **patterns and relationships.**

Writing and You. Writers often share information about patterns and relationships. A sports writer compares the records of two football teams and predicts the NFL champion. In a letter to the editor, a lawyer defines *individual rights* and defends a homeless person's right to vote. An advice columnist tells teenagers to consider location, size, and cost when choosing a college. What patterns and relationships do you observe?

As You Read. The following passage opens the novel *A Tale of Two Cities*. What patterns and relationships does Charles Dickens observe about the year 1775?

M.C. Escher, *Day and Night* (1938). Woodcut printed from 2 blocks, 15 1/2" × 26 3/4". © 1938 M.C. Escher/Cordon Art-Baarn-Holland.

from A Tale of Two Cities

by Charles Dickens

Charles Darnay and Sydney Carton both love Lucie Manette in the PBS production of *A Tale of Two Cities*.

It was the best of times, it was the worst of times, it was the age of wisdom, it was the age of foolishness, it was the epoch of belief, it was the epoch of incredulity, it was the season of Light, it was the season of Darkness, it was the spring of hope, it was the winter of despair, we had everything before us, we had nothing before us, we were all going direct to Heaven, we were all going direct the other way—in short, the period was so far like the present period, that some of its noisiest authorities insisted on its being received, for good or for evil, in the superlative degree of comparison only.

There were a king with a large jaw and a queen with a plain face, on the throne of England; there were a king with a large jaw and a queen with a fair face, on the throne of France. In both countries it was clearer than crystal to the lords of the State preserves of loaves and fishes, that things in general were settled for ever.

It was the year of Our Lord one thousand seven hundred and seventy-five.

Madame Defarge fights for the French peasants in the PBS production of *A Tale of Two Cities*.

Reader's Response

1. What is your personal response to these opening paragraphs? Do they make you curious about *A Tale of Two Cities*? Why?
2. Dickens writes of 1775 in terms of opposites: "the best of times" / "the worst of times." With a partner, try to think of some opposites that might describe this year—the one you are living in right now. When you write them down, imitate Dickens' style.

Writer's Craft

3. Many of the patterns and relationships that Dickens sees in the year 1775 are **paradoxes**, statements that appear to be contradictory but that are actually true. How can it be both the "best of times" and the "worst of times"? What other paradoxes can you find in these paragraphs?
4. When you examine patterns and relationships, you are classifying information, and one method of classification is comparison/contrast. What does Dickens compare and contrast in this passage?
5. *A Tale of Two Cities* is a novel, and Dickens' primary aim is to create literature. However, he also shares information in this introduction. What do you learn about British and French royalty? about the year 1775?

Strategies for Writing to Inform

When your purpose is to inform, *classification* is one strategy you can use. Classification—examining patterns and relationships—includes comparison/contrast, definition, and division (dividing a group into subgroups).

Although this chapter will focus on classification, you can, as the following examples show, use any of the four writing strategies when your purpose is to inform.

Narration: on a history test, writing about events leading up to the firing on Fort Sumter; reporting on the highlights of a high school soccer game.

Description: in world literature class, describing the treasure of the Anglo-Saxon ship found at Sutton Hoo; in a report for art history class, describing the paintings of Henry Tanner.

Classification: in a science report, comparing and contrasting cells seen through a microscope; defining free verse for an essay exam in English.

Evaluation: explaining to a friend why you enjoy reading mystery novels more than historical fiction; writing a review of last night's rock concert for the school paper.

LOOKING AHEAD

In the main assignment in this chapter, you'll write a comparison/contrast essay in order to inform. As you work through the assignments, keep in mind that a comparison/contrast essay

- points out relationships or patterns
- examines two or more subjects
- focuses on the subjects' similarities or differences or both

Writing a Comparison/Contrast Essay

Identifying Your Subjects, Purpose, and Audience

You make comparisons every day of your life. For example, you think about the plot, the actors, and the reviews you have read; and then you decide to see a Kevin Costner movie instead of a Tom Cruise movie. You have made your decision on the basis of comparisons and contrasts. Comparing and contrasting is a familiar thought process, so common that you hardly think about it; but it is a valuable technique, for both decision making and writing.

Subjects. In real life, subjects for comparison/contrast often present themselves. Your history exam has a question asking you to compare two forms of government, or your boss at the supermarket asks whether you think Phil would do a good job at the checkout counter. Your task, then, is not to find a subject, but to decide how to handle the subjects given you.

Sometimes, however, you have to identify your own subjects for comparison/contrast. Your English teacher may ask you to write a paper comparing two characters or two novels or two poems: Your task is to decide which two to compare. Or, you may be writing an article about high school graduation rates and realize that it might be useful to compare today's rates with those of some other time period or some other country. When you are in this kind of situation, use these criteria for selecting subjects:

- The two subjects should have something in common. For example, Japanese and Chinese porcelain are both Asian and they are both a ceramic art form.
- The two subjects should have some significant differences. There is no point in comparing two identical subjects.
- Your subjects should interest you.
- Information about your subjects should be fairly accessible.

Purpose and Audience. No matter what your aim in writing—expository, self-expressive, persuasive, literary—you can use comparison/contrast to examine your topic. In the main part of this chapter, you are focusing on using comparison/contrast to inform, which is an expository aim.

When your *purpose* is to inform, you want to be able to give your audience new information or a new way of looking at old information. For example, the differences between former Presidents Ronald Reagan and Jimmy Carter are obvious; but if you can point out some similarities between them, you may be able to help your audience understand these two leaders in a new way.

And that's the most important point to remember about your *audience* as well. Your task is to give them new and interesting information. To accomplish that task, you need to have some sense of what they already know. You don't want to lose your readers by taking them too far beyond what they know, nor do you want to bore them with a rehash of facts that are familiar to them.

Drawing by Jonik; © 1991 The New Yorker Magazine, Inc.

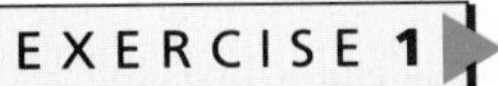

Speaking and Listening: Finding Subjects for Comparison/Contrast

With two or three classmates, survey the nonprint media for possible comparison/contrast subjects. As you work, make a list of possible subjects, and then share the list with other groups. You might try these activities:

1. Check movie titles in video stores and in TV program listings. Think about comparing and contrasting styles of directors and actors, sequels, or movie remakes.
2. Review music videos. You might compare and contrast different styles of videos, videos ten years ago and today, or different videos by the same performer.
3. Watch TV news programs or listen to radio news broadcasts. Think about comparing and contrasting the announcers themselves, political figures in the news, or terms that come up in the news (like *recession* and *depression*).
4. Compare and contrast subjects from TV programs such as situation comedies—perhaps the actors themselves, common themes in programs, or past programs and those of today.

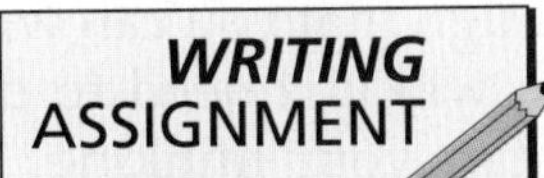

PART 1:

Choosing Subjects for Comparison/Contrast

You have a choice. What two subjects do you want to compare and contrast? Perhaps you are interested in ice hockey, movies of the 1950s, or one of the nonprint media ideas you explored in Exercise 1. Choose two subjects that have something in common but that also have enough differences to be interesting. Keep your audience (probably your classmates and your teacher) in mind, as well as your informative purpose.

The word *compare* might be confusing. Sometimes it means just "find similarities," and sometimes it means both "find similarities" and "find differences." Before you write an essay or answer a test question asking you to compare, be sure you know what you are being asked to do.

Planning a Comparison/Contrast Essay

According to some historians, the Duke of Wellington said the Battle of Waterloo was won on the playing fields of Eton (a school for young Englishmen that he attended). Similarly, your success in writing a comparison/contrast essay is won, in a sense, long before you struggle with your first draft.

Gathering Information

Sources of Information. Once you know what subjects you are going to compare and contrast, you need to think about the kind of information you will include. One ingredient of a good informative paper is *comprehensiveness*—you need to be sure you supply all important information. For example, if you were writing a newspaper article about a fire, it would be important to include the location.

For some subjects (two music videos, perhaps, or two of your teachers), you may know enough that you can write without further research. Perhaps you will just need to do a little brainstorming or freewriting to start your thinking. For subjects that are not as familiar to you, however, you will need to look for additional information. Although your comparison/contrast essay is not a formal research paper, you may need to consult experts in the field, and print and nonprint sources in your library or media center. (For more help with sources of information, see pages 446–449.)

Relevance of Information. Not all information that you find about your subjects will be equally useful, significant, or *relevant*—that is, relating to your specific subjects. What is significant and relevant will depend on the focus of your comparison. For example, if you are comparing and contrasting the childhoods of two presidents, the fact that one of them took piano lessons might be relevant. However, if you are comparing the two presidents' foreign policy efforts, the piano lessons are probably unimportant.

Richard M. Nixon

Harry S Truman

The following example shows how one writer gathered information for an essay comparing and contrasting a woman of the 1890s and a woman of the 1990s.

HERE'S HOW

POINT OF COMPARISON/ CONTRAST	WOMAN OF 1890s	WOMAN OF 1990s
Careers	*teacher, low wages; had to quit when she got married*	*almost any career available; typical example is lawyer*
Education	*education for social skills; only a few women's colleges available*	*scholarships, any school, any degree*
Leisure/Clothing	*bicycle riding, but only in ladylike clothes; ten yards of fabric in a bathing suit*	*jogging, swimming, any sport available; business suits and sweats, bikinis, slacks, and shorts*
Marriage	*all control in hands of husband; no appliances, no help with housework; no career outside marriage*	*continues in career; at least to some extent, shares duties of house-keeping and child care with husband*

CRITICAL THINKING

Analyzing Subjects for Their Relevant Features

To ***analyze*** something means to examine its parts. When you compare and contrast subjects, the important parts you want to examine are the *relevant features* of the subjects.

Here's how to determine the relevant features of your subjects.

- *Determine the basis for comparison.* Subjects for comparison/contrast should share a meaningful similarity; they should belong to a common group.
- *Think about your specific purpose.* In this chapter, your main purpose is to inform readers; but more specifically, what kind of information about your two subjects do you want to share with readers?

EXAMPLE **Subjects: Alexander the Great and Napoleon**

- *Alexander the Great and Napoleon were both men, they were both great military leaders, and both were associated with famous women. The fact that they were both men isn't meaningful—so are millions of other people. Their careers as military leaders and their associations with famous women are meaningful.*

- *One purpose might be to give information about the two men as military leaders. Features that are relevant to this purpose include (1) military training and background, (2) military strategies, and (3) victories and defeats.*

CRITICAL THINKING EXERCISE: Analyzing Subjects for Relevant Features

With two or three of your classmates, analyze the following sets of subjects for their relevant features. Begin by deciding what meaningful common groups the two subjects belong to (do some research if you're not familiar with the subjects). Then, decide on a specific purpose for comparing and contrasting the two subjects. Finally, identify three or four relevant features for each set of subjects.

EXAMPLE Subjects: Elizabeth Cady Stanton, Susan B. Anthony
Common group: Women's rights leaders

Relevant features: family background, role as social reformer, role as president of national women's suffrage organization

1. the Arctic and the Antarctic
2. the octopus and the argonaut (paper nautilus)

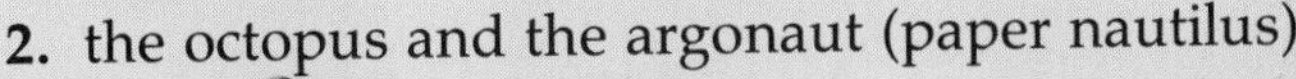

3. Martin Luther King, Jr., and Mohandas Gandhi
4. the University of Florida and the University of Chicago
5. Doris Lessing and Nadine Gordimer

PART 2:
Gathering Information

Now it is time to gather information to support the topic you selected in Part 1 of the Writing Assignment (page 217). Since you will probably have to do some research, it will be helpful to make a chart like the one on page 219. Write your two subjects at the top of the chart, the points of comparison/contrast, and the information you have gathered.

Developing a Thesis Statement

A comparison/contrast essay may focus on similarities, differences, or both similarities and differences. The thesis statement, which is usually a one- or two-sentence summary of your thesis (main idea), should indicate that focus. Here are three examples of such thesis statements.

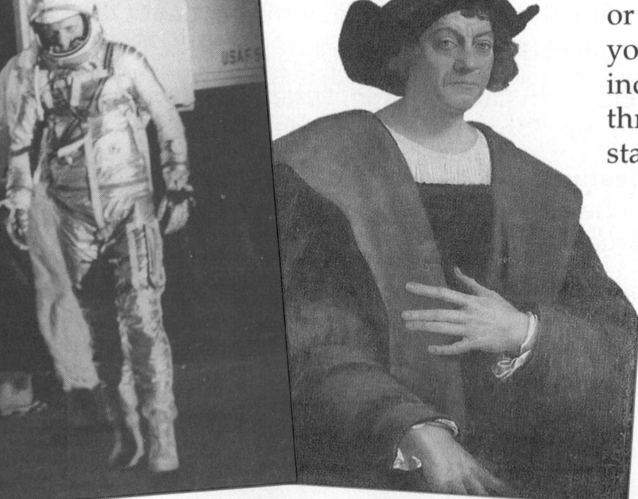

EXAMPLES *Stressing likenesses*: Almost five hundred years separated Christopher Columbus's sea voyage and Alan Shepard's space flight, but these two explorers faced many of the same challenges.

Stressing differences: Although Christopher Columbus and Alan Shepard both charted courses into the unknown, the results of their voyages were quite different.

Balancing likenesses and differences: The challenges faced by Christopher Columbus and Alan Shepard were similar, but the results of their voyages were worlds apart.

In this chapter, you are writing to inform, but sometimes you compare and contrast in order to make a point. For example, you can share information about the programs of two colleges, or you can try to prove that college *x* is better than college *y*. For more help with explaining and proving, see Chapter 7.

Arranging Information

After identifying relevant features and gathering information, your next step is to arrange your information so that the patterns and relationships are clear for your readers. Here are two common ways to organize comparison/contrast essays.

- The ***block method.*** With the block method, you present all the relevant features for the first subject and then all the relevant features for the second subject. If you use this method, which is more suitable for short papers than for longer ones, be sure to discuss the features in the same order for each subject.
- The ***point-by-point method.*** With this method, you arrange the essay by relevant features, focusing on one feature at a time. You discuss the feature for one subject and then for the other subject, and then go on to the next feature. This method works well with longer essays, but be sure to present the two subjects in the same order for each feature.

The chart on the next page shows both methods in action; the subjects are two poets, Anne Bradstreet and Sylvia Plath.

Sylvia Plath

BLOCK METHOD	POINT-BY-POINT METHOD
Subject 1: Anne Bradstreet Feature 1: Personal life and marriage Feature 2: Poetic themes and style Feature 3: Influence on other poets Subject 2: Sylvia Plath Feature 1: Personal life and marriage Feature 2: Poetic themes and style Feature 3: Influence on other poets	Feature 1: Personal lives and marriages Subject 1: Anne Bradstreet Subject 2: Sylvia Plath Feature 2: Poetic themes and style Subject 1: Anne Bradstreet Subject 2: Sylvia Plath Feature 3: Influence on other poets Subject 1: Anne Bradstreet Subject 2: Sylvia Plath

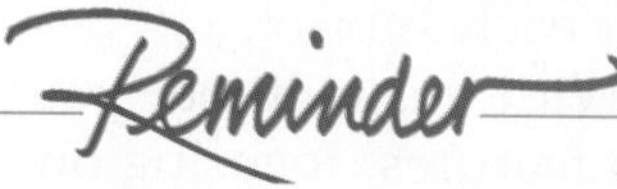

Plan your comparison/contrast essay by

- analyzing your subjects to find their relevant features
- gathering information about the relevant features
- writing a thesis statement that identifies the subjects and the main idea
- arranging your information in the block method or the point-by-point method

PART 3:
Writing a Thesis Statement and Arranging Information

Now that you have the information you need for your comparison/contrast essay, develop a thesis statement to guide you through the rest of the writing process. Then organize your information according to the method—block or point-by-point—you plan to use in drafting your paper.

Writing Your First Draft

Once you have completed the prewriting stage of your essay, you are ready to shape the results into a first draft. Remember, however, that you may have to move back and forth between drafting and prewriting. In the middle of your first draft, for example, you might discover that you need to go back and collect more information about one of your subjects. Keep in mind that this movement between stages is natural.

The Structure of a Comparison/Contrast Essay

In an informative comparison/contrast essay, your aim is to convey new and interesting information as clearly as possible. To do this, you usually need a fairly straightforward introduction, body, and conclusion.

Introduction	■ Immediately grabs readers' attention ■ States the thesis
Body	■ Identifies similarities and/or differences between the subjects ■ Uses block method, point-by-point method, or some variation
Conclusion	■ Brings essay to clear, definite close ■ May restate thesis

If you need more information about structuring your essay, review the material in the chapter **Understanding Composition Structure,** pages 99–121.

The example on the following pages is taken from a book, but it has most of the characteristics of an essay and illustrates the use of comparison/contrast to inform. The writer is sharing information about an experience common to many Japanese Americans during World War II. Soon after the Japanese bombing of Pearl Harbor and the United States' entry into World War II, more than 110,000 Japanese Americans were placed in internment camps. As you read, notice how the writer contrasts warm and loving mealtimes at home with the starkness of mealtimes in camp.

A PASSAGE FROM A BOOK

from Farewell to Manzanar

by Jeanne Wakatsuki Houston and James D. Houston

INTRODUCTION
Attention grabber

At seven I was too young to be insulted. The camp worked on me in a much different way. I wasn't aware of this at the time, of course. No one was, except maybe Mama, and there was little she could have done to change what happened.

BODY
SUBJECT 1:
Mealtimes before camp

Feature 1:
Household setting

It began in the mess hall. Before Manzanar, mealtime had always been the center of our family scene. In camp, and afterward, I would often recall with deep yearning the old round wooden table in our dining room in Ocean Park, the biggest piece of furniture we owned, large enough to seat twelve or thirteen of us at once. A tall row of elegant, lathe-turned spindles separated this table from the kitchen, allowing talk to pass from one room to the other. Dinners were always noisy, and they were always abundant with great pots of boiled rice, platters of home-grown vegetables, fish Papa caught.

Feature 2: Family interaction

He would sit at the head of this table, with Mama next to him serving and the rest of us arranged around the edges according to age, down to where Kiyo and I sat, so far away from our parents, it seemed at the time, we had our own enclosed nook inside this world. The grownups would be talking down at their end, while we two played our secret games, making eyes at each other when Papa gave the order to begin to eat, racing with chopsticks to scrape the last grain from our rice bowls, eyeing Papa to see if he had noticed who won.

SUBJECT 2: Mealtimes at camp
Feature 1: Mess-hall setting

Now, in the mess halls, after a few weeks had passed, we stopped eating as a family. Mama tried to hold us together for a while, but it was hopeless.

Feature 2: Family separation—details

Granny was too feeble to walk across the block three times a day, especially during heavy weather, so May brought food to her in the barracks. My older brothers and sisters, meanwhile, began eating with their friends, or eating somewhere blocks away, in the hope of finding better food. The word would get around that the cook over in Block 22, say, really knew his stuff, and they would eat a few meals over there, to test the rumor. Camp authorities frowned on mess hall hopping and tried to stop it, but the good cooks liked it. They liked to see long lines outside their kitchens and would work overtime to attract a crowd.

Younger boys, like Ray, would make a game of seeing how many mess halls they could hit in one meal period – be the first in line at Block 16, gobble down your food, run to 17 by the middle of the dinner hour, gulp another helping, and hurry to 18 to make the end of that chow line and stuff in the third meal of the evening. They didn't *need* to do that. No matter how bad the food might be, you could always eat till you were full.

Kiyo and I were too young to run around, but often we would eat in gangs with other kids, while the grownups sat at another table. I confess I enjoyed this part of it at the time. We all did. A couple of years after the camps opened, sociologists studying the life noticed what had happened to the families. They made some recommendations, and edicts went out that families *must* start eating together again. Most people resented this; they griped and grumbled. They were in the habit of eating with their friends. And until the mess hall system itself could be changed, not much could really be done. It was too late.

Feature 2: Family separation—consequences

My own family, after three years of mess hall living, collapsed as an integrated unit. Whatever dignity or feeling of filial strength we may have known before December 1941 was lost, and we did not recover it until many years after the war, not until after Papa died and we began to come together, trying to fill the vacuum his passing left in all our lives.

SUBJECT 3: Mealtimes after camp

The closing of the camps, in the fall of 1945, only aggravated what had begun inside. Papa had no money then and could not get work. Half of our family had already moved to the east coast, where jobs had opened up for them. The rest of us were relocated into a former defense workers' housing project in Long Beach. In that small apartment there never was enough room for all of us to sit down for a meal. We ate in shifts, and I yearned all the more for our huge round table in Ocean Park.

Return to SUBJECT 1: Mealtimes before camp

Soon after we were released I wrote a paper for a seventh-grade journalism class, describing how we used to hunt grunion before the war. The whole family would go down to Ocean Park Beach after dark, when the grunion were running, and build a big fire on the sand. I would watch Papa and my older brothers splash through the moonlit surf to scoop out the fish, then we'd rush back to the house where Mama would fry them up and set the sizzling pan on the table, with soy sauce and horseradish, for a midnight meal. I ended the paper with this sentence: "The reason I want to remember this is because I know we'll never be able to do it again."

CONCLUSION

Final comment

You might say it would have happened sooner or later anyway, this sliding apart of such a large family, in postwar California. People get married; their interests shift. But there is no escaping the fact that our internment accelerated the process, made it happen so suddenly it was almost tangible.

EXERCISE 2 Analyzing the Organization of a Comparison/Contrast Essay

After reading the passage on pages 226–229, think about the way in which the information is organized. Then get together with two or three classmates to discuss your answers to the following questions.

1. What technique do the writers use to grab the reader's attention in the first paragraph?
2. Why do you think the writers chose the block method rather than the point-by-point method for organizing their material? How does this method help to stress the writers' main point?
3. In the body of the passage, the writers focus on family mealtimes before, during, and after internment; but much more than mealtime customs was affected by internment. What larger issue about the camps do the mealtime examples suggest?
4. Before the war, the family ate together as a unit. How does this behavior at mealtime contrast with what happened in the camp? How does it contrast with what happened after the family left the camp?
5. In the next-to-the-last paragraph, the writers introduce an incident that relates to their first subject, mealtimes before camp. Why do you think the writers include this incident here rather than during the earlier discussion of mealtimes before camp?
6. Does this example meet the test of comprehensiveness for sharing information? Does any important information seem to be missing?

A Basic Framework for a Comparison/Contrast Essay

The passage you have just read from *Farewell to Manzanar* uses the block method of organization, but the Writer's Model that follows uses the point-by-point method. Notice that the writer of the following model covers only two subjects, not three, and does not go back to material covered earlier in the essay. It is also a fairly balanced presentation: The subjects receive a nearly equal amount of attention. You may want to use the following essay as a model for your own essay.

A WRITER'S MODEL

A Day in Two Lives

INTRODUCTION
Attention grabber

Jennifer jumps out of a hot, steamy shower, blow-dries her hair, catches the morning news on TV while she dresses, grabs her attaché case, and darts out the door. Her great-great-grandmother Emily would have been amazed, and maybe just a little envious, at this show of independence.

Thesis statement

Jennifer's self-reliant approach to life in the 1990s is startlingly different from Emily's restricted life back in the 1890s.

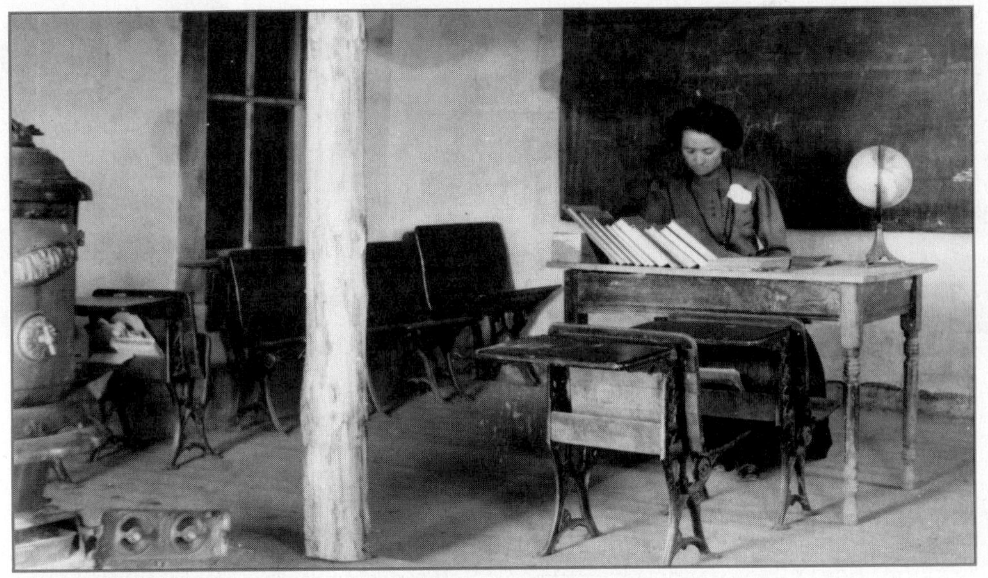

Montana Historical Society, Helena

BODY
Feature 1: Opportunities
SUBJECT 1

Although there are still areas of male dominance, Jennifer's generation has reached levels of achievement unattainable by women in Emily's day. Jennifer is free to make her own choices and to pursue whatever career she wishes. Of course, women in the nineteenth century achieved distinction in many areas, but compared with Jennifer,

SUBJECT 2

Emily had few opportunities and civil rights. In some parts of the country, she couldn't own property. She couldn't vote in national elections. And holding high public office was totally out of the question.

Feature 2: Careers
SUBJECT 1
SUBJECT 2

By 8 o'clock, Jennifer is at her desk at the large law firm where she is a law clerk. She is working and studying hard to prepare for the bar examination that will make her a full-fledged lawyer. Emily, on the other hand, worked as a schoolteacher, for wages that were low even for those days. She had none of the fringe benefits that Jennifer takes for granted and no chance for advancement.

Feature 3: Education
SUBJECT 1
SUBJECT 2

Merit scholarships and part-time jobs helped Jennifer get through college and law school. She chose to study law, but she had had her choice of any major at the undergraduate and graduate levels. Emily also attended college, but it did little to prepare her for any career other than teaching. For most women in the 1890s, the main focus of a college education was to learn the social skills necessary for becoming a good wife. The only exception was education at a handful of private women's colleges, available only to those with a considerable amount of money.

Feature 4: Marriage
SUBJECT 1

At noon, Jennifer meets her fiancé, Richard, for lunch. The couple intends to put off marriage until both are better established in their careers. After marriage, Jennifer will continue to practice law.

SUBJECT 2

She and Richard will share the duties of housekeeping and, later, of child care. With Emily and Fred, it was quite different. After they married, Emily turned the management of her life over to Fred. She had no control over the size of her family, and there were very few appliances to take the drudgery out of housework. It never occurred to her that her husband might share in any household responsibilities except to bring home a paycheck.

Feature 5: Leisure/clothes
SUBJECT 1

After work, Jennifer quickly changes out of her business suit and into her sweats. She leaves her apartment for a three-mile run around the park. On a warm summer afternoon, she may go to the nearby lakeshore to swim or sunbathe.

SUBJECT 2

Back in the 1890s, Emily had taken up the new bicycle-riding craze, but she didn't think of working up a sweat, nor would she have worn what she considered to be unladylike clothes. Actually, Emily and her friends thought they were quite daring in the new, less restrictive clothing that came into style during the Gay Nineties. But her daring bathing suit took up to ten yards of fabric, and she would have been shocked at the sight of Jennifer in her bikini.

Feature 6: Civic involvement
SUBJECT 1

In the evening, Jennifer spends a couple of hours stuffing envelopes and making phone calls for her friend María Gonzalez, who is running for the city council. Jennifer is deeply concerned with

SUBJECT 2

issues involving the homeless. Emily was also concerned about the world around her. She often attended meetings of the New York Consumers' League, where she heard horrifying stories about young women working in department stores under conditions that made Emily's life seem grand. These women worked from 7:45 a.m. to midnight, six days a week, often under dangerously unsafe conditions. The women received no vacation, no benefits, and earned a mere two dollars a week. They talked about organizing a strike to improve their lot.

Feature 7: Lifestyles
SUBJECT 1

After work, which ends at 4:30 p.m., Jennifer pops a load of laundry into her automatic washer. She slips a tape into her VCR and settles back in air-conditioned comfort to enjoy a dinner that took her five minutes to heat in her microwave oven. Later, she sets her clock radio and goes to bed.

SUBJECT 2

Emily, by contrast, had to spend a full hour preparing dinner for her family over a coal-burning stove. With no modern appliances, preparing and cleaning up after a meal was tedious and time-consuming. Emily had little time for leisure. She wrote a couple of letters, then read Harper's Weekly magazine before turning out the gas lights and going to bed.

CONCLUSION
Significance of the comparison/contrast

Obviously, Jennifer's life in the 1990s is much different from Emily's a hundred years earlier. Yet it is partly because of Emily's generation that Jennifer's life is what it is today. The women of the 1890s were among those who began to demand and force change. They fought for civil rights, political rights,

Final thought

and human rights. The struggles and occasional triumphs of these women were the greatest legacy they could leave to Jennifer and her generation.

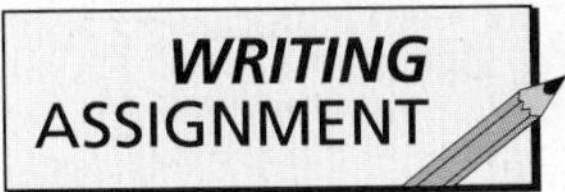

PART 4:
Writing a First Draft

Now you can make use of all your careful planning and thinking as you attempt to get a rough draft down on paper. Use the information you have gathered as a guide, but don't let it be a straitjacket. For example, you may need to stop and look for more information. It is important that you not be too critical at this point: Allow yourself the freedom to experiment a little. When you finish your draft, put it aside for a while.

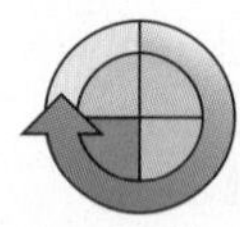

Evaluating and Revising

If you saw the original manuscript of nearly any great writer, you'd probably be surprised. In most cases, you'd find it to be a mass of handwritten corrections, additions, deletions, word changes, and other improvements. An experienced writer is usually a careful self-editor.

But experienced writers also know that there are advantages in having someone else read and evaluate their work. They often ask professional editors, family members, or friends to read their manuscripts and recommend changes. You, also, will find it helpful to have someone else read and comment on your draft. Remember, the ultimate test of any piece of writing is how the audience responds.

The following chart can help you, and anyone you have asked to read your paper, be a better editor. The first step is to read over the essay as objectively as possible, asking the evaluating questions in the left-hand column. If the answer to any question is no, try correcting the problem with the revising technique suggested in the right-hand column.

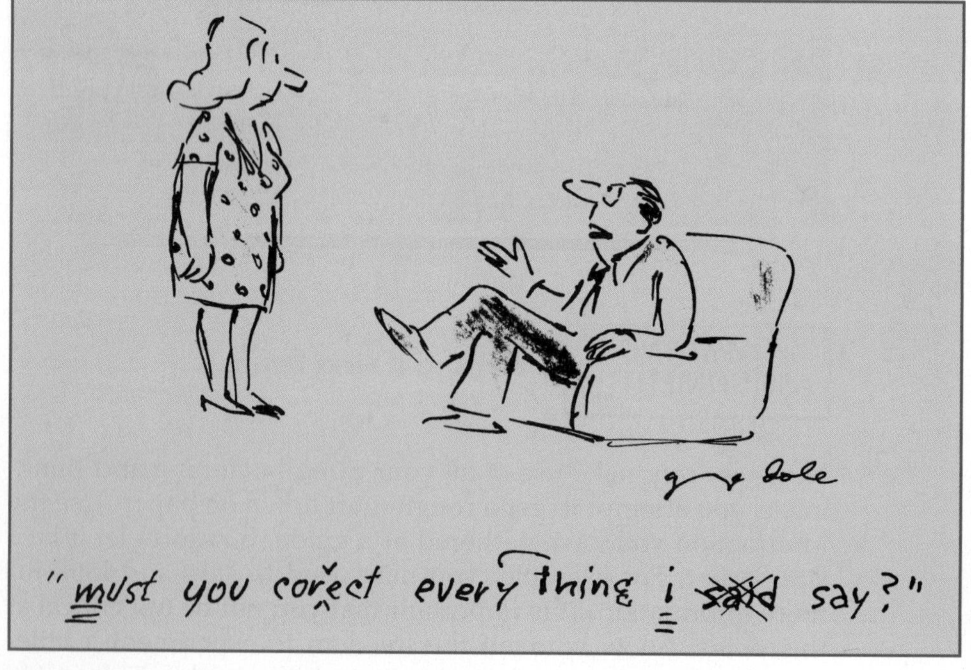
"must you corect every thing i ~~said~~ say?"

By permission of George Dole.

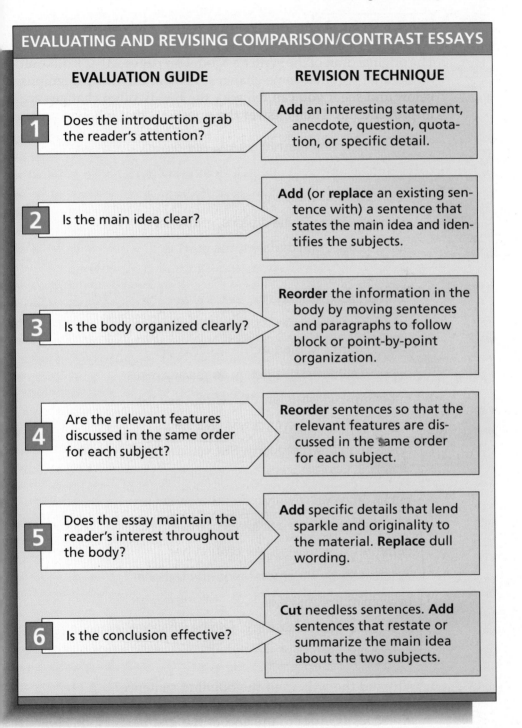

EVALUATING AND REVISING COMPARISON/CONTRAST ESSAYS

	EVALUATION GUIDE	REVISION TECHNIQUE
1	Does the introduction grab the reader's attention?	**Add** an interesting statement, anecdote, question, quotation, or specific detail.
2	Is the main idea clear?	**Add** (or **replace** an existing sentence with) a sentence that states the main idea and identifies the subjects.
3	Is the body organized clearly?	**Reorder** the information in the body by moving sentences and paragraphs to follow block or point-by-point organization.
4	Are the relevant features discussed in the same order for each subject?	**Reorder** sentences so that the relevant features are discussed in the same order for each subject.
5	Does the essay maintain the reader's interest throughout the body?	**Add** specific details that lend sparkle and originality to the material. **Replace** dull wording.
6	Is the conclusion effective?	**Cut** needless sentences. **Add** sentences that restate or summarize the main idea about the two subjects.

EXERCISE 3 Analyzing a Writer's Revisions

The original draft of the Writer's Model on pages 231–235 (like all first drafts) required some changes. Look at the two paragraphs below and see if you can tell why the handwritten changes are improvements. Then answer the questions that follow.

~~Here is how Jennifer starts her day.~~ **cut**

Jennifer jumps out of a hot, steamy shower, blow-dries her hair, catches the morning news on TV while she dresses, grabs her attaché case, and darts out the door. Her great-great-grandmother Emily would have been amazed, and maybe just a little envious, at this show of independence. Jennifer's self-reliant approach to life in the 1990s is startlingly different from Emily's restricted life back in the 1890s. **add**

Of course, women in the nineteenth century achieved distinction in many areas, but compared with Jennifer, Emily had few opportunities and even fewer civil rights. She couldn't own property. She couldn't vote in national elections. **add** And even thinking about holding high public office was totally out of the question. Although there are still areas of male dominance, Jennifer's generation has reached levels of achievement unattainable by women in Emily's day. Jennifer is free to make her own choices and pursue whatever career she wishes. **reorder**

1. Why did the writer cut the opening sentence?
2. Why was it important to add the sentence beginning *Jennifer's self-reliant approach* to the end of the first paragraph? How does the new sentence help to focus the essay?

3. Why did the writer add *in national elections* to the sentence in the second paragraph about Emily's not being able to vote?
4. Why did the writer move the last two sentences in the second paragraph to the beginning of the paragraph? [Hint: What method of organization is the writer using?]

PART 5:

Evaluating and Revising Your Comparison/Contrast Essay

Be a critic—of your own work and of a classmate's. Begin by evaluating your own essay, using the chart on page 237 for reference. What changes would improve your essay? Then exchange papers with another student and use the questions from the chart to evaluate each other's essays. Consider your partner's comments and your own observations as you determine where you might add, cut, replace, or reorder words, sentences, or paragraphs. To correct any problems that have been identified, change a word or sentence here and there or, if necessary, begin a whole new draft.

Proofreading and Publishing

Proofreading. You wouldn't go out on a date without taking one last look in the mirror before heading for the door; and when you finish revising an essay, it needs that one last piece of checking, too. It is always important to look for mistakes in spelling, capitalization, punctuation, grammar, and usage. (See page 49 for **Guidelines for Proofreading.**)

MECHANICS HINT

Hyphens in Compound Adjectives

Although hyphenated adjectives are not unique to comparison/contrast essays, you may have noticed several in the Professional Model and the Writer's Model.

> "A tall row of elegant, *lathe-turned* spindles separated this table from the kitchen. . . ."
>
> She is working and studying hard to prepare for the bar examination that will make her a *full-fledged* lawyer.
>
> Emily, by contrast, had to spend a full hour preparing dinner for her family over a *coal-burning* stove.

A ***compound adjective*** is two or more single words acting as a single adjective, working together to create a meaning that is different from their separate meanings. A compound adjective is usually composed of a noun and a past or present participle. When a compound adjective precedes the word it modifies, you usually hyphenate it. You do not usually hyphenate a compound adjective that follows the noun it modifies.

> It was a coal-burning stove.
> The stove was coal burning.

 REFERENCE NOTE: For more information about hyphens with compound adjectives, see page 953.

Publishing. When you write to inform, you need an audience to share the information with. Here are two ways you might publish your comparison/contrast essay.

- Try this game. In a small group, each writer names his or her two subjects. The writer then reads from his or her comparison/contrast essay about the features of only *one* of the subjects. (With the block method of organization, this is easy; with the point-by-point method, it's more complex, but certainly manageable.) The other students use their general knowledge to try to supply the missing information about the features of the second subject.
- Present your essay orally in class as a dialogue. Find a partner who will read the information on one subject; you will read the information on the other subject. This works best if you have two copies of the paper, with each reader's part marked with a highlighter pen. Ask the class for comments and questions on the presentation. This is an excellent way to find out how clearly you have communicated your main idea as well as the relevant features of the two subjects.

PART 6:
Proofreading and Publishing Your Comparison/Contrast Essay

Read your paper over carefully one last time, looking for any remaining errors in spelling, capitalization, punctuation, or usage. Make whatever corrections are needed. Then share your paper with others, using one of the publishing ideas suggested above or an original idea of your own.

WRITING WORKSHOP

An Extended Definition

In your comparison/contrast essay, you used the strategy of classification to inform: You identified the common group the two subjects belonged to before you examined their relationship to each other. You also use classification when you define a word. First, you identify the general category the word belongs to (a *chore* is a type of job or work). Then, you identify its relationship to other words in the same category by examining characteristics that distinguish the word from those other words. (A *chore* is a type of job or work that's assigned to be done on a regular basis, especially around the home.)

An ***extended definition*** may begin with the basic definition of the word, or the writer may assume that readers already know the basic definition. The extended definition goes beyond the basic definition by adding details such as examples, facts, word origins, quotations, anecdotes, descriptions, and opinions. For example, following is an extended definition of *chores*. As you read, notice the kinds of details the writer uses to explain what chores are.

Doing Chores

by August Heckscher

I have been doing chores, being for a brief spell alone in a house that recently was astir with bustle and echoed with the voices of a gathered family. For those who may be in some doubt as to the nature of chores, their variety, their pleasures and their drudgery, I am prepared to deliver a short disquisition.

The first point about chores is that they are repetitive. They come every day or thereabouts, and once done they require after a certain time to be done again. In this regard a chore is the very opposite of a "happening"—that strange sort of event which a few years back was so much in fashion. For a happening was in essence unrepeatable; it came about in ways no one could predict, taking form from vaporous imaginings or sudden impulse. Chores, by contrast, can be foreseen in advance; for better or worse, I know that tomorrow I must be re-enacting the same small round of ritualistic deeds; and they arise, moreover, from practical necessities, not from poetic flights.

A second point about chores is that they leave no visible mark of improvement or progress behind them. When I am finished, things will be precisely as they were before – except that the fires will have been set, the garbage disposed of, and the garden weeded. In this, they are different from the works which optimistically I undertake. Ozymandias may have been presumptuous, but he was essentially right when he looked about him and said: "*See how my works endure!*" A work, once achieved, leaves a mark upon the world; nothing is ever quite the same again. The page of a book may have been printed or a page of manuscript written; a sketch, a poem, a song composed; or perhaps some happy achievement reached in one of the more evanescent art forms like the dance or cooking. All these have an existence of their own, outside of time, and at least for a little while live on in the mind of their creator and perhaps a few of his friends.

The well-meaning wife, seeing her husband about his chores, will miss the character of his performance. "Henry loves to cut wood," she will say; "he positively dotes on controlling the flow of waste from dinner-table to compost heap." The wife is perhaps trying to appease an unnecessary sense of guilt at seeing her spouse engaged in mundane efforts. The fact is, he doesn't love doing chores. But neither does he feel humiliated or out of sorts for having to do them. The nature of a chore is that it is neither pleasant nor unpleasant in itself; it is entirely neutral – but it is obligatory.

Neutral — and yet I must confess that with their repetition, and perhaps because of their very inconsequence, chores can in the end evoke a mild sort of satisfaction. Here, as in more heroic fields of endeavor, a certain basic craft asserts itself. To do what must be done neatly, efficiently, expeditiously — "without rest and without haste" — lights a small fire deep in the interior being and puts a man in good humor with the world. Santayana described leisure as "being at home among manageable things"; and if he was right we who are the chore-doers of the world are the true leisure classes. At least one can be sure that no chore will defeat us; none will raise insuperable obstacles, or leave us deflated as when the divine muse abandons her devotee.

A man I know became seduced by the minor pleasure of doing chores — or at any rate by the absence of pain which they involve — and could be seen from morning till nightfall trotting about his small domain, putting everything in order, setting everything to rights that the slow process of time had disturbed. He was perhaps going too far. To season chores with work, and to intersperse them with a few happenings, is the secret of a contented existence. Fortunate the man or woman who achieves a just balance between these three types of activity — as I have been able to do by good chance, and for a little space of time.

For Better or For Worse copyright 1989 Lynn Johnston Producti

1. In the second, third, fourth, and fifth paragraphs, the writer gives important characteristics of chores. What characteristic does he give in each of those paragraphs?
2. What do you think the writer means by "happenings" in the second paragraph? by "works" in the third para-

graph? by "work" in the sixth paragraph? According to the writer, how are chores different from "happenings"? from both kinds of "work"?

3. What kinds of details (example, quotation, anecdote, and so on) does the writer use to extend the definition?
4. Informative writing should provide new information. What information about chores is new or different?
5. This writer used a definition to inform. How might you use a definition to express yourself? to persuade?

Writing an Extended Definition

Prewriting. Choose an idea or term that interests you and that can't be easily defined in a single sentence. Here are some suggestions:

the ideal job	blues music	fun
true love	winners and losers	fairness (justice)
"street smart"	adult	success

Think of examples, quotations, facts, anecdotes, comparisons, contrasts, or other kinds of details to extend the definition. Gather details from dictionaries, encyclopedias, magazines, or friends. Keep your audience in mind as you decide what information to use.

Writing, Evaluating, and Revising. In your first paragraph, write one or two sentences briefly identifying the general class to which the subject belongs and telling how it is different from all other items in this general class. Then extend your definition with the details (examples, quotations, facts, and so on) you have gathered. Since this is an essay, don't forget to include a concluding paragraph.

Exchange papers with a partner and ask for comments. Is the definition informative? Are there enough specific details? Revise your essay as necessary to improve it.

Proofreading and Publishing. Proofread your paper to correct errors in spelling, grammar, usage, and punctuation. Then get together with classmates to decide how to publish your essays. You might want to make a class dictionary of extended definitions or read them aloud in class.

WRITING WORKSHOP

An Essay of Division

In this chapter you have worked with two forms of the strategy of classification: comparison/contrast and definition. A third form is often just called classification, but it is really another form of classification—***division.*** In this form of classification, you start with a large group and break it into subclasses or categories.

Division is especially important in science. Classification systems have been developed for animals, plants, and minerals, as well as storms, bodies of water, viruses, and many other items. In a division essay, remember to do two things:

- identify the principle of division (the subgroups or categories to be used)
- divide the whole subject into subgroups, or categories

For example, suppose you are asked to classify the large group, or class, of aquatic mammals. Subgroups, or categories, include whales and dolphins, seals, and sea cows.

In the following excerpt the writer assumes you already know what a tarantula is. But in order to explain a specific aspect of tarantula behavior, he classifies information into three categories. As you read, look for the categories and subcategories (divisions of categories) he discusses.

from "The Spider and the Wasp"

by Alexander Petrunkevitch

. . .[All] spiders, and especially hairy ones, have an extremely delicate sense of touch. Laboratory experiments prove that tarantulas can distinguish three types of touch: pressure against the body wall, stroking of the body hair, and riffling of certain very fine hairs on the legs called trichobothria. Pressure against the body, by the finger or the end of a pencil, causes the tarantula to move off slowly for a short distance. The touch excites no defensive response unless the approach is from above where the spider can see the motion, in which case it rises on its hind legs, lifts its front legs, opens its fangs and holds this threatening posture as long as the object continues to move.

The entire body of a tarantula, especially its legs, is thickly clothed with hair. Some of it is short and woolly, some long and stiff. Touching this body hair produces one of two distinct reactions. When the spider is hungry, it responds with an immediate and swift attack. At the touch of a cricket's antennae the tarantula seizes the insect so swiftly that a motion picture taken at the rate of 64 frames per second shows only the result and not the process of capture. But when the spider is not hungry, the stimulation of its hairs merely causes it to shake the touched limb. An insect can walk under its hairy belly unharmed.

The trichobothria, very fine hairs growing from disklike membranes on the legs, are sensitive only to air movement. A light breeze makes them vibrate slowly, without disturbing the common hair. When one blows gently on the trichobothria, the tarantula reacts with a quick jerk of its four front legs. If the front and hind legs are stimulated at the same time, the spider makes a sudden jump. This reaction is quite independent of the state of its appetite.

These three tactile responses—to pressure on the body wall, to moving of the common hair, and to flexing of the trichobothria—are so different from one another that there is no possibility of confusing them. They serve the tarantula adequately for most of its needs and enable it to avoid most annoyances and dangers. But they fail the spider completely when it meets its deadly enemy, the digger wasp *Pepsis*.

From "The Spider and the Wasp" by Alexander Petrunkevitch from *Scientific American*, August 1952.

1. What aspect of tarantulas' behavior does the writer discuss?
2. Into what three categories does the writer divide the subject?
3. Which categories are further divided into subcategories? What are these subcategories?

Writing an Essay of Division

Prewriting. Choose a subject to write about that lends itself to division. It should be a subject with subgroups or categories, not an object with parts. For example, you could look at the subject of automobiles and analyze the different types of automobiles. In a division essay, you would not, however, break an individual car down into the transmission, wheels, radio, windows, and so on. (To do this would be to create a description.)

You may have more than one layer of division in your essay. For example, the first layer under automobiles might include the categories of passenger cars, minivans, and trucks. The second layer (subcategories) might divide passenger cars into sports cars, sedans, and station wagons.

If you have trouble thinking of a subject, you might try one of these:

- Pretend that you have been asked to help a Russian high school start a collection of music popular with American teenagers. Describe several types of music the library should include, and for each type, suggest specific performers and recordings.
- Survey your classmates who are going on to college. Find out whether they are going to a four-year state university, a two-year community college, a private four-year college, or some other form of post–high school education. Also ask why they have made the choices they made. Organize your findings according to the four categories of post–high school education.

To plan your paper, think about everything you already know about your topic, and list possible categories and subcategories. Don't worry if you can't think of subcategories; some subjects just don't have any. Research additional details and facts, and organize your information by category and subcategory. Keep your audience in mind as you decide what background information to include.

Writing, Evaluating, and Revising. To help readers follow your ideas, discuss one category at a time, including its subcategories. When you have finished your first draft, exchange papers with a classmate and ask for comments. Is the topic divided into two or more distinctly different categories (and possibly subcategories)? Are characteristics of each category and subcategory clearly identified? Are there enough details and examples? Revise your essay to clarify ideas and add information.

Proofreading and Publishing. Check for mistakes in spelling, usage, and mechanics, and make a clean copy. Brainstorm ideas for sharing essays. For example, the junior class might be interested in an essay on colleges, and a science class might be interested in an essay on fossils.

MAKING CONNECTIONS

TEST TAKING

Using Analogy

An ***analogy*** is a special kind of comparison—it points out the similarities between two basically unlike subjects. You can often use an analogy to explain a complex subject by comparing it to something familiar. To explain how a human heart works, for example, you might compare it to a pump.

How is voting like taking an exam? That's the analogy used in the following introduction for an essay about voting.

> Voting is much like taking an important exam. Both require preparation, and both can have long-lasting effects. Pulling just any lever or punching any hole is as foolish as randomly marking every answer on a test. Chances are that you'll make more bad decisions than good ones. It's just as important to study the candidates and their positions on issues as it is to learn the material that will be covered on a test. It's even better if you've been actively involved in both processes all along so that you don't make last-minute decisions. More than one election has been won or lost by just one vote, just as tests have been passed or failed by a single point. Voting is a duty as well as a right, and it's your duty to be informed about candidates and issues.

Try writing a paragraph of analogy to explain a complex idea or subject. You might want to use one of the following suggestions or think up two subjects of your own. Just be certain that the subjects are basically unlike each other, but share enough characteristics to make the analogy meaningful.

1. first date—first day of school
2. army ants—human army
3. the game of chess—war

4. green plant during photosynthesis—a factory
5. running a 28K marathon—baby-sitting seven two-year-olds for a whole day

COMPARISON/CONTRAST IN HUMOR

Have you ever thought about what makes a good humorous cartoon or joke? Often humor is based on ***irony,*** which is really a contrast between what we expect (or are led to expect) and what actually occurs. In the cartoon here, the humor is created by the contrast, or difference between, what the person thinks is happening and what really is happening.

LESS CHOLESTEROL
REGULAR CHECKUPS
NO NICOTINE
NO ALCOHOL
LOW SODIUM
MODERATE EXERCISE
NO SUGAR

Get together with a partner and do a reading survey of cartoons in newspapers and magazines. Your goal is to analyze twenty-five to thirty cartoons to determine whether their humor is based on comparison/contrast. When you return to class, discuss your findings with the whole class and share some of the best cartoons you found. Do some cartoonists seem to rely more on comparison/contrast than others? Which ones?

Now that you have studied humorous cartoons, brainstorm for ideas for a cartoon you could create yourself. Don't forget to take advantage of contrasts and irony. When your cartoon is finished, share it with others in your class.

7 WRITING TO EXPLAIN

Making Things Clear

SEQUENCE OF EVENTS

1. (lower right) The acrobat on stilts balances on a catapult using a pole handed to him by an assistant.
2. (lower right corner) Two men leap from a platform onto the catapult, propelling the acrobat on stilts high into the air.
3. (center) The acrobat, still wearing the stilts, does a somersault in the air.
4. (lower left) The acrobat lands, balanced on his stilts, which bow slightly from the impact.

Why has the grizzly bear become almost extinct? How will you be affected by attending a small college? a large university? Questions like these abound in your everyday life. In an attempt to **make things clear,** you look for explanations. "A huge star collapses into itself and causes a black hole." "Serious bone changes can result from a lack of vitamin D, produced by sunlight."

Writing and You. Writers often try to explain things. An environmentalist explains the effects of the 1989 *Valdez* oil spill in Alaska. A reporter for the school newspaper explains why a school policy has been changed. What questions do you have that explanations might make clear?

As You Read. In prescientific ages, people sought explanations for natural phenomena from folk tales and myths. What explanation does the following Native American myth give for the characteristics of the rabbit and the owl?

Dr. Harold E. Edgerton, *Moscow Circus* (1963), Photograph.

WHY THE OWL HAS BIG EYES

An Iroquois Myth
retold by Richard Erdoes and Alfonso Ortiz

▼▼▼

"I want nice long legs and long ears like a deer, and sharp fangs and claws like a panther."

▼▼▼

Raweno, the Everything-Maker, was busy creating various animals. He was working on Rabbit, and Rabbit was saying: "I want nice long legs and long ears like a deer, and sharp fangs and claws like a panther."

"I do them up the way they want to be; I give them what they ask for," said Raweno. He was working on Rabbit's hind legs, making them long, the way Rabbit had ordered.

Owl, still unformed, was sitting on a tree nearby and waiting his turn. He was saying: "Whoo, whoo, I want a nice long neck like Swan's, and beautiful red feathers like Cardinal's, and a nice long beak like Egret's, and a nice crown of plumes like Heron's. I want you to make me into the most beautiful, the fastest, the most wonderful of all the birds."

Raweno said: "Be quiet. Turn around and look in another direction. Even better, close your eyes. Don't you know that no one is allowed to watch me work?" Raweno was just then making Rabbit's ears very long, the way Rabbit wanted them.

Owl refused to do what Raweno said. "Whoo, whoo," he replied, "nobody can forbid me to watch. Nobody can order me to close my eyes. I like watching you, and watch I will."

Then Raweno became angry. He grabbed Owl, pulling him down from his branch, stuffing his head deep into his body, shaking him until his eyes grew big with fright, pulling at his ears until they were sticking up at both sides of his head.

"There," said Raweno, "that'll teach you. Now you won't be able to crane your neck to watch things you shouldn't watch. Now you have big ears to listen when someone tells you what not to do. Now you have big eyes—but not so big that you can watch me, because you'll be awake only at night, and I work by day. And your feathers won't be red like cardinal's, but gray like this"—and Raweno rubbed Owl all over with mud—"as punishment for your disobedience." So Owl flew off, pouting: "Whoo, whoo, whoo."

Then Raweno turned back to finish Rabbit, but Rabbit had been so terrified by Raweno's anger, even though it was not directed at him, that he ran off half done. As a consequence, only Rabbit's hind legs are long, and he has to hop about instead of walking and running. Also, because he took fright then, Rabbit has remained afraid of most everything, and he never got the claws and fangs he asked for in order to defend himself. Had he not run away then, Rabbit would have been an altogether different animal.

As for Owl, he remained as Raweno had shaped him in anger—with big eyes, a short neck, and ears sticking up on the sides of his head. On top of everything, he has to sleep during the day and come out only at night.

". . . I want a nice long neck like Swan's, and beautiful red feathers like Cardinal's, and a nice long beak like Egret's, and a nice crown of plumes like Heron's."

▼▼▼

Reader's Response

1. Folk tales and myths were created by people who wanted an explanation for natural phenomena they had observed. Modern science has provided many explanations, but many phenomena are still unexplained. In your journal, make a list of natural phenomena you would like to have explained.
2. What are some other myths that explain natural phenomena? For example, how does the Greek myth of Apollo driving his golden chariot explain the rising and setting of the sun? How does the myth of Demeter and Persephone explain the seasons?

Writer's Craft

3. What physical attributes of rabbits does this myth attempt to explain?
4. What were the effects of Everything-Maker's anger? The writers explain these effects twice. How does the repetition strengthen—or weaken—the telling of the story?
5. You may think of myths and folk tales as children's stories; but, in fact, they are generally stories created by adults for adults. As such, they reveal a great deal about the culture in which they originated. What does "Why the Owl Has Big Eyes" tell you about the Iroquois culture?

Strategies for Writing to Explain

When you are writing to explain, you may use any of the four basic strategies of writing—narration, description, classification, evaluation. For example, the preceding myth uses narration, the strategy you use to explain how things happen, or change, over time. The following examples identify explanations that reflect each of the four basic writing strategies.

Narration: in a history paper, recounting the causes of the Revolutionary War; writing an apology to another school explaining why the team was hours late for a swimming meet.

Description: describing the culture of the Iroquois and giving evidence to show how their heritage thrives today; in a story, describing the slum a character lives in and providing details to show the poverty.

Classification: defining the term *music video* and using examples and facts to distinguish among subjects and styles; explaining the attributes of different kinds of sharks and using details to illustrate the differences.

Evaluation: defending your choice of a new job to your parents and providing data to prove that your choice is valid; giving your opinion about a new movie and backing it up with specific details and examples.

LOOKING AHEAD

In the main assignment in this chapter, you will use the strategy of narration in an essay to explain causes and/or effects. As you work, keep in mind that a cause-and-effect explanation

- focuses on a particular situation or event
- provides an answer to one or both of these questions: Why did it happen? (What caused it?) What were the effects?
- gives evidence to support the explanation

Writing a Cause-and-Effect Essay

Considering Topic, Purpose, and Audience

An Appropriate Topic. You can take almost any idea or situation, apply a little curiosity to it, and come up with an appropriate *topic* for a cause-and-effect essay. Here are some examples to show how this works:

- One of the most popular books ever published is Margaret Mitchell's *Gone with the Wind.* Why? What caused it to be so popular?
- U.S students, many critics say, can no longer compete with students from Japan and other industrialized countries. If this statement is true, what caused the situation? What will the future effects be?
- Whales shouldn't be taken from their natural habitats, say many experts. Why? What happens when whales are put on display in gulfariums?

As the examples on the previous page illustrate, an appropriate topic for cause-and-effect essays begins with a *situation* or *condition* (the popularity of *Gone with the Wind,* the decline in American education) and then asks *Why?* and/or *What's the result?*

If you are still bewildered about how to find a good topic, look for changes. Anything that represents **change**—a trend, an invention, a physical or political shift—necessarily has both cause and effect. Combine a changing situation with your own personal interest and you have a topic with potential.

Purpose and Audience. Your purpose in examining causes and effects could be to persuade, to express yourself, or to create a literary work. In this chapter, though, your main *purpose* will be to explain. When you explain anything, you try to clarify it and supply evidence that proves what you say. An explanation is not valid without sound evidence, such as facts, to support it. For now, your *audience* includes your teacher and classmates. As you begin your research and writing, look for information that appeals to their interests. Treat your readers as thoughtful, mature people who won't accept an explanation without sound evidence to back it up.

Explaining is just one of the categories of the ***expository*** purpose, or aim, for writing. The other categories are informing and exploring. When you ***explain,*** you use facts and other forms of evidence to prove that your explanation is sound. When you ***inform*** (see Chapter 6), you share facts and ideas with your readers. When you ***explore*** (see Chapter 9), you attempt to discover facts and evidence.

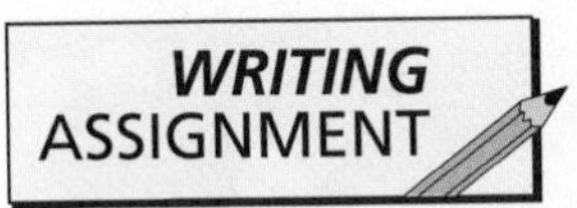

PART 1:

Choosing a Topic

What ideas do you have for cause-and-effect topics? Observe what is changing in your environment—home, school, or city. Brainstorm about pastimes and subjects you enjoy, looking for a change—a situation or event that makes you ask *Why?* or *What's the result?*

Planning a Cause-and-Effect Explanation

Your explanation won't be clear to your readers unless it is first clear to you. That means that you will have to form a ***thesis,*** or main idea; gather information about it; and decide how best to arrange your ideas for your readers.

Identifying Your Thesis

Writers sometimes decide on a thesis, or main idea, as soon as they have chosen a topic. For example, you hear that African elephants are in danger of becoming extinct, and you decide to write about the causes. Other times, writers may simply know that a situation exists—high insurance rates for teenage drivers, for example—and gather information about it before deciding on a thesis.

A cause-and-effect explanation may focus on causes, effects, or both. The ***thesis statement,*** which is usually a one-sentence summary of your thesis, should indicate the focus. The following thesis statements show three different focuses on the same situation:

Causes: Three major factors prompt teenagers to sign up for volunteer work in the community.

Effects: While the number of teenage volunteers may be small, the impact of their services is large.

Causes and Effects: Teenagers have different reasons for doing volunteer work, but the effects of their work are generally significant.

Identifying Sources

For some topics, you will be your own best source of information. If you have done volunteer work yourself, for example, you can draw on your own personal experience and knowledge for information about the reasons why teenagers are volunteering for community work. For other topics, you may need to use some of the following techniques to gather information from outside sources.

- Interview people to take advantage of their experience and knowledge.
- Read magazines and newspapers to find facts and figures about current situations.
- Read encyclopedias and library books for background information about topics of general interest.

Investigating Causes and Effects

Your aim in writing will be to explain; but before you can do that, you have to discover the causes and effects of the situation or condition. Although you may know some of them at the time you identify your topic, it is important to identify and investigate *all* possible causes and effects. Otherwise, you may miss something very important.

Causes. Why do birds rub ants on their backs? Why have historians begun using the term *Middle Ages* rather than *Dark Ages*? These are the kinds of questions you ask yourself when you explore causes. You can start by asking *Why did this happen?* and listing every likely cause that you uncover. Later, when you have completed your investigation, you can select the causes that you think merit discussion. The following questions will help you thoroughly investigate causes:

- What are the obvious causes?
- Is there a main, or most important, cause? What is it?
- What is the most recent cause?
- What causes occurred in the distant past?

Effects. What are the effects of not studying? One direct effect might be poor grades, but there may be other effects as well, ones that aren't as immediately obvious. You might not get into college, or you might not get a scholarship. When you investigate effects, ask yourself, *What are the results?* and list every possible effect you can think of. As with causes, wait until you have completed your investigation and then discard any effects that seem to be unrelated or unsupportable. These questions will help you investigate effects:

- What are the most obvious effects?
- Are there any hidden effects? What are they?
- What was (or will be) the first effect?
- What might be the future effects?

Cause-and-Effect Chains. During your investigation of the situation, you also need to look for a possible ***cause-and-effect chain.*** In such a chain, one event or situation causes an effect, then that effect becomes a cause for an additional effect, and so on. For example, a fire produces dangerous gases that cause health problems. The health problems cause people to move away, and their moving in turn causes a recession in the local economy. If such a chain exists, it may become an important part of your explanation.

Machine for Washing Dishes

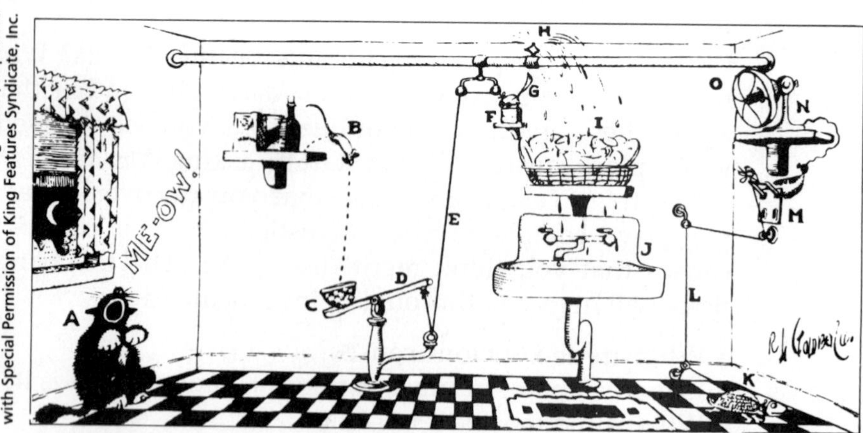

The professor turns on his think-faucet and dopes out a machine for washing dishes while you are at the movies.

When spoiled tomcat (**A**) discovers he is alone, he lets out a yell which scares mouse (**B**) into jumping into basket (**C**), causing lever end (**D**) to rise and pull string (**E**) which snaps automatic cigar-lighter (**F**). Flame (**G**) starts fire sprinkler (**H**). Water runs on dishes (**I**) and drips into sink (**J**). Turtle (**K**), thinking he hears babbling brook babbling, and having no sense of direction, starts wrong way and pulls string (**L**), which turns on switch (**M**) that starts electric glow heater (**N**). Heat ray (**O**) dries the dishes.

If the cat and the turtle get on to your scheme and refuse to cooperate, simply put the dishes on the front porch and pray for rain.

When you are exploring causes and effects, you need to avoid an error in thinking called ***false cause and effect.*** You can't assume that a cause-and-effect relationship exists just because one thing precedes another; there must be a valid connection between them.

FALSE CAUSE AND EFFECT

My computer broke the day after I bought those new disks. The disks must have caused the problem.

The only connection here is sequence, or timing, of the events. A more likely cause might be moisture or crumbs in the keyboard.

Providing Believable Support

If people continue using hair spray at the rate they now use it, the earth will become five degrees warmer by the year 2000. Do you believe that statement? An important part of an explanation is the support, or evidence, that proves your explanation is valid. You won't stand a chance of supporting your explanation unless you have sufficient, accurate, and reliable evidence.

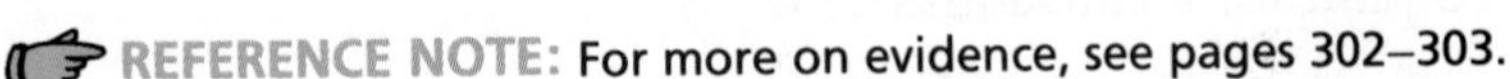

REFERENCE NOTE: For more on evidence, see pages 302–303.

Sufficient Evidence. What is *enough* evidence? The answer is, "Whatever it takes to prove your point." Sometimes one example may be enough; at other times, you may need some statistics as well as two or three examples to prove that a certain cause or effect exists. Your task is to be sensitive to your audience's doubts and to make sure that you have a reasonable amount of support. Your evidence may consist of facts, statistics, examples, or anecdotes, but you need to have enough of it.

Accurate Evidence. Whether you are quoting an expert or a magazine article, citing statistics, or giving an example, you need to be accurate. If you mean to say that the average American throws away five pounds of trash a day and instead say fifty pounds, your audience will begin to question your entire explanation. Take notes accurately, and be sure you get both the numbers and the words right.

Reliable Evidence. Reliable evidence comes from a "trustworthy" source. You or your neighbor, for example, may speak reliably about the effects of your neighborhood street becoming one-way, but unless you are scientists, you would not be reliable sources for an explanation of how climatic changes led to dinosaur extinction. And don't assume everything that is printed is reliable. Make sure that any magazine or newspaper you use, for example, has a reputation for using trustworthy sources.

To plan for a cause-and-effect essay

- identify a thesis that focuses on causes, effects, or both
- record information about secondary sources so you can cite them in your paper
- look for multiple and/or hidden causes and effects
- look for evidence to prove that the cause or effect exists

EXERCISE 1 **Speaking and Listening: Gathering Information About Causes and Effects**

Mr. and Mrs. Smith have died and left each of the one thousand residents of Nowhere, U.S.A., one million dollars. What caused the Smiths to make this donation? What might be the effects of this sudden wealth on the residents of this town? Get together with a small group of your classmates and discuss possible answers to these questions. Try to think of at least two likely causes of the Smiths' generosity and two effects the money might have on the residents of the small town. Then identify information that would support each cause and each effect. When you finish, share your causes and effects and supporting evidence with other groups.

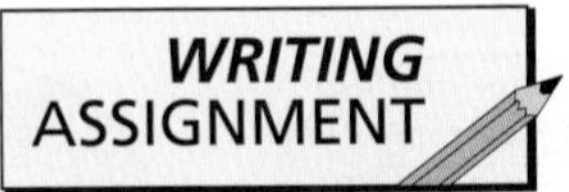

PART 2:
Planning Your Cause-and-Effect Explanation

You are now ready to begin planning your own cause-and-effect explanation. If you are using the topic you chose in Writing Assignment, Part 1, you probably already have some idea about the answers to one or both of these questions about your topic: *Why? What's the result?* Brainstorm or freewrite (see pages 22–24) to find additional possible causes or effects, and look for others in sources such as books, magazines, tapes, or interviews. At the same time, look for evidence that supports each cause or effect. At some point, identify your focus—causes, effects, or both—and write your thesis statement.

Organizing Information

The focus of your essay—causes, effects, or causes and effects—helps to determine how to organize your information. A map that shows the relationship between causes and effects is a useful organizational aid at this point, and the following example shows one writer's map for an essay on the causes of a dangerous intersection.

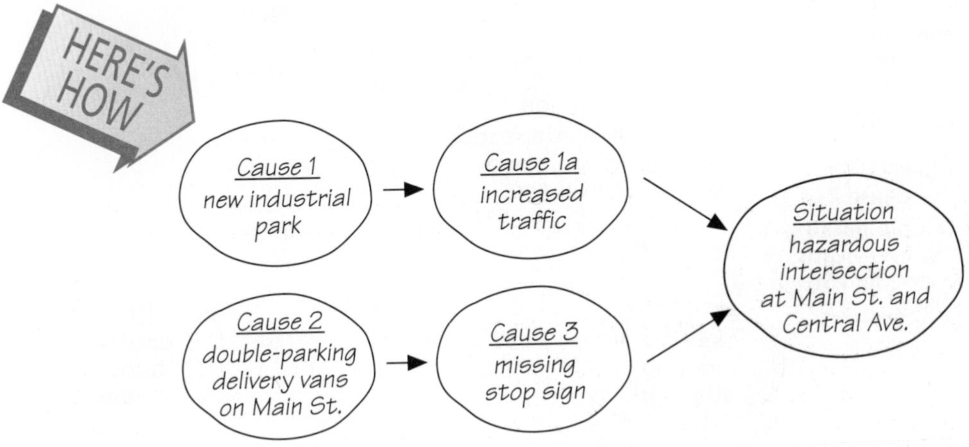

The following examples illustrate mapping for essays with other focuses.

Focusing on Effects

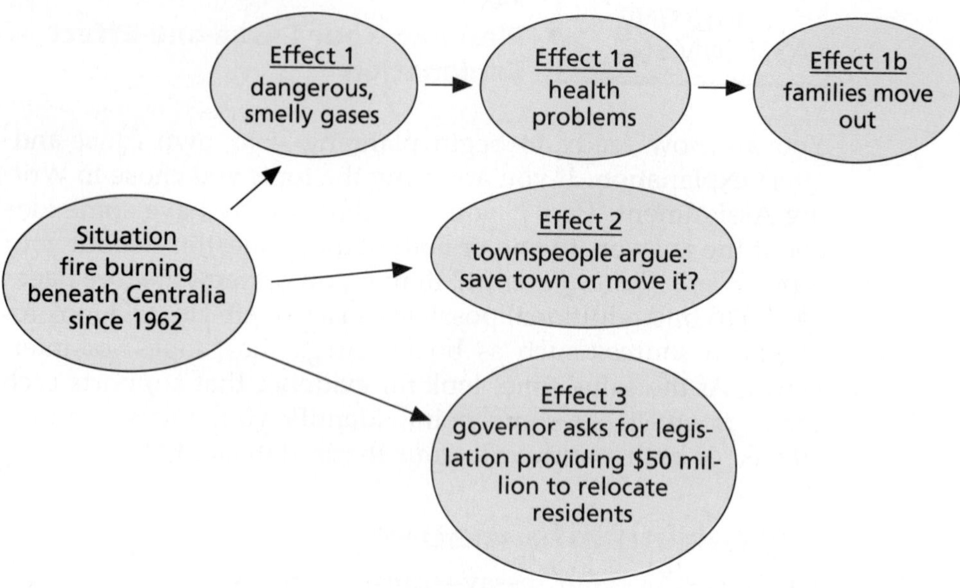

Focusing on Causes and Effects

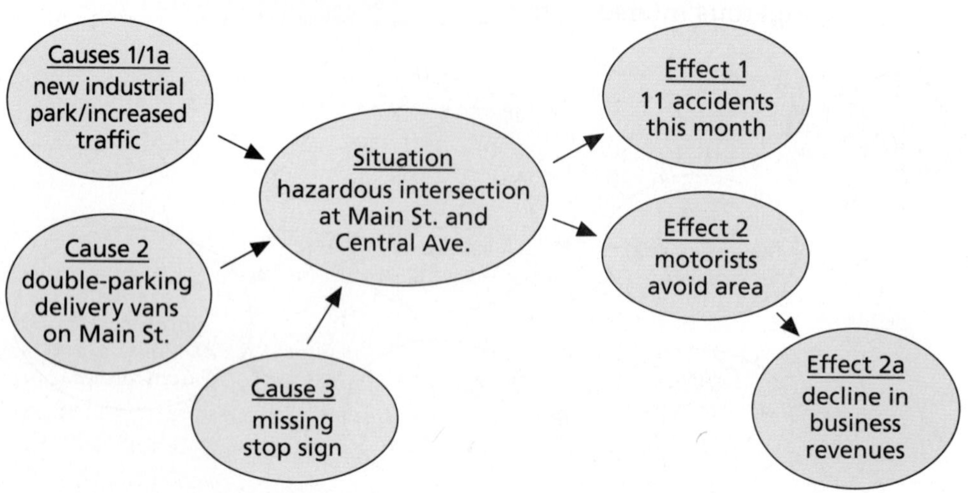

Focusing on a Chain of Causes and Effects

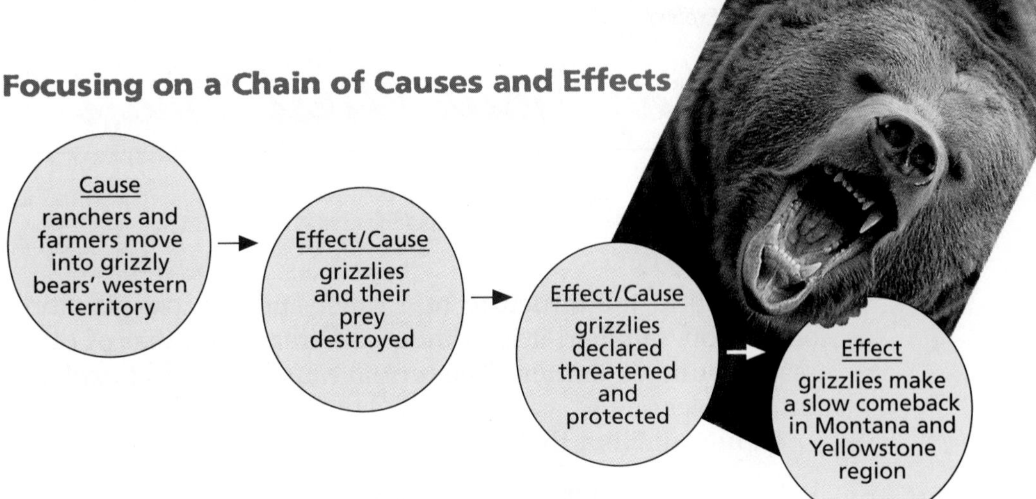
Cause
ranchers and farmers move into grizzly bears' western territory
Effect/Cause
grizzlies and their prey destroyed
Effect/Cause
grizzlies declared threatened and protected
Effect
grizzlies make a slow comeback in Montana and Yellowstone region

Arranging Causes and Effects. Naturally, it only makes sense to discuss causes before effects, but which cause do you list first when you have two or three causes? Out of three effects, which do you list first and which last? In most cases, use ***order of importance,*** listing the least important cause or effect first and building up to the most important one at the end. However, when a situation has developed over a long period of time, producing one effect after another, it's often best to use ***chronological order.*** The fire in Centralia, Pennsylvania, is such a topic. And when you are putting your causes and effects in order, remember to discuss the supporting evidence for each cause or effect before moving on to the next cause or effect.

REFERENCE NOTE: See pages 74, 79–82, and 86–87 for more information on order of importance and chronological order.

WRITING
ASSIGNMENT

PART 3:
Organizing Your Information

When you completed Writing Assignment, Part 2, you had a thesis statement and a great deal of information about causes and effects, probably jotted down on note cards or paper in no certain order. The next step is to arrange that information in an order that will make sense to readers. Depending on your focus—causes, effects, or causes and effect—use one of the patterns on pages 265–266 to make a map that you will use as a guide for writing your essay.

Writing Your First Draft

The Structure of a Cause-and-Effect Explanation

You will find the structure of a cause-and-effect explanation comfortably familiar; it isn't much different from that of other essays you have written. The typical cause-and-effect explanation includes

an **introduction** that

- captures your reader's attention
- identifies the situation or event you're explaining
- provides important background information
- identifies your thesis

a **body** that

- explains the causes and/or effects of the situation
- uses facts, examples, anecdotes, and statistics to support, or prove, each cause or effect
- has a clear organization

a **conclusion** that

- sums up the explanation
- possibly, refers to the introduction
- possibly, predicts future changes or effects

In the essay on the next page, Harold Krents writes about a situation he knows well—his blindness—and its effects on the sighted members of society. Krents moves from the "nuisance" effects to a more serious effect: the belief that a blind person can't practice law.

"I'm not sure I understand the process of writing.... The brain slowly begins to function in a different way, to make mysterious connections."

Elizabeth Hardwick

A CAUSE-AND-EFFECT ESSAY

Darkness at Noon

by Harold Krents

INTRODUCTION
Attention grabber

Blind from birth, I have never had the opportunity to see myself and have been completely dependent on the image I create in the eye of the observer. To date it has not been narcissistic.

BODY
Effect 1

Evidence—example

There are those who assume that since I can't see, I obviously also cannot hear. Very often people will converse with me at the top of their lungs, enunciating each word very carefully. Conversely, people will also often whisper, assuming that since my eyes don't work, my ears don't either.

Evidence—anecdote

For example, when I go to the airport and ask the ticket agent for assistance to the plane, he or she will invariably pick up the phone, call a ground hostess and whisper: "Hi, Jane, we've got a 76 here." I have concluded that the word "blind" is not used for one of two reasons: Either they fear that if the dread word is spoken, the ticket agent's retina will immediately detach, or they are reluctant to inform me of my condition of which I may not have been previously aware.

Effect 2
Evidence—examples

On the other hand, others know that of course I can hear, but believe that I can't talk. Often, therefore, when my wife and I go out to dinner, a waiter or waitress will ask Kit if "*he* would like a drink" to which I respond that "indeed *he* would."

Evidence—anecdote

This point was graphically driven home to me while we were in England. I had been given a year's leave of absence from my Washington law firm to study for a diploma in law degree at Oxford University. During the year I became ill and was hospitalized. Immediately after admission, I was wheeled down to the X-ray room. Just at the door sat an elderly woman – elderly I would judge from the sound of her voice. "What is his name?" the woman asked the orderly who had been wheeling me.

"What's your name?" the orderly repeated to me.

"Harold Krents," I replied.

"Harold Krents," he repeated.

"When was he born?"

"When were you born?"

"November 5, 1944," I responded.

"November 5, 1944," the orderly intoned.

This procedure continued for approximately five minutes at which point even my saint-like disposition deserted me. "Look," I finally blurted out, "this is absolutely ridiculous. Okay, granted I can't see, but it's got to have become pretty clear to both of you that I don't need an interpreter."

"He says he doesn't need an interpreter," the orderly reported to the woman.

Effect 3
Evidence—examples

The toughest misconception of all is the view that because I can't see, I can't work. I was turned down by over forty law firms because of my blindness, even though my qualifications included a cum laude degree from Harvard College and a good ranking in my Harvard Law School class.

The attempt to find employment, the continuous frustration of being told that it was impossible for a blind person to practice law, the rejection letters, not based on my lack of ability but rather on my disability, will always remain one of the most disillusioning experiences of my life.

Future effect/ cause

Fortunately, this view of limitation and exclusion is beginning to change. On April 16 [1976], the Department of Labor issued regulations that mandate equal-employment opportunities for the handicapped. By and large, the business community's response to offering employment to the disabled has been enthusiastic.

Future effect anticipated

I therefore look forward to the day, with the expectation that it is certain to come, when employers will view their handicapped workers as a little child did me years ago when my family still lived in Scarsdale.

Evidence—anecdote

I was playing basketball with my father in our backyard according to procedures we had developed. My father would stand beneath the hoop, shout, and I would shoot over his head at the basket attached to our garage. Our next-door neighbor, aged five, wandered over into our yard with a playmate. "He's blind," our neighbor whispered to her friend in a voice that could be heard distinctly by Dad and me. Dad shot and missed; I did the same. Dad hit the rim: I missed entirely: Dad shot and missed the garage entirely. "Which one is blind?" whispered back the little friend.

CONCLUSION

Prediction about future

I would hope that in the near future when a plant manager is touring the factory with the foreman and comes upon a handicapped and nonhandicapped person working together, his comment after watching them work will be, "Which one is disabled?"

EXERCISE 2 **Analyzing a Cause-and-Effect Essay**

After you have finished reading Harold Krents's essay, meet with two or three classmates to discuss these questions.

1. How well do you think Krents explained the effects of being blind? What examples or anecdotes did you find particularly convincing?
2. Krents says that the effects of blindness might be different in the future. What cause does he give for this change?
3. In your own words, explain the main idea of the essay.
4. Does Krents use chronological order or order of importance to present the effects in his essay? Why do you think he chooses the order he does?
5. Most of Krents's evidence consists of examples and anecdotes drawn from his own experience. Do you think this type of evidence is sufficient to support Krents's explanation? Explain your answer.

A Framework for a Cause-and-Effect Essay

In writing about his blindness, Krents makes use of several writers' options—extended anecdotes, witty quips, dialogue, and concise descriptions of scenes and people. The following essay, which focuses on causes, is written in a simpler, more straightforward fashion. You may wish to use this model when you write your own essay.

A WRITER'S MODEL

Why Teenagers Volunteer

INTRODUCTION
Attention grabber

Situation

Thesis statement

Typical teenagers have no interest in helping others. That is what some people believe, but it is not true. According to a Gallup survey, more than 12 million teenagers volunteer an average of 3.2 hours per week. Why do teenagers donate their time? As a teenage volunteer myself, I had some ideas, but I decided to find out what other teenage volunteers think. The three major reasons teenagers I interviewed in our school had for volunteering were to help people, to do something they enjoyed, or to learn new skills.

BODY
Cause 1

Evidence—examples

Over half (51 percent) of the volunteers enlisted simply because they wanted to help other people. The teenagers in this group became aware that certain needs or problems existed, and they realized they could make a difference. For the most part, the needs the volunteers discovered involved people--including disabled, poor, young, and elderly individuals. Sometimes, the volunteers had direct contact with the people they helped. They ran errands, helped with housework, mowed yards, and so on. Other times, the work involved community

improvement, such as removing graffiti or turning an ugly vacant lot into a neighborhood garden.

Cause 2

Another common reason (45 percent) for volunteerism was enjoyment of work. Most students began volunteering in order to help others, but they continued to volunteer because they discovered along the way that they really enjoyed what they were doing. One girl, a junior, said, "I didn't realize how bored I was until I started working with the Youth Volunteer Corps. I help out in a soup kitchen for the homeless, and the time flies. I know I would be bored again if I quit volunteering." A sophomore boy said, "I started volunteering in the first place because my parents insisted on it. Then I found I really liked it. I work in a daycare center, and the kids really like me. I'd feel terrible if I had to give it up now."

Evidence—quotes

Cause 3

Evidence—examples and quote

A third reason for volunteering, given by 33 percent of the teenagers interviewed, was a desire to learn new skills and to grow as a person. One junior boy said that he felt he needed to develop better skills in working with other people. Working as a part of a team to clean and maintain the town's beaches was one way he could gain useful experience. A senior girl volunteered to work in the gift shop of the local art museum. She wanted to help the art museum in a time of severe budget cuts, but she also wanted to learn more about the arts. She said, "I know what I'm learning at the museum will help me as I study to be a sculptor."

CONCLUSION
Restatement of thesis

As these interviews show, teenage volunteers are enthusiastic about their work. The main reason they volunteer is to help others and to help their communities, but many also volunteer because they feel a need to do interesting work or develop their

Reference to introduction

own skills and abilities. But whatever their motivation, these young men and women are destroying the myth of the self-centered teenager; they are showing the world that they care.

The essay you've just read focuses on causes only and adheres to the following simple framework for a cause-and-effect essay.

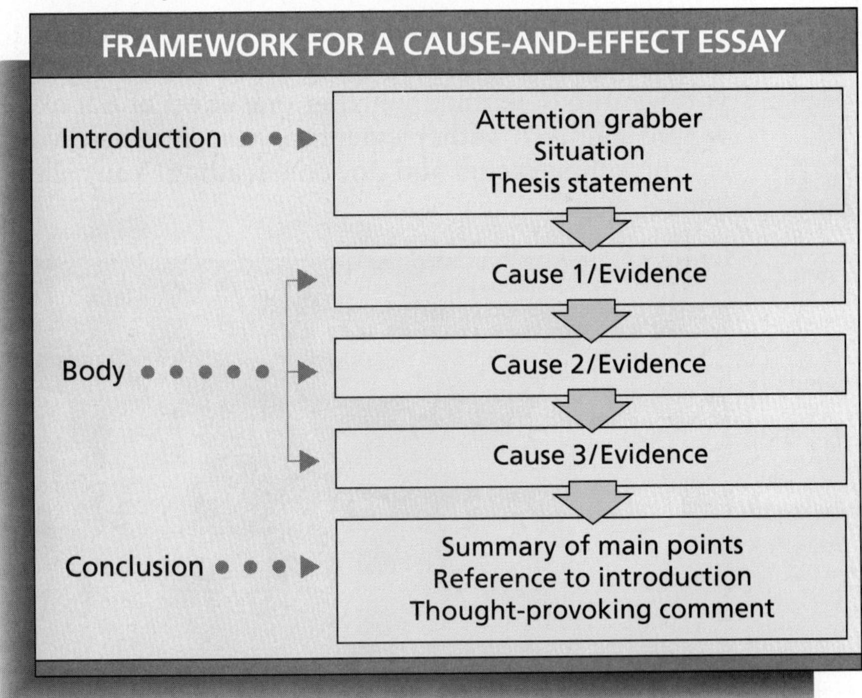

FRAMEWORK FOR A CAUSE-AND-EFFECT ESSAY
Introduction
Attention grabber
Situation
Thesis statement
Body
Cause 1/Evidence
Cause 2/Evidence
Cause 3/Evidence
Conclusion
Summary of main points
Reference to introduction
Thought-provoking comment

If your essay focuses on effects only, or on both causes and effects, you can use the same framework. Just substitute effects (or causes and effects) for causes in the body of the framework.

CRITICAL THINKING

Using Induction

When you write cause-and-effect explanations, you examine evidence and then draw conclusions about the causes or effects of a situation. This kind of reasoning is called ***induction.*** It always moves from a set of data, or evidence, to a general conclusion, or generalization. In other words, it moves from the specific to the general. Here's an example of inductive thinking.

Specific Instances:
The car is not in the driveway.
No lights are on in the house.
Several days' worth of newspapers are lying in the yard.

Generalization: No one is home.

You use induction when you examine evidence to determine whether a cause or effect exists. For example, suppose you want to determine whether one effect of not exercising is weight gain. To gather evidence, you interview your health and nutrition teacher and do some reading. You collect the following data.

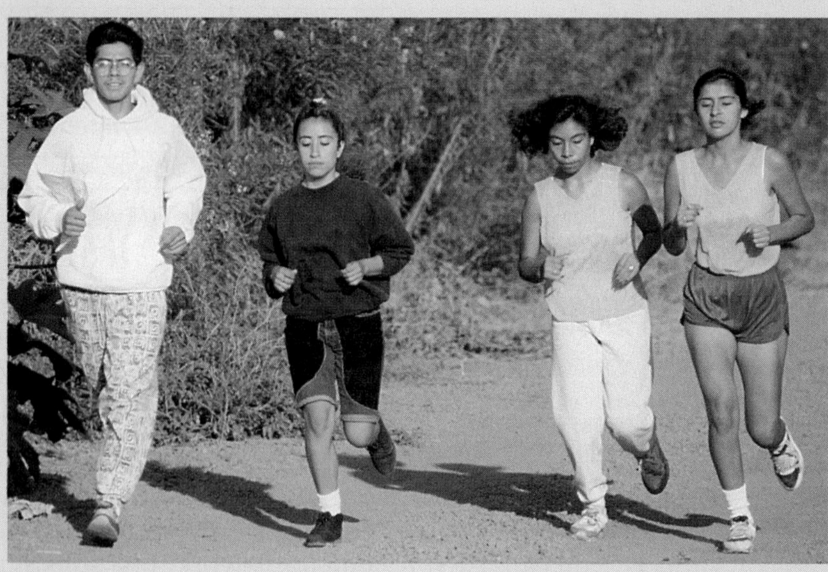

The health and nutrition teacher says that lack of exercise contributes to problems with obesity.

A nutritionist writing in the *New York Times* says that people who don't exercise are much more likely to be overweight.

A representative of the President's Council on Physical Fitness comments that exercise is the surest way to keep weight under control.

Generalization: One effect of no exercise is likely to be weight gain.

Not all generalizations are valid, however, and most readers will not accept invalid generalizations. To be valid, a generalization should meet four criteria.

1. **Enough evidence supports the generalization.** The amount of evidence that you need depends on the population you are generalizing about. If you are generalizing about students in your school, you would naturally need less evidence than if your generalization is about all teenagers in the United States.
2. **The evidence comes from trustworthy sources.** If you are generalizing about the effects on teenagers of taking two years of a foreign language, students who have completed two years of a language would be trustworthy sources. If, on the other hand, your topic is the effects of fluoridation on teeth, you would need to interview dental care experts or read secondary sources.
3. **All the evidence leads to the same generalization.** If trustworthy sources say that lack of exercise has nothing to do with weight gain, then you can't draw the conclusion that it does.
4. **The generalization is not stated in absolutes.** You can't say, for example, that lack of exercise *always* results in weight gain.

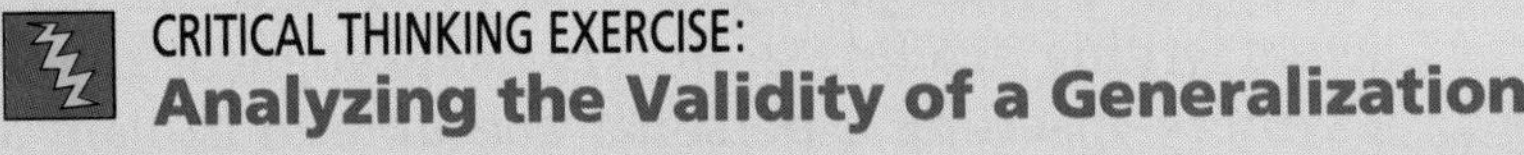

CRITICAL THINKING EXERCISE:

Analyzing the Validity of a Generalization

With a partner, read the following inductions and analyze them to decide what is necessary to make each generalization valid. What kind of research is needed? What sources might be trustworthy? When you have finished your analysis, exchange ideas with other students in your class.

1. *Topic:* "the effects of the senior prom"
   John spent $210 last year on the prom.
   I spent a lot, too.
   Generalization: Everybody spends too much money on the senior prom.

2. *Topic:* "the effects of teenagers' driving"
   Three drivers in the senior class had accidents last month.
   My car insurance costs $100 a month.
   Generalization: Teenagers have more accidents than drivers in almost any other category.

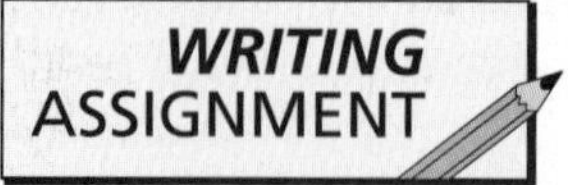

PART 4:

Writing Your First Draft

With your preparations complete, you now are ready for the actual writing of a first draft. Try using some of your options as a writer—inserting a personal anecdote to explain a cause or using a vivid example or shocking statistic to boost your audience's interest. You don't have to start your draft at the beginning—you may choose to begin with the body, then go back and add the introduction and conclusion later.

Evaluating and Revising

After finishing your draft, let it sit for a few days. Then use the chart on page 281 to identify and correct weaknesses in your draft. Answer each question in the left-hand column, and use the revision techniques in the right-hand column to correct any weaknesses.

EXERCISE 3 Analyzing a Writer's Revisions

With a partner, study the changes the writer made in the first draft of a paragraph from the model, pages 273–275. Answer the questions that follow to analyze the revisions.

Over half (51 percent) ~~Many~~ of the volunteers enlisted ~~for another reason~~ simply because they wanted to help other people. The teenagers ~~throughout the country are~~ in this group became aware that certain needs or problems exist~~ed~~, and they realize~~d~~ they ~~can~~ could make a difference. For the most part, the needs the volunteers discovered involved people--including disabled, poor, young, and elderly individuals. Sometimes, the volunteers had direct contact with the people they helped. They ran errands, helped with housework, mowed yards, and so on. Other times, the work involved community improvement, such as removing graffiti or turning an ugly vacant lot into a neighborhood garden.

replace

replace

replace

add/replace

add

1. Why did the writer change *Many* to *Over half (51 percent)*?
2. How does the replacement at the end of the first sentence make the explanation clearer?
3. What is the reason for the changes in the second sentence? [Hint: Review inductive thinking, pages 276–277.]
4. Why did the writer add additional information to the last sentence? How does this information make the explanation more acceptable to the audience?

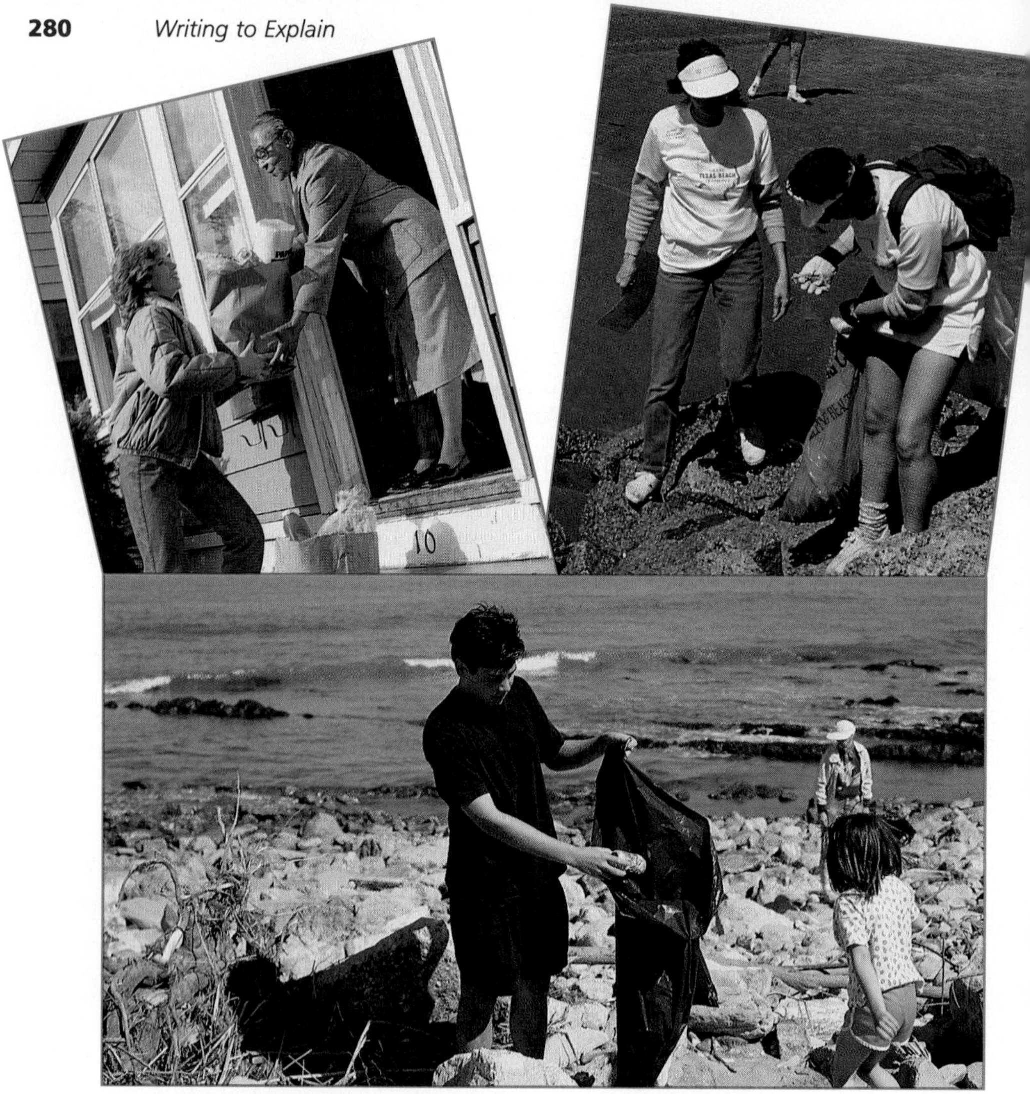

PART 5:

Evaluating and Revising Your Essay

Reread your essay and, with the help of the evaluating and revising chart on page 281, decide what changes are needed. Mark the spots that need improving. What might you add, cut, reorder, or replace? Then, exchange papers with a classmate and use the chart once more to evaluate each other's essays. Finally, revise your essay, using both your classmate's and your own observations to improve it. Make the changes on either your hard copy or word processor.

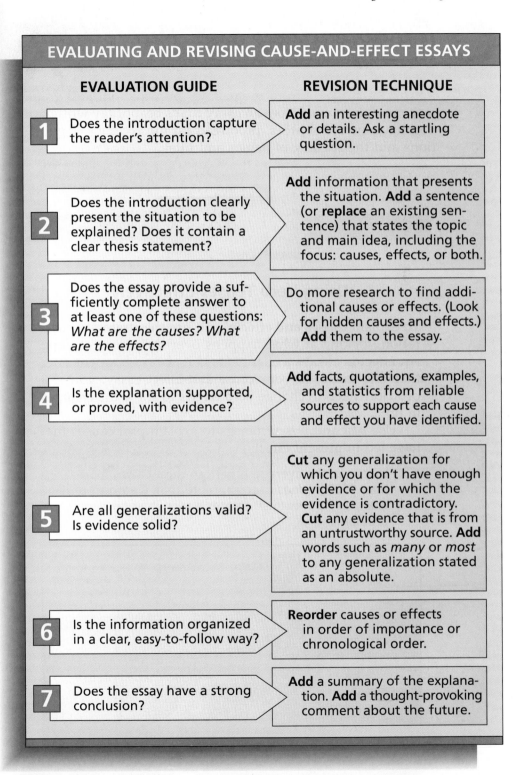

EVALUATING AND REVISING CAUSE-AND-EFFECT ESSAYS

	EVALUATION GUIDE	REVISION TECHNIQUE
1	Does the introduction capture the reader's attention?	**Add** an interesting anecdote or details. Ask a startling question.
2	Does the introduction clearly present the situation to be explained? Does it contain a clear thesis statement?	**Add** information that presents the situation. **Add** a sentence (or **replace** an existing sentence) that states the topic and main idea, including the focus: causes, effects, or both.
3	Does the essay provide a sufficiently complete answer to at least one of these questions: *What are the causes? What are the effects?*	Do more research to find additional causes or effects. (Look for hidden causes and effects.) **Add** them to the essay.
4	Is the explanation supported, or proved, with evidence?	**Add** facts, quotations, examples, and statistics from reliable sources to support each cause and effect you have identified.
5	Are all generalizations valid? Is evidence solid?	**Cut** any generalization for which you don't have enough evidence or for which the evidence is contradictory. **Cut** any evidence that is from an untrustworthy source. **Add** words such as *many* or *most* to any generalization stated as an absolute.
6	Is the information organized in a clear, easy-to-follow way?	**Reorder** causes or effects in order of importance or chronological order.
7	Does the essay have a strong conclusion?	**Add** a summary of the explanation. **Add** a thought-provoking comment about the future.

Proofreading and Publishing

Proofreading. Errors in spelling, punctuation, and grammar can detract even from an essay that's beautifully written. If you have quoted sources, proofread for the accuracy of quotations and the spelling of names and titles.

GRAMMAR HINT

Using Verb Tenses Effectively

To explain causes and effects, you use the strategy of narration, looking at what happens over the course of time. An effect is always a change, and it always happens later than the cause. In your cause-and-effect essay, you will probably need to change verb tenses to show the changes in time.

Use *past* and *present* tenses to explain past causes that have led to present effects.

> Last year, the average American **threw** away more than 1500 pounds of trash. More than 8 percent of it **was** plastic. This trash **creates** a monumental disposal problem.

Use *present, present progressive,* and *future* tenses to explain present causes that may lead to future effects.

> Garbage **is piling** up around us. Each American **throws** out between four and five pounds of trash each day. This **includes** everything from empty bottles to old refrigerators. At this rate, our landfills **will be** full within a few years.

 REFERENCE NOTE: For more information about verb tenses, see pages 788–799.

Publishing. When you write an essay for English class, your teacher and classmates probably read your essay. However, to really feel like a writer, you need to go beyond that immediate audience. Here are some suggestions for sharing your writing with a wider audience.

- Share your essay with an expert on the topic you have explained. That person might be willing to discuss how your explanation fits in with his or her knowledge of the situation.
- Present your explanation orally. Convert your written essay to a speech and present it to your class, an assembly or club in your school, or a community group that would be interested in your topic.

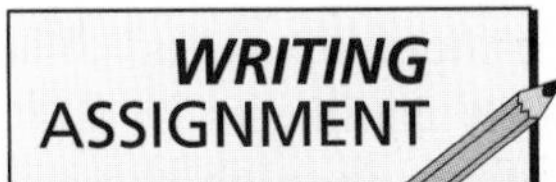

PART 6:
Proofreading and Publishing Your Essay

Proofread your essay carefully and correct any errors you find. Then make a final clean copy and share what you have written with at least one other person. Use the suggestions you've just read or an idea of your own for finding a wider audience.

WRITING WORKSHOP

A Process Explanation

While a cause-and-effect essay uses the strategy of narration to explain *why*, a *process explanation*, or *analysis*, uses the strategy of narration to explain *how* or *how to*. Instructions of any sort are examples of one type of process explanation. They explain how to *do* something: how to cook a great meal, how to make yourself glamorous, how to get into the college of your choice. A second type of process explanation explains how a process *works:* how your body digests food, how a car speedometer clocks speed, how snakes shed their skins.

As the name implies, a ***process analysis*** breaks down a process into steps or stages and then explains each one in the order the steps occur (or should occur). The following excerpt is a good example of writing that explains how something works. It is part of an article on heat disorders, and it tells how the human body regulates its temperature.

> The body temperature of warm-blooded animals is regulated by a tiny control center in the brain called the hypothalamus. When a person's blood rises above 98.6 degrees Fahrenheit, the hypothalamus sends chemical messages that prompt the heart to pump more blood and dilate the blood vessels, especially the tiny capillaries in the upper layers of the skin. More blood flows through these surface vessels so that excess heat will drain off into the cooler atmosphere by heat conduction. At the same time water diffuses through the pores of the skin (called insensible perspiration because the water evaporates before you see it and the skin remains dry).
>
> If this is not adequate to cool the blood, the hypothalamus signals the sweat glands to pour out larger amounts of water and heat in what is called sensible perspiration, or sweating. When perspiration evaporates, heat energy is

needed to change the liquid to vapor. This heat comes from your skin; that is why sweating helps to cool your body.

Jane E. Brody, *Jane Brody's "The New York Times" Guide to Personal Health*

1. What changes (or stages) does the writer describe, and when do they occur?
2. How does the writer make the sequence clear?
3. What supporting details does the writer include, and how do these help the reader understand the process?

Writing a Process Explanation

Prewriting. What process can you explain? Have you learned about a process in social studies or science class—how a prime minister is elected in England? how mitosis occurs in cells? how whales sing? Perhaps you have learned a complex process while working at your part-time job or participating in a sport or hobby—how a retail franchise works, how a sail catches the wind and powers a sailboat. Choose a process you know something about and, to avoid boring yourself and your readers, one that you think is interesting.

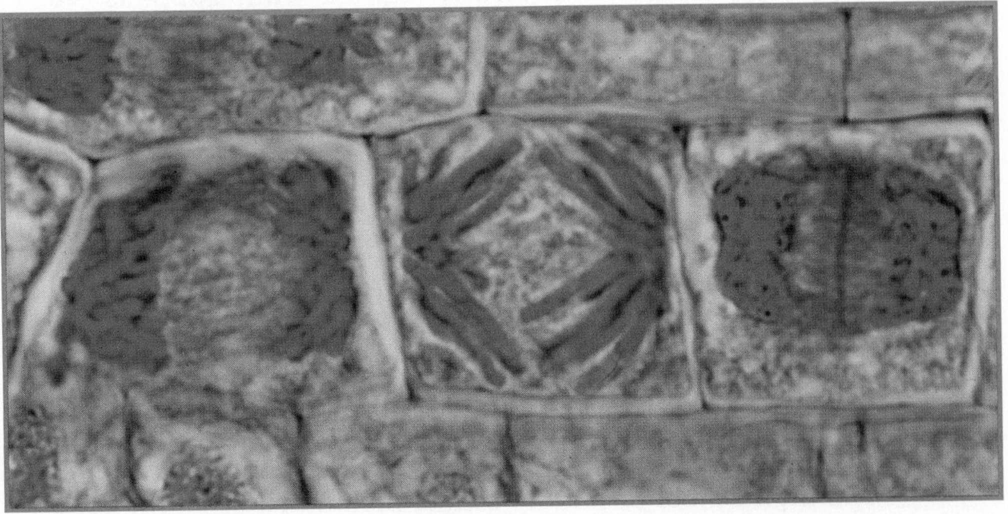

Begin to analyze the process involved, breaking it down into separate stages or steps and putting them in the order in which they occur. If you aren't positive about all the stages and their sequence, do some research. Talk to an expert or find a book or article on your topic. At some point in your planning, think about the terms you will need to define as well as any visual diagram or chart that would be helpful to your readers.

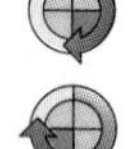

Writing, Evaluating, and Revising. Write a first draft that opens with an attention-grabbing statement or detail. Include in your introduction any important background information, such as definitions of unfamiliar terms. Then explain the steps or stages of the process in order, providing supporting details that clearly explain what happens. To make the order of the process clear, use transitional words such as *first, second, next, then,* and *finally*.

After writing, ask one or two classmates to read your first draft and give you feedback. Can they follow what occurs during the process? Are there any parts where they became lost or confused? Use your classmates' responses to help you revise your essay.

Proofreading and Publishing. Proofread the spelling, grammar, and punctuation in your revised draft. (See the guidelines for proofreading on page 49.) To share your essay, you might work with your classmates to create a "process encyclopedia," a booklet including all of your process analyses, with appropriate diagrams and illustrations. The high school or middle school media center might keep your booklet as reference material for younger students.

MAKING CONNECTIONS

USING CAUSE AND EFFECT IN PERSUASION

Your main assignment in this chapter was to write an explanation of causes and effects; it was an attempt to explain and prove objectively, rather than an attempt to persuade—to change the attitudes or behavior of your audience. However, an explanation of causes and effects is often a significant part of a persuasive argument. Many persuasive editorials and letters to the editor, for example, base their arguments on causes that need to be remedied or on the potential effects of some policy or situation. Following is part of a persuasive letter that Abigail Van Buren ("Dear Abby") wrote to her readers on the occasion of the 1991 Great American Smokeout. The cause she identifies is smoking; what effects does she identify?

> DEAR READERS: Tomorrow, Nov. 21, 1991, will mark the 15th Annual Great American Smokeout, a one-day campaign to encourage smokers to quit smoking for 24 hours, just to prove they can do it.
>
> Last year, 19 million smokers tried to quit for the day. This represents 38 percent of the nation's 50 million smokers. Breast cancer used to be the biggest killer for women. But the No. 1 cause of cancer death among women and men today is lung cancer. Tobacco claims one life every 13 seconds. An estimated 143,000 will die of lung cancer in 1991.
>
> And now, a word about smoking-related diseases—emphysema, chronic bronchitis and heart disease: This year an estimated 434,000 will die from one of these. This total exceeds the number of U.S. battle deaths in World War II—nine times as many people who die in automobile accidents every year.
>
> A congressional study has reported that health costs from the adverse effects of smoking have reached a new

> high of $100 billion a year in increased medical bills and lost productivity. The loss in death and disability cannot be measured. . . .
>
> LOVE, ABBY

How often do writers and speakers identify causes and effects in order to persuade? Get together with a partner and conduct a survey. Find five persuasive pieces—speeches, letters to the editor, editorials, or ads. Read each example and answer the following questions:

- How many of the examples refer to causes and effects in order to support an opinion or position?
- Do the references to causes and effects strengthen the argument? Why or why not?
- Of the five examples you studied, which is the most persuasive? The least persuasive? Why?

EXPLANATIONS ACROSS THE CURRICULUM

Cause and Effect in Science

What are the effects of acid rain? What caused the dinosaurs to die out? What causes cancer? How will advanced robotics and computers affect our lives? What would be the effects of a large-scale nuclear war?

Much of scientific research is concerned with an investigation of causes or effects, and many scientific reports explain the results of those investigations. For example, Carl Sagan and a number of other scientists attempted to identify possible effects of a large-scale nuclear war. As you read the following excerpt from an article reporting the results of that research, notice the effects Sagan identifies.

> The results of our calculations astonished us. In the baseline case, the amount of sunlight at the ground was reduced to a few percent of normal—much darker, in daylight, than in a heavy overcast and too dark for plants to

make a living from photosynthesis. At least in the Northern Hemisphere, where the great preponderance of strategic targets lies, an unbroken and deadly gloom would persist for weeks.

Even more unexpected were the temperatures calculated. In the baseline case, land temperatures, except for narrow strips of coastline, dropped to minus 25° Celsius (minus 13° Fahrenheit) and stayed below freezing for months—even for a summer war.

Carl Sagan, from "Nuclear War and Climatic Catastrophe: A Nuclear Winter"

Whether or not you go into one of the scientific professions, scientific research will be important in your life. Research will, or may, find cures for life-threatening diseases, discover how to protect the environment for your children, identify ways to feed the fast-growing population of our world. What scientific issues are important to you, and what have scientists already learned about their causes and effects?

Get together with two classmates and select one scientific issue or phenomenon you all find interesting and think is important. Using library and community resources (see pages 440–441), research the topic to determine what experts say are the causes and/or effects of this issue or phenomenon. Then, prepare a three-part report: Part 1, explanation of the phenomenon or issue; Part 2, the causes and/or effects that have been identified by experts; and Part 3, a summary and projection of future actions to be taken. Finally, share what you've learned in an oral presentation to your class or an interested community organization, with each member of your group taking responsibility for one of the three parts.

8 WRITING TO PERSUADE

Taking a Stand

We all have pet peeves, little things that bother us but are not worth getting upset about. Every now and then, though, an issue comes up that we feel we just can't let slip by. We decide we have to say something, to let others know our opinion. We have to **take a stand.**

Writing and You. Writers often take a stand. Powerful columnists pressure lawmakers to take action or to change their positions on sensitive issues. Critics build or threaten artists' careers with their reviews. People just like you argue, complain, encourage, and urge others on in letters to newspapers and magazines. On what issue are you ready to take a stand?

As You Read. In the following article, writer Stephen King tackles an issue personally important to him in more ways than one: children's exposure to horror on TV. As you read, look especially at the examples he uses to persuade readers that his opinion has merit.

Ben Shahn, *For All These Rights We've Just Begun to Fight* (1946). Lithograph in colors (poster), 28 1/4" × 38 3/4". Collection of the New Jersey State Museum, Trenton, N.J. Gift of Mr. & Mrs. Michael Lewis, FA1969.156. © 1993 Estate of Ben Shahn / VAGA N.Y.

from "NOW YOU TAKE 'BAMBI' OR 'SNOW WHITE'— THAT'S SCARY!"

by Stephen King

Read the story synopsis below and ask yourself if it would make the sort of film you'd want your kids watching on the Friday- or Saturday-night movie:

A good but rather weak man discovers that, because of inflation, recession and his second wife's fondness for overusing his credit cards, the family is tottering on the brink of financial ruin. In fact, they can expect to see the repossession men coming for the car, the almost new recreational vehicle and the two color TVs any day; and a pink warning-of-foreclosure notice has already arrived from the bank that holds the mortgage on their house.

The wife's solution is simple but chilling: kill the two children, make it look like an accident and collect the insurance. She browbeats her husband into going along with this homicidal scheme. A wilderness trip is arranged, and while wifey stays in camp, the father leads his two children deep into the Great Smoky wilderness. In the end, he finds he cannot kill them in cold blood; he simply leaves them to wander around until, presumably, they will die of hunger and exposure.

The two children spend a horrifying three days and two nights in the wilderness. Near the end of their endurance, they stumble upon a back-country cabin and go to it, hoping for rescue. The woman who lives alone there turns out to be a cannibal. She cages the two children and prepares to roast them in her oven as she has roasted and eaten other wanderers before them. The boy manages to get free. He creeps up behind the woman as she stokes her oven and pushes her in, where she burns to death in her own fire.

You're probably shaking your head no, even if you have already recognized the origin of this bloody little tale (and if you didn't, ask your kids: they probably will) as "Hansel and Gretel," a so called "fairy tale" that most kids are exposed to even before they start kindergarten. In addition to this story, with its grim and terrifying images of child abandonment, children lost in the woods and imprisoned by an evil woman, cannibalism and justifiable homicide, small children are routinely exposed to tales of mass murder and mutilation ("Bluebeard"), the eating of a loved one by a monster ("Little Red Riding-Hood"), treachery and deceit ("Snow White") and even the specter of a little boy who must face a black-hooded, ax-wielding headsman ("The 500 Hats of Bartholomew Cubbins," by Dr. Seuss).

"I watched, appalled, dismayed and sweaty with fear, as Snow White bit into the poisoned apple while the old crone giggled in evil ecstasy."

I'm sometimes asked what I allow my kids to watch on the tube, for two reasons: first, my three children, at 10, 8, and 4, are still young enough to be in the age group that opponents of TV violence and horror consider to be particularly impressionable and at risk; and second, my seven novels have been popularly classified as "horror stories." People tend to think those two facts contradictory. But . . . I'm not sure that they are.

Three of my books have been made into films, and at this writing, two of them have been shown on TV. In the case of "Salem's Lot," a made-for-TV movie, there was never a question of allowing my kids to watch it on its first run on CBS; it began at 9 o'clock in our time zone, and all three children go to bed earlier than that. Even on a weekend, and even for the oldest, an 11 o'clock bedtime is just not negotiable. A previous *TV GUIDE* article about children and frightening programs mentioned a 3-year-old who watched "Lot" and consequently suffered night terrors. I have no wish to question any responsible parent's judgment—all parents raise their children in different ways—but it did strike me as passingly odd that a 3-year-old should have been allowed to stay up that late to get scared.

But in my case, the hours of the telecast were not really a factor, because we have one of those neat little time-machines, a videocassette recorder. I taped the program and, after viewing it myself, decided my children could watch it if they wanted to. My daughter had no interest; she's more involved with stories of brave dogs and loyal horses these days. My two sons, Joe, 8, and Owen, then 3, did watch. Neither of them seemed to have any problems either while watching it or in the middle of the night—when those problems most likely turn up.

"Like their elders, children have a right to experience the entire spectrum of drama. . . ."

I also have a tape of "Carrie," a theatrical film first shown on TV about two and a half years ago. I elected to keep this one on what my kids call "the high shelf" (where I put the tapes that are forbidden to them), because I felt that its depiction of children turning against other children, the lead character's horrifying embarrassment at a school dance and her later act of matricide would upset them. "Lot," on the contrary, is a story that the children accepted as a fairy tale in modern dress.

Other tapes on my "high shelf" include "Night of the Living Dead" (cannibalism), "The Brood" (David Cronenberg's film of intergenerational breakdown and homicidal "children of rage" who are set free to murder and rampage), and "The Exorcist." They are all up there for the same reason: they contain elements that I think might freak the kids out.

Not that it's possible to keep kids away from everything on TV (or in the movies, for that matter) that will freak them out; the movies that terrorized my own nights most thoroughly as a kid were not those through which Frankenstein's monster or the Wolfman lurched and growled, but the Disney cartoons. I watched Bambi's mother shot and Bambi running frantically to escape being burned up in a forest fire. I watched, appalled, dismayed and sweaty with fear, as Snow White bit into the poisoned apple while the old crone giggled in evil ecstasy. I was similarly terrified by the walking brooms in "Fantasia" and the big, bad wolf who chased the fleeing pigs from house to house with such grim and homicidal intensity. More recently, Owen, who just turned 4, crawled into bed with my wife and me. "Cruella DeVille is in my room," he said. Cruella DeVille is, of course, the villainess of "101 Dalmatians," and I suppose Owen had decided that a woman who would want to turn puppies into dogskin coats might also be interested in little boys. All these films would certainly get G-ratings if they were produced today, and frightening excerpts of them have been shown on TV during "the children's hour."

Do I believe that all violent or horrifying programming should be banned from network TV? No, I do not. Do I believe it should be telecast only in the later evening hours, TV's version of the "high shelf"? Yes, I do. Do I believe that children should be forbidden all violent or horrifying programs? No, I do not. Like their elders, children have a right to experience the entire spectrum of drama, from such warm and mostly unthreatening programs as *Little House on the Prairie* and *The Waltons* to scarier fare. It's been suggested again and again that such entertainment offers us a catharsis—a chance to enter for a little while a scary and yet controllable world where we can express our fears, aggressions and possibly even hostilities. Surely no one would suggest that children do not have their own fears and hostilities to face and overcome; those dark feelings are the basis of many of the fairy tales children love best.

Do I think a child's intake of violent or horrifying programs should be limited? Yes, I do, and that's why I have a high shelf. But the pressure groups who want to see all horror (and anything smacking of sex, for that matter) arbitrarily removed from television make me both uneasy and angry. The element of Big Brotherism inherent in such an idea causes the unease; the idea of a bunch of people I don't even know presuming to dictate what is best for my children causes the anger. I feel that deciding such things myself is my right—and my responsibility.

TV Guide

Reader's Response

1. Do Stephen King's arguments convince you that only parents have the right to decide what their children are allowed to watch on TV? Why or why not? Discuss in class how you would feel, and act, as a *parent.*
2. What movie or TV show has frightened you badly or kept you from sleeping? What about it frightened you? How old were you? Did this affect the type of movies or TV shows you watched afterward?

Writer's Craft

3. Not until late in the essay does King explicitly state his opinion, or stand. What (and where) is this statement?
4. Before this, you implicitly know King's position because he's advancing support for it—reasons, especially in the form of factual examples. What are these examples? Do they have a logical or emotional impact? At the end of the excerpt, what reasons does King hammer home?
5. Where in the essay do you think King's writing—his word choice or style—is an effective part of his persuasion?
6. How well does King answer people on the other side of the issue—people who want to further restrict or ban horror on television? What arguments of theirs does he meet, and how? Are there any strong opposing arguments that he does *not* address?

Strategies for Persuasion

Like Stephen King, writers who persuade want to change people's minds and, sometimes, their actions. He chose, effectively for his issue, to write an essay in the popular magazine *TV Guide*. Persuasive writing, however, shows up in many different forums and forms: books, newspapers, speeches, advertisements, editorials, sermons, business proposals, résumé cover letters. There are many ways to develop a persuasive message. Here are some examples.

Narration: telling about a close call with death in an automobile accident to convince people of the benefit of air bags; telling about missing out on getting concert tickets to persuade others to plan ahead and buy tickets early.

Description: describing the features of a car to persuade someone to buy it; describing an artist's works to persuade your parents to go with you to a gallery.

Classification: comparing two methods of lawn care to convince the public works department that one is safer for city residents and the environment; defining the term *individualism* to convince school officials not to require school uniforms.

Evaluation: evaluating a movie to convince your friends that they should rent it for the evening; forming an opinion about lowering the voting age and writing to your representative supporting or opposing it.

In this chapter, you will write a persuasive essay in your main writing assignment. Your primary writing and thinking strategy will be evaluation. Keep in mind that persuasive essays

- state the writer's position, or opinion, about an important issue
- provide convincing support for the writer's stand
- refute significant opposing positions

Writing a Persuasive Essay

Choosing an Issue

Look around. What's going on in your life? in your community? in the world? Chances are you are surrounded by many ***issues,*** topics about which people have opposing opinions.

How do you feel about the government guaranteeing everyone a free college education? Should the manufacturing of items be banned if they can't be recycled? Should animal experimentation be abolished? There are at least two sides to each of these questions. Any one of them would make a good topic for a persuasive essay.

The issue you choose to write about, however, should also mean something to you personally. You need to get fired up, or you won't be able to fire up other people. Here are some points to keep in mind as you look for a topic that's right for you:

- Choose an issue that is important and interesting to you. It should be one you have a strong belief about, or at least a strong curiosity about.
- Make sure it's a real issue, not just your personal preference. You will have to be able to gather outside evidence to convince others. (You may think ballet surpasses all other dance forms, but you will never be able to persuade a modern dance lover that modern dance is an inferior art. It's a matter of taste.)

- Be sure your issue is arguable, that many people can and will disagree about it. (You may feel strongly that teenagers shouldn't hitchhike, but few people are real proponents of hitchhiking.)

Identifying Your Thesis

In a persuasive essay, the ***thesis*** of your paper—the main point you want to get across—is your opinion, or position, on the issue. This thesis is called a ***proposition*** or ***position statement.*** Writing your position statement in a sentence or two is an important prewriting step. It helps you stay on track as you gather information and as you draft.

POSITION STATEMENTS

Schools should abolish grades as a way of judging performance.

Passive resistance is the only acceptable way to protest.

Mohandas Gandhi (center), proponent of passive resistance

No single country should control any part of the world's oceans.

Laws should limit violence on television.

Sometimes you have not completely decided what your position is when you pick a topic. You may choose an issue because you feel that it is important and want to know more about it. Or, you may be leaning to one side of the issue without actually knowing enough about it to draw a final conclusion. Gathering information about the topic and writing the essay will help you explore your own opinion. By the time you are through, you may have strengthened your original belief or may even have changed your opinion. (For more on writing to explore, see Chapter 9, pages 344–387.)

EXERCISE 1 **Speaking and Listening: Identifying Issues in the News**

Controversial may be a word that some people dread, but journalists love it. Watch or listen to television or radio newscasts for a few days. Jot down examples of every major issue on which there are opposing sides. Is Congress debating an important new law? Is your city council talking about changing the animal leash laws? Are employees picketing a local business? Try to make a list of at least five current local, national, or international issues. Be prepared to identify each issue and to briefly describe opposing positions.

PART 1:
Choosing a Topic

What do you want to speak out about? Besides using news reports, you can find issues in the pictures or advertisements of newspapers and magazines. Also check your journal, or brainstorm with a classmate. Think about any time recently when you said, "In my opinion . . ." or "I really believe . . ." Jot down a few ideas, and choose the one you care most about. Write your position statement, and then check it closely. Be sure you state an idea or an opinion that might be disputed by at least some reasonably intelligent people—otherwise, there's no need to persuade anyone.

Developing Support

Notice the heading of this section. It's not called "Gathering Information" (although you will certainly be doing that); it is named "Developing **Support.**" In this stage of planning your persuasive essay, your job is to make your opinion as strong and appealing as possible. That calls for some very deliberate planning.

Thinking About Purpose, Audience, and Tone

Remember that the whole *purpose* for writing persuasion is to convince others that they should come around to your way of thinking. Sometimes you also want them to *do* something: You want action to follow belief. With such a clear-cut, personal impact in mind, you definitely have to think long and hard about *audience.*

Who are the readers you are trying to convince? Is there a single group, or are there several different groups—all with their own interests and opinions? Some readers may not know very much about the issue; others may be ready to fight to the finish. It is up to you to explore who these groups are, what they care about, and how they feel about the issue. You will want to know what points you can agree on and what arguments they will use to oppose you.

And—not surprisingly—when you want someone to agree with you or do something for you, the *tone* or *style* you adopt plays a significant role. In most persuasion (think of advertising, speeches, editorials, letters to the editor), an informal tone and everyday speech are expected and have been proved to be effective. Purely to convince, you use whatever tone fits your topic and will affect the audience: You can be personal, impassioned, or even comic.

In some persuasive essays, though, an informal tone isn't appropriate. A school assignment, for example, may call for a logical, reasoned argument about an issue. In that type of paper, you will need to use a formal, serious tone.

Using Logical Appeals

Logical appeals are appeals to reason, to clear thinking; and they are important in any persuasive essay. An ad, for example, may disregard logic entirely (many do!), but an essay can't. Readers expect you to have good ***reasons*** for your opinion; they expect to learn *why* you believe as you do.

Position Statement: Penalties for oil spills should be more severe.

Reasons: Oil spills may permanently damage the environment.

Oil companies will improve safety measures if their profits are threatened.

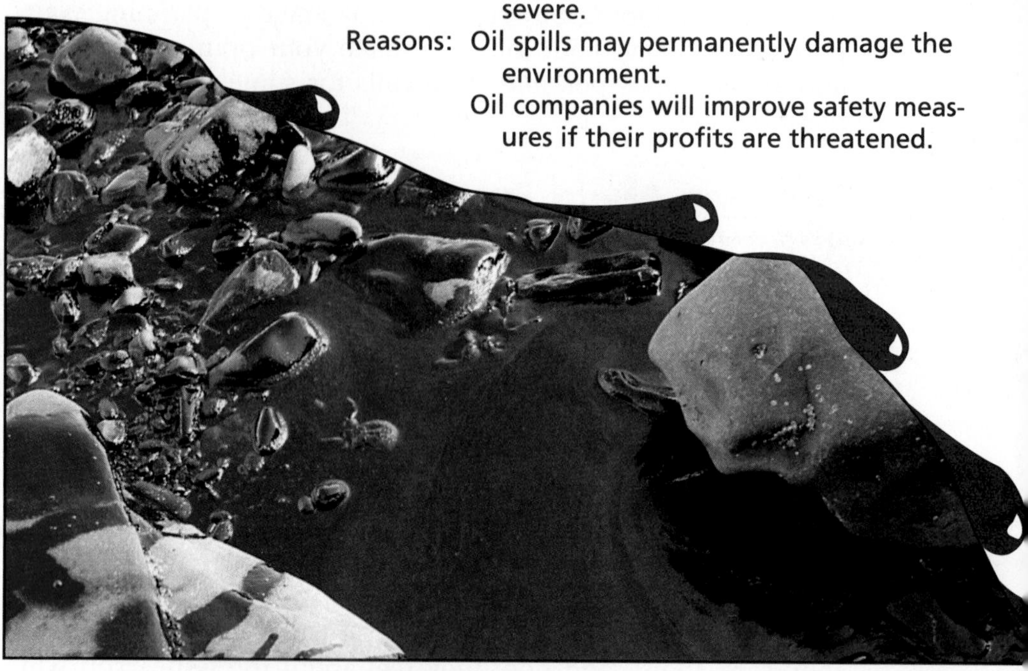

But most people want more than reasons: They want ***evidence,*** or proof, to back up the reasons. Here are two basic forms of evidence:

- ***Facts:*** statements that can be proved by testing, personal experience, or verification from reliable sources. Statistics, examples, and ***anecdotes*** (brief stories, often based on personal experiences) may be used as factual evidence.

  It is estimated that for every million metric tons of oil transported annually, about one metric ton is lost to spillage.

  A study of spill effects in the Caribbean found that coral organisms were severely hurt and coastal environments such as mangrove thickets were wiped out, along with the creatures that inhabited them.

Some companies that have paid large fines—especially in highly publicized cases—have released public statements of new procedures they will follow to prevent oil spills.

- ***Expert Testimony:*** statements by people who are recognized authorities on the issue.

In her book *Silent Spring,* Rachel Carson, marine biologist and environmentalist, wrote, "The most alarming of all man's assaults upon the environment is the contamination of air, earth, rivers, and sea with dangerous and even lethal materials. This pollution is for the most part irrecoverable; the chain of evil it initiates not only in the world that must support life but in living tissues is for the most part irreversible."

When you are gathering evidence from outside sources, make sure the source is reliable and not unfairly biased. Because your topic is inherently controversial, you should check facts and expert opinion in more than one source. If your sources aren't sound, your logical appeals can fail.

Using Emotional Appeals

People tend to make decisions with their hearts as well as their minds. Knowing what your audience cares about gives you a chance to appeal to their emotions. For example, there is a good reason why advertisers so often use children in their commercials. What better way to sell long-distance telephone service than by showing a lonely grandparent receiving a call from an adorable grandchild?

You usually don't have to look far for an idea for an ***emotional appeal.*** In fact, because some examples and details appeal to the emotions as well as to logic, you will probably discover some emotional appeals when you are looking for logical appeals. For example, the following details about the Alaskan oil spill are factual, but they also arouse strong feelings.

Following the Alaskan oil spill, the beaches were littered with thousands of otters and birds, slowly freezing to death after their protective fur and feathers were drenched with the black, foul-smelling oil.

This example shows you another potent emotional tool in persuasion: *language*. Words can have great power, especially those with ***connotative meanings:*** the feelings or attitudes that a word suggests. If you are calling for stronger penalties against those responsible for oil spills, you will want to gather statistics about environmental effects, but you will bring those statistics to frightening life when you describe feathers "drenched" (not just "covered") with "black, foul-smelling oil" (not just "oil") or otters "slowly freezing to death" (not just "dying"). Suddenly, the incident is real. People care.

Powerfully charged words such as these must be used carefully, however. Use them only to emphasize important points. It is okay to shock, but you don't want to overdo it. Your purpose is to appeal to your audience's emotions, but you want to be seen as credible, not extreme.

Using Ethical Appeals

Establishing your own credibility and character is also a specific type of appeal: the ***ethical appeal.*** If you are to convince people of anything, people must believe in you, the writer. They must believe that you can be trusted; that you are fair, that you know what you are talking about; that you are sensitive, responsible, and sincere. Rather than hoping readers will assume these qualities, the careful persuader exhibits them.

For example, you help establish your sense of fairness by considering different sides of an issue. Let's say your essay calls for drastic cuts in the benefits members of Congress receive. Although some people might agree that legislators, as public servants, should work for minimum wage without special benefits, many business people and political insiders would consider this argument foolish. You may gain credibility with these audiences by writing:

> As we begin to bring Congressional expenditures into line, we must be careful not to go overboard. Members of Congress must be able to support their families, must be able to maintain homes in Washington as well as in their home states. But they cannot be allowed to become independently wealthy at taxpayers' expense.

In this way, you exhibit common sense and show that you are not calling for irresponsible or radical action.

A different ethical appeal might show your readers your respect for them, as actor and director Woody Allen does in arguing against the colorization of black and white movies.

> I believe the people who are coloring movies have contempt for the audience by claiming, in effect, that viewers are too stupid and too insensitive to appreciate black and white photography—that they must be given, like infants or monkeys, bright colors to keep them amused.

By making it clear that he does not share this opinion, Allen both counters the opposition and shows his own sensitivity.

A persuasive essay differs from ***formal argument,*** a line of reasoning that attempts to explain or prove by logic. Research reports, business proposals, and some school essays require formal argument. They are strictly logical, thorough, and fair, looking at all available evidence, whether favorable or unfavorable. Most examples of persuasion in books, newspapers, and public speaking, however, aren't formal arguments. Their purpose is to persuade, not to prove by logic. In a persuasive essay you can select the most favorable evidence, appeal to emotions, and use style to sway your readers. Your single purpose is to be convincing.

EXERCISE 2 Identifying Logical, Emotional, and Ethical Appeals

Work with others as a team to analyze the appeals in different examples of persuasion. Collect a good sampling—advertisements, editorials, and letters—and pinpoint logical, emotional, and ethical appeals. (Don't forget to consider music and/or visuals in ads.) Prepare a group report by considering these questions for each example: Who is the probable audience? Which appeal(s) predominates? (Give examples.) Why do you think each appeal was chosen? How well do you think it works? Why?

Hi and Lois reprinted with special permission of King

I NEED SOMETHING CRISPY AND CRUNCHY AND BURSTING WITH FLAVOR

HAVE A CARROT STICK

3-12

CHANCE BROWNE

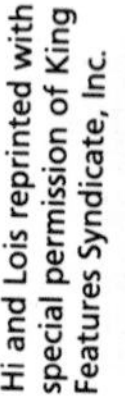

Hi and Lois reprinted with special permission of King Features Syndicate, Inc.

EXERCISE 3 Choosing Effective Appeals

The most effective appeals are the ones most persuasive to a particular audience. Study the four position statements that follow and the audience for each. In an essay, what particular support might convince these readers? Would you emphasize a certain type of appeal? For each position statement, develop at least one logical appeal (reason and evidence), emotional appeal (details/language), and ethical appeal (testimony to the writer's good character).

1. **Position Statement:** State lotteries conducted for any purpose should be abolished.
   Audience: state legislators

2. **Position Statement:** Every school day should begin with students singing the national anthem.
   Audience: PTA members

3. **Position Statement:** The city should not build a new municipal building.
   Audience: city council

4. **Position Statement:** Fasting is a dangerous way to try to lose weight.
   Audience: students your own age

Identifying Opposing Positions

When you chose your issue, you knew others would disagree with you. And you have to be ready for that opposition. Before writing, you should anticipate strong opposing arguments and plan your response, called a ***refutation.*** Your audience analysis and research are two good sources of opposing reasons.

Although you are not required to cover all opposing positions in a persuasive essay, refutation is usually an important strategy. Addressing the strongest opposing views strengthens your own argument and helps you select the most convincing support possible. You may even find an opposing position that you believe has merit. Admitting this in your essay is called ***conceding a point.*** It won't hurt you. Sometimes, it even helps, because it shows your fairness and openness. (Remember that establishing your credibility with your readers is an important part of persuasive writing.) In effect, your concession is an ethical appeal.

One way to pull together your support for a position statement is to make a chart like the one shown on the following page. Notice that the writer has included a position statement and that the audience is clearly identified. Next, the reasons and supporting evidence for the writer's position are listed. Finally, the writer has anticipated the most significant opposition positions and has collected a number of arguments to counteract these opposing ideas.

Position statement: The United States should require mandatory national service of young people after high school graduation.

Audience: general public

Logical, Emotional, and Ethical Appeals:

Reasons	*Evidence*
• *Public wants youth to help provide vital services.*	*Polls: majority want mandatory service* *Bills proposed for "national service"* *Nunn-McCurdy bill linking college aid to service*
• *All teenagers will receive benefits.*	*College-bound: more career choices; maturity; broader life perspective (emotional appeal)* *Work force: learn skills to get jobs; incentive to study*
• *Young people will become better citizens.*	*Serving others wherever assigned, they will see beyond narrow concerns, gain responsibility (emotional appeal)* *Joseph Duffey to World Future Society: summary of advantages*

Opposing Positions	*Refutations*
• *U.S. can't afford it.*	*Military—billions to recruit, reenlist* *Cold War and arms race money could be redirected; good for economy* *Teen unemployment statistics; chronic unemployment, crime more costly (emotional appeal)*
• *Young people are too self-centered; they will fight or avoid service.*	*Not "me generation": environmental and social concerns, Persian Gulf Conflict support (emotional appeal)*
• *Difficult to make workable.*	*Conceded, but concerned citizens can and must do it (ethical appeal)*

The types of appeals can overlap. A factual example may be emotionally persuasive. Evidence can show your reasonableness, or ethical stance. In fact, emotional appeals are possible *whenever* you use language, and ethical appeals are most often coupled with other support. In an essay the three types of appeals aren't always strictly separated.

Organizing Support

In a persuasive essay an effective, easy-to-follow plan of organization is to present your logical, emotional, and ethical appeals first, followed by opposing positions and refutations.

- **Order of Importance.** You can present your appeals by ***order of importance,*** beginning or ending with your strongest appeal—strongest in the eyes of *your audience.*
- **Chronological Order.** Sometimes, a ***cause-and-effect chain,*** or ***chronological order,*** works best—for example, to propose or attack a course of action.
- **Logical Order.** ***Comparison and contrast*** is often used to present opposing positions and refutations. You may present all objections first, then your refutations. Or, you may present and refute the positions one by one.

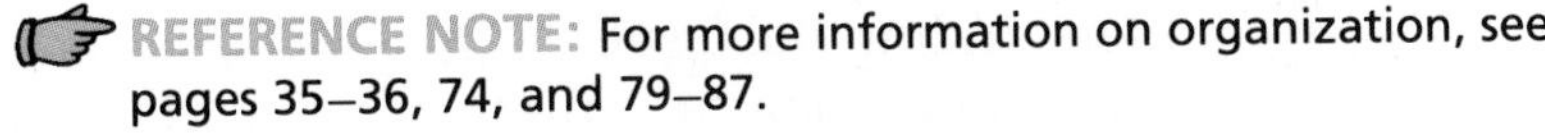
REFERENCE NOTE: For more information on organization, see pages 35–36, 74, and 79–87.

In planning and organizing your support

- identify logical appeals to support your position statement
- identify emotional and ethical appeals appropriate for your topic and audience
- identify significant opposing positions and plan your refutations
- select an order for your support that will be clear and convincing

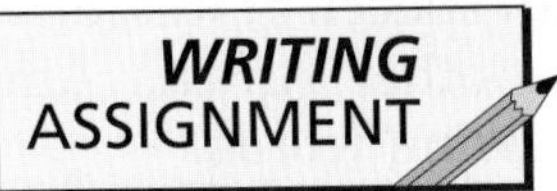

PART 2:
Identifying and Organizing Support

Brainstorming, clustering, and freewriting are all good ways to start building support for your opinion. Next, explore available resources. Keeping your audience in mind, remember to look for opposing arguments. Use your notes to make a chart like the one on page 308. Then, review: Do you have enough information? Are your appeals on target for the audience? Are your refutations realistic? Finally, decide how you will organize your support. What order will have the greatest impact?

Writing Your First Draft

The Basic Elements of Persuasion

In many ways, you make your own rules when you plan your persuasive essay. You can be in favor of something or against it. You can choose your evidence and kinds of appeals. You can refute a long list of opposing positions, just one or two, or none at all. It's up to you.

Yet you are working with basic elements that are easily incorporated into composition form (pages 99–121), with a clear introduction, body, and conclusion.

- **Introduction:** You begin by presenting your opinion, or position, and providing any background necessary for understanding the issue.
- **Body:** You use logical, emotional, and ethical appeals to develop your support; and you present opposing positions with your refutations.
- **Conclusion:** You end your essay by reemphasizing your position, perhaps summing up your most important ideas, repeating your strongest argument, or giving a ***call to action***—something your audience should do.

Persuasion and Style

Language is a powerful tool for changing people's minds and influencing their actions. In the 1960s, Cesar Chavez brought hope to migrant workers with these words: "We . . . stood tall outside the vineyards where we had stooped for years." And Paul Robeson, in his valedictorian speech at Rutgers University in 1919, attempted to persuade other African Americans to fight for the future with the following words.

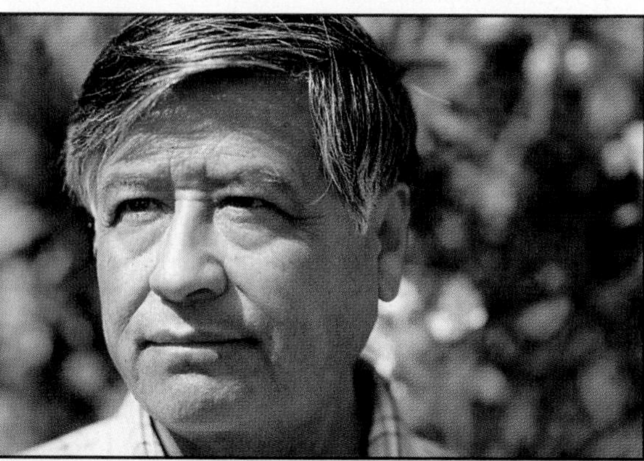

Cesar Chavez

On ourselves alone will depend the preservation of our liberties and the transmission of them in their integrity to those who will come after us. And we are struggling on, attempting to show that knowledge can be obtained under difficulties; that poverty may give place to affluence; that obscurity is not an absolute bar to distinction and that a way is open to welfare and happiness to all who will follow the way with resolution and wisdom; that neither the old-time slavery, nor continued prejudice need extinguish self-respect, crush manly ambition, or paralyze effort; that no power outside of himself can prevent man from sustaining an honorable character and a useful relation to his day and generation. We know that neither institutions nor friends can make a race stand unless it has strength in its own foundation; that races like individuals must stand or fall by their own merit; that to fully succeed they must practice the virtues of self-reliance, self-respect, industry, perseverance, and economy.

Paul Robeson

It is not just Robeson's ideas that are stirring; it is also his ***style*** that makes his ideas persuasive. When used well, style can be a powerful component in persuasion. In other words, it's not just what you say, but how you say it. Following are three stylistic techniques that are effective in persuasion.

Repetition. Paul Robeson begins each of a series of clauses with *that*. The repetition creates a dramatic expectation, focuses attention on his ideas, and unites those ideas to make one major point: that no obstacles, no matter how great, can destroy the integrity of anyone determined to overcome them.

Rhythm. Read the excerpt again, concentrating on its sound. The rhythm—the beat, or music—is rolling, stately, and formal. Robeson's audience was an academic one at a very formal occasion. At a different occasion with a different audience, his rhythm might have been faster and more informal, with drum bursts of words building in energy. You can create the rhythm you want through words' sounds and stressed syllables, their arrangement in phrases, the length of your sentences, and repetition.

Language. You won't convince readers if you lose them or put them off—both of which can happen if you use inappropriate language. Robeson's speech is an example of persuasion using formal language; his audience expected this relatively formal word choice and style. However, when the audience doesn't have this set of expectations, informal language can have a positive appeal. Readers or listeners feel you are speaking directly to them in language they understand. That's one of the ways advertising reaches out to an audience. In persuasive writing, it is important to recognize what kind of language will make your audience feel comfortable and responsive to your ideas; in other words, talk their language!

WRITING NOTE

Sentence fragments used inadvertently or carelessly can interfere with communication; but—in the hands of a skilled writer—fragmented sentences can create an energetic rhythm and emphasize important points. They can be an effective stylistic device. However, before using fragments deliberately in school papers, be sure your teacher feels you are ready to experiment with sentence style.

The following essay, written by filmmaker Woody Allen, shows its directness—a decided jolt—in the title. As you read, pay attention to the essay's content, tone, and style. What do you expect the tone to be? Is your expectation accurate?

A PERSUASIVE ESSAY

The Colorization of Films Insults Artists and Society

by Woody Allen

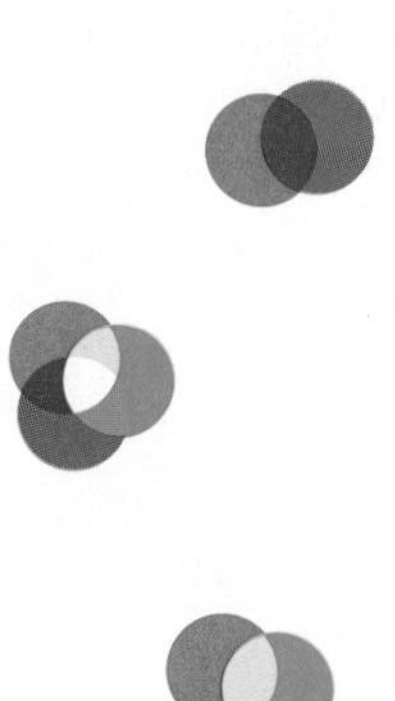

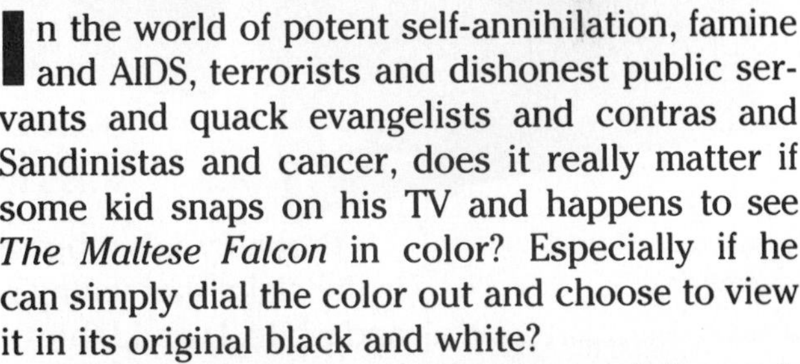

INTRODUCTION
Attention grabber

In the world of potent self-annihilation, famine and AIDS, terrorists and dishonest public servants and quack evangelists and contras and Sandinistas and cancer, does it really matter if some kid snaps on his TV and happens to see *The Maltese Falcon* in color? Especially if he can simply dial the color out and choose to view it in its original black and white?

BODY

Background information

I think it does make a difference and the ramifications of what's called colorization are not wonderful to contemplate. Simply put, the owners of thousands of classic American black and white films believe that there would be a larger public for the movies, and consequently more money, if they were reissued in color. Since they have computers that can change such masterpieces as *Citizen Kane* and *City Lights* and *It's A*

Ethical appeal

Wonderful Life into color, it has become a serious problem for anyone who cares about these movies and has feelings about our image of ourselves as a culture.

Conceding a point

Emotional appeal

I won't comment about the quality of the color. It's not good, but probably it will get better. Right now it's like elevator music. It has no soul. All faces are rendered with the same deadening pleasance. The choices of what colors people should be wearing or what colors rooms should be (all crucial artistic decisions in making a film) are left to caprices and speculations by computer technicians who are not qualified to make those choices.

Charlie Chaplin (left) in *City Lights;* Jimmy Stewart and Donna Reed (above) in *It's a Wonderful Life*

Opposing position/ Refutation

Probably false, but not worth debating here, is the claim that young people won't watch black and white. I would think they would, judging from the amount of stylish music videos and MTV ads that are done in black and white, undoubtedly after market research. The fact that audiences of all ages have been watching Charlie Chaplin, Humphrey Bogart, Jimmy Stewart, Fred Astaire—in fact, all the stars and films of the so-called Golden Age of Hollywood—in black and white for decades with no diminution of joy also makes me wonder about these high claims for color.

Ginger Rogers and Fred Astaire (below) in *Swing Time*; Katharine Hepburn and Humphrey Bogart (right) in *The African Queen*

Opposing position/ Refutation

Another point the coloroids make is that one can always view the original if one prefers. The truth is, however, that in practical terms, what will happen is that the color versions will be aired while token copies of the original black and white will lie around preserved in a vault, unpromoted and unseen.

Emotional appeal

Another aspect of the problem that one should mention (although it is not the crucial ground on which I will make my stand) is that American films are a landmark heritage that do our nation proud all over the world, and should be seen as they were intended to be. One would wince at defacing great buildings or paintings, and, in the case of movies, what began as a popular entertainment has, like jazz music, developed into a serious art form. Now, someone might ask: "Is an old Abbott and Costello movie art? Should it be viewed in the same way as *Citizen Kane*?" The answer is that it should be protected, because all movies are entitled to their personal

Logical appeal

Emotional appeal

Opposing position/ Refutation

integrity and, after all, who knows what future generations will regard as art works of our epoch?

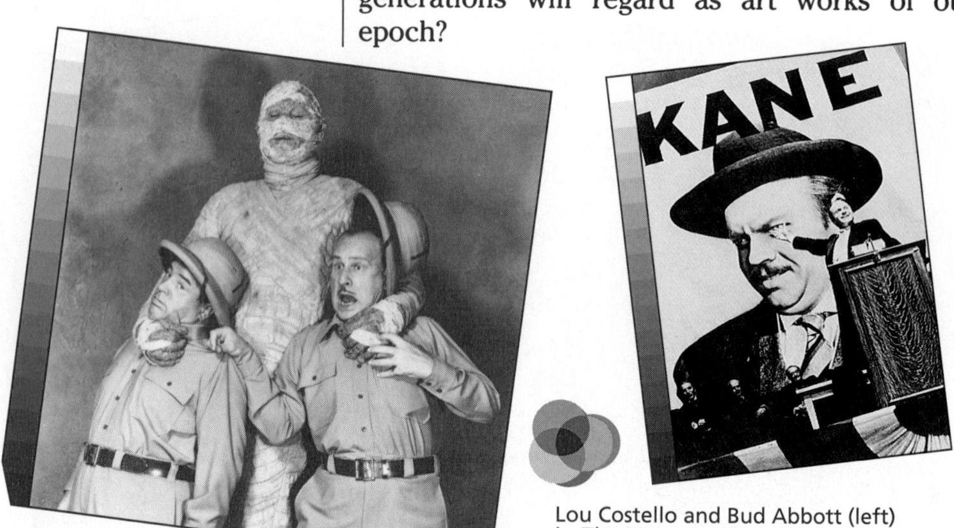

Lou Costello and Bud Abbott (left) in *The Mummy*; Orson Welles (above) in *Citizen Kane*

Opposing position/ Refutation

Yet another question: "Why were directors not up in arms about cutting films for television or breaking them up for commercials, insulting them with any number of technical alterations to accommodate the television format?" The answer is that directors always hated these assaults on their work but were powerless to stop them. As in life, one lives with the first few wounds, because to do battle is an overwhelmingly time-consuming and pessimistic prospect.

Logical appeal

Emotional appeal

Still, when the assaults come too often, there is a revolution. The outrage of seeing one's work transformed into color is so dramatically appalling, so "obvious"—as against stopping sporadically for commercials—that this time all the directors, writers and actors chose to fight.

Logical and emotional appeals

But let me get to the real heart of the matter and to why I think the issue is not merely one that affronts the parties directly involved but has a larger meaning. What's at stake is a moral issue and how our culture chooses to define itself. No one should be able to alter an artist's work in any way whatsoever, for any reason, without the artist's consent. It's really as simple as that.

Logical appeal

Position statement

Logical appeal

John Huston has made it clear that he doesn't want *The Maltese Falcon* seen in color. This is his right as an artist and certainly must be his choice alone. Nor would I want to see my film *Manhattan* in color. Not if it would bring in 10 times the revenue. Not if all the audiences in the world begged or demanded to see it that way.

Ethical appeal

I believe the people who are coloring movies have contempt for the audience by claiming, in effect, that viewers are too stupid and too insensitive to appreciate black and white photography—that they must be given, like infants or monkeys, bright colors to keep them amused. They have contempt for the artist, caring little for the moral right these directors have over their own creations. And, finally, they have contempt for society because they help define it as one that chooses to milk every last dollar out of its artists' work, even if it means mutilating the work and humiliating the culture's creative talent.

Emotional appeal

Humphrey Bogart (left) in *The Maltese Falcon*; Woody Allen and Mariel Hemingway (below) in *Manhattan*

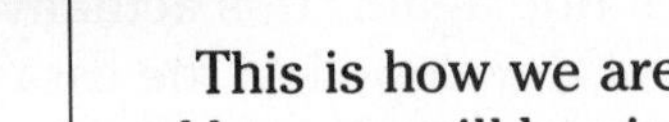

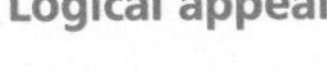

Logical appeal

This is how we are viewed around the world and how we will be viewed by future generations. Most civilized governments abroad, realizing that their society is at least as much shaped and identified by its artists as by its businessmen, have laws to protect such things from happening. In our society, merchants are willing to degrade

Emotional appeal

anything or anyone so long as it brings in a financial profit. Allowing the colorization of films is a good example of our country's regard for its artists, and why I think the issue of moral rights requires legislative help and protection.

CONCLUSION
Additional background

The recent Federal copyright decision says that if a human being uses a certain minimum amount of creativity in coloring a black and white film, the new color version is a separate work that can be copyrighted. In short, if a man colors *Citizen Kane,* it becomes a new movie that can be copyrighted. This must be changed. How?

Call to action

By making sure that Representative Richard A. Gephardt's film integrity bill is passed. It would legalize the moral rights of film artists and, in the process, make colorization without consent illegal.

Emotional appeal

It is, after all, a very short step to removing the score from *Gone With the Wind* and replacing it with a rock score under the mistaken notion that it will render it more enjoyable to young people.

The New York Times

EXERCISE 4 Analyzing the Elements of a Persuasive Essay

Get together with two or three other students to discuss the following questions about Woody Allen's essay.

1. Did you hold an opinion about the colorization of movies before you read Allen's essay? How do you feel about the issue now? Did Allen convince you?
2. Look at Allen's title again. It is actually an appeal, a statement of support developed in the essay. What kind of appeal is it? Where does it occur in the essay? What's your opinion of the title?
3. Which of the opposing arguments do you think were the strongest? How well do you think Allen refuted each of them? Can you think of any other opposition to Allen's position?

4. Find and list all of Allen's reasons for his position. Which is obviously the most important to him? How can you tell?
5. Allen often uses the word *artist*. What point do you think he is trying to make by repeating this word? What other stylistic techniques do you notice?
6. The style of this essay is typical of persuasion. Where does Allen use repetition for effect? Where does he address the audience directly? What is the effect of the sentence fragments he uses? What other examples of persuasive style can you find in the essay?

A Basic Framework for a Persuasive Essay

Woody Allen combines the elements of a persuasive essay in unique ways. For example, he begins with opposing arguments. After the title, his position is clearly implied from the start of the essay but not explicitly stated until near the end. His tone, while heartfelt, is sometimes sarcastic—not usually a winning attitude.

Your essay is likely to be different, not taking so many risks or unexpected turns. The Writer's Model that follows provides a framework you can study and use. As you read, pay attention to your own responses. You are part of a definite, concerned audience for this opinion. Do you agree with the writer?

A WRITER'S MODEL

Mandatory National Service for
America's Youth: The Time Has Come

INTRODUCTION

Sentence fragment used to grab attention

Graduation day--what high school student doesn't look forward to it? A handshake, a diploma, tears and laughter, and it's all over. It's time to move on, to grow up. Many graduates will go on to some type of higher education, some will enter the work force, and others will combine the two. A few will drift, trying to find their places in the world.

Style/Break in rhythm

Very few will be totally prepared for any of these challenges.

Transition from high school into the real world is one of the most significant periods in a young

Logical appeal

Joseph Duffey, chancellor of the University of Massachusetts at Amherst, summed up these advantages in a speech to the World Future Society:

> At its best national service . . . offers young people a chance to grow and mature at a critical stage in their development that cannot be accomplished in the schoolhouse or the workplace. Youth Service--as opposed to all other kinds of service--can teach lessons that redound to personal success in work, as citizens of the community and as examples to the generations that follow.

Opposing position/ Refutations

Logical appeals

Many opponents of national service don't see benefits, though; they see expense, just one more big government program the United States can't afford. Consider, however, that our military services spend a billion dollars a year trying to recruit new volunteers and another billion in reenlistment pay to keep them. And they are still falling short of their recruitment targets. National service would save some of this cost.

Style/Repetition (*Consider*)

Consider, too, our changing world. The Cold War and arms race are not the priorities they once were. It's time to divert some of those defense dollars into labor and service programs. These are dollars that will be reinvested in our economy by those who benefit from them, both the young people and those they help.

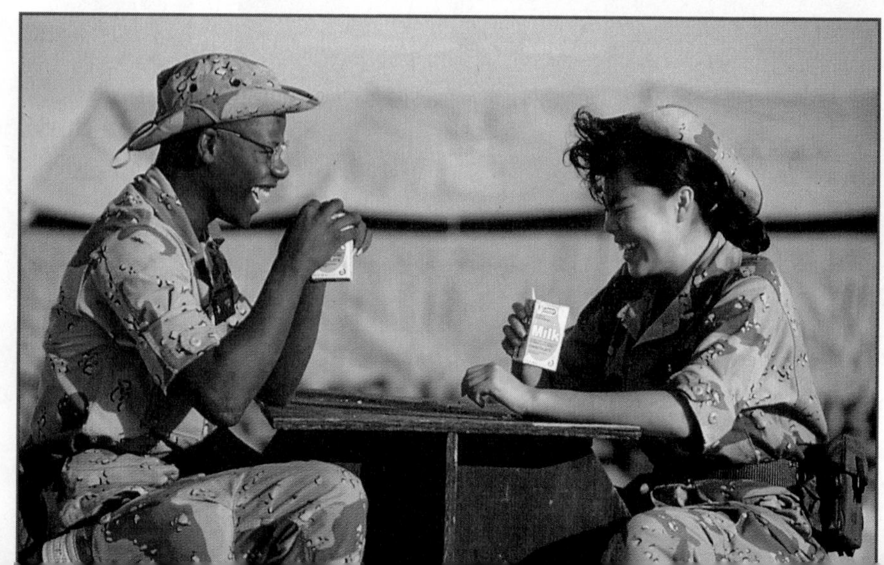

Logical and emotional appeals

Consider, too, unemployed teens. In January of 1990, the U.S. unemployment rate was 5.2 percent. At the same time, teenage unemployment was 14.5 percent; for minority teens, the rate soared to 26.7 percent. If teens don't learn useful skills through experience, many could become chronically unemployed. The resulting costs of welfare and crime are, ultimately, far greater than the costs of giving young people the challenge and opportunity to serve their country.

Opposing position/ Refutation

Logical and emotional appeal

Style/Repetition and rhythm

Some opponents reply that the challenge and opportunity aren't wanted: young people are too self-centered, too unconcerned to participate willingly in such a program. They'll fight it or shirk their duties. But the "me generation" was another generation, not this one. Young people today are open to being better citizens: They know the environment is threatened and only people can save it. They proved their patriotism in the Persian Gulf Conflict. They reject the fates of joblessness and drug addiction.

CONCLUSION Conceding a point/ Ethical appeal

Yes, setting up a workable program will be difficult. Congress and concerned citizens will have to work extremely hard to get past the politics, opposition, and bureaucracy. But it can, and must, be done.

Call to action

The time for mandatory national service for all young people is now. You can do your part by writing to your U.S. senator and representative. Let them know that you support national service and urge them to find a way to make it happen. Do you care about the future of our country and youth? Then act. It will be a national service.

No two persuasive essays are alike. The author of "Mandatory National Service for America's Youth: The Time Has Come" presented three main reasons and refuted two opposing arguments. Your essay may be different, depending upon your issue, the line of reasoning you develop, and the points you must refute. One way to put your thoughts in order is to use a basic framework like the one that follows.

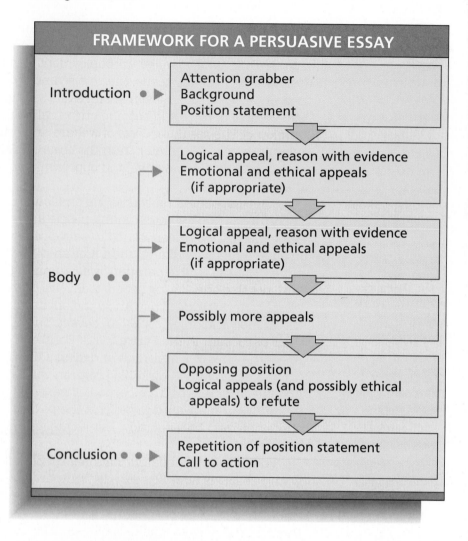

FRAMEWORK FOR A PERSUASIVE ESSAY

Introduction ▶
- Attention grabber
- Background
- Position statement

Body ▶
- Logical appeal, reason with evidence
Emotional and ethical appeals
(if appropriate)
- Logical appeal, reason with evidence
Emotional and ethical appeals
(if appropriate)
- Possibly more appeals
- Opposing position
Logical appeals (and possibly ethical appeals) to refute

Conclusion ▶
- Repetition of position statement
- Call to action

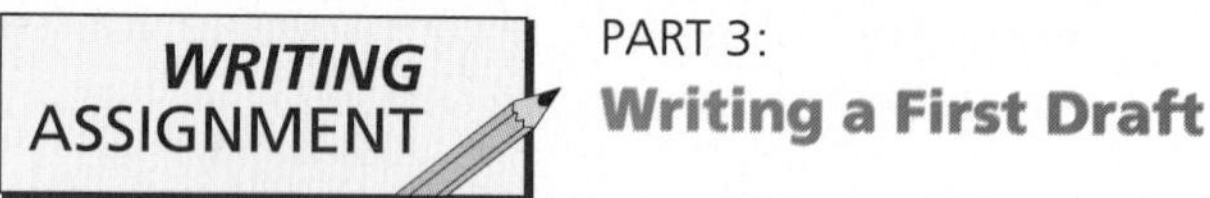

PART 3:

Writing a First Draft

If you've chosen your topic well, you should be itching to give people a piece of your mind—in a way that will change their minds. But even if you are feeling some pre-draft dread of starting (it happens to everyone), you have only to follow the guides you have created: your position statement, chart of support, and plan of organization. Also repicture your audience: Speak directly to these readers as you write. And let your persuasive language flow. Try to put some power in your style.

Evaluating and Revising

Becoming your own critic is the essence of evaluating and revising any paper, but for a persuasive paper, your role-playing of a reader is a little different. You have to become someone who *definitely* doesn't share your opinion, someone who may be ready to pick your argument to pieces. Will it hold up? In addition to evaluating other elements of your writing, you'll need to focus on logic, or reasoning.

CRITICAL THINKING

Evaluating Your Reasoning

When you are writing a persuasive essay, you don't have to be absolutely fair. You certainly aren't taking a neutral position—you're taking a stand. Some evidence may be one-sided; some emotion is allowed.

You must, however, provide logical support for your position statement because reasoning is essential to your essay. Avoid logical ***fallacies*** that look like reasons, but aren't. They are mistakes of logic, and you don't want them in your essay. While some readers may think hastily and be convinced by a fallacy, critical readers will not. They may decide you don't think well *or* are trying to fool them—and either opinion pokes holes in your persuasiveness. Watch out for these fallacies.

1. **Hasty Generalization.** A hasty generalization is a conclusion based on insufficient evidence or one that ignores exceptions. Sometimes broad generalizations can be made acceptable by using qualifying words like *many*, *most*, *generally*, and *some*.

Hasty Generalization	Television game shows exploit contestants by appealing to greed.
Acceptable Generalization	Many television game shows exploit contestants by appealing to greed.

2. **Attacking the Person.** This technique is formally called an *ad hominem* fallacy (Latin for "to the person"); informally, it's "name-calling." It avoids the real issue, attacking instead people who support the issue.

Attacking the Person	The only people who want television cameras in the courtroom are thrill-seeking busybodies.
Facing the Issue	Some people support television cameras in the courtroom because they believe that the public has a right to view all public trials.

3. **False Authority.** Just because a person is an authority in one field does not mean that person is an authority in all fields. Nor does a strong concern and opinion on an issue make someone an authority. Expert testimony is valuable only when it comes from someone knowledgeable about the topic in question.

False Authority	Michelle Van, president of the Downtown Merchants Association, says the proposed museum and auditorium will not interfere with traffic flow in the area.
Relevant Authority	City traffic engineers report that traffic on streets surrounding the proposed site is still far below maximum levels set in the city plan.

4. **Circular Reasoning.** Reasoning is circular when the reason offered for an opinion is simply the opinion stated in different words.

Circular Reasoning	No one country should control the world's oceans because the oceans belong to all countries.
Acceptable Reasoning	The world's oceans must be accessible to all. International treaties guarantee all nations their fair share of the oceans' resources and their ships the right to unrestricted travel on the open seas.

5. **Either-Or Reasoning.** This fallacy assumes that every issue has only two possible sides. Usually, there are many different choices or positions that fall between the extremes.

Either-Or Reasoning	Either we limit population growth or we starve.
Realistic Reasoning	Unchecked population growth threatens the world's ability to adequately feed future generations.

6. **Non Sequitur.** In Latin, *non sequitur* means "it does not follow." In this fallacy, statements or ideas are presented as logically connected but in fact are not. One is not a logical consequence of the other.

Non Sequitur	Our increasingly mobile society demands a higher speed limit.
Logical Connection	A higher speed limit will aid commerce by allowing truckers to shorten delivery times and increase total deliveries.

CRITICAL THINKING EXERCISE:
Evaluating Reasoning

Here is a chance to test your ability to find errors in reasoning. Each of the following statements has a logical flaw. Identify which of the six fallacies each statement exhibits, and then write a logical statement to replace it.

1. Unless the government loosens its restrictions on new medicines, thousands of people will continue to die needlessly.
2. According to former state representative Isao, students should learn more noncompetitive sports, such as swimming, golf, and jazz dancing—sports that last a lifetime.
3. Our country needs a national health plan because a national system is the solution to our problems.
4. Bingo should be made illegal since so many elderly people are players.
5. After-school sports are becoming increasingly dangerous. Last season one player had serious injuries, which included a broken leg and a dislocated shoulder.
6. The advocates of a higher sales tax do not care that it will be a bigger burden on poor and middle-income people than on the rich.
7. No one will be harmed if the fur industry dies.
8. People who live in the suburbs don't understand the problems of our cities.
9. If this city doesn't reelect our mayor, everyone should just leave town on the next train because it just won't be worth living here anymore.
10. The driving age in this state should be raised to twenty-one. The governor was nearly run down by a reckless teenage driver last month.

The following chart is an overall evaluation and revision guide for your essay. Ask yourself each numbered question in the left-hand column. If you find the weakness in your essay, use the revision technique suggested in the right-hand column to correct the problem.

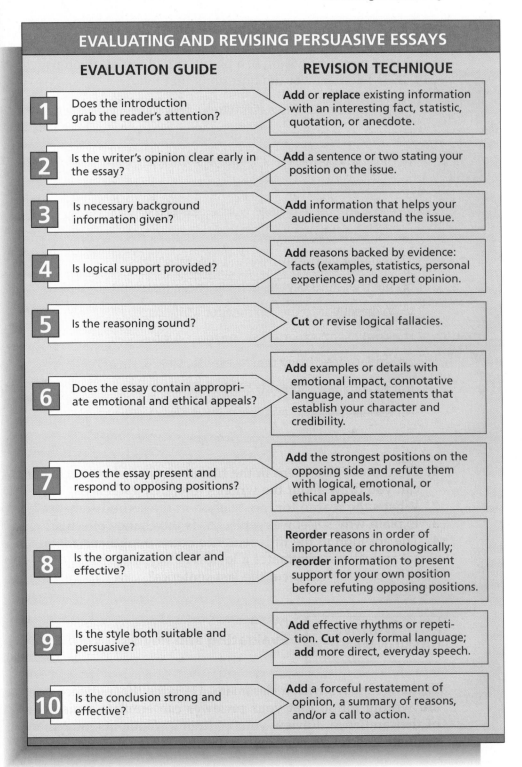

EVALUATING AND REVISING PERSUASIVE ESSAYS

	EVALUATION GUIDE	REVISION TECHNIQUE
1	Does the introduction grab the reader's attention?	**Add** or **replace** existing information with an interesting fact, statistic, quotation, or anecdote.
2	Is the writer's opinion clear early in the essay?	**Add** a sentence or two stating your position on the issue.
3	Is necessary background information given?	**Add** information that helps your audience understand the issue.
4	Is logical support provided?	**Add** reasons backed by evidence: facts (examples, statistics, personal experiences) and expert opinion.
5	Is the reasoning sound?	**Cut** or revise logical fallacies.
6	Does the essay contain appropriate emotional and ethical appeals?	**Add** examples or details with emotional impact, connotative language, and statements that establish your character and credibility.
7	Does the essay present and respond to opposing positions?	**Add** the strongest positions on the opposing side and refute them with logical, emotional, or ethical appeals.
8	Is the organization clear and effective?	**Reorder** reasons in order of importance or chronologically; **reorder** information to present support for your own position before refuting opposing positions.
9	Is the style both suitable and persuasive?	**Add** effective rhythms or repetition. **Cut** overly formal language; **add** more direct, everyday speech.
10	Is the conclusion strong and effective?	**Add** a forceful restatement of opinion, a summary of reasons, and/or a call to action.

EXERCISE 5 Analyzing a Writer's Revisions

Study the writer's revision of a paragraph of the essay on pages 319–323. Then answer the questions that follow.

> No matter how it is structured, mandatory national service could directly benefit ~~us~~ young people, not just the country. All teenagers will gain~~, even though opponents argue the price is too high~~. Those going on to college will be exposed to career choices they may not have considered. They'll also gain maturity and a perspective on life that goes beyond ~~school~~ the four walls of a classroom. Those planning to go directly into the job market will learn valuable skills that may help them escape the trap of "no experience--no job; no job--no experience." They may even discover a field they want to study further. ~~If national service isn't begun, we'll produce a nation of impractical or unemployed people.~~

replace / cut / replace / add / cut

1. From the replacement in the first sentence, what conclusion can you draw about the writer's intended audience?
2. What's the reason for the deletion in the second sentence?
3. Explain why *school* was replaced. Is the change effective?
4. The addition in the fifth sentence both strengthens a logical appeal and eliminates a logical fallacy. How?
5. Why did the writer cut the last sentence?

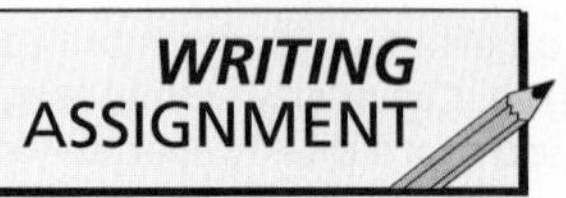

PART 4:

Evaluating and Revising Your Essay

Exchange essays with a classmate. Describe the audience you are writing for so that your reviewer can emulate a member of that audience. Review your partner's comments, and then evaluate and revise your own paper.

Proofreading and Publishing

Proofreading. In a very real sense, careful proofreading can strengthen the ethical appeal of your paper. Readers aren't likely to see you as a thoughtful, concerned person if your paper is sloppy or peppered with mistakes. Always take time to make mechanics, usage, and grammar as sound as your reasoning.

MECHANICS HINT

Using Commas with Parenthetical Expressions

Some common expressions are particularly useful in persuasive writing because they draw the reader's attention to a logical, emotional, or ethical appeal: *I believe (think, know, hope,* and so on*); I am sure; in fact; naturally; in my opinion; for example; to tell the truth.* Most of the time these expressions are parenthetical: that is, they are not essential to the main idea of the sentence. They are included to qualify or to add emphasis. When you want the reader to pause when reading and to recognize that an expression is parenthetical, set it off with commas.

In fact, the National and Community Service Act was passed in November 1990.

However, these expressions do not always have to be used parenthetically. When you want such expressions to be read as an essential part of the sentence, omit the commas.

A bill to create a national service program was in fact passed in November 1990.

REFERENCE NOTE: For more help with the use of commas in parenthetical expressions, see pages 914–915.

Publishing. If you want to convince people that you are right, you have to put your essay out there for them to read. Here are two ideas for publishing.

- Send a copy of your essay to a magazine that deals with the issue you wrote about. Reference books such as *Writer's Market* explain how to submit articles to magazines.
- Make your opinion a multimedia event. Create a poster on which you surround your essay with newspaper and magazine photographs or illustrations that highlight your major points. Ask permission to display your poster at an appropriate public location, such as a library, community theater, city hall, or school lobby.

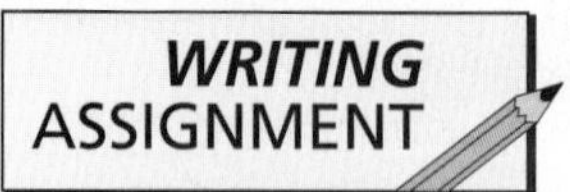

PART 5:
Proofreading and Publishing Your Persuasive Essay

Proofread and correct your paper so that its appearance and form give a clear message: Believe in me. Then use one of the publishing ideas above, or an idea of your own, to get it to the audience whose belief in your ideas really matters.

A STUDENT MODEL

Does an after-school job enhance a teenager's life, or is it just a burden to avoid? As the following persuasive papers show, either stance can be convincingly supported. Martha Delgado and Greg Robertson, both students at Valley High School in Albuquerque, New Mexico, take opposing sides on the issue. Martha says no to after-school jobs, while Greg says yes. What do you think? Who convinces you?

All Work and No Play
by Martha Delgado

It's nine o'clock when the front door opens. Another hard day of work has finally come to an end. "All work and no play" comes to mind as the working student climbs the stairs to his room. Since the student started working, there has been no time for anything besides work. He seems like a different person now that he has an after-school job. I believe that students should not have after-school jobs.

First of all, working has an effect on any student's social life. Having a job is too time-consuming, so students aren't able to enjoy life as teenagers. This is the time for students to live life fully and to be with friends. This is the time to take advantage of one's youth, not the time to spend life working when it's not really necessary.

Some people think that students should work because they begin to earn money. What's the rush? Why should students start working so soon when they're going to have the rest of their lives to earn money? Besides, when students do earn money, they usually end up spending it on things that are of no importance. About 83 percent of students surveyed said that they usually spend their money on entertainment. So what do students actually gain from earning their own money at such an early age? Students who don't work can manage just as well as students who do. This I know for a fact because I am one of the nonworking students.

Most important, working has an effect on grades. Many students' grades begin to drop because they don't have time to do homework. They arrive home from work too tired. The only thing on their minds is sleep. Many students usually arrive home at a late hour, so they really don't have time to do their homework. As a result, students don't work up to their full educational capacity.

Working after school is harmful as well as unnecessary. The high school years are not the years to work, but the years to enjoy life. If you agree, call or write your school board committee. If we--as people who care--take a stand, we can make a difference. Be one of these people.

"Get a Job!"
by Greg Robertson

Every week, many students give up their Saturday and Sunday afternoons to work and make money. Instead of sleeping late or "hanging out" with their friends, these youths are out in the working world getting a taste of how the real world works. I believe this shows responsibility. It also shows the community that not all young men and women are troublemakers with nothing to do.

A good reason for young men and women to have jobs is their self-esteem. When students have worked a couple of days a week and receive their paychecks, they feel good about themselves. They feel as though they have done a good deed, and they want to do it again!

Many people argue that when a person is young, a job consumes too much time. They say that young people waste the money they make on useless items. It is true that some of the weekly paycheck goes for recreation, but many students save money for school, use it to pay car insurance, or just put it in a savings account for future use. This is also a useful skill to learn because all people have to learn how to "pinch their pennies."

Students who have jobs are definitely doing themselves a favor. They are gathering experience for possible future jobs, and a good job is a wonderful thing to put on a résumé.

Having students in the workplace is a very good idea. It helps the student and the community. If YOU are a student who would like to be involved in the workplace, contact one of the agencies that help teens find jobs, such as "Dial-A-Teen" and "The Youth Employment Agency." Be part of the responsible (and richer) teens in your community. Go out and GET A JOB!

WRITING WORKSHOP

A Satire

Searching for persuasive issues showed you that people have a good many ideas about things that are wrong with our society and should be changed. In the main assignment in this chapter, you used logical, emotional, and ethical appeals to persuade. ***Satire*** is a form of persuasive writing that seeks to bring about change and reform through humor and wit. Satirists ridicule the failings of individuals, social and political institutions, and society in general in order to persuade people that reform—in thought or action—is needed.

Satirists often rely on distortion and exaggeration to get their points across. Their tone can be either gentle and smiling or biting and angry. They may use almost any form of writing—a poem, a novel, a short story, a song's lyrics, a play, an essay.

One of the most famous—and biting—satirists was Jonathan Swift. In his book *Gulliver's Travels,* Swift takes aim at many human failings, including the damaging inclination to fight over trivial matters. He describes two countries that were at war for three years. And for what? One country thought eggs should be cracked at the large end; the other thought they should be cracked at the small end. In the essay "A Modest Proposal," Swift ridicules those who complain about beggars yet offer no solution. He offers this satiric solution to the unpleasant sight of poor children begging in the street: Eat them!

Satire is still a flourishing and effective persuasive art, practiced by modern satirists such as Garry Trudeau, the creator of the "Doonesbury" comic strip; the writers and creators of the television series *M.A.S.H.;* essayist Fran Lebowitz; and a host of others. One well-known satirist is Art Buchwald, a syndicated newspaper columnist. As you read "The Killers," think not only about what he is satirizing but about the "support" he presents for his position.

The Killers

by Art Buchwald

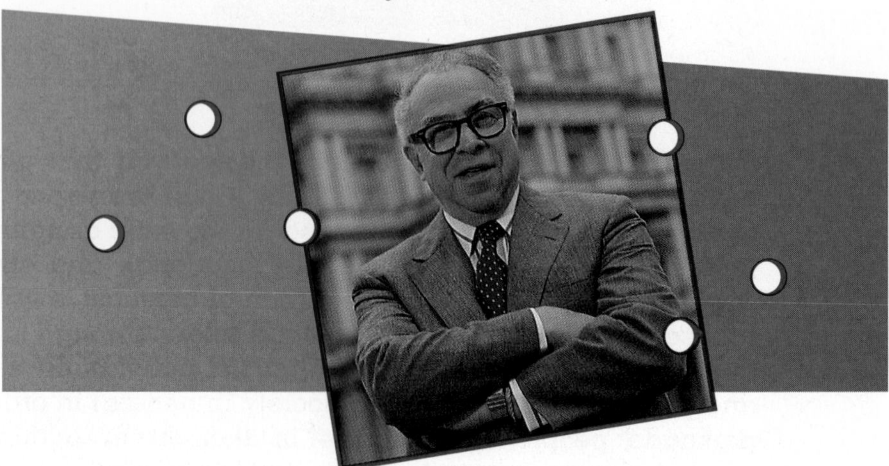

What fascinates me about films depicting so much violence is not the shooting, knifing, and garroting of the good guys as well as the bad guys, but the damage done to innocent people who just happen to be on the scene.

When I watch Sly Stallone, Clint Eastwood, Arnold Schwarzenegger, and Charles Bronson blowing up buildings, smashing cars, and spraying lead with submachine guns, the first thing that comes to mind is how much hurt they inflict on everyone else in the film.

The other night I said out loud in the theater, "Is this type of picture worth it?"

"Of course it's worth it," the man in the next seat said. "It teaches the audience that violence must be met with violence."

"But look at what's up on the screen. The Super-American has wrecked six cars and an orphanage to get the bad guy. He's driving like a madman. Who is going to pay for the wrecked automobiles and the buildings that the Super-American is senselessly destroying?"

"The Super-American's liability insurance company," the man said.

"But the Super-American didn't even stop to see if the bystanders were hurt."

"What would you want him to do, hold up the movie? You have to have continuous action in this kind of film. And when you do that, a lot of innocents are going to get hurt."

"How about the Super-American's car going right through a fruit market and mowing down a Chinese laundry. Doesn't anyone in the theater care about the fruit dealer and the laundryman?"

The man said, "That's nothing compared to the Super-American wiping out some of the country's worst villains. The only reason the Super-American is pursuing evil is because the police have failed in their job."

"Good enough, but why did he blow up the Senior Citizens' apartment building with dynamite? The bad guy still got away and now twenty families have no place to live."

"It's just a movie," the man said.

"Then why are all the kids in the theater cheering?"

The man said, "Because they identify with the Super-American—a lone warrior fighting the battle to rid the world of rot."

"If you believe in law and order, how do you feel about the Super-American hitting the bad guy over the head with a fire extinguisher?"

"The Super-American won't do it for long. As soon as he can grab the Uzi submachine gun, he'll fill the bad guy's stomach full of lead."

"Why doesn't the Super-American just turn him over for trial?"

"How can he after what they did to his brother?"

"I didn't know they did anything to the Super-American's brother."

"It was in the coming attractions. They cut it out in the final version so that they could spend more time showing the Super-American setting the villain on fire."

I said, "I can't believe what I'm seeing. The Super-American just pushed a crowded bus off the pier so that he could improve his line of fire to the hospital ship."

"You really pick up on every little thing, don't you?" the man said.

"What must our children think? They probably believe that what they see on the screen is the real thing."

"When you have every top-grossing male star in Hollywood fighting to do one of these pictures, then you realize that vigilantism is here to stay," he said.

"Even if the Super-American doesn't care a fig about constitutional rights?"

"If the audience doesn't care, why should he?"

from *I Think I Don't Remember*

1. Did you find this satire funny? Why or why not?
2. Clearly Art Buchwald is satirizing violence in the movies, but is that all? Read closely: What other aspects of America or American life are criticized through the actions of the "Super-American"? Explain your answer.
3. What details does Buchwald use to make his points? Are they realistic and believable or exaggerated? Explain.
4. Buchwald developed his satire as a dialogue between himself and another moviegoer. Why would he do this? [Hint: How does dialogue relate to an important part of your persuasive essay?] How else could he have developed this satire?
5. ***Verbal irony,*** saying one thing but meaning the opposite, is frequent in satire. Did Buchwald intend "It's just a movie" ironically? Explain.
6. Where in the satire does Buchwald try to include readers directly in the issues he's examining—to make them feel responsible? Is it effective?

Writing a Satire

Prewriting. What social or political situation seems to you unjust, harmful, or a threat to important values? What would you like others to think more about: the homeless? the power of the Supreme Court? the excessive amount of money students spend on proms? Then: How can you *make fun* of the situation? What elements lend themselves to ridicule? How can you use humor to persuade readers of the need for reform?

You have several choices for the form of your satire. For example, you could write an essay in which you make "serious" outrageous suggestions, a dialogue like Buchwald's (or one between two invented people), or a short comic story (for example, "The Unforgettable Prom Date").

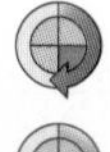

Writing, Evaluating, and Revising. Remember that while your topic is serious, your tone should be humorous and tongue-in-cheek or sarcastic and biting. Use exaggeration, silly details, and unexpected points of view; use language that suits your purpose (and characters, if any), whether slangy, ridiculously formal, or deadpan. You don't have to make a direct position statement, but be sure action, details, or dialogue communicate your concerns. Think about whether you want to incorporate an indirect call to action: a suggestion of what readers can do.

Try your satire out on others. Do they get it? Are they amused? Ask them for suggestions for clarifying your targets or adding humor. After evaluating your satire, revise it as needed.

Proofreading and Publishing. Make a clean, corrected final copy. The school newspaper and the local paper's op-ed page are good forums for a satirical essay. Your satire might also be turned into a funny skit for the class (think of satiric television programs like *Saturday Night Live*). Satire is common on radio, too, so see if local stations are interested. Finally, start each class period with a different student's satire until all are read or performed.

MAKING CONNECTIONS

ANALYZING PERSUASION IN AN ADVERTISEMENT

We all know that advertising manipulates us. It isn't all logical. It plays on emotions—both desires and fears. And yet we respond to it, we enjoy it, we *buy things* because of it. Why? How do advertisers make us pick up a particular brand of deodorant? eat in a certain restaurant or see a certain movie? contribute to an organization or vote for a candidate?

With a partner or a group, become an advertising analyst. Choose two ads from different media: print, television, radio, and direct mail (the advertisements that come unsolicited in the mail). Then analyze, and give an oral report on, the persuasion you find, showing the ads or describing them thoroughly. Here are some guides for your investigation:

- What product, service, or cause is the ad selling? What *value or feeling* is being "sold"? How?
- Who seems to be the primary audience for the ad? How can you tell?
- What logical appeals are used (reasons, factual evidence, expert testimony)? How sound are they?
- How are emotional appeals made? Look at language, visuals (consider content, color, style), music, celebrities.
- Which, if any, of the following appeals are used?

  Bandwagon appeal—suggests that you should buy the product because everyone else is buying it.

  Snob appeal—appeals to your desire to be rich, brainy, famous, and generally better than other people.

  Veiled threat—hints that something bad will happen to you if you don't buy the product (you'll lose your girlfriend because of bad breath, for example).

- What ethical appeals do you find—ways that the advertiser shows fairness, good character, or concern for the audience?
- Does the ad work? Why or why not?

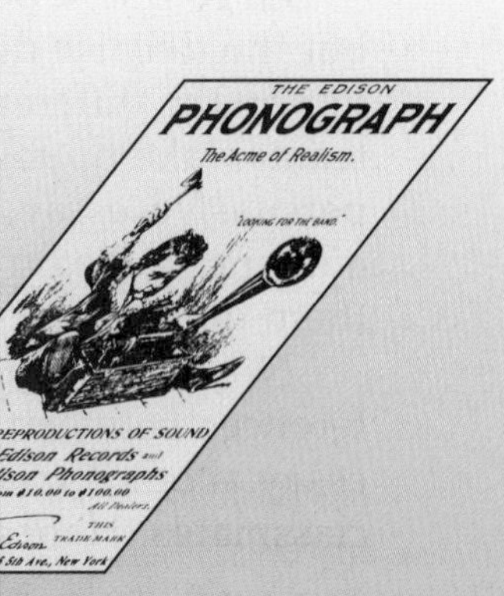

SPEAKING AND LISTENING

Persuasion and Debate

What does a debate have in common with a persuasive essay? The debater, like the writer of an essay, is taking a stand, trying to convince an audience to accept his or her position on an issue.

The proposition in a debate is much like the position statement in a persuasive essay. For example:

Position Statement:	All new urban road construction should include bicycle paths.
Debate Proposition:	Resolved, that all new urban road construction should include bicycle paths.

Of course, a persuasive essay is written and a debate is oral, but the debater does have to plan and write a speech. A more important difference is that in a debate, two people, or two teams, take opposite sides on an issue. When you wrote your persuasive essay, you assumed that some members of your audience were on the opposite side; but you didn't have to face them directly.

Now that you have thought about the similarities and differences between debating an issue and writing a persuasive essay about it, plan to take part in a debate with some of your classmates. Here are some suggestions for getting started:

1. In class discussion, create a list of propositions to debate (use the form in the example on the previous page). You could pick up some of the issues from the persuasive essays you wrote earlier in this chapter.
2. Decide whether you will debate in pairs or teams, and sign up for propositions. Your sign-up sheet should include an affirmative position and a negative position—that way you will have a pair or team on both sides of the issue.
3. Review the material on debating on pages 1001–1006, and plan your debate. After you have finished planning and rehearsing, hold the debate in your classroom.

PERSUASION AND THE MEDIA

Writing a Letter to the Editor

Sometimes, the editorial page of a newspaper or magazine is the most entertaining and interesting page in the publication. Letters to the editor are particularly interesting. People from all walks of life get their gripes and convictions off their chests, and usually they are trying to persuade others to agree with them.

They write for various reasons. They may be upset about an editorial; they may wholeheartedly agree or strenuously disagree with an article; they may want to start a debate; they may even be taking strong issue with a previous letter to the editor.

Have you ever written to a publication in response to something you read? If not, you now have a chance. Spend a few days looking over the letters to the editor in your local newspaper or a favorite magazine. Find a letter that stirs up your feelings. Does it make you angry? Do you think the person is totally off base or right on target? Or do you have a different slant on the issue that you think readers should consider?

When you write your letter, think about everything you have learned in this chapter about persuasion. Remember, however, that this is just a letter—not an essay—so be brief. Many publications give requirements about form and submission. You have a much better chance of being published if you follow the guidelines. If your letter makes it into print, bring a copy of the publication to class. Then check out future issues of the publication. Someone else may respond to what you wrote.

Shoe, by Jeff MacNelly, reprinted by permission: Tribune Media Services.

9 WRITING TO EXPLORE

Asking Questions, Seeking Answers

On October 14, 1947, Chuck Yeager climbed into his X-1 plane and became the first human being to fly faster than the speed of sound. Both Yeager and the people watching this momentous event wondered: What will happen at supersonic speed? Will the plane vibrate to pieces, sending the pilot to his death? People always **ask questions** about the mysteries and problems around them. And as they do, they **discover** new answers, solutions.

Writing and You. Explorations may start in your mind, but often they turn into words on a page. For example, historian Barbara Tuchman asked questions about World War I and then wrote *The Guns of August*. What problems and solutions have you explored?

As You Read. Some people explore problems through poems. What problem does the following sonnet explore?

Julius Ciss, *Brainstorm on the Future.* Acrylic on canvas, 20″ × 30″. The Image Bank.

Sonnet 29

by William Shakespeare

When, in disgrace with fortune and men's eyes,
I all alone beweep my outcast state,
And trouble deaf heaven with my bootless cries,
And look upon myself, and curse my fate,
Wishing me like to one more rich in hope,
Featured like him, like him with friends possessed,
Desiring this man's art and that man's scope,
With what I most enjoy contented least;
Yet in these thoughts myself almost despising,
Haply I think on thee—and then my state,
Like to the lark at break of day arising
From sullen earth, sings hymns at heaven's gate;
For thy sweet love remembered such wealth brings
That then I scorn to change my state with kings.

READER'S RESPONSE

1. When you're "down" or "depressed," is there someone or something that can raise your spirits? Explain.
2. Many people believe that part of Shakespeare's greatness lies in his exploration of timeless themes and feelings. Even though the sonnet was written about 400 years ago, do you understand and identify with the feelings it expresses? Why or why not?

WRITER'S CRAFT

3. When you write about a problem you've explored, you may describe the problem or explain a solution for it. In which lines of the sonnet does the speaker express his problem? In which lines does he identify a solution? What is the solution?
4. Part of exploring a problem may involve identifying its different causes and effects. What is causing the speaker's problem? What are its specific effects?
5. In this poem Shakespeare explores a personal problem. Would the poem work as well if he explored a problem that affected more people? Why?
6. Shakespeare's primary aim in creating this sonnet was, of course, to create literature. Exploring a problem was secondary. What other pieces of literature can you think of that show someone exploring a problem?

Ways to Explore

Writers like William Shakespeare explore problems in many different ways. The exploration may be in writing, or it may take place entirely in the writers' minds. But once writers uncover an insight or develop a new idea, they usually want to share it with others and perhaps even convince them to share their way of thinking. Exploratory writing, combined with informative or persuasive writing, may appear in newspapers, magazines, speeches and sermons, business proposals, and books.

There is more than one way that exploratory writing can be developed. Here are some examples.

Narration: tracing the genetic history of your family to discover why you look the way you do; studying the events that preceded the savings and loan crisis to discover how future financial crises might be avoided.

Description: describing your missing car to help the police locate it; describing a skin rash to your doctor.

Classification: comparing and contrasting two possible solutions to rising crime in your city; identifying two sources of funding—community and corporate—as you explore solutions to the problem of getting new football uniforms.

Evaluation: asking questions about candidates for local office before voting; explaining why you have decided to go to college or join the army or get a job after graduation.

LOOKING AHEAD

In the main writing assignment in this chapter, you will use the strategies of narration and classification to explore a problem and its possible solutions in an essay. As you work, keep in mind that a problem-solution essay

- identifies and explores a problem
- identifies, explores, and evaluates solutions to the problem
- explains (and proves) how to solve the problem

Writing a Problem-Solution Essay

Exploring Problems

Although you may not be exploring new continents or theories, your daily conversations, thinking, and writing are still filled with exploration. In exploring a personal problem, you often write for yourself—in a journal entry, for example (or a sonnet!). But when you explore a problem that involves others, you often present your findings to an audience in the form of an essay. In this chapter you will study models of this type of exploration and write an essay exploring a problem and a solution.

Identifying a Problem

Like most people, you probably have your share of problems, but most personal problems are not appropriate for a problem-solution essay. When you are planning to share the results of your exploration with others, you need to identify a problem that is common to many people. For example, a quarrel with your kid brother is too personal, but many readers might be interested in the causes and effects of sibling rivalry.

As you consider possible problems for exploration, check the significance of each problem by asking

- Does it affect a number of people?
- Is it important to the people it affects?

HINTS FOR IDENTIFYING APPROPRIATE PROBLEMS

- **Address your concerns at the grass-roots level.** If you're concerned about environmental issues, you might explore a problem such as waste disposal or clean water in your community. Or, if you are worried about education, you might explore a problem such as falling test scores or student apathy in a local school.

(continued)

HINTS FOR IDENTIFYING APPROPRIATE PROBLEMS *(continued)*

- **Address personal concerns that you share with others.** If you are worried about the crime rate and its effect on your family, you might explore a problem such as the rising crime rate or the understaffed police force. Or, if your concern is the worsening economy and its effect on your family, you might explore rising college costs or the lack of affordable housing.
- **Address problems that are solvable.** You probably can't make much progress in English class toward bringing peace to the Middle East or ending poverty in Central America.

EXERCISE 1 **SPEAKING AND LISTENING: Identifying Problems**

What issues concern people in your school and community? One way to find out is by attending open meetings of groups such as the school board, the city council, the student council, the local council on aging, and so on. Another way is to watch the broadcasts of such meetings on local cable TV. Or, you may gather information on local issues by reading newspaper reports or watching TV reports. Make a list of three or four problems that you identify in this way. With your classmates, decide which problems affect a large number of people.

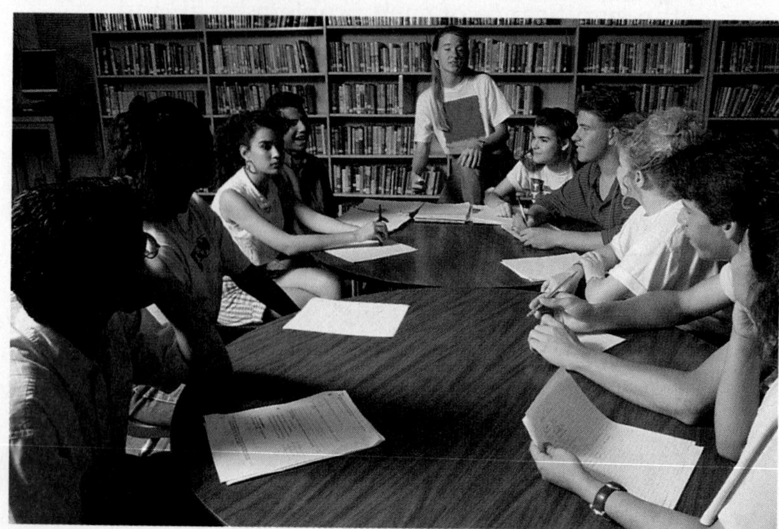

Investigating a Problem

Before you can find a solution for your problem, you must first understand the problem itself. But problems aren't easy! They are, by definition, "complicated" or "difficult" situations. For this reason, they will require some careful study on your part.

Often when you look more deeply into a problem, you will discover that you need more information. You can use a variety of prewriting techniques to investigate your problem: brainstorming and asking yourself questions to discover what you already know; reading, listening, observing, and questioning to discover what other people think about the problem. You may have to go to the library or interview some people who are likely to be knowledgeable about the problem. (See pages 21–28 for more help with these techniques.) For example, if you were exploring the problem of rising costs of a college education, you might go to the library and look for recent newspaper or magazine articles on the topic. You might also talk to someone in your high school guidance office to find out whether rising costs are affecting local students.

CRITICAL THINKING

Analyzing Problems

One way to investigate a problem thoroughly is to analyze it with the four different viewpoints, or strategies, mentioned earlier: description, narration, classification, and evaluation.

Description What is the problem?
How widespread is it?

Narration What is its history?
What are its causes?
What are its effects?

Classification How is the problem similar to other problems?
How is the problem different from other problems?
What are the major parts of the problem?

Evaluation Is the problem important? Why?

The following examples show how you might use these strategies to gather information about the problem, *the rising costs of college.*

Description: Cost increasing faster than most consumers' abilities to pay

Narration: During '80s, increases outpaced inflation
1991–1992—average in-state tuition and fees up 12% at 4-year colleges and 13% at 2-year colleges
One cause, inflation; another cause, cuts in local and national funding for education
Students obviously affected; also long-range prospects for country—fewer college graduates

Classification: '90s, like housing and medical costs—increasingly unaffordable for many, government subsidies being cut
Parts of the problem—tuition, fees, housing

Evaluation: Importance—limits opportunities for many young Americans

CRITICAL THINKING EXERCISE:
Analyzing a Problem

Is student apathy a problem in your high school? Is there a parking lot or street near your school that's too congested? Do school buses have to pick some students up hours before classes begin? Select one of these problems (or a problem of

your own choosing) to analyze. Then, working with a partner, use each of the four strategies—description, narration, classification, evaluation—to gather information about the problem. In a short paragraph, summarize what you learn from your analysis.

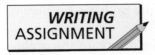

PART 1:
Identifying and Investigating a Problem

What are your concerns? Brainstorm a list of possible problems, including the ones you identified in Exercise 1 (page 350). The problems may affect your school or your community, or they may be of national and international significance. Then, evaluate the list to decide which problem would make the best topic for your essay (be sure that the problem is interesting and important to you). Once you've decided on a problem, use a variety of sources and find out everything you can about it. Finally, use the strategies that you read about in the Critical Thinking section (pages 351–352) to analyze the problem.

Exploring Solutions

Now that you are an expert on the problem you have chosen, it's time to turn your attention to the solutions. Most problems don't have easy solutions—if they did, they wouldn't be problems. Your job is to investigate all the possible solutions and then to decide which solution is the best one.

Identifying Possible Solutions

If your problem has been around for a while, somebody has probably already tried to solve it. One useful bit of exploration, then, is to investigate the solutions of others. But don't stop there—use freewriting, brainstorming, clustering, or imagining to create your own solutions. The following questions will help you get started.

STRATEGIES FOR ANALYZING POSSIBLE SOLUTIONS

Ideas of Others

1. What solutions to the problem have already been tried?
2. How effective have they been?
3. If the past solutions weren't effective, why not?
4. What solutions are currently being proposed?

Your Own Ideas

1. Can some of the causes of the problem be eliminated? How?
2. What can be done about the effects of the problem?
3. Is there any part of the problem that seems especially difficult to solve? Why?
4. Which part of the problem is simplest to solve? Why?
5. What is the strangest way you can think of to solve the problem? the easiest way? the most popular way?

It is possible to find creative solutions to problems that, on the surface, seem almost not to have a solution. For example, a college student named Wendy Kopp explored the problem of

teacher shortages in inner cities and rural communities. As part of her senior thesis, she proposed the creation of a national teacher corps that would recruit, train, place, and support outstanding recent college graduates from all academic majors and backgrounds to commit a minimum of two years to teach in urban and rural public schools. Her solution became a reality with a program called Teach for America.

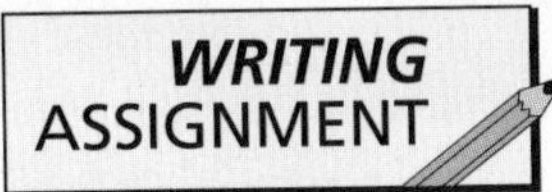

PART 2:
Identifying Possible Solutions

Using the strategies on page 354, analyze the solutions others have proposed to the problem you investigated in Writing Assignment, Part 1 (page 353). Then explore your own ideas. Make a list of every possible way you can find or think of to solve the problem. At this point, don't censor any solutions, even those that may seem a bit ridiculous at first. Even the silliest solution can contain the germ of a good idea.

Finding the Best Solution

There are solutions, but there are rarely *perfect* solutions. And, in the absence of a perfect solution, you still need to make a decision about the best solution. Asking yourself questions like the following ones can help you find the best solution.

1. **What are the strengths and weaknesses of each solution?** Every solution will have some strengths and some weaknesses. Make a chart for yourself like the one on page 356, listing each solution and its strengths and weaknesses. Does any one solution seem to have more strengths and fewer weaknesses?

2. **Which solution is the most practical?** Solutions may be impractical in terms of money or other resources that it would take to carry them out, in terms of time needed, or for many other reasons. Which solution would be the easiest to implement?
3. **Which solution has a comparative advantage?** A solution has a comparative advantage if it appears to offer more than other solutions do. For example, if a solution appears to be the fairest one or the one that will do the most good for the most people, then it has a comparative advantage over the others.

The following chart shows how one writer analyzed possible solutions for the problem of declining reading abilities.

HERE'S HOW

Possible Solutions	Advantages	Disadvantages
Hire additional teacher's aides to work one-on-one with students in the classroom.	Students would get more practice and help with reading skills.	Budgets are tight, and taxes are already high in the county.
Adopt a "book buddy" program, pairing older students with younger students.	Creates more opportunities to read, provides role models, promotes self-esteem of older students.	The students will not be able to identify and help each other with reading difficulties.
Library outreach program in day-care facilities or after-school programs.	Creates additional reading experiences; uses time spent in day-care facilities or after-school programs more effectively.	Library might need additional funding for staff; doesn't reach students who are at home.
Practicality Providing more teacher's aides is not practical because it would cost more money. There just isn't any more money available in the school budget at this time.		
Comparative Advantage The "book buddy" system and library/day-care program are fairer because, used together, they will reach more children and they will not place an additional burden on the county's taxpayers.		

Developing a Compromise Solution. What do you do if two solutions seem equally good for different reasons or if none of your solutions seems to work? First, check to see that you aren't falling into the either-or trap. With the problem of rising costs for college, for example, don't assume that a student either has to pay $20,000 a year to attend the state university or not go to college. And don't assume that a student has to work either full time or not at all. A compromise solution might be that a student could attend a community college, live at home, and work part time for the first two years and then transfer to the state university and take out government loans for the last two years.

Finding Different Solutions for Different Parts of the Problem. Sometimes, one solution or one compromise just doesn't cover the problem. If your problem has several different causes or affects several different populations, you may need to address these differences with separate solutions. Think of your own life, for example. If the problem is that you are getting a low grade in Spanish IV, a discussion with your teacher may reveal that the problem has two parts: (1) You aren't doing your homework regularly, and (2) you aren't participating in class discussion. One solution—getting a calendar to write down homework assignments and then remembering to do them—is not enough. You also need a solution for your lack of class participation.

Listing Necessary Steps

Unfortunately, even the most brilliant solution won't automatically put itself into place. You usually have to develop a plan, working toward a solution step by step. Think in specific, practical terms. Decide exactly what has to be done, how it is to be done, and in what order it is to be done. If you can identify the process involved in carrying out the solution, you can be fairly certain of its practicality. For example, setting up a district-wide "book buddy" program to give younger children more role models for reading might involve the following steps:

1. Develop and conduct a short orientation for fifth- and sixth-graders at each school. Cover the program's goals and older students' roles and responsibilities.

2. Set up the mechanics of the program: Pair each fifth-grade class with a kindergarten class, each sixth-grade class with a first-grade class. Have teachers create pupil pairs consisting of one older and one younger student, and schedule one half-hour meeting time per week for the program.
3. Monitor the program: Get feedback from teachers and students.
4. Evaluate the program's effectiveness. Monitor future test scores.

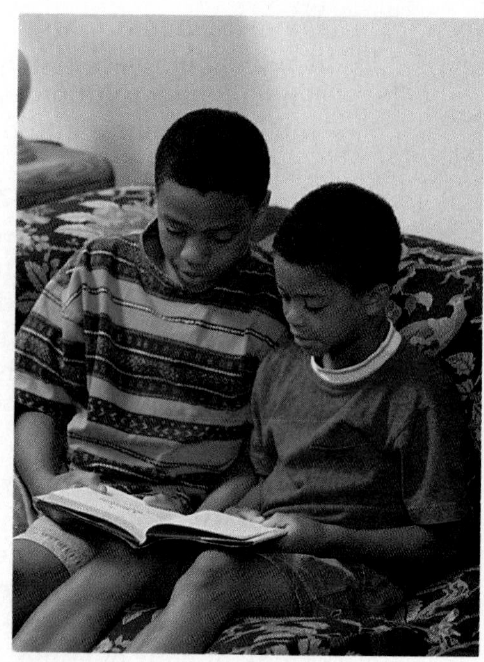

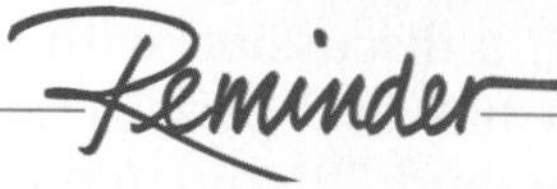

When exploring solutions

- explore the solutions of others and create your own
- consider each solution's strengths and weaknesses, practicality, and comparative advantages
- identify the best solution(s) for the problem
- list the necessary steps to implement the solution

PART 3:
Identifying Your Best Solution and Listing Necessary Steps

Before you decide on the best possible solution to the problem you have explored, make a chart like the one on page 356, listing the possible solutions and their strengths and weaknesses. Analyze the solutions, also, for practicality and comparative advantage. On the basis of your analysis, choose the best solution to the problem. When you've identified the best solution, list the steps necessary to implement it.

Planning Your Problem-Solution Essay

So far, you have been exploring a problem and its solutions—the focus has been on your own explorations. Now it's time to shift your attention to sharing what you have learned with others.

Considering Purpose, Audience, and Tone

Purpose. Your purpose up to this point has been to explore a problem and solution. When you begin to write your essay, your *purpose* shifts to explaining and proving. You explain and prove what you've discovered in your exploration. You might explain, for example, the nature of the problem and the possible solutions. Readers will also expect you to prove that the problem is serious and the solution you have found is the best one.

Audience and Tone. The exploration itself is as much for your own information as for that of your audience. However, when you begin to think about how to present what you have discovered, your *audience* now becomes very important. These questions will help you address their concerns.

- **What does your audience already know about this problem? How do they react to it?** If readers don't know about the problem or aren't affected by it, you may have to spend more time showing them that the problem really exists or that it is important to solve it.
- **What solutions might your audience favor?** Some readers may favor a solution you have rejected. In this case, you'll need to explain the disadvantages of your rejected solutions carefully.
- **What objections might your audience have to your solution?** Some readers may be quick to point out the flaws in your solution, so you'll need to explain its value thoroughly and attempt to answer their possible objections.

In writing your essay, use objective language that reflects your open, honest exploration of the problem—stay away from words that carry emotional overtones. However, because you are recounting a personal exploration, you may put yourself into your essay, referring to your own experience in the exploration. Another aspect of *tone* in exploratory writing is *tentativeness.* You may not always be certain that you've found the perfect solution, for example, and in that case you may use words like *appears, seems,* or *perhaps* to qualify your statements.

Providing Support

Evidence—in the form of facts, statistics, examples, and reasons—will help you explain and prove

- that a serious problem exists
- that the solutions you reject won't work
- that your solution is the best one

Readers usually require specific evidence before they are convinced. For example, suppose you want to prove that a problem exists with dumping garbage into a community lake. Readers tend to be suspicious of such vague statements as "A lot of garbage got dumped into Lake Osawaga last year." Instead, they prefer precise information: "The lake patrol office estimates that approximately a quarter of a ton of garbage was dumped in Lake Osawaga last year."

You have probably already collected some evidence through your analysis of the problem. When you analyzed possible solutions—their strengths, weaknesses, practicality, and comparative advantages—you found even more evidence. Now, to provide support, you may want to do some more research to find other facts, statistics, examples, and reasons. Be certain that the sources you use are reliable. A *reliable* source is trustworthy—the information you find there can usually be believed. Reliable sources are magazines like *Time* and *Newsweek,* major newspapers, and experts who have studied the problem carefully and objectively.

If you are proposing a new solution, you may not have solid facts to prove its worth. But you can still provide reasons and, possibly, a model as proof. For example, for the problem of latchkey children, you may not know exactly how many such children will benefit from your proposed solution of an afternoon activity program. But you can offer readers this good reason: Organized recreational activities are better for young children than unsupervised TV viewing. You can also use a similar, successful program in another community as a model of how and why your solution will help to solve the problem.

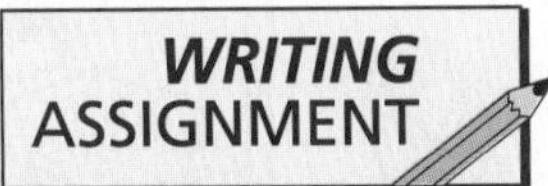

PART 4:

Planning Your Problem-Solution Essay

First, plan your problem-solution essay by jotting down the evidence—facts, statistics, examples, reasons—that you will use to explain, and prove, the problem and its seriousness. Then, list each solution you are rejecting and a major disadvantage of each. Finally, list the evidence that helps to prove that your solution is the best one, and list the steps needed to implement it. If necessary, do more research to fill in gaps of evidence. And be sure to think about the objections your readers are likely to have. If they've never heard about the problem, for example, you may need more evidence that it exists.

Writing Your First Draft

The Elements of a Problem-Solution Essay

Problem-solution essays, like most other kinds of essays, may follow different patterns. Most problem-solution essays, however, have the following elements:

- an explanation of the problem
- evidence of the problem's seriousness
- a description of the proposed solution
- a list of steps to implement the solution
- discussion of the disadvantages of rejected solutions
- evidence to support the solution and to counter possible objections

The amount of space you devote to each of these parts can vary according to the concerns of your readers. If they have never heard of the problem, for example, you may spend more time discussing it. The nature of the problem and its solution(s) may also influence your presentation. For instance, if a fairly straightforward problem has a very complex solution, you may devote more time to discussing the solution than to discussing the problem. Regardless of the emphasis, however, the introduction should include an interesting opening that focuses the reader's attention on some aspect of the problem.

The major emphasis in the following essay by Isaac Asimov is not the solution, but the problem itself—explaining its causes and effects and proving its significance. As you read "The Villain in the Atmosphere," think about why Asimov may have given the problem this amount of emphasis.

A PROBLEM-SOLUTION ESSAY

The Villain in the Atmosphere

by Isaac Asimov

INTRODUCTION
Attention-grabbing statement of problem

The villain in the atmosphere is carbon dioxide. It does not seem to be a villain. It is not very poisonous and it is present in the atmosphere in so small a quantity that it does us no harm. For every 1,000,000 cubic feet of air there are only 340 cubic feet of carbon dioxide – only 0.034 percent.

What's more, the small quantity of carbon dioxide in the air is essential to life. Plants absorb carbon dioxide and convert it into their own tissues, which serve as the basic food supply for all of animal life (including human beings, of course). In the process, they liberate oxygen, which is also necessary for all animal life.

BODY

But here is what this apparently harmless and certainly essential gas is doing to us:

Analysis of problem/ Examples

The sea level is rising very slowly from year to year. The high tides tend to be progressively higher, even in quiet weather, and storms batter at breakwaters more and more effectively, erode the beaches more savagely, batter houses farther inland.

Possible future effects

In all likelihood, the sea level will continue to rise and do so at a greater rate in the course of the next hundred years. This means that the line separating ocean from land will retreat inland everywhere. It will do so only slightly where high land abuts the ocean. In those places, however, where there are low-lying coastal areas (where a large fraction of humanity lives) the water will advance steadily and inexorably and people will have to retreat inland.

Virtually all of Long Island will become part of the shallow offshore sea bottom, leaving only a

Additional examples of effects

line of small islands running east to west, marking off what had been the island's highest points. Eventually the sea will reach a maximum of two hundred feet above the present water level, and will be splashing against the windows along the twentieth floors of Manhattan's skyscrapers. Naturally the Manhattan streets will be deep under water, as will the New Jersey shoreline and all of Delaware. Florida, too, will be gone, as will much of the British Isles, the northwestern European coast, the crowded Nile valley, and the low-lying areas of China, India, and the Soviet Union.

It is not only that people will be forced to retreat by the millions and that many cities will be drowned, but much of the most productive farming areas of the world will be lost. Although the changes will not be overnight, and though people will have time to leave and carry with them such of their belongings as they can, there will not be room in the continental interiors for all of them.

As the food supply plummets with the ruin of farming areas, starvation will be rampant and the structure of society may collapse under the unbearable pressures.

And all because of carbon dioxide. But how does that come about? What is the connection?

Causes

It begins with sunlight, to which the various gases of the atmosphere (including carbon dioxide) are transparent. Sunlight, striking the top of the atmosphere, travels right through miles of it to reach the Earth's surface, where it is absorbed. In this way, the Earth is warmed.

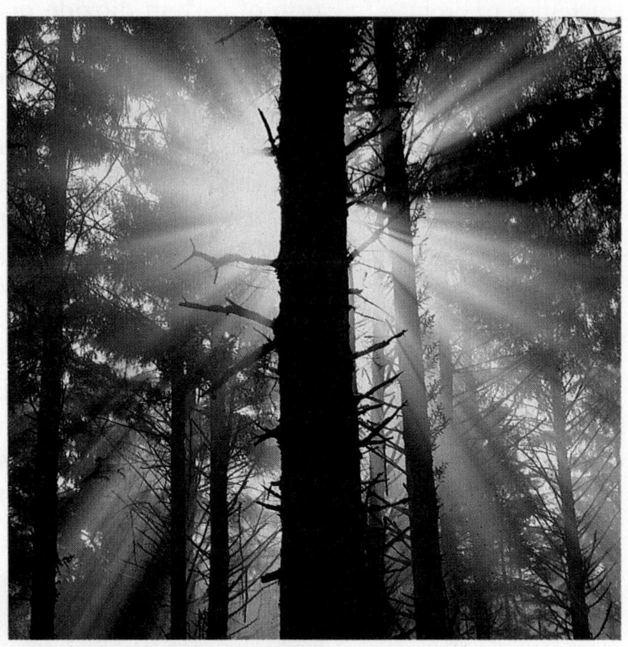

The Earth's surface doesn't get too hot, because at night the Earth's heat radiates into space in the form of infrared radiation. As the Earth gains heat by day and loses it by night, it maintains an overall temperature balance to which Earthly life is well-adapted.

Explanation of causes

However, the atmosphere is not quite as transparent to infrared radiation as it is to visible light. Carbon dioxide in particular tends to be opaque to that radiation. Less heat is lost at night, for that reason, than would be lost if carbon dioxide were not present in the atmosphere. Without the small quantity of that gas present, the Earth would be distinctly cooler on the whole, perhaps a bit uncomfortably cool.

This is called the "greenhouse effect" of carbon dioxide. It is so called because the glass of greenhouses lets sunshine in but prevents the loss of heat. For that reason it is warm inside a greenhouse on sunny days even when the temperature is low.

Explanation of problem/ Statistics

We can be thankful that carbon dioxide is keeping us comfortably warm, but the concentration of carbon dioxide in the atmosphere is going up steadily and that is where the villainy comes in. In 1958, when the carbon dioxide of the atmosphere first began to be measured carefully, it made up only 0.0316 percent of the atmosphere. Each year since, the concentration has crept upward and now it stands at 0.0340 percent. It is estimated that by 2020 the concentration will be about 0.0660 percent, or nearly twice what it is now.

Causes and effects

This means that in the coming decades, Earth's average temperature will go up slightly. Winters will grow a bit milder on the average and summers a bit hotter. That may not seem frightening. Milder winters don't seem bad, and as for hotter summers, we can just run our air-conditioners a bit more.

But consider this: If winters in general grow milder, less snow will fall during the cold season. If summers in general grow hotter, more snow will melt during the warm season. That means that, little by little, the snow line will move away from the equator and toward the poles. The glaciers will retreat, the mountain tops will grow more bare, and the polar ice caps will begin to melt.

Exploration of causes and effects

That might be annoying to skiers and to other devotees of winter sports, but would it necessarily bother the rest of us? After all, if the snow line moves north, it might be possible to grow more food in Canada, Scandinavia, the Soviet Union, and Patagonia.

Still, if the cold weather moves poleward, then so do the storm belts. The desert regions that now exist in subtropical areas will greatly expand, and fertile land gained in the north will be lost in the south. More may be lost than gained.

It is the melting of the ice caps, though, that is the worst change. It is this which demonstrates the villainy of carbon dioxide.

Something like 90 percent of the ice in the world is to be found in the huge Antarctica ice cap, and another 8 percent is in the Greenland ice cap.

In both places the ice is piled miles high. If these caps begin to melt, the water that forms won't stay in place. It will drip down into the ocean and slowly the sea level will rise, with the results that I have already described.

Even worse might be in store, for a rising temperature would manage to release a little of the carbon dioxide that is tied up in vast quantities of limestone that exist in the Earth's crust. It will also liberate some of the carbon dioxide dissolved in the ocean. With still more carbon dioxide, the temperature of the Earth will creep upward a little more and release still more carbon dioxide.

All this is called the "runaway greenhouse effect," and it may eventually make Earth an uninhabitable planet.

Clarification of problem

But, as you can see, it is not carbon dioxide in itself that is the source of the trouble; it is the fact that the carbon dioxide concentration in the atmosphere is steadily rising and seems to be doomed to continue rising. Why is that?

Causes

To blame are two factors. First of all, in the last few centuries, first coal, then oil and natural gas, have been burned for energy at a rapidly increasing rate. The carbon contained in these fuels, which has been safely buried underground for many millions of years, is now being burned to carbon dioxide and poured into the atmosphere at a rate of many tons per day.

Some of that additional carbon dioxide may be absorbed by the soil or by the ocean, and some might be consumed by plant life, but the fact is that a considerable fraction of it remains in the atmosphere. It must, for the carbon dioxide content of the atmosphere is going up year by year.

To make matters worse, Earth's forests have been disappearing, slowly at first, but in the last couple of centuries quite rapidly. Right now it is disappearing at the rate of sixty-four acres per minute.

Whatever replaces the forest – grasslands or farms or scrub – produces plants that do not consume carbon dioxide at a rate equal to that of forest. Thus, not only is more carbon dioxide being added to the atmosphere through the burning of fuel, but as the forests disappear, less carbon dioxide is being subtracted from the atmosphere by plants.

Final clarification of problem

But this gives us a new perspective on the matter. The carbon dioxide is not rising by itself. It is people who are burning the coal, oil, and gas, because of their need for energy. It is people who are cutting down the forests, because of their need for farmland. And the two are connected, for the burning of coal and oil is producing acid rain which helps destroy the forests. It is *people*, then, who are the villains.

What is to be done?

Solutions

First, we must save our forests, and even replant them. From forests, properly conserved, we get wood, chemicals, soil retention, ecological health—and a slowdown of carbon dioxide increase.

Second, we must have new sources of fuel. There are, after all, fuels that do not involve the production of carbon dioxide. Nuclear fission is one of them, and if that is deemed too dangerous for other reasons, there is the forthcoming nuclear fusion, which may be safer. There is also the energy of waves, tides, wind, and the Earth's interior heat. Most of all, there is the direct use of solar energy.

Comparative advantage

All of this will take time, work, and money, to be sure, but all that time, work, and money will be invested in order to save our civilization and our planet itself.

CONCLUSION

After all, humanity seems to be willing to spend *more* time, work, and money in order to support competing military machines that can only destroy us all. Should we begrudge *less* time, work, and money in order to save us all?

EXERCISE 2 **Analyzing a Problem-Solution Essay**

You've probably heard the term *greenhouse effect* before. But did you realize the seriousness of the problem? Read and review Isaac Asimov's essay, and then, meet with two or three classmates to discuss these questions.

1. What does Asimov do in his introduction to get his readers' attention?
2. Most of the essay is devoted to an analysis of the problem. Why do you think Asimov spends so much time explaining the problem and so comparatively little time explaining the solution? [Hint: This essay was written in 1968.]
3. One approach Asimov takes to analyze the problem is to discuss possible future effects of carbon dioxide in the atmosphere. What else does Asimov do to analyze the problem?
4. In his opening sentence, Asimov states that carbon dioxide is the "villain," or problem, but later in the essay he clarifies the problem further. According to Asimov, who or what is the real villain? Why do you think he waits so long to make this clarification?
5. What solutions does Asimov propose to the problem? What is the comparative advantage of those solutions?

A Framework for a Problem-Solution Essay

Asimov's essay is a little unusual in that most of it is devoted to the problem. Problem-solution essays may follow many different patterns. The following Writer's Model illustrates a basic pattern that you may want to follow in your own essay.

A WRITER'S MODEL

Our Children Can't Read

INTRODUCTION
Attention grabber

Is Brown County's population less intelligent than it used to be? When I first saw headlines such as "Reading Scores Decline Fifth Year in a Row" or "Study Shows Average Reading Scores Drop Five

Points in Ten Years," I was tempted to answer yes. These reading scores, so widely reported in the newspaper and on television, are based on reading tests given to third- and fifth-grade students. The scores are, in fact, falling. Our children do not read as well as children did ten years ago. But it is not because the children are less intelligent.

Statement of the problem

BODY

Analysis of the problem

What has caused this decline in reading abilities over the last ten years? Local elementary school teachers and administrators, as well as nationally recognized experts on the teaching of reading, say that the problem is not just in Brown County; it is a national one. Nor is it a problem with a single, clear-cut cause. Most educators agree that students are not as motivated to read as they once were, but the reasons for the lack of motivation are unclear.

Possible causes for lack of motivation

Some educators cite statistics on two-career families and single-parent families and suggest that parents just don't have as much time to read to their children as they used to. Others tell me that what has changed is our society's perception of the importance of reading. Television and other electronic entertainment and information services are grabbing the attention and time of adults and children alike. Still other educators say that the demographics of our society are changing. Fewer adults are literate, and as a result, there are fewer parents who can serve as role models by reading to their children.

Whatever the reason, it seems that children who don't see others read and who don't read themselves

aren't very likely to realize the value of reading. This does appear to be the case in Brown County. Interviews with 20 local elementary-school teachers indicate that many of Brown County's young children today are not very interested in learning to read. If a lack of role models and experience is partially responsible for our students' declining reading abilities,

Discussion of solutions

Practicality of solutions

Comparative advantage

then what are the solutions? In an ideal world with limitless funding, we can all think of many wonderful solutions. But budgets are tight and taxes already high here in Brown County, so the real question becomes "What solutions are possible within our existing institutions?" Fortunately, there seem to be several, relatively inexpensive remedies that might help solve the problem.

Solutions for lack of role models

To provide more models of readers for young children, all the Brown County schools could adopt the "book buddy" program. Ms. Gladow's third-grade class at Horne Elementary already participates in this program, and according to Ms. Gladow, it is one of her students' favorite activities. The program

Necessary steps

works like this: each kindergarten and first-grade class is paired with a fifth- or sixth-grade class. Then each younger child is paired with an older one. Once a week for thirty minutes, the two classes meet, and the "book buddies" spend time reading and talking about books of their own choice. This program gives the younger children additional reading role models, and it gives the older children an important sense of self-esteem as well.

Marginally literate and illiterate parents might also become reading role models for their children. Our library, which already sponsors a literacy

Program model

program, could expand its services to include an adult/child literacy program like one already operating in Indiana, Pennsylvania. According to a recent <u>School Library Journal</u> article, volunteer tutors in this program are trained to help parents

Necessary steps

learn to read with their children. Once a week, parents meet one-on-one with a tutor at the library and learn to read one easy-reading book. Then,

during the last fifteen minutes of class, each parent reads this book to his or her child or children.

Necessary steps

Many parents are too busy to read regularly for pleasure and so don't serve as role models for their children. Ms. Atkins, the reading specialist at Culvert Elementary, urges them to find other ways to be role models for reading. For example, she suggests that parents read recipes or directions aloud to children while fixing meals. Or, parents might read washing instruction tags aloud while sorting laundry.

Solutions for lack of experience

Children with more reading role models will also get more experience with reading. To create additional reading experiences, the library could modify and extend its services. For example, it could begin an outreach program for day-care facilities and providers. Rather than hold story hours only in the library, librarians could regularly visit day-care sites for story hours. In addition, the library could begin a special program for home day-care providers, creating specially prepared boxes of age-appropriate books for them to check out. Furthermore, if the library does begin the parent/child literacy program, the children of parents in the program could attend a story hour during the time their parents are being tutored.

Counter for possible objection

Experts may say that children who lack role models in reading and experience with reading also need extra instruction in reading skills. Teachers already provide this instruction, of course, but they often don't have the extra time that children with reading problems need. Using high school volunteers as tutors would solve that problem. High school students who have at least a C average could volunteer for thirty minutes each week, during their study hall or lunch period. Volunteer school-bus drivers would take the high school students to the elementary schools. A survey of two hundred high school students indicates that 80 percent of them would volunteer. And most of the elementary school teachers are enthusiastic about the prospect of more volunteers.

Statistic

CONCLUSION

The solutions aren't drastic. Adopt a "book buddy" program. Set up an adult/child literacy program. Create a library outreach program. Create a high school volunteer-tutor program. These programs cost almost nothing and ask of us only our time. Will they work? The children of this country are its most precious resource. Programs such as these might help us preserve that resource.

WRITING NOTE

Your facts and ideas will carry more weight with your readers if they know your information comes from reliable sources. Notice that "Our Children Can't Read" credits its information informally by naming sources within the paper. You might also use parenthetical citations and a list of Works Cited. Either method is acceptable as long as you acknowledge your sources. (For more help with crediting sources, see Chapter 11, Writing a Research Paper.)

Here is a framework you might use to develop your essay. "Our Children Can't Read" follows this framework.

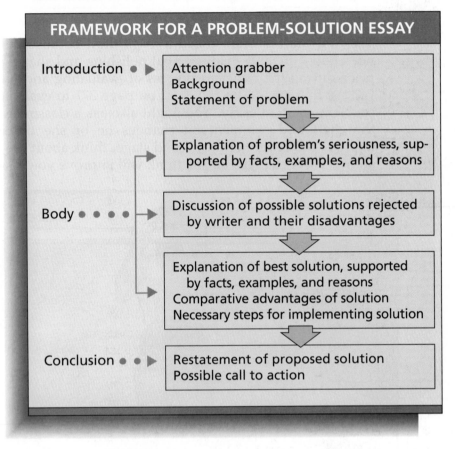

FRAMEWORK FOR A PROBLEM-SOLUTION ESSAY

Introduction	Attention grabber Background Statement of problem
Body	Explanation of problem's seriousness, supported by facts, examples, and reasons
	Discussion of possible solutions rejected by writer and their disadvantages
	Explanation of best solution, supported by facts, examples, and reasons Comparative advantages of solution Necessary steps for implementing solution
Conclusion	Restatement of proposed solution Possible call to action

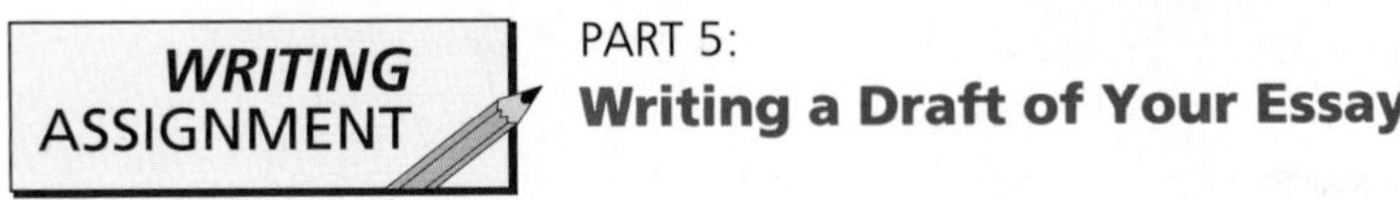

PART 5:
Writing a Draft of Your Essay

You have given some thought to planning your essay (in your work for Writing Assignment, Part 4, page 361). Now put your thoughts down on paper, using the framework above as a guide in writing your first draft. As you write, keep your readers in mind. Think about how you can best explain and prove to them that the problem is serious and that your proposed solution is both good and workable. Then, if possible, let your draft sit for a day or two before moving to the evaluating and revising stage.

Evaluating and Revising

The first draft is often called a *rough* draft because the ideas need polishing and shaping. That polishing and shaping takes place during the two-step process of evaluating and revising. For the first stage, use the chart on page 377 to evaluate your problem-solution essay. You might also ask a classmate to use the chart and comment on changes he or she thinks will improve the draft. For the second stage, think about the evaluations: What changes do *you* think will improve your essay?

Drawing by Dan Krovatin.

You can use the following chart to evaluate and revise your problem-solution essay. Begin by asking yourself each question in the left-hand column. If the answer is no, then use the revision technique suggested in the right-hand column.

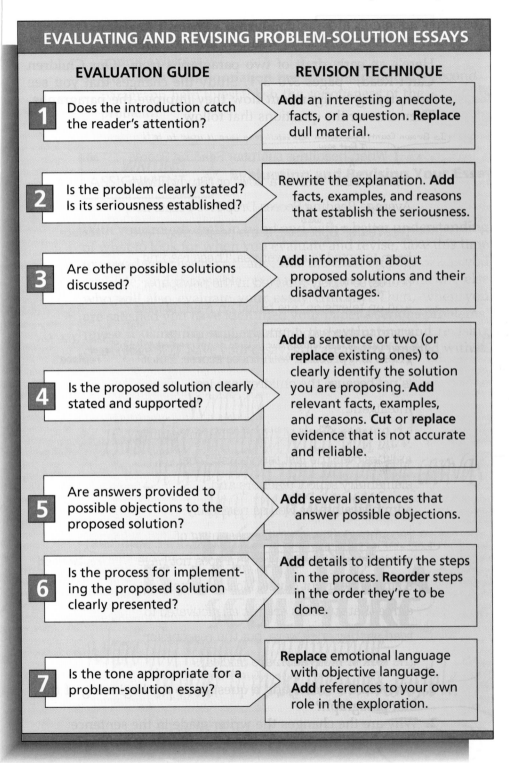

EVALUATING AND REVISING PROBLEM-SOLUTION ESSAYS

EVALUATION GUIDE	REVISION TECHNIQUE
1 Does the introduction catch the reader's attention?	**Add** an interesting anecdote, facts, or a question. **Replace** dull material.
2 Is the problem clearly stated? Is its seriousness established?	Rewrite the explanation. **Add** facts, examples, and reasons that establish the seriousness.
3 Are other possible solutions discussed?	**Add** information about proposed solutions and their disadvantages.
4 Is the proposed solution clearly stated and supported?	**Add** a sentence or two (or **replace** existing ones) to clearly identify the solution you are proposing. **Add** relevant facts, examples, and reasons. **Cut** or **replace** evidence that is not accurate and reliable.
5 Are answers provided to possible objections to the proposed solution?	**Add** several sentences that answer possible objections.
6 Is the process for implementing the proposed solution clearly presented?	**Add** details to identify the steps in the process. **Reorder** steps in the order they're to be done.
7 Is the tone appropriate for a problem-solution essay?	**Replace** emotional language with objective language. **Add** references to your own role in the exploration.

Proofreading and Publishing

Proofreading. After you have worked hard on a paper, it would be a shame if your audience failed to appreciate your effort because of minor errors. What if they decide, fairly or unfairly, that you can't know much about the problem you have explored because you have misspelled words or made mistakes in subject-verb agreement? That's why it is always important to take the time to give your essay a shine and polish.

Publishing. Solutions to problems do no good if no one knows about them. There are many ways to share a problem-solution essay with an audience, but here are two ideas you might try with your own paper.

- Use the desktop publishing features of a personal computer to create a broadside sheet (a sheet of paper printed on one or both sides and folded for distribution) from your essay. Distribute the broadside to people affected by the problem.
- Present your essay as an oral proposal before a group that has the power to solve the problem. Or, present it as a proposal before your classmates. Can you get them concerned about the problem?

MECHANICS HINT

Punctuating Subordinate Clauses

When explaining problems and their solutions, you need to make relationships between ideas clear. You may want to show, for example, that a problem has certain causes or that a solution has certain effects. You can do this by using subordinate clauses that begin with conjunctions such as *because, if, after, as long as, since, while.* Set off an introductory subordinate clause with a comma.

EXAMPLES **If** a lack of role models and experience is partially responsible for our students' declining reading abilities, then what are the solutions?

As long as children have models of readers and experience with reading, they will likely be interested in learning to read.

But it is not **because** the children are less intelligent.

 REFERENCE NOTE: For more information on punctuating introductory subordinate clauses, see page 913.

PART 7:

Proofreading and Publishing Your Essay

After carefully proofreading your essay and correcting any errors, make arrangements to share it with an audience.

WRITING WORKSHOP

Personal Exploration

In the main writing assignment for this chapter, you wrote a problem-solution essay. A suitable topic for this type of essay is a problem that affects a number of people. Exploring the problem and its possible solutions often leads you on an outward exploration: to books or articles or videotapes or to other people for their information and ideas. In contrast, a personal exploration requires an *inward* investigation into your own experiences, thoughts, and feelings.

In the following piece, Ralph Ellison explores an experience that brings him face to face with a personal dilemma. What does he discover about himself in his exploration?

from An Extravagance of Laughter

by Ralph Ellison

But for all their noise and tension, it was not the subways that most intrigued me. For although a pleasant way to explore the city, my rides in New York buses soon aroused questions about matters that I had hoped to leave behind. And yet the very fact that I encountered little on Northern buses that was distressing allowed me to face up to a problem which had puzzled me down South: the relationship between Southern buses and racial status. In the South you occupied the back of the bus, and nowhere *but* the back, or so help you God. So being in the North and encouraged by my anonymity, I experimented by riding *all* over New York buses, excluding only the driver's seat—front end, back end, right side, left side, sitting or standing as the route and flow of passengers demanded. *And,* since those were the glorious days of double-deckers, both enclosed and opened, I even rode *top*side.

Thus having convinced myself that no questions of racial status would be raised by where I chose to ride, I asked myself whether a seat at the back of the bus wasn't actually more desirable than one at the front. For not only did it provide more leg room, it offered a more inclusive perspective on both the interior and exterior scenes. I found the answer obvious and quite amusing, but then, as though to raise to consciousness more serious questions that I had too long ignored, the buses forced a more troubling contradiction upon my attention. Now that I was no longer forced by law and compelled by custom to ride at the back and to surrender my seat to any white who demanded it, what was more desirable—the possibility of exercising what was routinely accepted in the North as an abstract, highly symbolic (even trivial) form of democratic freedom, or the creature comfort which was to be had by occupying a spot from which more of the passing scene could be observed? And in my own personal terms, what was more important—my own individual comfort, or the exercise of the democratic right to be squeezed and jostled by strangers? The highly questionable privilege of being touched by anonymous whites—not to mention reds, browns, blacks, and yellows—or the minor pleasure afforded by having a maximum of breathing space? Such questions were akin to whether you lived in a Negro neighborhood because you were forced to do so, or because you preferred living among those of your own background. Which was easy to answer, because having experienced life in mixed neighborhoods as a child, I preferred to live where people spoke my own version of the American language, and where misreadings of tone or gesture were less likely to ignite lethal conflict.

1. Why do you think it is important to Ellison that he have the experience of riding in different places on the buses?
2. What problem, or question, does Ellison's freedom on the buses allow him to explore?
3. In what ways does Ellison suggest that, in the future, he will sit in the rear, rather than the front, of the buses?
4. Often, personal expressions are private; the writer does not intend to share what he or she discovers. Although Ralph Ellison's exploration is personal, in what way(s) does it also speak to you as a reader?

Writing About Self-Exploration

Prewriting. In the preceding excerpt, Ralph Ellison explores an issue that has become personal for him: What is more important, being comfortable or exercising a symbolic form of freedom? He is concerned with his own responses, his own reactions, rather than those of any larger group of people.

For your personal exploration, look for an issue or problem that affects you in a personal way, and one in which you are not sure of your response. For example, you know that college tuition is rising and low-cost loans are getting harder to find, but how are you going to respond to that problem? Or, if you and your best friend are vying for the same position on the baseball team or the same scholarship, how will you handle this problem? How will the competition affect you?

Writing, Evaluating, and Revising. Begin with a specific experience that highlights the issue or problem you will be exploring—talking to the bank about school loans, talking to the coach about positions on the baseball team. Then begin the exploration of the problem, what it means to you, and how you think you will respond. What, for example, will you do if you can't get a college loan? What will you do if your best friend wins and you lose?

If you feel comfortable doing so, have others read your draft. Ask them to summarize in their own words what your chosen problem or issue seems to mean to you. If their impression is different from the one you wish to create, revise your draft to make the meaning clearer. If your draft is too personal to share, put it aside. In a few years, you might enjoy looking back on this important part of yourself.

Proofreading and Publishing. If you intend to share your writing, check for and correct any errors. You may want to publish your work by sharing it with your family, friends, or a trusted adult. Put your essay aside in a safe place where you can find and reread it as the years go by.

"Your vision will become clear only when you can look into your own heart.... Who looks outside, dreams; who looks inside, awakes."

Carl Jung

MAKING CONNECTIONS

SPEAKING AND LISTENING

People in all fields explore problems and look for solutions:

- A roofer investigates a leaking roof and asks, "What's causing the leak? How can it be fixed?"
- A nurse has a patient with a high fever and asks, "What is causing the fever? How can this patient be stabilized?"
- A computer programmer who must make a program more user-friendly asks, "What applications were hard to access? How can procedures be simplified?"

In general, the methods that people in different fields use in their explorations are similar to the methods you used in this chapter, but their specific approaches may vary. You might find it interesting to learn how some of these people approach problem solving. Why not interview people in different fields of work and find out? Begin by asking these two questions:

1. What are some examples of problems that people in your field attempt to solve?
2. How do you approach solving these problems? (Do you look at different solutions? How do you decide which is the best solution? How do you get others to accept that solution?)

You and your classmates might enjoy sharing the information you gather. What similarities and differences do you notice in the problem-solving techniques you've heard about?

PROBLEM SOLVING ACROSS THE CURRICULUM

Literature

Problems and solutions have a central role in much of the literature you read. Without a problem (or conflict), you wouldn't have a very interesting plot in a story, novel, or play. What would *Romeo and Juliet* be without the long-standing Capulet-Montague family feud? What would *The Odyssey* be without Odysseus's dilemma involving Scylla and Charybdis? And solutions are often part of the resolution of the work. For example, after their children's deaths, the lords Capulet and Montague finally agree to peace, and Odysseus chooses to "hug Scylla's rock."

Kirk Douglas (below) in *Ulysses* (1954); Leonard Whiting and Olivia Hussey (right) in *Romeo and Juliet* (1968).

Working with one or two classmates, choose a work of fiction, a play, or a film, and analyze its problem-solution structure. Answer these questions about the work:

1. What character or characters are experiencing a problem?
2. What is the problem? Describe it as precisely as you can.
3. Does the character (or do the characters) consider different solutions to the problem? What are the solutions?
4. What is the final solution to the problem?
5. Do you think this is the best solution? Why or why not?

Present your answers in class, and compare your ideas with those of your classmates.

10 WRITING ABOUT LITERATURE

Reading and Responding

Have you ever laughed at the words in a comic strip? ever gotten angry at the words in an editorial? Whenever you are **reading,** you are also **responding**—with pleasure, annoyance, anger, boredom, or in some other way. In a similar way, you respond to music, to movies, to everything you see and hear.

Writing and You. Sometimes, you move beyond a personal response to writing critically about a work. You look at the parts of the work—the book, poem, or play—to understand how it is put together and what it means. In the same way, a film reviewer analyzes a movie—the script, the acting, the direction—and writes a review of the movie. Has a movie (or book, play, concert) review ever helped to shape your opinion?

As You Read. The following review of the movie *Hamlet,* with Mel Gibson, focuses on the acting. After reading the review, would you want to see the movie?

Bruce McGaw, *Books* (1958). Oil on canvas, 11 1/16″ × 13 5/8″. Courtesy of The Delman Collection, San Francisco.

A review of Mel Gibson's Hamlet

He did it

by Amy Taubin

It may not be called *Mel Gibson Plays Hamlet,* but really, why would anyone go except to find out if "Mel" can pull it off. So it's a little like giving the plot away to say, yes he does, and very nicely too. Never less than forthright and well-spoken, Gibson's performance, once it gets going, is also witty, intelligent, and full of emotional surprises. Of the 30-odd Hamlets I've seen, his is certainly the most straight-talking. Gibson respects the verse without letting it overwhelm him; he has a way of making familiar lines sound not only spontaneous but effortlessly clear.

"Never less than forthright and well-spoken, Gibson's performance, once it gets going, is also witty, intelligent, and full of emotional surprises."

No less admirable is the fact that Gibson refuses to rely on his glamour to get him through. This Hamlet is unremarkable physically: short, plain-faced, and pale-eyed. At a certain point, one even begins to wish that his body were more expressive—but the fault lies less with the actor than with his director, Franco Zeffirelli.

Zeffirelli's overriding goal seems to involve cramming as many lines as possible into two hours. No one, including the star, is allowed on camera unless his/her lips are moving. The only exceptions take place in the scenes that Zeffirelli *adds* to the play—the funeral of Hamlet's father, the execution of Rosencrantz and Guildenstern—in some sort of desperate attempt at creativity. These are played in total silence—dumb, as it were.

If Zeffirelli has any concept of the play itself, it's not evident on the screen. For some inexplicable reason—perhaps it's cold in this medieval castle—the actors are constantly on the move. With the exception of Paul Scofield's fiercely exhausted Ghost and Stephan Dillane's ganglingly innocent Horatio, the other supporting roles are given short shrift by actors who are variously miscast, incompetent, or not bothering. In the last category are Ian Holm's Polonius and Alan Bates' smarmy but lethargic Claudius.

As for Glenn Close, her Gertrude is brittle, girlishly coy, and well-bred—i.e., a disaster. Without a Gertrude who's doting and sexually desirous, the familial intrigue makes

". . . Paul Scofield's fiercely exhausted Ghost . . ."

"As for Glenn Close, her Gertrude is brittle, girlishly coy, and well-bred—i.e., a disaster."

absolutely no sense. And since Zeffirelli has stripped the text of its political content (if something is rotten in Denmark, its citizens don't seem to have noticed), it's hard to figure out what the fuss is about. Gibson, potentially, is Hamlet as undercover cop, feigning madness in order to gather evidence against his father's murderer. But since the performance happens in a vacuum, it never quite adds up.

If you have any doubts about why he did it, Shakespeare provides Gibson with several unique opportunities; not only does he speak in verse, he also dies.

The Village Voice

Reader's Response

1. If you have seen this movie, tell why you agree or disagree with the reviewer. If you haven't seen it, explain how you responded to another Shakespearean play or movie.
2. Suppose you have always disliked Shakespeare. Then you read this review. Would you go to see this movie? Why?

Writer's Craft

3. Whose performance does Taubin like best in the movie *Hamlet*? What reasons does she give to support her opinion?
4. Whose performance does Taubin like least? What reasons does she give to support that opinion?
5. Do you think the reviewer backs up her opinions with enough evidence? Give some examples to support your answer.

"Gibson, potentially, is Hamlet as undercover cop, feigning madness in order to gather evidence against his father's murderer."

Purposes for Writing About Literature

The title of Taubin's review, "He Did It," shows that her purpose is partly informative, telling readers that Mel Gibson succeeds in his performance as Hamlet. But her purpose may also be partly persuasive—she's attempting to persuade you to accept her opinion of the film.

Here are examples of the four basic purposes you might have when writing about literature or one of the other arts.

Self-Expressive: freewriting in your journal about a poem you especially like; writing to a friend about the way you wish a new novel had ended.

Informative: writing an analysis of Joseph Conrad's style as demonstrated in *The Secret Sharer;* writing an essay comparing ancient Japanese and Chinese poetry.

Persuasive: writing the author of a popular book to protest his or her portrayal of female characters; writing a review of the latest novel by Gabriel García Márquez for the library newsletter to persuade other students to read it.

Literary: writing a dialogue between you and a character in your favorite romance or science fiction story; writing a new ending to a play.

LOOKING AHEAD

In this chapter, your main writing assignment will be a critical, or literary, analysis. Your purpose in writing this analysis will be to inform and to explain. As you work through the chapter, keep in mind that an effective critical analysis

- starts with a careful reading of the work
- identifies the writer's main idea, or thesis, about the work
- uses examples from the work to support, or prove, the main idea

Writing a Critical Analysis

Reading and Responding to Literature

Your first reaction to what you have read is usually a personal response; perhaps you are puzzled by part of a poem, or you know you would like to read a story again. Your next reaction may be a feeling that you need, or want, to study the literature more critically and thoughtfully.

Starting with Personal Response

Maybe you are crazy about football games and reggae music and don't understand why your best friend prefers hockey and rap. It's the same with literature; people respond differently to everything they read. There is no right or wrong to personal response—it's as unique as you are.

To discover your own response, you need to become aware of your reactions, of the way a work of literature is affecting you. Any of the following strategies will help you identify your reactions or feelings about a piece of literature and respond to it.

STRATEGIES FOR RESPONDING TO LITERATURE

1. Freewrite in a journal about characters, ideas, and scenes that relate to your own experiences, knowledge, or memories.
2. Picture scenes in your mind. If you think in pictures rather than words, draw what the author describes.
3. Talk about your response with others who read the same work, discussing what you liked and disliked.
4. Respond creatively. Write a new ending to the work, or tell what happens to a character years later. Change the genre—make a poem into a short story, a play into a poem, and so on. Change the time and place—for example, rewrite a Renaissance poem as a modern poem.

The following short story was written by Nadine Gordimer, a South African who won the 1991 Nobel Prize for literature. As you read the story, be aware of your personal response. Does the main character's experience remind you of any experience in your own life or the life of someone you know?

A SHORT STORY

The Soft Voice of the Serpent

by Nadine Gordimer

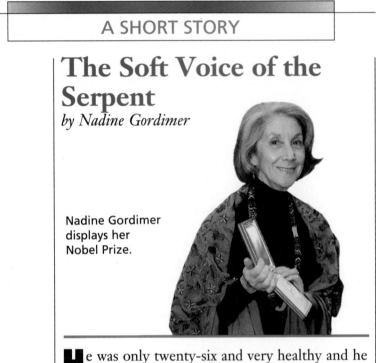

Nadine Gordimer displays her Nobel Prize.

He was only twenty-six and very healthy and he was soon strong enough to be wheeled out into the garden. Like everyone else, he had great and curious faith in the garden: "Well, soon you'll be up and able to sit out in the garden," they said, looking at him fervently, with little understanding tilts of the head. Yes, he would be out . . . in the garden. It was a big garden enclosed in old dark, sleek, pungent firs, and he could sit deep beneath their tiered fringes, down in the shade, far away. There was the feeling that there, in the garden, he would come to an understanding; that it would come easier, there. Perhaps there was something in this of the old Eden idea; the tender human adjusting himself to himself in the soothing impersonal presence of trees and grass and earth, before going out into the stare of the world.

The very first time it was so strange; his wife was wheeling him along the gravel path in the sun and the shade, and he felt exactly as he did when he was a little boy and he used to bend and hang, looking at the world upside down, through his ankles. Everything was vast and open, the sky, the wind blowing along through the swaying, trembling greens, the flowers shaking in vehement denial. Movement . . .

A first slight wind lifted again in the slack, furled sail of himself; he felt it belly gently, so gently he could just feel it, lifting inside him.

So she wheeled him along, pushing hard and not particularly well with her thin pretty arms — but he would not for anything complain of the way she did it or suggest that the nurse might do better, for he knew that would hurt her — and when they came to a spot that he liked, she put the brake on the chair and settled him there for the morning. That was the first time and now he sat there every day. He read a lot, but his attention was arrested sometimes, quite suddenly and compellingly, by the sunken place under the rug where his leg used to be. There was his one leg, and next to it, the rug flapped loose. Then looking, he felt his leg not there; he felt it go, slowly, from the toe to the thigh. He felt that he had no leg. After a few minutes he went back to his book. He never let the realization quite reach him; he let himself realize it physically, but he never quite let it get at *him.* He felt it pressing up, coming, coming, dark, crushing, ready to burst — but he always turned away, just in time, back to his book. That was his system; that was the way he was going to do it. He would let it come near, irresistibly near, again and again, ready to catch him alone in the garden. And again and again he would turn it back, just in time. Slowly it would become a habit, with the reassuring strength of a habit. It would become such a habit never to get to the point of realizing it, *that he never would realize it.* And one day he would find that he had achieved what he wanted: *he would feel as if he had always been like that.*

Then the danger would be over, for ever.

In a week or two he did not have to read all the time; he could let himself put down the book and look about him, watching the firs part silkily as a child's fine straight hair in the wind, watching the small birds tightroping the telephone wire, watching the fat old dove trotting after his refined patrician grey women, purring with lust. His wife came and sat beside him, doing her sewing, and sometimes they spoke, but often they sat for hours, a whole morning, her movements at work small and unobtrusive as the birds', he resting his head back and looking at a blur of sky through half closed eyes. Now and then her eye, habitually looking inwards, would catch the signal of some little happening, some point of colour in the garden, and her laugh or exclamation drawing his attention to it would suddenly clear away the silence. At eleven o'clock she would get up and put down her sewing and go into the house to fetch their tea; crunching slowly away into the sun up the path, going easily, empowered by the sun rather than her own muscles. He watched her go, easily . . . He was healing. In the static quality of his gaze, in the relaxed feeling of his mouth, in the upward-lying palm of his hand, there was annealment . . .

One day a big locust whirred dryly past her head, and she jumped up with a cry, scattering her sewing things. He laughed at her as she bent about picking them up, shuddering. She went into the house to fetch the tea, and he began to read. But presently he put down the book and, yawning, noticed a reel of pink cotton that she had missed, lying in a rose bed.

He smiled, remembering her. And then he became conscious of a curious old mannish little face, fixed upon him in a kind of hypnotic dread. There, absolutely stilled with fear beneath his glance, crouched a very big locust. What an amusing face the thing had! A lugubrious long face, that somehow suggested a bald head, and such a glum mouth. It looked like some little person out of a Disney cartoon. It moved slightly, still looking up fearfully at him. Strange body, encased in a sort of old-fashioned creaky armour. He had never realized before what ridiculous-looking insects locusts were! Well, naturally not; they occur to one collectively, as a pest—one doesn't go around looking at their faces.

The face was certainly curiously human and even expressive, but looking at the body, he decided that the body couldn't really be called a body at all. With the face, the creature's kinship with humans ended. The body was flimsy paper stretched over a frame of matchstick, like a small boy's homemade aeroplane. And those could not be thought of as legs — the great saw-toothed back ones were like the parts of an old crane, and the front ones like — like one of her hairpins, bent in two. At that moment the creature slowly lifted up one of the front legs, and passed it tremblingly over its head, stroking the left antenna down. Just as a man might take out a handkerchief and pass it over his brow.

He began to feel enormously interested in the creature, and leaned over in his chair to see it more closely. It sensed him and beneath its stiff, plated sides, he was surprised to see the pulsations of a heart. How fast it was breathing . . . He leaned away a little, to frighten it less.

Watching it carefully, and trying to keep himself effaced from its consciousness by not moving, he became aware of some struggle going on in the thing. It seemed to gather itself together in muscular concentration: this co-ordinated force then passed along its body in a kind of petering tremor, and ended in a stirring along the upward shaft of the great back legs. But the locust remained where it was. Several times this wave of effort currented through it and was spent, but the next time it ended surprisingly in a few hobbling, uneven steps, undercarriage — aeroplanelike again — trailing along the earth.

Then the creature lay, fallen on its side, antennae turned stretched out towards him. It groped with its feet, feeling for a hold on the soft ground, bending its joints and straining. With a heave, it righted itself, and as it did so, he saw — leaning forward again — what was the trouble. It was the same trouble. His own trouble. The creature had lost one leg. Only the long upward shaft of its left leg remained, with a neat round aperture where, no doubt, the other half of the leg had been attached.

Now as he watched the locust gather itself again and again in that concentration of muscle, spend itself again and again in a message that was so puzzlingly never obeyed, he knew exactly what the creature felt. Of course he knew that feeling! That absolute certainty that the leg was there: one had only to lift it . . . The upward shaft of the locust's leg quivered, lifted; why then couldn't he walk? He tried again. The message came; it was going through, the leg was lifting, now it was ready – now! . . . The shaft sagged in the air, with nothing, nothing to hold it up.

He laughed and shook his head: He *knew* . . . Good Lord, *exactly* like – He called out to the house – "Come quickly! Come and see! You've got another patient!"

"What?" she shouted. "I'm getting tea."

"Come and look!" he called. "Now!"

". . . What is it?" she said, approaching the locust distastefully.

"Your locust!" he said. She jumped away with a little shriek.

"Don't worry – it can't move. It's as harmless as I am. You must have knocked its leg off when you hit out at it!" He was laughing at her.

"Oh, I didn't!" she said reproachfully. She loathed it but she loathed to hurt, even more. "I never even touched it! All I hit was air . . . I couldn't possibly have hit it. Not its leg off."

"All right then. It's another locust. But it's lost its leg, anyway. You should just see it . . . It doesn't know the leg isn't there. God, I know exactly how that feels . . . I've been watching it, and honestly, it's uncanny. I can see it feels just like I do!"

She smiled at him, sideways; she seemed suddenly pleased at something. Then, recalling herself, she came forward, bent double, hands upon her hips.

"Well, if it can't move . . ." she said, hanging over it.

"Don't be frightened," he laughed. "Touch it."

"Ah, the poor thing," she said, catching her breath in compassion. "It can't walk."

"Don't encourage it to self-pity," he teased her.

She looked up and laughed. "Oh you – " she parried, assuming a frown. The locust kept its solemn silly face turned to her. "Shame, isn't he a funny old man," she said. "But what will happen to him?"

"I don't know," he said, for being in the same boat absolved him from responsibility or pity. "Maybe he'll grow another one. Lizards grow new tails, if they lose them."

"Oh, *lizards,*" she said. " – But not these. I'm afraid the cat'll get him."

"Get another little chair made for him and you can wheel him out here with me."

"Yes," she laughed. "Only for him it would have to be a kind of little cart, with wheels."

"Or maybe he could be taught to use crutches. I'm sure the farmers would like to know that he was being kept active."

"The poor old thing," she said, bending over the locust again. And reaching back somewhere into an inquisitive childhood she picked up a thin wand of twig and prodded the locust, very gently. "Funny thing is, it's even the same leg, the left one." She looked round at him and smiled.

"I know," he nodded, laughing. "The two of us . . ." And then he shook his head and, smiling, said it again: "The two of us."

She was laughing and just then she flicked the twig more sharply than she meant to and at the touch of it there was a sudden flurried papery whirr, and the locust flew away.

ELEMENTS OF POETRY *(continued)*	
Symbol—a person, place, thing, or event that has meaning in itself but that also stands for something else	What person, place, thing, or event seems to stand for something else? How do the symbols relate to the meaning of the poem? Does the title suggest a symbol?
Theme—an underlying idea or insight that the poem reveals about life and people	Does the poem examine any common problem or life experience? What message, or theme, does the poem suggest?

ELEMENTS OF FICTION	
Character—a person (sometimes an animal or thing) in a story or novel	What is the contribution of the characters to the development of the plot? How does the main character change during the story, and what does this change have to do with the theme? What do the characters' physical descriptions or the way they talk, act, or think suggest about their motivations and personifications?
Point of view—the perspective or vantage point from which a story is told	Does the story have a first-person or third-person (omniscient or limited) narrator? Through whose eyes do you see the events in the story? How much does the narrator know? What does the choice of narrator add to the theme or meaning of the story? How does it affect characterization?

(continued)

ELEMENTS OF FICTION *(continued)*	
Plot—the events that follow each other and cause other events to happen	Is the plot predictable, or are there surprises along the way? What is the central problem, or ***conflict,*** of the story? How does the outcome of the story relate to *theme,* or meaning?
Setting—the time and place of the story	How do the time and place contribute to the plot and theme of the story? What details help you imagine the setting? Does the setting suggest a tone or mood?
Theme—an underlying principle, idea, or insight that the work reveals about life and people	Does the work reveal a lesson or insight about life? Who learns this lesson? What passages provide the clearest expression of the theme? To what extent does the theme seem "universal"?

Using Critical Reading Strategies. One part of reading literature critically is knowing what to look for—the elements you have just read about. A second part of reading critically is knowing which strategies to use in order to read carefully and thoughtfully. You can use the following strategies along with your knowledge of literary elements to develop a good critical reading of a story or poem.

STRATEGIES FOR READING CRITICALLY

1. After you have read the story or poem once, go back and read it again. Each time you read it, you'll find something new.
2. Carry on a dialogue with the author by making notes to yourself as you read. Make a copy of the story or poem for yourself so you can mark it up or use self-sticking note papers to mark important details.

(continued)

STRATEGIES FOR READING CRITICALLY ***(continued)***

3. Jot down notes about the elements in the work and underline or circle phrases or sentences that answer the questions in the elements charts (pages 403–405).
4. Look carefully at the title. Often it's like a piece of a puzzle: The words are a clue to the theme of the story.
5. Talk about the work with others who have read it. Exchange ideas and compare your understanding of the story with theirs. You don't have to agree with other people's interpretations, but you should be able to back up your ideas with quotations and other evidence from the story.

Here are critical reading notes that one writer made while reading the first part of "The Soft Voice of the Serpent." Notice how the writer carries on a dialogue with the author of the story.

He was only twenty-six and very healthy and he was soon strong enough	*What's wrong with him?*
to be wheeled out into the garden. Like everyone else, he had great and curious faith in the garden:	*Third-person limited point of view.*
"Well, soon you'll be up and able to sit out in the garden," they said, looking at him fervently, with little understanding tilts of the head.	*Is the garden a symbol? What could it stand for?*
Yes, he would be out . . . in the garden. It was a big garden enclosed in old dark, sleek, pungent firs, and he could sit deep beneath their tiered fringes, down in the shade, far away.	*Irony—"out . . . in the garden" he's not facing the world. Garden stands for safety, being protected from life?*
There was the feeling that there, in the garden, he would come to an understanding; that it would come easier, there. Perhaps there was something in this of the old Eden idea;	*What understanding? Related to the theme? Eden—could the serpent in the title be like the snake in Eden?*
the tender human adjusting himself to himself in the soothing impersonal presence of trees and grass and earth, before going out into the stare of the world.	*The world sounds mean, very different from life in the garden.*

CRITICAL THINKING

Analyzing the Elements of a Story

Analyzing is a critical thinking skill that involves a careful study of a subject to see what it is like. It usually requires a study of the parts or pieces that make up the whole.

That's why the essay you are writing in this chapter is called a ***literary analysis;*** it involves a careful study of a work of literature. If you were analyzing your school, you might look at these parts: teachers, students, classrooms, instructional materials, and so on. The parts of a piece of literature are its basic elements, the ones in the charts on pages 403–405.

CRITICAL THINKING EXERCISE:

Analyzing a Story

In Exercise 1 you shared your personal responses to "The Soft Voice of the Serpent." Now practice the critical thinking skill of analysis by rereading the story and using the following questions to analyze its elements. You can also use the questions in the chart on pages 404–405 to analyze the story. After you have finished your analysis, get together with a small group and discuss your analyses.

1. How does the main character change during the story? What does this change have to do with the meaning of the story?
2. What is the point of view of the narrator? How does the choice of narrator affect the story?
3. What is the central conflict of the story? How does the outcome of the conflict relate to the meaning of the story?
4. How does the setting affect the plot and theme of the story?
5. What is the theme of the story? How does it apply to people other than the man in the garden?

PART 1: Responding and Reading Critically

Before you write a literary analysis of a story, you need to find a story you can work with. Browse through a literature anthology or short story collection to find a story that meets these criteria: (1) you won't mind reading it several times and (2) it appears to be well written and worth the time it will take to analyze it. After reading the story the first time, use one of the strategies for responding to literature on page 394. Then read the story critically, asking yourself the questions on the elements of fiction chart (pages 404–405). Jot down notes about your answers to the questions.

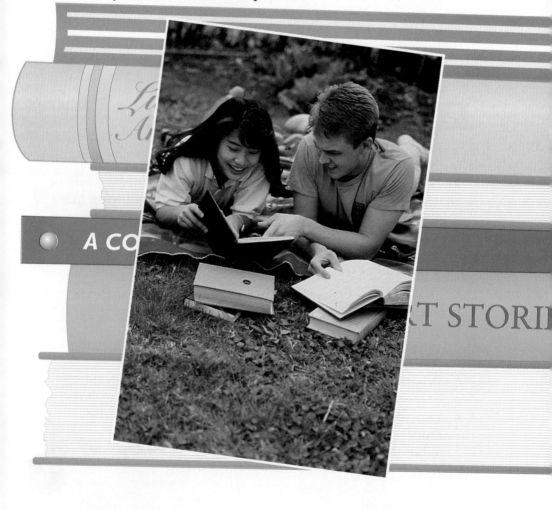

Planning Your Critical Analysis

You could begin by writing down everything you know about your story, but your critical analysis will be more effective if you give some thought to planning. Think about why you are writing, who you are writing for, and what your main idea will be.

Thinking About Purpose, Audience, and Tone

When you write a critical analysis, your *purpose* is to write exposition—to explain the meaning of the work and to convince readers that your explanation is sound. Think about your *audience* as you plan your analysis. It's important to give readers enough information to understand your ideas about the story, without giving them information they already know.

The *tone* of a critical analysis is usually more formal than the reviews you might read in a newspaper or magazine. Try to avoid using first-person pronouns such as *I* and *we,* contractions, and colloquial expressions (such as "the *kids* in the story"). Focus on being objective and serious.

Finding a Focus for Your Analysis

In a short essay, it would be difficult to analyze all the elements of a story, so you should focus on the elements that seem the strongest. It is often useful to start with the theme of the story, because the theme is the key to the meaning of any literary work. Then you can add a discussion of other elements as they contribute to the development of theme. For example, you might

- analyze the role of plot and characters in developing the theme
- analyze how a particular point of view helps to bring out the theme
- analyze how setting or mood controls the plot and helps to develop the theme

PEANUTS reprinted by permission of UFS, Inc.

Developing Your Thesis Statement

A critical analysis, like other essays, has a main idea, or ***thesis,*** that is usually stated in one or two sentences—the ***thesis statement.*** The thesis statement that you write now will be a preliminary guide to your thinking and writing. As you collect evidence and draft your essay, you may find that your preliminary thesis statement is either too broad or too narrow; and if that happens, you will revise it.

The first step in developing a thesis (and a thesis statement) is to decide which elements you want to focus on in your critical analysis. The second step is to decide how those elements relate to the theme of the story and write a statement that summarizes this "interpretation." Here are some examples of thesis statements.

- In Julia Alvarez' story "Daughter of Invention," the theme—that old ways must give into new American ways—is brought out most clearly in the character of the mother, who changes dramatically. [focus on theme and character]
- The theme of Alice Walker's story "Everyday Use" is how people use their pasts. This theme becomes clear through the conflicts between two sisters and through the first-person point of view of the mother, who relates her own links to the past. [focus on theme, plot, and point of view]
- In Nadine Gordimer's story "The Soft Voice of the Serpent," the theme of illusion's being inevitably overthrown by reality is brought out primarily through characterization, setting, and plot. [focus on theme, setting, characterization, and plot]

PART 2:
Finding a Focus and a Thesis

It may seem early, at this point, to decide on a focus and a thesis for your analysis, but remember that you can always change your mind later. For now, decide which elements you want to focus on in the story you have selected. Then you will need to decide what main idea you want to explain and prove in your analysis, and write out that main idea in the form of a thesis statement.

Gathering Support for Your Thesis

In a literary analysis, your readers expect you to support, or prove, your thesis. Support for your thesis is comprised of (1) the major points you will make to explain the thesis and (2) the evidence or proof that you supply to demonstrate that your points are valid. The following example illustrates how this works.

> *Thesis Statement*: Nadine Gordimer reveals a theme of illusion versus reality through the setting, characterization, and plot of "The Soft Voice of the Serpent."
>
> *Major Point*: Gordimer's characterization of the man in the wheelchair contributes to the theme of illusion versus reality.
>
> *Evidence to Show Validity of Point*: The man in the wheelchair has the illusory hope that he "never would realize" (397) that he has lost his leg.

Which comes first—your sense of the major points you want to make or the evidence to back them up? That's rather like the chicken and the egg. Sometimes you'll have a sense of the major points and then go looking for the evidence. At other times, your search for evidence will lead you to the discovery of a point you want to make. Most of the evidence comes from the ***primary source,*** the work itself. However, you might also find evidence in ***secondary sources,*** reference materials such as books about authors and their works, encyclopedias, and periodicals.

REFERENCE NOTE: For more information on secondary sources, see pages 448–449.

STRATEGIES FOR GATHERING INFORMATION

1. Reread the work of literature, thinking about the major points you will make in support of your thesis and looking for details and quotations to back them up.
2. As you read, make notes on note cards or sheets of paper.
3. Copy quotations exactly, and include the page numbers (for a story) or lines (for poetry) where the quotations appear.
4. Jot down information about the author, title, and place and date of publication so that you can give credit to your sources in your paper. (You want to avoid plagiarizing.)
5. Be certain that each piece of evidence is specific, not just a restatement of the thesis, and that it is related to the main idea.

Organizing Support

The evidence you gather may make sense to you, but it won't make sense to your readers unless it is organized in a sensible way. There are, however, several effective methods of organizing your material, and your choice of method will depend largely on the nature of your thesis.

For example, if you were writing about the symbolism of the garden in "The Soft Voice of the Serpent," you might divide your information into two groups—one group with points about the garden and another group with points about the real world. This is an example of ***logical order;*** related ideas are grouped together. On the other hand, if you were writing about the author's development of the main character, you might use ***chronological*** (time) ***order*** to organize examples that illustrate how the character changes during the course of the story. Yet another thesis might call for arrangement of information by ***order of importance,*** placing your most important point first or last. Then choose a method that works with your thesis.

REFERENCE NOTE: For more help with organizing ideas and details, see pages 35–36, 74, and 79–87.

As you gather and organize your support

- identify your focus and keep it in mind
- find specific evidence to back up each major point you plan to discuss
- make sure your evidence is related to your thesis
- if necessary, find information about the author and/or the story in secondary sources
- arrange your ideas in a sensible order

WRITING ASSIGNMENT

PART 3:
Gathering and Organizing Ideas

Reread the story you have chosen, this time taking notes about the elements you intend to focus on and the points you want to make in your critical analysis. (For help, use the strategies for critical reading on pages 405–406.) Also, if you're using any secondary sources, take notes from them. Next, jot down your major points and their supporting evidence in the form of an early plan (see pages 104–105). If any part of the plan looks skimpy, go back to your sources to collect more evidence; then decide what order you will use to present your information.

Writing Your First Draft

The Structure of a Critical Analysis

When you write a literary analysis, you can use the basic structural pattern of a composition (Chapter 3), with a few special considerations:

- In your **introduction** you need to identify the work's title and author, as well as your thesis. You may also have to provide background information about the author or a brief summary of the work if it is essential to an understanding of your thesis.
- In the **body** of the essay, you need to state your major supporting points and the evidence (details and quotations from the work) you are using as proof. You will also need to explain the connection between each quotation and the major point it supports or proves. Typically, you will need one or more paragraphs to develop each major point.
- In your **conclusion** you can synthesize your ideas, perhaps summarizing your major points or restating your thesis.

MECHANICS HINT

Incorporating Supporting Evidence

The evidence you use to support your thesis statement often includes direct quotations. Follow these guidelines when quoting from a literary work or a secondary source.

1. Enclose direct quotations in quotation marks. Be sure the quotation appears in your paper exactly as it appears in the published work. Periods and commas usually go inside the closing quotation marks.
2. Use a slash (/), with a space before and after it, to indicate the end of a line of poetry.
3. Use ellipses (. . .) to indicate an omission.

4. If the quotation is more than four typed or written lines, set it off by beginning a new line and indenting it ten spaces from the left-hand margin. Do not add quotation marks.
5. At the end of each quotation, place the page number in parentheses.

EXAMPLE Gordimer makes the point explicitly in the opening paragraph:

> Perhaps there was something in this of the old Eden idea; the tender human adjusting himself to himself in the soothing impersonal presence of trees and grass and earth. . . .

REFERENCE NOTE: For more information on using quotation marks and ellipses, see pages 935–939 and 941–943.

A Basic Framework for a Critical Analysis

The following Writer's Model is a critical analysis of "The Soft Voice of the Serpent" (pages 395–402). As you read it, see if you can identify the literary elements the writer focuses on to support the thesis statement.

A WRITER'S MODEL

A Locust in the Garden

INTRODUCTION
Title and author

Reference to theme of story
Thesis statement

Although the words <u>illusion</u> and <u>reality</u> never appear in Nadine Gordimer's "The Soft Voice of the Serpent," those two words accurately point to the theme of the story. Gordimer's "curiously human" (398) locust in the garden, with its "solemn silly face" (401), has lost a leg, just like the protagonist, but is not defeated. The locust's sudden flight from an Eden-like garden setting teaches the protagonist that he must abandon illusion and face reality. This theme of illusion versus reality is brought out primarily through setting, characterization, and plot.

BODY
Major point: Setting

The serpent in the story's title and the heavy emphasis on the garden setting suggest a parallel with the Old Testament story about Adam and Eve and their loss of innocence. Gordimer makes this point explicitly in the opening paragraph:

Long quotation from work

> Perhaps there was something in this of the old Eden idea; the tender human adjusting himself to himself in the soothing impersonal presence of trees and grass and earth. . . . (395–396)

Quotations from work to support interpretation of garden as a temporary shelter from reality

But such an Eden cannot last, either in the Bible or in the author's fictional setting, and the "tender human" (395) must eventually go "out into the stare of the world" (396).

The story alludes again and again to the sheltering comfort of the garden. The man tries to maintain an illusion that nothing serious has happened to him, that in time he will "feel as if he had always been like that" (397). The garden is his refuge against reality.

Quotation from work

Major point: Character

Gordimer's characterization of the man also contributes to the theme of illusion versus reality. In the garden setting, the man has plenty of time to think. What he tries to think about is anything not related to his missing limb. He reads to avoid considering his physical loss; and when his attention strays to "the sunken place under the rug where his leg used to be" (396), he represses the thought. His illusory hope is that he "never would realize" (397) he has lost his leg. Life will then be normal: the danger will be over.

Quotation from work to illustrate how the character is portrayed

Paraphrase

Throughout most of the story, the man focuses on mental avoidance. From childhood, the man remembers the flowers shaking "in vehement denial" (396). In the wheelchair, he feels the realization of loss "ready to burst" (396), but he always turns away, "just in time, back to his book" (396). He watches his wife "going" (not "walking") for tea. She is "empowered by the sun rather than her own muscles" (397). Only with the appearance

Quotations from work to illustrate character's illusions

of the injured locust does the man begin to admit his plight. He identifies with the locust. "It's as harmless as I am," he says (400).

Major point: Plot

The twin illusions of the garden as sanctuary and of mental avoidance as therapy are shattered by the progress of the plot. Gordimer's locust in the garden (much like the Bible's serpent in Eden) is the central plot device. The maimed locust, seemingly so like the maimed man, does not give in to its apparent fate--"I'm afraid the cat'll get him," the wife says (401). The comparison fails suddenly and startlingly when the locust flies away. The reality is that the locust can still face "the stare of the world" (396). It is not fated to die or even languish because of its injury. Somehow the man in the wheelchair will have to find a way to gain the same assurance. When his wife asks him about the locust's flight, he says, "Don't be a fool," more to himself, perhaps, than to her. Reality has set in.

Quotations from work to show how reality replaces illusions

CONCLUSION
Quotation from secondary source

The critic John Barkham, in reviewing Nadine Gordimer's first book of short stories, notes that "Miss Gordimer is a subtle writer who makes her points delicately and obliquely" (176). That observation is certainly true of "The Soft Voice of the Serpent," the title story in the book Barkham is reviewing. Various interpretations of the story are possible. The one that seems the most logical is that the injured locust's whirring flight from the garden (of Eden?) shows the protagonist that he must face reality and give up his illusion of achieving wholeness without effort or pain.

Restatement of thesis

When you write your own literary analysis, you may wish to model your essay on this literary analysis of "The Soft Voice of the Serpent." After you have gathered and organized your critical reading notes about the literary work you plan to write about and are ready to write your own first draft, review the preceding essay's major points. You will find that it is based on the following framework.

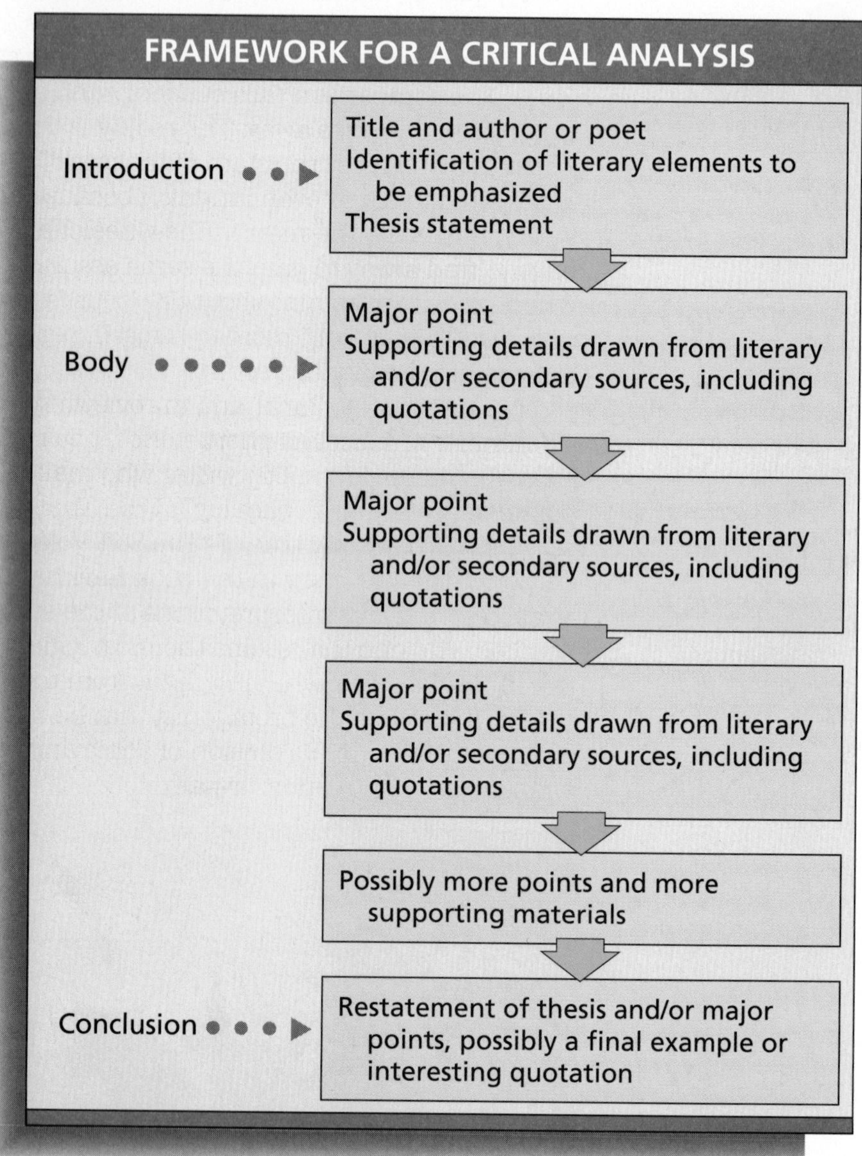

FRAMEWORK FOR A CRITICAL ANALYSIS
Introduction
Title and author or poet
Identification of literary elements to be emphasized
Thesis statement
Body
Major point
Supporting details drawn from literary and/or secondary sources, including quotations
Major point
Supporting details drawn from literary and/or secondary sources, including quotations
Major point
Supporting details drawn from literary and/or secondary sources, including quotations
Possibly more points and more supporting materials
Conclusion
Restatement of thesis and/or major points, possibly a final example or interesting quotation

In writing a critical analysis of a short story, there is a strong temptation to summarize the plot of the story. Resist it. Your job is to analyze the story, not condense it. You may need some background information about the story or the author in your introduction, but you probably won't need a thorough plot summary.

PEANUTS reprinted by permission of UFS, Inc.

PART 4:
Writing the First Draft of Your Critical Analysis

You have the thesis statement, notes, and plan you worked on in Parts 2 and 3 of the Writing Assignment. Using those materials—as well as the pattern provided in the Writer's Model and framework—write your first draft. Don't let the task intimidate you, however. You will have a chance later to revise your draft.

Evaluating and Revising

There comes a time when you have gone as far as you can go with thinking, planning, and getting your first draft on paper. And you've probably seen that drafting a critical, or literary, analysis has been like drafting any other kind of paper—you've pulled information, ideas, and details together without being overly concerned about having a perfect finished product. Now's the time, however, to think about the finished product.

No matter how good a writer you are, your first draft can be improved with revision. Use the chart on page 422 to guide your evaluation of your literary analysis. Ask yourself the questions in the left-hand column; then use the revision suggestions in the right-hand column.

EXERCISE 2 Analyzing a Writer's Revisions

Here is the first draft of the first paragraph of the writer's model on pages 415–416. In a small group, discuss the writer's reasons for making the handwritten changes shown here. Answer the questions that follow.

Although the words illusion and reality never appear in (Nadine Gordimer's) "The Soft Voice of the Serpent," those two words accurately point to the theme of the story. Gordimer's ("curiously human" [398]) locust in the garden, with its ~~funny~~ ("solemn silly") face, ([401]) has lost a leg, just like the protagonist, but is not defeated. The locust's sudden flight from an Eden-like garden setting teaches the protagonist that he must abandon illusion and face reality. This theme of illusion versus reality is brought out ~~by the author all the way through the story~~ (primarily through setting, characterization, and plot.) ~~Illusion versus reality is an important theme.~~

add

add

replace/add

replace

cut

1. In the first sentence, why did the writer add the words *Nadine Gordimer's*?
2. In the second sentence, why did the writer add *"curiously human" (398)*? How does this addition help to strengthen the writer's explanation?
3. In the second sentence, why did the writer replace *its funny face* with *its "solemn silly face" (401)*?
4. In the next-to-the-last sentence, why did the writer replace the words *by the author all the way through the story* with the words *primarily through setting, characterization, and plot*? [Hint: Review pages 409–410.]
5. Why did the writer cut the last sentence?

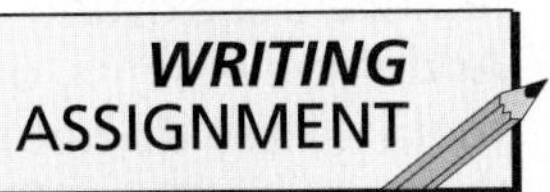

PART 5:
Evaluating and Revising Your Essay

Stanley Ellin, a writer of mystery short stories, used to revise each of his tales up to a dozen times. You won't have to do that for this assignment, but you will have to do some careful revision. Exchange papers with a classmate (or else work in small groups) to evaluate each other's first drafts. Using the suggestions in the chart on page 422 as a guide, make specific suggestions for changes or corrections. When you get your own paper back, evaluate and think about the evaluations of others. Make whatever changes you think will improve your essay.

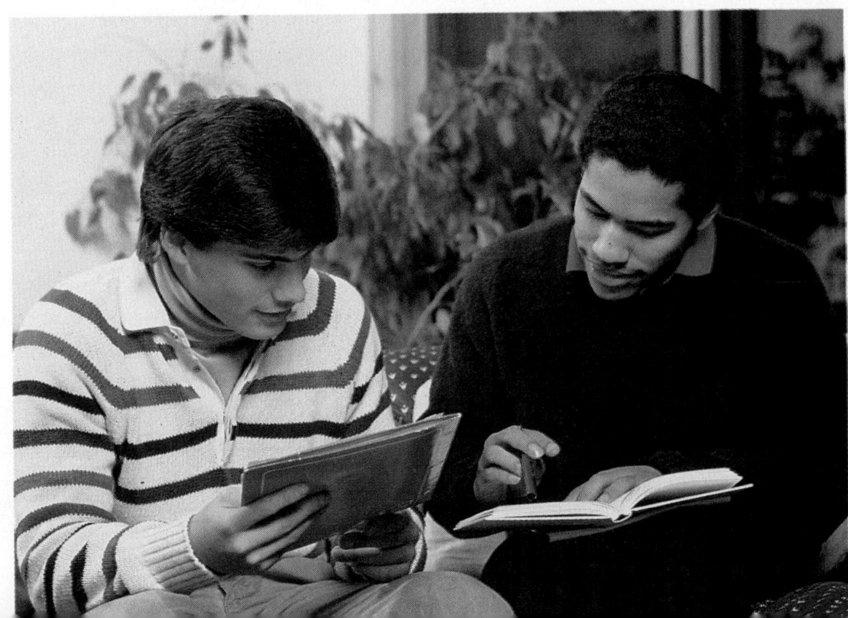

EVALUATING AND REVISING CRITICAL ANALYSIS ESSAYS

	EVALUATION GUIDE	REVISION TECHNIQUE
1	Does the introduction identify the title and author and give necessary background information?	**Add** the title and author; add any interesting, relevant information about the author and work, as necessary, to help readers understand your analysis.
2	Does a clear and precise thesis statement appear in the introduction? Does it clearly state the main idea and the elements to be discussed?	**Add** a thesis statement or **replace** the existing one. **Add** the elements, or **reorder** them if they do not match the organization of the essay.
3	Does the essay identify major points that support the thesis?	**Add** statements identifying the relationship between the evidence you have gathered and your thesis about the story.
4	Does the body give ample supporting evidence? Is the evidence specific and relevant?	**Add** evidence from the literary work or from secondary sources. **Cut** useless or repetitious evidence.
5	Is the organization of the essay clear and consistent?	**Reorder** ideas and evidence to follow a sensible order, such as chronological order or order of importance.
6	Does the conclusion effectively reinforce the thesis of the essay?	**Add** a sentence or sentences to summarize the main points or restate your thesis about the work.

Proofreading and Publishing

Proofreading. Although all of your revisions will clarify and strengthen the content of your paper, they will probably make something of a mess of it, too. Therefore, before you make the final, clean copy of your critical analysis essay, check for errors in spelling, capitalization, punctuation, grammar, and usage. Use this textbook and a good dictionary for reference.

Publishing. There are many ways to publish your paper so that it reaches a wider audience. Here are two possibilities:

- Ask your teacher to help you locate reading groups or literary groups within your community. Many such groups exist, often in conjunction with larger organizations such as churches, synagogues, social clubs, fraternal orders, and so on. Try getting in touch with one such group to see whether its members have read—or might consider reading—the story you have analyzed. If the response is favorable, attend the group's meeting and share your analysis of the story.
- Find other students who would like to create a collection of literary analyses. Arrange the essays by author and by story. Offer the collection to the school library as a resource for people who are looking for information about short stories.

When you proofread your essay of literary analysis, check the tense of the verbs you have used. To refer to events in a work of literature, you use the ***literary*** (sometimes called ***historical***) ***present*** tense. It's as if you are standing in the middle of the story (or poem or novel) and the action is happening all around you.

EXAMPLE Realization **creeps** up on him, but he **rejects** it before it **makes** him fully aware of his situation.

PART 6:
Proofreading and Publishing Your Essay

Search diligently for errors. Reread your essay word for word, making sure you haven't left out any words or written the same word twice in a row—*the the,* for example. (For some reason, little words like *a, an, the, to, of, on,* and *in* often get dropped or duplicated by mistake.) When you have corrected every mistake you can find, publish your essay, using one of the suggestions you have just read or an idea of your own.

A STUDENT MODEL

Robert Browning, an English poet of the Victorian Period, mastered the dramatic monologue, a poem in which the speaker is clearly someone other than the poet. In the following essay, Kerry Cookson analyzes the use of first-person point of view in Browning's "Porphyria's Lover." Kerry, who attends Oak Ridge High School in Orlando, Florida, also offers you this very sound advice for writing about literature: "Don't put in a lot of unnecessary gibberish."

"Porphyria's Lover"
by Kerry Cookson

The speaker in "Porphyria's Lover," by Robert Browning, is not of sound mind. Because of this, the first-person point of view is ideal for revealing the speaker's insanity. The speaker proves his psychosis through his actions, his motives, and his description of the weather.

First of all, the speaker is sitting in the dark and cold. He is doing absolutely nothing. Even when his lover walks through the door and embraces him, he doesn't move. However, because of Porphyria's embrace--her show of love--the speaker comes to the realization that Porphyria loves him. He says, "at last I knew / Porphyria worshiped me." To hold onto this moment, the speaker strangles Porphyria. These actions show clearly that he can't be in his right mind. The speaker's tone is so matter-of-fact and nonchalant that we see his madness clearly when he says, "and all her hair / In one long yellow string I wound / Three times her little throat around, / And strangled her." If the poem were written in the third person, this particular statement wouldn't reveal the speaker's true feelings.

The first-person point of view also allows the speaker to reveal that his motives are insane. He kills the woman he loves just so he can capture the moment. "That moment she was mine," he says, but he doesn't feel he can keep her love forever if she's alive. He wants to dominate Porphyria. His jealousy overtakes his being.

Finally, through his description of the weather, the speaker proves himself insane: "The rain set early in tonight, / The sullen wind was soon awake." His use of the word sullen depicts his brooding resentment. He resents Porphyria for not giving up her life to please and obey him. Describing the wind, he says, "It tore the elm-tops down for spite." The speaker's spite is his malicious ill-will to hurt others.

Throughout this poem, the speaker shows that he is quite psychotic. Because "Porphyria's Lover" is written in the first person, the speaker is able to prove his insanity in his actions, motives, and descriptions of the weather.

"[The] most important tribute
any human being can pay
to a poem or a piece of prose
he or she really loves...
is to learn it by heart.
Not by brain, by heart;
the expression is vital."

GEORGE STEINER

WRITING WORKSHOP

Parody

You have probably heard the truism "Imitation is the sincerest form of flattery." But the truth of that statement depends on the imitator's attitude: Is it genuinely respectful or comically mocking? In literature, a ***parody*** is a humorous imitation of a work or a style. Like a critical analysis, a parody is a response to literature, but it makes its point through ridicule—soft or sharp—and exaggerated mimicry.

Parody is an ancient form, going back at least to the Greek dramatist Aristophanes in the fifth century B.C. However, it's alive and well today: in *Saturday Night Live*'s and *Mad Magazine*'s parodies of commercials, sitcoms, and movies; in comedians' impressions of politicians, singers, and songs; in *The Naked Gun*'s parody of hard-boiled, hard-shooting cop movies. In all of these examples, the parodists make you laugh at their targets by exaggerating distinctive elements, whether language, mannerisms, characters, or subject matter.

A literary parody may imitate a particular work, writer, or school of writing. Miguel de Cervantes parodied courtly romances in *Don Quixote*. E. B. White parodied Ernest Hemingway's novel *Across the River and into the Trees* (and Hemingway's fiction in general) in "Across the Street and into the Grill." And in the following poem, George A. Strong parodies Henry Wadsworth Longfellow's well-known poem *The Song of Hiawatha*. Read aloud Longfellow's verse and then Strong's parody, and think about two questions: How does Strong make absolutely sure you'll "get" the parody? How does he make you laugh?

from The Song of Hiawatha

by Henry Wadsworth Longfellow

He had mittens, Minjekahwun,
Magic mittens made of deer-skin;
When upon his hands he wore them,
He could smite the rocks asunder,
He could grind them into powder.
He had moccasins enchanted,
Magic moccasins of deer-skin;
When he bound them round his ankles,
When upon his feet he tied them,
At each stride a mile he measured!

"The Modern Hiawatha"

by George A. Strong

When he killed the Mudjokivis,
Of the skin he made him mittens,
Made them with the fur side inside,
Made them with the skin side outside,
He, to get the warm side inside,
Put the inside skin side outside;
He, to get the cold side outside,
Put the warm side fur side inside.
That's why he put the fur side inside,
Why he put the skin side outside,
Why he turned them inside outside.

1. Since a parody has to be a close imitation, any good parody of a poem will duplicate its sounds. Besides copying *The Song of Hiawatha*'s singsong rhythm, Strong focuses on the many repetitions of words and phrases. What are some of Longfellow's repetitions? How does Strong exaggerate this style?
2. Often a parody's comedy involves applying the writer's style (recognizable but exaggerated) to a considerably "lowered" subject matter. How does Strong make fun of the *content* of *The Song of Hiawatha*?
3. What would you say is Strong's opinion of *The Song of Hiawatha*? Do you agree? Does Strong make you see this famous poem in a new way, or is his parody simply amusing and entertaining? Explain.

Writing a Literary Parody

Prewriting. Now, think of a writer or literary style that you could enjoy making fun of. Look through school texts and your own library. Perhaps you'll choose a favorite author, someone whose works and ways with words you know inside out; or a poem you've been assigned several times and never want to read again; or a form, like detective fiction, that seems full of comic possibilities.

Then ask yourself (1) *What makes this work, writer, or form distinctive?* and (2) *How can I make these elements laughable?* The charts on pages 403 and 405 will help you focus on important literary elements. When you've settled on the main elements of your parody, plan your story, poem, or play, keeping it to a manageable length. (Your creation can be a "condensed version" of the original.)

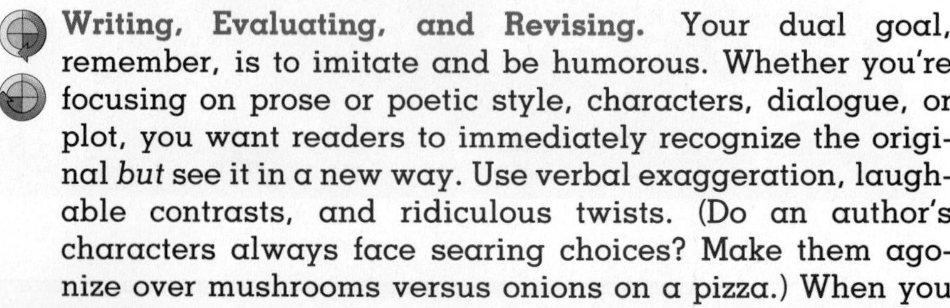

Writing, Evaluating, and Revising. Your dual goal, remember, is to imitate and be humorous. Whether you're focusing on prose or poetic style, characters, dialogue, or plot, you want readers to immediately recognize the original *but* see it in a new way. Use verbal exaggeration, laughable contrasts, and ridiculous twists. (Do an author's characters always face searing choices? Make them agonize over mushrooms versus onions on a pizza.) When you have a draft, definitely try it out on others. Do they instantly see the parody? Are they laughing? Use their suggestions and your own review to sharpen the comedy and mimicry.

Proofreading and Publishing. Correct errors, and make a clean copy of your parody. If several writers in your class have parodied brief poems, you could create a book with the original poems and parodies appearing on facing pages. But don't neglect live performances. You can bring out even more humor in a poem through your delivery (voice, gestures, facial expressions, timing), and you can use a story or scene from a play for classroom skits or readers' theater.

Shoe, by Jeff MacNelly, reprinted by permission: Tribune Media Services.

MAKING CONNECTIONS

SPEAKING AND LISTENING

A Critical Review

What Amy Taubin did in this chapter's opening selection—discuss a movie and advise people whether to see it—is something you have no doubt done, too. You are offering at least a casual critical review whenever you say, "I kept my eyes closed through at least half of *A Teenage Nightmare Too Horrible to Watch.* Especially the anteater scenes. You've got to see it!"

In a real review, you do the same thing but more thoroughly: You combine a critical analysis of a work's elements—similar to the literary analysis you've done—with an evaluation, or judgment, about whether it's worth watching or reading. Readers of a review also rely on you to give a brief summary or description of the work, without giving away too much.

Because perceptions of and judgments about art frequently vary, some popular movie review programs on television feature two reviewers. For example, Roger Ebert and Gene Siskel review the same film independently and then surprise each other with their face-to-face reviews. Whether sparks fly or two thumbs go up or down harmoniously is part of the viewer's fun.

Gene Siskel and Roger Ebert

Joel Siegel

Work with a partner to do a team review of a movie, play, or television special. Use these guidelines:

1. Set a time limit of three to five minutes for each review.
2. Write your review in a more informal style than your critical analysis for this chapter. As a rule, reviews are more casual, using the first-person viewpoint and colloquial language.
3. In your introduction, identify the film, program, or play; the writer, director, and main actors; and the general plot or theme.
4. Make the analysis of elements the meat of your review, with as many supporting details and examples as possible.
5. Close with your overall judgment of the work, thumbs up or thumbs down, strong points and weak.
6. After both reviews, take thirty to forty-five seconds for a final comment, reacting to your partner's review.

EVALUATING LITERATURE

Writing a Critical Analysis of a Poem

Everything you've done in writing about a short story prepares you well for writing about a poem, but of course there are differences between prose and poetry. The two you may immediately think of (with either pleasure or a bit of anxiety) are poetry's *music* and its often *figurative, highly compressed language:* The sounds and syntax of poetry *are* unique. Here are two tips to add to your strategies for reading a poem.

- Read a poem aloud. Use the punctuation to hear its rhythm; let its sounds linger in your mouth. [Remember: Sound is physical.]
- Paraphrase passages to clarify meanings. You can put figures of speech into your own words or change unusual word order into everyday speech patterns. Your paraphrases will *not* be poetry, but they can help you unravel difficulties and come back to the poetry.

Try writing a critical analysis of a poem you have read and found interesting. Use the chart of poetry elements on pages 403–404 to study the poem, and then determine what you will focus on in your analysis. Your focus will, of course, be dependent on the poem you choose, but here are some examples:

- how sound effects create a specific tone
- what the images show you about the speaker's emotions
- how figurative language helps develop the poem's theme

After you have determined the focus of your analysis, you can follow the same process you used to write an analysis of a story—identify a thesis, find and organize support, write, evaluate and revise, proofread and publish. Since poetry is meant to be read aloud, you might want to combine an oral reading of your poem with an oral presentation of your analysis.

EVALUATING LITERATURE

Using Deductive Reasoning

At the beginning of this chapter you read a review of *Hamlet*, and in one of the other connections, you did a team review of a movie, play, or television show. One characteristic of a review is that it includes an evaluation, or judgment, of the work. Such evaluations are examples of **deductive reasoning.** (See pages 276–277, for information about inductive reasoning.)

In deductive reasoning, you start with a general rule or general knowledge, and then you apply it to a specific situation or instance. Finally, you draw a conclusion about that specific instance. A classic deductive argument is stated in the form of a *syllogism:*

Major Premise All seniors on the soccer team will receive a letter jacket.
Minor Premise Danielle is a senior on the soccer team.
Conclusion Danielle will receive a letter jacket.

Major Premise All animals need water.
Minor Premise Camels are animals.
Conclusion Camels need water.

Major Premise It is the duty of every American citizen eighteen and older to vote in every election.
Minor Premise Juan Rivera is an eighteen-year-old American citizen.
Conclusion It is Juan Rivera's duty to vote in every election.

When you evaluate something—whether it is a work of literature, a movie, or a CD player—you use a similar reasoning process. For example:

Major Premise A good short story has a tight plot and believable characters.
Minor Premise Eudora Welty's "A Worn Path" has a tight plot and believable characters.
Conclusion "A Worn Path" is a good story.

Keep in mind two important points about deductive thinking: (1) If your major premise is incorrect, your conclusion will be incorrect, and (2) if your readers don't agree with your major premise, they may not agree with your conclusion.

Now get together with two classmates and try some deductive thinking. Begin by selecting two poems to evaluate. Then review the elements of poetry on pages 403–404 and use them, as well as your own experience with poetry, to determine a major premise, or general rule, about the characteristics of good poetry. After you have agreed on your major premise, apply it to each poem, and then draw a conclusion about each poem. State your deductive thinking in the form of two syllogisms and share them with the rest of your class.

11 Writing a Research Paper

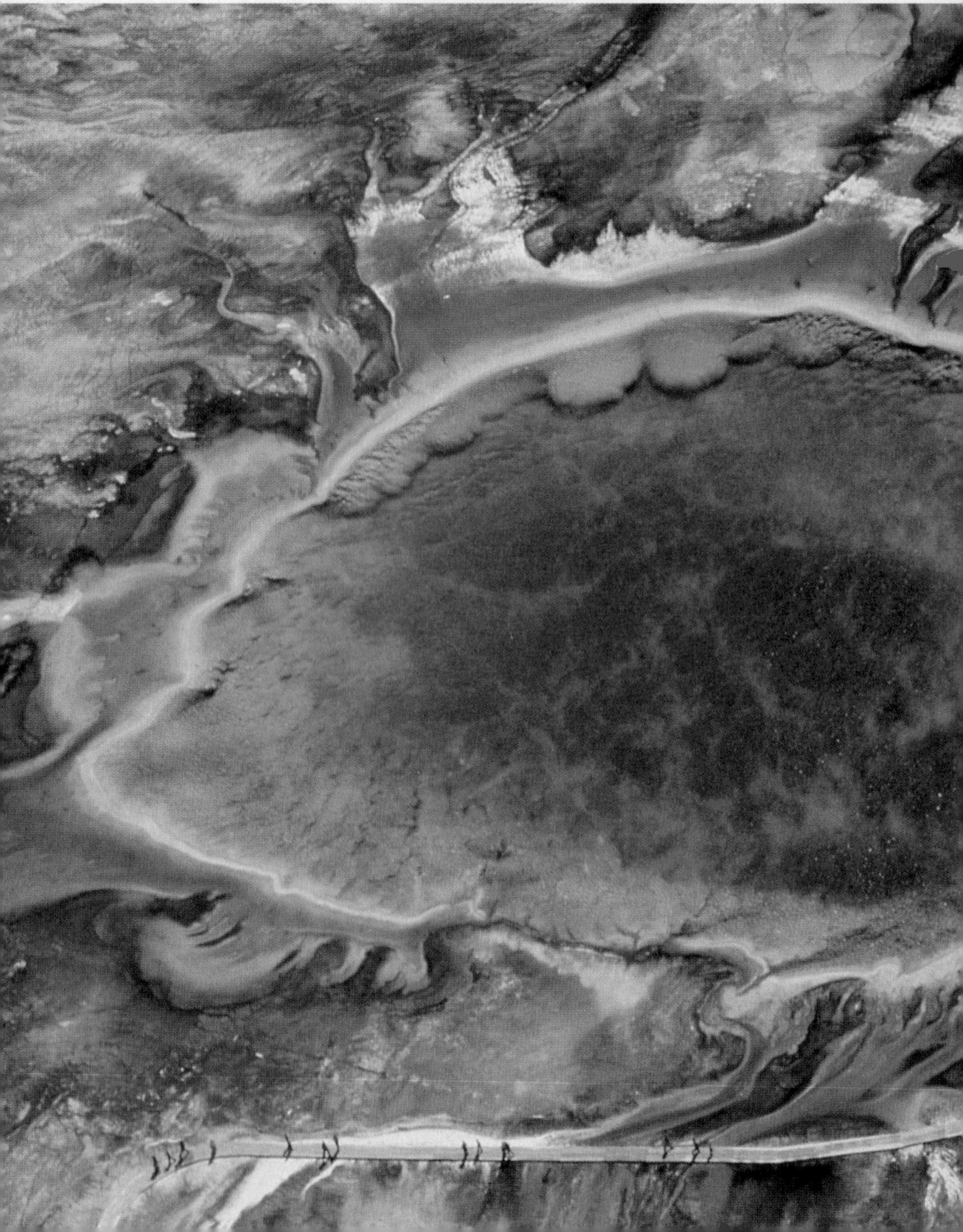

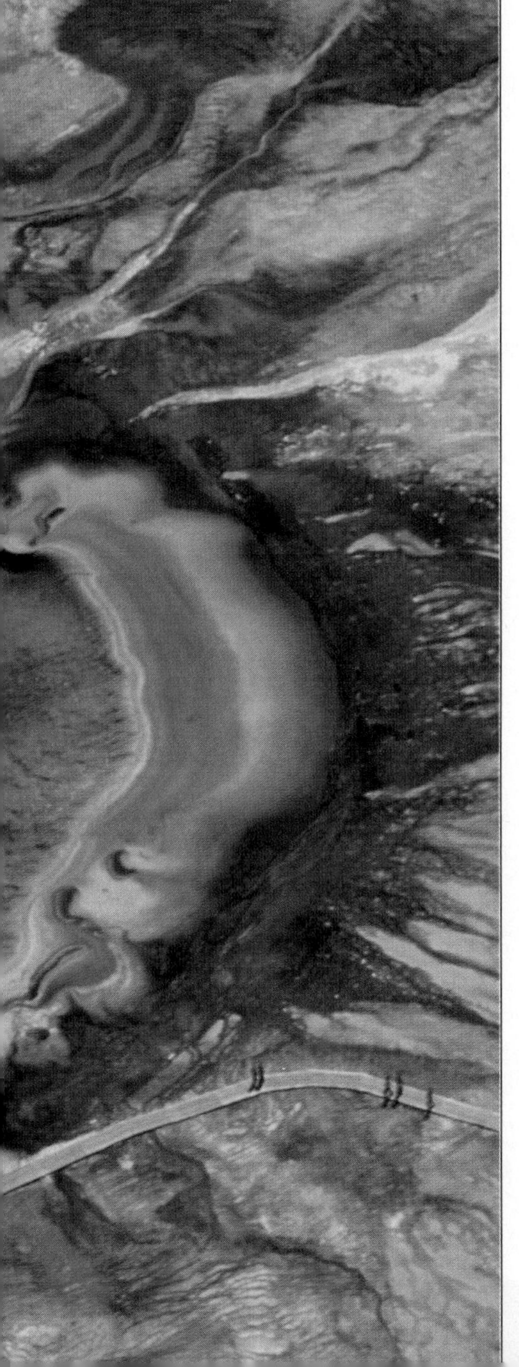

Exploring Your World

When you think of the world's explorers, you probably don't think of zoologists or secretaries or reporters. You think of people who set sail in uncharted waters or scale treacherous peaks. But many people **explore the world** in other adventurous, if usually more close-to-home, ways: They listen, observe, experiment, and read.

Writing and You. Reports of research are as varied as the explorations themselves. The zoologist writes an article about elephant communication; the secretary writes a memo detailing options for a new office telephone system; the reporter produces a radio program about a state mental hospital. How can these researchers find their information?

As You Read. Some explorations, like the following one about "elephant talk," are triggered by curiosity, mystery, and a keen eye—or ear. What techniques did these researchers use to explore the elephant's mysterious world?

Paul Chesley © 1980, *Grand Prismatic.* Photograph of Yellowstone Thermal Spring. Paul Chesley Photographers/Aspen.

from

ELEPHANT TALK

by
Katharine Payne

Spend a day among elephants, and you will come away mystified. Sudden, silent, synchronous activities—a herd taking flight for no apparent or audible reason, a mass of scattered animals simultaneously raising ears and freezing in their tracks—such events demand explanation, but none is forthcoming.

Some capacity beyond memory and the five senses seems to inform elephants, silently and from a distance, of the whereabouts and activities of other elephants.

I stumbled on a possible clue to these mysteries during a visit to the Metro Washington Park Zoo in Portland, Oregon, in May 1984. While observing three Asian elephant mothers and their new calves, I repeatedly noticed a palpable throbbing in the air like distant thunder, yet all around me was silent.

Only later did a thought occur to me: As a young choir girl in Ithaca, New York, I used to stand next to the largest, deepest organ pipe in the church. When the organ blasted out the bass line in a Bach chorale, the

". . . I repeatedly noticed a palpable throbbing in the air like distant thunder, yet all around me was silent."

whole chapel would throb, just as the elephant room did at the zoo. Suppose the elephants, like the organ pipe, were the source of the throbbing? Suppose elephants communicate with one another by means of calls too low-pitched for human beings to hear?

Half a year later the World Wildlife Fund, the Cornell Laboratory of Ornithology, and friends in the Cornell biology department helped me, Bill Langbauer, and Liz Thomas return to the zoo to test this idea. We recorded near the elephants for a month. Then we made electronic printouts and saw that we had recorded 400 calls—three times as many as we'd heard.

Elephant sounds include barks, snorts, trumpets, roars, growls, and rumbles. The rumbles are the key to our story, for although elephants can hear them well, human beings cannot. Many are below our range of hearing, in what is known as infrasound.

The universe is full of infrasound: It is generated by earthquakes, wind, thunder, volcanoes, and ocean storms—massive movements of earth, air, fire, and water. But very low frequency sound has not been thought to play much of a role in animals' lives. Intense infrasonic calls have been recorded from finback whales, but whether the calls are used in communication is not known.

Why would elephants use infrasound? It turns out that sound at the lowest frequencies of elephant rumbles (14 to 35 hertz, or cycles per

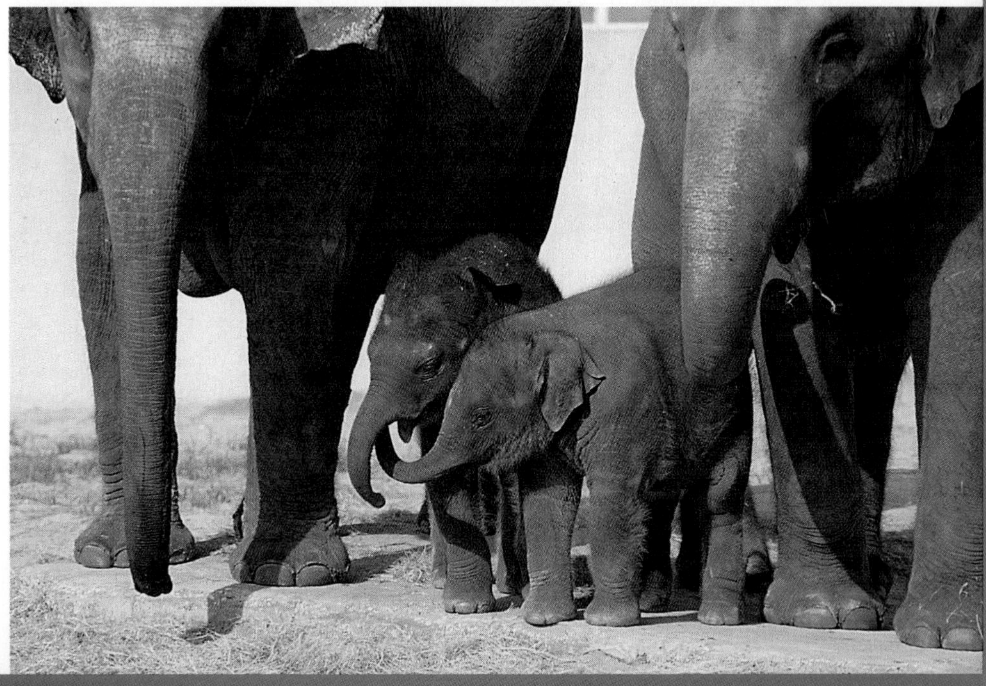

second) has remarkable properties—it is little affected by passage through forests and grasslands. Does infrasound, then, let elephants communicate over long distances?

Suddenly we realized that if wild elephants use infrasound, this could explain some extraordinary observations on record about the social lives of these much loved, much studied animals.

National Geographic

Reader's Response

1. Sometimes a seemingly insoluble mystery has a perfectly reasonable explanation, such as the one here: the elephants' use of infrasound for communicating. Think of something that you once regarded as a mystery but later came to understand. Explain how you or someone else solved the mystery.
2. A different observer at the Metro Washington Park Zoo might have concluded that elephants have extrasensory perception (ESP). What are your views on ESP? Is there such a thing? Do you know anyone who seems to have ESP?

Writer's Craft

3. Katharine Payne's research began because she was observant: She noticed something she wasn't expecting. What kind of observing did she and her colleagues do during the research? What details in the article show that reading was also part of their research?
4. This article was written for *National Geographic,* a magazine for the general public. But Payne probably also wrote reports of the research for scientists or scientific groups such as the Cornell Laboratory of Ornithology, which helped fund the research. How might a report written for scientists be different from "Elephant Talk"? What information or details might Payne delete? What different kinds of information might scientists want?

Strategies for Developing Research

The amount of information available on most topics is overwhelming. Businesses, government agencies, politicians, news reporters, and advertisers bombard you daily with facts and opinions and the results of research. Many of the reports you see are *informal,* like Katharine Payne's. An informal report doesn't use footnotes or provide a detailed list of sources. A *formal report,* like the one you'll be writing in this chapter, differs in that it always contains documentation, providing a detailed answer to the question "Where does this information come from?" Here are some examples of the various ways to develop research reports, whether formal or informal.

Narration: reporting on events in a recent presidential campaign; writing a biographical report about your favorite writer.

Description: describing the murals of Mexican artist Diego Rivera; describing a sod house on the prairie frontier.

Classification: reporting on the components of a telecommunications network; comparing and contrasting the judicial systems of the United States and England.

Evaluation: reporting the results of safety tests on crash-test dummies; reporting findings on the effects of irradiating food.

LOOKING AHEAD

In this chapter you will write a formal research report. You will also conduct and report on experimental research and make an informal report about a historical figure. In your formal paper, you'll present the results of your research using the strategy of either narration or classification. Keep in mind that a formal research report

- gives factual information about a topic
- presents information from several sources
- documents its sources of information

Writing a Research Paper

Finding a Research Topic

To find a research subject, you may automatically think, "First stop: library." The impulse is natural. Libraries are repositories of research and information, and going to that bank of books is a strategy that won't fail you. But it's not your only option.

Discovering Subjects

Think for a minute about what's in a library and how it got there. *People* wrote, compiled, drew, filmed, or recorded all of it. They probably used a library at some point, but they didn't necessarily start there. Where were they when curiosity hit and wouldn't go away? At home, at work, at sea, at a movie? Where were they when they noticed something they had to know more about? In a courthouse, a desert, a gallery? The whole world is a repository of research ideas, and you have complete freedom to use it. The best idea for a research paper is one that grabs *you*. Following are some ideas for starting your search.

SOURCES FOR RESEARCH SUBJECTS

- **Everyday curiosity:** Have you ever wondered how something works or why it happened as it did? Would you like to understand animation? the Underground Railroad?
- **Personal experiences:** What have you seen, done, or accomplished that might provide a subject for research—a trip to the Everglades? a gymnastics competition?
- **Friends and relatives:** Does someone you know do something interesting or unusual? Is she a television director? Is he a dietitian for cancer patients?
- **Entertainment:** Don't think of television, radio, movies, and sports as just diversions. What draws your imagination and interest—reggae music? modern police methods? baseball legends?

(continued)

SOURCES FOR RESEARCH SUBJECTS *(continued)*

- **Books, newspapers, magazines, documentary videotapes:** What do you linger over when you go to the library? Browse through the card (or on-line) catalog, the *Readers' Guide to Periodical Literature,* or other indexes and see what catches your attention—women's rights? medicine? ballet?

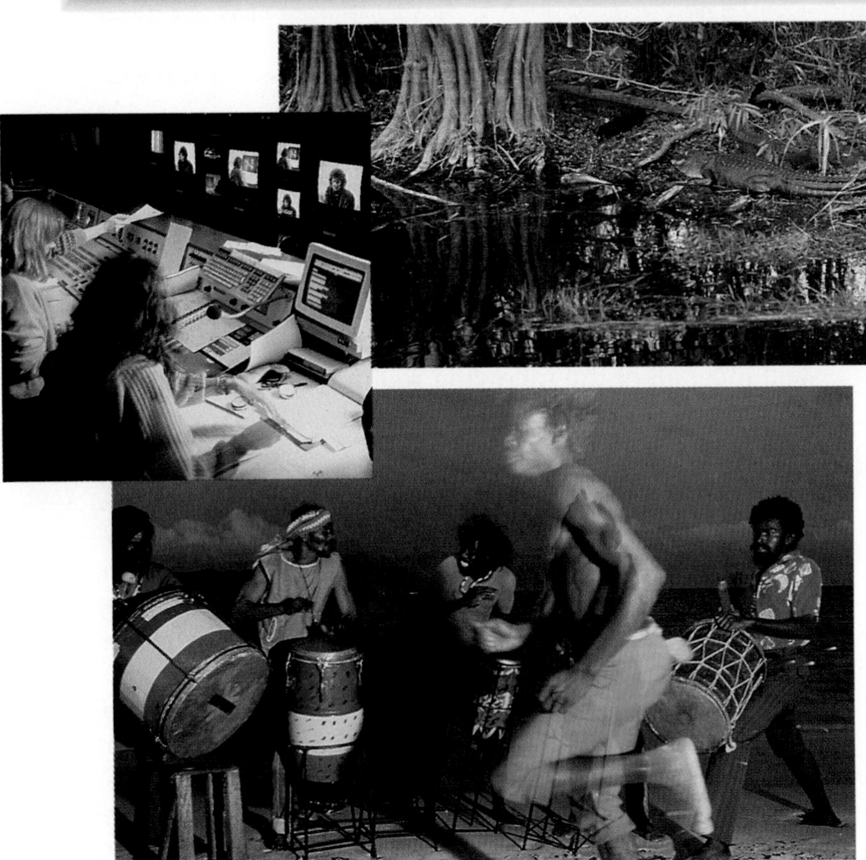

Identifying a Suitable Topic

Your first idea may be quite general—for example, Jane Austen, the Super Bowl, folk music, Native American culture. Since a typical high school research report is five to ten typed pages (check with your teacher for specific requirements), you will have to limit your subject to a workable topic.

You're looking for an aspect of the subject that appeals to you and that can also be covered well (that is, thoroughly) in a paper—not a book. You may be able to limit the subject from your own knowledge, but you can also look for subtopics in the *Readers' Guide*, card catalog, or encyclopedias. Keep pushing yourself to *be more specific.*

Subject:	*Native Americans*
Be more specific!	*Native Americans in the past*
Be more specific!	*the Iroquois League*
Be more specific!	*how the League worked as a government*
Limited topic:	*the influence of the Iroquois League on the form of the United States government*

Besides being manageable and personally appealing, your topic must be appropriate for a research report. A good topic will meet all of the following requirements.

CHECKLIST FOR A SUITABLE TOPIC

1. Can you find at least five sources of information, including books, articles, and nonprint sources? Beware of topics that are too recent ("last month's high school dropouts") or too technical or unusual ("the incidence of rabies among wild dogs in India").
2. Is the topic an objective one? You cannot report on your personal experiences or opinions. You may, for example, write a paper about "triathlete training and competition" but not about your experiences in meets.
3. Can you make the topic appealing to your audience? Interest is important for readers, not just for you. If your topic is written about often ("crucial Civil War battles") or on first impression dry ("the invention and manufacture of squeeze tubes"), what approach will give it life for your audience?

EXERCISE 1 Evaluating Topics for Research

Which of the following topics are suitable for a five- to ten-page research report? Get together with a partner and discuss the merits of each topic. For each one that isn't suitable, explain why. Is it too broad? Does it fail a test in the checklist on page 442? Also suggest a more limited or usable topic.

1. urban renewal in Newark, New Jersey
2. the problem of slavery in America
3. how Labrador retrievers are trained to detect drugs smuggled as cargo
4. my year as an exchange student in Japan
5. a new immunological cancer treatment reported in the current issue of the *New England Journal of Medicine*

Shoe, by Jeff MacNelly, reprinted by permission: Tribune Media Services.

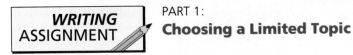

PART 1: Choosing a Limited Topic

Have you ever complained that you don't get to *choose* what to study in school? Well, whether the complaint's true or not, this is definitely one chance to choose, to study something that *you* want to learn. The source ideas on pages 440–441 give you ways to develop personal fascinations into research topics. The only director of this research project is you: Just remember to choose a topic that is specific and to satisfy the requirements on page 442. When you have chosen a topic, save it for later use.

Developing a Research Plan

Thinking of yourself as a project director is a good idea. Research—on any topic—is such a wide-open adventure that you have to have a plan, a direction. Since you don't want to go into the library and still be there when the paper's due, you need some solid methods for setting up and carrying out your research.

Considering Purpose, Audience, and Tone

Purpose. What do you want to accomplish? You actually have a dual *purpose* in writing a research report—discovering information for yourself and sharing new information with an audience. What you'll give readers will not be a jumble of facts and ideas, or even an orderly list of them: It will be a synthesis, a bringing together of the pieces of information you uncover into a whole. So be ready to make sense of what you find.

Audience. Your readers will usually be your teacher and your classmates, but don't limit yourself to that audience alone. You can plan your paper for a specific *audience* from the outset. For example, if you are writing about educational methods in Japan, you may want the state legislature's education committee to read it. Whoever your readers are, they are looking for information, for a better understanding of the topic. You need to take them *beyond* what they already know. You also need to interest them: Look for surprising details or an unusual twist to old information.

Tone. Adding interest to your report, however, doesn't mean using slang, exclamation marks, or flowery descriptions. The *tone* of a formal report should be serious but not stuffy: Think of yourself as an authority who really wants to communicate to others. To create this impression, you will have to sound objective. You can accomplish this by avoiding the use of the first-person pronouns *I, me,* or *my*. The use of *I* is appropriate in many kinds of writing, even in informal reports, but not in a formal research report.

EXERCISE 2 **Speaking and Listening: Analyzing the Audience for Your Report**

Companies, organizations, and even politicians often use a technique called *focus groups* to research a market before they put a new product, idea, or campaign before the public. The focus groups allow them to get the reactions of a small sample of people typical of the final audience. Form a focus group with five or six classmates, and test your topic. Tell the group briefly what your limited topic is and what you expect to cover in your report. If you have a special audience in mind, describe it, and have the others role-play its members. Ask them these questions, take notes on answers, and also let them question you. Take turns presenting and responding.

1. What do you know about this topic already? How did you learn it?
2. What interests you most about the topic? What questions about it would you like to have answered?
3. Does the topic seem boring to you? Why or why not?
4. If you were given this topic, how would you approach it?

Developing Research Questions

No matter how new to you a topic is, your mind isn't a blank about it. You chose it because you are curious, because you have questions about it, and those questions can guide you as you gather information. You can also generate research questions by brainstorming or by using the *5W-How?* questions: *Who? What? When? Where? Why?* and *How?* Remember that these questions are initial guides; you may ask others later. Following are some initial questions one writer brainstormed about the topic of the Iroquois League and the founding of the U.S. government.

What was the Iroquois League? When and how did it begin? What was its purpose?

Besides being a confederation (union), did the League have other similarities to the United States?

What did our nation's founders know about the Iroquois League? Did any of the founders ever acknowledge Iroquois contributions to the new government?

Do historians think the Iroquois League influenced the founders' ideas? If so, how?

Getting an Overview and Finding Sources

Your actual research starts with a quick overview of your topic. You already know *something* about it, of course, or you couldn't have gotten this far; but you need a solid grasp of the basic shape of the topic before plunging into specifics. One way to get a quick overview is to read one or two articles in encyclopedias or other reference books about your topic or, if it is highly limited, about related topics. For example, when researching "recent drug therapies for mental illness," you could look up "psychiatry" or "schizophrenia." Sometimes a videotape, an audiotape, or an expert (a teacher, librarian, parent, or neighbor) can give you a good overview, too. During this preliminary work you may think of other research questions, and you may find good suggestions for other sources.

Once you have an adequate overview and are ready to look for specific sources of information, remember to explore both *print* and *nonprint* sources in your *library* and *community*.

SOURCES OF INFORMATION	
LIBRARY	
SOURCE	WHAT TO LOOK FOR
Card catalog or on-line catalog	Books, recordings, audiotapes, and videotapes (Print and audiovisual listings are in separate catalogs in some libraries.)

(continued)

SOURCES OF INFORMATION *(continued)*	
LIBRARY	
SOURCE	WHAT TO LOOK FOR
Readers' Guide to Periodical Literature or an on-line index	Magazine and journal articles, indexed by subject and author (*InfoTrac*® is one well-known computerized index.)
Indexes to newspapers, essays, and articles	Articles from major newspapers, such as *The New York Times;* possibly local newspapers (Newspapers are frequently on microfilm.)
Specialized reference books	Encyclopedias of special subjects, such as the *Reference Encyclopedia of the American Indian;* almanacs; atlases; biographical references like *Current Biography*
Vertical file	Pamphlets and clippings, often on subjects of local interest, arranged by subject
Microfilm or microfiche	Indexes to major newspapers, back issues of some newspapers and magazines
COMMUNITY	
Colleges, historical societies, museums	Libraries, exhibits, experts, special collections, records
Local, state, and federal offices	Statistics, politicians' voting records, recent or pending legislation, surveys, reports, pamphlets, experts
Newspaper offices	Clippings, files on local events and history (Call to see if research is permitted.)

Evaluating Sources of Information. As the preceding chart shows, many sources are available to you. How do you know which ones to use? You can tell whether a source will be useful or not by applying the "4R" test.

1. **Relevant.** The source must contain information *directly* related to your topic. You can check the table of contents and index of a book and skim articles. Videotapes and audiotapes sometimes provide a written summary; and for some books, useful summaries and excerpts of reviews will appear in *Book Review Digest.*
2. **Recent.** Always use sources that are as current as possible. In many fields, research findings change rapidly. Even for a topic that doesn't rely on data and experiments, you should read the most recent publications about it because they will often show you which older sources of information are still important.
3. **Reliable.** The source must be accurate. A respected newspaper or periodical, such as *The Washington Post* or *Smithsonian,* or a respected scholar can generally be counted on to have facts straight. If in doubt about a source, consult a librarian or expert and look for the authors most often quoted on the topic or listed in the bibliographies of other sources.
4. **Representative.** If there are two opposing viewpoints on your topic, you need to look at sources with information and opinions on both sides of the issue. As a researcher, you must examine and present all relevant information, even if you finally draw a conclusion that one side's position is stronger.

Using Primary and Secondary Sources. A ***primary source*** is firsthand, original information. It may be a letter, a speech, or a literary work. It may be eyewitness testimony, a personal remembrance, an autobiography, a historical document, or information gathered from firsthand interviews or surveys. For example, in a report on the Iroquois League and the founding of the United States, a letter on the subject written by Benjamin Franklin is a primary source. You will want to use primary sources if they're available on your topic, but remember that the *R's* of *reliable* and *representative* apply to them too. A primary source could be mistaken or show bias. To be able to judge, research widely.

A ***secondary source*** contains secondhand or indirect information, but that does not mean such sources are unimportant. An encyclopedia entry, an expert's opinion, a magazine article, and a biography are all secondary sources. In fact, the research report you are now working on will be a secondary source about your topic for other researchers, just as the book *The Indians of Northeastern America* is a secondary source for a paper on the Iroquois League. You'll use secondary sources in virtually any research project, with the mix between primary and secondary sources depending mainly on the topic.

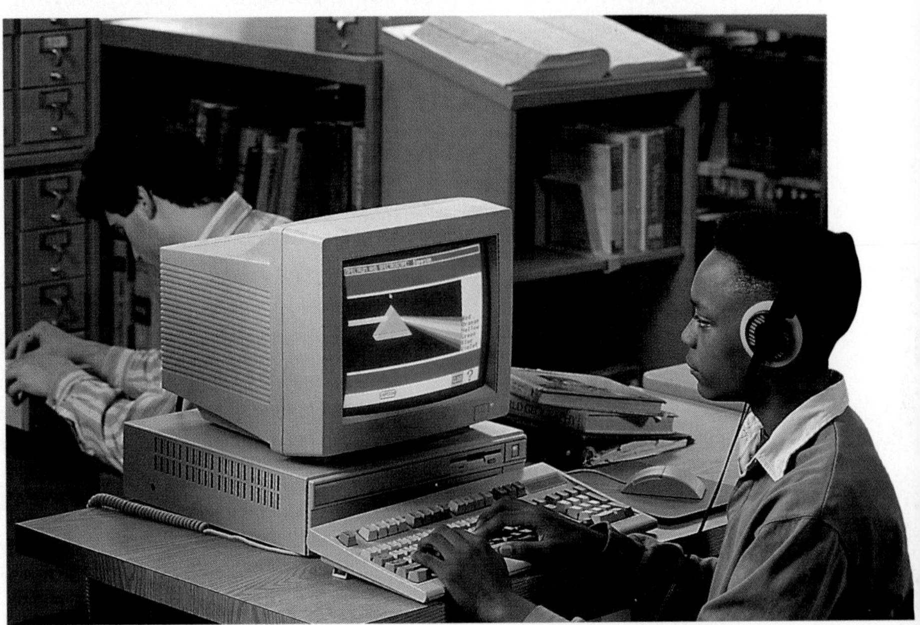

Listing Sources of Information. When people read your research report, they expect answers to the question "How do you know that?" In a *Works Cited* list at the end of your report, you will provide full information about every source you used—in a very precise format. Consequently, always carefully record information about sources *as you use them*. Otherwise, you may find yourself running back to the library or making a hasty, last-minute phone call to track down source information.

The best way to keep track of sources is to make a ***source card,*** or ***bibliography card,*** on a 3″ × 5″ index card for every source you decide to examine. You can use notebook paper, but cards are easier to handle, add to, and sort into alphabetical order for the Works Cited list. You'll also save time later if you record the information in final format (see the Works Cited examples on pages 476–480).

The format for recording source information shown in this chapter is that of the Modern Language Association (MLA). Your teacher may want you to follow a different format; but whatever system you use, pay close attention to *information required, styling* (capitalization, underlining, and so on), and *punctuation.*

GUIDELINES FOR SOURCE CARDS

1. **Number your sources.** To save time during note taking, assign a number to each source. Then you can write the number, rather than author and title, when you are taking notes.
2. **Record all publishing information.** Take down everything you *might* need: title and subtitle, an editor or translator, volume number, original publication year, revised edition year, and so on. You may have more than you need for the Works Cited list, but you won't have to backtrack for a tiny piece of missing information. (See the sample entries on pages 476–480 for the kinds of information required.)
3. **Note the call number or location.** This information will save you time if you must go back to a source later.

SAMPLE SOURCE CARD

8

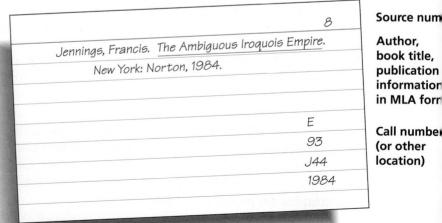

Jennings, Francis. The Ambiguous Iroquois Empire.

New York: Norton, 1984.

E
93
J44
1984

Source num

Author, book title, publication informatio in MLA forr

Call numbe (or other location)

To develop a research plan

- create a list of questions to guide your research
- gain a quick overview of your topic from general reference sources
- find specific information sources in the library or community
- use the "4R" test to evaluate the sources (pages 447–448)
- record all publishing information about your sources on index cards

PART 2:
Finding, Evaluating, and Listing Sources of Information

As director of research, you now need to identify sources of information for the topic you selected in the Writing Assignment, Part 1 (page 443). Follow the basic steps listed in the Reminder above, but allow yourself some flexibility to work with your topic. For example, the best overview for your topic may come from some knowledgeable person, not an encyclopedia. Try to find five or six different, acceptable information sources, of whatever type; and when you have a good list together, save it for later use.

Researching Your Topic

The word *search* is three fourths of the word *research*, which is an appropriate proportion: The diligent search for specific information is often the major part of a research project. The time you spend finding the facts, examples, opinions, and quotations you need to produce a strong and convincing report will be time well spent—provided that you take good notes.

Taking Notes

Careful note taking is vital to a good paper. Take notes thoughtfully but sparingly—you can't write down everything. Referring to your research questions will keep you focused on needed information. Use 4″ × 6″ cards (or single sheets of paper) so that you have ample space but can also easily sort information later. You'll take two main kinds of notes: (1) *summaries or paraphrases* and (2) *direct quotations*.

Summaries and Paraphrases. In most of your notes, you'll use your own words. A ***summary*** is a very brief statement, in your own words, of a source's main ideas. For example, you might summarize the relevant ideas in a two-page encyclopedia article on a single note card. A ***paraphrase*** is a restatement that retains more details. Often you'll want to note important details such as names, places, dates, and statistics; they're necessary and effective in a good report. For note-taking purposes, summaries and paraphrases don't have to be written in complete sentences. (See pages 1082–1085 for information on more formal uses of summaries and paraphrases.) You save space and time by using abbreviations, phrases, lists, and sentence fragments.

Direct Quotations. Use a ***direct quotation*** only when an idea is particularly well phrased or intriguing, or when you want to be sure of technical accuracy. When writing down a direct quotation, copy each word and punctuation mark carefully. *Always* enclose direct quotes in quotation marks on your note card (even if you expect to paraphrase them later) so that when you write your report, you'll remember that these words are the author's, not your own.

GUIDELINES FOR NOTE CARDS

1. **Use a separate note card (or sheet of paper) for each source and for each main idea.** If a card has information from two sources or unconnected items, you will have trouble sorting and grouping the notes later.
2. **Write the source number in the upper right-hand corner and the page number(s) at the bottom of the note.** Both numbers are essential for correct documentation. The number you have assigned to the source is your key to all publication data on the source card. And if you use the note's information, you will have to supply the page number(s) in your paper.
3. **Write a label showing the main idea at the top of the card.** The labels will let you see content at a glance.
4. **Reread the note to make sure you understand it.** Abbreviations and other shortcuts are fine, but be sure you can "translate" them. Check for clarity now—not later, when you're trying to draft.

Here's an excerpt from *The Indian Heritage of America* (page 95), by Alvin M. Josephy, Jr., followed by a sample note card on the information. The researcher has given this source the number *14*.

> However it was originally achieved, the League of the Five Nations in practice rested on the organization of Iroquois political life, in which women held a special and important position. The foundation of Iroquois society was the "fireside," comprised of the mother and all her children. Each fireside, in turn, was part of a larger *ohwachira,* a group of related families in which relationships were traced through mothers. Two or more *ohwachiras* composed a clan, and the various clans within a tribe constituted the nation. All authority stemmed ultimately from the *ohwachiras* and the women who were at their heads. They named the male delegates and *ohwachira* representatives in clan and tribal councils, as well as the fifty sachems, or peace chiefs, who made up the ruling council of the Five Nations.

SAMPLE NOTE CARD

The League 14

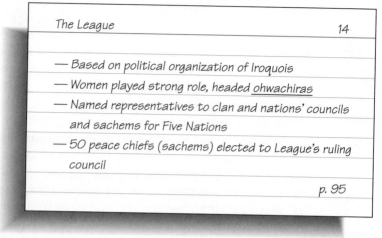

— *Based on political organization of Iroquois*
— *Women played strong role, headed* *ohwachiras*
— *Named representatives to clan and nations' councils and sachems for Five Nations*
— *50 peace chiefs (sachems) elected to League's ruling council*

p. 95

EXERCISE 3 **Taking Notes**

The following excerpt is from an article in *Science* magazine called "Dinosaurs and Friends Snuffed Out?" by Richard A. Kerr. It appears on page 160 of the January 11, 1991, issue. Take notes on the article for a research report, answering the questions listed before the excerpt. Make a minimum of three note cards (give the source number as 2), and include in your notes at least one direct quotation.

1. Who are Luis Alvarez and Walter Alvarez?
2. What is their theory about why dinosaurs became extinct?
3. Why did paleontologists object to the Alvarezes' theory?

In the 10 years since Nobel Laureate Luis Alvarez, his son Walter Alvarez, and their colleagues made the controversial suggestion that an asteroid impact wiped out the dinosaurs and a host of other species 66 million years ago, their hypothesis has won many adherents. Most geologists now agree, for example, that an asteroid or a comet did indeed strike at the right time. But one important group of scientists held back: the paleontologists.

Early on, the keepers of the fossil record protested that such a biological catastrophe was nonsense. Even if there was a gigantic impact, they said, it didn't have anything to do with the demise of the dinosaurs. The fossil record clearly showed that the plants and animals that had dominated Earth for tens to hundreds of millions of years before the asteroid struck died out gradually, species by species, over millions of years, not suddenly as the impact hypothesis predicted.

Now, more and more paleontologists are coming around to the idea of a catastrophic impact. As paleontologist Peter Ward of the University of Washington puts it, "The old saw was that [species] went out gradually, but as specialists begin to look more closely, they're finding otherwise." What's convinced them are new, intensive field studies. Not that the new records can be used to prove that a given species went out during "one bad weekend," as the impact advocates would have it. But what had appeared in some cases to be a gradual depletion of species turns out to be an artifact of the way paleontology has usually been done. "About 100 years too late, people are looking at what [the fossil record] really means," adds paleontologist David Raup of the University of Chicago. "This is a marvelous time. People are asking new questions and using new tools."

The primary new tool in studying mass extinctions is the sort of exhaustive field work the Alvarezes and their supporters had advocated for years. The fossil record had been read traditionally from specimens returned from the field for a variety of studies, none of them being the detection of sudden extinctions. The Alvarezes and others argued that this was simply too imperfect a means of telling whether a particular group of animals had petered out before the impact struck or was getting along just fine, thank you, until the moment of destruction.

Most paleontologists dismissed these arguments. Neither Luis Alvarez nor his son was a fossil expert; Luis, who died in 1988, was a physicist, and Walter is a geologist.

Richard A. Kerr, *from* "Dinosaurs and Friends Snuffed Out?"

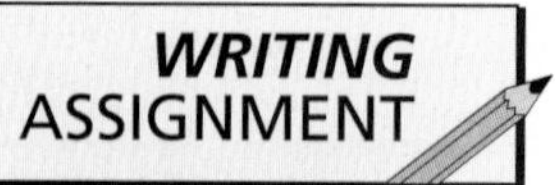

PART 3:
Taking Notes for Your Report

In this assignment you'll take notes for your report—something that will take some time and is very important. Before starting, review your research questions. Let them guide you to significant information. Remember to enclose direct quotations within quotation marks so you won't be confused later about whether or not the words are your own, and double-check all spelling and punctuation. A final wise step is to recheck all notes and source cards before returning any library materials. Do you understand them? Do they seem complete?

CRITICAL THINKING
Drawing Conclusions

Part of a researcher's task is to make sense of a great deal of information. You can't always simply report; sometimes you have to ***draw conclusions,*** to arrive at reasonable ideas about facts, opinions, and theories that you find. Controversial topics may even call for conclusions about opposing positions. This is the case in the Writer's Model you'll read on pages 463–469. The writer's research reveals that some experts believe the Iroquois League influenced America's government but others don't.

However, drawing conclusions can occur throughout a paper, not just in disputes. For example, the writer researching the Iroquois League discovered the following facts about Benjamin Franklin and then drew the conclusion that follows.

Facts:
In 1744, Franklin attended a meeting in which the League's leaders advised colonists to join together as the Iroquois had done. One chief showed that five arrows bound with sinew could not be broken, while a single arrow could.

In 1750, Franklin wrote to a friend that the colonies needed a union like the Iroquois Confederation.

In 1754, Franklin proposed the Albany Plan, a forerunner of the Articles of Confederation; that plan had similarities to the League's organization. An Iroquois was invited to the Albany meeting.

John Kahionhes Fadden, "Tree of Peace." Acrylic on canvas, 1987. Courtesy Akwe:kon Journal, Cornell University, Ithaca, New York.

Conclusion:
Benjamin Franklin is a clear link between the Iroquois League and the founding of our nation. He knew and admired the League's government and suggested it as a model for the colonies. He very likely brought these ideas to the Constitutional Convention.

When you are drawing conclusions, use these guidelines:

1. **Examine *all* the information, and gather more if it seems insufficient.** If you try to reach a conclusion without enough facts, you may make a *hasty generalization* that ignores exceptions (see page 325).
2. **State your conclusion in precise language.** The conclusion above says that Franklin is a "clear link," not that his experiences *prove* that the U.S. government is based on the Iroquois League. Also use qualifying words (notice *very likely* in the conclusion's last sentence); they can make broad statements acceptable and useful.

CRITICAL THINKING EXERCISE: Drawing Conclusions

Graphs, tables, and charts provide a good opportunity to practice drawing conclusions because they present "raw data"—uninterpreted facts. You'll frequently find a graph or chart in your research, and to present its information in your paper, you will have to draw conclusions for readers. Study the three graphs below; then answer the questions following the graphs.

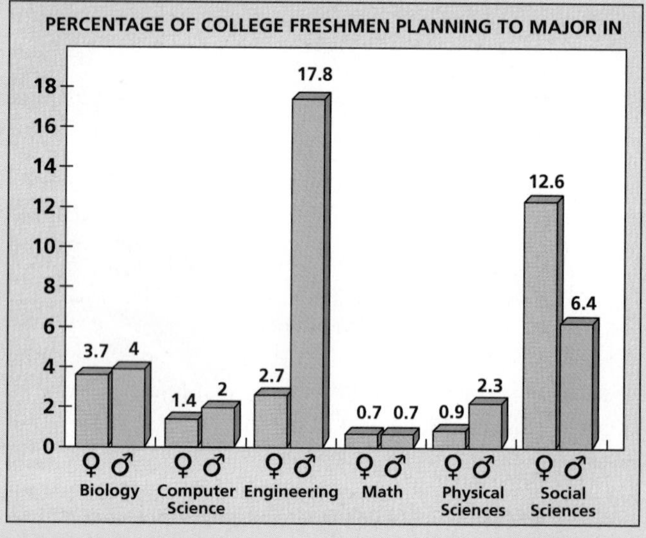

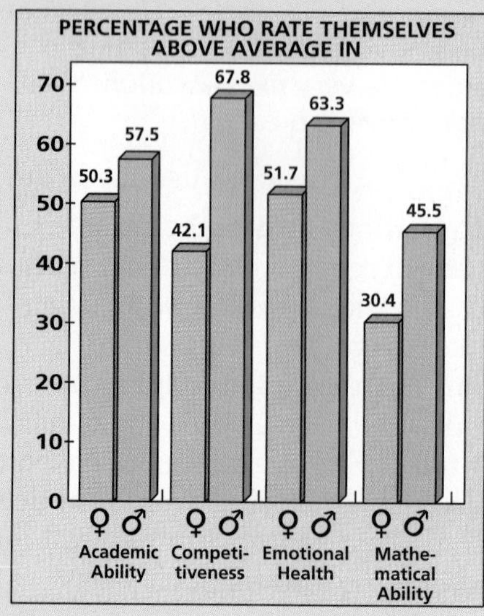

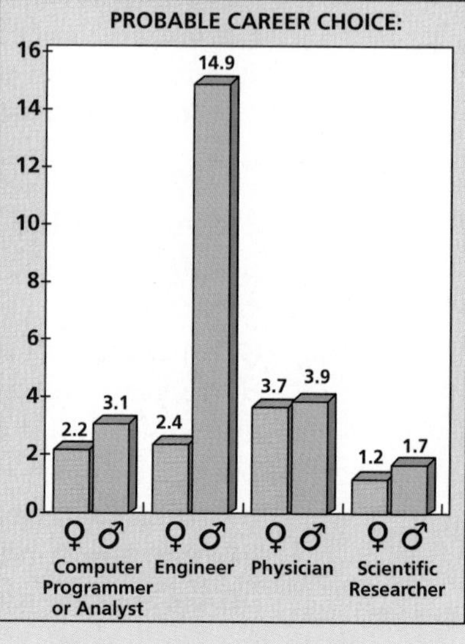

1. What conclusion(s) could you draw about the differences between men and women regarding the field of engineering?
2. What conclusion(s) could you draw about the self-image of male and female first-year students?
3. Based on the information in these graphs, would the following conclusion be valid? "In their first year of college, men have somewhat greater academic abilities, drive, and emotional health than women have."
4. Should the date of the survey be given when you draw conclusions about these graphs in a paper? Why or why not?

Graphs and charts can be useful in research reports because they allow you to condense information into a compact form. Often, putting numerical data or other detailed information into sentences and paragraphs is cumbersome—for you and your readers. Instead, you can refer readers to a chart's data while discussing its meaning in your paper. Whether you use a chart from a source or create your own, check the *MLA Handbook* (or a style guide your teacher specifies) for mechanics of form and of crediting a source.

Writing a Thesis Statement

Your ***thesis statement*** is a sentence or two telling the main idea of your paper. Like drawing a conclusion, writing a thesis statement is an act of ***synthesis,*** reviewing and pulling together all your information to say what the paper is about. A thesis statement guides you as you write by helping you focus on information that should directly support or develop the thesis. Of course, a thesis statement at this point is *preliminary:* It may change as you draft and revise the paper.

SAMPLE THESIS STATEMENTS

Because the Iroquois League had an influence on the founders of the United States, important similarities exist between the League and the U.S. government.

There are a number of parallels between the lives of the English novelist Jane Austen and the American poet Emily Dickinson.

Some computer games help to develop critical thinking skills, such as evaluating, making inferences, and drawing conclusions.

REFERENCE NOTE: For more information on writing thesis statements, see pages 100–101.

Making an Outline

Even though you've organized many papers before, the mass of information that you collect for a research report may make you dread this necessary step. Don't. Note cards (or notes on single sheets of paper) actually help accomplish your main tasks of grouping and ordering.

The labels on your notes allow you to sort notes into stacks by main ideas. You can go through each stack, deciding which ideas to use or set aside, whether "substacks" are possible, and what order will present the information clearly. Cards make arranging and rearranging information easier.

However, it is also helpful to make an outline on paper so that you have an overview of your writing plan. You can make an ***informal outline*** for planning; but after your paper is complete, your teacher may want you to prepare a final outline, which serves as a table of contents. This final ***formal outline*** must follow standard outline format, as shown in the following model. (The following model shows a partial outline. Note that formal outlines often omit the introduction and conclusion.)

America's Legacy from the Iroquois League

I. Iroquois League
  A. Founding, members, and purpose
    1. Date: about 1500
    2. Legend of Deganawidah's vision
    3. Union of five (then six) nations: Mohawk, Oneida, Onondaga, Cayuga, Seneca (Tuscarora, 1722)
    4. Establishment of peace, rights, and law
  B. Great Law of Peace, or constitution
    1. Joint laws, rules, and customs
    2. Oral transmission
    3. First written version, about 1850
    4. English translation by Seth Newhouse, 1880
  C. Council of sachems (chiefs)
    1. Fifty sachems
      a. Appointment by clan mothers
      b. Apportionment by heritage and power
    2. One vote per tribe
    3. Unanimous decisions
II. Parallels between Iroquois League and U.S. government
  A. etc.

 REFERENCE NOTE: To review outline form, see pages 105–106.

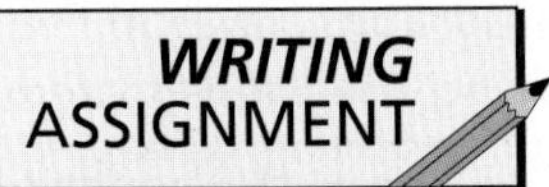

PART 4:

Writing a Thesis Statement and Outlining

This is a time to look in two directions—back at the information you have collected and ahead to the paper you plan to write. You have been "in the field," as some researchers say, collecting information. Now take a look at what you have and write a preliminary thesis statement, identifying the main thing you want readers to know about your topic. Then decide how to organize and create an informal outline. When you have finished this assignment, you'll be ready to think about drafting.

Writing Your First Draft

Source cards, stacks of note cards, a thesis statement, and a preliminary outline—you have everything you need to begin writing. If you've done your work carefully up to this point, you should be able to transform your notes and ideas into sentences and paragraphs with relative ease. The important thing is to dive in.

A research paper does have unique elements, however, as the following chart shows. Notice that a research paper, like many longer pieces of writing, such as most compositions, includes an introduction, body, and conclusion.

ELEMENTS OF A RESEARCH REPORT	
Formal outline (optional)	Some teachers request a formal outline of the final content of the report.
Title	The title of the report, sometimes on a separate page, can be interesting but should also communicate the topic. (Your teacher may recommend a title-page format.)
Introduction	The introduction captures the reader's attention and curiosity.
Thesis statement	A statement of the main idea appears early in the report, usually in the introduction. Its wording may not be the same as the preliminary thesis statement.
Body	The body paragraphs develop the main ideas supporting the thesis statement.
Conclusion	The conclusion brings the paper to a convincing end, usually by restating or summarizing the main idea.
Works Cited list	This list appears on a separate page (or pages) at the end of the report. It provides complete publication information for each source cited in the report.

Notice the listed elements in the Writer's Model that follows, as well as the way the writer weaves facts, quotations, and summaries of information into a unified essay. In the paper, you will see source information, or ***citations*** (covered in detail on pages 471–475), in parentheses.

A WRITER'S MODEL

America's Legacy from the Iroquois League

INTRODUCTION

Author named, TV interview, no pages

Striking quotation

In 1991, television journalist Bill Moyers interviewed Oren Lyons, chief of the Onondaga nation and a professor of American studies at the State University of New York at Buffalo. Chief Lyons mentioned the upsurge of American-inspired democracy throughout the world and commented, "But America got it from the Indians. America got the ideas of democracy and freedom and peace here."

Thesis statement

Lyons's statement may seem extreme, but he is not alone in believing that Native Americans, particularly the Iroquois, influenced the colonists who founded the United States. In 1988, which was the two hundredth anniversary of the signing of the U.S. Constitution, a joint Congressional resolution stated that

Indented quotation

> the confederation of the original Thirteen Colonies into one republic was influenced by the political system developed by the Iroquois Confederacy as were many of the democratic principles which were incorporated into the Constitution itself. (United States)

Despite an official resolution, many people do not know about this influence. What was the Iroquois Confederacy? What parallels between it and the American government have historians found? What contacts did Iroquois and colonial leaders have?

BODY
Iroquois League

The Iroquois Confederacy, a union of five (later six) nations, is said to have originated about 1500. It is known by several names: the Iroquois League, League of the Houdenosaunee, and Five Nations. According to legend, a Mohawk prophet named Deganawidah had a vision of a Great Peace that would unite the warring Iroquois nations into one people (Bjorklund 57; Moquin 20).

Two sources cited

Legend of founding
Details

In Deganawidah's vision, a huge evergreen tree, rooted firmly in the earth, reached "through the sky to the land of the Master of Life" (Farb 97). The roots of this tree of peace were the Iroquois nations: the Mohawks, Oneidas, Onondagas, Cayugas, and Senecas. (The Tuscaroras joined in 1722.) Deganawidah convinced the separate nations to form a union with the goal to advance "peace, civil authority, righteousness, and the great law" ("Iroquois League").

Direct quotation, no author

Great Law of Peace

The League did create an unwritten but detailed Great Law of Peace, or constitution, that was passed down through the generations. It was first put into writing about 1850; and in 1880, Seth Newhouse, a Seneca, wrote an English version that fully spells out the League's laws, rules, and customs (Moquin 20).

Council
Details (summary)

The constitution empowered a council of fifty sachems, or chiefs, to make decisions about affairs among nations. Traditionally, these sachems were chosen by each nation's powerful clan mothers; but beginning in the seventeenth century, leadership ability was favored over family relationships (Johansen, Forgotten 26). The number of a nation's sachems depended on heritage and power, with the smallest but most feared group, the Onondaga, having the greatest number (Spencer et al. 384; Bjorklund 58). However, in decisions about League actions, each nation had one vote, which was internally decided by its sachems. League decisions had to be unanimous.

More than one title in Works Cited

Four or more authors

Parallels between League and U.S. government

An obvious parallel between the Iroquois League and the federal government is union itself. The League was a strong confederation of nations

Unity

that were related by language and culture but had a history of being separate and quarrelsome (Jennings 362-63). The thirteen American colonies were likewise separate and sometimes at odds. First the Articles of Confederation, in 1781, and then the Constitution of the United States created a strong union of these formerly divided colonies.

Noninterference in nations/states

Common knowledge, no citation

Also, the League dealt only with issues concerning all the nations, primarily matters involving safety and defense. It did not interfere in the internal affairs of member nations (Bjorklund 59; Farb 98). Similarly, the U.S. Constitution spells out the powers delegated to the federal government, including national defense, reserving all other powers to the states' own governments.

Delegates' procedures

Author and title named in text

Both the Iroquois and U.S. constitutions established a representative government of delegates, and several historians have noted likenesses between Iroquois and Congressional procedures. Bruce E. Johansen explains in Forgotten Founders that the Great Law of Peace spelled out a "complex system of checks and balances," with the Senecas and Mohawks called the "older brothers," the Cayugas and Oneidas the "younger brothers," and the Onondagas the "firekeepers" (24-25).

Paraphrase

Encyclopedia article, no page needed

Negotiation was highly structured, and Johansen compares the younger and older brothers to a "two-house congress" and says, "The Onondagas filled something of an executive role, with a veto that could be overridden by the older and younger brothers in concert" (25). Alvin M. Josephy, Jr., also points out that Senate and House of Representative conferees use methods similar to those of the Iroquois sachems when they work out compromise bills (35). It was through "elaborately ritualized systems" that the League worked through disagreements to unanimous decisions ("Iroquois League").

Amendments, nondiscrimination

Finally, scholars have noted the Great Law's provisions for amendments and for accepting other peoples into the union (Johansen, Forgotten 24-25; Bjorklund 62). Like the framers of the U.S. Constitution, the Iroquois provided a mechanism for changing their law, and they made "no bars on the basis of race or national origin." Two colonial men were actually given full citizenship in the Confederacy (Johansen, Forgotten 24).

Opposing views

Of course, the League and America's new government were not identical, and not everyone agrees that the Iroquois League was a direct model or had an important influence. Michael Newman, a political journalist, maintains that "Western civilization, beginning in Greece" was a closer model for the founders (17). He has pointed out differences in the Iroquois and U.S. systems, also noting that a respected Constitutional scholar, Michael Kammen, does not support the idea that the Iroquois influenced the writing of the Constitution (17). Kammen's books, A Machine That Would Go of Itself: The Constitution in American Culture and The Origins of the American Constitution: A Documentary History, in fact do not discuss the Iroquois League.

Other models

Expert opinion

Entire books cited

Differences in system

Specific examples

The differences Newman highlights are that the sachems were appointed, not elected; that representation on the Council wasn't proportional; and that Council votes had to be unanimous (17).

Historians who support the theory of Iroquois influence, however, do not claim that no differences existed. Peter Farb, for example, has pointed out additional differences: that the League did not have the power to impose taxes and did not have its own military to enforce its decisions (98). As Johansen replied to Newman's article, the point is not that colonial leaders tried to "copy" the Great Law but that Native Americans helped "shape the thoughts of our Founders" (Letter).

Rebuttal: Influence, not imitation

One-word quotation

Transition to new main topic

Newman's position, however, seems even to reject this idea. In his view, the writers of the Constitution had "nothing" to gain by "looking to the New World for inspiration" (17-18). Nevertheless, Newman does not discuss the considerable contact between colonial leaders and the Iroquois.

Contact between Iroquois and founders

The 1988 Congressional resolution states that "the original framers of the Constitution, including, most notably, George Washington and Benjamin Franklin, are known to have greatly admired the concepts of the Six Nations of the Iroquois Confederacy" (United States).

Benjamin Franklin's knowledge of Iroquois League

Benjamin Franklin is an especially clear link between the two political systems, as history documents. He was Pennsylvania's representative to the Iroquois Nations and, as clerk of the Assembly, served as recording secretary at a 1744 meeting between leaders of the Six Nations and the Virginia, Maryland, and Pennsylvania colonies (Johansen, Letter). Here sachems advised the colonial governors to join together as the Iroquois had. One chief took a single arrow in his hand and snapped it easily. Then he took five arrows bound together with a deer sinew; they could not be broken.

Franklin's opinions

There is no question that Franklin found the Iroquois League impressive. On March 20, 1750, he wrote to James Parker, his friend and fellow printer:

Primary source

> It would be a strange thing if Six Nations . . . should be capable of forming a scheme for such a union, and be able to execute it in such a manner as that it has subsisted ages and appears indissoluble; and yet that a like union would be impracticable for ten or a dozen English colonies, to whom it is more necessary and must be more advantageous, and who cannot be supposed to want an equal understanding of their interests. (444)

Early plan

Native American participation

In 1754, Franklin proposed his important Albany Plan of Union for the American colonies; the Plan resulted from a meeting at which Tiyanoga, an Iroquois chief, was an invited adviser (Johansen, Letter). Franklin's plan called for a Grand Council made up of delegates from the colonies. The number of delegates from each colony would vary, depending not on population but on the amount of money each colony gave to the general treasury (Adler 522-23). The Albany Plan failed, but it planted the seeds for the Articles of Confederation and the U.S. Constitution.

Additional evidence of contact and knowledge

Franklin and others who wrote the Constitution and earlier plans for union may not have specified--in historical documents--that they were using Native American political concepts and laws, but they did consider them. Records show that colonial leaders purposely studied many examples of union. Stephen L. Schechter, executive director of the New York State Bicentennial Commission, said,

Quotation from an indirect source

"They contemplated examples from Europe, examples from Greco-Roman times, examples from the Bible. And they also looked at Native American examples, particularly the Iroquois Confederacy" (qtd. in "Iroquois Constitution").

CONCLUSION

Writer's conclusion

Many Americans today are only dimly aware of the characteristics of the Iroquois League, not realizing that the United States may owe a debt to the Six Nations for America's political heritage. That debt cannot be measured exactly, but historians agree that "democratic government, brotherhood in society, and equality of rights were . . . characteristic" of the Native American culture that colonial leaders came to know in some detail (Bjorklund 156).

Restatement of thesis

The Iroquois League gave our nation's founders a living example of successful union; and it is understandable why some historians believe that our government--

Clincher/vivid quotation

which has so inspired other nations--was not necessarily "cut entirely from European cloth" (Johansen, Letter).

Works Cited

Adler, Mortimer J., ed. The Annals of America. Vol. 1. Chicago: Encyclopaedia Britannica, 1968.

Bjorklund, Karna L. The Indians of Northeastern America. New York: Dodd, 1969.

Farb, Peter. Man's Rise to Civilization as Shown by the Indians of North America from Primeval Times to the Coming of the Industrial State. New York: Dutton, 1968.

Franklin, Benjamin. "To James Parker." 20 Mar. 1750. Letter in Benjamin Franklin: Writings. New York: Library of America, 1987.

"Iroquois Constitution: A Forerunner to Colonists' Democratic Principles." New York Times 28 June 1987, sec. 1: 40.

"Iroquois League." New Encyclopaedia Britannica: Micropaedia. 1990 ed.

Jennings, Francis. The Ambiguous Iroquois Empire. New York: Norton, 1984.

Johansen, Bruce E. Forgotten Founders: Benjamin Franklin, the Iroquois and the Rationale for the American Revolution. Ipswich: Gambit, 1982.

---. Letter. New Republic 19 Dec. 1988: 4.

Josephy, Alvin M., Jr. The Indian Heritage of America. New York: Knopf, 1968.

Kammen, Michael. A Machine That Would Go of Itself: The Constitution in American Culture. New York: Knopf, 1987.

---. The Origins of the American Constitution: A Documentary History. New York: Penguin, 1986.

Lyons, Oren. Oren Lyons: The Faithkeeper. By Bill Moyers. Public Affairs Television. WNET, Newark. 3 July 1991.

Moquin, Wayne, ed., with Charles Van Doren. Great Documents in American Indian History. New York: Praeger, 1973.

Newman, Michael. "Founding Feathers: The Iroquois and the Constitution." New Republic 7 Nov. 1988: 17-18.

Spencer, Robert F., et al. The Native Americans. New York: Harper, 1977.

United States. Cong. House Committee on Interior and Insular Affairs. House Report 100-1031. 100th Cong., 2nd sess. H. Res. 331. Washington: GPO, 1988.

Using Quotations

When you use information from sources in your paper, most of it will be summarized. By summarizing, you shape the information to the needs of your own writing *and* avoid boring readers with strings of quotations. However, direct quotations are important for variety and will sometimes make your point better or more vividly than a summary. Following are some ways to use quotations smoothly.

GUIDELINES FOR USING QUOTATIONS

1. **Quote one or more whole sentences, introducing them in your own words.**

   EXAMPLE Chief Lyons commented, "But America got it from the Indians. America got the ideas of democracy and freedom and peace here."

2. **Quote part of a sentence within a sentence of your own.**

   EXAMPLE Bruce E. Johansen explains that the Great Law spelled out a "complex system of checks and balances" (Forgotten 24).

3. **Quote only a few words (or even just one word) within a sentence of your own.**

   EXAMPLE These historians do not believe the writers of the Constitution tried to "copy" the Great Law (Johansen, Letter).

4. **Use ellipsis points (three spaced periods) to show you've omitted words from a quotation.** You may want to alter a quotation to shorten it or make it fit grammatically into your text. If so, you must use ellipsis points for words deleted within a sentence or for any deletion that makes a partial sentence from the source appear to be a complete sentence.

   EXAMPLE Johansen explains that "The retention of internal sovereignty within the individual colonies . . . closely resembled the Iroquoian system" (Forgotten 71-72).

(continued)

GUIDELINES FOR USING QUOTATIONS *(continued)*

5. **Set off longer quotations as "blocks."** For quotations of four lines or more, start a new line, indent the entire quotation ten spaces from the left margin, continue to double-space, and do not use quotation marks.

   EXAMPLE See the quotation from Benjamin Franklin's letter on page 467.

Documenting Sources

Documentation, giving credit to your sources, is an important part of writing a research report. How can you tell whether to give credit or not? Here are some *do*'s and *don't*'s.

GUIDELINES FOR CREDITING SOURCES

1. **Do** credit the source of each quotation (unless it's very widely known, such as George Bush's "Read my lips").
2. **Do** credit the source of information from scientific studies, surveys, and polls and other sources of unique or little-known information. (Doing so also lends credibility to sources of information unfamiliar to your audience. You want your audience to accept the information you present.)
3. **Do** credit any original theory, opinion, or conclusion. You must not present another person's ideas as your own, even if you are paraphrasing them. (See the discussion of plagiarism on the next page.)
4. **Don't** credit facts that appear in standard reference works or several sources. For example, the names of the nations in the Iroquois League are given in most encyclopedias and do not need documentation. And if several history books state that League votes had to be unanimous, you do not need to credit this information.
5. **Don't** credit common, or general, knowledge. For example, you don't have to document the fact that oil spills damage the environment or that Washington, D.C., does not have Congressional representatives.

Avoiding Plagiarism. Caution! If you use someone else's *words or ideas* without giving proper credit, you're guilty of ***plagiarism.*** Plagiarism is a serious offense, and your teacher will view it as such. Be scrupulous about crediting not only direct quotations but also restatements of the original ideas of others. Don't use another person's phrases or exact sentence structure unless you enclose the material in quotation marks. When in doubt about plagiarism, give credit.

Using Parenthetical Citations. The source references in parentheses in the body of the Writer's Model are called ***parenthetical citations.*** The purpose of a parenthetical citation is to give the reader just enough information to find the full source listing on the Works Cited page. Often, the author's last name and the page numbers are all that is needed, but here are some exceptions to that rule.

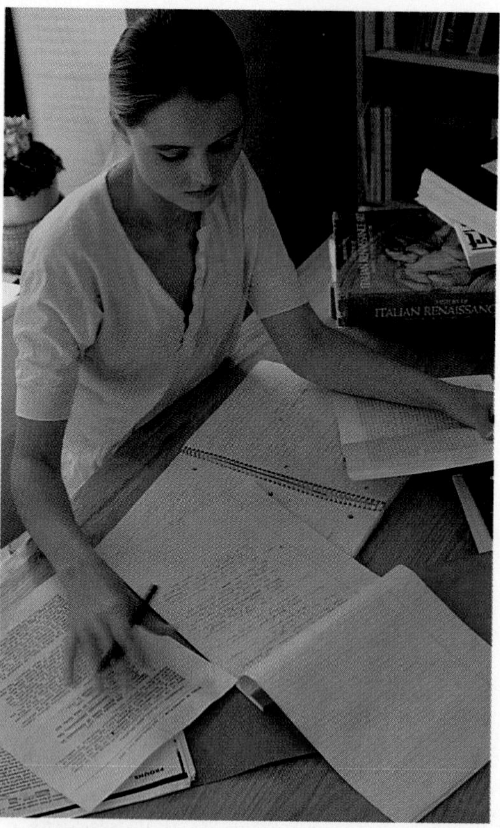

- A nonprint source such as an interview or audiotape will not have a page number.
- A print source of fewer than two pages (such as a one-page letter) will not require a page number.
- If you name the author in your sentence, you need give only the page number (for print sources of more than one page) in parentheses: Michael Newman, a political journalist, maintains that "Western civilization, beginning in Greece" was a closer model for the founders (17).
- If the author has more than one work in the Works Cited list, you will also have to give a short form of the title so readers will know which work you are citing: (Johansen, Forgotten 24) or (Johansen, Letter).

The following chart defines and illustrates the basic forms of parenthetical citations.

BASIC CONTENT AND FORM OF PARENTHETICAL CITATIONS

These examples assume that the author or work has not been named in introducing the source information.

Works by one author Author's last name and a page reference	(Farb 97)
Works by more than one author All author's last names (or first author and *et al.* if over three) and a page reference	(Richter and Merrill 78) (Spencer et al. 384)
Multivolume works Author's last name plus volume and page(s)	(Prucha 2: 115-16)
Works with a title only Full title (if short) or a shortened version and a page reference	(World Almanac 394) ("Iroquois League" 5)
Literary works published in many editions Author and title above, but with other identifying information, such as act, scene, and line numbers	(Shakespeare, Tempest III. 2. 51-52)
Indirect sources *Qtd. in* ("quoted in") before the source and a page reference	(qtd. in Newman 17)
More than one work Citations, with page numbers, separated by semicolons	(Bjorklund 57; Moquin 20)

There are rules of form about placement of citations, too. Again, use both the following chart and the Writer's Model for examples.

PLACEMENT OF CITATIONS

1. Put the citation close to the information it documents, but try not to interrupt sentences. Place it at the end of a sentence or at another point of punctuation.
2. Place the citation *before* the punctuation mark of the sentence, clause, or phrase you're documenting.

   EXAMPLE The League was a strong confederation of nations that were related by language and culture but had a history of being separate and quarrelsome (Jennings 362-63).

3. For a direct quotation that ends a sentence, place the citation *after* the quotation mark but *before* the end punctuation mark.

   EXAMPLE The Onondagas were the "firekeepers" (Johansen 24).

4. For an indented quotation, place the citation **two spaces after the final punctuation mark.**

   EXAMPLE See pages 463 and 467.

An alternative to the parenthetical citation system is citation by numbered *footnotes* or *endnotes.* Footnotes and endnotes are identical, except that a ***footnote*** goes at the bottom of the page where the source is cited, while ***endnotes*** are listed together on a separate page at the end of the report.

In using either type of note, place the note number in the text where a parenthetical citation would otherwise appear. The first time a work is cited, give full publication information in the note. Thereafter, use a short form. If your teacher wants you to use footnotes or endnotes, you'll need guidelines showing further examples of form.

EXAMPLE

Number in body of paper	In the giant tree a vigilant eagle searched for anyone who threatened to disturb the Great Peace.[7]
Note (full form)	[7] Karna L. Bjorklund, The Indians of North-eastern America (New York: Dodd, 1969) 61.

Listing Works Cited. The list of ***Works Cited*** contains all the sources that you cite in your paper. *Works Cited* is a broader term than ***Bibliography,*** which refers only to printed information. Don't include in the list sources that you looked at but did not refer to. (Some teachers, however, may want you to list *all* sources consulted. If so, prepare a ***Works Consulted*** list.)

GUIDELINES FOR PREPARING THE WORKS CITED LIST

1. **Center the heading *Works Cited* on a separate page from your report.**
2. **Begin each entry on a separate line.** Start the first line of the entry at the left margin. Then indent the second and subsequent lines five spaces. Use double-spacing.
3. **Alphabetize the sources by the authors' last names.** If a source has no author, alphabetize it by the first word of the title, ignoring an initial *A, An,* or *The.*
4. **If you list two or more sources by the same author, put the author's name only in the first entry.** For subsequent entries, put three hyphens where the author's name would be, followed by a period (- - -.).

EXERCISE 4 Using Sources

Work with a partner to practice using direct quotations, summaries, and paraphrases of material from sources, as well as parenthetical citations. Using the source information in the directions for Exercise 3 (page 454) and its excerpt about the extinction of dinosaurs, complete the tasks that follow on the next page. For each task item, include a parenthetical citation.

1. Write a sentence that summarizes Luis and Walter Alvarez's theory about what caused the extinction of dinosaurs. Include a few words of direct quotation in the sentence.
2. Write two sentences explaining the paleontologists' objection to the Alvarezes' theory. Make your first sentence a direct quotation of the first sentence in paragraph two, introduced with the author's name.
3. Write a paragraph about what paleontologists are doing now. Include part of the quotation by David Raup of the University of Chicago.

PART 5:
Writing Your First Draft

Use your outline and note cards to write a first draft of your research report. Before you begin, recheck the list of elements on page 462, and then concentrate on getting ideas down on paper. *Do* insert parenthetical citations—without stopping your flow too much. You only need to get a basic reference in: You can add, delete, and correct form in the citations later. Finally, draft a Works Cited list of the sources you actually credit in the paper, *using the guidelines that follow to prepare it.*

SAMPLE ENTRIES FOR LIST OF WORKS CITED

These sample entries, which use MLA style, are a reference for preparing your Works Cited list. Notice that you include page numbers only for articles in periodicals or for other works that are part of a whole work, such as one essay in a book of essays.

Standard Reference Works
When an author or editor is credited in a standard reference work, that person's name is written first. Otherwise, the title of the book or article appears first. Page and volume numbers aren't needed if the work alphabetizes entries. For common reference works, the edition year is sufficient publication information.

(continued)

SAMPLE ENTRIES FOR LIST OF WORKS CITED *(continued)*

ENCYCLOPEDIA ARTICLE

Smith, Whitney. "Great Seal of the United States." Encyclopedia Americana. 1990 ed.

"Iroquois League." New Encyclopaedia Britannica: Micropaedia. 1990 ed.

ARTICLE IN A BIOGRAPHICAL REFERENCE BOOK

Amacher, Richard E. "Benjamin Franklin." Dictionary of Literary Biography. Ed. Emory Elliott. Vol. 24. Detroit: Gale, 1984. 125-47.

Books

Use shortened forms of publishers' names. For the words *University* and *Press* use *U* and *P*.

ONE AUTHOR

Graymont, Barbara. The Iroquois in the American Revolution. Syracuse: Syracuse UP, 1972.

TWO AUTHORS

Deloria, Vine, Jr., and Clifford M. Lytle. The Nations Within: The Past and Future of American Indian Sovereignty. New York: Pantheon, 1984.

THREE AUTHORS

Gosnell, Cullen B., Lane W. Lancaster, and Robert S. Rankin. Fundamentals of American Government: National, State, and Local. New York: McGraw, 1957.

FOUR OR MORE AUTHORS

Spencer, Robert F., et al. The Native Americans. New York: Harper, 1977.

NO AUTHOR SHOWN

Report on Indian Education. Washington: American Indian Policy Review Commission, Task Force Five, 1976.

EDITOR OF A COLLECTION OF WRITINGS

Tooker, Elisabeth, ed. An Iroquois Sourcebook: Political and Social Organization. New York: Garland, 1985.

(continued)

SAMPLE ENTRIES FOR LIST OF WORKS CITED *(continued)*

TWO OR THREE EDITORS

Foster, Michael, Jack Campisi, and Marianne Mithun, eds. Extending the Rafters: Interdisciplinary Approaches to Iroquoian Studies. Albany: State U of New York P, 1984.

TRANSLATOR

Chateaubriand, François René de. Travels in America. Trans. Richard Switzer. Lexington: U of Kentucky P, 1969.

Selections Within Books

FROM A BOOK OF WORKS BY ONE AUTHOR

Wilson, Edmund. "The Seneca Republic." Apologies to the Iroquois. New York: Vintage, 1959. 169-97.

FROM A BOOK OF WORKS BY SEVERAL AUTHORS

Hallowell, A. Irving. "The Backwash of the Frontier: The Impact of the American Indian on American Culture." The Frontier in Perspective. Ed. Walker D. Wyman and Clifton B. Kroeber. Madison: U of Wisconsin P, 1957. 231-58.

FROM A COLLECTION OF LONGER WORKS (NOVELS, PLAYS)

Duberman, Martin. The Colonial Dudes. The Best Short Plays 1973. Ed. Stanley Richards. Radnor: Chilton, 1973. 291-317.

[*The Colonial Dudes* is a play included in *The Best Short Plays 1973.*]

Articles from Magazines, Newspapers, and Journals

FROM A WEEKLY MAGAZINE

Adler, Jerry. "The Genius of the People." Newsweek 25 May 1987: 46-47.

FROM A MONTHLY OR QUARTERLY MAGAZINE

Zobel, Hiller B. "How History Made the Constitution." American Heritage Mar. 1988: 54+.

[The + sign means the article isn't on consecutive pages.]

(continued)

SAMPLE ENTRIES FOR LIST OF WORKS CITED *(continued)*

NO AUTHOR SHOWN

"Revenge of the Senecas." Time 2 July 1990: 27.

FROM A SCHOLARLY JOURNAL

Day, Gordon M. "Iroquois: An Etymology." Ethnohistory 15 (1968): 389-402.

FROM A DAILY NEWSPAPER, WITH A BYLINE (LINE IDENTIFYING THE WRITER)

Grimes, William. "The Indian Museum's Last Stand." New York Times 27 Nov. 1988, sec. 6: 46+.

FROM A DAILY NEWSPAPER, WITHOUT A BYLINE

"Iroquois Constitution: A Forerunner to Colonists' Democratic Principles." New York Times 28 June 1987, sec. 1: 40.

UNSIGNED EDITORIAL FROM A DAILY NEWSPAPER, NO CITY IN PAPER'S TITLE

"Supreme Injustice." Editorial. Star-Ledger [Newark, NJ] 6 Oct. 1991: 17.

Other Sources

PERSONAL INTERVIEW

Whitecrow, Gloria. Personal interview. 15 Aug. 1991.

TELEPHONE INTERVIEW

Hauptman, Laurence M. Telephone interview. 5 Oct. 1991.

PUBLISHED INTERVIEW WITH TITLE

Johnson, Elias. "Origin of the Five Nations." Cry of the Thunderbird: The American Indian's Own Story. Ed. Charles Hamilton. Norman: U of Oklahoma P, 1972.

RADIO OR TELEVISION INTERVIEW WITH TITLE

Lyons, Oren. Oren Lyons: The Faithkeeper. By Bill Moyers. Public Affairs Television. WNET, Newark. 3 July 1991.

(continued)

SAMPLE ENTRIES FOR LIST OF WORKS CITED *(continued)*

UNPUBLISHED LETTER

Franklin, Benjamin. Letter to Count de Bouffon. 19 Nov. 1787. Library of Congress, Manuscript Division, Washington.

UNPUBLISHED THESIS OR DISSERTATION

Richards, Cara E. "The Role of Iroquois Women: A Study of the Onondaga Reservation." Diss. Cornell U, 1957.

CARTOON

Wilson, Gahan. Cartoon. Gahan Wilson's America. New York: Simon and Schuster, 1985. 32.

SPEECH OR LECTURE

Prucha, Francis Paul. "The Indians in American Society: Self-Determination." Thomas I. Gasson Lecture. Boston College, 13 Mar. 1985.

RECORDING

Sainte-Marie, Buffy. "Native North American Child." Native North American Child: An Odyssey. Vanguard, VSD 79340, 1974.

FILM, FILMSTRIP, OR VIDEOTAPE

Drums Along the Mohawk. Dir. John Ford. With Claudette Colbert, Henry Fonda, Edna May Oliver, and John Carradine. Twentieth Century Fox, 1939.

[The title, director, distributor, and year are standard information. You may add other information, such as performers.]

TELEVISION OR RADIO PROGRAM

Benjamin Franklin Alive. With Bill Meikle. PBS. WGBH, Boston. 19 Sept. 1988.

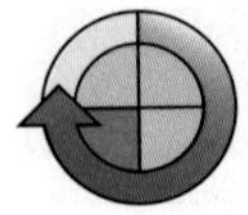

Evaluating and Revising

Break the process of evaluating and revising into steps: First focus on content, then on organization, and finally on clarity and style. Be sure to use the chart on page 482.

EXERCISE 5 Analyzing a Writer's Revisions

Here is the first draft of a paragraph from the model on page 464. Study the revisions and answer the questions.

The constitution empowered a council of fifty sachems (, or chiefs,) to make decisions about affairs among nations. Traditionally, these sachems were chosen by each nation's powerful clan mothers; but ~~"during the seventeenth and eighteenth centuries, chiefs were elected outside this hereditary structure on the basis of their leadership qualities"~~ beginning in the seventeenth century, leadership ability was favored over family relationships (Johansen, Forgotten 26). The number of a nation's sachems depended on ~~being upper class plus tough,~~ heritage and power, with the smallest but ~~scariest~~ most feared group, the Onondaga, having the greatest number (Spencer et al. 384; Bjorklund 58). However, in decisions about League actions, each nation had one vote, which was internally decided by its sachems. League decisions had to be unanimous.

Revision
add
replace
replace
replace
add
add

1. The writer made two additions to the paragraph's content. How does each addition help the reader?
2. The writer replaces a direct quotation in the second sentence. Is the change an improvement? Why?
3. Why were the replacements made in the third sentence?
4. The writer made an addition to one citation. Why?

EVALUATING AND REVISING RESEARCH REPORTS

	EVALUATION GUIDE	REVISION TECHNIQUE
1	Does a thesis statement appear early in the report?	**Add** a statement to the introduction that gives your report's main idea.
2	Is the report developed with sufficient sources that are relevant, reliable, recent, and representative?	**Add** facts, examples, or expert opinions. **Cut** or **replace** outdated or questionable information. **Add** sources to balance controversial views.
3	Is the report clear, interesting, and suitable for its audience?	**Add** needed background information and explanations. **Add** interesting, unusual, or surprising details.
4	Is the tone of the report appropriate?	**Replace** words or phrases that make your report sound too casual.
5	Are ideas and information stated mainly in the writer's own words?	**Cut** unnecessary quotations. **Replace** sentences in which your wording is too close to that of the source.
6	Does all the information relate directly to the topic and thesis?	**Cut** information that doesn't develop your main ideas.
7	Has proper credit been given for each source of information?	**Add** proper documentation for quotations, others' ideas, and information that is unique or not general knowledge.
8	Does documentation follow the style recommended by your teacher?	**Replace** and correct as necessary to follow MLA style or another professional style.

GRAMMAR HINT

Varying Sentence Structure

It's very possible to write a long paper, full of information, that is energetic and easy to read. One way to do that is to vary the types of sentences you use. By paying attention to how your sentences work together and using different sentence structures, you can create variety both in length and in rhythm.

EXAMPLES

Simple sentence: one independent clause. *It did not interfere in the internal affairs of member nations.*

Compound sentence: two or more independent clauses connected by a conjunction or semicolon. *Then he took five arrows bound together with a deer sinew; they could not be broken.*

Complex sentence: one independent clause and one or more subordinate clauses. *As Johansen replied to Newman's article, the point is not that colonial leaders tried to "copy" the Great Law.*

Compound-complex sentence: two or more independent clauses and at least one subordinate clause. *Lyons's statement may seem extreme, but he is not alone in believing that Native Americans influenced the colonists who founded the United States.*

REFERENCE NOTE: For more information on sentence structure, see pages 686–687.

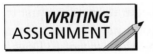

PART 6:
Evaluating and Revising Your Report

Ask someone else to read your report, and pay close attention to reactions and suggestions. Using the guidelines on page 482, continue to revise until you're satisfied that your report is tightly organized, well focused, clear, and interesting.

Proofreading and Publishing

Proofreading. Besides your usual proofreading, a research paper requires a careful check for accuracy in citations and the Works Cited entries. Keep the reference lists on pages 473 and 476–480 beside you as you work. You might also want to exchange papers with a classmate, for some peer proofreading. You might catch errors in each other's papers that your familiarity with your own work doesn't allow you to notice.

Publishing. A research paper is a real achievement, a testimony to hard work, persistence, and thought. So do think about ways to share it with others. Brainstorm with your class about imaginative publishing, and consider these possibilities:

- During your research, you may have come across people or groups that would have a special interest in your subject. For example, the researcher writing about the Iroquois saw a number of references to the Association on American Indian Affairs. The Association might appreciate a copy of "America's Legacy from the Iroquois League" for its files. Who might like to have a copy of your report?
- Your research report may serve as a writing sample to accompany a college-entrance application or a job application. If you use your report for this purpose, make sure it fits the requirements given by the college or business organization.

PART 7:
Proofreading and Publishing Your Report

When you're proofreading, a separate reading just for citations and the Works Cited list is a good idea. (Check for mechanics, but also make sure citations and the list *match:* Does every citation have an entry in *Works Cited*? Do authors or titles appear the same way in both places?) But don't neglect errors in your writing itself. When you have a clean, professional-looking paper, show it off to someone, perhaps using one of the two publishing ideas listed above.

A STUDENT MODEL

You can apply your research skills to any topic, as Jennifer Guild—a student at Nashua High School in Nashua, New Hampshire—shows in her research paper on birth order and personality. Notice how the following excerpts both develop support for her thesis and provide a thought-provoking conclusion. And Jennifer has this to say about writing a research paper: "Keep track of where your notes are from!"

Birth Order
by Jennifer Guild

Your birth order, whether you were born first, second or later in your family, has a powerful influence on the kind of person you will be. It also affects the kind of person you will marry, the type of occupation you will choose, and even the type of parent you will be (Leman 11). The patterns set in motion by birth order don't prescribe what must occur; they simply describe tendencies that may need to be recognized or overcome (Withers 58). This paper illustrates what some researchers suggest about how oldest, only, middle, and youngest children are affected by their birth order.

Birth order characteristics appear to be set by age five. They tend to start over with the next child when there exists a large age difference of five or more years between siblings. Birth order traits develop as coping strategies a child uses to feel comfortable in his or her particular position in the family. These coping strategies include to be pleasing, to be perfect, to be strong, or to try hard (Isaacson 5).

Some only children develop birth order characteristics while trying to avoid excessive attention from their parents and while playing alone without the company of siblings. Shy and self-conscious around their peers, onlies are used to considerate treatment from their parents and other adults. Thus, their feelings are easily hurt when other children are rude. Not having siblings to relate to or play with, onlies automatically identify with their parents and come to think of themselves as small adults (Spock 38). Only children tend to pick up characteristics of their same-sex parent. Onlies are often most comfortable alone, yet they tend to be well-adjusted individuals (Withers 59). . . .

Firstborn children tend to be more serious in their approach to life and are likely to be jealous of their younger siblings' easy popularity (Spock 38). Usually the more studious of the children, firstborns may be considered overachievers. Relatively quiet and reserved, self-assured firstborns may become perfectionists and worriers who find it difficult to take criticism or tolerate other's mistakes. They may be slow to make friends, perhaps being content with only one companion (Withers 59). Firstborn children may identify more readily with parental authority because, among other things, they are often put in charge of younger siblings. Through this identification, firstborns absorb the norms and values of society in ways that subsequent children do not. "The older child gets responsibility. He's the company man," says University of Michigan psychologist Robert Zajonc (Denworth 76). . . .

Middle children, in contrast to onlies and oldest children, tend to make friends more quickly. Unlike firstborns, they identify with other children and share their eager playfulness. In fact, they're so eager to make friends that they easily overlook the impolite behavior of other children and win them over with their innate friendliness. Middle children are not generally self-conscious; they tend to be more at ease with themselves and the world (Spock 38). Middle children are less likely to take initiative or achieve the high academic standards of an only or an oldest child. They are more anxious and self-critical than others (Withers 59). "The general conclusion of all research studies done on birth order is that middle children will probably be somewhat opposite of firstborns" (Leman 117). . . .

Lastborn children may carry the yoke of not being taken very seriously, first by their families and then by the world. Lastborns are acutely aware that they are the youngest, smallest, weakest, and least equipped to cope with life. Lastborns instinctively know and understand that their knowledge and ability carry far less weight than that of their older brothers and sisters. The older kids always laugh at the baby who still believes blindly in fantasies like Santa Claus and the Tooth Fairy. It's no wonder the lastborns grow up with an "I'll show them!" attitude (Leman 133-136). . . .

Birth order continues to be revealing when you look at who's in what occupation. All seven astronauts in the original Mercury program were firstborns in their families (Leman 11). James Watson and Francis Crick were the pair of firstborns who won the 1962 Nobel Prize in physiology or medicine, for explaining the makeup of DNA. Fran S. Sullaway, a historian of science at MIT, says, "Nobel Prizes are given for solving clever puzzles. That's something firstborns are good at. Firstborns tackle officially sanctioned puzzles while later borns flock to the untried and novel" (Denworth 76).

Birth order can give great insight and may be helpful in understanding others. Not every aspect of birth order psychology may apply to every individual, but for the most part, birth order does have an effect on people's personalities. Look at the understanding of birth order as a tool, allowing conflicts with others to be an opportunity for growing.

WRITING WORKSHOP

Informal Research: Investigating Unsolved Mysteries

All those television shows aside, detectives are not the only ones who love a good mystery. Researchers do, too. In fact, the world's fascinating, unsolved mysteries probably make researchers out of many people: Exploring *why* and *how* can be a lively career.

Think of the mysteries that have never been solved. No one can say for sure how the huge statues on Easter Island, some of them weighing more than fifty tons, got there or what purpose they served. Nor can anyone explain what was seen in some well-documented sightings of UFOs (unidentified flying objects). Researchers have devised theories attempting to explain these mysteries, but no one yet knows the full truth. (A ***fact*** can be proved true or false by observation or verification in references. A ***theory*** is a possible explanation that, despite all existing evidence, can't be—or hasn't yet been—proved true.)

You yourself can be a researcher of unsolved mysteries by investigating both the known facts of a mysterious phenomenon and the theories advanced by other researchers to explain these facts. For example, on pages 454–456 you read about one of the world's great unsolved mysteries—why dinosaurs became extinct—and took notes on a theory proposed by Luis and Walter Alvarez. The Alvarezes believe that when an asteroid hit the earth with tremendous impact, the resulting changes in climate and weather killed the dinosaurs. But not all scientists agree. For a research report, you could inform readers about the extinction mystery and the different theories advanced to explain it.

For this writing assignment, you'll choose one of the following unsolved mysteries, or find one of your own, and write a research report about it. Discussing unsolved mysteries in class may lead to other topics.

- What was the purpose of Stonehenge?
- Did King Arthur and the Knights of the Round Table really exist?
- Are sasquatches (or the Abominable Snowman) real?
- What caused Amelia Earhart's plane to go down in the South Pacific?
- For what reason(s) did the Nazca in Peru construct earthen lines, trapezoids, and giant animal figures?
- Does the Loch Ness Monster actually exist?
- What happened to the crew of the *Mary Celeste*?

Writing an Informal Research Report

Prewriting. Consult at least three sources, being sure to evaluate them using the "4R" test (pages 447–448). If you can find a TV documentary on the mystery (check your video store), it may provide a good overview. Don't forget to keep accurate source information for documentation. To guide your research and note taking, use the following questions:

1. What is the mystery? What facts and reputable personal reports have brought it to light?

2. What theory or theories explain the mystery? What evidence do the researchers use to support their ideas?
3. What conclusions, if any, can *you* draw? Is one theory more believable? Why? (This theory *may* be your own.) Does solving the mystery seem probable or not? Why?

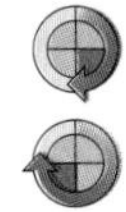

Writing, Evaluating, and Revising. At the beginning of your report, give background information for understanding the mystery and the theories about it. This material may include dates, places, statistics, and facts about people important to the research. Then, devote at least one paragraph to each theory. Finally, give and explain your opinion. You might judge one theory more plausible and well supported. You might speculate on the new facts or discoveries needed to *prove* a theory to be true—that is, to change it from theory to fact. (Remember visuals for this report. You may want to include charts, illustrations, or photographs.)

Since this report is informal, it is not necessary to use formal citations and a Works Cited page to credit sources. As in many magazine and newspaper articles, you can simply identify the source within the body of your report. For example, here is the way you might handle a source of information on the Loch Ness monster:

> According to Mary Cardenes of Earth's Mysteries, "The sightings of the Loch Ness monster have increased considerably in the last five years."

You can use the guidelines on page 482 to evaluate and revise your paper. Exchange papers with a partner or small group, and ask your partner-editor to note anything that puzzles him or her and to point out unanswered questions.

Proofreading and Publishing. After proofreading your writing and checking the accuracy of your references to sources, share your report as part of an "Unexplained Mysteries" display in the library or classroom. Presenting your findings in an oral report is another good idea. Your class could set up a lecture series or speakers' bureau for other classes and/or for younger students.

REFERENCE NOTE: See pages 992–998 for detailed suggestions on how to prepare and present an oral report.

MAKING CONNECTIONS

RESEARCH ACROSS THE CURRICULUM

Science: Experimental Research

Generally speaking, the kind of research you've been doing in this chapter involves finding information that other people have discovered using a variety of research methods. You assemble this information into a well-developed report and perhaps add your own conclusions.

Experimental research is different. It involves *designing and conducting* experiments to yield information about specific areas of interest. The researcher first determines what question he or she wants to answer and then carefully structures the experiment, controls its operation, records and tabulates the results (often numerical data), and writes a report.

Experimental research isn't restricted to laboratories. Deborah Tannen, for example, is a language researcher interested in comparing the ways men and women communicate. In her book *You Just Don't Understand: Women and Men in Conversation,* she reports on experimental research that has yielded these findings:

- Women use tag questions far more frequently than men. A tag question is a statement with a brief question tacked on at the end: "She's a fine actress, isn't she?"
- Men sit in relaxed postures (sprawling, taking up room) in both all-male and mixed gender groups; women sit in relaxed postures with other women but draw in to "lady-like" postures in mixed-gender groups.

Do these findings seem accurate? Experiment for yourself to find out—that's what other researchers in a field have done whenever new studies have been published. An important task of experimental research is attempting to verify information by ***replicating*** a study: performing the same or a similar experiment to see if the same results occur. Working with others, use the steps listed on the next page:

1. Design and conduct one of the following experiments. Use the directions as a guide, working out details with your group. If possible, consult a teacher familiar with research design. *The participants in the research cannot know what you are studying.*
   a. **Tag questions**: Count male and female tag questions in a mixed-gender group conversation for at least 30 minutes. You might observe a class discussion (with the teacher's permission), a public meeting, or a television talk show. Write *F* or *M* for each speaker, with a check mark for each tag question used.
   b. **Body posture**: Observe—if possible, videotape—three small-group meetings that you arrange: men alone, women alone, both together. You might ask for volunteers for an experimental discussion group on any topic (don't reveal your actual research objective). Devise a labeling system for "relaxed" and more "reserved" postures (again, use *F* and *M*), and take careful notes.
2. Review your data, and create tables or charts to show your findings. Think about different ways to present the information. For example, you may show total "counts" for each gender; you may calculate percentages (what percentages of male and female speakers used tag questions?); you may create comparison charts.
3. Write a report that describes the experiment, presents the data, and draws conclusions based on the data (see the Critical Thinking activity on pages 456–459).

SPEAKING AND LISTENING

History: Biography in Action

Curiosity about the lives of famous people, whether heroes or villains, is natural. What were they like—in life, not just in the pages of a history book or encyclopedia? What would they have to say if you could talk to them? Use your imagination and research to find out.

Choose a historical figure, from any age and any country, that you would like to learn more about. Read a full-length biography or several detailed articles about that person's life, and, if they are available, use films and videos as sources, too. Then prepare yourself to appear before the class, not as yourself, but as the famous person you've studied (and become). Costumes and props are fine, but your main purpose is to take questions from the class in an interview format. Here are some basic questions you should be ready to answer about "yourself" as that historical figure:

1. When and where were you born?
2. Who were your parents, and what were they like? (Also, sisters and brothers?)
3. What are some of the unusual or memorable experiences you had as a child and as a young adult?
4. What did you do that made you famous? What was your life like during the period when you achieved your greatest accomplishment?
5. What was your greatest mistake?
6. What about your life isn't generally known?
7. What person in your life had the greatest influence on you?
8. What do you think of the way the world is today? What would you like to change?

Encourage your audience to ask additional questions, and be prepared for imaginative questioning tactics.

12 English: History and Development

LOOKING AHEAD

Every English word you use—from *aardvark* to *zucchini*—has its own place in the history of the language. This chapter will lead you on a journey through that history, giving you a close look at some people, places, times, and events in the amazing story of English. As you work through the chapter, you will learn

- where English comes from
- how English has grown and developed
- how English is used throughout the world today

A Various Language

Like people and their cultures, languages change and develop over time. English used to sound and look very different from the way it does now. If you had lived in England a thousand years ago, you might have taken part in a conversation like the one on the next page.

That exchange from *Aelfric's Colloquy* is the English half of an English-Latin conversation for use by students of Latin in tenth-century England. The modern equivalent would be this:

Why don't you go fishing on the ocean?
Sometimes I do, but not often, because on the ocean I have to do a lot of rowing.
Would you like to catch a whale?
Not me!
Why?
Because it's a dangerous thing to catch a whale!

The English of a thousand years ago is so different from the language we speak that it is like a foreign tongue to us. However, we can still recognize some similarities between that form (called *Old English* or *Anglo-Saxon*) and our English. If we go back farther, though—say seven thousand years—the language would be so different that we would not call it English at all, but give it a different name (*Proto-Indo-European*).

A language changes gradually as it is passed on from one generation to the next. We change the words we use, the way we pronounce and spell them, and the way we put them together to make sentences. One cause of those changes is the fact that we meet speakers of other languages and imitate them. Over the centuries, English speakers have met speakers of Latin, Danish, French, Dutch, Spanish, German, and many other languages, and have taken something from each of those languages to make English marvelously complex and varied.

As a result of English speakers coming into contact with other languages around the world, English itself has grown in different directions in various places. Today, English takes many different forms in countries all over the planet.

The history of English can be divided into four main periods: *Pre-English, Old English, Middle English,* and *Modern English.* The following time line shows approximately when English moved from one period to the next. It also shows which languages had the most influence on the early development of English.

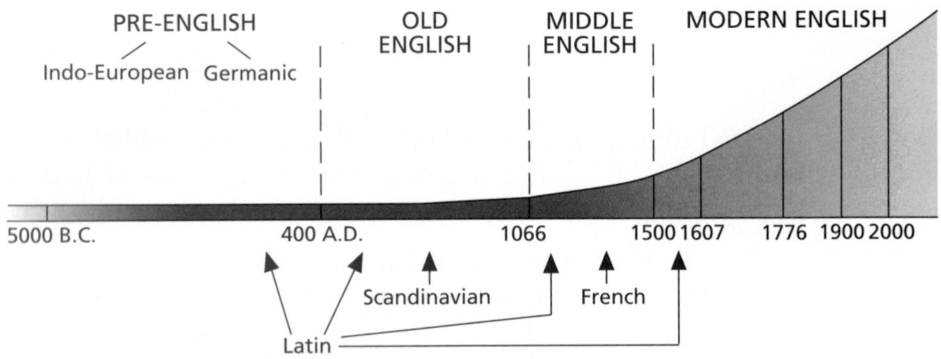

The Origins of English: Pre-English

About seven thousand years ago, the language we call ***Proto-Indo-European*** was spoken in Asia Minor or in southeast Europe—we are not sure exactly where. It was the ancestor of most of the languages of Europe and many of those of north India and Iran, and for that reason we name it *Indo–* (for India) and *European.* (*Proto–* means "first or earliest.")

Speakers of Proto-Indo-European migrated over all of Europe and south central Asia. One group of migrants settled along the coast of the North Sea, in what today is northern Germany. They consisted of several tribes—the Angles, Saxons, and Jutes. Their version of Proto-Indo-European, called ***Germanic,*** is the ancestor of present-day English.

While the Anglo-Saxons (as those tribes are collectively called) were living in northern Europe, they got to know another Indo-European people on their south, the Romans. From the Romans, they borrowed a number of Latin words (along with the things the words name), such as *wine* (*vinum*), *cheese* (*caseus*), *pepper* (*piper*), *kettle* (*catillus*), and *sack* (*saccus*).

Words that one language borrows from another are called ***loanwords.*** The chart on the next page shows the origins of some present-day English words.

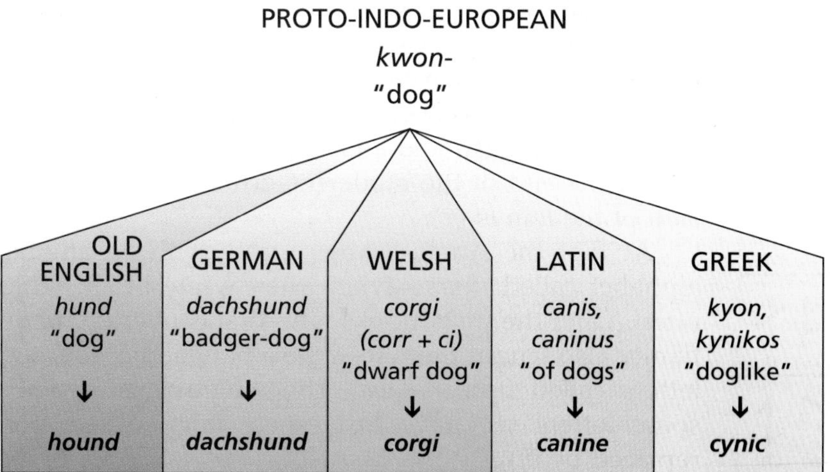

Old English

The Anglo-Saxons did not stay in northern Germany. Some of them took jobs with the Roman army, to work as mercenaries in the British Isles. Southern Britain and its native population of Celts had earlier been conquered by the Emperor Claudius and made into a province of the Roman Empire, but the northern part of the island was inhabited by a fierce, independent people called the Picts.

The Picts had a disconcerting habit of stripping naked, painting themselves blue, and howling as they charged down from the hills to raid their southern neighbors. To prevent such unwanted visits, the Roman Emperor Hadrian built a wall across northern England and hired troops, such as the Angles and Saxons, to keep the Picts on the other side. They succeeded in keeping the Picts under control, but in the long run the Anglo-Saxons turned out to be even more of a problem to the Celts.

After the Romans gave up ruling Britain, the Anglo-Saxons stayed on, and kin of theirs from the Continent arrived to join them. These Germanic peoples took over the south of the main island of Britain and called it after themselves, Engla land—the land of the Angles—or as we know it today, England. They also called their language *Englisc;* we call it ***Old English.***

The English of the Anglo-Saxons sounded very different from our English. They used sounds we have lost, as in their

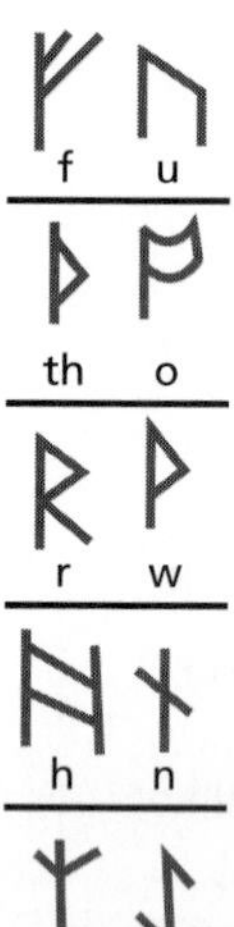

word *cniht,* which meant "boy" but has come to us with a changed meaning as *knight.* In Old English *cniht* had an initial *c* or *k* sound, which we continue to spell although we do not pronounce it. We also keep an unpronounced *gh* in the spelling, where Old English had an *h* representing a throaty sound like that at the end of the modern German word *ich* (a strong version of the *h* in *huge*).

At first the Anglo-Saxons wrote with an angular-looking alphabet called *runes*—when they wrote at all, which wasn't often. Later the Irish monks who first converted them to Christianity also taught them to write a handsome, rounded form of letters called *insular hand.* The Anglo-Saxons' alphabet had some letters we have lost, such as þ, called *thorn* (today replaced by *th*).

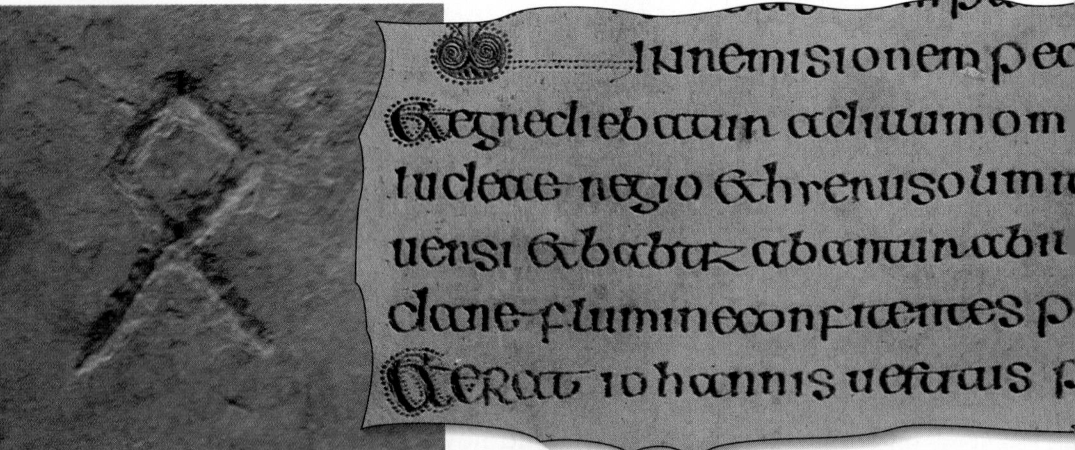

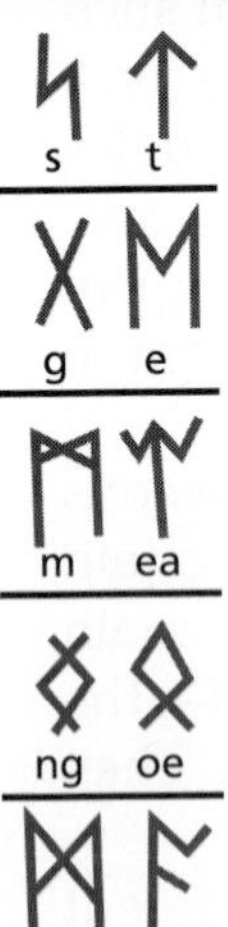

Many Old English words differed in spelling and pronunciation from those we use. For example, in Old English the verb *fish* was spelled *fix, fics,* or *fisc.* The Anglo-Saxons also had some words we have lost completely, such as *fon* or *gefon* for "take" or "catch," and they lacked a great many words we have, such as *dangerous* (instead of which they used *plyhtlic,* that is, "plightly"). Some words have changed meaning, like *cniht* (*knight*) mentioned earlier.

Old English words also had endings to relate them to other words in a sentence. For example, the verb *fish* took different forms depending on its subject.

ic fixe *or* fisce = I fish
þu fixast *or* fiscast = you fish
we fixiaþ *or* fisciaþ = we fish

Although English has changed over the centuries, many of our most familiar, everyday words are still native English—words that have been used by English speakers as far back in the past as we can see or imagine. Most of these words have changed their pronunciation and spelling, and many have changed their meanings, too. Yet their old forms are recognizable from their modern ones.

OLD ENGLISH	PRESENT-DAY ENGLISH
finger	finger
fot	foot
broþor	brother
hnutu	nut
hlaf (meaning "bread")	loaf
tun (meaning "enclosed place")	town

EXERCISE 1 Identifying Changes in Our Language

Here is a word-by-word translation of the Old English conversation at the beginning of this chapter. Using this literal translation to help you, compare the Old English version with its Modern English equivalent on page 495. What differences do you find in words, spellings, word combinations, and word order? What similarities do you see?

Forhwi ne fixast þu on sæ?
For-why not fishest thou on sea?

Hwilon ic do, ac seldon, forþam micel rewyt me ys to sæ.
Sometimes I do, but seldom, because much rowing to-me is at sea.

Wylt þu fon sumne hwæl?
Wilt thou catch some whale?

Nic.
Not I. [*Nic* is a contraction of *ne ic.*]

Forhwi?
For-why?

Forþam plyhtlic þingc hit ys gefon hwæl.
Because dangerous thing it is to-catch whale.

EXERCISE 2 Identifying Original Forms of Words

Look up each of the following words in a dictionary that gives etymologies (word origins). What did the word look like in Old English? Has its meaning changed since Old English times? If so, what did it originally mean?

1. heaven
2. dream
3. bread
4. elbow
5. starve

After they had been converted to Christianity by monks from Rome, the English borrowed many more Latin words. Many of these were for religious matters, but some were for other things. Following are examples of words that came into English from Latin. Notice the changes these words underwent on their way to Modern English.

Latin	Old English	Modern English
presbyter	preost	priest
apostolus	apostol	apostle
schola	scol	school
portus	port	port
butyrum	butere	butter

Old English also formed some compound words by imitation of Latin. Some of these compounds have survived. For example, *gospel* comes from the Old English compound *godspel*, meaning "good story," after Latin *evangelium*, from a Greek word meaning "good news." Other compound words have gone by the wayside, for example, the Old English *leorningcniht* meaning "learning-boy, student, disciple."

England was invaded by Vikings from Scandinavia several times in the ninth to eleventh centuries. Large numbers of these Northmen, or Norse, as they were also called, settled among the English. The Norse introduced into Old English Scandinavian words such as *give, skin, take, want,* and *window* (originally *vindauga,* "wind eye"), as well as the pronouns *they, them,* and *their*. The corresponding Old English words had been *giefan, hyd* (which survives as *hide*), *niman, willan* (which survives as *will*), *eagþyrl* ("eye-hole"), and the pronouns *hie, hem, heora*.

Middle English

In 1066 yet another group of Norse conquered England. Called the Normans ("northern people"), they had earlier settled in France and learned French. The Normans began the process of introducing a great many French words into the English language. *Army, court, government, literature, mirror,* and *service* are a few of those words.

The Norman Conquest marks the beginning of the ***Middle English*** period. During much of the Middle English period, English was used only by the common people for everyday matters. The important languages of the country were French and Latin, in which affairs of government, education, religion, law, and literature were expressed. In the fourteenth century, English began to be used for important purposes again, but by then English speakers had forgotten the native English words for many specialized subjects. And so they found it easiest to borrow large numbers of French and Latin words to use in talking about these matters.

Following are some more examples of French and Latin loanwords from the Middle English period:

FRENCH	cité	contrée	juge	libraire
ENGLISH	city	country	judge	library

LATIN	mercurius	scriba	sub poena ("under penalty")
ENGLISH	mercury	scribe	subpoena

EXERCISE 3 The Origin of Words

Look up each of the following words in a dictionary that gives etymologies (word origins). Which of the words came from Old English and which from French? What conclusions might you draw about the difference in life between English and French speakers in early medieval England?

1. admiral
2. attorney
3. fowler
4. plow
5. profession
6. shepherd
7. sheriff
8. soldier
9. tailor
10. weave

Modern English

Despite the Scandinavian and Norman French invasions of England, the Anglo-Saxons were relatively protected and isolated in England for nearly 1,200 years. Most of them were illiterate; they had little need to write or read because books were copied by hand and therefore were much too expensive for ordinary people.

Near the end of the fifteenth century, however, printing was introduced to England. The printing press had appeared in Germany in the late 1430s, and by 1455, Gutenberg had printed the Bible in Latin. In 1475 William Caxton published the first English book on a printing press in Belgium; it was a translation of a French work about the legends of the Trojan War. Two years later, Caxton began publishing books in England. Cheap books became readily available, and, as a result, communication and the English language were forever changed.

Handwritten manuscripts were produced slowly and expensively. Each copy was unique—at least slightly, and often greatly, different from every other. The printing press, on the other hand, allowed many identical copies of the same work to be produced cheaply. For the first time, anyone could have books to read, and many people could read the same text. The mass production of books and the resulting increase in literacy helped standardize the English language and make universal education possible.

In the sixteenth century, while the revolution of the printing press was still fresh, some English people got an itch to travel and see whether they could make their fortunes in foreign lands. The first of these adventurers and explorers were little more than pirates. They were sanctioned by the English government because they directed their piracy against other governments (like that of Spain, with whom Queen Elizabeth I had been feuding).

The Granger Collection, New York

Eventually, though, some English people traveled abroad for another reason—to settle in new lands. A little more than a hundred years after Columbus had stumbled upon the Western Hemisphere in 1492, the English decided they would try to plant some colonies there, too. They got into the colonial game rather late: Spain, Portugal, and France had all been busy sending out explorers, shipping over settlers, and exploiting the resources of the New World, while the English stayed cozily at home. The first successful English settlement in America was at Jamestown, Virginia, in 1607; the next was at Plymouth, Massachusetts, in 1620.

Edibles from the New World

Can you imagine life without french fries or catsup, mashed potatoes or spaghetti sauce? Potatoes and tomatoes, like many other common foods, were unknown in Europe before they were imported from the Americas. More often than not, the words used to name these foods were new to the Europeans, too.

Spanish explorers in the Americas discovered the white, or "Irish," potato among the Incas at the end of the sixteenth century. The English borrowed their name for this vegetable from the Spanish. The Spanish word was *patata,* a variant of the West Indian word for sweet potato.

Tomato comes from the language of the Nahuatl, a native people of Mexico and Central America. The Nahuatl word *tomatl* came into Spanish as *tomate,* and the English adapted the spelling in 1753.

The English colonies in America were the beginning of the British Empire. When those colonies broke away and declared themselves a single, independent nation, that action had two effects on the English language. First, the United States formed its own variety of standard English, different from the standard English of England. This new variety, ***American English,*** then proceeded to develop in its own direction. Second, deprived of their American colonies, the British were motivated to establish new colonies elsewhere. This colonization process encouraged the growth not only of the British Empire but also of British English.

The British began building an empire around the globe. British settlers and traders went to Canada, the Caribbean, India, Australia, New Zealand, South Africa, and many other places, taking the English language with them wherever they traveled. At the same time, Americans were spreading out into the West, gradually filling the area between the Atlantic and the Pacific that became the forty-eight continental states. As a result of these two expansions, English soon became the most widely dispersed language in the world, as well as one of the most widely used languages.

Meanwhile, back in England, the Industrial Revolution of the late eighteenth and early nineteenth centuries introduced more efficient methods of manufacturing. The combination of abundant goods and worldwide commerce helped spread the English language still further and make it into an important international tongue.

American English

The early American settlers, like colonists everywhere, changed their language by necessity. For example, they had to find names for some animals they had never encountered before. One such animal was a nocturnal creature with a ringed, bushy tail and black marks around its eyes that made it look like a bandit wearing a mask. It was a complete novelty to the English settlers, who asked the Algonquians of Virginia what they called it. The answer was something like *ärähkun,* which the settlers imitated as *raccoon.*

The settlers also saw another animal, a large bird with a splendid tail, which seemed very exotic to the English. Because exotic things were associated with the Orient or the Middle East, the colonists called this bird a *turkey fowl* after the country of Turkey. The raccoon has a borrowed name and the turkey an imaginative, invented one.

In other cases, the settlers adapted old words to new uses. In England, the word *creek* was used for a small bay or harbor on the seacoast. When the settlers arrived in the New World, they often landed at creeks, in the older English sense. But because those "creeks" were frequently the mouths of streams, the settlers used the word *creek* not just for the inlet by the sea but also for the stream that emptied into it, and for any tributary of a larger river.

The differentiation of American English from British English was greatly accelerated after the Declaration of Independence in 1776 and the success of the American Revolution. The citizens of the new country were proud of their land and wanted to be independent culturally as well as politically. As they set about building a new nation, they were also building a new literature and a new variety of the language.

In the late 1800s, Americans began to turn their attention to areas outside the continental United States. During the twentieth century, the nation has become an increasingly important international power. As a result, American English has exerted increasing influence on other varieties of English and other languages throughout the world. At the same time, these languages have been influencing American English.

Among the words and expressions that America has contributed to the English language are these:

arm-twisting	jalapeño pepper
charge card	maple syrup
fluorescent lamp	possum

EXERCISE 4 Identifying Americanisms

Which of the following words are Americanisms—words that entered the English language in the United States? To find out, look up each word in a dictionary that identifies Americanisms. (A good one is *Webster's New World Dictionary,* which labels each Americanism with a star.)

1. blintz
2. blizzard
3. dishwasher
4. fingerprint
5. ghostwriter
6. motel
7. pretzel
8. smog
9. tom-tom
10. waffle

English Around the World

Today, English has three kinds of users. First, there are those who speak it as their native language. They include all or much of the populations of the United States, Canada, the United Kingdom, Ireland, Australia, New Zealand, South Africa, Jamaica, and a number of other countries.

Second, there are those who use English frequently, often every day, as a second language. For example, India has two official languages, Hindi and English, and fourteen regional languages, some of which are completely unrelated to Hindi. Speakers of the latter languages in India prefer to use English for official use, rather than Hindi. English is used as a first or second language more widely around the world than any other language.

Third, some people use English occasionally or for special purposes. It is the main language of international commerce, communication, transportation, entertainment, science, technology, and scholarship around the world. A Norwegian pilot landing an airplane in Greece talks to the airport controller in English. A Japanese businessperson dealing with an Arabian sheik conducts negotiations in English. A Dutch student of physics reads textbooks and journal articles written in English. As a result, about seven hundred million people use English fluently, and half again as many use it with lesser degrees of fluency.

With so many people using English in so many places around the world, it is inevitable that new varieties and uses of the language should develop. For example, in India, English speakers talk about a *lakh,* which is "a hundred thousand" or loosely "a very large number," and call a popsicle *ice-candy.* They also say things like "Today is hot like anything," meaning "It is very hot today."

Some people think that because of such new varieties, English will break up into a number of different and mutually incomprehensible languages. That is exactly what happened to Latin some 1,500 years ago, when Italian, Spanish, French, Portuguese, Romanian, and other Romance languages began to develop out of local dialects of Latin. It also happened to Proto-Indo-European much earlier, and has happened to many other languages throughout history.

However, today circumstances are different. All languages change constantly. They have to, in order to adapt to changes in human knowledge and society. But if speakers of a language communicate with each other freely, their language will change in the same way for all of them over a period of time. The big difference between us and sixth-century speakers of Latin is the improvement in our communication and transportation. We can travel from the United States to Europe overnight, and we can talk with people on the other side of the globe almost instantaneously by means of telephone signals bounced off a satellite.

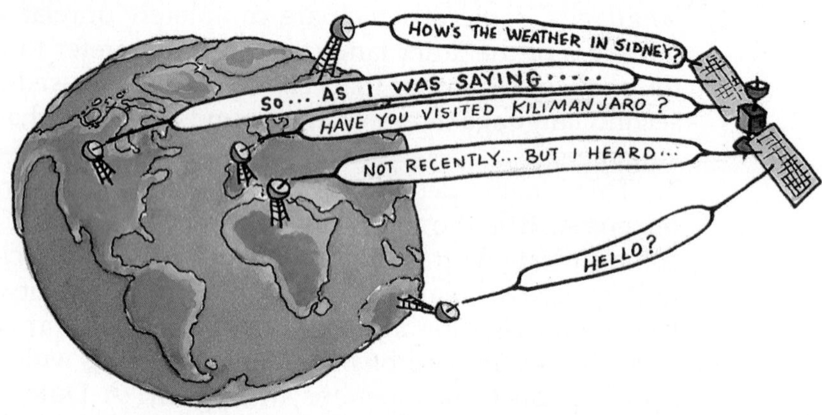

Local varieties of English are developing and will certainly continue to do so. But an international variety of the language is also developing. Because those who use that international variety communicate frequently with each other, it will stay relatively uniform. And it will influence the local varieties so that they do not turn into separate languages. What we are likely to see in the future is an international English that is pretty much the same all over the earth. Many local subvarieties of English will flourish, but they will be related to the central international variety as planets are to the sun.

EXERCISE 5 Speculating on the Future of English

You are an English-speaking person in the year 2500. What does your language look and sound like? How is it different from the English of the 1990s? Write a dialogue between two people discussing entertainment, sports, business, travel, or a similar subject. Write it in the kind of English you think might be used in the future. For your dialogue you might invent new words, new spellings for words, and new uses for old words.

Varieties of International English

The two major national varieties of English are American English and British English. About two thirds of the native speakers of English are Americans, and the United States and the United Kingdom together account for more than 85 percent of the world's native speakers of the language.

American and British versions differ somewhat in pronunciation or accent. They have quite a few differences in informal and specialized vocabulary but not many important ones in grammar. Americans and Britons have very little difficulty in understanding each other's writing and not much in understanding each other's speech.

Here are some differences in word choice between the two main national varieties of English.

British	American
beetroot	beet
biscuit	cracker or cookie
block of flats	apartment building
cornet	ice-cream cone
drawing pin	thumbtack
fiddle	swindle, cheat
hire (a car)	rent (a car)
jelly	jello
mash	mashed potatoes
polling day	election day
rota	duty roster, work schedule
sister	nurse
toffee-nosed	snobbish, stuck-up
zip	zipper

Each national variety of English has its own distinctive characteristics. The differences among the varieties are strongest in slang and informal language. In Australia, people say *g'day* for "hello," and they talk about having a *barbie* ("barbecue"), drinking *lollywater* ("a soft drink"), and eating a *sanger* ("sandwich"). In New Zealand, a driver may hit a *judder bar* ("speed-breaker, a bump in the road to slow down traffic") on the way to buy some *kitset furniture* ("ready-to-assemble furniture").

EXERCISE 6 Identifying Words from Other Varieties of English

Here are some words from other varieties of English around the world. The meanings and origins of these words are given in the second and third columns in jumbled order. See whether you can match each word to its meaning and origin. Try to guess and to use elimination before you look the words up in a dictionary.

Word	Meaning	Origin
colleen	club	Australian
dinkum	yearly festival	Australian
eisteddfod	food	British
hols	good, first-rate	British
kraal	hideaway, nook	Indic
loch	lake	Irish
pukka	true, genuine	Irish
shillelagh	holiday	Scottish
snuggery	village, stockade	South African
tucker	young woman	Welsh

Dialects of American English

The language we use tells much about us—our home locality, ethnic background, education, gender, and age. Language variation that tells such things about us, thus helping to identify who we are, is called ***dialect.*** The two main types of dialect are *regional dialects* and *ethnic dialects.*

Regional Dialects. Language varies from place to place. Geographical differences in a major variety of English are called ***regional dialects.***

In the United States, there are four main dialect regions in the eastern half of the country: *Northern, North Midland, South Midland, and Southern.* In the West, there is less regional distinctiveness. Within each of the major regions, there are also local dialects. In the North, Bostonians talk differently from New Yorkers; in the South, Charlestonians talk differently from New Orleanians. So too in Britain, there are major regional dialects like those of Scotland, Wales, and Southern England. And there are local variations, too: Liverpudlians (from Liverpool) don't talk like Glaswegians (from Glasgow) or Tynesiders (from Newcastle).

This chart shows some features of pronunciation, vocabulary, and grammar that distinguish one regional dialect in American English from another.

FEATURES OF REGIONAL DIALECTS

	NORTHERN	NORTH MIDLAND	SOUTH MIDLAND	SOUTHERN
PRONUNCIATION	"greassy"	"greassy"	"greazy"	"greazy"
	"hahg"	"hahg" or hog	hog	"hawg"
	"pahked cah"	parked car	parked car	"pawked caw"
WORD CHOICE	burlap bag or gunny sack	burlap bag	burlap bag	burlap bag or croker sack
	pail	bucket	bucket	bucket
	devil's darning needle	snake feeder	snake doctor	skeeter hawk
GRAMMAR	quarter of/to	quarter to	quarter till	quarter till/to
	you, youse	you	you, you'uns	you, y'all

Ethnic Dialects. In addition to regional dialects, there are also ***ethnic dialects***—the dialects of special communities that have preserved some of their heritage from the past.

The most prominent ethnic dialect in the United States is that of African Americans. It unites some features of West African languages with others from conservative varieties of early Southern speech and yet others developed by the African American community itself. Some features are *aunt* pronounced "ahnt," "He be sick" (meaning a continuing, rather than a temporary, illness), and *tote,* "carry" (of African origin, but now common in all Southern use).

Not all African Americans use the ethnic dialect associated with their group, and some features of the dialect turn up in other speech communities, too. So the boundaries of such an ethnic dialect, like those of geographical dialects, are fluid.

The second most prominent American ethnic dialect is Hispanic English, with three subvarieties: Mexican-influenced English in the Southwest; Cuban-influenced English in Florida; and Puerto-Rican-influenced English in New York City and, of course, in Puerto Rico. Early Hispanic influence in the West introduced such words as *vamoose* for "leave quickly" (from Spanish *vamos,* "let's go"), *hoosegow* for "jail" (from *juzgado,* "courtroom"), and *mesa* ("table").

Today, Spanish-influenced English sometimes uses English words with the meanings of similar Spanish words. For example, speakers of a Hispanic dialect may use *apple* with the meaning of "city block," since the Spanish word for apple, *manzana,* can also mean "city block." And Hispanic speakers may use *direction* with the meaning of the Spanish word *dirección* ("address").

EXERCISE 7 Identifying Dialect Differences

The following descriptions identify things that have different names in different parts of the United States. What word do you use for each thing? Do you know any other words for the same thing? Read each description to a friend, neighbor, or relative who grew up in another part of the United States (or another country) than you did. Note any differences between that person's word choice and your own.

1. a small town or rural area remote from the city
2. a porch or covered entrance outside a house
3. peanuts
4. what you say when you want to claim something as yours
5. a thick drink made of ice cream, milk, and flavoring blended together.

Standard English

Standard English is the most useful and the most widely used variety of English. Unlike a dialect, it is not limited to a particular place or group. It is used all over the United States (and even all over the world) by people of all backgrounds without indicating what place or group they belong to. It is the one variety of English that belongs to everybody.

The term *standard English* applies more to writing than to speech, especially in the United States. Standard English is especially appropriate for communicating with a general audience and with anyone outside a familiar circle of family and friends. It is the language of public affairs and education, publication and television, science and technology, business and government.

Nobody needs to use standard English all the time, but everybody should be able to use it when it is the appropriate variety to use. Dictionaries and grammar handbooks record the rules and guidelines of standard English for ready reference. You can find some of these rules and guidelines in the **Handbook** in this textbook. The **Handbook** uses the labels *standard* and *nonstandard* to identify differences between standard English and other varieties of English. *Nonstandard* doesn't mean wrong language. It means language that is inappropriate in situations where standard English is expected.

REFERENCE NOTE: For more about standard English, see page 842.

International Games

Sports terms are as international as the games themselves. Although each nation may specialize in a few sports, many sports are played—and talked about—around the world. As a result, a single sport may use terms from several different languages.

1. What sport or game uses each of the following terms? What language does each term come from? Use a dictionary to help you find out.
   a. hotdogging, schuss, slalom
   b. davit, luff, yaw
   c. caddie, niblick, par
2. Choose a sport or game you are interested in, and write down at least four terms used in it. Where do the terms come from?

13 Style in Writing

LOOKING AHEAD

Behind each effortless-sounding piece of writing is a real person who chose words with care. Professional writers develop style the same way you do—one word at a time. In this chapter, you will work on your style by

- adapting your writing to audience, situation, and aim
- experimenting with voice and tone
- choosing clearer, livelier words
- sidestepping some common obstacles to style

What Is Your Style?

Whether you are applying for a job, writing a history paper, or describing a movie to a friend, you make choices about what words to use and how to use them. The choices you make add up to your *style*. ***Style*** is your way of adapting your language to suit different occasions.

When you speak and write, you adapt your language to

- your aim—the purpose behind your words
- your attitude—the way you feel about your subject
- your audience—the people who will hear or read your words
- your situation—the time and place

Depending on the writing you do, some of these factors may be more important than others. For example, in personal journal entries, you write for yourself without worrying about how other people might react to your words. In a persuasive essay, though, you always keep your audience in mind, choosing words for their likely effects on readers. As you develop style in many different kinds of writing, you'll also develop greater sureness about word choice.

Adapting Style to Aim

Read the following four sentences about the same event. Notice how in each case, a change in aim brings a change in language.

INFORMATIVE	In a sellout concert at Carnegie Hall last night, popular singer Raul Fisher performed selections from his first album.
PERSUASIVE	By all means, plan to attend this brilliant young musician's demonstration of technical mastery and contemporary showmanship.
EXPRESSIVE	Fisher's got an awesome light show—I felt like I was on another planet. Intense sounds, too—he laid down riffs that made me look to make sure my feet were still on the floor.
LITERARY	Onto the most venerable stage in American music history stepped a young man about to smash the barriers between traditional and contemporary music, bringing listeners to their feet in thunderous approval.

REFERENCE NOTE: For more about these four aims of writing, see pages 7 and 19.

Voice and Tone

People have distinctive voices when they write just as they do when they speak. ***Voice*** in writing is the unique sound and rhythm of a writer's language—a writer's personal way of talking to the reader. Voice is an important part of style because it gives a ring of honesty and authority to writing. It helps the reader imagine a real person speaking from the page.

Your personal voice can shine through in any kind of writing, from a science report to a thank-you note. Most often, you will want to write in a voice that sounds like you. Sometimes, though, you may want to imitate someone else's voice—for example, when you write a short story from the point of view of a particular narrator.

Like your speaking voice, your writing voice can express many different attitudes and feelings, or ***tones.*** It can sound happy, angry, sad, serious, sentimental, objective, horrified, offhand, sarcastic—however you want it to sound.

When you speak, you raise, lower, and otherwise alter your voice to express how you feel about your subject. But when you write, your words, sentence structure, and punctuation do all the work. That's why careful word choice is the key to creating tone.

In the following passage, N. Scott Momaday creates a happy, festive tone as he describes a Navajo celebration.

> The outriders were men and women and youths on handsome horses in glossy leather trappings and rich saddle blankets, the men in big hats and fine boots and bright silk and satin shirts, the women in velveteen blouses, long, pleated skirts, and red moccasins. They all wore silver and turquoise and coral—concha belts, necklaces, bracelets, and rings which flashed and glinted and gleamed in the sun. And their voices, as I hear them even now—the singing and the laughter—carried along the train like a long, rising and falling woodwind music. . . .
>
> N. Scott Momaday, *The Names*

Notice how Momaday creates tone by using words that suggest pleasant sensations: *handsome, glossy, rich, silk, velveteen, satin, bright*.

Now read a passage with a very different tone from Momaday's. In this passage, Paul Theroux describes a tree in Malaysia called "The Midnight Horror." (The corolla are the petals of the tree's flowers.) What is the overall feeling of the passage? What words help create the tone?

> During the day the tree looked comic, a tall simple pole like an enormous coatrack, with big leaves that looked like branches—but there were very few of them. It was covered with knobs, stark black things; and around the base of the trunk there were always fragments of leaves that looked like shattered bones, not human bones.
>
> At night the tree was different, not comic at all. It was Ladysmith who showed me the underlined passage in his copy of Professor Corner's *Wayside Trees of Malaya.* Below the entry for *Oroxylum indicum* it read, "Botanically, it is the sole representative of its kind; aesthetically, it is monstrous. . . . The corolla begins to open about 10 P.M., when the tumid, wrinkled lips part and the harsh odor escapes from them. By midnight, the lurid mouth gapes widely and is filled with stink. . . . The flowers are pollinated by bats which are attracted by the smell and, holding to the fleshy corolla with the claws on their wings, thrust their noses into its throat; scratches, as of bats, can be seen on the fallen leaves the next morning. . . ."
>
> Paul Theroux, *The Consul's File*

EXERCISE 1 **Creating Tone**

Write two descriptions of a familiar place or scene—for example, a shopping mall, a football game, or a neighborhood park. In the first description, use neutral language that doesn't reveal your feelings about your subject. In the second description, use language that does show your attitude—affection, humor, disdain, or whatever. Ask a classmate to read your two paragraphs and describe the tone of each.

Formal to Informal

Like your clothes, your language can be formal, informal, or somewhere in between. Often, you adapt the level of formality in your language without thinking about it. For example, your language is naturally more formal in an English essay than it is in a note to a friend. Sometimes, though, you must take extra care to be sure that your language is appropriate and consistent. You want to be sure that your words have the effect you intend.

Whether you use formal or informal language depends on the situation. Following are some of the appropriate uses for ***formal English*** and ***informal English.***

WRITING	
Formal	Informal
serious essays, official reports, research papers, some literary criticism, and speeches on serious or solemn occasions	personal letters, journal entries, newspaper and magazine articles, and some nonfiction books, novels, short stories, and plays
SPEAKING	
Formal	Informal
banquets, dedication ceremonies, addresses, presentation ceremonies	everyday conversation at home, school, work, and recreation

The following chart gives some examples of formal and informal English usage.

FEATURES OF FORMAL AND INFORMAL ENGLISH			
WORDS			
FORMAL	EXAMPLE	INFORMAL	EXAMPLE
longer	*intelligent*	**shorter**	*smart*
rare	*incendiarism*	**common**	*arson*
precise	*unimpressive*	**fuzzy**	*so-so*
specialized	*apiarist*	**general**	*beekeeper*
serious	*Please calm down.*	**offhand**	*Cool it!*
restrained	*very commendable*	**exaggerated**	*fantastic*
PRONUNCIATION			
FORMAL	EXAMPLE	INFORMAL	EXAMPLE
slower	*Get out of the way.*	**faster**	*Getouttatheway!*
precise	*How do you know?*	**relaxed**	*How d'ya know?*
SPELLING			
FORMAL	EXAMPLE	INFORMAL	EXAMPLE
in full	*should not*	**contractions**	*shouldn't*
conventional	*though*	**unconventional**	*tho*
GRAMMAR			
FORMAL	EXAMPLE	INFORMAL	EXAMPLE
complex	*The woman who wrote the story was Jamaican.*	**compound**	*The woman was Jamaican, and she wrote the story.*
complete	*It is chilly today.*	**fragmentary**	*Chilly today.*
explicit	*What he just did was amazing.*	**implied**	*Amazing!*

Formal language usually creates a serious tone. For example, notice the tone of the following formal passage.

> Benjamin Joshua Baker, Charlotte County's first black educator, had a thousand children but none bearing his name. They were his students who revere his memory through periodic reunions of the Baker Academy of Punta Gorda.
>
> *Charlotte Sun Herald*

For informal situations, your language will tend to have a friendlier, more personal tone.

> "Hit him? What would she want to hit him for?"
>
> "I don't know," said Mr. Delahanty. "I don't know that she did hit him. Maybe she kicked him. Anyway, his mother seems to think the boy's been damaged in some way."
>
> "Damaged," repeated Mrs. Delahanty angrily. "Damaged! Why, Cress is too tender-hearted to hurt a fly. She shoos them outside instead of killing them. And you sit there talking of hitting and kicking."
>
> Jessamyn West, "Then He Goes Free"

Always consider your audience and situation before you "dress up" or "dress down" your language. In informal situations, a formal style may sound stiff or unfriendly. At a formal occasion, casual language may be considered disrespectful.

Informal English Usage

Colloquialisms and *slang* are two kinds of expressions that give flavor to informal English.

Colloquialisms are the everyday words and phrases of conversational language. If you say that the home team "bit the dust" in last night's basketball game, you are using a colloquialism. If you tell a friend that you "couldn't care less" about new fashions, you are using a colloquialism.

Colloquialisms are most common in casual conversation. However, they also have a place in expressive and creative writing. Notice how the writers of the following sentences use colloquialisms to get their points across.

> We had our irregularities; but every family has something or other out of whack.
>
> Josephine Humphreys, *Rich in Love*
>
> I used to get all revved up.
>
> Philip Booth, *The New Yorker*

When Booth uses the term "revved up," he makes the reader think of fast cars, loud engines, and the exhilaration of racing. Imagining those things helps the reader understand the kind of excitement that Booth is talking about. But if you were writing a letter to a prospective employer, you would not say that you are "*all revved up* about this *big deal* job."

Slang consists of new words, or old words used in new ways, that are vivid and colorful. Almost any group of closely associated people creates slang. For example, students and musicians are constantly devising slang words, some of which are eventually used by the general public. Some slang words have been around for centuries—for example, the slang word *lousy* dates back to 1690. However, most slang is short-lived. It rides a crest of popularity and then is quickly replaced.

Here are a few expressions that are considered slang. How many do you recognize? What expressions do you use to mean the same things?

chill out: relax
awesome: very good
weirdo: a strange person
nuts: crazy
bummer: disappointing
stupid money: money spent unwisely
lame: weak, pathetic
zone out: relax

Shoe, by Jeff MacNelly, reprinted by permission: Tribune Media Services.

Slang is considered highly informal and is inappropriate in most kinds of writing. However, like colloquial language, slang sometimes has a place in expressive and creative writing. For example, in fictional dialogue, slang can help make your characters sound like real people.

EXERCISE 2 **Identifying Formal and Informal English**

Read a newspaper or magazine article on a topic that interests you. Is the article written in formal or informal English? What words, expressions, and sentences make the writer's language seem more formal or more informal? Give at least five examples.

Levels of Meaning

The effect that a word has on its audience is part of the meaning of the word. A word can have different meanings for different people and in different situations. Understanding the effects that your words have will help you make better choices when you write.

Specific Words

The English language is full of general nouns and verbs. The word *house* is a general noun that could refer to any number of specific dwellings: a brick row house, an apartment house, a split level, a prefab, an adobe hut, a mobile home, a farmhouse.

General words tend to weaken your writing because they call up only a vague picture in your reader's mind. Take, for example, the sentence "I went to the store." Is it a 5 & 10, a hardware store, a grocery, a deli, or a boutique? Even the verb *went* could be more specific—did the speaker *walk, run, dash, meander, fly?* Maybe the speaker *rode* the streetcar or *drove*.

Compare the following pairs of passages. Notice how the specific words in the second version give readers better, clearer, more interesting information.

a. If we don't do something, those people will keep putting waste water into the lake.
b. If we don't protest, XYZ Corporation will continue its irresponsible dumping of over one hundred thousand tons of industrial waste water into the once-crystal waters of Rabbit Lake.

a. Add some cloves, some cinnamon, and some vanilla.
b. Add one-quarter teaspoon cloves, one-half teaspoon cinnamon, and one teaspoon vanilla.

a. About half way between West Egg and New York the motor road goes alongside the railroad to avoid an ash dump.
b. "About half way between West Egg and New York the motor-road hastily joins the railroad and runs beside it for a quarter of a mile so as to shrink away from a certain area of land. This is a valley of ashes—a fantastic farm where ashes grow like wheat into ridges and hills and grotesque gardens. . . ."

F. Scott Fitzgerald, *The Great Gatsby*

The more specific a description is, the more realistic it will seem. The more realistic it seems, the more impact it will have on an audience. When Shakespeare wrote *Julius Caesar,* he didn't have a character say that ghosts were *talking* in the streets. The character reported that "ghosts did *shriek* and *squeal* about the streets."

Vivid Words

Vivid words are specific words that appeal to the senses. A well-chosen vivid word can make a dramatic impression on your readers. When your audience can see, hear, touch, taste, and smell what you are describing, your writing will come alive. If you compare writing that does not use vivid words to writing that does, the contrast is like the difference between a black-and-white film and a color film.

The following passages are from Edward Abbey's essay "The First Morning," which is about his job as a park ranger in Utah. Each passage by Abbey is preceded by a passage that says basically the same thing but uses general words that do not create sensory images.

a. Some birds are near the rock, making noises.
b. "Three ravens are wheeling near the balanced rock, squawking at each other and at the dawn."

a. The birds call and flap their wings. I smell breakfast cooking.
b. "The ravens cry out in husky voices, blue-black wings flapping against the golden sky. Over my shoulder comes the sizzle and smell of frying bacon."

"Birds . . . making noises" does not help you see or hear the birds, but "ravens . . . squawking" does. In the same way, "I smell breakfast cooking" does not call to mind a specific smell, but "Over my shoulder comes the sizzle and smell of frying bacon" creates a specific sensory image of sound and odor.

EXERCISE 3 **Using Vivid Words**

Here are five dull sentences that don't say much. Rewrite each sentence to express the same idea in specific, vivid language. Add as many words and details as you wish.

1. Xavier's car is full of stuff.
2. I smelled dinner cooking.
3. The dog went after a rabbit.
4. At night I hear the sound of traffic through my window.
5. The cars moved toward the starting line.

Nonsexist Language

Nonsexist language is language that applies to people in general, both male and female. When you are referring to humanity as a whole, nonsexist expressions are more appropriate than gender-specific ones. For example, you might use the nonsexist terms *humanity, human beings,* and *people* instead of the gender-specific term *mankind.*

In the past, many skills and occupations excluded either men or women. Expressions like *seamstress, stewardess,* and *mailman* reflect those limitations. Now that most jobs are held by both men and women, language is adjusting to reflect this change.

Following are some widely used nonsexist terms that you can use to replace the older, gender-specific ones.

Gender-Specific	Nonsexist
businessman	executive, businessperson
chairman	chairperson
deliveryman	delivery person
fireman	firefighter
foreman	supervisor
housewife	homemaker
mailman	mail carrier
manmade	synthetic
manpower	workers, human resources
may the best man win	may the best person win
policeman	police officer
salesman	salesperson
steward, stewardess	flight attendant
watchman	security guard

Connotations

Before you use a word, you need to know both its denotation and its connotations. ***Denotation*** is the strict dictionary definition of a word. ***Connotations*** are the emotions and associations that a word may suggest. Not all words have connotations. For most people, *look, paper, set,* and *table* suggest no particular emotions or associations. But words such as *skinny, slender, glare, gray, intellectual,* and *spring* do.

Connotations become attached to words through everyday usage and common experience. For example, each of the following words for dwellings has similar connotations for many people.

WORDS	CONNOTATIONS
log cabin	simplicity, strength, the pioneer past, Abraham Lincoln
lodge	country retreats, hunting
shack	poverty, shabbiness
chalet	skiing, snow, Switzerland

When you choose your words, be aware of their connotations. Suppose you want to write about someone who is not working. You might refer to that person as *unemployed, out of work, at leisure,* or *between jobs.* None of these terms have strongly negative connotations. However, if you describe the person as a *freeloader* or a *moocher,* your word choice will prompt your readers to associate negative feelings with the person.

Connotations help set the tone of writing. When a writer's attitude changes, his or her word choice changes, too. For example, during the Boer War in South Africa, the British fought the Boers, descendants of the Dutch colonists. During the earlier days of the war, the British press described the Boers as "sneaking and skulking behind rocks and bushes." But when the British forces learned to imitate the Boers' tactics for veld warfare, the press described the British as "cleverly taking advantage of cover."

EXERCISE 4 **Responding to Connotations**

Many animal names have strong associations for us, whether or not we feel strongly about the animals themselves. What would each of the following names call to mind if it were used to describe a person? Identify the animal habits or mannerisms, real or legendary, that account for each word's effect.

1. owl
2. worm
3. lamb
4. mouse
5. ox
6. skunk
7. cat
8. fox
9. weasel
10. wolf

Loaded Words

Words and phrases that have strong connotations, either positive or negative, are called ***loaded words.*** Because they appeal to emotions, loaded words can bias people for or against something. For example, if prospective car buyers hear a salesperson describe a car as a *roomy luxury sedan,* they might want to test-drive the car. But if they hear someone else describe the car as an *oversized, overpriced gas-guzzler,* they will probably hesitate to consider the purchase.

Advertisers, politicians, salespeople, and writers of newspaper editorials all use loaded words to influence their audiences. Writers of literary works often use loaded words to get readers emotionally involved with situations and characters. Even writers of informative articles and news reports do not always use objective language.

Here are two reports of a trial. If you read these accounts in two different newspapers, what would you guess about each newspaper's point of view?

The first newspaper's account:

> In the courtroom this morning, weary but attentive jurors listened somberly to Tasha Jones's long-awaited testimony. The room was deathly silent as Jones, one of the few witnesses to the robbery, described in detail what she saw.

The second newspaper's account:

> In the courtroom this morning, exhausted jurors struggled to remain attentive through the fourth and last witness's account of the robbery. According to one observer, even the judge, Roland Foster, glanced at his watch several times during Tasha Jones's long, rambling testimony.

Use loaded words with care. Intelligent readers recognize them as attempts to manipulate emotions and therefore view them with suspicion. When you do use loaded words, remember that your readers will associate these feelings with your subject. Avoid any words that might leave your audience with the wrong impression.

EXERCISE 5 **Using Loaded Words**

You have just attended a fancy banquet. Write two descriptions of your seven-course meal. In the first, use language that will make your readers wish they had been there. In the second, use words that will convince them they were better off eating TV dinners at home.

Jargon

Jargon is language that has a special meaning for a particular group of people. Jargon most often appears in informative writing. However, you will find jargon wherever people share an occupation, a hobby, or a field of study. Military personnel, computer users, editors, truck drivers, doctors, astronauts, and baseball players all have their own specialized vocabularies. Properly used, jargon is a valuable tool because it compresses complex information into a precise word or two.

SAILING	*fox:* several ropes twisted together
HORSE SHOWS	*in and out:* two fences situated twenty-five feet apart over which a horse and rider jump, touching the ground after the first fence
AVIATION	*check the runway:* to fly at high speed with wheels up just above an airstrip
FILM	*cut:* to stop filming
PSYCHOLOGY	*constellation:* several thoughts having a relationship to one another and centered on one idea

Don't use jargon unless you are sure that your audience will understand the terms. Often, jargon might as well be a foreign language to people outside a field of interest. When you write a description of an experiment for your science instructor, you might say that "the compound entered an excited state." However, if you describe the experiment to someone who is not familiar with physics, just say "the water began to boil."

EXERCISE 6 Revising Jargon

You're probably more familiar with jargon than you think. Rewrite each of the following sentences, replacing the italicized jargon with clear, plain English that anyone would understand. If you're in doubt about the meaning of a word, use a dictionary. (In most dictionaries, jargon uses of words are labeled with the field of interest they apply to.)

1. The poker player cracked a smile as he laid down a *flush*, but he changed his expression when his opponent displayed a *full house*.
2. The football league drafted two new *backs* from the state university.
3. At the start of the season, with only three *tko's* under his belt, the contender knocked out the reigning champion of five years.
4. When we spotted the school of dolphins, the pilot *peeled off* and *banked right* to give us a closer look.
5. This film is *fast*.

Don't Cramp Your Style

Some kinds of words and expressions get in the way of an effective style. They weaken your writing by boring or confusing your reader. You can bring clarity and interest to your writing by eliminating these stumbling blocks to style. First, though, you need to identify the words and expressions that give you trouble. This section of the chapter will help you do just that.

Misused Words

Many words sound so much alike or seem so close in meaning that they're easily confused with one another. For clear writing, it's important to know the differences in meaning between similar words. Don't leave your readers wondering what you meant to say. As you revise and proofread, use a dictionary to check the spellings and meanings of words you're not sure about. Then choose words that say exactly what you mean.

Following are some pairs of easily confused words. Note any words that you've had trouble with, and look them up in a dictionary. You might keep your own list of tricky words and their definitions as a reference for when you revise and proofread.

disinterested	affect	famous	set
uninterested	effect	notorious	sit
principal	allusion	imply	emigrate
principle	illusion	infer	immigrate

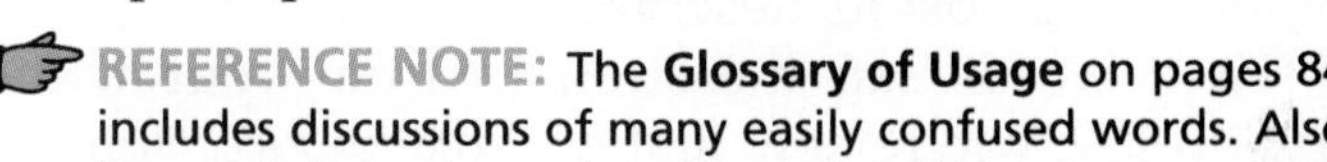
REFERENCE NOTE: The **Glossary of Usage** on pages 842–862 includes discussions of many easily confused words. Also see the lists and discussions of easily confused words on pages 784–787 and 816–817.

EXERCISE 7 **Choosing the Correct Words**

For each of the following sentences, choose the word in parentheses that has the correct meaning. Use a dictionary to check the meanings of any words you're not sure about.

1. By constantly (*flouting, flaunting*) the rules, Charles ended up thrown out of the game.
2. An ugly, (*livid, vivid*) red welt appeared where the mare's lead rope had burned the girl's hand.
3. The ambassador (*respectfully, respectively*) approached the Queen and asked her to read the message from his government.

4. From the look on his face, I (*inferred, implied*) that the party had been a disaster.
5. By drawing an (*anthology, analogy*) between birds and dinosaurs, he explained the development of the dolphin.
6. The black, swollen clouds gathering over our heads told us that rain was (*immanent, imminent*).
7. If they do not reach a settlement out of court, their lawyers will (*persecute, prosecute*).
8. By milking poisonous snakes for their venom, snake handlers help scientists make (*anecdotes, antidotes*) to snakebites.
9. After hearing Mrs. Abeyto's arguments, the committee (*capitalized, capitulated*) to her demands.
10. The judge agreed to shut down the plant after we presented (*credible, credulous*) evidence that the owners were violating environmental protection laws.

Tired Words

A ***tired word*** is one that has become vague and bland from overuse. The word *great* is a good example of a tired word. Used to refer to everything from a sandwich to a Nobel Prize winner, it has lost its descriptive power.

Tired words sap the strength from your writing. If you write in a movie review that a movie is *nice,* you aren't telling your readers much. Is the movie inspiring, heartwarming, or true-to-life? Or is it so-so, lackluster, or overly sentimental? Chances are, your readers won't be in a hurry to buy tickets and judge for themselves.

With every tired word you use, you lose an opportunity to develop an exact, vivid description of your subject. Keep your readers' attention by using lively, specific words.

Clichés

A ***cliché*** is a tired expression. The word *cliché* comes from a French word for a master printing plate used to print thousands of impressions. Each impression is identical, but each is just a little less sharp than the last. And finally the master plate, the cliché, is so worn down that it is thrown away.

The English language contains thousands of clichés. Many are figures of speech—metaphors, similes, or personifications. Others are hyperboles—exaggerations for special effect. Here are a few clichés based on figurative language.

EXAMPLES clear as crystal the long arm of the law
hungry as a horse Father Time
a dog's life wise as an owl

Some clichés come to us so naturally that we use them without thinking. That's the problem with clichés. They keep us from being original—from seeing and describing things in new ways. They may be handy in conversation, but they are too dull to be effective in writing. Watch for clichés as you evaluate and revise your writing. Try to create vivid, unique expressions to replace them.

EXERCISE 8 Replacing Tired Words

For each tired word in italics, suggest two effective replacements. (You may suggest other ways to reword a sentence, too.)

1. For two weeks last summer, we hiked through the mountains of Switzerland and saw all that *great* scenery.
2. After Kito bought the rusted chassis of an old roadster and completely restored it, no one could doubt that he was a *good* mechanic.
3. My stepmother is a *nice* person who always has time to talk to my sister and me.
4. This computer program is really *neat;* all you have to do is tap a key to bring up dozens of synonyms on the screen.
5. She thought it was a *good* movie because the ending came as a complete surprise.
6. "Look out!" he said as we met the watchful eyes of a tiny tan beast sitting in the corner yard, "That's a *bad* dog!"
7. It was a *nice* day, but all I could think about was the root canal that the dentist said I had to have.
8. The field trips make this a *great* course for anyone interested in botany.
9. Did Mr. Méndez take you up in that *terrific* twin-engined plane of his?
10. He ran *well,* finishing first by over twenty yards.

EXERCISE 9 **Writing an Original Description**

You are an alien sent to observe and record the habits and environments of Earth creatures. Write a paragraph describing a person, thing, or event you have witnessed. Some possible topics follow. Use words that will help your readers see, hear, feel, smell, or taste what you are describing. Because you aren't familiar with any of the clichés Earthlings use, you will have to come up with original ways to describe your topic.

1. a cat chasing a squirrel
2. someone mowing a lawn
3. a concert
4. a family eating spaghetti at a restaurant
5. a violent thunderstorm

Mixed Idioms and Metaphors

An ***idiom*** is an expression that can't be taken literally. It says one thing but means another. For example, if your brother says "I lost my head," you don't expect to see him walking around headless. And if you hear that "Stephanie fell for Carlos," you don't think that Carlos was supposed to fall down but Stephanie did it for him. Like *fall for,* many idioms are also colloquialisms.

A ***metaphor*** is a figure of speech that describes one thing by comparing it to another, basically different thing. The *roof of the mouth,* the *arm of the chair,* the *foot of the table,* and the *nose of the plane* are all metaphors. William Shakespeare's "All the world's a stage," Emily Dickinson's "'Hope' is the thing with feathers," and "The Lord is my shepherd" from Psalm 23 also are metaphors.

It's important to use idioms and metaphors correctly and consistently. If you mix up idioms or metaphors, you may confuse your readers or create unintentionally funny mental images. For example, if you say "we've been sold up the creek" (a mix of the idioms *up a creek* and *sold down the creek*), readers won't know what you mean. And if you say that "the woman flapped her arms and barked for silence," your mixed metaphor will create a picture of somebody who is birdlike and doglike at the same time.

Gobbledygook

Gobbledygook is wordy, puffed-up language. Awkward and confusing, it obscures rather than clarifies meaning. You can recognize gobbledygook by its strings of long, complicated words and long, complicated sentences. At first glance, gobbledygook may seem impressive. But on a closer look, it is like a balloon filled with hot air. For example, here is a famous little proverb restated in gobbledygook.

> A plethora of culinary specialists has a deleterious effect upon the quality of purées, consommés, and other soluble pabula.

In plain English this says:

> Too many cooks spoil the broth.

Can you translate the following gobbledygook into the plain English of the original proverb?

> A mobile section of petrified matter agglomerates no bryophytes.

Gobbledygook is an enemy of style because it confuses your audience and buries your natural voice. It can even make readers wonder if, underneath all those words, you have anything real to say. Stick to clear, straightforward language in your writing. Use simple words instead of complicated ones, and use only as many words as you need to make your point.

REFERENCE NOTE: For more about reducing wordiness in writing, see pages 588–592.

The reason Verbal SAT scores are at an all-time low.

Euphemisms

Euphemisms are indirect, agreeable words used in place of direct words that might seem offensive to people. Most euphemisms are used as a courtesy. For example, instead of saying that your best friend's dog is "hyperactive," you might say the animal is "frisky." During dinner at a neighbor's house, you might refer to a strange dish as "interesting" or "unusual" rather than "odd" or "bizarre."

Following are some of the euphemisms you might hear, read, or use in everyday life:

EUPHEMISM	MORE DIRECT TERM
additional revenues	higher taxes
deceased	dead
correctional institution	prison
offender	criminal
faux	imitation
memorial garden	cemetery
misrepresentation	lie
powder room	toilet

Euphemisms eliminate negative connotations that might interfere with a writer's aim. If government officials want to persuade people to accept higher taxes, they might refer to the proposed plan as "revenue enhancement." If a press agent's job is to announce a nuclear power plant explosion without causing panic, he or she might call the explosion an "energetic disassembly."

Like the examples in the paragraph above, many euphemisms have nothing to do with courtesy. Instead, their purpose is to mislead people by hiding unpleasant truths or misrepresenting important facts.

Euphemisms are appropriate whenever you want to show courtesy and tact. However, keep in mind that their indirectness tends to weaken your writing. Also, euphemisms might cause readers to wonder if you are being honest with them. Use direct language whenever you can. Check your writing for any euphemisms that you can replace with more straightforward terms.

EXERCISE 10 Revising Gobbledygook and Euphemisms

How good are you at translating gobbledygook and euphemisms? First, figure out what the writer of the following passage is really saying. (You may need to use a dictionary.) Then, rewrite the passage in plain, straightforward language. You may use either formal or informal English.

Congratulations! Our office is happy to inform you that your neighborhood has been selected to be the recipient site of a new refuse management facility that will serve the entire county.

This new service center features an ivy-covered brick barrier encompassing the entire campus and rising to a height of over ten feet. Our studies tend to indicate that this buffer will ensure that the center's schedule of ceaseless activities become an almost noiseless and invisible part of your everyday life.

No expense has been spared and every effort has been made to incorporate the latest technology and an elegant design into this modern campus specializing in the rapid oxidation of flammable refuse. We are proud to report that our projections anticipate that residents will enjoy the virtually clean, odorless, and nearly invisible operation of this vital utility for the remainder of this century and well into the next.

Aim for Style

You are reading the newspaper one afternoon after school. As you turn the pages to the local section, a photograph catches your eye. You are surprised to see a classmate of yours holding a very dirty seagull. Curious, you read the article that follows.

Volunteers Save Sea Birds

Thursday's oil spill left hundreds of sea birds dead and dying along the coast. Drenched with sticky black oil, the birds that were still alive floundered along the shore, unable to swim or fly. But thanks to the efforts of students, retirees, and dozens of other concerned community members, many of these birds are being saved.

On Friday morning, volunteers chased, coaxed, and captured over one hundred unwilling birds and rushed them to East Side Community Center. There, teams of volunteers helped clean the oil from the birds' wings, using special detergents and other supplies donated by local merchants. About one hundred birds are now recovering in captivity.

Aim: Persuasive

You've decided to recruit volunteers from your school to help save the sea birds. Write a brief speech persuading your classmates to work all weekend capturing and cleaning the injured birds. To gain your friends' help, you will need to stir their emotions. You will also need to offer them reasons why they should sacrifice their free time. Choose your words carefully to make your speech convincing. Then use the following checklist to help you revise your speech for effectiveness and style.

Revision Checklist

- Is your tone appropriate for your aim and your audience?
- Is your language clear and to the point?
- Have you weighed your words for their connotations?
- Have you used specific words that create a vivid picture of the birds' plight?

Aim: Expressive

You are one of the volunteers who helped catch, cage, and wash the oil-soaked sea birds. How do you feel knowing you've saved lives? Do you think all the hard work was worthwhile?

Write a letter to a friend or a relative describing your part in the rescue operation and explaining how you feel about the experience. Help your reader imagine and understand your experiences and feelings. You may use either formal or informal English—whichever you think is appropriate for your audience.

14 Writing Clear Sentences

LOOKING AHEAD

Clear, smooth sentences are basic to any writer's style. In this chapter, you will learn how to improve both the style and the sense of your sentences by

- using sentence structure to show the relationships between ideas
- expressing parallel ideas in parallel form
- recognizing and removing obstacles to clarity in your writing

Ways to Achieve Clarity

You write for many different purposes. Maybe you want to give a friend your recipe for chili, to persuade other students that you're the best choice for class treasurer, to describe how the first crisp day of fall makes you feel. No matter what your purpose is, you want to communicate your meaning clearly for your readers (or just for yourself).

One of the best ways to bring clarity to your writing is to sharpen the focus of your sentences. You can bring your sentences into focus by *coordinating* and *subordinating* ideas.

Coordinating Ideas

When two or more ideas carry the same weight in a sentence, they are called ***coordinate*** ideas. (*Coordinate* means "equal-ranked.") To show that two ideas are coordinate, you link them with a connecting word and/or with appropriate punctuation.

> He felt some light object fall across his palm**,** **and** his fingers closed upon a match. [comma and coordinating conjunction]
>
> H. G. Wells, "The Man Who Could Work Miracles"

> It was so quiet**;** the bees hummed and the river water played the pebbles, the rocks, and the hollows. [semicolon]
>
> Maxine Hong Kingston, *The Woman Warrior*

Different connectives show different kinds of relationships between ideas. Following are some connecting words you can use to show *addition, contrast, choice,* and *result.*

ADDITION	CONTRAST	CHOICE	RESULT
also and besides both . . . and likewise	but however nevertheless still yet	either . . . or neither . . . nor nor or otherwise	accordingly consequently hence therefore

You can use connecting words to join words, phrases, independent clauses (clauses that express complete thoughts), or subordinate clauses (clauses that don't express complete thoughts). The result is a compound element in your sentence.

CONTRAST Yolanda **stumbled** over the second hurdle **but recovered** to win the race. [compound verb]

CHOICE **Either Mr. Chávez or Ms. Hutchins** will drive us to the match. [compound subject]

ADDITION Every successful football team has a quarterback who is **strong, quick, and agile.** [compound predicate adjective]

RESULT Your entire premise is faulty**;** **therefore,** I cannot accept the rest of your argument. [compound sentence]

Be sure to choose a connective that shows the correct relationship between the linked ideas. Otherwise, your meaning may not be clear to your readers.

UNCLEAR Hector checked the movie listings, and he couldn't find the show times for *The Slime*.

CLEAR Hector checked the movie listings, **but** he couldn't find the show times for *The Slime*. [contrast]

UNCLEAR Keep the stove on low heat, yet the eggs will burn.

CLEAR Keep the stove on low heat; **otherwise,** the eggs will burn. [choice]

MECHANICS HINT

Punctuation in Compound Sentences

When you use a coordinating conjunction to join two independent clauses, put a comma before the conjunction unless the clauses are very short.

We played volleyball in the back yard for a while**,** and then we got ready to barbecue.
Janna cooked and Rico set the table.

When you use a conjunctive adverb to link independent clauses, put a semicolon before the connecting word.

Kiko did poorly on the midterm**;** however, she got an A on the final exam.

REFERENCE NOTE: For more about punctuating compound sentences, see pages 686, 907, and 928–929.

EXERCISE 1 **Using Appropriate Connectives**

Complete each of the following sentences by deciding which connecting word(s) will best fit in the blank(s). Give the correct punctuation to go with the connective you choose.

EXAMPLE **1. Matthew Henson was a famous black navigator ____ explorer.**

1. *and*

1. Henson had very little formal education or other advantages ____ he overcame these limitations and became the first explorer to reach the North Pole.
2. Admiral Robert E. Peary led the 1909 expedition to the Pole ____ Henson, his assistant, may have been the first to set foot on the Pole.

3. Radio and satellite communications had not yet been invented ____ the world did not learn of the expedition's success until months after the event.
4. Peary and Henson met in 1888 ____ they worked and traveled together for twenty-three years.
5. They journeyed first to the tropical climates of Central America ____ then to the frozen lands of the Arctic.
6. When they began their trek to the North Pole, ____ Peary ____ Henson were familiar with the harsh Arctic climate.
7. They had already led seven Arctic expeditions ____ their final goal was to reach the Pole.

8. Henson had learned the ways of native Arctic people ____ he knew how to survive in the cold.
9. Fierce winds ____ blinding snow made travel extremely difficult.
10. The explorers returned from their mission exhausted ____ triumphant.

Subordinating Ideas

Sometimes you will want to show that one idea in a sentence is more important than another. To make your main idea stand out, you can downplay the less important ideas. Ideas that are given lower rank in a sentence are called ***subordinate*** ideas.

One way to subordinate an idea is to place it in a ***subordinate clause.*** Used as part of a sentence, a subordinate clause elaborates on the thought expressed in an independent clause.

EXAMPLES James, **who has seen all of the *Star Trek* movies,** chose *The Wrath of Kahn* as his favorite.
Sara likes *The Voyage Home* best **because it warns against the extinction of endangered species.**

The kinds of subordinate clauses you will use most often are *adverb clauses* and *adjective clauses.*

REFERENCE NOTE: For more about the types of subordinate clauses, see pages 675–683.

Adverb Clauses

An ***adverb clause*** modifies a verb, an adjective, or another adverb in a sentence. You introduce an adverb clause with a subordinating conjunction such as *although, after, because, if, when,* or *while.* The conjunction shows how the adverb clause relates to the main clause. Usually, the conjunction shows a relationship of *time, cause or reason, purpose or result,* or *condition.*

TIME At Bonanza Creek, **while our socks dried by the fire,** we fished for arctic grayling.

Barry Lopez, *Crossing Open Ground*

CAUSE OR REASON **Because we had no other name for her,** we called her Baby.

Jeanne Larsen, *Silk Road*

PURPOSE OR RESULT	Rage made him weak, **so that he stumbled.**

Carson McCullers, *The Heart is a Lonely Hunter*

CONDITION	He ran so hard that he could feel the sweat fly from his head and arms, **though it was winter and the air was filled with snow.**

N. Scott Momaday, *House Made of Dawn*

The following chart lists subordinating conjunctions you can use to show each kind of relationship.

TIME	CAUSE	PURPOSE	CONDITION
after as before since until when whenever while	as because even though since unless whereas if while	in order that so that that	although provided that though

You can place an adverb clause at either the beginning or the end of a sentence. Read the sentence aloud with the clause in each position to see which sounds better. When you place an adverb clause at the beginning, be sure to put a comma after the clause.

EXERCISE 2 Choosing Appropriate Subordinating Conjunctions

Each of the following sentences is missing a subordinating conjunction. First, decide what the relationship is between the independent clause and the subordinate clause. Then, give a subordinating conjunction that clearly shows the relationship.

1. ____ you buy a rare manuscript, make sure it's authentic.
2. William Henry Ireland was a highly successful forger ____ he was only a teenager at the height of his exploits.

3. Ireland started forging Shakespeare manuscripts ____ his father had a keen interest in them.
4. ____ he forged a document, Ireland had to do careful research on the details that would make it look genuine.

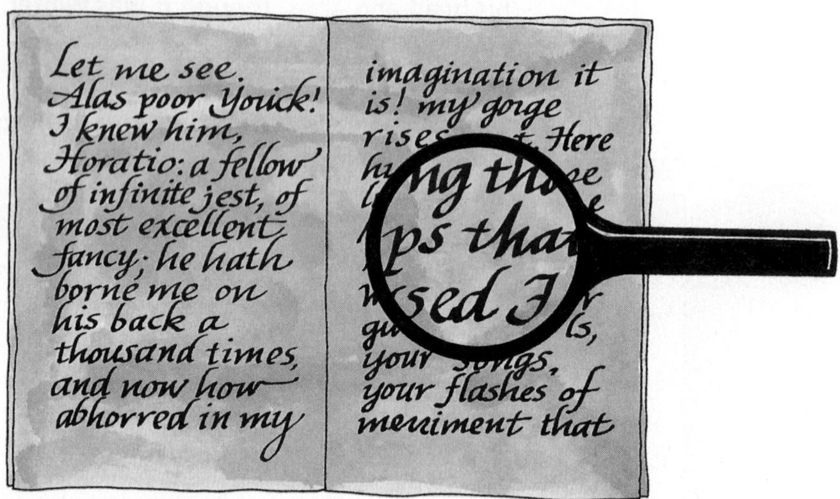

5. He used special blends of ink ____ the forged manuscript would look older than it really was.
6. ____ he trusted his son, Ireland's father published a collection of the forged manuscripts.
7. Scholars became more and more skeptical ____ Ireland could no longer defend himself against their accusations.
8. Ireland published a confession ____ the documents were proven to be fraudulent, and his father's health declined.
9. ____ Ireland tried to ease his father's disappointment, the older man died in disgrace in the middle of the scandal.
10. ____ Ireland himself died in 1835, the art of forgery obviously did not die with him.

EXERCISE 3 Revising Sentences by Inserting Adverb Clauses

Using the photos on the next page to help spark your imagination, revise each of the following sentences by adding an adverb clause at the beginning or the end of the sentence. Use a different subordinating conjunction for each sentence. [Note: Remember to add a comma if you place the clause at the beginning.]

EXAMPLE **1.** White-water rafting is fun.
1. *White-water rafting is fun because it's full of surprises.*

1. We tried some of the calmer rapids.
2. We learned how to maneuver in faster rapids.
3. You should try this exciting sport sometime.
4. The guide describes the high points of the upcoming rapids.
5. Some of the best white-water rapids are in Virginia.

Adjective Clauses

You can also subordinate an idea by placing it in an ***adjective clause,*** a subordinate clause that modifies a noun or a pronoun in a sentence. An adjective clause usually begins with *who, whom, whose, which, that,* or *where.*

> I propped myself against the brick wall of the schoolhouse, **where the school delinquent found me.**
>
> Henry Louis Gates, Jr., "A Giant Step"

Before you use an adjective clause in a sentence, you need to decide which idea in the sentence you want to subordinate. Suppose you want to combine these two ideas in one sentence:

> Ishmael Reed helped found the Yardbird Publishing Company in 1971. He considers himself as much a publisher as a writer.

If you want to emphasize that Reed helped found Yardbird, put that information in an independent clause and the other information in an adjective clause.

> Ishmael Reed, **who considers himself as much a publisher as a writer,** helped found the Yardbird Publishing Company in 1971.

If you want to emphasize that Reed is both a publisher and a writer, put the information about Yardbird in an adjective clause.

> Ishmael Reed, **who helped found the Yardbird Publishing Company in 1971,** considers himself as much a publisher as a writer.

REFERENCE NOTE: For more about combining sentences by subordinating ideas, see pages 574–577.

EXERCISE 4 Subordinating Ideas by Using Adjective Clauses

Change the emphasis in each of the following sentences. Emphasize the idea that is now in the subordinate clause, and subordinate the idea that is now in the independent clause. [Hint: You may have to delete or add some words or change the word order.] Which version sounds better and clearer to you?

1. The word *alphabet,* which comes from the Greek letters *alpha* and *beta,* refers to a series of signs used to write a language.
2. The Egyptians, who developed their alphabet around 3000 B.C., had several hundred signs for words and syllables.

3. The Greeks, who borrowed symbols from the Phoenician alphabet, improved on earlier alphabets by using separate signs for vowel sounds.
4. The Roman alphabet, which is the one we use to write English today, comes from the Greek alphabet.
5. Roman stonecutters, who had to make the alphabet practical for carving, simplified the letters and added graceful finishing strokes called serifs.

Correcting Faulty Coordination

In everyday speech, we tend to be casual about stringing together ideas with *and.* In writing, though, it's important to clearly show the relative importance of ideas. If you use a coordinating conjunction to join ideas of unequal importance, you end up with ***faulty coordination.***

To avoid faulty coordination, check each compound sentence to make sure the ideas in it are really equal in importance. If they aren't, subordinate the less-important idea by placing it in a subordinate clause or a phrase. You may need to rearrange some words in the sentence.

FAULTY The tiny sand crab was the same color as the sand, and it could hardly be seen.

BETTER **Because it was the same color as the sand,** the tiny sand crab could hardly be seen. [adverb clause]

FAULTY Wild horses are beautiful, inspiring animals, and they make their home on the islands of Chincoteague and Assateague.

BETTER Wild horses, **who make their home on the islands of Chincoteague and Assateague,** are beautiful, inspiring animals. [adjective clause]

FAULTY The light was at the end of the pier, and it showed us how far we had walked.

BETTER The light **at the end of the pier** showed us how far we had walked. [prepositional phrases]

FAULTY Tama was the lifeguard on duty that day, and she saved the drowning child.

BETTER Tama, **the lifeguard on duty that day,** saved the drowning child. [appositive phrase]

REFERENCE NOTE: For more about using phrases in sentences, see pages 652–667.

EXERCISE 5 **Revising Sentences by Correcting Faulty Coordination**

Faulty coordination blurs the focus in each of the following sentences. Revise each sentence by placing one of the ideas in a subordinate clause or a phrase. [Hint: You may need to add or delete some words or change the punctuation.] Make sure each revised sentence shows the appropriate relationship between the two ideas.

1. Mackinac Island is located in a channel between Lake Michigan and Lake Huron, and it is my favorite place to visit.
2. People get around mostly by bicycle and by horse and carriage, and automobiles are not permitted on the island.
3. It was the first morning of our visit, and we woke to the click-clack of horses' hooves on the street below.
4. I had some mechanical problems with my bike, but I still enjoyed my ride, and the ride was around the island.
5. Mackinac Island's Grand Hotel is one of the oldest hotels in the United States, and the movie *Somewhere in Time* was filmed there.

Using Parallel Structure

For clear meaning and smooth rhythm in a sentence, it's important to place equal ideas in the same grammatical form. For example, pair an adjective with an adjective, a prepositional phrase with a prepositional phrase, and a noun clause with a noun clause. When you use the same grammatical form for equal ideas, you create ***parallel structure.***

He had come to tell his brother **that power corrupts, that a man who fights for justice must himself be cleansed and purified, that love is greater than force.**

Alan Paton, *Cry, the Beloved Country*

He was the **weather-beaten, brown-faced, black-eyed** Cupid of the community.

Jovita González, "The Mail Carrier"

She hadn't expected that, because he was shy and seemed more at home **with his hogs** than **with people.**

Bobbie Ann Mason, "Memphis"

Use parallel structure when you link coordinate ideas.

FAULTY My favorite camping activities are fishing and to hike. [gerund paired with infinitive]

PARALLEL My favorite camping activities are **fishing** and **hiking.** [gerund paired with gerund]

FAULTY Mari's sculpture projects reveal her talent and that she has patience. [noun paired with noun clause]

PARALLEL Mari's sculpture projects reveal **that she is talented** and **that she has patience.** [noun clause paired with noun clause]

Use parallel structure when you compare or contrast ideas.

FAULTY Water-skiing no longer interests me as much as to go scuba diving. [gerund contrasted with infinitive]

PARALLEL **Water-skiing** no longer interests me as much as **scuba diving.** [gerund contrasted with gerund]

FAULTY In figure skating, style is just as important as that you have technical expertise. [noun paired with noun clause]

PARALLEL In figure skating, **style** is just as important as **technical expertise.** [noun paired with noun]

Use parallel structure when you link ideas with correlative conjunctions (*both . . . and, either . . . or, neither . . . nor, not only . . . but also*).

FAULTY The medicine woman was revered not only for her healing abilities but also because she possessed wisdom. [prepositional phrase correlated with adverb clause]

PARALLEL The medicine woman was revered not only **for her healing abilities** but also **for her wisdom.** [prepositional phrase correlated with prepositional phrase]

Be sure to place correlative conjunctions directly before the parallel terms. Otherwise, your sentence may sound awkward and unclear.

UNCLEAR Those interested in stage acting can either join the drama club or the community theater.

BETTER Those interested in stage acting can join **either** the drama club **or** the community theater.

UNCLEAR The team both felt the satisfaction of victory and the disappointment of defeat.

BETTER The team felt **both** the satisfaction of victory **and** the disappointment of defeat.

When you create parallel structure, you often need to repeat an article, a preposition, or a pronoun before each of the parallel terms to make your meaning clear. Notice how the first version of each of the following sentences might be misread.

UNCLEAR Before the meeting I talked with the secretary and treasurer.

BETTER Before the meeting I talked with **the** secretary and **the** treasurer.

UNCLEAR The old diaries revealed more about that era in history than the man who wrote them.

BETTER The old diaries revealed more **about** that era in history than **about** the man who wrote them.

Sometimes you will need to add a few words to the second part of the parallel structure to clarify your meaning.

UNCLEAR We enjoyed the music of the opening band more than the featured band.

BETTER We enjoyed the music of the opening band more than **that of** the featured band.

EXERCISE 6 Revising Sentences by Correcting Faulty Parallelism

Some of the following sentences are unclear because they lack parallel structure. Revise each faulty sentence by putting parallel ideas into the same grammatical form. Add, delete, and replace words as necessary. [Note: Remember to check the placement of correlative conjunctions.] If a sentence is already in parallel form, write *C*.

1. When Thomas "Fats" Waller was a child, his favorite pastimes were singing for his family and to pretend to play the piano.
2. At the suggestion of Waller's older brother and because an uncle helped to finance it, the family finally got a real piano at home.
3. His parents hired a music teacher for him, but Fats was more interested in learning by ear than to take lessons.

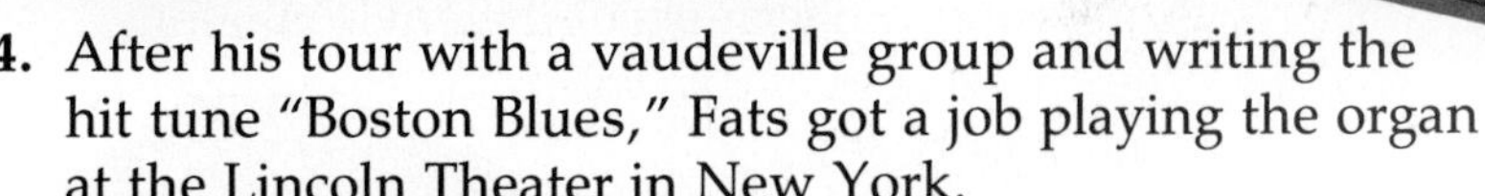

4. After his tour with a vaudeville group and writing the hit tune "Boston Blues," Fats got a job playing the organ at the Lincoln Theater in New York.
5. He became a favorite there, not only for his musical talents but also because he had a sense of humor.
6. James P. Johnson, a well-known Harlem pianist, taught Fats the secrets of symmetry and style.
7. Waller was as successful at writing full-length musical revues as he was as a performer.
8. In 1928, Fats participated in a concert at Carnegie Hall called "Musical History of the Negro," which was a rousing success both artistically and as far as finances.
9. His jazz combo "Fats Waller and His Rhythm Boys" was a hit in both its live performances and on record.
10. Later in his career, Waller received as much praise for his work in film as when he did live performances.

REVIEW A Revising Paragraphs for Clarity

The following paragraphs are confusing because they contain faulty coordination and faulty parallelism. Use the methods you've learned in this chapter to make each faulty sentence smoother and clearer. [Hint: You may need to add, delete, or rearrange some words in the sentences.]

Simon J. Ortiz is an Acoma Pueblo, and he writes eloquently about the experiences of Native Americans. His poems and short stories are infused with Native American history, mythology, and philosophical. Ortiz uses simple, direct language, and his language reflects the oral storytelling tradition of his heritage. Ortiz often employs a sorrowful tone, but he tempers his writings with humor and being optimistic.

Going for the Rain was Ortiz's first full-length collection of poems, and it was published in 1976. Going for the Rain depicts a journey that begins in the traditional Native American world, goes through present-day America, and returning to its origin. In these poems Ortiz expresses concern not only for his own people but also American society as a whole.

The collection A Good Journey is similar to Going for the Rain both in structure and theme. The poems in A Good Journey describe Native American history and expressing concern about the environment. The conclusion of this volume is as hopeful as his other works.

Acoma Pueblo Indian Pottery

Obstacles to Clarity

In this part of the chapter, you will learn how to check your writing for some common obstacles to clarity: *sentence fragments, run-on sentences,* and *unnecessary shifts.*

Sentence Fragments

A sentence expresses a complete thought. If you punctuate a part of a sentence as if it were a whole sentence, you create a ***sentence fragment.*** Fragments are usually confusing in writing because the reader has to puzzle out the missing information.

FRAGMENT Photographed families who were victims of the Great Depression. [missing subject]
SENTENCE **Dorothea Lange** photographed families who were victims of the Great Depression.

FRAGMENT After the flood, the barn roof in pieces in the yard. [missing verb]
SENTENCE After the flood, the barn roof **lay** in pieces in the yard.

FRAGMENT We observing the bacteria through a powerful microscope. [missing helping verb]
SENTENCE We **were** observing the bacteria through a powerful microscope.

FRAGMENT When she won three gold medals in track at the 1960 Olympics. [not a complete thought]
SENTENCE **Wilma Rudolph became famous** when she won three gold medals in track at the 1960 Olympics.

Phrase Fragments

A ***phrase*** is a group of words that doesn't have a subject and its verb. If a phrase gets separated from the sentence it belongs with, it becomes a ***phrase fragment.***

FRAGMENT I found my sister in the den. **Making origami swans out of blue and green paper.** [participial phrase fragment]
SENTENCE I found my sister in the den making origami swans out of blue and green paper.

FRAGMENT The Miami chief Little Turtle was born near the Eel River. **In the Midwest.** [prepositional phrase fragment]

SENTENCE The Miami chief Little Turtle was born near the Eel River in the Midwest.

FRAGMENT They got together all the supplies they would need. **To make the canoe trip go smoothly.** [infinitive phrase fragment]

SENTENCE They got together all the supplies they would need to make the canoe trip go smoothly.

FRAGMENT Coretta brought her two favorite kites. **A stunt kite and a parafoil kite.** [appositive phrase fragment]

SENTENCE Coretta brought her two favorite kites, a stunt kite and a parafoil kite.

Subordinate Clause Fragments

A ***subordinate clause*** has a subject and a verb but doesn't express a complete thought. Unlike an independent clause, a subordinate clause can't stand on its own as a sentence.

FRAGMENT Some lizards used to be killed for their skins. **Which were used to make wallets and handbags.** [adjective clause fragment]

SENTENCE Some lizards used to be killed for their skins, which were used to make wallets and handbags.

FRAGMENT I had nightmares. **After I watched that scary movie.** [adverb clause fragment]

SENTENCE I had nightmares after I watched that scary movie.

EXERCISE 7 Revising to Eliminate Fragments

Some of the following items contain phrases or clauses that have been separated from the sentences they belong with. Fix each fragment by attaching it to the independent clause. [Note: You may need to move or add some words.] If the item is already correct, just write *C*.

1. Elizabeth Blackwell was born in 1821. And died in 1910.
2. In 1832 her parents immigrated with their eight children to New York. To escape an unpleasant social and political situation in Bristol, England.

3. Because of the financial plight of her family. Blackwell and her mother established a boarding school.
4. A friend of Blackwell's encouraged her to become a doctor. At first, Blackwell totally rejected this suggestion.
5. Eventually, Blackwell became interested in the idea of becoming a doctor. Leading her to investigate the possibility of a woman studying medicine.
6. She became even more determined to follow her friend's advice. After she was told that it would be impossible for a woman to become a doctor.
7. In 1847 Elizabeth Blackwell was granted admission to the Medical Institution of Geneva College. Which is today known as Hobart College.
8. She became the first woman in the United States to earn an M.D. degree. When she graduated in 1849 at the head of her class.
9. Elizabeth was not content with these honors. She spent the next two years doing graduate work in Europe.
10. In 1857 Elizabeth Blackwell established the New York Infirmary for Women and Children, a hospital staffed by women. She opened the hospital on May 12, the birthday of her friend Florence Nightingale.

A complete sentence is usually the best and clearest way to express a thought. However, experienced writers sometimes use fragments for stylistic effect. For example, in the following passage, notice how each fragment creates a single, precise image in your mind. The fragments make sense because they are clearly related to the complete sentence before them.

> Silently, wallowing in the pleasures of conspiracy, we take the bead purse from its secret place and spill its contents on the scrap quilt. Dollar bills, tightly rolled and green as May buds. Somber fifty-cent pieces, heavy enough to weight a dead man's eyes. Lovely dimes, the liveliest coin, the one that really jingles. Nickels and quarters, worn smooth as creek pebbles. But mostly a hateful heap of bitter-odored pennies.
>
> Truman Capote, "A Christmas Memory"

You can use fragments occasionally in expressive and creative writing such as journal entries and short stories. For example, you might use fragments in dialogue to capture the natural sounds of your characters' speech. You can also use fragments in classified ads and other types of writing where an informal, shorthand style is appropriate. However, avoid fragments in informative writing such as research papers and reports. Because your readers expect formal, straightforward language in this type of writing, fragments may interfere with your aim.

Run-on Sentences

A ***run-on sentence*** is just the opposite of a fragment. It is made up of two complete sentences run together as if they were one sentence. Like fragments, run-ons usually occur when you're writing in a hurry. Most run-ons are ***comma splices***—two complete thoughts that have only a comma between them. Other run-ons, called ***fused sentences,*** have no punctuation between the two thoughts.

The following examples show four ways to correct run-ons.

RUN-ON	Bill "Bojangles" Robinson worked in motion pictures from 1929–1943, the films he made with Shirley Temple were very popular.
CORRECT	Bill "Bojangles" Robinson worked in motion pictures from 1929–1943**. T**he films he made with Shirley Temple were very popular. [two sentences]
RUN-ON	We were fifteen minutes late, the concert hadn't started yet.
CORRECT	We were fifteen minutes late**, but** the concert hadn't started yet. [compound sentence with comma and coordinating conjunction]
RUN-ON	Everybody dreams at night, dreaming is a normal part of the sleep cycle.
CORRECT	Everybody dreams at night**;** dreaming is a normal part of the sleep cycle. [compound sentence with semicolon]
RUN-ON	We struggled to set up the tent the mosquitoes ate us alive.
CORRECT	We struggled to set up the tent**; meanwhile,** the mosquitoes ate us alive. [compound sentence with semicolon plus conjunctive adverb]

EXERCISE 8 **Revising Run-on Sentences**

The following items are confusing because they're run-ons. Revise each run-on by using one of the methods you've learned in this section. Use each of the four methods at least once.

1. Some friends and I are making a movie, it will be on videotape.
2. We saved up our money then we rented a camcorder from an electronics store.
3. We're still revising some parts of the script, we've already written most of the scenes.
4. The sets will be simple most of the scenes will be shot in Joe's back yard.
5. We want to shoot a pool-party scene at the neighborhood swimming pool, we'll need to recruit some of our friends as "pool-party extras."

Unnecessary Shifts in Sentences

For clarity, it's usually best to stick with the same subject and the same verb form throughout a sentence. An unnecessary shift in subject or in verb form can make a sentence awkward to read.

Shifts in Subject

Sometimes, especially in short compound sentences, a shift in subject is necessary to express your intended meaning. In the following sentence, the shift in subject is natural.

NATURAL SHIFT I knocked on the door, but no one answered.

Most often, though, a shift in subject is awkward and unnecessary. In the following examples, notice that each sentence is much clearer when it has the same subject throughout.

AWKWARD Team members should be at the locker room by 5:30 so that you can pick up your uniforms.
BETTER **Team members** should be at the locker room by 5:30 so that **they** can pick up **their** uniforms.

AWKWARD Fishers from around the country visit the Ontario lakes, where fish are found in abundance.
BETTER **Fishers** from around the country visit the Ontario lakes, where **they** find fish in abundance.

Shifts in Verb Tense and Voice

Changing verb tense or voice in mid-sentence can also create awkwardness and confusion. Stick to the tense and voice you start with unless you have a good reason for changing.

AWKWARD Carl gave us a ten-minute lecture about recycling, but then he tosses his aluminum can into the trash. [shift from past tense to present tense]
BETTER Carl **gave** us a ten-minute lecture about recycling, but then he **tossed** his aluminum can into the trash. [past tense throughout]

AWKWARD Volunteers made the dangerous journey after dark, but no wolves were encountered. [shift from active voice to passive voice]
BETTER Volunteers **made** the dangerous journey after dark but **encountered** no wolves.

A shift in voice usually causes a shift in subject, too. Notice that in the last example, the shift from active to passive voice results in a shift from the subject *volunteers* to the subject *wolves*.

REFERENCE NOTE: If you're not sure about the difference between active and passive voice, see pages 800–804.

Often, the best way to correct a shift in voice and subject in a compound sentence is to create a compound verb. Just omit the second subject and place the second verb in the same voice as the first. You may also need to delete a comma when you take out the second subject.

AWKWARD Margaret Walker worked for the Federal Writers' Project for four years, and then graduate studies were pursued at the University of Iowa.

BETTER **Margaret Walker worked** for the Federal Writers' Project for four years and then **pursued** graduate studies at the University of Iowa.

EXERCISE 9 Eliminating Unnecessary Shifts in Subject and Verb

Most of the following sentences contain unnecessary shifts from one subject to another or from one verb to another. Revise each awkward sentence to make it flow more smoothly. You may need to add, delete, or rearrange some words. If a sentence doesn't need improving, write *C*.

1. *Windwalker* is a 1980 film that portrayed the cultures of the Cheyenne and Crow people.
2. Set in the late 1700s, the film informs the viewer about traditional Native American values.
3. In the film, a dying Cheyenne warrior tells his grandchildren the story of his life.

4. Before he can die, he must find his long-lost son, and the telling of his story must be finished.
5. A Crow warrior, who said he considers Windwalker an enemy for life, kidnapped Windwalker's son.
6. The Crow warrior developed his vengeful feelings when the woman of his choice marries Windwalker instead of him.
7. Trevor Howard stars as Windwalker, and an excellent performance is delivered by him.
8. One will enjoy seeing this film if you like breathtaking cinematography and suspenseful action scenes.
9. Very little dialogue is contained in the film; the visual elements largely speak for themselves.
10. Native American music helps set the tone for each sequence and for the film as a whole.

REVIEW B **Revising Paragraphs for Clarity**

Fragments, run-ons, and unnecessary shifts in subjects and verbs make the following paragraphs awkward and unclear. Using the methods you've learned, revise the sentences to eliminate these obstacles to clarity. Notice how much smoother the paragraphs sound when you're finished.

Dorothy West began writing stories when she was seven, and several Boston Post prizes were won by her while she was a teenager. Opportunity published West's story "The Typewriter." Which later appeared in The Best Short Stories of 1926.

West born in Boston but eventually settled in New York City, there West met many writers of the Harlem Renaissance. Including Zora Neale Hurston and Langston Hughes. In the early 1930s, she edited Challenge, a magazine that published the works of young writers.

After West's magazine ventures failed. She took a job as a welfare investigator in Harlem, she later joined the Federal Writers' Project. She became a contributor to the New York Daily News. Which published many of her stories. In 1945, West moved to Martha's Vineyard, where her only novel, The Living Is Easy, was written.

Parallel Structure in Poetry

For many professional writers, parallel structure is an important stylistic tool. Parallelism creates natural rhythm and flow in both prose and poetry.

In the following stanza, notice that a string of parallel phrases follows the preposition *between*. How does the parallel structure help form the rhythm of this stanza?

> On visiting days with aunts and uncles,
> I was shuttled back and forth—
> between Chavez bourgeois in the city
> and rural Lucero sheepherders,
> new cars and gleaming furniture
> and leather saddles and burlap sacks,
> noon football games and six packs of cokes
> and hoes, welfare cards and bottles of goat milk.
>
> Jimmy Santiago Baca,
> *Martín and Meditations on the South Valley*

Think of a time that is vivid in your memory. It may be a period from your childhood or a more recent event. Perhaps there is a certain place that you especially like (or even dislike). What are the details surrounding this memory or place? Why does it stand out for you? What objects, smells, or people come to mind when you think about it?

Write a one-stanza poem, modeled after the stanza above, describing the topic you've chosen. Use parallel structure to present the sensory details, and concentrate on making the words and phrases flow smoothly.

15 Combining Sentences

LOOKING AHEAD

By using sentence-combining techniques, you can add detail to your sentences and variety to your writing style. In this chapter, you will learn how to combine sentences by

- inserting words and phrases
- coordinating ideas
- subordinating ideas

Combining for Variety

Sometimes a short, simple sentence can have just the effect you want. But if you use only short sentences, you probably won't hold your reader's attention for very long. Notice that the following passage, which contains only short sentences, sounds dull and choppy.

The sinking of the *Titanic* was one of the worst maritime disasters in history. The *Titanic* was the largest ship of its time. It was the most luxurious ship of its time. The *Titanic* was on its maiden voyage. The ship struck an iceberg. The iceberg was located off the Grand Banks of Newfoundland. The accident happened on the night of April 14, 1912. The night was clear and cold. The *Titanic*'s hull had sixteen watertight compartments. The iceberg punctured five compartments. The ship sank in less than three hours.

When some of the short sentences are combined to create longer, more varied ones, the passage sounds smoother and more interesting.

The sinking of the *Titanic*, the largest and most luxurious ship of its time, was one of the worst maritime disasters in history. On the clear, cold night of April 14, 1912, the ship, which was on its maiden voyage, struck an iceberg off the Grand Banks of Newfoundland. The iceberg punctured five of the sixteen watertight compartments in the ship's hull, and the ship sank in less than three hours.

Sentence-combining techniques can help you create lively, detailed sentences that read smoothly. You can combine related sentences to improve your style in any kind of writing.

Inserting Words and Phrases

Sometimes a sentence adds only a little information to a more important idea before or after it. Instead of giving the small detail a sentence of its own, you can insert it into the other sentence as a word or phrase. By combining the sentences, you'll eliminate extra words and repeated ideas.

FOUR SENTENCES The archaeologist agreed to an interview. She agreed readily. She was elated by her discovery. It was a recent discovery. [Notice how many words are repeated.]

ONE SENTENCE **Elated by her recent discovery,** the archaeologist **readily** agreed to an interview.

or

The archaeologist, **elated by her recent discovery, readily** agreed to an interview.

You may see several possibilities for the placement of the words or phrases you are inserting. Just make sure your combined sentence sounds smooth and expresses the meaning you intend. Watch out for awkward, confusing combinations like this one: *Readily, the archaeologist agreed, elated by her recent discovery, to an interview.*

Single-Word Modifiers

Before you take a word from one sentence and insert it into another sentence, check to make sure the word can act as a modifier in the second sentence. You may need to change the word into an adverb or adjective before you insert it.

USING THE SAME FORM

ORIGINAL Angela de Hoyos is a Mexican American poet. She is an award-winning poet.

COMBINED Angela de Hoyos is an **award-winning** Mexican American poet.

ORIGINAL De Hoyos has spoken out against racism and social oppression. She has spoken out publicly.

COMBINED De Hoyos has spoken out **publicly** against racism and social oppression.

CHANGING THE FORM

ORIGINAL She was involved in the revolution of the 1960s. It was a revolution of the culture.

COMBINED She was involved in the **cultural** revolution of the 1960s.

ORIGINAL In her poetry de Hoyos often explores themes through humor. The humor is based on irony.

COMBINED In her poetry de Hoyos often explores themes through **ironic** humor.

Prepositional Phrases

Usually, you can insert a prepositional phrase without any change in form.

ORIGINAL Jason likes science fiction novels. He likes the ones with fantastical creatures.

COMBINED Jason likes science fiction novels **with fantastical creatures.**

Sometimes you can change a part of one sentence into a prepositional phrase and then insert it into the other sentence.

ORIGINAL Science fiction stretches the imagination. It contains thought-provoking concepts.
COMBINED Science fiction stretches the imagination **with thought-provoking concepts.**

EXERCISE 1 Combining Sentences by Inserting Adjectives, Adverbs, and Prepositional Phrases

Combine each of the following groups of short sentences by inserting adjectives, adverbs, or prepositional phrases into the first sentence. [Hint: You may need to change the forms of some words before you insert them.] Read your combined sentences aloud to make sure they're clear.

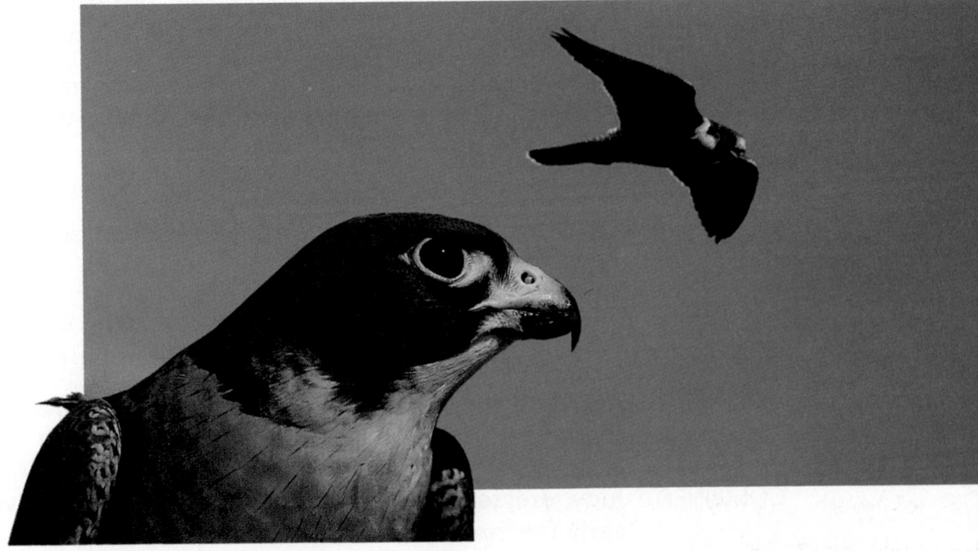

EXAMPLE **1.** Peregrine falcons soar. They soar gracefully. They soar near their nests.
1. *Peregrine falcons soar gracefully near their nests.*

1. Peregrine falcons became scarce. They became scarce in the United States. They became scarce because of the pesticide DDT.
2. No breeding pairs remained. No pairs remained in the eastern United States. The breeding pairs were gone by 1970.

3. Scientists have reintroduced peregrine falcons. These scientists are from Cornell University. The falcons are wild. The scientists have reintroduced the falcons to the eastern United States. They have reintroduced the falcons under controlled conditions.
4. A ban on DDT has helped the falcons. The ban has been effective. It has been a considerable help.
5. Peregrines are hatching eggs. The peregrines are in the eastern wilderness. It is the first time they are hatching eggs since the 1950s.

Participial Phrases

A ***participial phrase*** contains a participle and its modifiers and complements. Participial phrases act as adjectives in a sentence. They help develop concrete details that elaborate on a sentence's main idea. You can use participial phrases to add interest to your writing.

> Sometimes their mother sat in the room behind them, sewing, or **dressing their younger sister,** or **nursing the baby, Paul.**
>
> James Baldwin, "The Rockpile"

REFERENCE NOTE: For more about participles and participial phrases, see pages 657–658.

Often, you can take a participial phrase from one sentence and insert it into another sentence without a change in form.

ORIGINAL Judy arrived early for the "Syndicated TV Shows" theme party. She was dressed as Alice from *The Brady Bunch.*

COMBINED Judy, **dressed as Alice from *The Brady Bunch,*** arrived early for the "Syndicated TV Shows" theme party.

Sometimes you can create a participial phrase by changing the verb of a sentence into a participle. Then you can insert the phrase into another sentence.

ORIGINAL A Gilligan impersonator stumbled in the door a few minutes later. He carried a coconut and a homemade fishing pole.

COMBINED A Gilligan impersonator, **carrying a coconut and a homemade fishing pole,** stumbled in the door a few minutes later.

Place a participial phrase close to the noun or pronoun you want it to modify. Otherwise, you may give your sentence a meaning you don't intend. Notice how the placement of the modifier makes a difference in the meaning of the following sentence.

MISPLACED **Wrapped in silver paper, Samantha tried to guess the contents of the box.**

CORRECT **Samantha tried to guess the contents of the box wrapped in silver paper.**

EXERCISE 2 Combining Sentences by Using Participial Phrases

Combine each of the following pairs of sentences by reducing one sentence to a participial phrase and inserting the phrase into the other sentence. In some of the pairs, you'll need to change a verb form into a participle first. You may also have to delete some words from a participial phrase to avoid an awkward combination. Be sure to use correct punctuation.

EXAMPLE **1.** Marian Anderson demonstrated her love for music at an early age. She sang in the church choir.
1. *Singing in the church choir, Marian Anderson demonstrated her love for music at an early age.*

1. Anderson traveled to Europe to study for a year when she was twenty-two. She was awarded a fellowship to do this.
2. Anderson became famous. She was well received by audiences all over Europe.
3. She returned to the United States for a recital in 1935. She won the praise of American opera lovers as well.

4. Anderson sang on the steps of the Lincoln Memorial in protest on Easter morning of 1939. She had been banned from singing at Constitution Hall because she was black.
5. Seventy-five thousand people came to hear the Easter morning concert. They expressed their disapproval of the discriminatory treatment.

UPI/Bettman

Appositive Phrases

An ***appositive phrase*** is made up of an appositive and its modifiers. It adds detail by identifying or explaining a noun or pronoun in a sentence. For clear meaning, insert an appositive phrase directly before or after the noun or pronoun it explains.

> The gang met every morning in an impromptu car-park, **the site of the last bomb of the first blitz.**
>
> Graham Greene, "The Destructors"

MECHANICS HINT

Punctuating Appositive Phrases

Set an appositive phrase off from the rest of the sentence with a comma (or two commas if you place the phrase in the middle of the sentence).

> Canterbury**, the ancient religious center of Great Britain,** attracted many pilgrims during the Middle Ages.

REFERENCE NOTE: For more about punctuating phrases in sentences, see pages 909–915.

You can combine sentences in a variety of ways by using appositive phrases.

TWO SENTENCES Hernando De Soto was a Spanish explorer of the 1500s. He led the first European expedition to reach the Mississippi River.

ONE SENTENCE **A Spanish explorer of the 1500s,** Hernando De Soto led the first European expedition to reach the Mississippi River.

or

Hernando De Soto, **leader of the first European expedition to reach the Mississippi River,** was a Spanish explorer of the 1500s.

In the second combination, the verb *led* was changed into the noun *leader* to create the appositive phrase. Notice that each combination emphasizes a different idea.

EXERCISE 3 Combining Sentences by Using Appositive Phrases

To combine the following pairs of sentences, turn one of the sentences into an appositive phrase and insert it into the other sentence. Be sure to check your punctuation.

EXAMPLE **1. Elizabeth Bowen became one of the leading fiction writers in England after World War I. She was a native of Ireland.**

1. ***Elizabeth Bowen, a native of Ireland, became one of the leading writers in England after World War I.***

1. In *The Death of the Heart* the protagonist is a sensitive teenage girl. *The Death of the Heart* is one of Bowen's best-known novels.
2. Bowen was a nurse in World War I and an air-raid warden during World War II. Bowen wrote about the psychological effects of war on civilians.
3. Writer Doris Lessing describes people attempting to find meaning in life. She is a sensitive observer of social and political struggles.
4. In *Going Home,* Doris Lessing writes about a return visit to Rhodesia. *Going Home* is an autobiographical narrative.
5. Toni Morrison is one of America's most celebrated novelists. Morrison won the Pulitzer Prize for her best-selling novel *Beloved*.

REVIEW A **Combining Sentences**

The following paragraphs sound choppy because they contain many short sentences. Combine some of the sentences by using the methods you've learned. Use your judgment about which sentences to combine and how to combine them. When you're finished, the paragraphs should have a smoother, livelier style.

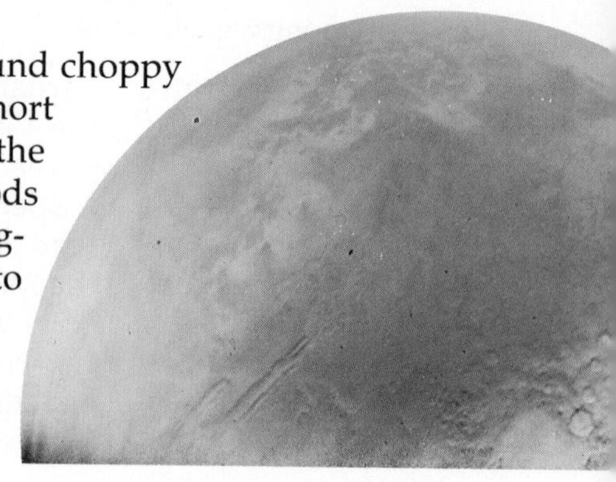

Mars is the only planet whose surface can be seen in detail. It can be seen from the earth. The planet is reddish in color. It was named after the ancient Romans' red god of war. Mars travels in an elliptical orbit. It travels around the sun. It maintains a distance from the sun of at least 128 million miles.

Part of the planet's surface is covered with craters. These craters were caused by meteors. Mars also has canyons and gorges. The gorges are deep. Such features seem to support the view that large quantities of water once flowed on the planet's surface. This is the view of some scientists. Mars also has plains. The plains are windblown. They are covered by sand dunes and rocks. The rocks are jagged.

Coordinating Ideas

You can join equally important words, phrases, or clauses by using coordinating conjunctions (such as *and, but, or, for, yet*) or correlative conjunctions (such as *both . . . and, either . . . or, neither . . . nor*). When you combine sentences in this way, you will usually create a compound subject, a compound verb, or a compound sentence.

ORIGINAL Angelo displayed leadership ability at the meeting. Suzanne also displayed leadership ability at the meeting.

COMBINED **Both Angelo and Suzanne** displayed leadership ability at the meeting. [compound subject]

ORIGINAL Many cerebral palsy victims lead active lives. They become productive members of society.

COMBINED Many cerebral palsy victims **lead active lives and become productive members of society.** [compound verb]

ORIGINAL Toshi executed a quick move toward the basket. Her opponent blocked the shot.

COMBINED Toshi executed a quick move toward the basket, **but** her opponent blocked the shot. [compound sentence]

To form a compound sentence, you can also link independent clauses with a semicolon and a conjunctive adverb or just a semicolon.

> Winston had never made the smallest effort to verify this guess**;** **indeed,** there was no way of doing so.
>
> George Orwell, *1984*

> The beautiful church took years to build**;** thousands of adobe are in those thick walls.
>
> Nina Otero, "The Bells of Santa Cruz"

REFERENCE NOTE: You can find a more detailed discussion of coordination on pages 541–542.

EXERCISE 4 Combining Sentences by Coordinating Ideas

Combine each of the following pairs of sentences by creating a compound subject, a compound verb, or a compound sentence. Make sure the connective you use shows the proper relationship between the ideas.

1. Between 1840 and 1850, Canton Province in China experienced severe economic problems. Large numbers of Chinese peasants emigrated to the United States.
2. During the 1850s, more than 41,000 Chinese made their way to this country. They joined the great "gold rush" of that time.

3. Most of these early Chinese immigrants found no gold. They found no well-paying work.
4. They came seeking prosperity. They found only hard work and discrimination.
5. The transcontinental railroad system was being built in the 1850s. Cheap labor was in great demand.
6. Ten thousand laborers built the Union Pacific railroad. Nine thousand of them were Chinese.
7. The railroad builders of America initially favored Chinese immigration. The sentiment changed when the railroad system was finished.
8. In 1869, the tracks of the Central Pacific joined those of the Union Pacific in Ogden, Utah. Thousands of Chinese were thrown out of work.
9. Most new immigrants in the nineteenth century lacked education. They possessed few skills.
10. Despite their hardships, many Chinese immigrants stayed in the United States. They began to call it home.

Subordinating Ideas

When two related sentences contain ideas of unequal importance, you can combine the sentences by placing the less-important idea in a subordinate clause (an *adjective clause,* an *adverb clause,* or a *noun clause*). The use of subordination will help show the relationships between the ideas.

In the following sentences, notice how each subordinate clause begins with a connecting word that shows how the clause relates to the main idea.

Nettie, **who was quickly bored in those days,** began to break up straw and drop it into her lunch pail. [adjective clause]

Roseanne Coggeshall, "Peter the Rock"

As his hearing got fuzzier, he accused more and more people of whispering. [adverb clause]

John Steinbeck, *The Winter of Our Discontent*

Brave Orchid thought **that her niece was like her mother, the lovely, useless type.** [noun clause]

Maxine Hong Kingston, *The Woman Warrior*

REFERENCE NOTE: For more about subordination, see pages 544–545.

Adjective Clauses

An ***adjective clause*** modifies a noun or pronoun and usually begins with *who, whose, which, where,* or *that.* To combine sentences by using an adjective clause, first decide which sentence you want to subordinate. Then, change that sentence into an adjective clause and insert it into the other sentence.

ORIGINAL Donner Pass cuts through the Sierra Nevada in eastern California. It lies 2,160 meters above sea level.

COMBINED Donner Pass, **which cuts through the Sierra Nevada in eastern California,** lies 2,160 meters above sea level.

or

Donner Pass, **which lies 2,160 meters above sea level,** cuts through the Sierra Nevada in eastern California.

MECHANICS HINT

Punctuating Adjective Clauses

Use a comma or commas to set off an adjective clause that is not essential to the meaning of the sentence.

ESSENTIAL The bicycle **that has the wider tires** is designed for riding on rugged surfaces.

NONESSENTIAL The bicycle, **which hasn't been well maintained,** has only one working brake.

REFERENCE NOTE: For more information on punctuating adjective clauses, see pages 909–910.

Adverb Clauses

An ***adverb clause*** modifies a verb, an adjective, or an adverb in a sentence. To form an adverb clause, add a subordinating conjunction (*although, after, because, if, when, where, while)* to the beginning of the sentence you want to subordinate. (You may also need to delete or replace some words to form the clause.) You can then attach the adverb clause to the sentence it's related to.

When you combine sentences by using an adverb clause, choose the subordinating conjunction carefully. Make sure it shows the proper relationship between the ideas in the adverb clause and the independent clause.

ORIGINAL The band played patriotic music. Fireworks burst into brilliant color across the night sky.
COMBINED The band played patriotic music **as fireworks burst into brilliant color across the night sky.**

ORIGINAL There may not be any racquetball courts open. In that case, we'll go to the park and play tennis.
COMBINED **If there are no racquetball courts open,** we'll go to the park and play tennis.

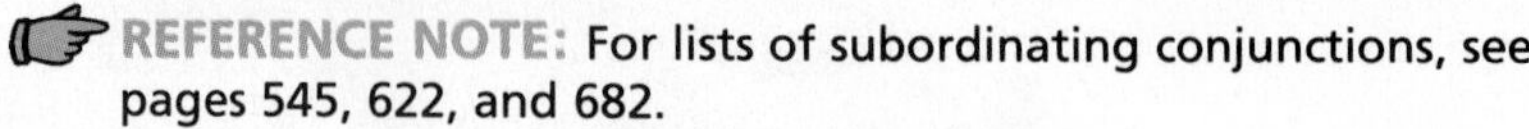
REFERENCE NOTE: For lists of subordinating conjunctions, see pages 545, 622, and 682.

Noun Clauses

A ***noun clause*** is a subordinate clause used as a noun. It usually begins with *that, what, whatever, why, whether, how, who, whom, whoever,* or *whomever.* Here are a few examples of noun clauses in sentences.

Whoever buys that car will be sorry. [noun clause as subject]
Many people don't realize **that actress Raquel Welch is part Hispanic.** [noun clause as direct object]
We can spend the money on **whatever we like.** [noun clause as object of preposition]

Sometimes you can drop the introductory word *that* from a noun clause without any confusion.

EXAMPLE My sister told us (that) ***The Rocketeer*** **was a fast-paced, exciting movie.**

You can combine sentences by turning one of the sentences into a noun clause and attaching it to the other sentence.

ORIGINAL Cactus plants are able to survive in the desert. The TV documentary explained it.
COMBINED The TV documentary explained **how cactus plants are able to survive in the desert.**

ORIGINAL The actress knew it. The role was right for her.
COMBINED The actress knew **that the role was right for her.**

EXERCISE 5 **Combining Sentences by Subordinating Ideas**

Combine each of the following pairs of sentences. Change one sentence into a subordinate clause and attach the clause to the other sentence. [Hint: You may need to add, delete, or rearrange some words.] Choose your connectives carefully, and check your combined sentences for correct punctuation.

1. Louise Erdrich writes in lyrical prose about the Native American experience. She is part Chippewa.
2. The Turtle Mountain Chippewa Reservation is the setting for her novel *Love Medicine*. Erdrich spent time there as a child.
3. Erdrich attended the Bureau of Indian Affairs boarding school. Both of her parents worked there.
4. Erdrich had close ties to the Chippewa community. She never really thought about her Native American heritage.
5. As a young adult Erdrich began to realize something. Her Native American heritage was important to her.
6. Erdrich's writing emphasizes the beauty and universality of the Native American experience. Critics have noted this about her writing.
7. Her eccentric characters take on a mythic quality. They struggle to overcome their problems.
8. Erdrich met her husband, Michael Dorris. Erdrich was attending Dartmouth College at the time.
9. Dartmouth was founded in 1769 under a charter that stressed the education of Native Americans. By 1972 it had graduated only twelve of them.
10. Dorris has collaborated closely with Erdrich on her works. He is also part Native American.

REVIEW B **Combining Sentences by Coordinating and Subordinating Ideas**

Use either coordination or subordination to combine each of the following pairs of sentences. You may see more than one way to combine a sentence pair. Just write the combination that sounds best to you.

EXAMPLE **1.** *Amazing Stories* was the first science fiction magazine. Hugo Gernsback began publishing it in 1926.

1. Amazing Stories, *which Hugo Gernsback began publishing in 1926, was the first science fiction magazine.*

1. Some science fiction contains outlandish speculation. It has to seem somewhat believable in order to be effective.
2. *Frankenstein* is an early example of science fiction. The novel describes the scientific creation of human life.
3. H. G. Wells's *The Time Machine* offers thought-provoking social criticism. *The Time Machine* describes a devastated future world.
4. Some critics did not accept science fiction as serious literature. Major authors in the early twentieth century often included science fiction in their works.
5. Today science fiction has many supporters. They hold annual conventions and present awards for the best writing.

REVIEW C Revising a Paragraph by Combining Sentences

Here's a chance to put all of your sentence-combining skills to the test. The following paragraph is made up of short, choppy sentences. Using the methods you've learned, combine the short sentences into longer sentences. [Note: In some cases you'll be combining more than just two sentences.] Your combined sentences should add variety and improve the style of the paragraph. Remember to check for correct punctuation.

Mount Saint Helens erupted in May 1980. It is near Vancouver, Washington. The eruption was sudden. The explosion had a force over five hundred times that of an atomic bomb. It tore the top off the mountain. It threw ash high into the air. The explosion and resulting mudslides caused more than thirty deaths. The explosions and mudslides left many people homeless. The mud killed hundreds of deer and elk. The mud turned Spirit Lake into a mudhole. Much of the ash fell to earth within a few days. A cloud of dust remained. This cloud was over much of the Northern Hemisphere. People saw spectacular sunrises and sunsets for years. The sunrises and sunsets were rose-colored. The color was due to solar rays striking microscopic particles of ash.

Writing for Different Audiences

Think back to when you were first learning to read. The books you read in those days used mostly short, simple sentences. Now that you're a more accomplished reader, you'd probably become bored or impatient with that type of writing. You're looking for more richness and variety in what you read as well as in what you write.

Writing a Children's Story

It's a week before an important holiday. You've been working after school at a day-care center. One of the teachers has asked you to plan a special holiday activity for the children. You've decided to have a story hour in which you tell the children a short, simple story about the upcoming holiday. Write a brief, entertaining story to tell the children. Your story might tell about the origin of the holiday, or it might just illustrate the meaning and spirit of the holiday. Feel free to draw from your own memories and experiences as you write the story. (For help with planning and writing a story, see pages 169–199.) Be sure to use clear, short sentences that the children will understand.

Writing a Story for Your Peers

Your high school has caught the holiday spirit, too. The editor of the school newspaper is compiling a special holiday issue. Write a different version of your holiday story to submit for publication in the paper. Revise the story so that it will hold the interest of readers your age. You may want to add or replace details. Use sentence-combining techniques to adapt the style of your writing for an older audience. Craft lively, detailed sentences that are fun to read.

16 Improving Sentence Style

LOOKING AHEAD

This chapter will give you some practice in revising your sentences for style. As you work through the chapter, you will learn ways to

- vary sentence beginnings and sentence structures
- reduce wordiness in sentences

Revising for Variety

As you evaluate and revise your writing, it's important to read your sentences with an eye for style. Notice how the sentences fit together. Do they add up to lively, natural-sounding paragraphs or dull, stilted ones? If your writing sounds dull, you probably need to vary the beginnings and the structures of some of your sentences.

As you read the following passage, notice how the varied sentences work together to form a smooth, effective paragraph.

> Bring out the tall tales now that we told by the fire as the gaslight bubbled like a diver. Ghosts whooed like owls in the long nights when I dared not look over my shoulder; animals lurked in the cubbyhole under the stairs where the gas meter ticked. And I remember that we went singing carols once, when there wasn't the shaving of a moon to light the flying streets. At the end of a long road was a drive that led to a large house, and we stumbled up the darkness of the drive that night, each one of us afraid, each one holding a stone in his hand in case, and all of us too brave to say a word. The wind through the trees made noises as of old and unpleasant and maybe webfooted men wheezing in caves. We reached the black bulk of the house.
>
> Dylan Thomas, *A Child's Christmas in Wales*

Varying Sentence Beginnings

Most sentences begin with a subject followed by a verb.

EXAMPLES **I sprained** my ankle the first time I went ice-skating.
That cat is a finicky eater.

There's nothing wrong with this basic subject-verb pattern—except that it begins to sound monotonous after a while. You can improve the style of your writing by beginning some sentences with introductory words, phrases, and clauses instead of with subjects. At the same time, you can make more effective connections between related sentences.

In each example below, the first version of the sentences is clear. But notice that the revision brings the ideas into sharper focus by shifting the emphasis in the second sentence.

BLAND The lacrosse team qualified for the state finals. The players never stopped practicing from the minute they got the news.

BETTER The lacrosse team qualified for the state finals. **From the minute they got the news,** the players never stopped practicing.

BLAND Marion was shy in the classroom. She came into her own, however, on the stage.

BETTER Marion was shy in the classroom. **On the stage,** however, she came into her own.

Sometimes the best way to vary sentence beginnings is to reduce a short sentence to an introductory word, phrase, or clause and attach it to another sentence. Here's where your sentence-combining skills come in handy.

BLAND The novel put me to sleep after an hour of reading. It is long and dull.

BETTER **Long and dull,** the novel put me to sleep after an hour of reading.

REFERENCE NOTE: For more about combining sentences, see pages 564–577.

You can begin sentences in many different ways. The following chart gives some examples.

VARYING SENTENCE BEGINNINGS
SENTENCE CONNECTIVES
Almost everyone watches television. **But** how many people really know how a television set works? I don't mind lending you my new book. **However,** you must promise to give it back.
APPOSITIVES
An enormously complex mechanism, the human brain contains between 10 and 100 billion nerve cells. **A merchant sailor for ten years,** Jim knew every important port in the world.
SINGLE-WORD MODIFIERS
Methodically, Mrs. Williams worked the calculus problem on the board. **Shivering,** we warmed our chapped hands by the fire. **Large and heavy,** the water-dwelling manatee can eat over one hundred pounds of plants in a day.
PHRASE MODIFIERS
From the window of the plane, Marisol saw her family waving goodbye.

(continued)

VARYING SENTENCE BEGINNINGS *(continued)*
PHRASE MODIFIERS *(continued)*
Tiring rapidly, Joe decided to save his strength for the final set. **To win the essay prize,** Tanya worked late every night.
CLAUSE MODIFIERS
Because no one saw the crash, investigators had to depend on evidence found in the wreckage. **Although the investigators had little to go on,** they were successful in uncovering the cause of the crash.

Sentence connectives like *and, but,* and *however* can help you make transitions between ideas. Usually, these connecting words link ideas within a sentence. Sometimes, though—especially in informal writing—you may use one at the beginning of a sentence for variety and emphasis. For example, notice how Robert Cormier uses a sentence connective for emphasis in the following passage.

> You drive out in your father's Le Mans doing seventy-five on the pike and all you're doing is visiting an old lady in a nursing home. A duty call. And then you find out that she's a person. She's *somebody.*
>
> Robert Cormier, "The Moustache"

Use sentence connectives sparingly and carefully. Be sure that the connective you use shows the appropriate relationship between your ideas.

EXERCISE 1 Varying Sentence Beginnings

Here's a chance to practice varying sentence beginnings. Revise each sentence so that it begins with an appositive or with a single-word, phrase, or clause modifier.

1. Michael Jordan, one of the most exciting players in the National Basketball Association, is the leading scorer for the Chicago Bulls.
2. He darts aggressively past defensive players and scores basket after basket.
3. Jordan practiced hard to become the star he is today.
4. Jordan had to work to overcome a lack of self-confidence as a teenager, although today he radiates self-assurance.
5. Jordan, self-conscious and shy, was convinced he was so unattractive that he would never get married.
6. He was embarrassed by his awkwardness and rarely dated in high school.
7. He chose to attend the University of North Carolina and was determined to succeed in a major college basketball program.
8. Jordan was named All-American Player and College Player of the Year during his years at the University of North Carolina.
9. Jordan acknowledges that his knowledge and ability seemed to come together at the pro level, although his college career was outstanding.
10. Jordan, smiling happily, agrees that he has traveled a long way from his days as a gawky teenager.

Varying Sentence Structure

When you revise your writing for style, it isn't always enough to vary your sentence beginnings. It's also important to vary your sentence structures. That means using a mix of simple, compound, complex (and sometimes compound-complex) sentences.

REFERENCE NOTE: For information about the four types of sentence structures, see pages 686–687.

Read the following short paragraph, which contains only simple sentences.

Quasars are the brightest, most distant objects in the sky. For decades they have puzzled and intrigued astronomers. Quasars may hold important clues to the birth and formation of galaxies. Astronomers believe this. Astronomers first observed quasars in 1960. By the mid-1970s they knew of hundreds of these objects. With the help of the huge new Keck Telescope in Hawaii, astronomers hope to discover the power source of quasars. Quasars give off as much energy as 100 trillion stars.

Now, read the revised version of the paragraph. Notice how the writer has made the paragraph smoother by including a variety of sentence structures.

Quasars are the brightest, most distant objects in the sky. For decades they have puzzled and intrigued astronomers, who believe quasars may hold important clues to the birth and formation of galaxies. Astronomers first observed quasars in 1960, and by the mid-1970s they knew of hundreds of these objects. With the help of the huge new Keck Telescope in Hawaii, astronomers hope to discover the power source of quasars, which give off more energy than 100 trillion stars.

Complex sentences do more than add variety to your writing. They also help bring your thoughts into focus by emphasizing main ideas and subordinating less-important ones. For example, in the revised paragraph, notice how the complex sentence at the end makes a clearer connection between the last two ideas. As a subordinate clause, the information about the energy output of quasars explains why astronomers are eager to discover the power source.

REFERENCE NOTE: For more about subordinating ideas in sentences, see pages 544–548 and 574–577.

EXERCISE 2 Varying Sentence Structure

The writer of the following paragraph wants to make an important point, but too many simple sentences make the writing sound dull. Improve the paragraph by varying the structure of the sentences. Add, delete, or rearrange words wherever you need to.

I learned recently that companies can pay filmmakers to display name-brand products in films. I was shocked. Commercials shown before a feature film are annoying. Ads sneaked into the films themselves are downright unethical, though. People go to the movies expecting to enjoy a commercial-free film. They see an actor eating Brand X pizza or wearing Brand Y jeans. At the time, they don't realize that they are watching a paid advertisement. Filmmakers have a responsibility to make their audiences aware of these ads. They shouldn't have to interrupt a film to identify an ad. They should be required to list the advertisers in the credits.

REVIEW A **Varying Sentence Beginnings and Sentence Structure**

Using what you've learned about varying sentence beginnings and sentence structure, revise the following paragraph for style. Add, delete, and rearrange words wherever necessary to make the sentences more varied. Be careful to keep the original meaning of the paragraph.

> Toni Morrison, a gifted African American writer, has earned international acclaim for her works. She won the National Book Critics Circle Award for her third novel, Song of Solomon. She received the Pulitzer Prize for her fifth novel, Beloved. Beloved demonstrates Morrison's talent for portraying complex human emotions and relationships. It tells the story of a former slave haunted by tragic memories. Beloved is rich with vivid characterizations, like her other novels.

Revising to Reduce Wordiness

Don't make the mistake of thinking that the more words you use, the better your writing will sound. Extra words don't improve your style; they just get in your reader's way. Your writing is most effective when it is clear and concise—that is, free of the clutter of unnecessary words.

To avoid wordiness in your writing, keep these three points in mind.

- Use only the number of words you need to make your point.
- Avoid pretentious, complicated words where plain, simple ones will do.
- Don't repeat words and ideas unless it's absolutely necessary.

Sometimes you can fix a wordy sentence by taking out whole groups of unnecessary words. At other times you can revise by reducing clauses to phrases and both clauses and phrases to single words.

Eliminating Unnecessary Words

The following paragraph about computer viruses is an example of wordy writing. Lines have been drawn through the unnecessary words. First, read the paragraph aloud with the crossed-through words left in. Then, read the shorter, more concise version. Notice the difference the revisions make in the sound of the paragraph.

In the 1980s computer experts became aware of a dangerous type of program called a computer virus. A computer virus ~~by its very nature~~ is designed to alter or destroy data and to copy itself into other programs in the same computer or in other computers. Sometimes a virus removes and deletes information, and sometimes it simply inserts a message. Some mischievous programmers ~~who like to play jokes~~ design computer viruses as a joke ~~or a prank~~. Their type of virus might cause a humorous message to appear ~~in a funny way~~ on a computer's screen. However, some people design viruses ~~with the intent~~ to deliberately destroy data. In one well-publicized 1988 incident ~~that made all the newspapers~~, a computer virus crippled sixty thousand computers in a research network ~~in a matter of hours~~ overnight. Since the emergence of computer viruses, the U.S. government has passed strict laws making it illegal to introduce viruses into the computers of unwitting users ~~when they are not aware of it~~.

Following are some more examples of how less can be more when it comes to sentences. Can you see other ways in which the sentences might have been revised to reduce the wordiness?

WORDY **The game is played with tiny, little round balls that, in my opinion, I think, are made of steel.**

BETTER **The game is played with tiny balls that, I think, are made of steel.**

WORDY **Far away at a great distance, the small, diminutive shapes of the campers' tents were outlined in silhouette against the dark night sky.**

BETTER **Far away, the small shapes of the campers' tents were outlined against the night sky.**

EXERCISE 3 Revising Wordy Sentences

For each of the following sentences, ask: Does it have any unnecessary words? Does it repeat any ideas? If you answer "yes" to either of these questions, revise the sentence to reduce the wordiness. If a sentence is already concise, write *C*.

1. Most people have heard of William Shakespeare, the man many people call the greatest writer of all time.
2. Even though Shakespeare is famous throughout the world everywhere, we can't be certain about his physical appearance—that is, what he looked like.
3. From the portraits of Shakespeare that have survived and withstood the passage of time, he appears to have been a slim man of slight build and average height.
4. Artists rendered Shakespeare with well-proportioned features and expressive eyes.
5. Although we may never learn more about Shakespeare the man himself, we can continue to learn and gain information about Shakespeare the writer by studying his magnificent works.

EXERCISE 4 Revising a Paragraph by Eliminating Unnecessary Words

Revise the following paragraph to make it more concise. Eliminate unnecessary words, keeping the original meaning of each sentence. [Note: You may need to change some verb forms, too.]

Few athletes earn lasting reputations that endure outside the realm of sports. However, athlete and baseball player Roberto Clemente is remembered not only as a skilled athlete but also as a compassionate human being. A lifelong opponent of injustice and unfairness, Clemente, who was from Puerto Rico, fought prejudice in the major leagues and in every part of his life. In 1972 Clemente died in an accident in a plane crash on his way to help deliver supplies to the victims of a terrible, horrible earthquake in Nicaragua. His courage and bravery live on in the memories of his fans, who still think of him.

Reducing Groups of Words

Writing concisely means using only as many words as you need. You don't want to leave out words that clarify your meaning or add interest to your sentences. However, you do want to make sure that every word counts. The charts on this page and the next page give some examples of how you can trim away excess words from your writing.

CLAUSES REDUCED TO PHRASES	
CLAUSE	**When they were trapped by a cave-in,** the miners waited for rescuers.
PARTICIPIAL PHRASE	**Trapped by a cave-in,** the miners waited for rescuers.
CLAUSE	We decided **that we would get an early start.**
INFINITIVE PHRASE	We decided **to get an early start.**
CLAUSE	The teams **that had come from Missouri** were not scheduled to play the first day of the tournament.
PREPOSITIONAL PHRASE	The teams **from Missouri** were not scheduled to play the first day of the tournament.
CLAUSE	Her two dogs, **one of which is a collie and the other a spaniel,** perform different duties on the farm.
APPOSITIVE PHRASE	Her two dogs, **a collie and a spaniel,** perform different duties on the farm.

CLAUSES AND PHRASES REDUCED TO SINGLE WORDS	
CLAUSE	The performance **that was on Saturday** was the best.
WORD	**Saturday's** performance was the best.
CLAUSE	Laura is a runner **who never tires.**
WORD	Laura is a **tireless** runner.
PHRASE	**Cherishing the invitation,** I answered it promptly.
WORD	I answered the **cherished** invitation promptly.
PHRASE	She greeted everyone **in a cheerful manner.**
WORD	She greeted everyone **cheerfully.**

Following is a list of concise, one-word replacements for some common wordy phrases.

Wordy	Simpler
at which time	when
by means of	by
due to the fact that	because, since
in spite of the fact that	although
in the event that	if
the fact is that	actually

EXERCISE 5 Revising Sentences Through Reduction

Reduce the italicized clauses and phrases in the following sentences by deleting, replacing, and rearranging words. [Note: You may see more than one way to make a reduction.] Be sure to keep the original meaning.

1. Genetics, *which is the study of heredity,* began in 1866 when an Austrian monk *who was named Gregor Mendel* demonstrated the inheritance patterns of the garden pea.
2. The results of Mendel's studies went unnoticed until 1900, *at which time* Hugo De Vries in the Netherlands, Carl Correns in Germany, and Erich von Tschermak-Seysenegg in Austria discovered the work *of Mendel in a simultaneous way.*

3. *After they proved* that hybrid crops that are produced by selective breeding programs provide more food than nonhybrid plants, geneticists were able to increase the food supplies *of many nations.*
4. Selective techniques *of breeding* have also helped develop cattle, hogs, sheep, and poultry *that are healthier and more productive.*
5. Using the basic principles of genetics *that were established* in 1866, geneticists have introduced selective breeding *with success* around the world.

REVIEW **B**

Revising a Paragraph by Reducing Wordiness

Revise the following wordy paragraph. Eliminate unnecessary words and reduce clauses and phrases to make the paragraph concise. You should be able to make at least five reductions.

Needless to say, I am not one of those in the senior class who believe that the senior lounge should be closed during the week of exams. What I mean to say is that seniors need a place that is quiet and relaxing where they can escape the pressures that accompany exam week. If the lounge is closed during this time, it would mean that seniors would be forced to use the cafeteria, which is crowded, or the auditorium, which is noisy, for the purpose of relaxation. Furthermore, the use of the senior lounge during exam week is one of the few privileges that seniors are still able to enjoy here at East High. Not long ago the right of seniors to park cars in the parking area reserved for members of the faculty was recently taken away by the Student-Teacher Council. If more privileges are taken away, the morale of seniors will weaken.

Writing a College Admissions Essay

The admissions essay is one of the most important and challenging parts of your application to a college or university. In an admissions essay, you do much more than give factual information about yourself. You try to give the admissions officers a sense of who you are, what makes you special, and what unique qualities you have to offer the school. The admissions essay is your chance to stand out from the crowd of applicants. It's also a chance to demonstrate your writing skills. Just as you dress up for a face-to-face interview, you use your best writing form in an admissions essay. You want each sentence to be clear, lively, and concise.

Following is one student's successful admissions essay about a turning point in her life. As you read, pay attention not only to what the writer says but also to how she says it.

> When I was ten years old, I discovered that good things can come out of unpleasant experiences. One freezing-cold winter morning I woke up itching all over. I had chicken pox, and I had to stay home from school for a week. Those first few days were the worst days of my life. Embarrassed by those awful red bumps all over my face, I didn't even go outside. I just stayed in bed, watched TV, and felt sorry for myself. Then, one morning my mother came into my room with a dog-eared paperback. "This was your sister's favorite book when she was your age. Why don't you try reading for a little bit? It might take your mind off the itching." I sighed. Right then, reading was the last thing I felt like doing. Even my eyelids were puffed-up and itchy. But I decided anything was worth a try.
>
> The extraordinary thing that happened was that--practically overnight--I fell in love with reading. The book was The Wolves of Willoughby Chase by Joan Aiken. By the time I was well enough to go back to school, I had read it twice, cover to cover. It was about a girl my age whose

parents are thought to be lost at sea. Before being reunited with her parents at the end, she has a series of amazing adventures. And as I turned the pages, I was right there with her. I could hear the wolves howling at my heels as we ran through the dark woods after escaping from the orphanage. My mother was right. Huddled under the covers, I was so involved in the story that I almost forgot about my chicken pox.

That worn copy of The Wolves of Willoughby Chase has a place of honor on my bookshelf. Alongside it are many other books that have helped me through difficult times over the years. But as I've gotten older, I've discovered that books are more than just escapes. They are also passports into a larger world. With a book as your companion, you can travel anywhere, do anything, and be anyone. Someday I will write books of my own. By creating stories from my experience and imagination, I hope to give other people the enjoyment that my favorite authors have given me.

You've just finished filling out a college application form. You've given all the necessary factual information about yourself and your high school courses and activities. Now, you're ready to tackle the admissions essay. Write an essay telling something special about yourself that an application form wouldn't cover. (For help with writing a personal essay, see pages 130–159.) Take extra care with revising your essay. Pay special attention to your sentence style. Make sure all of your sentences are clear and concise and work together to form smooth paragraphs.

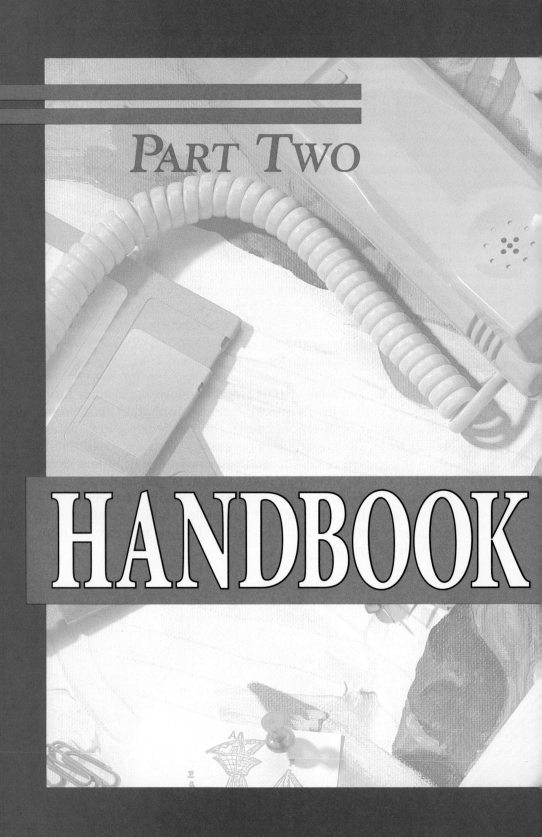

Part Two

HANDBOOK

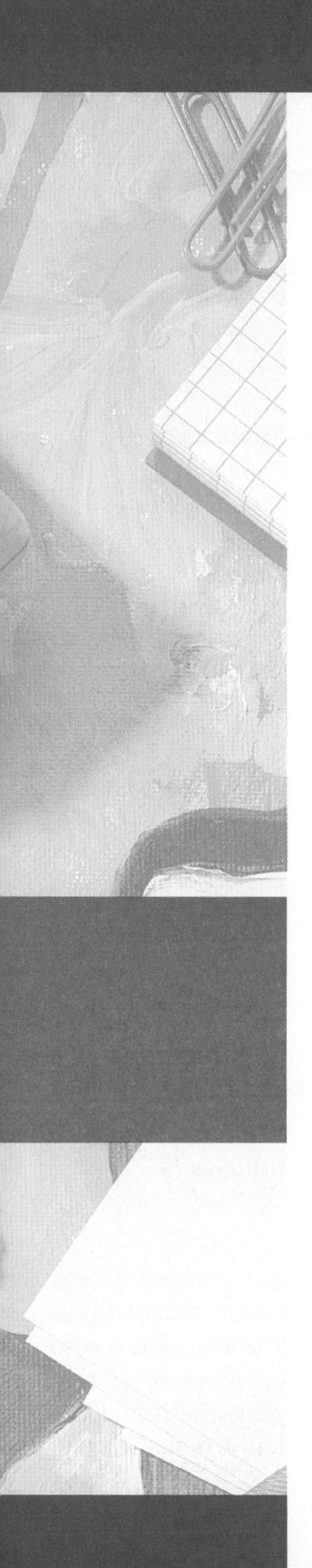

Grammar

Usage

Mechanics

17 The Parts of Speech

Identification and Function

Diagnostic Test

Identifying Parts of Speech

Identify each italicized word in the following paragraphs as a *noun*, a *pronoun*, an *adjective*, a *verb*, an *adverb*, a *conjunction*, a *preposition*, or an *interjection*.

EXAMPLE **Writing [1] *can* be a [2] *means* of self-discovery.**
1. *verb*
2. *noun*

For less [1] *than* what you might pay to see a movie [2] *you* can get to know yourself better. Simply purchase a [3] *blank* notebook and begin to keep a personal journal. You'll be amazed to see what you [4] *learn* [5] *about* yourself in just a short time.

Keeping a journal is [6] *easy,* [7] *for* there's only one rule: Date all entries. Writing four or five entries a week is a realistic goal;

[8] *usually* your mood will determine the length of each entry. One type of entry is the [9] *daily* log, in which you record [10] *what* you did and how you felt on a particular day. Another is a [11] *list* of your favorite songs, movies, and poetry. [12] *Most* [13] *important* are [14] *those* entries that have nothing to do with your exterior life and, instead, [15] *reveal* your inner life: your dreams, your thoughts, your questions, your goals, and your feelings. [16] *Because* the journal is a personal book, which [17] *no one* else reads, it becomes a place where you're free to say [18] *anything* you want. Rereading your entries [19] *later* will show you how you've changed.

If you're wondering [20] *whether* keeping a journal is worth the effort, [21] *well,* it certainly is. [22] *According to* one girl in [23] *Connecticut,* her journal is "the closest [she's] ever come to knowing [her]self." The journal is an adventure [24] *in* self-awareness. [25] *Try* keeping one yourself.

THE EIGHT PARTS OF SPEECH

noun	verb	conjunction
pronoun	adverb	interjection
adjective	preposition	

The Noun

17a. A ***noun*** is a word used to name a person, a place, a thing, or an idea.

PERSONS	carpenter, tourists, team, cousins, Faith Ringgold
PLACES	cities, theater, forest, neighborhood, Santa Fe
THINGS	telescope, bricks, birds, horseshoe, Liberty Bell
IDEAS	justice, creativity, power, opinions, Buddhism

GRAMMAR

Common Nouns and Proper Nouns

A ***common noun*** names any one of a group of persons, places, things, or ideas. A ***proper noun*** names a particular person, place, thing, or idea. Common nouns aren't capitalized (except when they begin a sentence or are part of a title); proper nouns, however, always are.

COMMON NOUNS	PROPER NOUNS
woman	Queen Isabella, Wilma Mankiller, Judith Baca
nation	Egypt, Mexico, Vietnam, New Zealand
event	Pan American Games, French Revolution, Academy Awards, Boston Tea Party
holiday	Martin Luther King Day, Patriots' Day, Fourth of July, Potlatch
language	Hebrew, Spanish, Bantu, Thai

 REFERENCE NOTE: For more on capitalizing proper nouns, see pages 875–877.

Concrete and Abstract Nouns

A ***concrete noun*** names an object or event that can be perceived by the senses. An ***abstract noun*** names a quality, a characteristic, or an idea.

CONCRETE NOUNS	sneeze, star, gravel, cinnamon, Beijing, Leaning Tower of Pisa, Woody Allen
ABSTRACT NOUNS	peace, civilization, honor, courage, Romanticism, Manifest Destiny

Collective Nouns

A ***collective noun*** names a group.

COLLECTIVE NOUNS	jury, band, family, class, flock, committee

Compound Nouns

A ***compound noun*** consists of two or more words used together as one noun. Some compound nouns are written as a single word, some as separate words, and others as hyphenated words.

ONE WORD	stairway, bookcase, Newfoundland
SEPARATE WORDS	lieutenant governor, ceiling fan, Golden Gate Bridge
HYPHENATED WORD	sister-in-law, jack-of-all-trades, stick-in-the-mud

NOTE: When you're not sure how a compound noun is written, look it up in a dictionary.

EXERCISE 1 **Identifying and Classifying Nouns**

Identify the nouns in each of the following sentences, and classify each noun as *proper* or *common* and as *concrete* or *abstract.*

1. In Japan many homes have a place of honor in which the family displays a favorite scroll or a vase of flowers.
2. Amalia Mesa-Bains and Michael Ríos are among the many Hispanic artists who launched their careers in the Mission District of San Francisco.
3. In one afternoon the crew repaired eleven helicopters.
4. We purchased tomatoes, lettuce, and corn grown by local farmers.
5. Congress debated the merits of the bill late into the night.
6. My goal is to visit every state in the United States.
7. Last summer our family drove from our home in Kansas City to Chicago in our new van.
8. Her excellent record as treasurer convinced a majority of the students to vote for her for president.
9. Blunt honesty, quick wit, and fierce loyalty are three of the strongest personality traits in Mark Twain's character Huck Finn.
10. The crowd roared as Chip sank the winning basket for the Falcons just one second before time ran out.

EXERCISE 2 **Identifying and Classifying Nouns**

Identify the twelve compound nouns and three collective nouns in the following sentences. Then classify each noun as *common* or *proper* and as *concrete* or *abstract*.

1. Did you do a double take when you saw this picture?

2. The juxtaposition of Egyptian landmarks with a seashore and a sign in Japanese writing is certainly an eye-opener.
3. Actually, the Sphinx and the pyramid are sand sculptures that a team of students from a high school in Japan built for the Kamakura Beach Carnival at Zaimokuza Beach.
4. Do you suppose the committee that judged the sculptures awarded the students' undertakings a prize?
5. The sightseers in front of the pyramid took a number of snapshots as keepsakes of the carnival.

The Pronoun

17b. A ***pronoun*** is a word used in place of a noun or of more than one noun.

The word that a pronoun stands for is called the ***antecedent*** of the pronoun.

EXAMPLE **The students complained to the principal about the dress code. They said he had not consulted them about it.** [The noun *students* is the antecedent of the pronouns *they* and *them;* the noun *principal* is the antecedent of the pronoun *he;* and the compound noun *dress code* is the antecedent of the pronoun *it.*]

 REFERENCE NOTE: See pages 718–720 and 754–760 for more information on antecedents.

A pronoun may also take the place of another pronoun or a verbal.

EXAMPLE **One** of the film projectors is broken. **It** is being repaired. [The pronoun *it* takes the place of the pronoun *one*.]
Jay enjoys hiking and camping; in fact, **they** are his two favorite pastimes. [The pronoun *they* takes the place of the gerunds *hiking* and *camping*.]

Personal Pronouns

A ***personal pronoun*** refers to the person speaking (*first person*), the person spoken to (*second person*), or the person or thing spoken about (*third person*).

	SINGULAR	PLURAL
First person	I, me, my, mine	we, us, our, ours
Second person	you, your, yours	you, your, yours
Third person	he, him, his, she, her, hers, it, its	they, them, their, theirs

EXAMPLES If **I** give **you my** address, will **you** write to **me**?
We told **them they** could go with **us**.

Some of the personal pronoun forms—*my, your, his, her, its, our, their*—are used before nouns in the same way that adjectives are used. In this book these words are called *possessive pronouns*. However, your teacher may prefer to have you call them *possessive adjectives*.

Reflexive and Intensive Pronouns

A ***reflexive pronoun*** refers to the subject of a sentence, directing the action of the verb back to the subject. An ***intensive pronoun*** emphasizes a noun or another pronoun.

GRAMMAR

The Adjective

17c. An ***adjective*** is a word used to modify a noun or a pronoun.

To modify means "to describe or to make more definite." Adjectives modify nouns or pronouns by telling *what kind, which one,* or *how many (how much).*

WHAT KIND?	**ripe** apples **blue** sky	**happy** child **loud** music
WHICH ONE?	**this** book **those** girls	**last** straw **next** step
HOW MANY?	**two** students **several** choices	**both** answers **many** people
HOW MUCH?	**some** news **more** money	**enough** time **less** trouble

An adjective usually precedes the word it modifies.

EXAMPLE The **tired** and **hungry** hikers straggled into camp.

For emphasis, however, a writer may place an adjective after the word it modifies.

EXAMPLE The hikers, **tired** and **hungry,** straggled into camp.

A ***predicate adjective*** is separated from the word it modifies by a linking verb.

EXAMPLES The hikers were **hungry** and **tired**.
The hikers felt **hungry** and **tired**.

 REFERENCE NOTE: See pages 642–643 for more information about predicate adjectives. For guidelines on using adjectives, see Chapter 25.

Articles

The most frequently used adjectives are *a, an,* and *the.* These words are called ***articles.***

A and *an* are ***indefinite articles;*** they refer to *any* one of a general group. *A* is used before words beginning with a consonant sound; *an* is used before words beginning with a vowel sound.

EXAMPLES Felipe added **a** tomato and **an** avocado to the salad.
It's **an** honor to be here.

Notice in the second example above that *an* is used before *honor* because the *h* in *honor* is not pronounced; *honor* is pronounced as though it began with a vowel. Remember that the *sound* of the noun, not the spelling, determines which indefinite article to use.

The is the ***definite article.*** It specifies a particular person, place, thing, or idea.

EXAMPLE We spent **the** hour discussing **the** revolution of **the** slaves that began in 1791 in Haiti.

Adjective or Pronoun?

In different contexts, a word may be used as different parts of speech. For example, the following words may be used as adjectives or as pronouns.

all	either	much	some	what
another	few	neither	that	which
any	many	one	these	whose
both	more	other	this	
each	most	several	those	

Remember that an adjective *modifies* a noun and that a pronoun *takes the place of* a noun.

ADJECTIVE **These** books are overdue. [*These* modifies the noun *books.*]

PRONOUN **These** are overdue. [*These* takes the place of the noun *books.*]

ADJECTIVE Ntozake Shange wrote **both** poems. [*Both* modifies the noun *poems.*]

PRONOUN Ntozake Shange wrote **both.** [*Both* takes the place of the noun *poems.*]

GRAMMAR

NOTE: In this book the words *my, your, his, her, its, our,* and *their* are called possessive pronouns. Since they precede nouns and tell *which one* or *whose,* some teachers prefer to call these words possessive adjectives.

EXAMPLES **my** job, **your** essay, **their** plans

Follow your teacher's instructions in labeling these words.

Nouns Used as Adjectives

Nouns are sometimes used as adjectives.

NOUNS	NOUNS USED AS ADJECTIVES
sofa	**sofa** cushion
hotel	**hotel** lobby
taco	**taco** salad
high school	**high school** senior
Marine Corps	**Marine Corps** cadet

NOTE: Remember that some pairs of nouns form compound nouns.

EXAMPLES paper clips, cable TV, time capsule, goal line

EXERCISE 4 Identifying Adjectives and the Words They Modify

Identify the adjectives and the words they modify in the following paragraph. Do not include articles (*a, an,* and *the*).

[1] William Least Heat-Moon's first book, *Blue Highways,* chronicled his journey across the United States in 1978. [2] That book attracted many readers and even made the bestseller lists. [3] In *PrairyErth,* Heat-Moon narrows his focus to a single Kansas county. [4] The book's unusual title comes from the shorthand term scientists use for the unique soils of the nation's central states. [5] Chase County lies in east central Kansas. [6] It is, as Heat-Moon says, "the most easterly piece of the American Far West." [7] A county with a population of 3,013 may seem an unlikely location for an examination of humans' place on this planet. [8] After all, the county has only two towns and

a few villages. [9] In many ways, though, Kansas is a microcosm of America. [10] And in Heat-Moon's proficient hands, Chase County reveals itself to be a microcosm of Kansas.

GRAMMAR

REVIEW A

Identifying Nouns, Pronouns, and Adjectives

Identify each italicized word in the following sentences as a *noun*, a *pronoun*, or an *adjective*. If a word is an adjective, give the word it modifies.

EXAMPLE **1.** *Everyone* in class is writing a poem about an *American* pioneer.
1. *Everyone—pronoun; American—adjective—pioneer*

1. Several students are writing *theirs* about people whose names are familiar to *many;* others have chosen people who they believe merit wider recognition.
2. After *much* thought, I have finally narrowed my choices to two *African American* women whom I admire.
3. Both of *these* women broke *new* ground in their fields—one in the performing arts and the other in the visual arts.
4. The fieldwork *that* Katherine Dunham (right) did as an anthropology student in the West Indies inspired her to incorporate elements of African and Caribbean folk culture into *modern dance.*
5. After touring the world for *several* decades, the dancer and choreographer founded the Katherine Dunham Children's Workshop in *East St. Louis,* Illinois, which she still directs.

GRAMMAR

6. Tributes to Dunham, *who* is now in her eighties, continue to pour in; for she is considered a true *dance* innovator.
7. My other *potential* choice is Barbara Brandon, who in 1991 became the first African American woman cartoonist to achieve syndication in the *mainstream* press.
8. As you can see below, Brandon's *cartoon strip* depicts life from the *perspective* of an African American woman.
9. Brandon pictures only the heads and, occasionally, the hands of her characters, *all* of whom are women; for she believes that women's bodies are displayed enough in the *media*.
10. As *you* might guess, *my* final choice of a subject will not be an easy one.

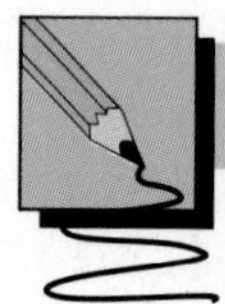

WRITING APPLICATION

Creating a Dictionary of New Words

There are over 450,000 words in the English language, yet we still don't have a word for everything. What, for instance, do you call your former best friend? or the feeling you have when a word is on the tip of your tongue but you can't quite remember it? What's more, many words in our language seem ill-suited to the things they stand for. For example, why do we drive on parkways and park in driveways? Fortunately for us, our language is readily open to change and adopts new words all the time to meet the needs of those who use it.

WRITING ACTIVITY

For a school project, you and your classmates have decided to create a dictionary of words that should exist but don't. Write a complete dictionary entry proposing a name for something that doesn't have one or that you think could be more aptly named. Give the new word's derivation, use, and part of speech.

Prewriting Use observation, brainstorming, or freewriting to come up with situations, things, places, thoughts, feelings, and qualities that could benefit from a new word. Then choose the one that appeals to you the most and create a word for it. Next, think of the information you will need for your dictionary entry. How is your new word spelled and pronounced? What is its part of speech, and what other forms does it have? What is the word's derivation? its definition(s)? (For more information about the content and form of dictionary entries, see pages 1038–1039.)

Writing Refer to your prewriting notes often as you write your first draft. Don't be concerned about using complete sentences. Consider including an example sentence that gives the word in context.

Evaluating and Revising As you reread your dictionary entry, check to make sure that your organization and tone are appropriate for a dictionary entry. Compare your entry with the sample one found on page 1038. Make any changes that you think will improve your entry.

Proofreading and Publishing Proofread your dictionary entry carefully. You and your classmates may want to gather together all of your dictionary entries and photocopy them or input them on a computer. The entries could then be alphabetized to create a new-word dictionary, which could be photocopied for the entire class.

The Verb

17d. A ***verb*** is a word used to express action or a state of being.

Action Verbs

An ***action verb*** expresses physical or mental activity.

PHYSICAL	speak	sleep	carry	give
MENTAL	think	imagine	dream	believe

(1) A ***transitive verb*** is an action verb that takes an *object*—a noun or a pronoun that tells *who* or *what* receives the action.

EXAMPLES The rain **lashed** the windows. [*Windows* receives the action of *lashed.*]
Amy Tan **writes** fiction. [*Fiction* receives the action of *writes.*]

(2) An ***intransitive verb*** is an action verb that doesn't take an object.

EXAMPLES The rain **fell.**
My cousin **arrived.**

Most English verbs can be either transitive or intransitive, depending on the context of the sentence.

EXAMPLES The chorus **sang** patriotic songs. [transitive]
The chorus **sang** beautifully. [intransitive]

NOTE: Most dictionaries group the definitions of verbs according to whether the verbs are used transitively (marked *v.t.* in most dictionaries) or intransitively (*v.i.*).

Linking Verbs

A ***linking verb*** is an intransitive verb that connects the subject with a noun, a pronoun, or an adjective that describes or identifies the subject. The word that is linked to the subject is called the *subject complement*.

EXAMPLES Marcy **looks** serious.
[*Serious* describes the subject *Marcy.*]

Wovoka **was** an influential Paiute prophet.
[*Prophet* identifies the subject *Wovoka.*]

REFERENCE NOTE: For more about subject complements, see pages 642–643.

NOTE: Linking verbs are sometimes called *state-of-being verbs* because they help make a statement about the subject's condition, or state of being.

COMMON LINKING VERBS			
FORMS OF *BE*			
am	be	will be	had been
is	can be	could be	shall have been
are	may be	should be	will have been
was	might be	would be	could have been
were	must be	has been	should have been
being	shall be	have been	would have been
OTHERS			
appear	grow	seem	stay
become	look	smell	taste
feel	remain	sound	turn

NOTE: The forms of *be* are not considered linking verbs when they're followed by words that tell *where* or *when.*

EXAMPLE You should have been **here yesterday.** [*Here* tells *where,* and *yesterday* tells *when.*]

Some of the other verbs listed above can be either linking verbs or action verbs, depending on the context of the sentence.

LINKING The alarm **sounded** shrill.
ACTION I **sounded** the alarm.

To determine whether a verb is a linking verb or an action verb, substitute a form of *be* or *seem.* If the sentence still makes sense, the verb is probably a linking verb.

LINKING The fabric **felt** soft. [*The fabric was soft* makes sense.]
ACTION I **felt** the fabric. [*I was the fabric* doesn't make sense.]

GRAMMAR

The Verb Phrase

A ***verb phrase*** consists of a main verb and at least one ***helping verb*** (also called an ***auxiliary verb***).

EXAMPLES **has played** [*Has* is a helping verb; *played* is the main verb.]
will be going [*Will* and *be* are helping verbs; *going* is the main verb.]

COMMON HELPING VERBS			
Forms of *be*	am were is	be are being	was been
Forms of *have*	has	have	had
Forms of *do*	do	does	did
Others	may might must	can shall will	could should would

A helping verb may be separated from the main verb.

EXAMPLES **Have** you **seen** Lorraine Hansberry's play *A Raisin in the Sun?*
You **should** not **miss** it.

REFERENCE NOTE: The word *not* and its contraction, *–n't,* are adverbs telling *to what extent;* they are never part of a verb phrase. See pages 616–617 for more information about adverbs.

EXERCISE 5 Identifying and Classifying Verbs and Verb Phrases

Identify the verbs and verb phrases in the following sentences. Then classify each verb or verb phrase as *transitive, intransitive,* or *linking.*

1. The Statue of Liberty, which has become a major American landmark, may be the best-known structure in the world.
2. It possesses a twofold appeal: It symbolizes human liberty, and it unfailingly awes the visitor by its colossal size.
3. Moreover, it has withstood the continuous assaults of time and weather.

4. Although Frédéric Auguste Bartholdi designed the statue, the supporting framework came from the drawing board of Alexandre Gustave Eiffel.
5. The copper-plated statue has an intricate iron framework that supports Liberty's familiar pose.
6. The statue itself was a gift from the people of France, but Americans paid the construction costs for the pedestal.
7. In newspaper editorials, Joseph Pulitzer persuaded the American people that they needed the statue.
8. The people agreed, and in 1886 the nation celebrated the dedication of the Statue of Liberty on what was then named Bedloe's Island in Upper New York Bay.
9. Bartholdi modeled Liberty's face after his mother's features.
10. Those features (*left*, before the mid-1980s restoration; and *right*, after) have remained symbols of quiet determination.

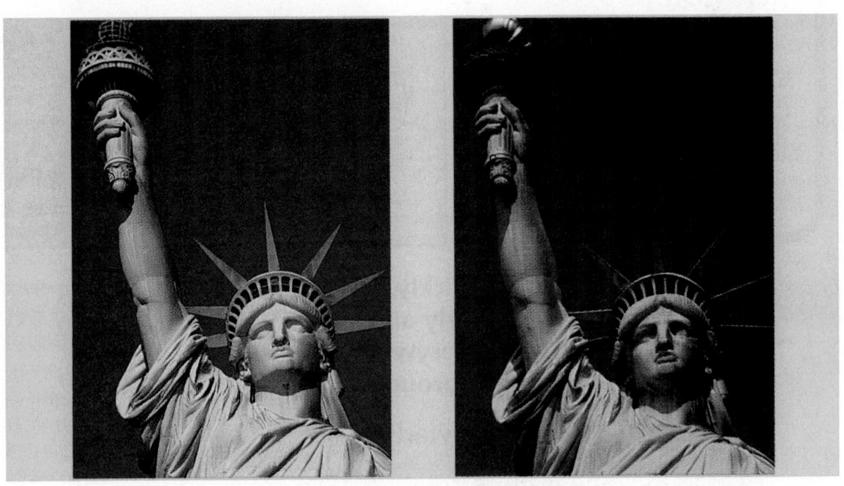

EXERCISE 6 Replacing General Verbs with Specific Ones

Rewrite the following dialogue twice, replacing each italicized verb with two more specific ones to create two different conversations.

1. "Let's *go* downtown after school," said Frank.
2. "I can't," said Aldo. "Tonight's the night I *cook*."
3. "Oh, yeah? What *are* you *making*?"
4. "It's one of my original concoctions; you should *try* it!"
5. "In that case, I have just one more question: When *are* you *serving*?"

The Adverb

GRAMMAR

17e. An ***adverb*** is a word used to modify a verb, an adjective, or another adverb.

Most adverbs modify by telling *how, when, where,* or *to what extent.* Adverbs are most commonly used to modify verbs and verb phrases.

"I've just read your latest book and found it fast moving, full of suspense, and very well written. You're probably just the person who could clear up something that's been puzzling me for years. What's an adverb?"

EXAMPLES She reads **quickly.** [*how*]
She reads **early** and **late.** [*when*]
She reads **everywhere.** [*where*]
She reads **thoroughly.** [*to what extent*]

Adverbs may modify adjectives.

EXAMPLES She is **quite** creative. [The adverb *quite* modifies the adjective *creative,* telling *to what extent.*]
This species is found on an **extremely** remote island. [The adverb *extremely* modifies the adjective *remote,* telling *to what extent.*]

Adverbs may also modify other adverbs.

EXAMPLES Florence Griffith-Joyner runs **remarkably** swiftly. [The adverb *remarkably* modifies the adverb *swiftly,* telling *to what extent.*]
It's **too** soon to know the results. [The adverb *too* modifies the adverb *soon,* telling *to what extent.*]

NOTE: The word *not* and its contraction, *–n't,* are classified as adverbs; they tell *to what extent.*

Nouns Used as Adverbs

Some nouns may be used as adverbs.

EXAMPLES **My parents left yesterday.** [The noun *yesterday* is used as an adverb, telling *when.*]
They will return home Saturday. [The noun *home* is used as an adverb, telling *where.* The noun *Saturday* is used as an adverb, telling *when.*]

In identifying parts of speech, label nouns used in this way as adverbs.

REFERENCE NOTE: For guidelines on using adverbs, see Chapter 25.

EXERCISE 7 Identifying Adverbs and the Words They Modify

Identify the adverbs and the words they modify in the following sentences. Be prepared to tell whether each adverb tells *how, when, where,* or *to what extent.*

1. American physicist Rosalyn Yalow helped develop an extremely sensitive biological technique.
2. Radioimmunoassay, which is now used in laboratories worldwide, readily detects antibodies and hormones.
3. Yalow writes, "If you ever have a new idea, and it's really new, you have to expect that it will not be widely accepted immediately."
4. In other words, most scientists do not leap excitedly from the bath crying "Eureka!" as Archimedes supposedly did.
5. Yalow and her colleague discovered radioimmunoassay accidentally while observing two patients.
6. After they carefully interpreted their observations, they arrived at their exciting discovery.
7. In 1977, though Yalow's collaborator had died, the Nobel Prize Committee awarded Yalow the undeniably prestigious Nobel Prize for medicine.
8. Radioimmunoassay eventually became a basic diagnostic tool in widely different areas of medicine.
9. According to Yalow, the technique was not quickly accepted because people ordinarily resist change.
10. She believes that progress can not be impeded forever and that good ideas are eventually accepted.

GRAMMAR

REVIEW B Identifying Parts of Speech

Identify the part of speech of each italicized word in the following paragraphs. Tell what word or words each adjective or adverb modifies.

[1] Diego Rivera is *chiefly* famous for his murals, but he was a prolific artist who *worked* in a wide variety of styles. [2] *This* landscape is an example of his early work; *it* was painted in 1904. [3] Rivera, *who* was born in Guanajuato, Mexico, in 1886, entered the San Carlos Academy of Fine Arts in Mexico City when he was *only* eleven. [4] In 1907, with the proceeds from his first *art* show, he made the *first* of several lengthy visits to Europe. [5] *There* he experimented with different approaches until he realized it was the fresco process, the art of painting on wet plaster, *that* best suited his artistic vision.

[6] *Two* of Rivera's lifelong interests *were* Mexican history and machinery. [7] *His* murals in the former palace of *Hernán Cortés* in Cuernavaca, in the state of Morelos, depict the history of Morelos from before the conquest by Spain until after the Mexican Revolution of 1910. [8] *One* of the works *that* Rivera created in the United States was a series of twenty-seven murals that the Detroit Arts Commission asked him to paint on subjects related to Detroit and the general theme of industrialization.

[9] Rivera was *controversial* in the United States because he included *political* themes in his work. [10] Ironically, capitalists attacked *him* for his affiliation with Communists, and Communists attacked him for accepting *commissions* from capitalists.

Diego Rivera, "La era", 1904, oil on canvas, 100 × 114.6 cm. Reproduction authorized por el Instituto Nacional de Bellas Artes y Literatura, Marte R. Gomez Collection (INBA)/The Detroit Museum of Art

The Preposition

17f. A ***preposition*** is a word used to show how a noun or a pronoun is related to some other word in the sentence.

Notice how changing the preposition in the following examples changes the relationship between *swam* and *raft*.

I swam **to** the raft.
I swam **from** the raft.
I swam **around** the raft.
I swam **past** the raft.
I swam **under** the raft.

Object of a Preposition

A preposition introduces a ***prepositional phrase.*** The noun or pronoun at the end of a prepositional phrase is the ***object of the preposition.***

EXAMPLES before **lunch** at the **game** throughout the **week**

REFERENCE NOTE: See pages 652–655 for more information on prepositional phrases.

Commonly Used Prepositions

about	beside	in	through
above	besides	inside	throughout
across	between	into	to
after	beyond	like	toward
against	but (meaning "except")	near	under
along		of	underneath
among	by	off	until
around	concerning	on	unto
at	down	out	up
before	during	outside	upon
behind	except	over	with
below	for	past	within
beneath	from	since	without

NOTE: Some of the words in this list may also be used as adverbs. Keep in mind that an adverb is a modifier, and it does not take an object.

ADVERB I'll meet you **outside** at noon. [*Outside* modifies *meet.*]

PREPOSITION I'll meet you **outside** the library. [*Outside* introduces a prepositional phrase ending with the object *library.*]

A preposition that consists of two or more words is a ***compound preposition.***

EXAMPLES Tena has been accepted by several private colleges **in addition to** both state universities.
As of today, she hasn't made her final choice.

Commonly Used Compound Prepositions		
according to	because of	in spite of
along with	by means of	instead of
apart from	in addition to	next to
aside from	in front of	on account of
as of	in place of	out of

EXERCISE 8 **Completing Sentences by Adding Prepositional Phrases**

Complete the following sentences by replacing each blank with a prepositional phrase.

1. Rob collects postcards ____.
2. ____ we collapsed.
3. We first heard the rumor ____.
4. ____ people had gathered to hear the concert.
5. I tiptoed ____ and listened quietly.
6. The deer darted quickly ____ and raced ____.
7. Everyone ____ applauded Branford Marsalis' solo.
8. Exhausted ____, the explorers pitched their tents ____ and planned the next day's work.
9. ____ the city council has voted to renovate the abandoned building ____ and turn it ____.
10. ____ I thought that something may have gone wrong ____.

The Conjunction

 A *conjunction* is a word used to join words or groups of words.

Coordinating Conjunctions

A *coordinating conjunction* connects words or groups of words that are used in the same way.

Coordinating Conjunctions						
and	but	for	nor	or	so	yet

EXAMPLES In A.D. 711, the Berbers **invaded** and **conquered** Spain. [*And* joins two words.]

We missed the opening scene, **but** we enjoyed the rest of the play. [*But* joins two groups of words.]

Correlative Conjunctions

Correlative conjunctions are pairs of conjunctions that join words or groups of words used in the same way.

Correlative Conjunctions		
both . . . and	either . . . or	whether . . . or
not only . . . but also	neither . . . nor	

EXAMPLES **Either** Fred **or** Manuela will bring music for the party. [*Either . . . or* joins two words.]

Not only did Garrett Morgan patent the first gas mask, **but** he **also** invented the automatic traffic signal. [*Not only . . . but also* joins two groups of words.]

Subordinating Conjunctions

A *subordinating conjunction* begins a subordinate clause, joining it to an independent clause.

GRAMMAR

Commonly Used Subordinating Conjunctions			
after	because	since	until
although	before	so that	when
as	how	than	whenever
as if	if	that	where
as much as	in order that	though	wherever
as though	provided	unless	while

EXAMPLES Many Native Americans are reluctant to reveal their traditional names for some places **because** the names have spiritual meaning.
I gasped **when** I saw the headline.

A subordinating conjunction may begin a sentence instead of coming between the groups of words it joins.

EXAMPLE **When** I saw the headline, I gasped.

REFERENCE NOTE: See pages 675–683 for more information about subordinate clauses.

EXERCISE 9 Identifying and Classifying Conjunctions

Identify the conjunction(s) in each of the following sentences, and tell whether each is a *coordinating conjunction,* a *correlative conjunction,* or a *subordinating conjunction.*

1. Our old car needs either a valve job or a new engine.
2. Before you write your paper, you must submit an outline.
3. Have you decided whether I'll take physics or economics?
4. During the Tang dynasty (618–906), China experienced not only a revival of Confucianism but also the development of specifically Chinese schools of Buddhism.
5. Thomas Hardy found a publisher for his poetry only after he had published more than a dozen novels.
6. Workers here pay city, state, and federal income taxes.
7. José Martí, a hero of the Cuban rebellion against Spain, was both a revolutionary leader and a great poet.
8. Mike enjoyed the movie as much as Sue did.
9. Are you going to the movies or to the concert?
10. When Liberia was founded in 1821, thousands of free African Americans moved there.

PICTURE THIS

Shipwrecked alone on this desert island, you have an ample supply of food and water, but no means of leaving the island. Fortunately, however, you also have a pencil, paper, and four bottles. Write four different messages to place in the bottles, explaining your predicament and requesting rescue. In your messages use a variety of coordinating, correlative, and subordinating conjunctions.

Subject: rescue notes
Audience: whoever finds each of the bottles
Purpose: to explain and persuade

The Interjection

17h. An ***interjection*** is a word used to express emotion. It has no grammatical relation to other words in the sentence.

EXAMPLES	ah	oh	well	whoops
	hey	ouch	whew	wow

GRAMMAR

EXERCISE 10 Completing Sentences by Adding Interjections

Complete the following conversation by replacing each blank with an appropriate interjection. Do not use any interjection more than twice.

"[1] ____, Mariana, why are you so edgy tonight?" Mrs. Montero asked her eighteen-year-old daughter.

"[2] ____, Mom, don't you remember? Tonight's the night KHOP announces who won the drawing for a free car."

"[3] ____, yes, how could I forget? You've been talking about it for months."

"[4] ____, Mom, it's only been two weeks, and—wait, that's the phone; I'll get it. Hello? This is Mariana Montero. What? [5] ____, are you kidding me? I did? Really?! [6] ____, you're serious! [7] ____! That's incredible! When can I pick it up? Tonight? [8] ____, that's great! I'll be there in twenty minutes! 'Bye—and thanks! [9] ____, Mom, will you drive me? [10] ____, just think: That's the last time you'll ever hear me say those words!"

The Same Word as Different Parts of Speech

17i. A word's part of speech is determined by how the word is used in a sentence.

EXAMPLES This **plant** is native to North America. [noun]
We **plant** tomatoes every year. [verb]
Bacteria cause many **plant** diseases. [adjective]

Marisa led, and we followed **after.** [adverb]
We crossed the finish line **after** Marisa. [preposition]
We crossed it **after** all the other runners did, too. [conjunction]

This pillow is filled with **down** from geese. [noun]
I've always wanted a **down** pillow. [adjective]
Put it **down;** it's too expensive. [adverb]
We can find cheaper pillows at the store **down** the street. [preposition]

REVIEW C Identifying Parts of Speech

Identify the part of speech of each italicized word in the following paragraphs.

[1] Did you know that millions of African Americans celebrate a *uniquely* American holiday *whose* roots lie in ancient Africa? [2] *Well,* they do; called Kwanzaa, which in Swahili means "the first fruits of the harvest," the holiday is observed *during* the week between Christmas and New Year's Day.

[3] Kwanzaa isn't a religious holiday or a substitute for Christmas *but* a celebration of black Americans' rich cultural *heritage.* [4] The holiday, which was created by Maulana (Ron) Karenga of California State University in Long Beach in 1966, *synthesizes* elements from a variety of *African* harvest festivals.

[5] Kwanzaa *focuses* on seven basic principles: unity, self-determination, collective work and responsibility, cooperative economics, purpose, *creativity,* and faith. [6] *Among* the symbols of the holiday *are* a straw mat for respect for tradition; an ear of corn for each child in the family; and a candleholder with seven green, red, and black candles for the continent of Africa. [7] *Each* day during the week family members light *one* of the candles and discuss one of the principles. [8] They *also* exchange simple gifts *that* reflect their heritage and eat foods from Africa and from the lands to which their ancestors were taken, such as the Caribbean and South America.

[9] Some families follow Karenga's original program for the holiday strictly, *while* others *freely* adapt it. [10] In some communities families gather for concerts and *dance* performances *like* this one, which took place in Los Angeles.

GRAMMAR

Review: Posttest 1

A. Identifying Parts of Speech

For each of the following sentences, identify every word or word group that is the part of speech indicated in parentheses.

1. If anyone calls me while I am out, will you please tell whoever it is that I can be reached at one or the other of these two numbers? (*pronoun*)
2. Although she lost both her sight and her hearing during childhood, Helen Keller later learned to communicate effectively with other people. (*noun*)
3. As much as we all had wanted to eat at the new French restaurant, we could not afford the prices. (*conjunction*)
4. Inca artisans were quite expert; among the works they left behind are elaborate jewelry and colorful tapestries. (*adverb*)
5. At the very beginning of the movie, many people in the audience were startled by the eerie sound effects that came toward them from all directions. (*preposition*)
6. This antique mantel clock chimes a delicate melody every quarter-hour. (*adjective*)
7. Do you think that the weather will finally turn cool once this low-pressure system moves through? (*verb*)
8. I developed extremely painful shin splints when I jogged much farther than I usually do. (*adverb*)
9. Oh, how beautifully Kathleen Battle and Jessye Norman sang in their concert at Carnegie Hall! (*interjection*)
10. Neither the coach nor the team members offered excuses for the loss, for they had done their best. (*conjunction*)

B. Identifying Parts of Speech

Identify the part of speech of each italicized word in the following paragraphs.

[11] When *it* opened in 1991, the Museum of Television and Radio became New York City's first new major museum *since* 1966. **[12]** The late William Paley, the *founder* of CBS, *established* the museum with contributions from the broadcasting industry. **[13]** The museum doesn't contain *everything* ever heard on radio or seen on TV, *for* many early programs were never copied, and some of those that were are missing or unplayable. **[14]** But *its* collection is *quite* extensive: twenty-five thousand TV programs, fifteen thousand radio shows, and ten thousand commercials. **[15]** *Whether* you want to hear Jack Benny in a comedy sketch from the 1930s *or* watch Billie Holiday in a live performance from the 1950s, you'll find the recording *here.* **[16]** In fact, the earliest material *dates* to 1920, *when* the nation's first radio station, KDKA in Pittsburgh, went on the air.

[17] Modern *technology* provides *easy* access to the museum's collection. **[18]** Simply answer a *few* questions and press a button *on* one of the computers that store the catalog. **[19]** *Instantly* a museum worker using the computer signals special machines in the basement, *which* automatically load the tapes. **[20]** Often by the time you've made *yourself* comfortable in one of the console rooms, the tape is *ready* for you to enjoy.

Review: Posttest 2

Writing Sentences Using Words as Specific Parts of Speech

Write two sentences for each numbered item, according to the following guidelines.

1. Use *right* as a noun and as an adjective.
2. Use *signal* as a noun and as a verb.
3. Use *home* as a noun and as an adverb.
4. Use *few* as a pronoun and as an adjective.
5. Use *that* as a pronoun and as an adjective.
6. Use *around* as an adverb and as a preposition.
7. Use *how* as an adverb and as a conjunction.
8. Use *well* as an adverb and as an interjection.
9. Use *for* as a preposition and as a conjunction.
10. Use *since* as a preposition and as a conjunction.

GRAMMAR

SUMMARY OF PARTS OF SPEECH

Rule	Part of Speech	Use	Examples
17a	noun	names	**Max** has an **idea** for our **party** on **Valentine's Day**.
17b	pronoun	takes the place of a noun or another pronoun	**Who** told **you this** is the **one that I** want for **myself**?
17c	adjective	modifies a noun or a pronoun	**Some nice** people bought **the big** house on **the next** block.
17d	verb	shows action or a state of being	**Are** you warm enough, or **do** you **need** a sweater?
17e	adverb	modifies a verb, an adjective, or another adverb	We need to find a **much** shorter route, or we'll arrive **too late**.
17f	preposition	relates a noun or a pronoun to another word	**As of** today we have only two weeks **of** school **before** graduation.
17g	conjunction	joins words or groups of words	**Both** Maria **and** I hope to be there **if** we can make it.
17h	interjection	shows emotion	**Hey!** What are you doing here?

18 The Parts of a Sentence

Subject, Predicate, Complement

Diagnostic Test

A. Identifying Subjects, Verbs, and Complements

Identify the italicized word or word group in each of the following sentences as a *subject*, a *verb*, a *direct object*, an *indirect object*, an *objective complement*, a *predicate nominative*, or a *predicate adjective*.

EXAMPLE 1. Have *you* seen Jim?
1. *subject*

1. Many fugitive slaves found *shelter* with the Seminoles of Spanish Florida.
2. The water in the bay feels quite *cold*.
3. Cheryl gave *me* her paper to read.
4. The Great Wall of China *is* one of that nation's oldest structures.
5. There are two *parts* to this test.

6. The coach named Yolanda *captain* of the team.
7. Please put the *dishes* away.
8. The mail carrier left *you* this letter.
9. From out of the darkness lumbered a huge, shaggy *creature.*
10. Lee Trevino is *one* of America's all-time best golfers.

B. Identifying Subjects, Verbs, and Complements

Identify the subject and verb in each sentence in the following paragraph. If a sentence has any complements, identify them as well, and indicate whether each is a *direct object,* an *indirect object,* an *objective complement,* a *predicate nominative,* or a *predicate adjective.*

EXAMPLE **[1] Manny and I visited Coney Island last weekend.**
1. ***subject—Manny, I; verb—visited; direct object—Coney Island***

[11] Along the coast of the Atlantic Ocean in Brooklyn, New York, lies Coney Island, a world-famous amusement park. **[12]** Until 1654, the island (now a peninsula) was the summer campground of the Canarsie and the Nyack peoples. **[13]** In that year, the Native Americans sold a group of Dutch settlers the island. **[14]** The Dutch named the island Conye (Dutch for "rabbit") because of the abundance of wild rabbits in the area. **[15]** In the 1820s, the island became popular as an ocean resort and throughout the nineteenth and early twentieth centuries grew increasingly lavish. **[16]** Among its many attractions were the mechanical horses and the 250-foot Parachute Jump of Steeplechase Park and the onion domes, minarets, and Japanese tea gardens of Luna Park. **[17]** Today, after years of neglect and a series of fires, the amusement area of this once-grand resort is only a five-block strip between Surf Avenue and the 80-foot-wide boardwalk along the ocean. **[18]** Yet ten million people still visit Coney Island each year. **[19]** Now Horace Bullard, the founder of a restaurant chain, is planning a major facelift for the area. **[20]** Bullard holds the rights to the former site of Steeplechase Park and envisions the park spectacularly beautiful once again.

The Sentence

18a. A ***sentence*** is a group of words that expresses a complete thought.

A thought is complete when it makes sense by itself.

EXAMPLES In many ways the development of the microprocessor has revolutionized technology.
When did Mexico achieve independence from Spain?
How quickly this year has passed!

Every sentence begins with a capital letter. The punctuation mark that follows a sentence depends on the purpose of the sentence.

REFERENCE NOTE: See pages 689–690 for more information on the purposes of sentences. See pages 899–901 for more on end marks.

A group of words that looks like a sentence but that doesn't make sense by itself is a ***sentence fragment.***

SENTENCE FRAGMENT Students representing sixty-one historically black universities and colleges.
SENTENCE Students representing sixty-one historically black universities and colleges competed in the knowledge bowl.

SENTENCE FRAGMENT The graduation ceremony scheduled for June 20.
SENTENCE The graduation ceremony is scheduled for June 20.

SENTENCE FRAGMENT Sponsors election-year debates.
SENTENCE The League of Women Voters sponsors election-year debates.

REFERENCE NOTE: For more information about sentence fragments, see pages 555–558.

EXERCISE 1 **Writing Complete Sentences**

Write five sentences summarizing the trends shown in the chart on the next page. Proofread each sentence to make sure that you have not included any sentence fragments.

EXAMPLE **1.** *The decline in shipments of long-playing records leveled off between 1983 and 1984.*

Changing Trends in Recorded Music

Numbers of compact discs, cassettes, long-playing records, and singles shipped by manufacturers.

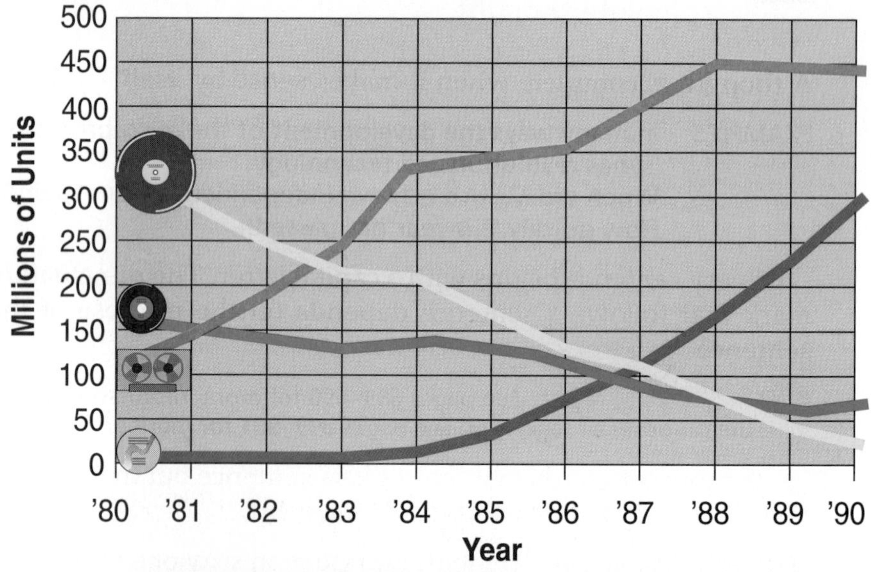

Source: Recording Industry Association of America

The Subject and the Predicate

18b. A sentence consists of two parts: the *subject* and the *predicate.* The ***subject*** tells *whom* or *what* the sentence is about. The ***predicate*** tells something about the subject.

EXAMPLES

Subject	Predicate
Jenny	laughed.
Rain	pelted the sailors.
Each of the amateur mimes	performed.

Predicate | Subject
Away on the breeze sailed | the dry leaves.

Predicate | Subject | Predicate
When did | Alex Haley | write *Roots?*

As you can see, a subject or a predicate may consist of one word or more than one word. In these examples, all the words labeled subject make up the ***complete subject,*** and all the words labeled predicate make up the ***complete predicate.***

The Simple Subject

18c. The ***simple subject*** is the main word or group of words that tells *whom* or *what* the sentence is about.

EXAMPLES The **view** from the observatory on the top floor of the building is extraordinary. [The complete subject is *The view from the observatory on the top floor of the building.*]

Lasting for eight days, **Hanukkah** celebrates the rededication of the temple in Jerusalem in 165 B.C. [The complete subject is *Lasting for eight days, Hanukkah.*]

The **Memorial Coliseum** in Los Angeles was filled to capacity. [The complete subject is *The Memorial Coliseum in Los Angeles.*]

REFERENCE NOTE: Compound nouns, such as *Memorial Coliseum,* are considered single nouns. Therefore, they may be used as simple subjects. For more about compound nouns, see page 601.

NOTE: In this book the term *subject* refers to the simple subject unless otherwise indicated.

The Simple Predicate

18d. The ***simple predicate*** is a verb or verb phrase that tells something about the subject.

EXAMPLES The crowd **surged** forward. [The complete predicate is *surged forward.*]

GRAMMAR

The victorious athletes **were** completely **surrounded** by admirers. [The complete predicate is *were completely surrounded by admirers.*]
Felipe **has** not yet **revealed** his plans. [The complete predicate is *has not yet revealed his plans.*]

NOTE: In this book, the term *verb* refers to the simple predicate (a one-word verb or a verb phrase) unless otherwise indicated.

REFERENCE NOTE: For more information about verbs and verb phrases, see pages 612–614.

The Compound Subject and the Compound Verb

18e. A ***compound subject*** consists of two or more subjects that are joined by a conjunction and have the same verb.

Compound subjects are usually joined by *and* or *or.*

EXAMPLES **East Germany** and **West Germany** have been reunited.
Did **Michelle** or **Chondra** lead the petition drive?
Hokkaido, Honshu, Shikoku, and **Kyushu** are the four main islands of Japan.

18f. A ***compound verb*** consists of two or more verbs that are joined by a conjunction and have the same subject.

Compound verbs are usually joined by *and, but,* or *or.*

EXAMPLES Mary McLeod Bethune **founded** Bethune-Cookman College and twice **served** as its president.
I **read** the book but **missed** the movie.
Would you rather **wash** the dishes or **dry** them?

Do not confuse a sentence containing a compound subject or compound predicate with a compound sentence.

EXAMPLES **Anna** and **Lyle will sing** and **do** a comedy routine. [compound subject and compound predicate]
Anna will sing, and **Lyle will do** a comedy routine. [compound sentence]

REFERENCE NOTE: For more information about compound sentences, see pages 686–687.

How to Find the Subject of a Sentence

To find the subject of a sentence, ask *Who?* or *What?* before the verb.

EXAMPLES In the auditorium **friends** and **relatives** of the graduates awaited the ceremony. [Who awaited? Friends and relatives awaited.]
Sharing the island of Hispaniola with Haiti is the **Dominican Republic.** [What is sharing? Dominican Republic is sharing.]

Keep the following four guidelines in mind whenever you are trying to find the subject of a sentence.

(1) The subject of a command or a request is always understood to be *you*, even if the word *you* does not appear in the sentence.

COMMAND Always document the source of a direct quotation. [Who documents? You document.]
REQUEST Please write soon. [Who writes? You write.]

If a command or a request contains a *noun of direct address*—a word naming the one or ones spoken to—the subject is still understood to be *you*.

EXAMPLE Frances, (you) walk the dog.

(2) The subject of a sentence is never in a prepositional phrase.

EXAMPLES A **committee** of students investigated the allegations. [Who investigated? Committee investigated. *Students* is the object of the preposition *of*.]
One of the parks in Austin, Texas, is named for the Mexican general Ignacio Seguín Zaragoza. [What is named? One is named. *Parks* is the object of the preposition *of*. *Austin* is the object of the preposition *in*.]
From the alley came the **wail** of a siren. [What came? Wail came. *Alley* is the object of the preposition *from*. *Siren* is the object of the preposition *of*.]

☞ REFERENCE NOTE: For more information about prepositional phrases, see pages 619–620 and 652–655.

(3) The subject of a question usually follows the verb or comes between the parts of a verb phrase.

EXAMPLES Are these **jeans** on sale? [What are on sale? Jeans are.]
When did **Thurgood Marshall** retire from the United States Supreme Court? [Who did retire? Thurgood Marshall did retire.]

To find the subject of a question, turn the question into a statement.

QUESTION Have you tasted sushi?
STATEMENT **You** have tasted sushi. [Who have tasted? You have tasted.]

QUESTION Is the cold war over?
STATEMENT The **cold war** is over. [What is over? Cold war is over.]

(4) *There* or *here* is never the subject of a sentence. In the following examples, *there* and *here* are adverbs telling *where.*

EXAMPLES There goes **Rebecca.** [Who goes? Rebecca goes.]
Here is your **receipt.** [What is? Receipt is.]

NOTE: *There* is not always an adverb. It may instead be an *expletive*—a word that fills out the structure of a sentence but does not add to the meaning.

EXAMPLE **There** will be a special broadcast on the coup tonight at 11:30 P.M.

EXERCISE 2 Identifying Subjects and Verbs

Identify each simple subject and verb in the following paragraphs. Include all parts of a compound word and all words in a verb phrase.

EXAMPLE [1] The miniature Japanese sculptures shown on the next page are called *netsuke.*
1. *subject—sculptures; verb—are called*

[1] This exquisite art form originated as a practical solution to an everyday problem. [2] During Japan's Tokugawa period (1615–1867), an integral part of the traditional costume of the new merchant class was a set of lacquerware boxes for medicines and spices. [3] The boxes were threaded onto the sash of the kimono and served as pockets for the otherwise pocketless garment.

[4] Originally just small, plain toggles of lightweight ivory or wood, the *netsuke* held the boxes in place along the sash.

[5] Under the feudal system then in effect, there were strict laws against any display of wealth by persons below the rank of *samurai*. [6] However, wealthy merchants wanted some obvious symbol of their success. [7] Over time, increasingly elaborate *netsuke* from the nation's finest artisans became that symbol.

[8] Eventually, the Japanese adopted Western clothing, with pockets. [9] As a result, both the small boxes and the *netsuke* became obsolete. [10] Today, collectors all over the world gladly pay large sums for specimens of these beautiful objects with the humble origin.

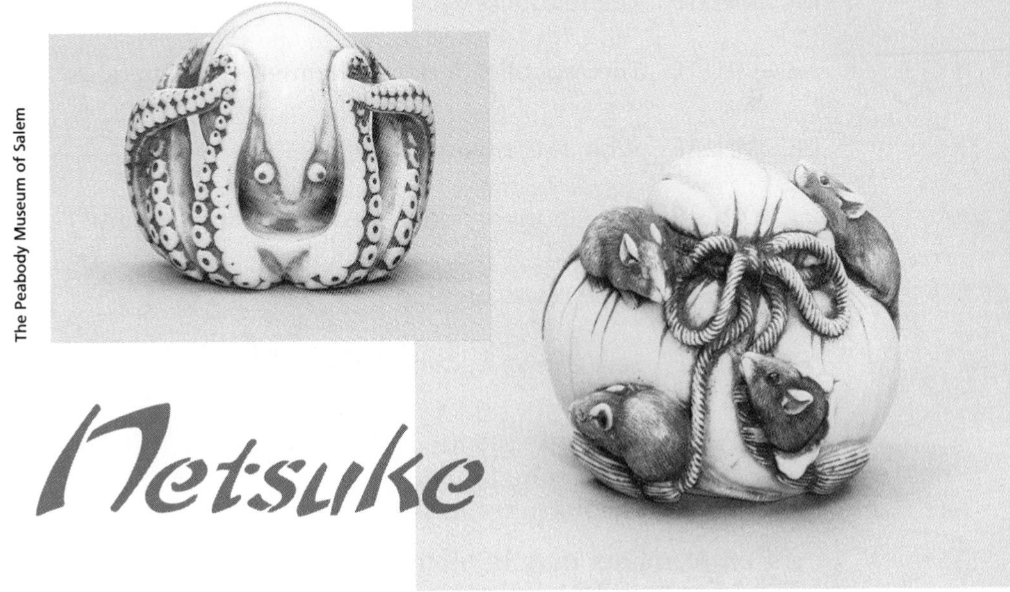

The Peabody Museum of Salem

The Peabody Museum of Salem

Complements

18g. A ***complement*** is a word or word group that completes the meaning of a predicate.

Some sentences are complete with only a subject and a verb.

EXAMPLES She won. (She = S, won = V)

(You) Look! ((You) = S, Look = V)

Other sentences require one or more complements to complete their meaning.

S V
INCOMPLETE **Judith Baca created**

S V C
COMPLETE **Judith Baca created the mural.**

S V
INCOMPLETE **They mailed**

S V C C
COMPLETE **They mailed me the information.**

S V
INCOMPLETE **The republics declared**

S V C C
COMPLETE **The republics declared themselves independent.**

S V
INCOMPLETE **Who in the world named**

S V C C
COMPLETE **Who in the world named the puppy Cerberus?**

S V
INCOMPLETE **Seiji Ozawa became**

S V C
COMPLETE **Seiji Ozawa became a successful conductor.**

S V
INCOMPLETE **The horse seems**

S V C
COMPLETE **The horse seems skittish.**

Complements may be nouns, pronouns, or adjectives. Be careful not to mistake an adverb for a complement.

ADVERB **Hatshepsut ruled ably.** [The adverb *ably* tells *how* Hatshepsut ruled.]

COMPLEMENT **Hatshepsut ruled Egypt during the early fifteenth century B.C.** [The noun *Egypt* completes the meaning of *ruled.*]

A complement is never in a prepositional phrase.

EXAMPLE **At first Hatshepsut ruled with her husband.** [The noun *husband* is the object of the preposition *with.*]

REFERENCE NOTE: See pages 619–620 and 652–655 for more information on prepositional phrases.

Direct Objects and Indirect Objects

18h. A *direct object* is a noun or a pronoun that receives the action of the verb or shows the result of the action. A direct object tells *whom* or *what* after an action verb.

EXAMPLES Mr. Martínez uses **newspapers** as supplements to our history text. [Uses what? Newspapers.]
The tornado leveled the **warehouse.** [Leveled what? Warehouse.]
I miss **you.** [Miss whom? You.]

A direct object may be compound.

EXAMPLES The concert starred **Wynton Marsalis** and **Marcus Roberts.**
The cat followed **Karen** and **me** home.

NOTE: For emphasis, a writer may place the direct object before the subject and the verb.

EXAMPLE What an eerie **sound** we heard! [Heard what? Sound.]

18i. An *indirect object* is a noun or a pronoun that comes between an action verb and a direct object. It tells *to whom* or *to what* (or *for whom* or *for what*) the action of the verb is done.

EXAMPLES The Swedish Academy awarded **Octavio Paz** the 1990 Nobel Prize in literature. [Awarded the prize to whom? Octavio Paz.]
Julie's part-time work experience landed **her** a full-time position. [Landed the position for whom? Her.]

Don't mistake an object of the preposition *to* or *for* for an indirect object.

INDIRECT OBJECT Clarice wrote **me** a letter.
OBJECT OF PREPOSITION Clarice wrote a letter to **me.** [*Me* is the object of the preposition *to.*]

An indirect object may be compound.

EXAMPLES The travel agent gave **Todd** and **Steve** their itinerary.
The incident earned my **sister** and **me** our nicknames.

GRAMMAR

PICTURE THIS

Now what are the earthlings doing? There's certainly nothing like this on your home planet. You're here to gather information for the "Earth" entry in the new edition of *Encyclopedia Galactica*. Surveillance cameras have shown that the strange activity shown here is highly popular in some areas of the planet. Write a description of what the earthlings are doing, and speculate about the meaning and purpose of their activities. In your encyclopedia entry, use at least three direct objects and two indirect objects.

Subject: a basketball game
Audience: readers of the *Encyclopedia Galactica*
Purpose: to inform

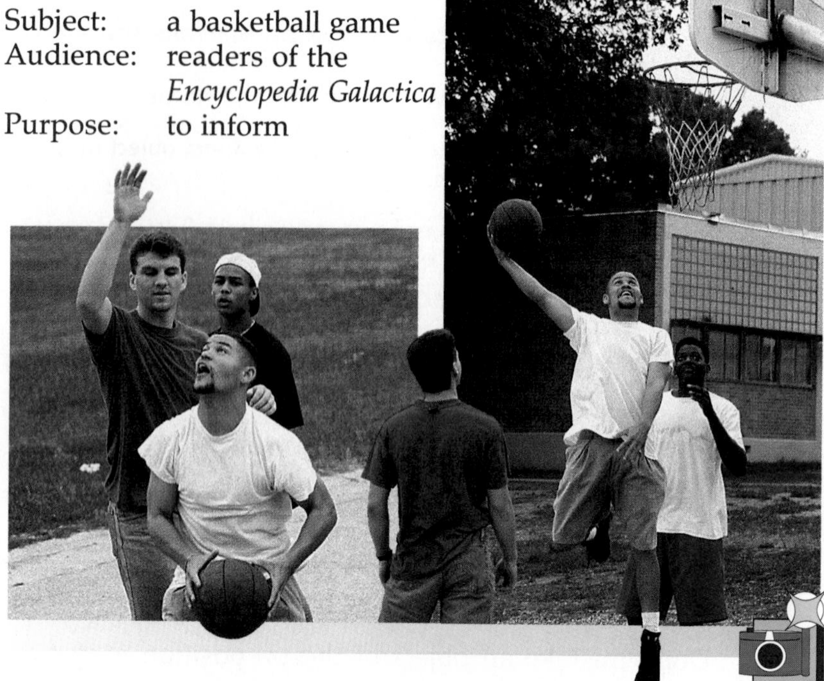

Objective Complements

18j. An ***objective complement*** is a word or word group that helps complete the meaning of an action verb by identifying or modifying the direct object.

An objective complement may be a noun, a pronoun, or an adjective.

EXAMPLES France named Miles Davis a **knight** in the Legion of Honor. [The noun *knight* identifies the direct object *Miles Davis.*]

Garfield considers the refrigerator **his.** [The possessive pronoun *his* modifies the direct object *refrigerator.*]

We have painted the house **blue.** [The adjective *blue* modifies the direct object *house.*]

Only a few action verbs take an objective complement. These verbs are *consider, make,* and any verbs that can be replaced by *consider* or *make,* such as *call, keep, name, find, choose, elect, appoint, paint, color,* and *render.*

EXAMPLES The referee called the line drive **foul.** [or *considered* the line drive foul]

The Supreme Court's 1954 decision rendered public-school segregation **unlawful.** [or *made* public-school segregation unlawful]

An objective complement may be compound.

EXAMPLES The stockholders elected her **president** and **chief executive officer.**

The lack of ventilation made the room **stuffy** and **uncomfortable.**

EXERCISE 3 Identifying Direct Objects, Indirect Objects, and Objective Complements

Identify each *direct object, indirect object,* and *objective complement* in the sentences in the following paragraphs.

[1] Recent advances in technology have made interactive television systems a reality. [2] The system shown here includes a remote-control converter box with a computer inside. [3] The computer gives viewers several options for the content of a program. [4] During a football game, for example, viewers can

EXAMPLE [1] **Arabesques are complex, elaborate designs of flowers, foliage, calligraphy, and geometric patterns.**

1. ***subject—Arabesques; verb—are; predicate nominative—designs***

GRAMMAR

[1] The arabesques on the left from the fortress-palace of the Alhambra in Granada, Spain, and the ones on the right from the king's palace in Fez, Morocco, illustrate a historic link

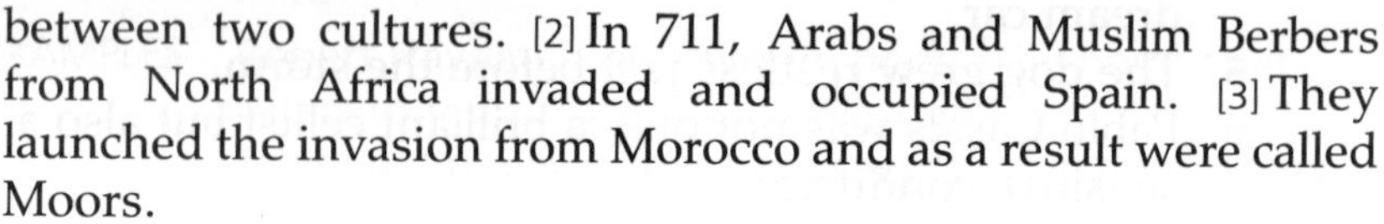

between two cultures. [2] In 711, Arabs and Muslim Berbers from North Africa invaded and occupied Spain. [3] They launched the invasion from Morocco and as a result were called Moors.

[4] The Moors' encouragement of commerce made Spain's major cities wealthy. [5] Meanwhile, the Moors' patronage of art, literature, and science rendered the cities centers of learning for Christian, Jewish, and Muslim scholars.

[6] Through reconquest, parts of Spain became Christian again as early as 1085. [7] At the end of the fifteenth century, Granada remained the Moors' last stronghold, until finally in 1492, it too fell to the forces of Ferdinand V and Isabella I. [8] Spain gave the Moors the choice of conversion to Christianity or expulsion from the country. [9] Nearly all of them rejected the idea of conversion and left. [10] Yet traces of their rich heritage still survive in the architecture, poetry, and music of Spain.

WRITING APPLICATION

Using Sentence Variety to Improve Style

Like a song, a piece of writing has rhythm. In addition to your choice of words, the structure and arrangement of your sentences create this rhythm. One way to avoid a monotonous rhythm is to vary the elements in each sentence. For example, try using a mixture of long and short subjects, use one-word verbs as well as verb phrases, or include an assortment of action verbs and linking verbs that require a variety of complements. Once in a while, begin a sentence with a phrase, a clause, or a single-word modifier instead of the subject.

As you read the following paragraph from a student's college admissions essay, notice the rhythm the writer creates by varying her sentences.

EXAMPLE When I tried out for the field hockey team in ninth grade, it was merely because a good friend of mine begged me to do it with her. The idea of spending 3 hours every day running around a field didn't particularly appeal to me, but for a friend I'd do anything. After 2 weeks, my friend quit. Quitting has always been anathema to me, but in this case it never entered my mind anyway. I was having fun. Those 3 hours of practice were the best part of my day. I loved being outside, and being physically active. Most importantly, I loved being with my teammates. Between studying and practicing the piano, I'd spend so much time alone that my time on the field became a welcome and necessary break in my day. Also, coming home at six o'clock every evening helped me to budget my time, since I knew I only had a few hours in which to complete my assignments.

George Ehrenhaft, from *Write Your Way Into College*

WRITING ACTIVITY

You have been looking through a number of college brochures. At last, you have found a school that seems right for you and have decided to apply for admission. Your application is complete except for one thing—the admissions essay. The essay instructions are as follows: In a short essay, tell about something that is important to you.

Prewriting First, you'll need to decide on a topic for your essay. Brainstorm a list of issues, ideas, and activities that are important to you. For example, do you especially enjoy (or dislike) a particular sport? Is playing music, writing science fiction, or doing volunteer work a significant part of your life? Choose the most engaging topic from your list. Then, decide whether the tone of your essay will be serious or light-hearted. Jot down facts, details, and examples to help develop your topic.

Writing Begin your essay with an attention-grabber. You might start with a brief anecdote, a thoughtful question, or a surprising statement. Then develop your topic with supporting examples, facts, and details. Explain your feelings and the reasons behind them. Sum up your ideas in a clincher paragraph. (For more about writing a personal essay, see pages 153–155.)

Evaluating and Revising Now that you've gotten your ideas down on paper, you can fine-tune the content, organization, and style of your essay. First, make sure that your thesis statement gives a clear focus to your essay. Then, check to be sure the body of your essay supports that thesis. Do your supporting paragraphs follow a clear, logical sequence? If not, revise or rearrange details. Next, evaluate the tone of your essay. (For a discussion of tone, see page 32.) Although you may write a humorous essay, you'll want to avoid a silly or sarcastic tone that might annoy the members of the admissions committee. Finally, check your sentence style. Have you varied the elements of your sentences to avoid a monotonous rhythm? During the revision process, you can ask a friend to read your essay and give you feedback and suggestions.

Proofreading Using standard English is very important in an admissions essay. Check your writing carefully for errors in usage, spelling, or punctuation. Be sure that you've used only complete sentences.

Review: Posttest 1

GRAMMAR

A. Identifying Subjects, Verbs, and Complements

Identify the italicized word or word group in each of the following sentences as a *subject,* a *verb,* a *direct object,* an *indirect object,* an *objective complement,* a *predicate nominative,* or a *predicate adjective.*

EXAMPLE **1. We *took* the shortest route.**
1. *verb*

1. The girls' gymnastics team unanimously elected Ming Chin their *captain.*
2. *Carlos Chávez* established the Symphony Orchestra of Mexico.
3. The antique dresser *was* carefully *moved* to a protected corner of the showroom.
4. Margaret wants a *set* of luggage for graduation.
5. On Fajada Butte in northwestern New Mexico is an ancient Anasazi solar *calendar.*
6. The director gave my *grandfather* a part in the play.
7. *Call* me after school.
8. Exercise keeps me *energetic.*
9. Since she won the Pulitzer Prize in 1983, Alice Walker has become a famous *writer.*
10. My mother is *taller* than any of her four sisters.

B. Identifying Subjects, Verbs, and Complements

Identify each italicized word or word group in the following paragraphs as a *subject,* a *verb,* a *direct object,* an *indirect object,* an *objective complement,* a *predicate nominative,* or a *predicate adjective.*

EXAMPLE **[1] In 1675, Spanish friar Juan Paiva recorded the *rules* of a major sports contest between the Apalachee and the Timucuan peoples of North Florida.**
1. *direct object*

[11] The arrival of a messenger in a raccoon costume was a *challenge* to a ballgame from the loser of the last game. **[12]** On acceptance of the challenge, *all* of the villagers traveled to meet their opponents. **[13]** In an all-night vigil before the game, elders of the host village interpreted their dreams and told the home *team* their predictions of the game's outcome. **[14]** Meanwhile, the visitors *made* a stew with rancid food, *mixed* it with decorative clays, and *painted* their bodies with the foul mixture as a deterrent to the other players.

[15] On game day, a village leader started *play* by tossing out a small, hard ball to teams of forty to fifty players on each side. **[16]** Suddenly, eighty to one hundred men *were scrambling* for a ball only about an inch in diameter! **[17]** The goal post in the center of an empty field was a ten- to fifteen-foot *pole* with an eagle's nest on top. **[18]** Teams scored one *point* for each throw of the ball against the pole and two *points* for each basket. **[19]** When one team had scored eleven points, the game was *over*. **[20]** According to historians, these rules probably made the average game a one- to two-hour *contest*.

Review: Posttest 2

Writing Sentences

Write your own sentences according to the following guidelines. In your sentences, underline the words you use as the italicized sentence parts. Use a variety of subjects, verbs, and complements in your sentences.

1. a sentence with a *compound subject*
2. a sentence with a *compound verb*
3. a sentence with a *direct object*
4. a sentence with a *compound direct object*
5. a sentence with an *indirect object* and a *direct object*
6. a sentence with a *compound indirect object* and a *compound direct object*
7. a sentence with a *predicate nominative*
8. a sentence with a *compound predicate adjective*
9. a sentence with a *direct object* and an *objective complement*
10. a sentence with a *direct object* and a *compound objective complement*

SEVEN COMMON SENTENCE PATTERNS

The subject and the verb produce one sentence pattern. The subject, the verb, and the various complements produce the other six sentence patterns.

S V
Velma painted.

S V D.O.
Velma painted a landscape.

S V I.O. D.O.
The judges gave Velma an award.

S V D.O. Obj. Comp. (Noun)
They considered her landscape a masterpiece.

S V D.O. Obj. Comp (Adj.)
They called the painting brilliant.

S V P.N.
Velma has become a celebrity.

S V P.A.
She is famous.

GRAMMAR

19 THE PHRASE

Kinds of Phrases and Their Functions

Diagnostic Test

A. Identifying Phrases

For each of the following sentences, identify the italicized phrase as an *adjective phrase*, an *adverb phrase*, a *participial phrase*, a *gerund phrase*, an *infinitive phrase*, or an *appositive phrase*. Do not separately identify a prepositional phrase that is part of a larger phrase.

EXAMPLE **1. For a split second, the football sat balanced *on the goal-post bar.***
1. *adverb phrase*

1. *Smiling broadly,* Anthony showed us the sizable amount of interest he has earned on his savings account.
2. Asked about enjoyable ways to both relax and get fit, the librarian recommended the new book *about tai chi.*
3. Gabriel García Márquez, *the brilliant Colombian novelist,* was awarded the Nobel Prize for literature in 1982.
4. Donya wants to ride her bicycle from Washington, D.C., *to Seattle, Washington.*

5. Kai's ambition is *to drive a tractor-trailer truck.*
6. Marnie made an appointment *to audition for a part in the play this morning.*
7. Many of us in biology class have mixed emotions *about dissecting frogs.*
8. *Moving their vehicles to the right,* all of the drivers let the ambulance pass.
9. *Watching closed-captioned television programs* is a joy for my cousin, who has a hearing impairment.
10. My friends *Alecca and Leon* sent me a postcard from Rome.

GRAMMAR

B. Identifying Phrases

For each sentence in the following paragraph, identify the italicized phrase as an *adjective phrase,* an *adverb phrase,* a *participial phrase,* a *gerund phrase,* an *infinitive phrase,* or an *appositive phrase.* Do not separately identify a prepositional phrase that is part of a larger phrase.

EXAMPLE **[1]** ***Wondering about different clothing terms,*** **Marcie went to the library to do some research.**

1. ***participial phrase***

[11] After a lively discussion in home economics class, Marcie wanted *to learn more about the history of fabrics, clothes, and clothing parts.* **[12]** One material *of special interest* to the entire class was Velcro. **[13]** In her research, Marcie discovered that the idea for Velcro is attributed to Georges de Mestral, *a Swiss hiker and engineer.* **[14]** *During an outing in the 1940s,* de Mestral started thinking about the burrs that stuck to his socks. **[15]** *Adapting the idea from nature,* de Mestral developed a pair of nylon tapes that fastened together. **[16]** The new material was called *Velcro,* a name that combines the French words *for velvet (velours) and hook (crochet).* **[17]** *Patented in 1955,* Velcro is widely used today instead of other fasteners such as zippers. **[18]** However, zippers were once considered high-tech in the fashion industry, and *learning about those devices* was Marcie's next goal. **[19]** The zipper, she found out, was patented in 1893 *by Whitcomb Judson* of Chicago. **[20]** The public was reluctant to try the new fasteners until the United States military decided *to use zippers on some uniforms during World War I.*

GRAMMAR

19a. A ***phrase*** is a group of words that is used as a single part of speech and does not contain a verb and its subject.

VERB PHRASE	**have been waiting** [no subject]
PREPOSITIONAL PHRASE	**during the storm** [no subject or verb]

REFERENCE NOTE: A group of words that has a subject and a verb is called a ***clause.*** For more about independent and subordinate clauses, see pages 674–683.

Prepositional Phrases

19b. A ***prepositional phrase*** begins with a preposition and ends with a noun or a pronoun called the ***object of the preposition.***

EXAMPLES **Did officials of the Smithsonian Institution** recently unveil plans **for a new museum**? [The compound noun *Smithsonian Institution* is the object of the preposition *of.* The noun *museum* is the object of the preposition *for.*]

According to them, the National African-American Museum may be open **by 1995.** [The pronoun *them* is the object of the preposition *According to.* The noun *1995* is the object of the preposition *by.*]

The object of a preposition may be compound.

EXAMPLE Do you know the Greek myth **about Daedalus and Icarus**?

Prepositional phrases are usually used as adjectives or adverbs. Occasionally, a prepositional phrase is used as a noun.

EXAMPLE **Before lunch** will be convenient. [*Before lunch* is used as a noun; it is the subject of the sentence.]

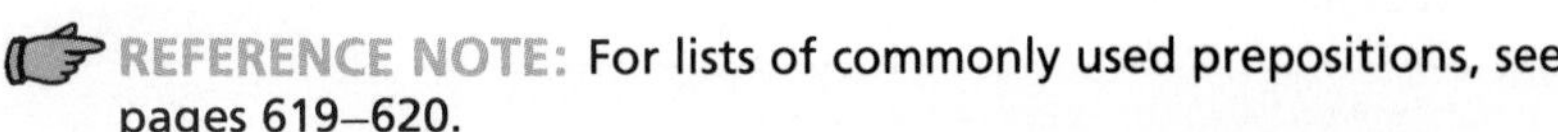

REFERENCE NOTE: For lists of commonly used prepositions, see pages 619–620.

The Adjective Phrase

19c. An ***adjective phrase*** is a prepositional phrase that modifies a noun or a pronoun.

An adjective phrase tells *what kind* or *which one.*

EXAMPLE One **of my friends** is making a film **about our senior year.** [*Of my friends* modifies the pronoun *one. About our senior year* modifies the noun *film.*]

An adjective phrase always follows the word it modifies. That word may be the object of another preposition.

EXAMPLE The film won't include all **of the students in our class.** [*Of the students* modifies the direct object *all. In our class* modifies *students,* which is the object of the preposition *of.*]

More than one adjective phrase may modify the same word.

EXAMPLE Instead, it will relate the adventures **of five students at school** and **in their neighborhood.** [The three phrases *of five students, at school,* and *in their neighborhood* modify the noun *adventures.*]

EXERCISE 1 Identifying Adjective Phrases and the Words They Modify

The following sentences contain ten adjective phrases. Identify each adjective phrase and the word it modifies.

1. New Guinea rivers, like the one shown on the next page, are popular areas for rafting enthusiasts.
2. As you can see, a series of nearly continuous rapids criss-crosses jungles of primeval beauty.
3. The twenty-eight major rapids on the Tua River make it a course for rafters with experience and courage.

4. Brilliantly colored butterflies brighten the riverbanks, and the metallic whine of cicadas almost drowns out the roar of the river.
5. The banks are a chaos of tumbled boulders and uprooted trees.

The Adverb Phrase

19d. An ***adverb phrase*** is a prepositional phrase that modifies a verb, an adjective, or an adverb.

An adverb phrase tells *how, when, where, why,* or *to what extent* (*how long* or *how far*).

An adverb phrase may modify a verb.

EXAMPLE **After the early 800s,** the Fujiwara family ruled **as regents in Japan for more than three hundred years.** [Each phrase modifies the verb *ruled. After the early 800s* tells *when, as regents* tells *how, in Japan* tells *where,* and *for more than three hundred years* tells *how long.*]

As this example shows, more than one adverb phrase can modify the same word. The example also shows that an adverb phrase, unlike an adjective phrase, can precede the word it modifies.

An adverb phrase may modify an adjective.

EXAMPLE Then the Minamoto, another family active **in court intrigues,** gained power. [*In court intrigues* modifies the adjective *active.*]

An adverb phrase may modify an adverb.

EXAMPLE The Fujiwara had ruled too complacently **for their own good.** [*For their own good* modifies the adverb *complacently.*]

EXERCISE 2 Identifying Adverb Phrases and the Words They Modify

Each of the following sentences contains at least one adverb phrase. Identify each adverb phrase and the word or words it modifies.

EXAMPLE 1. From this map, you can clearly tell the function of the Panama Canal.
1. *From this map—can tell*

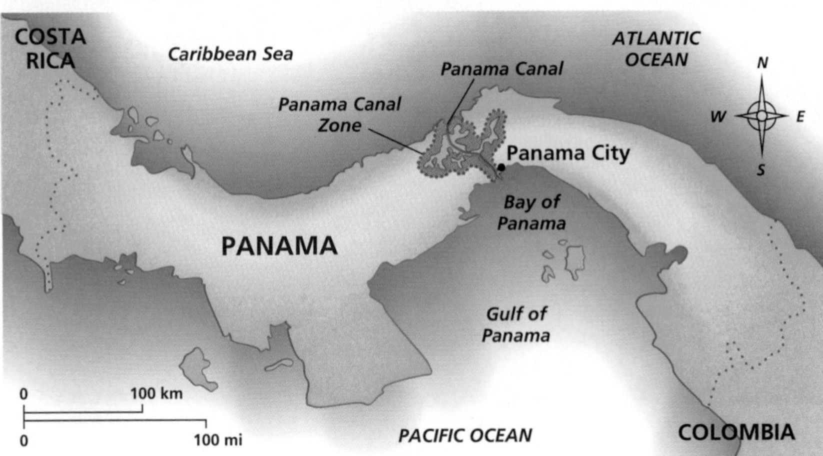

1. The canal, which is fifty-one miles long, links the Pacific Ocean to the Atlantic Ocean.
2. Ships can travel from ocean to ocean using the canal's elaborate series of locks that raise and lower the water levels.
3. Construction of the canal, an engineering marvel, began in 1904 and continued until 1914.
4. Of course, the builders faced many obstacles during the canal's construction.

5. Mosquitoes posed a major health risk throughout the area and had to be eliminated.
6. For the duration of the canal project, Dr. William C. Gorgas, an army surgeon, fought the mosquitoes.
7. With great efficiency, he drained swamps, fumigated buildings, and installed a pure water supply.
8. After the resignation of two chief engineers, President Theodore Roosevelt in 1907 appointed Army Lieutenant Colonel George W. Goethals to be chief engineer.
9. Goethals, active in all phases of canal construction, quickly gained the respect of workers.
10. This photograph shows some of the workers who dug through the mountains along the Continental Divide.

Verbals and Verbal Phrases

A ***verbal*** is a form of a verb used as a noun, an adjective, or an adverb. The three kinds of verbals are the *participle*, the *gerund*, and the *infinitive*.

A *verbal phrase* consists of a verbal and its modifiers and complements. The three kinds of verbal phrases are the *participial phrase*, the *gerund phrase*, and the *infinitive phrase*.

The Participle

19e. A ***participle*** is a verb form that can be used as an adjective.

Two kinds of participles are the *present participle* and the *past participle.*

Present participles end in *–ing.*

EXAMPLES The **freezing** rain made the road slick. [*Freezing,* a form of the verb *freeze,* modifies the noun *rain.*]

Bowing, the performers acknowledged the applause. [*Bowing,* a form of the verb *bow,* modifies the noun *performers.*]

Did I hear someone **knocking** on the door? [*Knocking,* a form of the verb *knock,* modifies the pronoun *someone.*]

Most past participles end in *–d* or *–ed.* Others are irregularly formed.

EXAMPLES First prize was an **engraved** trophy. [*Engraved,* a form of the verb *engrave,* modifies the noun *trophy.*]

The lab tested samples of water **taken** from wells in the area. [*Taken,* a form of the verb *take,* modifies the noun *water.*]

Rested and **relaxed,** we returned to work. [*Rested,* a form of the verb *rest,* and *relaxed,* a form of the verb *relax,* modify the pronoun *we.*]

REFERENCE NOTE: Because they are verbs, participles have different tenses. In addition to the present and past forms, they also have a present perfect form.

EXAMPLES having gone having been gone

For more about present perfect participles, see page 799.

Don't confuse a participle used as an adjective with a participle used as part of a verb phrase.

ADJECTIVE The Hispanic Association of Colleges and Universities, **founded** in 1986, is based in San Antonio, Texas.

VERB PHRASE The Hispanic Association of Colleges and Universities, which **was founded** in 1986, is based in San Antonio, Texas.

GRAMMAR

The Participial Phrase

19f. A ***participial phrase*** consists of a participle and all of the words related to the participle.

Participles may be modified by adverbs and may also have complements.

EXAMPLES **Grinning broadly,** Whoopi Goldberg accepted the Oscar. [The participial phrase modifies the compound noun *Whoopi Goldberg.* The adverb *broadly* modifies the present participle *Grinning.*]

Proclaiming his innocence, the candidate denied the charges. [The participial phrase modifies the noun *candidate.* The noun *innocence* is the direct object of the present participle *proclaiming.*]

Puzzled by their behavior, I asked for an explanation. [The participial phrase modifies the pronoun *I.* The adverb phrase *by their behavior* modifies the past participle *Puzzled.*]

Zimbabwe, **formerly named Rhodesia,** is in southern Africa. [The participial phrase modifies the noun *Zimbabwe.* The adverb *formerly* modifies the past participle *named.* The noun *Rhodesia* is the direct object of *named.*]

To prevent confusion, place participial phrases as close as possible to the words they modify.

MISPLACED **Stalking the squirrel,** I saw the cat out in the yard.
IMPROVED I saw the cat **stalking the squirrel** out in the yard.

REFERENCE NOTE: For more information about misplaced participial phrases, see pages 832–836. For information about the participial phrase as a sentence fragment, see pages 555–556.

 EXERCISE 3 **Identifying Participial Phrases and the Words They Modify**

Each of the following sentences contains at least one participial phrase. Identify each participial phrase and the word or words it modifies.

EXAMPLE **1.** Living far from the city, I developed an interest in nature at an early age.
1. *Living far from the city—I*

1. All of the students trying out for the soccer team have heard from the coach or her assistant.
2. Thanking us several times, the piano teacher returned the chairs borrowed for the recital.
3. Today's newspaper, printed last night, made no mention of the president's announcement.
4. Annoyed by the high prices, Mr. Sims has decided not to shop at that store anymore.
5. Addressing the senior class, the principal praised all of the students for their work on the clean-up campaign.
6. Having studied hard, Karen wasn't surprised that she did well on the Spanish test.
7. The movies showing at that theater are old ones released before 1940.
8. Cheered by the crowd, our school's Special Olympics team rushed onto the field.
9. Looking through the catalog, Earl found a Cajun cookbook.
10. Smiling shyly, Lynn showed us the pictures she had taken.

REVIEW A **Identifying Prepositional and Participial Phrases and the Words They Modify**

Identify each italicized phrase in the following sentences as a *prepositional phrase* or a *participial phrase.* Then give the word or words each phrase modifies. Do not separately identify a prepositional phrase that is part of a participial phrase.

EXAMPLE [1] ***Visiting friends in Los Angeles last year,*** **I became interested *in low-riders.***

1. ***participial—I; prepositional—interested***

[1] My friend Jorge told me that this unique form *of folk art* has been popular *for forty years or more.* [2] He said the term *low-rider* refers *to the automobile, its driver, and any passengers.* [3] *Making artistic statements with their automobiles,* many young Mexican American men *in the Southwest* spend both time and money on their cars. [4] First, a car is lowered *by several methods* so that its chassis just skims the pavement. [5] *After the height adjustment,* the car is embellished *with exterior paint and trim work.* [6] *Decorated elaborately,* Jorge's car, *shown on the next page,* is a good example *of a low-rider.* [7] When their cars are finished and spotlessly clean, riders drive slowly *through their communities.* [8] *Relaxing behind the steering wheel of his car,* Jorge is proud

when people admire the results *of his hard work.* [9] On sunny days, long caravans *of low-riders* may drive for hours *through the neighborhood.* [10] Low-riders *in some cities* have even formed clubs that work *with charitable organizations.*

The Gerund

19g. A ***gerund*** is a verb form ending in *–ing* that is used as a noun.

SUBJECT	**Fishing** requires great patience.
PREDICATE NOMINATIVE	Norene's trade is **welding.**
DIRECT OBJECT	Please stop **whispering.**
INDIRECT OBJECT	The team gave **winning** their best effort.
OBJECT OF PREPOSITION	In **answering,** give specific examples.

Don't confuse a gerund with a present participle used as an adjective or as part of a verb phrase.

GERUND	I remember **driving** from Florida to Texas last fall. [direct object of the verb *remember*]
PRESENT PARTICIPLE	**Driving** on long trips, we usually take turns behind the wheel. [adjective modifying the pronoun *we*]
PRESENT PARTICIPLE	We heard mostly country music on the radio while we were **driving.** [main verb in the verb phrase *were driving*]

NOTE: When you use a noun or a pronoun just before a gerund, use the possessive form.

EXAMPLES **Lee's** pitching won the game.
What did the teacher say about **your** missing the test yesterday?

The Gerund Phrase

19h. A ***gerund phrase*** consists of a gerund and all of the words related to the gerund.

Like participles, gerunds may have modifiers and complements.

EXAMPLES **Managing the restaurant efficiently** required lots of hard work. [The gerund phrase is the subject of the verb *required.* The noun *restaurant* is the direct object of the gerund *Managing.* The adverb *efficiently* modifies the gerund *Managing.*]

My cousin enjoys **working as a lifeguard.** [The gerund phrase is the direct object of the verb *enjoys.* The adverb phrase *as a lifeguard* modifies the gerund *working.*]

We were fined for **parking there.** [The gerund phrase is the object of the preposition *for.* The adverb *there* modifies the gerund *parking.*]

Her greatest achievement was **winning three gold medals.** [The gerund phrase is a predicate nominative explaining the subject *achievement.* The noun *medals* is the direct object of the gerund *winning.*]

EXERCISE 4 Identifying Gerund Phrases and Their Functions

Identify the gerund phrase in each of the following sentences as a *subject,* a *predicate nominative,* a *direct object,* an *indirect object,* or an *object of a preposition.*

EXAMPLE 1. Learning to type has been one of my most practical accomplishments.
1. *Learning to type—subject*

1. Solving crossword puzzles is one of Geraldo's favorite pastimes.
2. Sylvia's method of making decisions reveals a great deal about her.
3. My grandparents enjoy practicing their square dance routines with the Nicholsons.
4. In making any changes, please notify our secretary, Ms. Erikson.
5. Producing a movie for Mr. Matsuyama's cinematography course requires the ability to organize and communicate.
6. Ms. Sanapaw finished writing her paper.

7. Gaining the vote for women was Susan B. Anthony's mission.
8. One of the most interesting characteristics of bees is their dancing to communicate the location of food sources.
9. Hector earns money on the weekends by giving guitar lessons.
10. My brother's singing in the shower annoys everyone early in the morning.

GRAMMAR

PICTURE THIS

You are a publicist for Alaska's Division of Tourism. Your current project is to prepare a brochure about Misty Fiords National Monument, a beautiful wilderness reserve. From the many pictures taken by your staff photographer, you've chosen these to use in your brochure. Now, write two or three paragraphs based on the photos, describing some of the things visitors can see and do in the area. In your paragraphs, use at least five prepositional phrases, three participial phrases, and two gerund phrases.

Subject: Misty Fiords National Monument
Audience: readers of a travel brochure
Purpose: to inform; to persuade readers that Misty Fiords is a great place to visit

The Infinitive

19i. An ***infinitive*** is a verb form that can be used as a noun, an adjective, or an adverb. An infinitive usually begins with *to.*

NOUNS **To leave** now would be rude. [subject of *would be*]
No one wants **to stay.** [direct object of *wants*]
Her goal is **to win.** [predicate nominative identifying the subject *goal*]

ADJECTIVES She is the candidate **to watch.** [adjective modifying the noun *candidate*]
The one **to see** is the class president. [adjective modifying the pronoun *one*]

ADVERBS We came **to cheer.** [adverb modifying the verb *came*]
Is everybody ready **to go**? [adverb modifying the adjective *ready*]

NOTE: Don't confuse an infinitive with a prepositional phrase beginning with *to.* Remember that a prepositional phrase ends with a noun or a pronoun.

INFINITIVES	to go	to forget	to graduate
PREPOSITIONAL PHRASES	to them	to the party	to everyone

REFERENCE NOTE: Infinitives, like participles, have different tense forms. The preceding examples all contain present infinitives. There is also a present perfect infinitive form.

EXAMPLES **To have seen** Spike Lee would have pleased Jerome.
Elsa was disappointed not **to have been chosen.**

For more about present perfect infinitives, see pages 798–799.

The word *to,* the sign of the infinitive, is sometimes omitted.

EXAMPLES Let's [to] **wait** here.
The clowns made us [to] **laugh.**
Help me [to] **wash** the car.

The Infinitive Phrase

19j. An ***infinitive phrase*** consists of an infinitive and all of the words related to the infinitive.

Infinitives may have modifiers and complements.

GRAMMAR

EXAMPLES **To become a doctor** is her goal. [The infinitive phrase is the subject of the verb *is.* The noun *doctor* is the predicate nominative of the infinitive *to become.*]

They promised **to return soon.** [The infinitive phrase is the direct object of the verb *promised.* The adverb *soon* modifies the infinitive *to return.*]

We have time **to walk to the concert.** [The infinitive phrase modifies the noun *time.* The adverb phrase *to the concert* modifies the infinitive *to walk.*]

It's important **to be prompt for an interview.** [The infinitive phrase modifies the adjective *important.* The modifier *prompt* is the predicate adjective of the infinitive *to be.* The adverb phrase *for an interview* modifies the adjective *prompt.*]

NOTE: Unlike other verbals, an infinitive may have a subject. Such a construction is called an ***infinitive clause.***

EXAMPLES Everyone expects **Guadalupe to win the election.** [*Guadalupe* is the subject of the infinitive *to win.* The entire infinitive clause is the direct object of the verb *expects.*]

We asked **her to lead the discussion.** [*Her* is the subject of the infinitive *to lead.* The entire infinitive clause is the direct object of the verb *asked.*]

I found **everyone to be friendly.** [*Everyone* is the subject of the infinitive *to be.* The entire infinitive clause is the direct object of the verb *found.*]

Notice that the subject of an infinitive is in the objective case.

EXERCISE 5 Identifying Infinitive Phrases and Their Functions

Identify each infinitive phrase in the following sentences as a *noun,* an *adjective,* or an *adverb.* If a phrase is used as a noun, tell whether it is the *subject,* the *direct object,* or the *predicate nominative.* If the phrase is used as a modifier, give the word it modifies.

EXAMPLE **1.** I like to compose music for the guitar.
1. *to compose music for the guitar—noun, direct object*

1. To win an Olympic medal is the dream of every member of the women's ski team.
2. The candidate had the courage to speak on a controversial issue.

GRAMMAR

3. We went to Italy to see Michelangelo's statue *David*.
4. The Latin and French clubs try to work together on projects.
5. Martin Luther King's dream was that all people should be free to exercise their rights as American citizens.
6. Louis Pasteur experimented for many years to discover a method for preventing rabies.
7. The ability to speak distinctly is an advantage in job interviews.
8. To open the box required a hammer and a crowbar.
9. Alana's hobby is to spend hours each day developing original computer programs.
10. Marvella has always wanted to learn about photography.

REVIEW B **Identifying Prepositional, Participial, Gerund, and Infinitive Phrases**

Identify each numbered italicized phrase in the following paragraph as a *prepositional phrase,* a *participial phrase,* a *gerund phrase,* or an *infinitive phrase.* Do not separately identify a prepositional phrase, a verbal, or a verbal phrase that is part of a larger phrase.

EXAMPLE Actress Marlee Matlin has gained attention for [1] *championing the rights of people with hearing impairments,* and it almost seems she has made a career [2] *of tackling new challenges.*

1. *gerund phrase*
2. *prepositional phrase*

Matlin, who lost her hearing [1] *because of complications from childhood measles,* never let her deafness [2] *stand in her way.* [3] *Learning to sign, to read lips, and to speak* helped the young Matlin [4] *to communicate effectively* [5] *with a wide range* of people. [6] *Interested in acting,* she was soon performing [7] *in a children's theater group.* [8] *After high school,* she started on the road [9] *to Hollywood and stardom* by [10] *winning a supporting role* [11] *in a Chicago revival* of the play Children of a Lesser God. Film producers saw a tape [12] *of Matlin's performance* and wanted [13] *her to audition for a starring role.* [14] *Praised by the critics and the public alike,* Matlin's portrayal of a proud and independent deaf woman was magnificent. [15] *For her stellar performance,* Matlin won the Oscar for Best Actress [16] *at the 1987 Academy Award*

ceremonies. [17] *Turning her abilities to television,* Matlin starred in the movie Bridge to Silence. Later, she decided [18] *to try a full-time TV series* and costarred with Mark Harmon in Reasonable Doubt. [19] *Playing the role of a hearing-impaired assistant district attorney,* Matlin, [20] *shown here in a scene from the show,* usually signed but sometimes spoke her lines.

Appositives and Appositive Phrases

19k. An ***appositive*** is a noun or pronoun placed beside another noun or pronoun to identify or explain it.

An appositive usually follows the word it identifies or explains.

EXAMPLES My cousin **María** is an accomplished violinist.
Riboflavin, a **vitamin,** is found in leafy vegetables.

For emphasis, however, an appositive may come at the beginning of a sentence.

EXAMPLE A natural **leader,** Joseph Cinqué led the *Amistad* revolt.

19l. An ***appositive phrase*** consists of an appositive and its modifiers.

EXAMPLE My brother's car, **a sporty red hatchback with bucket seats,** has over 100,000 miles on it.

GRAMMAR

An appositive phrase usually follows the word it explains or identifies but may precede it.

EXAMPLE **Once a pagan feast,** Valentine's Day is now celebrated as a day of love.

 REFERENCE NOTE: For information on how to punctuate appositives, see pages 914–915. For a discussion of the use of appositives, see pages 570–571 and 740–741.

WRITING APPLICATION

Using Infinitive and Appositive Phrases in Business Writing

Infinitive and appositive phrases add variety and detail to sentences. Such phrases also help make writing more concise. Often, a writer can reduce a sentence to an appositive or infinitive phrase and insert the phrase into another sentence. As you read the following examples, notice how the writer eliminates unnecessary words by reducing the less-important sentence to a phrase.

ORIGINAL Mr. Jenkins of Jenkins' Sporting Goods donated a valuable, autographed baseball. He made this donation to help our fund-raiser.

COMBINED **To help our fund-raiser,** Mr. Jenkins of Jenkins' Sporting Goods donated a valuable, autographed baseball.

ORIGINAL Lakewood Cineplex donated a month's supply of movie passes. Lakewood Cineplex is the new movie theater in town.

COMBINED Lakewood Cineplex, **the new movie theater in town,** donated a month's supply of movie passes.

WRITING ACTIVITY

Every year your school holds a raffle to raise funds for special equipment and activities. This year's goal is to raise enough money for two new computers. As secretary of the student council, you've been asked to contact owners of local businesses and ask them to donate prizes for the raffle. Write a letter explaining the purpose of the raffle and

GRAMMAR

persuading the business owners to donate their products or services. You may want to give examples of donated prizes that helped raise money for the school last year. Include at least three infinitive phrases and two appositive phrases in your letter.

Prewriting First, invent some details about last year's raffle. List three or four interesting items that local businesses donated. Note how much money was raised and what the money was used for. Then, jot down specific information about the upcoming raffle, including when and where it's being held. Think about how you can convince business owners that they should donate prizes. You might explain that the names of contributors will be displayed prominently at the raffle, giving the businesses good publicity.

Writing Begin your letter by clearly stating your purpose for writing. Then give specific information about the raffle. Explain how local businesses helped make last year's raffle a success. Conclude by restating your request. Also, tell your reader whom to contact to make a donation.

Evaluating and Revising Make sure your letter says what you want it to say. Have you clearly explained the purpose of the raffle? Have you told your reader everything he or she needs to know about the event? Will your letter convince your reader that the raffle is a worthy cause? Also be sure that the form and the tone of your letter are appropriate for business correspondence. (See pages 1056–1059 for more about business letters.) Note any revisions you will need to make. You may want to ask an adult friend or family member to read your letter and to offer further suggestions for revision. As you revise your letter, look for short, choppy sentences that you could combine into longer, smoother ones. Be sure that you include at least three infinitive phrases and two appositive phrases.

Proofreading Errors in grammar, usage, spelling, or punctuation won't help your cause, so be sure to proofread carefully. Check that your letter follows the correct form for business letters. Also take care not to count prepositional phrases beginning with *to* as infinitive phrases.

GRAMMAR

REVIEW C **Identifying Prepositional, Verbal, and Appositive Phrases**

Identify each italicized phrase in the following paragraph as a *prepositional phrase*, a *participial phrase*, a *gerund phrase*, an *infinitive phrase*, or an *appositive phrase*. Do not separately identify a prepositional phrase that is part of a larger phrase.

Altamont Pass, [1] *an area of grassy hills* [2] *surrounding San Francisco Bay*, is producing a new cash crop. Energy entrepreneurs are hurrying [3] *to lease wind rights on acreage* [4] *throughout the Altamont*. One rancher owns several hundred acres [5] *dotted with tall white wind machines like the ones shown here*. [6] *Standing in rows on the windswept hills*, these machines are expected [7] *to produce electricity*. [8] *With any luck*, the wind-power industry may soon spread [9] *to other parts* of the country. The temperature differences [10] *between the cool coast and the hot valley* can create air surges [11] *funneling inland through natural gaps* [12] *like the Altamont*. According to some energy experts, there will be several hundred wind machines [13] *producing thirty million kilowatts per year*, the power [14] *used by 4,800 homes*. [15] *An economist and a trained engineer*, John Eckland has advocated [16] *generating electricity* by [17] *using these updated windmills*. Not until the oil shortages of the 1970s did a serious effort begin [18] *in the United States* [19] *to develop a wind industry*. Modern wind turbines may someday become as numerous [20] *in the United States* as windmills were in Holland.

Review: Posttest 1

A. Identifying Phrases

Identify the italicized phrase in each of the following sentences as a *prepositional phrase,* a *participial phrase,* a *gerund phrase,* an *infinitive phrase,* or an *appositive phrase.* Do not separately identify a prepositional phrase that is part of a larger phrase.

EXAMPLE **1. The sunlight shimmering *on the lake* was beautiful.**
1. *on the lake—prepositional phrase*

1. Juanita likes *to draw caricatures of her friends.*
2. *Arriving late at school,* Bill went to the office to get a pass.
3. *Made in Ireland,* Waterford crystal is admired throughout the world.
4. By *inventing the telephone,* Alexander Graham Bell assured himself a place in history.
5. Luciano Pavarotti, *the great Italian tenor,* received a hearty standing ovation at the end of his concert.
6. After the concert we saw them *looking in vain for a taxi.*
7. Raúl has the talent *to sculpt and design beautiful objects.*
8. "It is a pleasure to be here with you today," remarked the mayor *at the beginning* of her talk.
9. A number of pioneer women kept diaries and journals *of their experiences* settling the American wilderness.
10. *To speak freely on any issue* is a right guaranteed to all U.S. citizens.

B. Identifying Prepositional, Verbal, and Appositive Phrases

Identify each italicized phrase in the following paragraph as a *prepositional phrase,* a *participial phrase,* a *gerund phrase,* an *infinitive phrase,* or an *appositive phrase.* Do not separately identify a prepositional phrase or a verbal phrase that is part of a larger phrase.

EXAMPLE **[1] *For more than fifty years,* Thurgood Marshall worked [2] *to protect the rights of all people in the United States.***

1. *prepositional phrase*
2. *infinitive phrase*

[11] *Ranked at the top of his law school class,* Thurgood Marshall began law practice in Baltimore; and in 1936, he was selected **[12]** *to be a counsel for the National Association for the Advancement of Colored People.* From the start of his career, he believed strongly in **[13]** *using the U.S. Constitution to fight injustice.* **[14]** *Risking his life at times,* Marshall, **[15]** *the son of a schoolteacher,* won many civil rights cases **[16]** *before federal and state courts.* His arguments played an important role in **[17]** *convincing the Supreme Court* that "separate but equal" educational facilities were unconstitutional. **[18]** *During the Kennedy administration,* Marshall became a federal judge. **[19]** *After a two-year term* as U.S. solicitor general, he was nominated for the Supreme Court by President Lyndon Johnson. Marshall was the first African American **[20]** *to serve on the nation's highest court.*

Review: Posttest 2

Writing Sentences with Phrases

Write ten sentences according to the following guidelines.

1. Use *because of the rain* as an adverb phrase.
2. Use *from Puerto Rico* as an adjective phrase.
3. Use *running towards us* as a participial phrase.
4. Use *seen from a distance* as a participial phrase.
5. Use *building a fence* as a gerund phrase that is the object of a preposition.
6. Use *writing résumés* as a gerund phrase that is the subject.
7. Use *to dream* as an infinitive phrase that is the object of a verb.
8. Use *to sell* as an infinitive phrase that is a modifier.
9. Use *to study music* as an infinitive phrase that is the predicate nominative.
10. Use *our local newspaper* as an appositive phrase.

20 THE CLAUSE

The Function of Clauses

Diagnostic Test

A. Identifying and Classifying Clauses

Identify the italicized word group in each of the following sentences as an *independent clause* or a *subordinate clause*. Then classify each subordinate clause as an *adjective clause*, an *adverb clause*, or a *noun clause*.

EXAMPLE **1.** I hope *that the snow will be deep and solid enough for sledding.*
1. *subordinate clause—noun clause*

1. The violinist *whom I most enjoy hearing* is Itzhak Perlman.
2. This car is more fuel efficient *than the other ones.*
3. *The pitcher read the catcher's signals,* and then she struck out the hitter with a fastball.
4. *Where the city will build the new recycling center* has still not been decided.

5. *When champion golfer Juan Rodríguez was a boy,* he worked on a sugar-cane plantation in Puerto Rico.
6. Here is the savings bond *that Aunt Ruthie and Uncle Bob gave me for graduation.*
7. *Because his artwork received wide recognition,* Pablo Picasso became famous and wealthy.
8. As we walked along the road, *we saw the wheat waving in the wind.*
9. The Kimbell Art Museum, *which was designed by architect Louis Kahn,* is one of the leading attractions in Fort Worth.
10. During the quiz bowl, *whoever rings the buzzer first* gets to answer the question.

B. Classifying Sentences According to Structure

Classify each sentence of the following paragraph as *simple, compound, complex,* or *compound-complex* and then as *declarative, interrogative, imperative,* or *exclamatory.*

EXAMPLE [1] Walt Disney, who won many awards for his movies and cartoons, received the U.S. Presidential Medal of Freedom in 1964.

1. *complex—declarative*

[11] What simple beginnings great men and women often have! **[12]** Consider the life of famed animator Walt Disney, for example. **[13]** Although he was born in Chicago in 1901, Disney grew up on a farm in Missouri. **[14]** Disney loved farm life, and he paid particular attention to the animals, which he sketched constantly. **[15]** Surely you're not surprised that his early drawings were of farm animals! **[16]** Where do you think he got his ideas for Mickey Mouse, Donald Duck, and the other Disney-animated animals that are now household names? **[17]** During his school years, Disney and a friend enjoyed acting; indeed, they even performed a short-lived comedy routine together. **[18]** How fortunate it is that Disney's main interest remained art! **[19]** He continued to doodle, and later he attended several art institutes where he learned not only about drawing anatomical figures but also about drawing cartoons. **[20]** Is it any wonder that one of Disney's first jobs was to draw farm animals for an advertising company?

GRAMMAR

20a. A ***clause*** is a group of words that contains a subject and its predicate and is used as part of a sentence.

Every clause has both a subject and a verb. Not every clause expresses a complete thought, however.

SENTENCE **A sitar is an Indian stringed instrument that resembles a lute.**

CLAUSE **A sitar is an Indian stringed instrument.** [complete thought]

CLAUSE **that resembles a lute** [incomplete thought]

There are two kinds of clauses: the *independent clause* and the *subordinate clause.* Standing alone, an independent clause is a complete sentence. Like a word or a phrase, a subordinate clause acts as a single part of speech.

REFERENCE NOTE: Another type of clause—the infinitive clause—is discussed on page 664.

The Independent Clause

20b. An ***independent*** (or ***main***) ***clause*** expresses a complete thought and can stand by itself as a sentence.

EXAMPLES **Mexican artist José Guadalupe Posada** (S) **opposed** (V) **the dictatorship of Porfirio Díaz.** [one independent clause]

Posada (S) **attacked** (V) **the Díaz regime in his paintings,** and **he** (S) **made** (V) **thousands of inexpensive prints of his work.** [two independent clauses joined by *and*]

Posada's art (S) **helped** (V) **to stir the social unrest** that led to the overthrow of Díaz in the revolution of 1910. [an independent clause combined with a subordinate clause]

By itself an independent clause is simply called a sentence. It is called an independent clause only when it is combined with at least one other clause (independent or subordinate) to form a sentence.

The Subordinate Clause

20c. A ***subordinate*** (or ***dependent***) ***clause*** does not express a complete thought and cannot stand alone as a sentence.

EXAMPLES whoever knows the song
which is my favorite song
as we were singing

The meaning of a subordinate clause becomes clear only when the clause is combined with an independent clause.

Whoever knows the song may join in.
We sang "We Shall Overcome," **which is my favorite song.**
As we were singing, we joined hands and formed a circle.

EXERCISE 1 Identifying Independent and Subordinate Clauses

Identify the italicized word group in each of the following sentences as an *independent clause* or a *subordinate clause.*

1. Egyptology is the branch of learning *that is concerned with the language and culture of ancient Egypt.*
2. *Until the Rosetta Stone was discovered in 1799,* the ancient Egyptian language was an enigma to scholars.
3. A man named Bouchard, *who was a captain under Napoleon,* and some of his men found the stone near Rosetta, a city near the mouth of the Nile.
4. As you can see in this photograph of the Rosetta Stone, *it has three different kinds of writing inscribed on it.*

The Rosetta Stone, 196 B.C., British Museum, London. Bridgeman/Art Resource, N.Y., BAL2359.

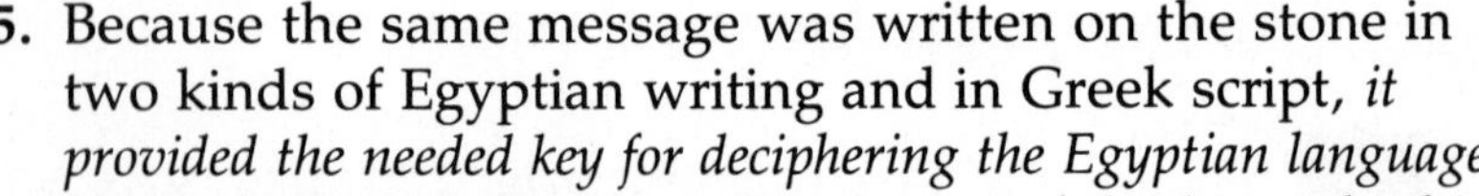

5. Because the same message was written on the stone in two kinds of Egyptian writing and in Greek script, *it provided the needed key for deciphering the Egyptian language.*
6. *When the Rosetta Stone was found,* part of the hieroglyphic portion was missing.
7. Scholars could easily read the Greek inscription, *which was nearly complete.*
8. *In 1816, Thomas Young isolated several hieroglyphics* that he took to represent names.

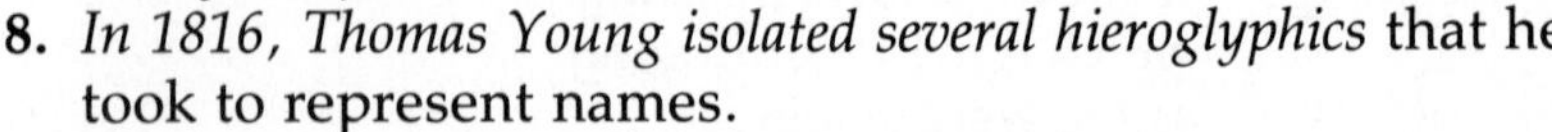

9. *The message* that was inscribed on the stone *was not very exciting.*
10. Since the priests of Egypt were grateful for benefits from the king, *they were commemorating the crowning of Ptolemy V.*

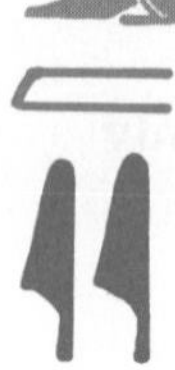

The Adjective Clause

20d. An ***adjective clause*** is a subordinate clause that modifies a noun or a pronoun.

An adjective clause always follows the word or words it modifies and tells *what kind* or *which one.*

EXAMPLES The report **that Diego wrote** was on the Battle of the Little Bighorn. [The adjective clause modifies the noun *report.*]

The Cuban Cultural Heritage Walk, **which is located in Hialeah, Florida,** honors Cuban artists in exile. [The adjective clause modifies the compound noun *Cuban Cultural Heritage Walk.*]

She is someone **whom I admire.** [The adjective clause modifies the pronoun *someone.*]

Relative Pronouns

An adjective clause usually begins with a ***relative pronoun***—a word that relates the clause to the word or words the clause modifies.

Relative Pronouns				
that	which	who	whom	whose

A relative pronoun does three things.

(1) It refers to a preceding noun or pronoun, the antecedent.
(2) It connects the adjective clause with the rest of the sentence.
(3) It performs a function within its own clause by serving as a subject, a direct object, an indirect object, or an object of a preposition in the adjective clause.

EXAMPLES Mr. Mendoza is a good counselor **who never betrays a confidence.** [The relative pronoun *who* relates the adjective clause to its noun antecedent *counselor* and serves as the subject of the verb *betrays.*]

Han-Ling is the one **whose essay took first place.** [The relative pronoun *whose* relates the adjective clause to its pronoun antecedent *one* and modifies the noun *essay* by showing possession.]

Have you practiced the speech **that you will give on Friday**? [The relative pronoun *that* relates the adjective clause to its noun antecedent *speech* and serves as the direct object of the verb *will give.*]

The mariachi band **in which I play** once performed for Governor Ann Richards. [The relative pronoun *which* relates the adjective clause to its noun antecedent *band* and serves as the object of the preposition *in.*]

An adjective clause may also begin with a relative adverb such as *when* or *where.*

EXAMPLES Dr. Martin Luther King, Jr., dreamed of the day **when freedom and justice would reign in the United States.** [The relative adverb *when* relates the adjective clause to its noun antecedent *day* and modifies the verb *would reign.*]

The site **where Dr. King delivered his great "I Have a Dream" speech in 1963** was the Lincoln Memorial in Washington, D.C. [The relative adverb *where* relates the adjective clause to its noun antecedent *site* and modifies the verb *delivered.*]

The relative pronoun or relative adverb is sometimes not expressed, but its meaning is understood.

EXAMPLES The vase [that] **my family brought from the Philippines** was made by my great-grandmother.

Do you remember the first time [when] **we met each other?**

Identifying Adjective Clauses and the Words They Modify

Identify each adjective clause in the following sentences. Then give the noun or pronoun that the adjective clause modifies. Be prepared to tell whether the relative pronoun or relative adverb is used as the subject, the direct object, the object of a preposition, or a modifier in the adjective clause.

1. The Mars of the nonscientist is a planet of the imagination, where an ancient civilization has left its mark and where maps blossom with romantic place names like Utopia and Elysium.
2. "Earthlings," who were awed by the planet's red glow in the evening sky, looked on Mars as a home for creatures who might someday cross cosmic barriers and visit planet Earth.
3. Such thinking was encouraged by an Italian astronomer who observed the planet through a telescope and saw a series of fine lines that crisscrossed its surface.
4. He called the lines *canali,* which is Italian for "channels"; this word was erroneously translated into English as "canals."
5. A planet where there are such canals must, of course, be inhabited by people who are capable of building not only canals but also the cities that presumably sprang up at their intersections.
6. Percival Lowell, the astronomer who founded the Lowell Observatory in Flagstaff, Arizona, brought new life to old myths about life on Mars with nonscientific observations most astronomers disputed.
7. Lowell reported a total of more than four hundred Martian canals, of which a considerable number were discovered by his own team of astronomers.
8. One writer whose interest was drawn to Mars was Edgar Rice Burroughs, whom many people know as the creator of Tarzan.
9. In his Martian books, Burroughs recounts the adventures of John Carter, who could get to Mars by standing in a field and wishing.
10. Burroughs' best-known literary successor is Ray Bradbury, who wrote *The Martian Chronicles,* published in 1950.

The Noun Clause

20e. A ***noun clause*** is a subordinate clause used as a noun.

A noun clause may be used as a subject, a predicate nominative, a direct object, an indirect object, or an object of a preposition.

Subject	**How students can apply for college loans** was the speaker's topic.
Predicate Nominative	My suggestion is **that we all meet again tomorrow.**
Direct Object	Many modern historians question **whether Columbus was truly the first European to explore the Americas.**
Indirect Object	Mrs. Romero offers **whoever completes additional assignments** extra credit.
Object of a Preposition	Write about **whomever you admire most.**

COMMON INTRODUCTORY WORDS FOR NOUN CLAUSES		
RELATIVE PRONOUNS		
that	which	whoever
what	whichever	whom
whatever	who	whomever
RELATIVE ADVERBS		
how	whenever	whether
if	where	why
when	wherever	

The word that introduces a noun clause may or may not serve a function in the noun clause.

EXAMPLES Tawana will do well at **whatever she attempts.** [The word *whatever* introduces the noun clause and serves as the direct object of the verb *attempts.*]

Does Luís think **that Puerto Rico will become a state someday?** [The word *that* introduces the noun clause but does not serve a function in its clause.]

Sometimes the word that introduces a noun clause is not expressed, but its meaning is understood.

EXAMPLES I think [that] **I. M. Pei is one of the judges of the design contest.**

Did you know [that] **the actor James Earl Jones was once a pre-med student?**

EXERCISE 3 Identifying Noun Clauses and Their Functions

Identify each noun clause in the following sentences, and tell whether it is a *subject*, a *direct object*, an *indirect object*, a *predicate nominative*, or an *object of a preposition*.

1. The problem is that my finances don't quite allow me to live in style; in fact, I'm broke!
2. Do you know what the referee says to the opponents at the start of a boxing match?
3. What I like most about Harriet is that she never complains.
4. Scientists disagree about why dinosaurs died out.
5. Sometimes I am amused and sometimes I am amazed by what I read in the newspaper's advice column.
6. I don't know how they decided who would be the leader.
7. What the dancers Agnes de Mille and Martha Graham did was to create a new form of American dance.
8. Can you please tell me where the Museum of African Art is located and what time it opens?
9. The radio station will give whoever can answer the next question one hundred dollars.
10. Through scientific research, psychologists have learned that everyone dreams during sleep.

EXERCISE 4 Distinguishing Between Adjective and Noun Clauses

Identify the subordinate clause or clauses in each of the following sentences. Tell whether each subordinate clause is used as an *adjective* or a *noun*. Be prepared to tell what word each adjective clause modifies and whether each noun clause is a subject, a predicate nominative, a direct object, an indirect object, or an object of a preposition.

1. The person in the photograph on the next page, Athelstan Spilhaus, found that toys are not meant only for children.

2. Spilhaus, an oceanographer, admits he has sometimes been unable to distinguish between his work and his play.
3. Some of the toys he collects are simply to be admired; his favorites are those that can be put into action.
4. Some of his collectibles are put into intensive care, where he skillfully replaces parts that have been damaged or lost.
5. Dr. Spilhaus says that a toy is anything that enables us to stop and refresh ourselves during our hectic lives.
6. What is appealing about some toys is that they can make us laugh.
7. I have read that many mechanical principles were first applied to playthings.
8. For example, the toy monkey shown here is activated by squeezing a rubber bulb that uses the same principle as the jackhammer that digs up our streets.
9. Only those who have lost touch with childhood question what a toy can be worth to a young boy or girl.
10. Ask someone who knows toys what their enchantment is worth.

The Adverb Clause

20f. An ***adverb clause*** is a subordinate clause that modifies a verb, an adjective, or an adverb.

An adverb clause tells *how, how much, when, where, why, to what extent,* or *under what conditions.*

EXAMPLES You look **as though you have a lot on your mind.** [The adverb clause modifies the verb *look,* telling *how* you look.]

Many Western artists were influenced by the Asian art they saw **while they were studying in Paris.** [The adverb clause modifies the verb *saw,* telling *when* the artists saw.]

Miriam Makeba attracts huge audiences **wherever she performs.** [The adverb clause modifies the verb *attracts,* telling *where* she attracts huge audiences.]

The conquest of Cuba was essential to the Spanish **because the island is strategically located at the entrance to the Gulf of Mexico.** [The adverb clause modifies the adjective *essential,* telling *why* the conquest of Cuba was essential to the Spanish.]

Davita likes classical music better **than I do.** [The adverb clause modifies the adverb *better,* telling *to what extent* Davita likes classical music.]

If you want to gain an understanding of Native American culture, read *Voices of Our Ancestors* by Dhyani Ywahoo. [The adverb clause modifies the verb *read,* telling *under what condition* you should read Ywahoo's book.]

Subordinating Conjunctions

An adverb clause is introduced by a ***subordinating conjunction***—a word that shows the relationship between the adverb clause and the word or words the clause modifies.

Common Subordinating Conjunctions

after	as though	since	when
although	because	so that	whenever
as	before	than	where
as if	if	though	wherever
as long as	in order that	unless	whether
as soon as	provided that	until	while

REFERENCE NOTE: The words *after, as, before, since,* and *until* may also be used as prepositions. See pages 619–620.

The Elliptical Clause

20g. Part of a clause may be left out when the meaning can be understood from the context of the sentence. Such a clause is called an ***elliptical clause.***

Most elliptical clauses are adverb clauses. In the following examples, the word or words in brackets may be omitted because they can be understood from the context.

EXAMPLES Australia is smaller **than the other continents** [are].
When [you are] **taking notes,** use your own words.

NOTE: Often the meaning of an elliptical clause depends on the form of the pronoun in it.

EXAMPLES I like Anne as much as **she** [likes Anne].
I like Anne as much as [I like] **her.**

REFERENCE NOTE: For more about the correct use of pronouns in elliptical clauses, see pages 741–742.

EXERCISE 5 Identifying Adverb Clauses and the Words They Modify

Identify the adverb clause in each of the following sentences. Give the word or words that the clause modifies. Be prepared to state whether the clause tells *how, how much, when, where, why, to what extent,* or *under what conditions.*

1. Because company was coming for dinner, Lola Gómez and her father prepared a special treat of Cuban-style black beans, one of their specialties.
2. After Lola had soaked a pound of black beans overnight, she drained them and covered them with fresh water to make the beans more easily digestible.
3. Before she lit the stove, she added some chopped onion and green pepper, a bay leaf, cilantro leaves, oregano, and salt pork to the beans.
4. While the beans were simmering, Mr. Gómez prepared the *sofrito,* which is a characteristic ingredient in many Latin American dishes.
5. Whenever a recipe calls for *sofrito,* you finely chop some onion, green pepper, and garlic.

6. Then you fry these vegetables in a little oil until they are tender, and add herbs and spices such as basil, cilantro, cumin, and black and white pepper.
7. As soon as the *sofrito* was ready, Mr. Gómez added it to the bean mixture.
8. He then crushed some of the beans against the side of the pot so that the bean mixture would become thicker.
9. When the mixture was thick, Lola put in a blend of vinegar and sugar, which gives the beans that extra "tang."
10. No one at the dinner table was more eager than I to enjoy a large helping of the Gómezes' special black beans.

REVIEW A **Identifying and Classifying Subordinate Clauses**

Identify the subordinate clause or clauses in each of the following sentences. Tell whether each one is used as an *adjective*, a *noun*, or an *adverb*.

1. When a group of scholars first applied computer science to the study of literature, their colleagues expressed what can only be described as polite skepticism.
2. What, they asked, would the computer do?
3. Scornful scholars argued that measuring the length of Hemingway's sentences was dreary enough when it was done without computers.
4. Would precise mathematical analyses of style determine whether Thomas More wrote one of Shakespeare's plays?
5. Initial studies made along these lines fueled controversy that raged for years.
6. Researchers now use computers whenever their projects involve such mechanical tasks as compiling an index or a bibliography.
7. Since all of ancient Greek is now stored on computers, scholars can make analyses that shed light on etymology.
8. There are some features of literary works that computers can identify faster than human readers can.
9. Of course, nowadays many students take advantage of computer technology when writing research papers about literature.
10. After writing their first drafts, students may then revise their papers using software programs that check spelling, grammar, and style.

PICTURE THIS

GRAMMAR

In your creative writing class, you've been experimenting with *magical realism,* a technique of fiction writing that interweaves fantastical details with realistic narrative. Since some of your most imaginative story ideas come from dreams, you've also been keeping a dream journal. You just woke from a dream in which you visited this mysterious city. Write a journal entry describing what you saw and experienced there. Include both realistic and fantastical details. In your journal entry, use at least five subordinate clauses.

Subject: a dream city
Audience: yourself
Purpose: to record a dream; to collect imaginative details for a story

El Greco (Domenicos Theotocopoulos) (1514–1614). *View of Toledo.* Oil on canvas. H: $47\frac{3}{4}$" W: $42\frac{3}{4}$". (121.3 × 108.6 cm). The Metropolitan Museum of Art, Bequest of Mrs. H. O. Havemeyer, 1929. The H. O. Havemeyer Collection (29.100.6).

Sentences Classified According to Structure

20h. Sentences are classified according to their structure as ***simple, compound, complex,*** or ***compound-complex.***

(1) A ***simple sentence*** has one independent clause and no subordinate clauses.

EXAMPLES **Great literature stirs the imagination.**
Located on an island in Lake Texcoco, Tenochtitlán was the capital of the Aztec empire and may have had more than 100,000 inhabitants in the 1500s.

(2) A ***compound sentence*** has two or more independent clauses but no subordinate clauses.

Independent clauses may be joined either by a comma and a coordinating conjunction (*and, but, for, nor, or, so,* or *yet*); by a semicolon; or by a semicolon and a conjunctive adverb or transitional expression.

EXAMPLES **In 1528, the Spanish explored the area near present-day Tampa, but Europeans did not begin settling there until 1823.** [two independent clauses joined by a comma and the coordinating conjunction *but*]
The Aswan High Dam is on the Nile River in Egypt; it is one of the world's largest dams. [two independent clauses joined by a semicolon]
We should leave early; otherwise, we will miss our bus. [two independent clauses joined by a semicolon and the conjunctive adverb *otherwise*]

Common Conjunctive Adverbs

also	incidentally	next
anyway	indeed	nonetheless
besides	instead	otherwise
consequently	likewise	still
finally	meanwhile	then
furthermore	moreover	therefore
however	nevertheless	thus

Common Transitional Expressions

after all	even so	in fact
as a result	for example	in other words
at any rate	for instance	on the contrary
by the way	in addition	on the other hand

NOTE: Don't confuse a simple sentence that has a compound subject or a compound predicate with a compound sentence.

EXAMPLES **The 1991 eruption of Mount Pinatubo destroyed many homes and led to the closing of Clark Air Base.** [simple sentence with compound predicate]
The 1991 eruption of Mount Pinatubo destroyed many homes, and it led to the closing of Clark Air Base. [compound sentence]

(3) A *complex sentence* has one independent clause and at least one subordinate clause.

EXAMPLES **Yiddish, which is a West Germanic language, is now spoken by millions of people all over the world.** [The independent clause is *Yiddish is spoken by millions of people all over the world.* The subordinate clause is *which is a West Germanic language.*]
After Napoleon I was defeated at Waterloo, he was exiled to Saint Helena. [The independent clause is *he was exiled to Saint Helena.* The subordinate clause is *After Napoleon I was defeated at Waterloo.*]

(4) A *compound-complex sentence* has two or more independent clauses and at least one subordinate clause.

EXAMPLES **The interest that you pay on a car loan will increase the actual cost of the car, so be sure to shop for the lowest interest rate.** [The two independent clauses are *The interest will increase the actual cost of the car* and *be sure to shop for the lowest interest rate.* The subordinate clause is *that you pay on a car loan.*]
Hong Kong has been a crown colony of Britain since 1898; however, it will revert to China when the lease expires in 1997. [The two independent clauses are *Hong Kong has been a crown colony of Britain since 1898* and *it will revert to China.* The subordinate clause is *when the lease expires in 1997.*]

GRAMMAR

EXERCISE 6 Classifying Sentences According to Structure

Classify each sentence of the following paragraphs as *simple*, *compound*, *complex*, or *compound-complex*.

EXAMPLE [1] **H. J. (Henry Jackson) Lewis is generally regarded as the first African American political cartoonist.**
1. *simple*

[1] During the late 1800s, H. J. Lewis drew political cartoons for *The Freeman*, which was the first illustrated African American newspaper. [2] Through his cartoons, Lewis frequently criticized the U.S. government's racial policies; however, he also produced nonpolitical ink drawings, sketches, and chalk plates. [3] If you examine this self-portrait of Lewis, you can see evidence of his artistic versatility, and you can get a sense of the atmosphere in which he worked.

Self-Portrait of Henry Jackson Lewis, Courtesy of the DuSable Museum of African American History, Chicago, Illinois.

[4] Lewis had to overcome many difficulties to achieve success as an artist, and parts of his life are shrouded in mystery. [5] Lewis was born into slavery in Mississippi and was badly burned and blinded in one eye when he was a toddler. [6] As a young man, he worked at various menial jobs until a Little Rock newspaper artist taught him how to draw. [7] It is known that Lewis made sketches for archaeological studies in Arkansas, Mississippi, Tennessee, and Louisiana in 1882 and 1883.

[8] The Smithsonian Institution now has most of these sketches, which include drawings of prehistoric Native American burial mounds. [9] Throughout his life, Lewis produced drawings for various publications. [10] Upon Lewis' death in 1891, *The Freeman*, the newspaper that had made him famous, praised his talent and mourned his loss.

Sentences Classified According to Purpose

20i. Sentences are classified according to purpose as ***declarative, imperative, interrogative,*** or ***exclamatory.***

(1) A ***declarative sentence*** makes a statement. All declarative sentences end with periods.

EXAMPLE **Homes should be made more accessible for people who have disabilities.**

(2) An ***imperative sentence*** gives a command or makes a request. Imperative sentences usually end with periods, but a very strong command may end with an exclamation point.

EXAMPLES **Please pay attention.**
Stop what you're doing and listen!

(3) An ***interrogative sentence*** asks a question. Interrogative sentences end with question marks.

EXAMPLES **What is the name of that song?**
Have you seen Alma?

NOTE: Any sentence may be spoken in such a way that it is interrogative. If so, it should end with a question mark.

EXAMPLES **Rex came back yesterday?** [Declarative becomes interrogative.]
Ask Ed? [Imperative becomes interrogative.]
What great news I got? [Exclamatory becomes interrogative.]

(4) An ***exclamatory sentence*** expresses strong feeling. Exclamatory sentences end with exclamation points.

EXAMPLES **How happy you look!**
What a surprise to see you here!

NOTE: **Any sentence may be spoken in such a way that it is exclamatory. If so, it should end with an exclamation point.**

EXAMPLES **You're home early!** [Declarative becomes exclamatory.]
Stop that racket! [Imperative becomes exclamatory.]
How do you expect me to react! [Interrogative becomes exclamatory.]

EXERCISE 7 **Classifying Sentences According to Structure and Purpose**

Classify each of the following sentences first according to its structure and then according to its purpose.

EXAMPLE **1. Look at this article I'm reading.**
1. *complex—imperative*

1. Are you aware that there is a huge worldwide demand for butterflies?
2. Millions are caught and sold each year to entomologists, museums, private collectors, and factories.
3. The plastic-encased butterflies that are used to decorate ornamental objects such as trays, tabletops, and screens are usually common varieties, many of which come from Taiwan, Korea, and Malaysia.
4. There is a difference, though, between collection practices there and what goes on in Papua New Guinea.
5. Papua New Guinea, which was administered by Australia until 1975, has taken advantage of a growing interest in tropical butterflies.
6. The butterfly rancher shown on the next page gathers, raises, and markets high-quality specimens, which are accompanied by scientific data.
7. Because biologists have not yet determined the life cycles of all of these butterflies, local villagers have become the experts; as a result, butterfly ranching has improved the country's economy.
8. Some butterfly specimens are quite small, but others are larger than an adult human hand.

9. The middle photograph shows butterflies emerging from cocoons that the rancher had gathered.
10. What rich, vibrant colors these butterflies have!

GRAMMAR

REVIEW B **Classifying Sentences**

Classify each of the following sentences first as *simple, compound, complex,* or *compound-complex* and then as *declarative, interrogative, imperative,* or *exclamatory.*

1. Have you discovered that imaginative teachers who are enthusiastic about their work can make school enjoyable for their students?
2. Last year, when I took a social studies elective, Law and Order, I found myself looking forward to fourth period each day.
3. What our teacher, Ms. Klein, did to make our course more interesting was to bring the outside world into the classroom.
4. In addition to having us watch the TV news and read the local newspaper, she invited guest speakers to share their experiences with us.
5. By the end of three months, the class had heard from a defense attorney, a prosecutor, and several local police officers; and we had interviewed the first FBI agent any of us had ever met.
6. Ms. Klein also arranged to have four prisoners, escorted by police, tell us about prison life.

GRAMMAR

7. After we had listened to their descriptions of their experiences, we all agreed that crime definitely does not pay!
8. In addition to bringing these people into the classroom, Ms. Klein set up a schedule of field trips, and she then took the classroom out into the world.
9. For example, on one of our trips, we visited the local jail; and on another, when we observed a jury trial, we spoke personally with the judge.
10. I am glad that I was in Ms. Klein's class, and I was very pleased when she was voted "Outstanding Educator of the Year."

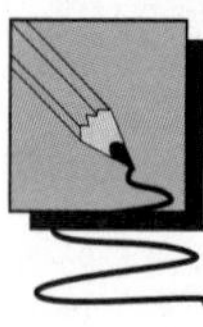

WRITING APPLICATION

Using End Marks to Reflect Attitude in an Interview

The main purpose of an interview is to gather information. However, unlike an encyclopedia or other reference source, people who are interviewed provide more than information on a subject—they provide their own unique and personal perspective on the subject. Often that perspective is reflected in the way a person speaks. A good interviewer, therefore, records not only *what* a person says but also *how* he or she says it—colloquial expressions, slang, and technical terms included.

Recording a person's exact words is easy enough with a tape recorder, but transcribing, or writing down, those words is a little more complicated. The interviewer must choose end marks that accurately reflect the speaker's attitude. In addition, it is the interviewer's job to decide where and how to break the flow of ideas into sentences. As you read the example below, notice how an interviewer recorded the speech of cowboy Jack Pate.

> "I think cowboys is as good a class a people as any. They might not have as much money as some but money don't mean everything. It's just whatever you're happy doing. I'll tell you one thing. Most cowboys—if they've got a dollar and you need it—you can shore get four bits of it.

> "Would I recommend it? Well, really I don't guess I would—but I wouldn't change my own life. Do what you're happy doing. It's poor pay and hard work but I think living outside and eating cow meat and gravy keeps you young!"
>
> Eliot Wigginton, Editor, from *"I wish I could give my son a wild raccoon."*

The passage above records both what Mr. Pate said and how he said it. The writer chose to use dashes to join some ideas together, but that is not the only way the passage could be punctuated. How might you punctuate the passage differently?

WRITING ACTIVITY

Is there a job you've always dreamed of doing? Maybe it's driving a truck, being an attorney, designing computer software, running a day-care center, practicing medicine, or even being a cowboy like Jack Pate. Well, now's your chance to learn what that "dream job" is all about. For a class project, you are to interview someone employed in a field that interests you. Find out what kind of training the person needed for his or her job and what a typical day on the job is like. If possible, arrange to visit the person's workplace. When you write your interview, use end marks to accurately reflect your interviewee's tone and attitude.

Prewriting First, brainstorm a list of interesting jobs. Choose the one that most appeals to you, and start looking for someone to interview. You may need to use the Yellow Pages or ask friends and family members to help you find a person working in the area you've chosen. Ask the person if he or she will grant you an interview either in person or over the phone. Be sure to explain the purpose of the interview. Set up a date and time to conduct it.

Next, prepare for your interview. Jot down a number of questions that you might ask about the person's job. Make your questions clear and specific, but avoid questions that could be answered with a simple yes or no. Instead, use the *5W–How?* questions listed on page 25.

When you conduct the interview, be friendly and polite. If you're planning to use a tape recorder, be sure to get the person's permission before you begin recording. Feel free

GRAMMAR

to redirect or add to your original questions as the interview progresses. Remember, an interview should have a personal flavor. Encourage your interviewee to tell any interesting anecdotes that reveal what his or her job is really like.

Writing Begin with a brief paragraph introducing your interviewee and telling the date and location of the interview. In writing the interview itself, you'll need to record the interviewee's responses exactly. You can leave out selected portions of the interview, but be sure to use ellipsis points to mark the omissions. (See pages 941–943 on the use of ellipses.) Don't "correct" the speaker's grammar or usage as you write. Instead, try to capture the actual sound of the person's speech. Use contractions wherever the speaker used them. If you think a spoken sentence won't be clear to readers, paraphrase it in brackets. As you write, choose end marks that accurately reflect the speaker's pauses, questions, and exclamations.

Evaluating and Revising Evaluate the written version of your interview for accuracy and clarity. Keep in mind the purpose of the interview—to gather information about an interesting job. With that aim in mind, you may want to omit some passages from the interview. However, don't change the meaning of any quoted material. If you are lacking needed information, you may have to call your interviewee and conduct a brief telephone interview.

Proofreading and Publishing Check your writing carefully against your tape or notes. Be sure that you've quoted the person exactly and that your punctuation accurately reflects contractions, pauses, questions, and exclamations. Check your end marks to make sure that they show the intended purpose of each sentence.

You and your classmates may want to collect the interviews in a booklet. Work together to write a brief introduction explaining the nature and purpose of the interviews. Also include an acknowledgment page thanking each of the contributors.

Review: Posttest 1

A. Identifying and Classifying Clauses

Identify the italicized clause in each of the following sentences as an *independent clause* or a *subordinate clause.* If a clause is subordinate, tell whether it is an *adjective clause,* an *adverb clause,* or a *noun clause.*

EXAMPLE **1. *While we were talking on the telephone,* my call-waiting light flashed.**
1. *subordinate clause—adverb clause*

1. *Tamara applied for the job last Monday,* and each day since then she has been waiting for a call from the company.
2. *The band played calypso and reggae music from the West Indies.*
3. Serious hikers know *that a topographical map is often useful in unfamiliar territory.*
4. Amelia Earhart, *who was the first woman to fly solo over both the Atlantic Ocean and the Pacific Ocean,* had great courage.
5. *Though he was a paraplegic because of injuries sustained in an auto accident,* Mr. Benoit was the best coach at Northeast High School.
6. As you wait, concentrate on *what you have to do to win.*
7. Since last year Erin and Jim have been rotating household tasks, and *as a result, each has become more understanding and more helpful.*
8. *Renowned underwater explorer Jacques-Yves Cousteau was ten years old* when he made his first dive.
9. How was I ever going to get the parts of the engine put back together *before my father got home*?
10. Lawrence, who transferred to our school last month, is taller *than the other boys on the team.*
11. Tired after a long day in the summer sun, the lifeguard reported *that there had been no accidents.*
12. In high school, Lori Garcia set an all-city scoring record in basketball, and *she later went to college on a scholarship.*
13. Can you tell me *why there is still famine in parts of the world*?
14. After World War II, President Harry Truman authorized the Marshall Plan, *which was a massive program designed to speed economic recovery in Europe.*

15. The Vietnam Veterans Memorial, a black granite wall engraved with the names of those *who died in the war in Vietnam,* was designed by Maya Ying Lin when she was a student at Yale University.

B. Classifying Sentences

Classify each of the following sentences first according to its structure and then according to its purpose.

EXAMPLE 1. **Did you know that some of the best-preserved Anasazi dwellings are at Mesa Verde National Park in Colorado?**

1. ***complex—interrogative***

16. *Anasazi* means "ancient ones," and that term accurately describes these cliff dwellers.
17. The Anasazi had a thriving culture around A.D. 1100.
18. They lived primarily in an area now called the Four Corners, where the states of New Mexico, Colorado, Utah, and Arizona converge.
19. These remarkable people built dwellings, some of which were several stories high, in the cliffs.
20. What unusual villages they created, and what views they had over the canyons!
21. Don't assume, however, that this fascinating civilization lasted as long as the Mayan and Aztec civilizations did.
22. The Anasazi disappeared completely around A.D. 1300.
23. Do you know why they disappeared?
24. Nobody does for sure, but anthropologists have several theories that may explain the disappearance.
25. A drought that lasted many years is one good possibility, but the Anasazi may have been driven from their villages by enemies or by changes in climate.

Review: Posttest 2

Writing a Variety of Sentence Structures

Write ten sentences according to the following guidelines.

1. Write an exclamatory simple sentence.

2. Write a simple sentence with a compound verb.
3. Write an interrogative compound sentence.
4. Write an imperative sentence.
5. Write a complex sentence with an adjective clause beginning with the relative adverb *where*.
6. Write a complex sentence with a noun clause used as the object of the main verb of the sentence.
7. Write a complex sentence with an adjective clause beginning with the relative pronoun *who*.
8. Write a complex sentence with an adverb clause beginning with the subordinating conjunction *because*.
9. Write a compound-complex sentence.
10. Write a complex sentence with an elliptical clause.

USAGE

21 AGREEMENT

Subject and Verb, Pronoun and Antecedent

Diagnostic Test

A. Identifying Verbs That Agree in Number with Their Subjects and Pronouns That Agree with Their Antecedents

Choose the word in parentheses that correctly completes each of the following sentences.

1. Neither of the pitchers (*was, were*) able to stop the Hawks from winning the baseball game.
2. "(*Is, Are*) mumps contagious?" I asked when my sister got the disease just two days before I was to star in our high school play.
3. Martin's greatest problem before a race (*is, are*) nerves.

4. One of the girls left (*her, their*) camera when she got off the train in Wyoming.
5. Coach Ruíz says that a team with too many superstars (*has, have*) trouble working as a unit.
6. Both of your answers (*is, are*) correct.
7. An adventure novel by French writer Alexandre Dumas, *The Three Musketeers* (*has, have*) been made into a movie many times.
8. When we got to the picnic grounds, we discovered that neither Josh nor Brandon had brought (*his, their*) radio.
9. My mother thought that twenty-five dollars (*was, were*) too much to pay for the designer T-shirt.
10. Our city is proud of (*its, their*) cultural activities.

B. Proofreading for Subject-Verb Agreement and Pronoun-Antecedent Agreement

Most of the sentences in the following paragraph contain errors in agreement between subjects and verbs or between pronouns and their antecedents. If a sentence contains an error, give the correct form. If a sentence is correct, write *C.*

[11] Most of us has some knowledge of the periods in European history known as the Middle Ages and the Renaissance. **[12]** Those times is the special interest of the Society for Creative Anachronism. **[13]** Members of this society, who is found all over the world, do more than study the Middle Ages and the Renaissance. **[14]** Every member takes a name and becomes a character appropriate to the society's historical period (A.D. 500 to A.D. 1500). **[15]** Popular characters in the society includes princes, princesses, lords, and ladies. **[16]** After joining, everyone is free to choose a new name and to re-create his or her favorite aspect of medieval life. **[17]** Each person can pursue their own interests. **[18]** For example, some people enjoys costuming, armor-making, calligraphy, and woodworking. **[19]** There is also some members who compete in tournaments to become monarchs of the society's kingdoms. **[20]** If you want to learn more about such historical activities in your area, the society usually displays their brochures at public Renaissance festivals.

Number

Number is the form of a word that indicates whether the word is singular or plural.

21a. A word that refers to one person or thing is ***singular*** in number. A word that refers to more than one is ***plural*** in number.

SINGULAR	employer	theory	woman	that	either	it
PLURAL	employers	theories	women	those	both	they

Most nouns that end in *s* are plural; most present-tense verbs that end in *s* are singular. Past-tense verbs (except *be*) have the same form in both the singular and the plural.

NOTE: The singular pronouns *I* and *you* almost always take plural verbs. The only exceptions are the forms *I am* and *I was.*

USAGE

Agreement of Subject and Verb

21b. A verb should agree with its subject in number.

(1) Singular subjects take singular verbs.

EXAMPLES The **child takes** an afternoon nap.
She cleans and **restores** old paintings.

(2) Plural subjects take plural verbs.

EXAMPLES The **children take** an afternoon nap.
They clean and **restore** old paintings.

A verb phrase, like a one-word verb, agrees in number with its subject. The number of a verb phrase is indicated by the form of its first auxiliary (helping) verb.

EXAMPLES The **Vietnam Veterans Memorial was** designed by Maya Lin. [singular subject and verb phrase]
The **Vietnam Veterans Memorial** and the **Civil Rights Memorial were** designed by Maya Lin. [plural subject and verb phrase]

Intervening Phrases and Clauses

21c. The number of the subject is not changed by a phrase or a clause following the subject.

EXAMPLES The **short stories are** by various contemporary Native American writers.

The **short stories** in this anthology **are** by various contemporary Native American writers. [The prepositional phrase *in this anthology* does not affect the number of the subject, *short stories.*]

Edmonia Lewis was the first African American woman to achieve renown for her sculpture.

Edmonia Lewis, whose subjects included John Brown and Abraham Lincoln, **was** the first African American woman to achieve renown for her sculpture. [The adjective clause *whose subjects included John Brown and Abraham Lincoln* does not affect the number of the subject, *Edmonia Lewis.*]

The number of the subject is also not affected when the subject is followed by a phrase that begins with an expression such as *along with, as well as, in addition to,* and *together with.*

EXAMPLES The **man** in the next apartment, as well as the people across the hall, **has lived** in the building since the mid-1970s. [singular subject and verb]

The **people** across the hall, as well as the man in the next apartment, **have lived** in the building since the mid-1970s. [plural subject and verb]

USAGE

EXERCISE 1 Identifying Subjects and Verbs That Agree in Number

For each of the following sentences, identify the subject of the verb in parentheses. Then choose the verb form that agrees in number with the subject.

1. The theory of plate tectonics (*has, have*) explained causes of earthquake activity throughout the world.
2. Enormous plates of rock (*is, are*) shifting constantly far beneath the earth's surface.
3. The movements, in addition to the pressure of molten rock, (*causes, cause*) the plates to collide.

4. The cause of most earthquakes (*is, are*) the sudden release of stress along a fault.
5. A ridge of these breaks (*is, are*) called a fault.
6. The pressure of colliding plates (*forces, force*) the rock to bend until it breaks.
7. The Richter scale, as well as other measurements, (*has, have*) been used to record the magnitude of earthquakes.
8. The tremors of the great San Francisco earthquake that occurred in 1906 (*was, were*) estimated to have measured 8.3 on the Richter scale.
9. California, with two major fault lines, (*has, have*) about ten times the world average of earthquake activity.
10. A map of the earth's plates, such as the one shown here, (*gives, give*) you a pretty good idea of why California has so many quakes.

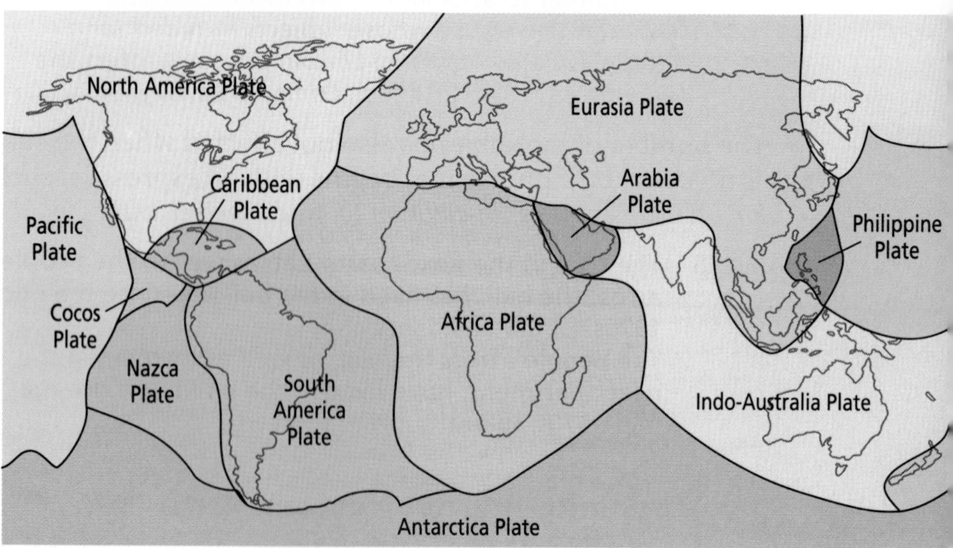

Indefinite Pronouns

21d. The following indefinite pronouns are singular: *anybody, anyone, anything, each, either, everybody, everyone, everything, neither, nobody, no one, nothing, one, somebody, someone,* and *something.*

EXAMPLES **Is anyone** in the audience a medical doctor?
Each of the boys **does** his own cooking.
Either of these videos **is** suitable for a four-year-old.

21e. The following indefinite pronouns are plural: *both, few, many,* and *several.*

EXAMPLES **Both** of the universities **offer** degrees in forestry.
Few on the committee ever **miss** a meeting.
Several of the students **have transferred.**

21f. The following indefinite pronouns may be singular or plural: *all, any, most, none,* and *some.*

These pronouns are singular when they refer to singular words. They are plural when they refer to plural words.

EXAMPLES **All** of the workout **seems** simple. [*All* refers to the singular noun *workout.*]
All of the exercises **seem** simple. [*All* refers to the plural noun *exercises.*]

Is any of the salad left? [*Any* refers to the singular noun *salad.*]
Are any of the vegetables left? [*Any* refers to the plural noun *vegetables.*]

Most of the plan **was** new to me. [*Most* refers to the singular noun *plan.*]
Most of the plans **were** new to me. [*Most* refers to the plural noun *plans.*]

None of the deck **is** missing. [*None* refers to the singular noun *deck.*]
None of the cards **are** missing. [*None* refers to the plural noun *cards.*]

Some of the show **was** hilarious. [*Some* refers to the singular noun *show.*]
Some of the acts **were** hilarious. [*Some* refers to the plural noun *acts.*]

EXERCISE 2 Identifying Subjects and Verbs That Agree in Number

For each of the following sentences, identify the subject of the verb in parentheses. Then choose the verb form that agrees in number with the subject.

1. Each of the pictures (*was, were*) in a silver frame.
2. One of my friends (*play, plays*) the tuba.

3. All of our belongings (*is, are*) carefully unpacked.
4. Some of these rare books (*has, have*) leather covers.
5. None of the people in the theater (*was, were*) sitting in the first two rows.
6. Every one of these computer games (*is, are*) on sale.
7. A few in my class (*was, were*) asked to help out.
8. The lack of funds (*present, presents*) a problem.
9. Everybody living in Lewis Heights (*go, goes*) to George Washington Carver High School.
10. A band with two trumpet players and thirty-five clarinetists (*sound, sounds*) terrible.

EXERCISE 3 Revising Subject-Verb Agreement in Sentences

Revise each of the following sentences according to the instructions in brackets after each sentence. Make any needed changes in the form of the verb.

EXAMPLE **1. Each of the contestants was confused by the question. [Change *Each* to *Several.*]**
1. *Several of the contestants were confused by the question.*

1. All of the fruit has been picked. [Change *fruit* to *oranges.*]
2. Each of us was angry about the election. [Change *Each* to *Many.*]
3. Has anybody joined the choir? [Change *anybody* to *any of the new students.*]
4. The committee leaves today for Washington, D.C. [Add *representing the farmers* after *committee.*]
5. Our team is going to Austin for the debate tournament. [Add *Three members of* before *Our team.*]
6. Most of the classrooms were equipped with new microcomputers. [Change *Most* to *None.*]
7. The pitcher was disappointed in the coach's decision. [Add *as well as the other players* after *pitcher*. Set off the addition with commas.]
8. Every one of the smoke detectors works fine. [Change *Every one* to *All but two.*]
9. Both of them usually hope that things will turn out for the best. [Change *Both of them* to *Everyone.*]
10. Some of her plan has been adopted. [Change *plan* to *ideas.*]

REVIEW A **Proofreading for Subject-Verb Agreement**

Most of the sentences in the following paragraph contain errors in subject-verb agreement. If a sentence contains an error, give the correct form. If a sentence is correct, write *C*.

[1] The history of the Hawaiian Islands tell of some interesting rulers. [2] Of course, none of these rulers is more amazing than King Kamehameha I. [3] This powerful leader, together with his followers, are credited with uniting the numerous islands into a kingdom in 1795. [4] Kamehameha I, whose family ruled the islands until 1872, was sometimes called the Napoleon of the Pacific. [5] Few of his descendants was more influential than King Kamehameha III. [6] No one deny that he helped the common people by permitting them to own land and by issuing a democratic constitution. [7] The musical interest of Hawaii's last two royal rulers, King Kalakaua I and Queen Liliuokalani, are fascinating. [8] Both of these monarchs was known as songwriters. [9] The queen, whose regal bearing is evident in this photograph, has several claims to fame. [10] One of these are having written the famous song *"Aloha Oe"* ("Farewell to Thee").

Compound Subjects

A ***compound subject*** is two or more subjects that have the same verb.

21g. Subjects joined by *and* usually take a plural verb.

EXAMPLES **Spanish** and **Quechua are** the official languages of Peru.

Hannah and **Dot have been** friends for years.

NOTE: Subjects joined by *and* may be considered a single item or may refer to the same thing. In such cases, a compound subject takes a singular verb.

EXAMPLES My next-door **neighbor** and best **friend is** from Mexico. [one person]
Macaroni and **cheese is** a nutritious main course. [one dish]

21h. Singular subjects joined by *or* or *nor* take a singular verb.

EXAMPLES A **jacket** or a **sweater is** warm enough for tonight.
Neither the **coach** nor the **trainer knows** the umpire.
Either **Soledad** or **Chen writes** the weekly editorial.

USAGE

21i. When a singular subject and a plural subject are joined by *or* or *nor,* the verb agrees with the subject nearer the verb.

EXAMPLES Either the **musicians** or the **singer is** off-key. [The singular subject *singer* is nearer the verb.]
Either the **singer** or the **musicians are** off-key. [The plural subject *musicians* is nearer the verb.]

Whenever possible, revise the sentence to avoid this awkward construction.

EXAMPLE Either the singer is off-key, or the musicians are.

NOTE: Formal usage requires a singular verb after a singular subject. Informal usage, however, often permits the use of a plural verb if the meaning is clearly plural.

FORMAL The director, as well as the star and several stage hands, was trapped in the theater fire.
INFORMAL The director, as well as the star and several stage hands, were trapped in the theater fire.

REFERENCE NOTE: For a discussion of formal and informal English, see pages 519–523. As you work the exercises in this chapter, follow the rules of formal standard usage.

EXERCISE 4 Identifying Verbs That Agree with Compound Subjects

Choose the verb form in parentheses that correctly completes each of the following sentences.

1. Del Rio and San Angelo (*is, are*) two Texas cities that have names of Spanish origin.
2. My books and tennis racket barely (*fit, fits*) in the locker.
3. Either my cat or the raccoons always (*eat, eats*) all the food by morning.
4. That blouse and scarf (*is, are*) a good combination.
5. Neither Mariah Carey nor Gloria Estefan, I believe, (*sing, sings*) that song.

REVIEW B Correcting Errors in Subject-Verb Agreement

Most of the following sentences contain verbs that do not agree with their subjects. If a verb does not agree with its subject, give the correct form of the verb. If a sentence is correct, write *C*.

1. One of the most precious resources in the nation is water.
2. The abundance and use of water vary greatly among the regions of the United States.
3. The water supply in every region comes from either surface water or underground water.
4. Unfortunately, neither overuse nor contamination of our water supplies has stopped completely.
5. After years of study, the pollution of lakes, rivers, and streams continue to be a serious problem.
6. Lake Erie, as well as the Potomac River and the Cuyahoga River, have been saved by clean-up efforts.

7. As you can see in the picture above, Lake Erie, which is bounded by several large, industrial cities, sparkle again.

8. The government, in addition to environmentalists, are also worried about the quality and abundance of ground water.
9. Aquifers, a source of ground water, is layers of rock, sand, and soil that hold water.
10. Billions of gallons of water is pumped out of the ground each day.
11. In some regions, drinking water for thousands of people come from aquifers.
12. Every one of the recent studies of aquifers has revealed contamination to some degree.
13. The causes of contamination are varied.
14. Salt for melting ice on city streets cause pollution.
15. The chemicals that sometimes leak out of a sewer system or waste dump contaminates aquifers.
16. Fertilizers and pesticides used widely all over the country also add pollutants to the water.
17. The extent of the damages from pollution are not known.
18. Another problem, according to scientists, is uncontrolled use of water sources.
19. Ground water in some areas are being used faster than the supply can be renewed.
20. Each one of the fifty states have a stake in preserving sources of water.

Special Problems in Subject-Verb Agreement

21j. When the subject follows the verb, as in questions and in sentences beginning with *here* and *there,* identify the subject and make sure that the verb agrees with it.

The verb usually comes before the subject in sentences beginning with *Here* or *There* and in questions.

EXAMPLES Here **is** the **book** you reserved.
Here **are** the **books** you reserved.

There **was** a **detour** on the interstate.
There **were** no **detours** on the interstate.

When **is Passover** this year?
When **are Passover** and **Easter** this year?

NOTE: Contractions such as *Here's, There's, When's,* and *Where's* incorporate the verb *is.* Use such contractions only with subjects that are singular in meaning.

NONSTANDARD	When's your finals?
STANDARD	When **are** your **finals**?
NONSTANDARD	Here's your gloves.
STANDARD	Here **are** your **gloves.**
STANDARD	Here**'s** your **pair** of gloves.

21k. Collective nouns may be either singular or plural.

A ***collective noun*** is singular in form but names a group of persons or things.

Common Collective Nouns

army	club	flock	squadron
assembly	committee	group	staff
audience	crowd	herd	swarm
band	family	jury	team
class	fleet	public	troop

A collective noun takes a singular verb when the noun refers to the group as a unit. A collective noun takes a plural verb when the noun refers to the parts or members of the group.

SINGULAR	The **class meets** Monday, Wednesday, and Friday. [The class meets as a unit.]
PLURAL	The **class** usually **bring** their calculators with them. [The members of the class bring separate calculators.]
SINGULAR	The **team has won** the semifinals. [The team won as a unit.]
PLURAL	The **team have voted** twenty-one to nothing to buy new uniforms. [The members of the team voted individually.]
SINGULAR	A **herd** of cattle **was stranded** by the flood. [The herd was stranded as a unit.]
PLURAL	The **herd** of cattle **were grazing** in the clover. [The cattle were grazing individually.]

USAGE

USAGE

21l. An expression stating an amount (such as a measurement, a statistic, or a fraction) may be singular or plural.

An expression stating an amount is

- singular when the amount is thought of as a unit
- plural when the amount is thought of as separate parts

EXAMPLES **Twenty-seven dollars is** all we've raised so far. [The amount refers to one unit. Notice that the entire expression *Twenty-seven dollars* is the subject.]

Twenty-seven **dollars were** counted out by the teller. [The amount refers to separate dollars. Notice that only the noun *dollars* is the subject. *Twenty-seven* is an adjective telling how many.]

Eight hours is now the standard workday throughout the United States. [one unit]

Eight **hours were** set aside for that miniseries about the Civil War. [separate hours]

REFERENCE NOTE: For information on using hyphens in expressions stating an amount, see page 953.

A fraction or a percent is singular when it refers to a singular word and plural when it refers to a plural word.

EXAMPLES **Two thirds** of my bibliography **has been typed.** [The fraction refers to the singular noun *bibliography.*]
Two thirds of my references **have been typed.** [The fraction refers to the plural noun *references.*]

Forty-two percent of the senior class **is planning** to go to college. [The percentage refers to the singular noun *class.*]
Forty-two percent of the seniors **are planning** to go to college. [The percentage refers to the plural noun *seniors.*]

Expressions of measurement (length, weight, capacity, area) are usually singular.

EXAMPLES **Two and fifty-four hundredths centimeters equals** one inch.
Seven pounds was the baby's weight at birth.
Ninety miles is the distance between Florida and Cuba.

REFERENCE NOTE: For information on when to spell out numbers and when to use numerals, see pages 973–974.

EXERCISE 5 **Identifying Subjects and Verbs That Agree in Number**

Choose the word in parentheses that correctly completes each of the following sentences.

1. Forty dollars (*is, are*) too much to pay for those jeans.
2. (*Where's, Where are*) my coat and boots?
3. There (*seems, seem*) to be something for everyone.
4. The newspaper staff (*has, have*) turned in all their stories.
5. One half of the receipts (*was, were*) found in a shoe box.
6. (*Here's, Here are*) the notes you took about the history and symbolism of Japanese pagodas.
7. Two thirds of the students (*intend, intends*) to go to trade school or college.
8. The orchestra (*specialize, specializes*) in the Big Band music of Count Basie and Duke Ellington.
9. A number of us (*think, thinks*) the test was hard.
10. Fifty miles (*is, are*) a long way to drive to work every day.

21m. The title of a creative work (such as a book, song, film, or painting) and the name of a country (even if it is plural in form) take a singular verb.

EXAMPLES ***Dust Tracks on a Road* is** Zora Neale Hurston's autobiography.

***Vermilion Lotuses* was** among the paintings by Chinese artist Chang Dai-chien exhibited at the Smithsonian Institution.

The **United Arab Emirates generates** most of its revenue from the sale of oil.

The United States of America belongs to both the United Nations and the Organization of American States.

USAGE

21n. The name of an organization usually takes a singular verb even if it is plural in form.

EXAMPLES **The United Nations has** its headquarters in New York City.

Is Benson Motors where you bought your car?

The names of some organizations may take singular or plural verbs. When the name refers to the organization as a unit, it takes a singular verb. When the name refers to the members of the organization, it takes a plural verb.

EXAMPLES The **Veterans of Foreign Wars was founded** in 1899. [The organization was founded in 1899.]

The **Veterans of Foreign Wars are leading** the parade. [The members of the organization are leading the parade.]

21o. Some nouns that are plural in form are singular in meaning.

(1) The following nouns always take singular verbs.

civics	genetics	mumps
economics	mathematics	news
electronics	measles	physics

EXAMPLES **Mumps is** usually more severe in adults than in children.

Economics was my mother's major in college.

(2) The following nouns always take plural verbs.

binoculars	pliers	shears
eyeglasses	scissors	trousers

EXAMPLES The **binoculars are** on the screened porch.
Have these **shears** ever **been sharpened**?

NOTE: Many nouns ending in *–ics,* such as *acoustics, athletics, ethics, politics, statistics,* and *tactics,* may be singular or plural in meaning. Generally, such a noun takes a singular verb when it names a science, a system, or a skill. It takes a plural verb when it names qualities, operations, or activities.

EXAMPLES Who said, "**Politics is** the art of the possible"?
Are your **politics** like those of your parents?

If you don't know whether a noun that is plural in form is singular or plural in meaning, check a dictionary.

21p. A verb should always agree with its subject, not with its predicate nominative.

EXAMPLES Quick **reflexes are** one requirement for becoming an astronaut.
One **requirement** for becoming an astronaut **is** quick reflexes.

The **highlight** of the evening **was** the compositions by Quincy Jones.
The **compositions** by Quincy Jones **were** the highlight of the evening.

21q. Subjects preceded by *every* or *many a* take singular verbs.

EXAMPLES **Every takeoff** and **landing is cleared** with the tower.
Many a runner finishes a marathon long after the winner.

21r. *Doesn't,* not *don't,* is used with singular subjects except *I* and *you.*

Remember that *doesn't* is the contraction for *does not* and that *don't* is the contraction for *do not*.

NONSTANDARD He don't live here anymore.
STANDARD **He doesn't** [does not] live here anymore.

USAGE

NONSTANDARD It don't look like rain.
STANDARD **It doesn't** [does not] look like rain.

NONSTANDARD Ruth don't know about the surprise party for her.
STANDARD **Ruth doesn't** [does not] know about the surprise party for her.

21s. When a relative pronoun (*that, which,* or *who*) is the subject of an adjective clause, the verb in the clause should agree with the word that the relative pronoun refers to.

EXAMPLE San Juan, **which is** the capital of Puerto Rico, is a major tourist destination. [*Which* refers to the singular noun *San Juan.*]
I know some people **who own** a Christmas-tree farm. [*Who* refers to the plural noun *people.*]

NOTE: When the relative pronoun is preceded by *one of those* [or *these* or another plural word] it takes a plural verb. When it is preceded by *the only one of those* [or *these* or another plural word] it takes a singular verb.

EXAMPLES Egypt is **one of the nations that border** the Red Sea.
Quebec is **the only one of the Canadian provinces that has** a majority of French-speaking citizens.

21t. The word *number* when followed by the word *of* is singular when preceded by *the*; it is plural when preceded by *a*.

EXAMPLES **The number** of volunteers **is** surprising.
A number of volunteers **are** signing up now.

EXERCISE 6 **Identifying Subjects and Verbs That Agree in Number**

For each of the following sentences, identify the subject of the verb in parentheses. Then choose the verb form that agrees in number with the subject.

1. Many a gymnast (*dreams, dream*) of winning a medal in the Olympic games.
2. Bao (*doesn't, don't*) remember what year her grandparents moved here from Vietnam.
3. Many critics agree that *Boyz N the Hood* (*offer, offers*) movie watchers a realistic look at inner-city life.

USAGE

4. The Chicago Cubs is a team that (*rallies, rally*) in the late innings.
5. Civics (*is, are*) supposed to be his best subject.
6. The Society of Procrastinators (*has, have*) postponed its annual meeting.
7. That was one of those jokes that (*offends, offend*) everyone.
8. The kitchen scissors (*was, were*) not on the counter this morning.
9. My favorite part of the movie (*was, were*) scenes in New York's Adirondack Mountains.
10. Every volunteer in the regional hospitals (*is, are*) being honored at the banquet.

REVIEW C **Correcting Errors in Subject-Verb Agreement**

Most of the sentences in the following paragraph contain verbs that do not agree with their subjects. If a verb does not agree with its subject, give the correct form of the verb. If a sentence is correct, write *C*.

[1] The White House, which has been home to all U.S. presidents since John Adams, is a national treasure. [2] The public, as you can see in this picture, like to view the White House and grounds when visiting Washington, D.C. [3] How many people actually tours the White House each year? [4] One million are a conservative estimate. [5] There's more than 130 rooms in the White House. [6] Of course, a tourist don't get to see all the rooms. [7] In fact, only seven rooms, including the State Dining Room, is open to the public on the official tour. [8] Many a party have been given in the East Room, another large reception area. [9] The White House chefs, who works in two kitchens, sometimes prepare food for more than one hundred people in a single day. [10] The presence in the White House of recreational facilities, such as a movie theater and a bowling alley, usually surprises some visitors.

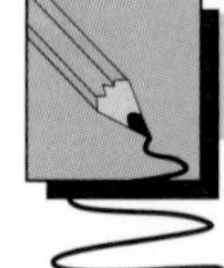

WRITING APPLICATION

Using Correct Subject-Verb Agreement in Formal Writing

By now you've learned that a word can mean different things in different contexts. For example, the same word can be a singular subject in one sentence and a plural subject in another. To determine the number of a collective noun, a plural noun, an expression of an amount, and a relative pronoun, you need to look at how each word is used. As you read the following paragraph, notice which subjects take singular verbs and which take plural ones.

> Ten years is a long time to stay friends with someone. Shawn Popovich, who has applied for a position at your summer camp, has been my best friend since the second grade. In addition to being a loyal friend, he is also a natural leader and athlete. Four years ago Shawn was the only freshman who made the cut for the varsity football team. This year, as a senior and captain of the team, he led us to victory in the state championship. But athletics isn't the only area in which Shawn stands out from the crowd. Last year he singlehandedly recruited more than a dozen volunteers from our school for the Big Brother/Big Sister program, which he and I still participate in. An openhearted, fun-loving person, Shawn earns the trust and admiration of children and adults alike. I know that the majority of the senior class share my high opinion of him.

What effect does this writer's careful use of subject-verb agreement have on you as a reader? What is your general impression of the writer? of his friend Shawn?

WRITING ACTIVITY

A friend of yours is applying for a summer job as a camp counselor and has asked you to write a letter of recommendation. Because you think highly of this person, you've agreed to write a letter explaining why he or she would make an excellent counselor. Write the letter of recommendation that you will send to the director of the summer camp. In your letter, follow the rules of formal standard English and pay particular attention to subject-verb agreement.

USAGE

Prewriting Take a few minutes to jot down a list of your friend's positive qualities and outstanding abilities. Focus on traits that you think would make your friend a good camp counselor. For example, does he or she work well with children? excel at a particular sport, craft, or academic subject? exhibit enthusiasm and team spirit? have a responsible attitude toward work? Think of specific examples that illustrate the qualities you've listed.

Writing Begin your letter by introducing yourself and stating your purpose. Tell how long you've known the person you're recommending. Then express your positive opinion of the person and his or her abilities. Be specific. You may want to give two or three brief examples to illustrate your friend's qualities. Or you may want to tell one interesting anecdote that achieves the same result. Resist the temptation to exaggerate your friend's achievements or abilities. Nobody expects him or her to be perfect, and an employer may become suspicious if an applicant sounds "too good to be true."

Evaluating and Revising Read through your letter once before you begin to revise it. Does it have the effect you want? Will it help your friend get the job? On a second reading, identify specific parts of the letter that need revising. Note any examples that don't illustrate your friend's qualities as well as they could. Also delete overly general statements such as "He's a great guy" or "She's a nice person." Replace colloquialisms or slang words with more formal expressions. (For help identifying colloquialisms and slang, see pages 521–523.) During your revision process, you may wish to ask a friend to read your letter and offer suggestions. Check to be sure you've followed the standard form for a business letter. (See pages 1056–1064.)

Proofreading Correct grammar, usage, punctuation, and spelling are extremely important in a letter of recommendation. Be sure to proofread your letter carefully. When you check for errors in subject-verb agreement, take extra care with collective nouns, plural nouns, expressions of an amount, and relative pronouns.

Agreement of Pronoun and Antecedent

A pronoun usually refers to a noun or another pronoun. The word to which a pronoun refers is called its ***antecedent.***

21u. A pronoun should agree with its antecedent in number and in gender.

(1) Singular pronouns refer to singular antecedents. Plural pronouns refer to plural antecedents.

EXAMPLES **Arthur Mitchell** founded **his** own ballet company.
Native Americans live **their** lives in harmony with the natural world around **them.**

(2) A few singular pronouns indicate gender. The singular pronouns *he, him, his,* and *himself* refer to masculine antecedents. The singular pronouns *she, her, hers,* and *herself* refer to feminine antecedents. The singular pronouns *it, its,* and *itself* refer to antecedents that are neuter (neither masculine nor feminine).

EXAMPLES **Rudolfo** stated **his** position clearly.
Maxine has already prepared **her** acceptance speech.
The **river** overflowed **its** banks.

21v. Singular pronouns are used to refer to the following antecedents: *anybody, anyone, anything, each, either, everybody, everyone, everything, neither, nobody, no one, nothing, one, somebody, someone,* and *something.*

These words do not indicate gender. To determine their gender, look in phrases following them.

EXAMPLES **Each** of these **women** runs **her** own business.
One of the **men** in the audience forgot **his** coat.

If the antecedent may be either masculine or feminine, use both the masculine and feminine pronouns to refer to it.

EXAMPLES **Everyone** should learn how to manage **his or her** money.
Each of the participants in the contest paid **his or her** own entry fee.

USAGE

You can often avoid the awkward *his or her* construction by substituting an article (*a, an,* or *the*) for the construction or by rephrasing the sentence, using the plural forms of both the pronoun and its antecedent.

EXAMPLES **Each** of the participants in the contest must pay **an** entry fee.
All of the **participants** in the contest must pay **their** own entry fees.

In conversation, plural pronouns are often used to refer to singular antecedents that can be either masculine or feminine.

EXAMPLES **Everyone** remembered **their** first day of school.
Each of the students read **their** poems.

This usage is becoming increasingly popular in writing. One reason for the growing use of this form is that using a singular pronoun with a singular antecedent that is clearly plural in meaning may be awkward or misleading.

MISLEADING **No one** failed the pop quiz because **he or she** had done **his or her** homework. [Since *no one* is clearly plural in meaning, the singular pronouns, though grammatically correct, are awkward.]

IMPROVED **No one** failed the pop quiz because **they** had done **their** homework.

MISLEADING **Everyone** in the band was so tired from the long bus ride that **he or she** did not play well.

IMPROVED **Everyone** in the band was so tired from the long bus ride that **they** did not play well.

21w. A plural pronoun is used to refer to two or more singular antecedents joined by *and.*

EXAMPLES **Hilda** and **Lupe** presented **their** reports.
After **Ethel, Jared,** and **Cam** ate lunch together, **they** went to **their** next class.

21x. A singular pronoun is used to refer to two or more singular antecedents joined by *or* or *nor.*

EXAMPLES Either **Paul** or **Diego** is willing to drive **his** car.
Neither **Sue** nor **María** brought **her** vacation photos with **her.**

21y. When a singular and a plural antecedent are joined by *or* or *nor,* the pronoun usually agrees with the nearer antecedent.

EXAMPLES Neither the **puppies nor** our full-grown **dog** likes **its** new toys.

Neither our full-grown **dog nor** the **puppies** like **their** new toys.

Whenever possible, revise the sentence to avoid such an awkward construction.

EXAMPLE The **puppies** don't like **their** new toys, and our full-grown **dog** doesn't like **its** new toys either.

NOTE: Sometimes following the rules results in another type of awkward or misleading sentence.

MISLEADING Either Anthony or Dolores is bringing her guitar. [The pronoun agrees in gender with the nearer of the two antecedents; however, the antecedents are of different genders.]

REVISED Either **Anthony** is bringing **his** guitar, or **Dolores** is bringing **hers.**

EXERCISE 7 Correcting Errors in Pronoun-Antecedent Agreement

Most of the following sentences contain pronouns that do not agree with their antecedents. If a pronoun does not agree with its antecedent, write the correct form of the pronoun. If a sentence is correct, write *C.*

EXAMPLE **1.** Neither Elena nor Barbara made any errors on their test.
1. *her*

1. Each of the skiers waxed their skis every morning before leaving the lodge.
2. All of the senior citizens enjoyed their trip to Boston, where they walked the Freedom Trail.
3. Every one of the reporters at the press conference asked their questions too quickly.
4. I believe that anybody should be free to express their opinion.
5. No one brought their camera to the party.
6. Both of the male soloists pronounced his words clearly.
7. Did any of the newborn kittens seem steady on its feet?

8. If anyone gets lost while exploring Salt Lake City, they should use the street maps available from the tour guide.
9. As far as I could see, each of the speakers made a mistake while presenting their argument during the debate.
10. One of the interesting quirks of American history is that neither President Gerald Ford nor Vice President Nelson Rockefeller was elected to his high office.

REVIEW D Proofreading Sentences for Pronoun-Antecedent Agreement

Most of the following sentences contain errors in pronoun-antecedent agreement. If a sentence contains an error in agreement, supply the correct form of the pronoun. If a sentence is correct, write *C*.

1. Each of the men says that they will help deliver the gift packages to the families.
2. One of those cars has their own factory-installed stereo.
3. The factory of the future will have robots working on its assembly line.
4. Either the Wilsons or Mrs. Kim will bring their camera.
5. Has either of the new students been assigned his locker?
6. Anyone who speaks a foreign language increases their chance for a high-paying job.
7. When the bank's computer breaks down, every one of the tellers holds their breath.
8. No one in the crowd had noticed the pickpocket stealing his wallet.
9. Neither Jason nor Maggie bought their shoes until they went on sale.
10. Brenda and Charlene read her report about Rosa Parks and the civil rights movement.

REVIEW E Proofreading for Correct Subject-Verb Agreement

Most of the sentences in the following paragraph contain errors in subject-verb agreement. If a sentence contains an error, supply the correct form of the verb. If a sentence is correct, write C.

[1] Many of today's moviegoers is familiar with the actor on the left in the photograph on the next page. [2] Doesn't Woody Allen's distinctive features make you smile? [3] *Bananas* are the

film from which this scene is taken. [4] At a recent film festival, the audience were shaking with laughter at this film and at *Don't Drink the Water,* another early hit by Allen. [5] The actor and director are generally regarded as one of America's most original talents. [6] Probably few of Allen's fans, though, know his real name. [7] Allen, whose films and writing frequently mirrors his own life, was born Allen Stewart Konigsberg in 1935 in Brooklyn, New York. [8] As a young man, Allen began writing comedy material for others, and many a television and screen star were his client. [9] The enthusiastic response to his jokes were one reason Allen started doing his own comedy routines in 1961. [10] If you're interested in Allen's successful film career, which began in 1962, there's many articles available in the library.

USAGE

REVIEW F

Revising Subject-Verb Agreement in Sentences

Revise each of the following sentences according to the directions given in brackets after each one. Make any needed changes in the forms of verbs.

1. A number of famous sports stars have made television commercials. [Change *A number of famous sports stars* to *Many a famous sports star.*]
2. Where's my book? [Add *and my pen* after *book.*]
3. Both of the candidates have promised to cut taxes. [Change *Both* to *Neither.*]
4. She writes neatly. [Add *is one of those people who* after *She.*]
5. Our basketball team has won the city championship. [Add *Neither our soccer team nor* at the beginning of the sentence.]
6. Nearly all people need at least one friend to confide in. [Change *all people* to *everyone.*]

7. A complete copy of your high school transcript is required by the state university. [After *transcript* add *together with a completed application form and an autobiographical essay*. Put a comma before *together* and after *essay*.]
8. The tigers are growling ferociously. [At the beginning of the sentence, add *Either the lion or*.]
9. The movie screen is hard to see. [At the beginning of the sentence, add *The captions on*.]
10. A day in the library is all the time I will need to finish my research. [Change *A day* to *Two days*.]

PICTURE THIS

You and two other aspiring comedians have volunteered to perform a clown skit at the local children's hospital. The skit will be part of a comedy show sponsored by a local volunteer group. To spark some ideas for your skit, you and your friends went to the circus to watch this professional clown troupe. Plan a funny skit that you and your friends could perform. Then write a letter proposing the skit to the director of the show. Tell what happens in the skit and what props are required. Also describe any audience participation that you think will make the show more fun for the children. In your description, use each of the following words at least once as the antecedent of a pronoun: *each*, *either*, *all*, *one*, and *somebody*. Be sure to proofread your writing for agreement of pronouns and antecedents.

Subject: a clown skit
Audience: the director of the the comedy show
Purpose: to inform; to persuade

Review: Posttest

A. Proofreading Sentences for Subject-Verb and Pronoun-Antecedent Agreement

Most of the following sentences contain errors in agreement. If a sentence contains an error, supply the correct form of the verb or pronoun. If a sentence is correct, write *C*.

USAGE

1. One of the South's most precious ecological treasures are the flatlands and estuary of Galveston Bay.
2. In September, the new teacher was delighted because the class were enthusiastic and cooperative.
3. One junior, as well as four seniors, have been invited to attend the Milford Youth Council next month.
4. The number of investors in companies that manufacture robots is increasing.
5. Twenty miles are quite far for someone to walk without stopping and resting.
6. Neither Charlotte nor Tyrone answered their telephone yesterday.
7. Anyone earning such a small salary will have difficulty paying their bills.
8. You may be surprised to know that many a city dweller grows vegetables in a backyard garden.
9. A completed application, in addition to a full financial statement, are required of all students seeking college scholarships.
10. Every file cabinet, bookcase, and desk drawer have been stuffed with books and papers.
11. Doesn't the boys get bonuses for their work?
12. Where there's people and excitement, you're sure to find Kazuo and Yori.
13. Public relations and advertising is exciting but frequently stressful work.
14. Do you know whether the Lesser Antilles are nearer to Puerto Rico or to Cuba?
15. Did you know that the city of Savannah, Georgia, has their own spectacular parade on Saint Patrick's Day?

B. Correcting Errors in Subject-Verb and Pronoun-Antecedent Agreement

Most of the sentences in the following paragraph contain errors in agreement. If a verb or pronoun is incorrect, give the correct form. If a sentence is correct, write *C*.

[16] There's a number of people and programs making life safer for endangered and threatened animals. **[17]** For example, many a preservation effort have been directed at saving eagles. **[18]** What, you may ask, is the biggest threats to eagles? **[19]** Most of the danger comes from hunters and expanding civilization. **[20]** Fortunately, eagles is one of the world's most admired animals. **[21]** As a result, many governments have passed laws to protect eagles and their habitats. **[22]** The United States, for example, have created sanctuaries for bald eagles and golden eagles. **[23]** The Philippine eagle, which are the rarest of these magnificent birds, receives special protection on the Philippine island of Mindanao. **[24]** Ethiopia, as well as some other countries, has planted trees for their eagles to use as nesting places. **[25]** Anybody who wants to know more about these and other preservation programs for eagles should consult their local library or conservation club.

22 Correct Pronoun Usage

Case Forms of Pronouns; Special Problems

Diagnostic Test

A. Selecting Correct Forms of Pronouns

For each of the following sentences, choose the correct pronoun form in parentheses.

EXAMPLE **1. José and (*her, she*) completed the math test first.**
1. *she*

1. Greg and (*I, myself*) both got our driver's licenses on the same day.
2. My Uncle Bill, (*who, whom*) I greatly admire, worked in the Peace Corps for two years after he had finished college.
3. As we waited at the starting line, I knew in my heart that the race was really going to be between Ted and (*I, me*).
4. At the town meeting, Ellen McCarthy asked, "If (*we, us*) citizens don't vote, how can we expect the situation to change?"

5. I thought Manuel was in Kansas City; so when he walked into the restaurant, I could hardly believe it was (*he, him*).
6. Even though we are twins, Janice has always been taller than (*I, me*).
7. Does anyone in this group know (*who, whom*) was using the computer after school yesterday?
8. Sometimes my parents have a low tolerance for (*me, my*) playing rock music, even though I play it in my room with the door closed.
9. "Does anyone dance better than (*she, her*)?" I wondered, as I watched Twyla Tharpe on the stage.
10. (*Who, Whom*) can describe the different shapes of Navajo hogans?

B. Proofreading a Paragraph for Correct Pronoun Usage

Most of the sentences in the following paragraph contain an error in pronoun usage. Identify each error, and then give the correct pronoun form. If a sentence is correct, write *C*.

[11] Jim Henson's gifts to all of we puppet fans were some of the most beloved characters in show business—Kermit the Frog, Miss Piggy, and the Cookie Monster, to name a few. **[12]** You probably know that Henson was the puppeteer who created the Muppets. **[13]** In the history of television, few puppeteers have been as successful as him. **[14]** Henson's associate Frank Oz and himself operated many of the Muppets. **[15]** Whom do you think spoke for Kermit on *Sesame Street* and *The Muppet Show* and in such movies as *The Muppets Take Manhattan?* **[16]** As you may have guessed, us Kermit fans were listening to Henson's voice. **[17]** Kermit and him started performing together in 1956 when Henson introduced his frog to the audience of the late-night TV show *Sam and Friends* in Washington, D.C. **[18]** Henson, whom originally fashioned Kermit out of an old coat and a split Ping-Pong ball, revolutionized puppetry. **[19]** Henson's ability to give each of his puppets a life of its own earned himself international renown and many awards. **[20]** When Henson died in 1990, people throughout the world mourned his passing.

Case

Case is the form that a noun or a pronoun takes to indicate its use in a sentence. In English, there are three cases: *nominative, objective,* and *possessive.*

The form of a noun is the same for both the nominative case and the objective case. For example, a noun used as a subject (nominative case) will have the same form if used as an object (objective case).

NOMINATIVE CASE The **ghost** of Banquo suddenly appeared. [subject]
OBJECTIVE CASE Only Macbeth saw the **ghost.** [direct object]

A noun changes its form for the possessive case, usually by adding an apostrophe and an *s.*

POSSESSIVE CASE What effect did the **ghost's** appearance have on Macbeth?

REFERENCE NOTE: For more information about forming possessive nouns, see pages 944–947.

Case Forms of Personal Pronouns

Unlike nouns, most personal pronouns have three forms, one for each case. The form a pronoun takes depends on its function in a sentence.

NOMINATIVE CASE **We** enjoyed reading *Macbeth.* [subject]
OBJECTIVE CASE Some of **us** had seen a performance of the play on PBS. [object of the preposition *of*]
POSSESSIVE CASE **Our** next assignment is to read *Othello.*

Within each case, the forms of the personal pronouns indicate *number, person,* and *gender.* ***Number*** is the form of a word that indicates whether it is *singular* or *plural.* ***Person*** is the form a word takes to indicate the one(s) speaking (*first person*), the one(s) spoken to (*second person*), or the one(s) spoken of (*third person*). ***Gender*** is the form of the word that indicates whether it is *masculine, feminine,* or *neuter* (neither masculine nor feminine).

PERSONAL PRONOUNS			
SINGULAR			
	NOMINATIVE CASE	OBJECTIVE CASE	POSSESSIVE CASE
FIRST PERSON	I	me	my, mine
SECOND PERSON	you	you	your, yours
THIRD PERSON	he, she, it	him, her, it	his, her, hers, its
PLURAL			
	NOMINATIVE CASE	OBJECTIVE CASE	POSSESSIVE CASE
FIRST PERSON	we	us	our, ours
SECOND PERSON	you	you	your, yours
THIRD PERSON	they	them	their, theirs

Notice in the chart that *you* and *it* have the same forms for the nominative and the objective cases. All other personal pronouns have different forms for each case. Notice also that only the third-person singular pronouns indicate gender.

MOTHER GOOSE AND GRIMM by Mike Peters, reprinted by permission: Tribune Media Services.

The Nominative Case

The personal pronouns in the nominative case—*I, you, he, she, it, we, they*—are used as subjects of verbs and as predicate nominatives.

22a. The subject of a verb is in the nominative case.

EXAMPLES **They** are playing backgammon.
We think that **she** deserves the Most Valuable Player award.

A subject may be compound, with a pronoun appearing in combination with a noun or another pronoun. To help you choose the correct pronoun form in a compound subject, try each form as the simple subject of the verb.

CHOICES: Gloria and (*he, him*) built a scale model of the Temple of the Magician. [*He built* or *him built*?]
ANSWER: Gloria and **he** built a scale model of the Temple of the Magician.

CHOICES: (*She, Her*) and (*I, me*) made all of the Aztec costumes for the pageant. [*She made* or *her made*? *I made* or *me made*?]
ANSWER: **She** and **I** made all of the Aztec costumes for the pageant.

22b. A predicate nominative is in the nominative case.

A predicate nominative follows a linking verb and explains or identifies the subject of the verb.

A pronoun used as a predicate nominative always follows a form of the linking verb *be: am, is, are, was, were, be,* or *been.*

EXAMPLES The one that you should appoint chairperson is **she.** [*She* follows *is* and identifies the subject *one.*]
The first speaker will be **he.** [*He* follows *will be* and identifies the subject *speaker.*]

As you can see, the predicate nominative and the subject of the verb indicate the same individual(s). To help you choose the correct pronoun form to use as a predicate nominative, try each form as the subject of the verb.

CHOICES: The best clog dancers are (*they, them*). [*They are* or *them are* the best clog dancers?]
ANSWER: The best clog dancers are **they.**

CHOICES: The composer of the sonata is (*she, her*). [*She is* or *her is* the composer?]
ANSWER: The composer of the sonata is **she.**

Like a subject, a predicate nominative may be compound.

EXAMPLES **The only seniors who volunteered were Elia and I.** [*Elia* and *I* follow *were* and identify the subject *seniors.*]

The managers of the new Thai restaurant are she and he. [*She* and *he* follow *are* and identify the subject *managers.*]

NOTE: Expressions such as *It's me, This is her,* and *It was them* are examples of informal usage. Though acceptable in everyday situations, such expressions should be avoided in formal speaking and writing.

REFERENCE NOTE: For more about predicate nominatives, see page 642.

EXERCISE 1 Using Pronouns in the Nominative Case

For each of the following sentences, give a personal pronoun that can be substituted for the word or words in brackets.

EXAMPLES **1.** Carl and [*Sue Ann*] are always happy.
1. *she*
2. Terri and [*first person singular*] were at the picnic.
2. *I*

1. Jorge and [*Mike*] are tied for third place.
2. [*Donna*] and her parents have moved to San Antonio.
3. [*First person plural*] will take the exam on Friday.
4. Can it be [*some choir members*] in that picture?
5. Either Ellen or [*Sally*] will be in charge.
6. The team and [*Mr. Knight*] have chartered a bus.
7. [*First person plural*] earned our trophies.
8. Neither [*Carolyn*] nor Michele has change for the bus.
9. Did you know that Greg and [*first person singular*] are leaving?
10. I am sure it was [*Ed*] and you on the dance floor.

The Objective Case

The personal pronouns in the objective case—*me, you, him, her, it, us, them*—are used as objects of verbs and as objects of prepositions.

22c. An object of a verb is in the objective case.

The object of a verb may be a *direct object* or an *indirect object*. A ***direct object*** follows a transitive verb and tells *whom* or *what* receives the action of the verb.

EXAMPLES Carmen has invited **me** to the fiesta. [*Me* tells *whom* Carmen has invited.]
The kittens were asleep until the sudden noise woke **them.** [*Them* tells *what* the noise woke.]

An ***indirect object*** comes between a transitive verb and a direct object and tells *to whom or what* or *for whom or what* the action of the verb is performed.

EXAMPLES His uncle brought **him** a poncho from Mexico. [*Him* tells *to whom* his uncle brought a poncho.]
Because the engine was running rough, Uncle Theo gave **it** a tune-up. [*It* tells *to what* Uncle Theo gave a tune-up.]

USAGE

An object of a verb may be compound. To help you choose the correct pronoun form in a compound object, read the sentence, using each form as a single object.

CHOICES: Mr. Osaka gave Karl and (*she, her*) the job. [*Mr. Osaka gave she* or *gave her*?]
ANSWER: Mr. Osaka gave Karl and **her** the job.

CHOICES: Celia showed (*he, him*) and (*I, me*) photographs of her vacation in Hawaii. [*Celia showed he* or *showed him*? *Celia showed I* or *showed me*?]
ANSWER: Celia showed **him** and **me** photographs of her vacation in Hawaii.

REFERENCE NOTE: For more information about objects of verbs, see page 639.

EXERCISE 2 **Using Pronouns in the Objective Case**

For each of the following sentences, give a personal pronoun that can be substituted for the word or words in brackets.

EXAMPLES **1.** I helped [*Rod*] and her with their projects.
1. *him*
2. Sonia and Molly sent [*first person singular*] a get-well card.
2. *me*

1. Did you tell the superintendent or [*Ms. Marshall*]?
2. [*Carla*] and [*Dave*] I would never doubt.
3. Leave [*first person plural*] alone for a while.
4. Carmen will be inviting both you and [*first person singular*] to the recital.
5. Did you see Lois or [*Andy*] today?
6. I sent the admissions director and [*her assistant*] a letter.
7. The coach chose Joan and [*Michelle and me*].
8. The principal should have notified [*Sven*] and Gail.
9. Ron just passed Tina and [*first person singular*] in the hall.
10. Please don't ask [*the athletes*] about today's game.

REVIEW A Selecting Correct Forms of Personal Pronouns

For each of the following sentences, choose the correct pronoun form in parentheses.

EXAMPLE 1. Paulo and (*her, she*) are my lab partners.
1. *she*

1. The guests thanked Rita and (*she, her*).
2. Gloria and (*I, me*) are giving a report on the relationship between the Shoshone people and the Mormon settlers in the 1800s.
3. That's (*he, him*) standing on the corner.
4. (*We, Us*) are learning about Hendrick Arnold, a scout who helped Texas win independence from Mexico.
5. What were you telling Chuck and (*we, us*) earlier?
6. Of course, I remember Monica and (*she, her*).
7. We knew the first guests to arrive would be (*they, them*).
8. Give (*we, us*) the message as soon as possible.
9. Jana and (*she, her*) are active members.
10. It's either you or (*he, him*) in the runoff.

REVIEW B Proofreading a Paragraph for Correct Pronoun Usage

Most sentences in the following paragraph contain errors in pronoun usage. Identify each error, and then give the correct pronoun form. If a sentence is correct, write *C*.

[1] At the start of track season, our coach told Sarah and I the story of famous sprinter Evelyn Ashford. [2] During high

school, Ashford had started running races against the boys at lunchtime, and eventually she beat they. [3] Later, champion coach Pat Connolly recognized the young runner as a great talent when she saw Ashford race at the University of California at Los Angeles in 1976. [4] In 1983 and 1984, Ashford set records in the women's 100-meter event, and her became the fastest woman in the world. [5] Our coach said that Ashford's speed—10.76 seconds for the 100-meter dash in 1984—amazed even he. [6] At the 1988 Olympic games Ashford hoped that she could better her record time. [7] The other competitors knew that the runner to beat that year was her. [8] Ashford's talent, hard work, and determination earned she a gold and a silver medal, but set no new records, at those games. [9] The athlete in this picture is her carrying the flag for the American team at the 1988 Olympics. [10] Don't you think she looks like a winner?

22d. **The object of a preposition is in the objective case.**

An ***object of a preposition*** comes at the end of a phrase that begins with a preposition.

EXAMPLES for **me** after **her** next to **them**
with **us** beside **him** between **you** and **me**

REFERENCE NOTE: For lists of prepositions, see pages 619–620.

An object of a preposition may be compound, such as in the phrase *between you and me.* To help you determine the pronoun form to use, read each form separately with the preposition.

CHOICES: Dwayne sat behind Norman and (*I, me*) at the jazz concert. [*Behind I* or *behind me*?]

ANSWER: Dwayne sat behind Norman and **me** at the jazz concert.

CHOICES: **Give the extra tickets to (*he, him*) and (*she, her*).** [*To he* or *to him*? *To she* or *to her*?]

ANSWER: **Give the extra tickets to him and her.**

EXERCISE 3 Selecting Pronouns as Objects of Prepositions

For each of the following sentences, choose the correct pronoun form in parentheses.

EXAMPLE **1. This letter is addressed to you and (*I, me*).**
1. *me*

1. The chess team sent a challenge to Don and (*he, him*).
2. The slide show was presented by my sister and (*I, me*).
3. We are planning to leave with (*they, them*) and Alice.
4. I dedicated my poem to both Marcia and (*she, her*).
5. Frank arrived right after Juanita and (*I, me*).
6. The responsibility has fallen upon (*we, us*).
7. Were you sitting near Tony and (*she, her*)?
8. The matter is strictly between Ms. James and (*they, them*).
9. Consuelo has been asking about you and (*she, her*).
10. Would you draw a cartoon for the girls and (*we, us*)?

REVIEW C Selecting Correct Forms of Personal Pronouns

For each of the following sentences, choose the correct pronoun form in parentheses. Then identify its use in the sentence—*subject of a verb, predicate nominative, direct object, indirect object,* or *object of a preposition.*

EXAMPLE **1. Leave the pamphlets with Kim and (*he, him*).**
1. *him—object of a preposition*

1. The coach chose Darrell and (*he, him*).
2. Luckily, the Smiths and (*we, us*) got tickets to Kathleen Battle's concert.
3. I haven't heard from Mark and (*she, her*) in ages.
4. It could be (*they, them*) across the street.
5. Ms. Grant, the Dodges, and (*she, her*) went to the Palos Verdes Peninsula for the day.
6. The mayor granted (*they, them*) an interview.
7. (*She, Her*) and Heather always sit in the last row.

8. Would you please stop bothering Simon and (*I, me*)?
9. Adele painted a picture for (*they, them*) and (*we, us*).
10. Jim Bob visited (*she, her*) and (*I, me*) in the hospital.

REVIEW D Proofreading a Paragraph for Correct Pronoun Usage

Most of the sentences in the following paragraph contain errors in pronoun usage. Identify each error, and then give the correct pronoun form. If a sentence is correct, write *C*.

[1] Looking through an old history book, Larry and me found this fascinating picture of four famous men. [2] Do you recognize any of they? [3] Of course, most of we are familiar with Thomas Edison and his inventions. [4] The man standing on the left is him. [5] Beside him on the old mill wheel are John Burroughs, Henry Ford, and Harvey Firestone. [6] Burroughs was an American naturalist and author; such books as *Birds and Poets* and *Field and Study* were written by he. [7] Ford, as you probably know, gave us the Model T in 1908 and helped usher in the age of the automobile. [8] Standing next to he is Firestone, who was head of the world's largest rubber company. [9] It surprised Larry and I to see these four noted Americans together. [10] Wouldn't it have been great to meet and talk with they at the old mill?

The Possessive Case

The personal pronouns in the possessive case—*my, mine, your, yours, his, her, hers, its, our, ours, their, theirs*—are used to show ownership or relationship.

22e. The possessive pronouns *mine, yours, his, hers, its, ours,* and *theirs* are used in the same ways that the pronouns in the nominative and objective cases are.

SUBJECT OF VERB	**Mine** has a flat tire.
PREDICATE NOMINATIVE	This floppy disk is **hers.**
OBJECT OF VERB	We haven't received **ours** yet.
OBJECT OF PREPOSITION	My mother wants to talk to **yours.**

22f. The possessive pronouns *my, your, his, her, its, our,* and *their* are used as adjectives before nouns.

EXAMPLES The subject of **my** report is the Inuit of Canada.
Her first novel was published in 1960.
Do you have **their** telephone number?

22g. A noun or a pronoun preceding a gerund is in the possessive case.

A ***gerund*** is a verb form that ends in *–ing* and functions as a noun.

EXAMPLES John objected to his **sister's** using his new computer. [*Sister's,* not *sister,* is used because John objected to the using, not to his sister.]
Their winning the Stanley Cup surprised us ice hockey fans. [*Their,* instead of *them* or *they,* is used because the winning, not they, surprised us.]

Do not confuse a gerund with a present participle, which also ends in *–ing.* A gerund serves as a noun, whereas a present participle serves as an adjective. A noun or a pronoun before a present participle is not in the possessive case.

EXAMPLES Suddenly, her Chihuahua started chasing a **boy** riding on a skateboard. [*Riding* is a participle that modifies the noun *boy.*]
We heard **them** talking in the hallway. [*Talking* is a participle that modifies the pronoun *them.*]

The form of a noun or a pronoun before an *–ing* word often depends on the meaning you want to express. If you want to emphasize the *–ing* word, use the possessive form. If you want to emphasize the noun or pronoun preceding the *–ing* word, avoid the possessive form. Notice the difference in meaning between the following sentences.

EXAMPLES Can you imagine **Dena's** riding a camel and **my** riding an elephant? [emphasis on *riding*]
Can you imagine **Dena** riding a camel and **me** riding an elephant? [emphasis on *Dena* and *me*]

REFERENCE NOTE: For more information about gerunds and present participles, see pages 657 and 660.

USAGE

EXERCISE 4 Using Possessive Pronouns

Complete each of the following sentences with an appropriate possessive pronoun. Do not use the same pronoun twice.

1. I admire the work of Edmonia Lewis; ____ sculptures of famous people are outstanding.
2. His car looks great, but ____ is in better running condition.
3. Nathan is a dedicated student, but ____ winning the science contest was a surprise.
4. If you let me, I'd like to borrow ____.
5. ____ rescuing the kitten certainly was a humane act.

WRITING APPLICATION

Using Possessive Pronouns with Gerunds

Most of the time, you probably can read a sentence aloud and "hear" which pronoun form is correct to use. Sometimes, though, you may need to examine the sentence more closely. Be especially careful with pronouns preceding an *–ing* word. Use the possessive case before a gerund and the objective case before a participle.

EXAMPLES I saw him studying for his American government exam this morning. [The sentence emphasizes *him,* not the studying. *Studying* is a participle modifying *him.*]

Emma teased Larry about his studying for exams at the last possible minute. [The sentence emphasizes the act of studying. The possessive pronoun *his* modifies the gerund *studying.*]

WRITING ACTIVITY

Exam week is approaching fast, and soon everyone will be busy studying for finals. To help students cope with test anxiety, the editor of your school's newspaper has decided to devote an entire issue to that subject. Write an article to submit for publication in the paper. In your article, present some helpful tips for students studying for exams. Your article may be humorous or serious. Use at least two pronouns preceding gerunds and three pronouns preceding participles. Be sure to check your writing for correct pronoun usage.

Prewriting Brainstorm a list of strategies that have helped you stay calm and collected through exams. If you wish, poll a number of other students about their "survival" strategies. From your notes, choose several of the most practical suggestions. Next, decide how you will present the information. You may want to give straightforward lists of "do's" and "don'ts" preceded by a brief introduction. Or you may want to tell a humorous story about an imaginary student preparing for exams. Whatever approach you use, be sure to organize your information in a rough outline.

Writing Refer to your prewriting notes and outline as you write your first draft. Begin with a lively, attention-grabbing opener. Remember: You want to inform as well as to entertain the reader. Even if you take a lighthearted tone, be sure to present some helpful information.

Evaluating and Revising Ask a friend or classmate to read your article. Is it helpful and interesting? Does it address the concerns of students preparing for exams? If not, add, cut, and revise details. Be sure you've used at least two gerunds and three participles preceded by pronouns.

Proofreading and Publishing Read through your article once, checking for errors in pronoun usage. Then proofread for other errors in grammar, usage, punctuation, and spelling. To publish your articles, you and your classmates may want to create a bulletin-board display for your classroom or for a widely trafficked area in your school.

USAGE

Special Pronoun Problems

Appositives

An ***appositive*** is a noun or a pronoun placed next to another noun or pronoun to explain or identify it.

22h. An appositive is in the same case as the word to which it refers.

EXAMPLES Both teachers, **Mr. Petrakis** and **she,** have agreed to coach the academic team. [*Mr. Petrakis* and *she* are in apposition with the subject *teachers.* Since a subject is always in the nominative case, an appositive to the subject is also in the nominative case.]

For two of the major roles in *Purlie Victorious,* the director chose us, **Joel** and **me.** [*Joel* and *me* are in apposition with the direct object *us.* Since *us* is in the objective case, an appositive to *us* is also in the objective case.]

To help you choose which pronoun form to use in a compound appositive, try each form in the position of the word it refers to.

CHOICES: Two seniors, Theo and (*she, her*), gave the speeches. [The appositive refers to *seniors,* the subject of the verb *gave. She gave* or *her gave*?]

ANSWER: Two seniors, Theo and **she,** gave the speeches.

CHOICES: The speeches were given by two seniors, Theo and (*she, her*). [The appositive refers to *seniors,* the object of the preposition *by. Were given by she* or *by her*?]

ANSWER: The speeches were given by two seniors, Theo and **her.**

Sometimes the pronoun *we* or *us* is followed by a noun appositive. To determine which pronoun form to use, try each form without the noun appositive.

CHOICES: (*We, Us*) senior citizens are in charge of the paper drive. [*We are in charge* or *us are in charge*?]
ANSWER: **We** senior citizens are in charge of the paper drive.

CHOICES: Coach Shapiro talked to (*we, us*) players about sportsmanship. [*Coach Shapiro talked to we* or *talked to us*?]
ANSWER: Coach Shapiro talked to **us** players about sportsmanship.

REFERENCE NOTE: For more about appositives, see page 666.

EXERCISE 5 **Selecting Pronouns to Use as Appositives**

For each of the following sentences, choose the correct pronoun form in parentheses.

1. The bus driver greeted (*we, us*) students with a smile.
2. Owen said that for the first time the basketball team had elected co-captains, Mario and (*he, him*).
3. Two students, Angela and (*she, her*), toured the Frederick Douglass National Historic Site in Washington, D.C.
4. Should (*we, us*) members of the fitness club sponsor the walk-a-thon?
5. The new mural in the cafeteria was painted by two seniors, Chad and (*he, him*).

Elliptical Constructions

An ***elliptical construction*** is a clause from which words have been omitted. The word *than* or *as* often begins an elliptical construction.

22i. A pronoun following *than* or *as* in an elliptical construction is in the same case as it would be if the construction were completed.

ELLIPTICAL The tenor sang louder **than he.**
COMPLETED The tenor sang louder **than he sang.**

ELLIPTICAL The accident hurt Tim as much **as her.**
COMPLETED The accident hurt Tim as much **as the accident hurt her.**

Be sure to use the pronoun case form that expresses the meaning you intend. Notice how the meaning of each of the following sentences depends on the form of the pronoun in the elliptical construction.

EXAMPLES **I think I helped Macaulay more than she.** [I think I helped Macaulay more *than she helped Macaulay.*]
I think I helped Macaulay more than her. [I think I helped Macaulay more *than I helped her.*]

EXERCISE 6 Selecting Pronouns for Elliptical Constructions

For each of the following sentences, add words to the elliptical clause to make its meaning clear. Include in the clause the correct pronoun form. [Note: In several sentences, either pronoun form may be correct, depending on how the elliptical clause is completed. Give both correct forms.]

EXAMPLE **1. I don't know Brenda as well as (*she, her*).**
1. *as well as she knows Brenda*
or
as well as I know her

1. Have you and the rest of your family lived in this area as long as (*they, them*)?
2. Nolan has worked longer than (*he, him*).
3. Eva is shorter than (*I, me*).
4. The senior class scored higher than (*they, them*).
5. The field trip next week will probably benefit Roger more than (*I, me*).
6. Is she six months older than (*I, me*)?
7. The results show that I do better on essay tests than (*he, him*).
8. Do they play handball as often as (*we, us*)?
9. I understand him better than (*she, her*).
10. Can Ms. Edwards tutor Paula as well as (*I, me*)?

Reflexive and Intensive Pronouns

Reflexive and intensive pronouns (sometimes called *compound personal pronouns*) have the same forms.

REFLEXIVE AND INTENSIVE PRONOUNS		
	SINGULAR	PLURAL
FIRST PERSON	myself	ourselves
SECOND PERSON	yourself	yourselves
THIRD PERSON	himself herself itself	themselves

A ***reflexive pronoun*** refers to another word that indicates the same individual(s).

EXAMPLES I hurt **myself.** [*Myself* refers to *I.*]
Clarice and Jane should be proud of **themselves.** [*Themselves* refers to *Clarice and Jane.*]

An ***intensive pronoun*** emphasizes another word that indicates the same individual(s).

EXAMPLES Simon **himself** developed both rolls of film. [*Himself* emphasizes *Simon.*]
Jorge and Kim installed the tape player in the car **themselves.** [*Themselves* emphasizes *Jorge* and *Kim.*]

NOTE: Unlike a reflexive pronoun, an intensive pronoun may be omitted from a sentence without a significant change in meaning.

EXAMPLE Tamisha herself washed and waxed the car.
Tamisha washed and waxed the car.

REFERENCE NOTE: The words *hisself* and *theirselves* are nonstandard usage. See page 854.

22j. A pronoun ending in *–self* or *–selves* should not be used in place of a simple personal pronoun.

Avoid using a pronoun ending in *–self* or *–selves* when there is no word that it can refer to or emphasize.

NONSTANDARD Mariah and myself went to the rodeo.
STANDARD Mariah and **I** went to the rodeo.

NONSTANDARD I know I can depend on Katrina and yourself.
STANDARD I know I can depend on Katrina and **you.**

EXERCISE 7 **Using Reflexive, Intensive, and Personal Pronouns**

Complete each of the following sentences with an appropriate pronoun. Label each pronoun you use as *reflexive, intensive,* or *personal.*

1. Will the principal ____ preside at the academic awards ceremony?
2. After the test I will wait for Linda and ____.
3. I bought ____ a Scottish kilt at the import store.
4. Mark and Ginger should be ashamed of ____ for forgetting your birthday.
5. Evelyn and ____ raked the leaves in the front yard.

USAGE

Who and *Whom*

Like most personal pronouns, the pronoun *who* (*whoever*) has three case forms.

NOMINATIVE	who	whoever
OBJECTIVE	whom	whomever
POSSESSIVE	whose	whosever

These pronouns may be used in two ways: to form questions and to introduce subordinate clauses. When they are used to form questions, they are called ***interrogative pronouns.*** When they are used to introduce subordinate clauses, they are called ***relative pronouns.***

22k. The form an interrogative pronoun takes depends on its use in the question.

Who is used as a subject of a verb or as a predicate nominative. *Whom* is used as an object of a verb or as an object of a preposition.

NOMINATIVE **Who** plays the part of Peter Pan in the film *Hook*? [*Who* is the subject of the verb *plays.*]
Who could it be? [*Who* is the predicate nominative identifying the subject *it.*]

OBJECTIVE **Whom** did Ella choose? [*Whom* is the direct object of the verb *did choose.*]
With **whom** did Aaron Neville sing the ballad? [*Whom* is the object of the preposition *with.*]

NOTE: In informal situations, *who* is often used in place of *whom* as an interrogative pronoun. In formal speaking and writing, however, the distinction between *who* and *whom* should be observed.

INFORMAL **Who** did you call?
FORMAL **Whom** did you call? [direct object]

INFORMAL **Who** is he baking the pita bread for?
FORMAL For **whom** is he baking the pita bread? [object of a preposition]

22l. The form a relative pronoun takes depends on its use in the subordinate clause.

When choosing between *who* and *whom* in a subordinate clause, follow these steps:

CHOICES: Nadine Gordimer, (*who, whom*) is famous for writing novels and short stories set in South Africa, won the Nobel Prize for literature in 1991.

STEP 1: Find the subordinate clause. In the sentence above, the subordinate clause is *(who, whom) is famous for writing novels and short stories set in South Africa.*

STEP 2: Decide how the relative pronoun is used in the clause—*subject, predicate nominative, object of the verb,* or *object of a preposition.* In the example sentence the relative pronoun serves as the subject of the verb *is.*

STEP 3: Determine the case for this use of the relative pronoun. A subject of a verb is in the nominative case.

STEP 4: Select the correct form of the relative pronoun. The nominative form of the relative pronoun is *who.*

ANSWER: Nadine Gordimer, **who** is famous for writing novels and short stories set in South Africa, won the Nobel Prize for literature in 1991.

CHOICES: Harry Houdini, (*who, whom*) audiences adored, performed daring escape tricks.

STEP 1: The subordinate clause is *(who, whom) audiences adored.*

STEP 2: The relative pronoun serves as the direct object of the verb *adored.*

STEP 3: A direct object is in the objective case.

STEP 4: The objective form of the relative pronoun is *whom.*

ANSWER: Harry Houdini, **whom** audiences adored, performed daring escape tricks.

Remember that the case of a relative pronoun is not affected by any word outside the subordinate clause.

CHOICES: A plaque will be given to (*whoever, whomever*) catches the most fish.

STEP 1: The subordinate clause is *(whoever, whomever) catches the most fish.*

STEP 2: The relative pronoun serves as the subject of the verb *catches,* not as object of the preposition *to.* The entire subordinate clause is the object of *to.*

STEP 3: A subject of a verb is in the nominative case.

STEP 4: The nominative form of the relative pronoun is *whoever.*

ANSWER: A plaque will be given to **whoever** catches the most fish.

REFERENCE NOTE: For more about subordinate clauses, see pages 675–683.

When choosing between *who* and *whom* to begin a question or a subordinate clause, do not be misled by a parenthetical expression consisting of a subject and a verb, such as *I think, he feels,* or *they believe.* Select the pronoun form you would use if the parenthetical expression were not in the sentence.

EXAMPLES **Who** do you suppose will win the election? [*Who* is the subject of the verb *will win.*]

Roberta is the student **who** Mr. Hines thinks should be a chemist. [*Who* is the subject of the verb *should be.*]

REFERENCE NOTE: For more information about parenthetical expressions, see pages 914–915.

EXERCISE 8 Using *Who* and *Whom* Correctly

For each of the following sentences, choose the correct pronoun form in parentheses. Then identify its use in the subordinate clause—*subject, predicate nominative, object of a verb,* or *object of a preposition.*

EXAMPLE 1. Can you tell me (*who, whom*) wrote *Bury My Heart at Wounded Knee*?

1. *who—subject*

1. The two people (*who, whom*) I like most are Will and Rosa.
2. Someone called, but I don't know (*who, whom*) she was.
3. With (*who, whom*) do you intend to go to the play?
4. Several of the women (*who, whom*) had served on other committees were considered for the position.

USAGE

5. (*Who, Whom*) did the scholarship committee choose?
6. Allen is the only person in school (*who, whom*), I believe, has lived in a foreign country.
7. I never found out (*who, whom*) the driver was.
8. It does not matter (*who, whom*) wins, as long as you do your best.
9. I found the person to (*who, whom*) this package belongs.
10. Ralph Bunche was a man (*who, whom*) many people respected for helping to found the United Nations.

PICTURE THIS

These behind-the-scenes volunteers worked hard to make the senior-class dance a success. As chair of the Dance Committee, you were responsible for recruiting the volunteers and organizing their efforts. Now, you'd like to thank the volunteers for their help. Write an open letter to your school's newspaper. In your letter, name each volunteer and explain the role he or she played in the preparations. Use the pronouns *who* and *whom* at least twice each in subordinate clauses and use *who* or *whom* in a question.

Subject: senior-class dance
Audience: readers of the school newspaper
Purpose: to inform; to express your thanks

REVIEW E Proofreading Sentences for Correct Pronoun Usage

Each of the following sentences contains an error in pronoun usage. Identify the error, and then give the correct pronoun form, according to the rules of formal standard usage.

1. Do you know who they gave the money to?
2. "We sprinters are better than the ones on Central High's team," Phillip said. "So why aren't we doing better than them?"
3. Oscar, whom I believe is the most adventurous member of our family, is backpacking in the Appalachians.
4. When Anna and I were young, us children loved to ride on the tractor with my father.
5. John and myself wish we could excel in both baseball and football like Bo Jackson.
6. Who did the teacher choose to give the first speech?
7. When Andrew and I study together, nobody else in our class does better than us.
8. Kyle was here looking for Josh and yourself.
9. When we heard that Ms. Cohen was going to retire, all three of we seniors felt sad.
10. The two people who you can always rely on are Dave and she.

REVIEW F Proofreading a Paragraph for Correct Pronoun Usage

Each sentence in the following paragraph contains an error in pronoun usage. Identify each error, and then give the correct pronoun form.

[1] Satoshi Yabuuchi is a modern Japanese sculptor whom works with wood. [2] Critics generally agree that few sculptors today are as inventive as him. [3] For example, look at the works by he on the following page. [4] Them are children's heads representing the seven days of the week. [5] Working with simple tools, Yabuuchi created they out of cypress. [6] Who do you know that could resist these engaging faces? [7] As you can see, Yabuuchi's imagination and sense of humor are important to himself. [8] Other modern Japanese wood sculptors and him use techniques that date back more than 1,500 years. [9] Yabuuchi, whom was born in 1953, first studied European

art but then became interested in wood carving and sculpture. [10] A number of works by himself also incorporate elements of American pop art.

Satoshi Yabuuchi/Courtesy of Gallery Kitano, Tokyo, Japan

Review: Posttest

A. Selecting Correct Forms of Pronouns

For each of the following sentences, choose the correct pronoun form in parentheses.

EXAMPLE **1.** After a pause, I heard Megan say into the phone, "Yes, this is (*she, her*)."
1. *she*

1. Last summer my friend Megan and (*I, me*) worked in a factory that produces microchips for computers.
2. Before we began, we made a pact that (*we, us*) teenagers would show the adults that we were responsible workers.

3. For the first two weeks, everything ran smoothly because our supervisor, Mr. Karas, was a person (*who, whom*) we thought was firm and just.
4. In fact, we were surprised by (*him, his*) showing interest in our progress and going out of his way to train us.
5. When Mr. Karas went on vacation, we doubted that his assistant, Ms. Sullivan, would be as firm as (*he, him*).
6. Our first mistake was in thinking that Mr. Karas and (*she, her*) would have different sets of standards.
7. We started giving (*us, ourselves*) ten extra minutes during our morning break a week after Ms. Sullivan took over.
8. One afternoon Ms. Sullivan walked up to us at our job stations and said, "Megan and Rick, until recently I had thought you were employees (*who, whom*) took pride in your work."
9. "If you're late again," she said calmly, "we, Mr. Karas and (*I, me*), will be looking for two new trainees for this station after he gets back."
10. The experience has really taught (*we, us*) some valuable lessons.
11. First, (*us, our*) deliberately taking extra time at the break was wrong.
12. Second, we had let Mr. Karas down because it was (*he, him*) who had hired us, trained us, and trusted us.
13. Third, we had mistakenly presumed that Ms. Sullivan wouldn't do her job as well as (*he, him*).
14. Fourth, we had let (*us, ourselves*) down by failing to do our best.
15. (*Who, Whom*) do you think were model employees the rest of the summer?

B. Proofreading a Paragraph for Correct Pronoun Usage

Most of the sentences in the following paragraph contain errors in pronoun usage. Identify each error, and then give the correct pronoun form. If a sentence is correct, write *C*.

[16] Do you know whom Tiberius Claudius Nero Germanicus was? **[17]** Such a long, elegant name certainly seems fitting for a Roman emperor, and that's exactly what he was. **[18]** Us modern readers and television watchers, as well as historians, know him simply as Claudius. **[19]** Robert Graves wrote about he in the popular novel *I, Claudius.* **[20]** Claudius, whom had a severe speech impediment, lived from 10 B.C. to A.D. 54. **[21]** Him becoming emperor in A.D. 41 troubled many Romans because they thought he was a fool and would be a weak ruler. **[22]** Claudius had not been an important government figure during the reigns of emperors Tiberius and Caligula, but he outlived both of they. **[23]** He was a more stable ruler than Caligula and accomplished more than him. **[24]** Claudius, who historians now generally praise, initiated many building programs, such as the huge Claudian Aqueduct. **[25]** In addition, many Roman civil and military accomplishments of the time are credited to himself.

USAGE

23 Clear Reference

Pronouns and Antecedents

Diagnostic Test

A. Revising Sentences to Correct Faulty Pronoun References

Revise each of the following sentences to correct ambiguous, general, weak, or indefinite pronoun references.

1. Dana is afraid of large dogs, but she doesn't let it show.
2. In Washington they have a subway system that is modern and efficient.
3. James saw Michael Jordan play basketball when he was ten years old.

4. My cousins showed a video of their trip to Puerto Rico, which made me want to go there.
5. In some classes you are given additional time to finish semester tests.
6. After the choir director asked Larry to sing the solo, he left the rehearsal room.
7. I think James Michener is a fine novelist; unfortunately, I don't own any of them.
8. In the program it describes the play as a lighthearted look at a serious subject.
9. The larger school won the geography competition at the convention, which didn't surprise us.
10. Beth wanted Laura to see the movie because she is a fan of Lou Diamond Phillips.

B. Revising Sentences to Correct Faulty Pronoun References

Revise the following sentences to correct each weak, general, ambiguous, or indefinite pronoun reference.

11. In the city library, they have a videotape about Martha Washington's early life and first marriage to a wealthy Virginia planter.
12. After Aaron Burr played matchmaker for Dolley Payne Todd and James Madison, she married Madison.
13. Abigail Adams is the only woman who was the wife of one president and mother of another, which is an interesting bit of First Lady trivia.
14. Julia Tyler supported her husband John Tyler's causes, especially the annexation of Texas, and that gave him strength.
15. In one book I read, it says that people accused Mary Todd Lincoln, who was from Kentucky, of opposing the Union, but she actually was a strong Unionist.
16. In addition to all of her social duties as First Lady, Edith Roosevelt, wife of Theodore Roosevelt, had to attend to her six children and the family's many pets, including cats, dogs, and snakes. It must have been a wild place.
17. Helen Taft was a determined woman who wanted her husband William Howard Taft to be president, and it paid off.

18. In the newspaper article it tells all about the "birthday calendar" that Mamie Eisenhower kept on her White House employees and about the presents and cakes she gave to them.
19. Jacqueline Kennedy helped her husband John Kennedy research and organize his book *Profiles in Courage.* This foreshadowed her later career as a book editor.
20. The comparison between Lady Bird Johnson and Eleanor Roosevelt is valid because she was an activist First Lady who visited 1960s War Against Poverty programs.

USAGE

One cause of ambiguity in writing is the use of pronouns without clear antecedents. A pronoun has no definite meaning in itself. Its meaning is clear only when the reader knows which word the pronoun refers to. This word is called the ***antecedent*** of the pronoun.

REFERENCE NOTE: For more information about pronouns and antecedents, see pages 602–605 and 718–720.

23a. A pronoun should refer clearly to its antecedent.

In the following examples, arrows point from the pronouns to their antecedents.

EXAMPLES Amy promised Brandon she would help him clean up the kitchen.

The Sánchezes have a new sailboat on which they intend to cruise to the Bahamas.

Handing Shina the novel, the librarian told her, "This won the Pulitzer Prize."

Often, an unclear pronoun reference is due to a lack of agreement between a pronoun and its antecedent.

UNCLEAR Eli is always thinking about computers. It seems to be his only interest.

CLEAR Eli is always thinking about computers. **They** seem to be his only interest.

REFERENCE NOTE: For more about agreement between pronouns and their antecedents, see pages 718–720.

Ambiguous Reference

23b. Avoid an ***ambiguous reference,*** which occurs when a pronoun can refer to either of two antecedents.

A simple way to correct some ambiguous pronoun references is to replace the pronoun with an appropriate noun.

AMBIGUOUS The partnership between Jones and Potter ended when he drew the firm's money from the bank and flew to Brazil. [To whom does *he* refer: *Jones* or *Potter*?]

CLEAR The partnership between Jones and Potter ended when Jones [*or* Potter] drew the firm's money from the bank and flew to Brazil.

If replacing the pronoun with a noun results in awkward repetition, rephrase the sentence to eliminate the ambiguous pronoun reference.

AMBIGUOUS The mayor appointed Ms. Vásquez chairperson of the committee because she was convinced of the need for an environmental study. [To whom does *she* refer: the *mayor* or *Ms. Vásquez*?]

CLEAR Convinced of the need for an environmental study, the mayor appointed Ms. Vásquez chairperson of the committee.

CLEAR Because Ms. Vásquez was convinced of the need for an environmental study, the mayor appointed her chairperson of the committee.

EXERCISE 1 Revising Sentences to Correct Ambiguous Pronoun References

Revise each of the following sentences to correct the ambiguous pronoun reference. [Note: A sentence may be correctly revised in more than one way.]

EXAMPLE **1.** As soon as Lucinda and Gwen arrived, we asked her to tell us about her trip to the Yukon.
1. *As soon as Lucinda and Gwen arrived, we asked Lucinda to tell us about her trip to the Yukon.*

1. Leta offered Molly a bowl of plantain porridge, which she thoroughly enjoyed.
2. One of the passengers told the bus driver that she didn't know the route very well.

3. Right after the accountant sent in a report to the treasurer, she became very much alarmed.
4. Raise the viewfinder to your eye, turning it slowly to the right until it is focused.
5. We removed the labels from the bottles and washed them.

General Reference

23c. Avoid a ***general reference,*** which occurs when a pronoun refers to a general idea rather than to a specific word or group of words.

USAGE

The pronouns commonly used in making general references are *it, that, this, such,* and *which.* To correct a general pronoun reference, either replace the pronoun with an appropriate noun or rephrase the sentence.

GENERAL Great ships were moving slowly up the harbor; tugs and ferryboats scurried in and out among them; here and there a white cabin cruiser sliced through the blue water under the suspension bridge. It was thrilling to a young farmer. [*It* has no specific antecedent.]

CLEAR The sight was thrilling to a young farmer.

GENERAL In her act Mariana told jokes, did impersonations, and sang comic songs. This amused her audience. [*This* has no specific antecedent.]

CLEAR Mariana amused her audience by telling jokes, doing impersonations, and singing comic songs.

EXERCISE 2 **Revising Sentences to Correct General Pronoun References**

Revise the following sentences to correct each general pronoun reference.

EXAMPLE
1. Carla was declared the winner of the debate, which didn't surprise me.
1. *That Carla was declared the winner of the debate didn't surprise me.*

1. In the 1800s, Spanish-language newspapers sprang up throughout the Southwest. This helped many Mexican Americans maintain ties to their culture.

2. Clarissa's four-year-old sister brought a frog inside and let it loose, which made Clarissa shriek.
3. I enjoyed the author's style and the type of characters she wrote about. It made me want to read her other books.
4. Rabbi Meyer came to the house daily, from which a sturdy friendship grew.
5. A great deal of effort went into planning that expedition, hiring the right people, and anticipating every emergency, which accounts for the success of the undertaking.

REVIEW A **Revising Ambiguous and General Pronoun References**

Revise the following sentences to correct each ambiguous or general pronoun reference.

1. Benito Pablo Juárez was a liberal reformer and president of Mexico during the 1860s and early 1870s, and he helped mold Mexico into a nation. That established Juárez as Mexico's foremost national hero.
2. Juárez, of Zapotec ancestry, was a serious, hard-working man, which is suggested in this photograph.
3. A professor who obviously had researched Juárez' life described his childhood in Oaxaca, his interest in law and social reforms, and his military successes. This kept the students' attention.
4. One of the students told the professor that he hoped he would write a biography of Juárez someday.
5. Juárez, a state governor in 1855, and General Santa Anna were on opposing sides, and he was exiled.
6. Juárez later returned to Mexico and joined the revolution to overthrow Santa Anna, who had seized control of the government. It was a brave and risky endeavor.

7. France installed Maximilian as emperor of Mexico in 1864, and Juárez moved his capital from Mexico City, but he was not popular.
8. Maximilian's government collapsed in 1867, which opened the way for Juárez to be reelected president.
9. Juárez was interested in education and helped to establish free public schools in Mexico. This, of course, had a major impact on Mexico's people.
10. José de la Cruz Porfirio Díaz overthrew Juárez' successor and governed Mexico longer than any other person. It was certainly a contrast to Juárez' government.

USAGE

Weak Reference

23d. Avoid a ***weak reference,*** which occurs when a pronoun refers to an antecedent that has not been expressed.

To correct a weak pronoun reference, either replace the pronoun with an appropriate noun or give the pronoun a clear antecedent.

WEAK The people want honest public servants, but many voters think that is not a virtue of any of the candidates. [The antecedent of *that* is not expressed.]

CLEAR The people want honest public servants, but many voters think that honesty is not a virtue of any of the candidates.

WEAK We spent the day on a fishing boat, but we didn't catch a single one. [The antecedent of *one* is not expressed.]

CLEAR We spent the day on a fishing boat, but we didn't catch a single fish.

CLEAR We spent the day on a fishing boat, trying to catch some fish, but we didn't catch a single one.

EXERCISE 3 Revising Sentences to Correct Weak Pronoun References

Revise each of the following sentences to correct the weak pronoun reference.

EXAMPLE **1.** We went to the card shop but didn't buy any.
1. *We went to the card shop but didn't buy any cards.*

1. I take many photographs with my camera and consider it an enjoyable hobby.
2. Being neighborly is important because you may need their help someday in an emergency.
3. Nguyen has become a virtuoso violinist, but he has never owned a valuable one.
4. Luisa is highly intelligent, but she hides it from people she doesn't know well.
5. Our guide said the Pueblo village was well worth seeing, but it would take three hours.

PICTURE THIS

What is it like to see the earth from space? to float free of gravity? to open a spacecraft hatch and gaze at the stars? You are one of the few people who know. A short while ago, you had your first mission in space. Now that you're back on earth, you're eager to answer everyone's questions. You've decided to write a letter describing some of the experiences you had on your mission. You'll send copies of the letter and of this picture of yourself in space to all your friends and relatives. In your letter, make sure that each pronoun you use clearly refers to its proper antecedent.

Subject: your first space mission
Audience: friends and relatives
Purpose: to inform; to express your thoughts and feelings

Indefinite Reference

23e. In formal writing, avoid the indefinite use of the personal pronouns *you, it,* and *they.*

An ***indefinite reference*** occurs when *you, it,* or *they* has no specific person or thing as its antecedent. To correct an indefinite reference, rephrase the sentence, eliminating the personal pronoun.

INDEFINITE In some countries, you don't dare express political views openly. [*You* does not refer to any specific person.]

CLEAR In some countries, people don't dare express their political views openly.

INDEFINITE In the magazine article, it describes the aftermath of the eruption of Mount Pinatubo. [*It* does not refer to any specific thing.]

CLEAR The magazine article describes the aftermath of the eruption of Mount Pinatubo.

INDEFINITE Each summer in Cherokee, North Carolina, they present the historical drama *Unto These Hills* outdoors.

CLEAR Each summer in Cherokee, North Carolina, the historical drama *Unto These Hills* is presented outdoors.

NOTE: The indefinite reference of *it* in expressions such as *it is raining, it seems,* and *it is late* is acceptable.

EXERCISE 4 **Revising Sentences to Correct Indefinite References**

Revise each of the following sentences to correct the indefinite references of personal pronouns.

1. In many households in India, they serve a flat, pancake-like bread called a *chapati.*
2. In large cities you often don't feel comfortable calling the mayor about problems.
3. In the newspaper article, it calls this presidential election the closest race in many years.

USAGE

4. Each summer in Round Top, Texas, they have an international music festival that is extremely popular.
5. In the telephone book, it lists only five music stores in the city.

REVIEW B

Revising Sentences to Correct Weak and Indefinite Pronoun References

Revise each sentence of the following paragraph to correct weak pronoun references and indefinite references of personal pronouns.

[1] Irish author Christy Brown (1932–1981) was extremely talented, but he had to overcome great physical challenges for it to be recognized. [2] In Brown's autobiography, *My Left Foot,* it tells about his lifelong struggle with cerebral palsy. [3] In some biographies, you don't become emotionally involved, but Brown's autobiography is very personal. [4] The public likes accurate film biographies, and that is a strong point of the movie *My Left Foot.* [5] In this scene from the movie, it shows actor Daniel Day-Lewis portraying Christy Brown. [6] In the movie, they show how Brown learned to write and type with his only functioning limb—his left foot. [7] Brown married in 1972 and her help contributed to Brown's improved muscular control. [8] Brown excelled as a writer, but it is sometimes difficult to locate them in libraries and bookstores in the United States. [9] Brown was acclaimed as a poet as well as a novelist, but I never read one. [10] In the card catalog it lists these books by Brown: *My Left Foot, Down All the Days, A Shadow on Summer,* and *Wild Grow the Lilies.*

Review: Posttest

A. Revising Sentences to Correct Faulty Pronoun References

The following sentences contain ambiguous, general, weak, and indefinite references of pronouns. Revise the sentences to correct each faulty pronoun reference.

EXAMPLE **1.** On this cruise, they serve meals without charge.
1. *On this cruise, meals are served without charge.*

1. Golf wouldn't cost me so much if I didn't lose so many in the rough.
2. The radiator was leaking badly; it ran all over the garage floor.
3. In the cabin he checked the fuel. In those days this might mean the difference between life and death.
4. She overcame her hip injury, which doctors had said was impossible.
5. Her spelling and sentence variety are not good, but most of it is due to carelessness.
6. Ruth saw Julie when she was in town last week.
7. In yesterday's editorial, it says that the mayor has failed to live up to his campaign promises.
8. The witness testified that she had seen the accused when she was eating dinner in the dining car, which convinced the jury that she had been on the train.
9. The library does not have enough copies of some of the books in greatest demand by students writing research papers, which makes it difficult to find the information you need.
10. In Washington they are skeptical about the success of the new farm program.

B. Revising Sentences to Correct Faulty Pronoun References

Revise the following sentences to correct each ambiguous, general, weak, or indefinite pronoun reference.

11. Scientist Carl Sagan has written and lectured extensively about the possibility of life on other planets, which has contributed to his appeal to the general public.

12. Johnny Carson liked Sagan's informal science lectures so much that he appeared many times on *The Tonight Show* after his first appearance in 1972.

13. Sagan came to be known as an expert in the study of extraterrestrial life, even though he has never seen one.

14. In Daniel Cohen's book *Carl Sagan: Superstar Scientist,* it tells about Sagan's childhood in Brooklyn and about his early fascination with the stars and planets.

15. As a boy, Sagan discovered the genre of science fiction, and he read them regularly.

16. At the University of Chicago, they had a highly regarded astronomy department, so Sagan enrolled there in 1951.

17. Sagan has been a consultant for many of NASA's major programs, including the *Mariner, Viking,* and *Voyager* planetary expeditions. This has resulted in such awards as the NASA Medal for Distinguished Public Service and the NASA Medal for Exceptional Scientific Achievement.

18. When my father saw Sagan on the popular television series *Cosmos,* he was greatly impressed.

19. Sagan's novel *Contact* explores a number of scientific and social issues that arise when extraterrestrial life makes contact with earthlings. Of course, this made me want to read some of his nonfiction books.

20. In this magazine, it says Sagan believes that the public's understanding of science is necessary for the good of the planet.

24 Correct Form and Use of Verbs

Principal Parts, Tense, Voice, Mood

Diagnostic Test

A. Choosing the Correct Verb Form

For each of the following sentences, choose the correct form of the verb in parentheses.

EXAMPLE **1.** In a hurry to go to work, I couldn't remember where I had (*laid, lain*) my keys.
1. *laid*

1. During the political rally, many of the balloons filled with helium (*burst, bursted*) as they rose from the ground.
2. Whenever Joan watches television, her Samoyed puppy (*lies, lays*) down at her feet.
3. If I (*was, were*) president, I would make world peace my first priority.
4. Mary Louise (*swam, swum*) the hundred-meter race in record time.

5. If I (*had, would have*) told the truth in the first place, the situation would have been much easier to handle.
6. (*Cooking, Having cooked*) a delicious Thanksgiving meal together, the newlyweds received many compliments from their guests.
7. The members of the second-place math team were upset because they (*hoped, had hoped*) to take first place.
8. Because we did not add the proper amount of yeast, the loaves of bread failed to (*raise, rise*).
9. The tree died after it (*was hit, had been hit*) by lightning.
10. The five riders are pleased (*to qualify, to have qualified*) for the equestrian team.
11. After I had (*wrote, written*) my autobiographical essay for my college application, I heaved a sigh of relief.
12. I wished that there (*was, were*) a good movie playing in town.
13. Because he had starred in four high school productions, David hoped (*to pursue, to have pursued*) an acting career.
14. (*Lie, Lay*) your work aside and relax for a few minutes.
15. In 1984, Joaquim Cruz, whose right leg is slightly shorter than his left leg, was overjoyed when he (*won, had won*) Brazil's first gold medal in the 800-meter run.

B. Revising Sentences by Correcting Verb Forms

Revise each sentence in the following paragraph by correcting any incorrect verb forms.

[16] For at least five thousand years, people been eating popcorn. **[17]** If you are like most of them, you probably falled in love with popcorn when you were a child. **[18]** The ancient Aztecs thought so highly of popcorn that they even use to wear it around their necks. **[19]** Centuries ago adult Native Americans probably would have been remembering popcorn as a source of delight and excitement in their childhoods. **[20]** After all, at that time popcorn was often simply throwed into a fire or roasted on a stick. **[21]** What a stir there must have been among the children when the kernels began to have popped clear of the fire! **[22]** Like children today, they probably would not be too bothered by the sand or dirt that the popcorn must have picked up. **[23]** Still, these early popcorn lovers were not plagued by duds, which can have broken your teeth and which had been the scourge of the popcorn industry until the 1950s. **[24]** That was when Orville Redenbacher and Charles Bowman successfully growed a variety of corn that just did not have very many duds. **[25]** When the big popcorn manufacturers rejected the new corn, Redenbacher started his own company, and as you probably know, he had experienced phenomenal success ever since.

Depending on their function, verbs may be classified as *action verbs* or *linking verbs* and as *main verbs* or *helping verbs*. For a discussion of these different kinds of verbs, see pages 612–614.

The Principal Parts of a Verb

24a. Every verb has four basic forms called its ***principal parts:*** the *infinitive,* the *present participle,* the *past,* and the *past participle.* All other verb forms are derived from these principal parts.

The following examples include *is* with the present participle and *have* with the past participle forms to indicate that helping verbs (forms of *be* and *have*) are used with those forms.

INFINITIVE	PRESENT PARTICIPLE	PAST	PAST PARTICIPLE
live	(is) living	lived	(have) lived
talk	(is) talking	talked	(have) talked
run	(is) running	ran	(have) run
rise	(is) rising	rose	(have) risen
hit	(is) hitting	hit	(have) hit

All verbs form the present participle in the same way: by adding *–ing* to the infinitive form. Not all verbs form the past and past participle in the same way, however. The way in which a verb forms the past and past participle determines whether it is classified as *regular* or *irregular*.

Regular Verbs

24b. A ***regular verb*** forms the past and past participle by adding *–d* or *–ed* to the infinitive form.

INFINITIVE	PRESENT PARTICIPLE	PAST	PAST PARTICIPLE
care	(is) caring	cared	(have) cared
remove	(is) removing	removed	(have) removed
suppose	(is) supposing	supposed	(have) supposed
match	(is) matching	matched	(have) matched
offer	(is) offering	offered	(have) offered
push	(is) pushing	pushed	(have) pushed

A few regular verbs have alternate past and past participle forms ending in *–t.*

INFINITIVE	PRESENT PARTICIPLE	PAST	PAST PARTICIPLE
burn	(is) burning	burned *or* burnt	(have) burned *or* burnt
dream	(is) dreaming	dreamed *or* dreamt	(have) dreamed *or* dreamt
leap	(is) leaping	leaped *or* leapt	(have) leaped *or* leapt

NOTE: The regular verbs *deal* and *mean* always form the past and past participle by adding *–t: dealt, (have) dealt; meant, (have) meant.*

When forming the past and past participle of regular verbs, don't make the common mistake of leaving off the *–d* or *–ed* ending. Pay particular attention to the forms of the verbs *ask, attack, drown, prejudice, risk, suppose,* and *use.*

NONSTANDARD We use to live in Bakersfield.
STANDARD We **used** to live in Bakersfield.

NONSTANDARD I was suppose to be home by now.
STANDARD I was **supposed** to be home by now.

REFERENCE NOTE: See page 513 for more about standard English.

SALLY FORTH, reprinted with special permission of North America Syndicate, Inc.

USAGE

Irregular Verbs

24c. An ***irregular verb*** forms the past and past participle in some other way than by adding *–d* or *–ed* to the infinitive form.

Irregular verbs form the past and past participle by

- changing vowels *or* consonants
- changing vowels *and* consonants
- making no change

	INFINITIVE	PRESENT PARTICIPLE	PAST	PAST PARTICIPLE
Vowel Change	sing	(is) singing	sang	(have) sung
Consonant Change	lend	(is) lending	lent	(have) lent
Vowel and Consonant Change	buy	(is) buying	bought	(have) bought
No Change	cost	(is) costing	cost	(have) cost

When forming the past and past participle of irregular verbs, avoid these common errors:

(1) using the past form with a helping verb

NONSTANDARD I have sang in the chorus for three years.
STANDARD I **have sung** in the chorus for three years.

(2) using the past participle form without a helping verb

NONSTANDARD I sung three solos this year.
STANDARD I **sang** three solos this year.

(3) adding *–d, –ed,* or *–t* to the infinitive form

NONSTANDARD This cassette costed only $6.95.
STANDARD This cassette **cost** only $6.95.

NOTE: If you're not sure about the principal parts of a verb, look in a dictionary. Entries for irregular verbs list the principal parts. If the principal parts are not listed, the verb is a regular verb.

The irregular verbs within each of the following groups form the past and past participle in a similar way.

COMMON IRREGULAR VERBS

GROUP I: Each of these irregular verbs has the same form for its past and past participle.

INFINITIVE	PRESENT PARTICIPLE	PAST	PAST PARTICIPLE
bind	(is) binding	bound	(have) bound
bring	(is) bringing	brought	(have) brought
build	(is) building	built	(have) built
buy	(is) buying	bought	(have) bought
catch	(is) catching	caught	(have) caught
creep	(is) creeping	crept	(have) crept
feel	(is) feeling	felt	(have) felt
fight	(is) fighting	fought	(have) fought
find	(is) finding	found	(have) found
fling	(is) flinging	flung	(have) flung
have	(is) having	had	(have) had
hold	(is) holding	held	(have) held
keep	(is) keeping	kept	(have) kept
lay	(is) laying	laid	(have) laid
lead	(is) leading	led	(have) led
leave	(is) leaving	left	(have) left
lend	(is) lending	lent	(have) lent
lose	(is) losing	lost	(have) lost
make	(is) making	made	(have) made
meet	(is) meeting	met	(have) met

(continued)

4. *bring* The holds of the ships ____ a cheap, new food source into a world of recurrent famine.
5. *catch* On a diet of corn, many of the world's poor ____ pellagra, a disease that affects the stomach, mind, and skin.
6. *build* Yet the peoples of Mexico and Central America had ____ healthy bodies on a steady diet of corn.
7. *make* When the women of Mexico and Central America ____ tortillas, they added some lime or ashes to the dough.
8. *stand* Then, after the mixture of corn, water, and lime or ashes had ____ for a few hours, the tortillas were shaped and cooked.
9. *have* Heated, this alkali solution ____ the ability to release not only corn's niacin but also its protein and calcium.
10. *lose* In European and African methods of preparation, corn had unfortunately ____ much of its essential nutrient value.

COMMON IRREGULAR VERBS

GROUP II: Each of these irregular verbs has a different form for its past and past participle.

INFINITIVE	PRESENT PARTICIPLE	PAST	PAST PARTICIPLE
arise	(is) arising	arose	(have) arisen
be	(is) being	was, were	(have) been
bear	(is) bearing	bore	(have) borne
beat	(is) beating	beat	(have) beaten *or* beat
become	(is) becoming	became	(have) become
begin	(is) beginning	began	(have) begun
bite	(is) biting	bit	(have) bitten
blow	(is) blowing	blew	(have) blown
break	(is) breaking	broke	(have) broken
choose	(is) choosing	chose	(have) chosen
come	(is) coming	came	(have) come
dive	(is) diving	dove *or* dived	(have) dived

(continued)

COMMON IRREGULAR VERBS *(continued)*			
GROUP II			
INFINITIVE	PRESENT PARTICIPLE	PAST	PAST PARTICIPLE
do	(is) doing	did	(have) done
draw	(is) drawing	drew	(have) drawn
drink	(is) drinking	drank	(have) drunk
drive	(is) driving	drove	(have) driven
eat	(is) eating	ate	(have) eaten
fall	(is) falling	fell	(have) fallen
fly	(is) flying	flew	(have) flown
forbid	(is) forbidding	forbade *or* forbad	(have) forbidden
forgive	(is) forgiving	forgave	(have) forgiven
forget	(is) forgetting	forgot	(have) forgotten *or* forgot
forsake	(is) forsaking	forsook	(have) forsaken
freeze	(is) freezing	froze	(have) frozen
get	(is) getting	got	(have) gotten *or* got
give	(is) giving	gave	(have) given
go	(is) going	went	(have) gone
grow	(is) growing	grew	(have) grown
hide	(is) hiding	hid	(have) hidden
know	(is) knowing	knew	(have) known
lie	(is) lying	lay	(have) lain
ride	(is) riding	rode	(have) ridden
ring	(is) ringing	rang	(have) rung
rise	(is) rising	rose	(have) risen
run	(is) running	ran	(have) run
see	(is) seeing	saw	(have) seen
shake	(is) shaking	shook	(have) shaken
shrink	(is) shrinking	shrank *or* shrunk	(have) shrunk
sing	(is) singing	sang	(have) sung
sink	(is) sinking	sank *or* sunk	(have) sunk

(continued)

USAGE

COMMON IRREGULAR VERBS *(continued)*			
GROUP II			
INFINITIVE	PRESENT PARTICIPLE	PAST	PAST PARTICIPLE
slay	(is) slaying	slew	(have) slain
speak	(is) speaking	spoke	(have) spoken
spring	(is) springing	sprang *or* sprung	(have) sprung
steal	(is) stealing	stole	(have) stolen
strike	(is) striking	struck	(have) struck *or* stricken
strive	(is) striving	strove *or* strived	(have) striven *or* strived
swear	(is) swearing	swore	(have) sworn
swim	(is) swimming	swam	(have) swum
take	(is) taking	took	(have) taken
tear	(is) tearing	tore	(have) torn
throw	(is) throwing	threw	(have) thrown
wake	(is) waking	woke	(have) woke, waked, *or* wakened
wear	(is) wearing	wore	(have) worn
weave	(is) weaving	wove	(have) woven
write	(is) writing	wrote	(have) written

EXERCISE 3 Using the Past and Past Participle Forms of Irregular Verbs Correctly

For each sentence in the following paragraphs, choose the correct one of the two verbs in parentheses.

[1] Years ago in Africa, languages like Bantu had no alphabet; therefore, nothing was (*wrote, written*) in these languages. [2] In fact, the musical quality of many African languages (*gived, gave*) them an intricacy unsuitable for written alphabets. [3] Consequently, drums (*sung, sang*) these languages throughout equatorial and southern Africa, and these songs acted as a kind of musical writing. [4] According to Janheinz Jahn, the use of

drums (*arose, arisen*) for communication at a distance. [5] Young Africans learned to "read" the different sounds of the drums and (*knew, known*) the meaning of these sounds in combinations, just as you were taught to read using the alphabet.

[6] The wide acoustic range of drums like the Yorubas' *dundun* (*gived, gave*) quick and easy access to a complex language. [7] By varying tone, pitch, and modulation, a skillful drummer (*striven, strove*) to re-create the sounds of his language. [8] With this meaningful music, he (*wove, woven*) the news of the day into an informative report. [9] At the speed of sound, his warnings, invitations, and other messages (*flew, flown*) over miles of jungle and plain. [10] With drum scripts that had been (*beat, beaten*) for decades, he sent information to interested listeners. [11] Many of the drum scripts eventually (*became, become*) classic epics. [12] As you can see, drummers were not just musicians; they (*been, were*) also teachers and historians. [13] Through them, generations of young Africans (*drank, drunk*) in the history of their ancestors.

[14] When European missionaries came to Africa, however, they (*forbidden, forbade*) the playing of drums. [15] Their prohibitions (*struck, stricken*) at the hearts of many African cultures. [16] Today, through disuse, almost all of the old drum scripts have been (*forgot, forgotten*). [17] Scholars, however, have (*maked, made*) recordings of many of the remaining scripts. [18] Sadly, many listeners have not (*spoke, spoken*) their native language in their whole lives; consequently, even verbal translations of the drum songs are meaningless to many Africans. [19] The power of the drums has (*went, gone*). [20] Like so much of ancient knowledge and wisdom, this marvelous system of communication has been (*forsaken, forsook*).

USAGE

EXERCISE 4 Using the Past and Past Participle Forms of Irregular Verbs Correctly

Most of the following sentences contain incorrect past or past participle forms of verbs. If a verb form is incorrect, give the correct form. If a sentence is correct, write *C*.

1. Benjamin Franklin may have gotten many of his ideas for the structure of our government from his observations of the League of the Iroquois.
2. She should not have drew a beard on that poster.

3. Why would anyone have stole your notebook?
4. I have ran too far to turn back now.
5. Tommy has growed two inches taller than I.
6. After 1922, other ancient treasures shrunk in significance when compared to the discoveries made in the tomb of Tutankhamen.
7. Last night, the noise from the party waked up the whole neighborhood.
8. I seen that movie several times.
9. Who throwed out my old comic books?
10. They have frozen a peck of green beans for next winter.
11. Henry done his best yesterday.
12. In the courtroom, the young man was sweared in to give testimony.
13. Jesse Owens' spectacular run at the 1936 Olympic games shaked the world.
14. Have you ever dove from the high board?
15. Thunder crashed, and wind blowed the candles out.
16. We should have chose seats closer to the stage.
17. Why have they tore up the newspapers?
18. How the ancient Mexicans' multicolored garments made of feathers must have shined in the sunlight!
19. He always rid the bus to school.
20. Has the bell rung yet?

REVIEW A **Proofreading for Correct Verb Forms**

For each sentence in the following paragraphs, find and correct any errors in verb forms.

[1] Many cultures have not forsaked their traditional ceremonies that mark the significant stages in a person's life. [2] For instance, when an Apache girl has came of age, she sometimes receives a Sunrise Ceremonial. [3] Through this ceremony, the young woman is forever separated from her girlhood and lead into womanhood. [4] Everything in the ceremony is suppose to remind the young woman of the deep spiritual meaning of her life. [5] Perhaps part of that meaning can be founded in the glad hearts of her many friends and family members who come to participate in the ceremony.

[6] Not long ago, Carla, the young woman in the photograph on the next page, and her mother seeked the blessings of a traditional Sunrise Ceremonial. [7] Complex preparations

had began months in advance. [8] During the winter, Carla's mother choose a campsite where Carla, her family, and her friends would live for two weeks according to the ways of their ancestors. [9] The crucial choice of godparents for the young woman also had been maked by Carla's mother. [10] Not surprisingly, she chose a couple who had keeped to the traditional Apache way of life. [11] By summer, Carla's mother and godparents had builded enough shelters at the campsite to house at least eight families.

[12] During Carla's ceremonial, many traditional songs were sang, thirty-two of them by one group of dancers alone. [13] The two cows that had been slew for the feasting were eaten. [14] In addition, Carla and her family gave away all of the gifts they had brung for the godparents and other friends. [15] Although young women used to dance all night, Carla danced for six hours at a time at her ceremonial. [16] Then she standed for seemingly endless hours in the burning sun. [17] Through it all, she worn a hot, heavy buckskin dress. [18] Surely, these tests of self-discipline teached Carla and everyone who attend the ceremony something about the endurance and strength that a woman needs to live as a proper Apache. [19] Finally, after offering a blessing, a medicine man gived Carla a cane, a reminder that she will not always be young. [20] In her old age, when the cane has became her constant companion, it will, no doubt, remind her of the strength of her youth.

COMMON IRREGULAR VERBS			
GROUP III: Each of these irregular verbs has the same form for its infinitive, past, and past participle.			
INFINITIVE	PRESENT PARTICIPLE	PAST	PAST PARTICIPLE
burst	(is) bursting	burst	(have) burst
cost	(is) costing	cost	(have) cost
cut	(is) cutting	cut	(have) cut
hit	(is) hitting	hit	(have) hit
hurt	(is) hurting	hurt	(have) hurt
let	(is) letting	let	(have) let
put	(is) putting	put	(have) put
read	(is) reading	read	(have) read
set	(is) setting	set	(have) set
spread	(is) spreading	spread	(have) spread

USAGE

EXERCISE 5 **Using the Past and Past Participle Forms of Irregular Verbs Correctly**

Most of the following sentences contain errors in the use of verbs. If a verb form is incorrect, give the correct form of the verb. If a sentence is correct, write *C*.

1. During the freeze last March, the water pipes at school bursted.
2. That dog would not have hurted a fly.
3. Yesterday evening, I had just putted dinner on the table when the phone rang.
4. Shaka Zulu led his warriors into battle, and soon news of Shaka's victory had spreaded throughout Zululand.
5. Have you ever cutted out a pattern before?
6. Have you read the assignment yet?
7. After art class, Jeremy and I setted our pottery out in the sun to dry.
8. The drought hitted the spring crops hard.
9. One chance remark had costed her the election.
10. Wisely, Francisca Henrique de Ribera letted the Andean natives treat her malaria attack with a powerful bark, now known as quinine.

REVIEW B

Proofreading for Correct Verb Forms and Usage

Most of the sentences in the following paragraphs contain errors in verb usage. If a verb is incorrect, give the correct form of the verb. If a sentence is correct, write *C*.

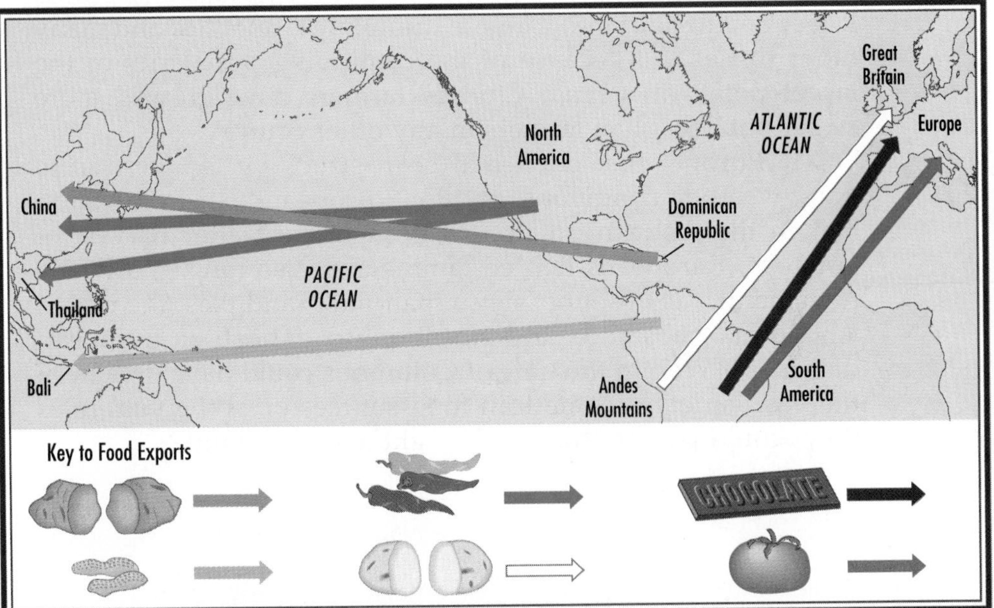

[1] Now that you've readed the map shown above, are you surprised by where these food products originated? [2] Perhaps you have ate some of these foods. [3] Like naturalized citizens, many food products have became vital, even characteristic, parts of their adopted nations. [4] Consequently, most people have forgot that key ingredients, such as tomato sauce on pizza, come from the Americas.

[5] Reports from early explorers putted cooks all over Europe into a creative frenzy. [6] When the explorers returned home, dozens of strange and exotic foods were suddenly maked available to Europeans. [7] Some of the foods that the explorers sended home include sweet potatoes, white potatoes, corn, peppers, tomatoes, avocados, vanilla, maple sugar, chocolate, peanuts, all sorts of beans (kidney, lima, snap, string, butter, pole, and navy), and a host of other welcome additions to a chef's larder. [8] So many new spices, fruits, vegetables, meats, and grains hitted the market that this period in history can be called a "Food Revolution."

USAGE

[9] In these unfamiliar foods, many peoples also founded new hope. [10] For example, the Chinese use to experience severe famine. [11] Countless lives had been losed due to the failure of rice crops. [12] However, with the introduction of the sweet potato, an alternative to rice arisen. [13] Sweet potatoes cost little and did well in poor soil. [14] Soon, cooks had putted sweet potato flour into Chinese dumplings, noodles, and many other dishes. [15] Because of the continuing popularity of the sweet potato in China, Chinese farmers have growed more sweet potatoes than farmers in any other country.

[16] Europe, too, often had been struck by famine due to poor weather conditions. [17] For Europeans, their salvation lain in the Andean potato. [18] With harvest after harvest of potatoes, Europeans fighted famine and also rang in a whole new menu. [19] In soups, stews, pancakes, and pies, the potato lended its substance and nutrition to a host of European dishes. [20] Who in the time of Columbus could have dreamt of the vast variety of American food sources or of the vital roles they would play in the world's fight against famine?

WRITING APPLICATION

Using Standard Verb Forms in Writing

Often, writers make errors in using the past and past participle forms of verbs because many nonstandard verb forms sound quite natural. When you proofread your writing for incorrect verb forms, don't rely on how a form sounds. Always check the sentence to determine which form—past or past participle—is called for.

EXAMPLES By April, the Eastside High Choir had (*gave, given*) four excellent performances at the town auditorium. [The helping verb *had* signals that the past participle form is called for.]

By April, the Eastside High Choir **had given** four excellent performances at the town auditorium.

The new telescope (*cost, costed*) almost exactly as much as we had raised at the school raffle. [The sentence requires the simple past form of *cost.*]
The new telescope **cost** almost exactly as much as we had raised at the school raffle.

To save time, identify the verbs that give you trouble and memorize their forms. Keep a dictionary handy to check any forms you're not sure about.

USAGE

WRITING ACTIVITY

The editor of your school's yearbook is planning a seniors-only feature. Interested seniors may submit one-paragraph descriptions of school or special events that helped make this year memorable. Selected descriptions, along with photographs, will be published as part of the feature. Write a paragraph to submit for publication. In your paragraph, include at least five irregular verbs from the lists on pages 769–770, 772–774, and 778. Be sure that you've used the correct past and past participle forms of verbs.

Prewriting Brainstorm a list of memorable moments in the school year. Focus on events in which a number of students participated. From your list choose the one event that you remember most vividly. What was the high point of the event? What made the moment special?

Writing As you write your first draft, name the event and give the time at which it occurred. Then describe the event, capturing the feeling or mood it inspired in your school. Include vivid sensory details to hold the reader's interest. Mention some of the people who helped make the event memorable.

Evaluating and Revising Ask a classmate who took part in the event to read your paragraph. Have you described the event clearly and captured its special flavor? Will your description help students remember the event in years to come? Note down your reader's comments and suggestions. Then add, cut, and revise details as necessary to improve your description. Replace bland adjectives, adverbs, and verbs with livelier, more expressive ones. Be sure that you've used at least five irregular verbs from the lists.

Proofreading and Publishing Read through your paragraph several times, checking for any errors in grammar, usage, spelling, or punctuation. Take extra care with the past and past participle forms of verbs. To publish your descriptions, you and your classmates can compile them in a mini-yearbook. You may want to include photographs or drawings to accompany the descriptions. Leave a few blank pages for future events.

USAGE

REVIEW C Using the Past and Past Participle Forms

For each of the following sentences, write the correct past or past participle form of the italicized word.

1. *creep* While the children were asleep, their father ___ into their room to kiss them good night.
2. *let* After breakfast, I ___ the cat outside.
3. *visit* Many Cheyenne, Arapaho, Shoshone, Blackfoot, Crow, and Sioux pilgrims have ___ the Big Horn Medicine Wheel in Wyoming, a ceremonial site for perhaps two thousand years.
4. *fling* Joyfully, he ___ his cap into the air.
5. *sting* Where had the bee ___ her?
6. *win* The baby's trusting smile ___ our hearts.
7. *think* At last, I had ___ of the perfect present for Amy.
8. *bear* We could not have ___ another moment of that awful music.
9. *swim* The frantic cat ___ desperately to the shore.
10. *blow* Even before the whistle had ___, they had seen the train coming.
11. *sink* After our long voyage, we gratefully ___ into the plush velvet chairs.
12. *hide* Someone had ___ one of my birthday presents at the back of the top shelf in a kitchen cabinet.
13. *set* That afternoon, we hurriedly ___ the table for the party.
14. *lie* During World War II, the success of England's military blood bank ___ in the capable hands of Dr. Charles Drew.

15. *hold* Only that morning, I had ____ the trembling bird in my hands.

16. *bite* The injured whale had obviously been ____ many times by sharks.

17. *lead* Boadicea, a queen in ancient Britain, ____ her people in a revolt against the Romans.

18. *cut* With one sure stroke, he had ____ his ties to his native country.

19. *throw* That horse has ____ everybody who has tried to ride her.

20. *break* The death of Mao Zedong ____ the rigid rule that had governed China for many years and opened the way for somewhat greater freedom for the Chinese people.

REVIEW D **Proofreading for Correct Verb Forms and Usage**

Most of the sentences in the following paragraphs contain errors in the use of verbs. If a verb form is incorrect, give the correct form. If a sentence is correct, write *C.*

[1] For over thirty years, my aunt has had a lacquerware plate similar to the one in this picture. [2] When I been a child, she displayed the plate on a low table in her living room in Tacoma, Washington. [3] Naturally, she forbidded me to touch her prized plate, and I respected her wish. [4] One day, however, my younger brother runned through the living room. [5] As he zoomed past the table, his foot accidentally hitted the leg. [6] In the blink of an eye, my aunt's beautiful plate falled

Song-Yuan Dynasties (13th century). Tray, brown and red lacquer with gilt background. H: 2.5 cm, 1 in. Diam: 22.5 cm, 9 in. #B83 M9. The Avery Brundage Collection. Asian Art Museum of San Francisco.

and spinned wildly on the floor. [7] After that, the plate, which was miraculously unbroken, sitted on the top shelf of my aunt's china closet.

[8] Ever since I first expressed an interest in lacquerware, my aunt has telled me more and more about its history and production. [9] Lacquerware has been make since around 300 B.C. [10] The art begun in China and later spreaded to Japan and then to the Western world. [11] To protect their trade, the tappers of lacquer in ancient China keeped their valuable knowledge of lacquer production secret. [12] Now we know that they drew the sap from lacquer trees, filtered it, and dried it to a thick, syrupy consistency. [13] Then they selled it to artists for its beauty and for its waterproofing ability.

[14] In the finer pieces of lacquerware, like this one, some two hundred coats of lacquer might have been spread over the plate. [15] For each coat, a thin film of lacquer was applied and then was leaved to dry thoroughly. [16] Consequently, the whole lacquering process sometimes taked as long as a year to complete. [17] Then, when the artist had chosed a design, the carving began. [18] Would you have devote a year's work to such an intricate design? [19] What confidence these artists must have feeled! [20] My aunt bought her plate years ago for only a few dollars; now, it has brought offers of many, many times the price that she payed.

USAGE

Six Troublesome Verbs

Lie and *Lay*

The verb *lie* means "to rest" or "to stay, to recline, or to remain in a certain state or position." *Lie* never takes an object. The verb *lay* means "to put [something] in a place." *Lay* usually takes an object.

INFINITIVE	PRESENT PARTICIPLE	PAST	PAST PARTICIPLE
lie (*to rest*)	(is) lying	lay	(have) lain
lay (*to put*)	(is) laying	laid	(have) laid

EXAMPLES Your car keys **are lying** on the kitchen counter. [no object]

The servers **are laying** a napkin on each diner's plate. [*Napkin* is the object of *are laying.*]

The valedictorian spoke of the challenges that **lay** before the graduates. [no object]

Last winter we **laid** seed on the ground for the wild birds. [*Seed* is the object of *laid.*]

The clothes to be ironed **have lain** in the basket all week. [no object]

The state legislators **have laid** the matter before the voters. [*Matter* is the object of *have laid.*]

EXERCISE 6 Choosing the Forms of *Lie* and *Lay*

For each of the following sentences, choose the correct verb form in parentheses.

1. If you are sick, you should be (*lying, laying*) down.
2. They (*lay, laid*) the heavy crate on the handcart.
3. Lucia's mother has always (*lain, laid*) a great deal of emphasis on bilingual education.
4. Amy (*lay, laid*) down for a while.
5. I left my gloves (*lying, laying*) on the counter.
6. She had just (*lain, laid*) down when the doorbell rang.
7. They (*lay, laid*) their plans before the committee.
8. The calf (*lay, laid*) on a pile of straw.
9. Kiyoshi (*lay, laid*) his paintbrush down and added more blue to his palette.
10. Don't leave your shoes (*lying, laying*) under the table.

Sit and *Set*

The verb *sit* means "to rest in an upright, seated position." *Sit* seldom takes an object. The verb *set* means "to put [something] in a place." *Set* usually takes an object.

INFINITIVE	PRESENT PARTICIPLE	PAST	PAST PARTICIPLE
sit (*to rest*)	(is) sitting	sat	(have) sat
set (*to put*)	(is) setting	set	(have) set

USAGE

EXAMPLES **Where should we sit?** [no object]
Where should I set this bag of groceries? [*Bag* is the object of *should set.*]

We **sat** in the bleachers behind the end zone at last night's game. [no object]
Liang **set** the platter of egg foo yong on the table. [*Platter* is the object of *set.*]

EXERCISE 7 Choosing the Forms of *Sit* and *Set*

For each of the following sentences, choose the correct verb form in parentheses.

1. After he had struck out, Pete (*sat, set*) on the bench.
2. Part of San Francisco's Chinatown (*sits, sets*) on an incline that overlooks the San Francisco Bay.
3. Where were the packages (*sitting, setting*) this morning?
4. We had (*sat, set*) our weary bones in the plush chairs.
5. In Japan people often (*sit, set*) on tatami instead of chairs.
6. They were (*sitting, setting*) placemats on the table.
7. It makes no difference to me where you (*sit, set*).
8. We (*sat, set*) down our packs and got out our map.
9. Mr. Carr told me to (*sit, set*) the equipment on his desk.
10. I may never know who had (*sat, set*) on my glasses.

USAGE

Rise and *Raise*

The verb *rise* means "to go up" or "to get up." *Rise* never takes an object. The verb *raise* means "to cause [something] to rise" or "to lift up." *Raise* usually takes an object.

INFINITIVE	PRESENT PARTICIPLE	PAST	PAST PARTICIPLE
rise (*to go up*)	(is) rising	rose	(have) risen
raise (*to lift up*)	(is) raising	raised	(have) raised

EXAMPLES Una **rose** from her desk and walked to the front of the classroom. [no object]
The players **raised** the coach onto their shoulders. [*Coach* is the object of *raised.*]

The number of women who work outside the home **has risen** steadily during the past decade. [no object]
The reporters **have raised** that issue at several press conferences. [*Issue* is the object of *have raised.*]

EXERCISE 8 Choosing the Forms of *Rise* and *Raise*

For each of the following sentences, choose the correct verb form in parentheses.

1. Air bubbles have been (*rising, raising*) to the surface.
2. Increasing the import duty will (*rise, raise*) retail prices.
3. The speaker (*rose, raised*) from her chair and took the mike.
4. This month, the star has been (*rising, raising*) in the east.
5. The rooster (*rises, raises*) early.
6. Before and during the Revolutionary War, many colonists worked hard to (*rise, raise*) public sentiment against King George III.
7. Balloons can (*rise, raise*) because they contain heated air, which is less dense than the surrounding air.
8. At the tribal council meeting, someone (*rose, raised*) the issue of land ownership within reservation boundaries.
9. Mist was (*rising, raising*) from the ground.
10. To make traditional challah, braid the bread dough after it has (*risen, raised*) for an hour.

REVIEW E Choosing the Forms of *Lie* and *Lay*, *Sit* and *Set*, and *Rise* and *Raise*

For each of the following sentences, choose the correct verb form in parentheses.

1. All week that box has (*lain, laid*) unopened on the desk.
2. We (*rose, raised*) our hats to salute the astronauts.
3. The injured deer (*lay, laid*) motionless in the road.
4. Our applications were (*lying, laying*) in front of the file.
5. Would you like to (*sit, set*) with us at the powwow?
6. I always (*lie, lay*) the phone book on this table.
7. We arrived late and had to (*sit, set*) at the top of the bleachers.
8. Kathy sang as she (*lay, laid*) the baby in the crib.
9. Clean up the mess that's (*lying, laying*) on your floor.
10. Last night's victory really (*rose, raised*) the team's spirit and confidence.

11. Our potbellied pig Oscar often (*lies, lays*) in my lap when I watch TV.
12. Fred should (*lie, lay*) on his side to stop snoring.
13. After the fire, the museum (*lay, laid*) in a heap.
14. Tempers (*rose, raised*) as the debate progressed.
15. In Washington, D.C., we will (*lie, lay*) flowers at the Vietnam Veterans Memorial.
16. Mrs. Nasser (*sat, set*) the tabbouleh and kibbe next to other traditional Lebanese foods.
17. If you (*sit, set*) the pie on the ledge, it may vanish.
18. Billows of dust (*rose, raised*) up from the field.
19. Haven't they (*sat, set*) down the piano yet?
20. You should (*lie, lay*) on a padded surface to do exercises.

USAGE

Tense

24d. The ***tense*** of a verb indicates the time of the action or state of being expressed by the verb.

Every verb has six tenses: *present, past, future, present perfect, past perfect,* and *future perfect*. These six tenses are formed from the principal parts of the verb. Listing all of the forms of a verb according to tense is called ***conjugating*** a verb.

CONJUGATION OF THE VERB *GIVE*			
PRINCIPAL PARTS			
INFINITIVE	PRESENT PARTICIPLE	PAST	PAST PARTICIPLE
give	(is) giving	gave	(have) given
PRESENT TENSE			
SINGULAR		*PLURAL*	
I give		we give	
you give		you give	
he, she, it gives		they give	

(continued)

CONJUGATION OF THE VERB *GIVE (continued)*	
PAST TENSE	
SINGULAR	*PLURAL*
I gave	we gave
you gave	you gave
he, she, it gave	they gave
FUTURE TENSE (*will* or *shall* + infinitive)	
SINGULAR	*PLURAL*
I will (shall) give	we will (shall) give
you will give	you will give
he, she, it will give	they will give
PRESENT PERFECT TENSE (*have* or *has* + past participle)	
SINGULAR	*PLURAL*
I have given	we have given
you have given	you have given
he, she, it has given	they have given
PAST PERFECT TENSE (*had* + past participle)	
SINGULAR	*PLURAL*
I had given	we had given
you had given	you had given
he, she, it had given	they had given
FUTURE PERFECT TENSE (*will have* or *shall have* + past participle)	
SINGULAR	*PLURAL*
I will (shall) have given	we will (shall) have given
you will have given	you will have given
he, she, it will have given	they will have given

Each tense has an additional form called the ***progressive form,*** which expresses continuing action or state of being. In each tense, the progressive form of a verb consists of the appropriate tense of *be* plus the verb's present participle. Some tenses also include one or more helping verbs.

Present Progressive	**am, is, are giving**
Past Progressive	**was, were giving**
Future Progressive	**will (shall) be giving**
Present Perfect Progressive	**has been, have been giving**
Past Perfect Progressive	**had been giving**
Future Perfect Progressive	**will (shall) have been giving**

Only the present and the past tenses have another form called the ***emphatic form,*** which shows emphasis. In the present tense, the emphatic form of a verb consists of *do* or *does* plus the verb's infinitive. In the past tense, the emphatic form consists of *did* plus the verb's infinitive.

Present Emphatic I **do** not **intend** to give up.
Although the grass is green, the lawn **does need** watering.

Past Emphatic The explorers suffered many hardships, yet they **did** finally **reach** their destination.

USAGE

The conjugation of the verb *be* is somewhat different from that of other verbs. Notice that only the present and past tenses of *be* have the progressive form and that none of the tenses has the emphatic form.

CONJUGATION OF THE VERB *BE*

PRINCIPAL PARTS

INFINITIVE	PRESENT PARTICIPLE	PAST	PAST PARTICIPLE
be	(is) being	was, were	(have) been

PRESENT TENSE

SINGULAR	*PLURAL*
I am	we are
you are	you are
he, she, it is	they are

Present Progressive: am, is, are being

PAST TENSE

SINGULAR	*PLURAL*
I was	we were
you were	you were
he, she, it was	they were

Past Progressive: was, were being

(continued)

CONJUGATION OF THE VERB *BE* *(continued)*	
FUTURE TENSE (*will* or *shall* + infinitive)	
SINGULAR	*PLURAL*
I will (shall) be	we will (shall) be
you will be	you will be
he, she, it will be	they will be
PRESENT PERFECT TENSE (*have* or *has* + past participle)	
SINGULAR	*PLURAL*
I have been	we have been
you have been	you have been
he, she, it has been	they have been
PAST PERFECT TENSE (*had* + past participle)	
SINGULAR	*PLURAL*
I had been	we had been
you had been	you had been
he, she, it had been	they had been
FUTURE PERFECT TENSE (*will have* or *shall have* + past participle)	
SINGULAR	*PLURAL*
I will (shall) have been	we will (shall) have been
you will have been	you will have been
he, she, it will have been	they will have been

The Uses of the Tenses

24e. Each of the six tenses has its own special uses.

(1) The ***present tense*** is used mainly to express an action or state of being that is occurring now.

EXAMPLES Ashley and Ira **wait** patiently for the bus. [present]
Ashley and Ira **are waiting** patiently for the bus. [present progressive]
Ashley and Ira **do wait** patiently for the bus. [present emphatic]

The present tense is also used

- to show a customary or habitual action or state of being
- to state a general truth—something that is always true
- to summarize the plot or subject matter of a literary work (such use is called the *literary present*)
- to make a historical event seem current (such use is called the *historical present*)
- to express future time

EXAMPLES After school I **wash** the breakfast dishes and **start** supper. [customary action]
In the Northern Hemisphere the summer solstice **occurs** when the sun is farthest from the equator. [general truth]
Countee Cullen **uses** traditional verse forms to explore African American themes. [literary present]
In 1520, Ferdinand Magellan **rounds** the southern tip of South America and **names** the ocean that **lies** before him the Pacific Ocean. [historical present]
The movie that **opens** tomorrow **runs** through next week. [future time]

USAGE

(2) The ***past tense*** is used to express an action or state of being that occurred in the past but did not continue into the present.

EXAMPLES I **stayed** at the library until closing time. [past]
I **was researching** the life of Timothy Thomas Fortune, a civil rights advocate in the 1800s. [past progressive]
My research **did provide** me with enough information for my paper on Fortune. [past emphatic]

NOTE: A past action or state of being may also be shown in another way.

EXAMPLE She **used to collect** stamps.

(3) The ***future tense*** is used to express an action or a state of being that will occur. The future tense is formed with *will* or *shall* and the verb's infinitive.

EXAMPLES I **will attend** the University of Iowa in the fall. [future]
I **will be attending** the University of Iowa in the fall. [future progressive]

NOTE: A future action or state of being may also be expressed by using

- the present tense of *be* with *going to* and the infinitive form of a verb

- the present tense of *be* with *about to* and the infinitive form of a verb
- the present tense of a verb with a word or phrase that expresses future time

EXAMPLES My aunt and uncle **are going to visit** the Philippines.
Mr. Campos **is about to open** the time capsule.
Finals **begin next Monday.**

(4) The ***present perfect tense*** is used mainly to express an action or a state of being that occurred at some indefinite time in the past. The present perfect tense always includes the helping verb *have* or *has.*

EXAMPLES I **have written** to the governor, but I **have** not **received** a reply. [present perfect]
Who **has been playing** my cassettes? [present perfect progressive]

NOTE: Avoid the use of the present perfect tense to express a *specific* time in the past. Instead, use the past tense.

NONSTANDARD *Prairie Schooner* has published a new short story by Louise Erdrich last month.
STANDARD *Prairie Schooner* **published** a new short story by Louise Erdrich last month.

The present perfect tense is also used to express action (or a state of being) that began in the past and continues into the present.

EXAMPLES The International Sister City program **has existed** for more than thirty-five years. [present perfect]
The program **has been pairing** cities in the United States with cities in other nations since 1956. [present perfect progressive]

(5) The ***past perfect tense*** is used mainly to express an action or a state of being that was completed in the past before some other past occurrence. The past perfect tense always includes the helping verb *had.*

EXAMPLES I finally remembered where I **had seen** a copy of Rufino Tamayo's mural *Nature and the Artist.* [The seeing occurred before the remembering.]
I **had been looking** through dozens of old magazines before I finally remembered to check the latest issue of *Smithsonian.* [past perfect progressive]

(6) The ***future perfect tense*** is used to express an action or a state of being that will be completed in the future before some other future occurrence. The future perfect tense always includes *will have* or *shall have.*

EXAMPLES By the time the bus **arrives,** we **will have waited** for an hour. [The waiting will occur before the arrival of the bus.]
By then, we **will have been waiting** for two hours. [future perfect progressive]

EXERCISE 9 **Understanding the Uses of the Six Tenses**

Identify the tenses of the verbs in each of the following pairs of sentences. Be prepared to explain how these differences in tense alter the meanings of the sentences.

1. Margo lived in Brazil for eight years.
   Margo has lived in Brazil for eight years.
2. Why had she gone to the theater?
   Why has she been going to the theater?
3. Have the directions been explained clearly?
   Had the directions been explained clearly?
4. Was she driving?
   Had she been driving?
5. As of June 30, they will have raised taxes twice this year.
   As of June 30, they will be raising taxes twice this year.

EXERCISE 10 **Understanding the Uses of the Six Tenses**

Identify which sentence in each pair correctly expresses the meaning given. Be prepared to name the tenses used in each sentence.

1. *Meaning:* John still works for Mr. Porzio.
   a. John has worked for Mr. Porzio for a year.
   b. John had worked for Mr. Porzio for a year.
2. *Meaning:* Ann Rosine could be on her way to Worcester right now or could be going later.
   a. Ann Rosine is moving to Worcester, Massachusetts.
   b. Ann Rosine will be moving to Worcester, Massachusetts.
3. *Meaning:* Jaime is still studying physics.
   a. Jaime has been studying physics since last summer.
   b. Jaime studied physics last summer.

4. *Meaning:* Alison takes a bus to work on a regular basis.
   a. Alison takes the bus to work.
   b. Alison is taking the bus to work.
5. *Meaning:* Ray was a bank officer at the age of twenty-four.
   a. When Ray turned twenty-five, he had been promoted to the position of bank officer.
   b. When Ray turned twenty-five, he was promoted to the position of bank officer.

PICTURE THIS

USAGE

The year is 2993. Due to a computer error, certain historical records have been erased from the World Archives. You are a member of the task force whose job is to travel back in time to collect factual information that will fill in the gaps in the record. Because you have a special interest in twentieth-century entertainment, you've slipped into this movie audience and put on a pair of the optical devices they're wearing. Take careful notes for your records. Describe the experience of viewing a movie, and also explain the purpose of wearing the strange devices. Compare this experience to one that you're familiar with in the thirtieth century. Be sure to use verb tenses that accurately express your meaning.

Subject: viewing a movie through 3-D glasses
Audience: people in the thirtieth century
Purpose: to inform

Special Problems in the Use of Tenses

Sequence of Tenses

24f. Use tense forms carefully to show the correct relationship between verbs in a sentence.

(1) When describing events that occur at the same time, use verbs in the same tense.

EXAMPLES The bell **rings,** and the classroom **empties.** [present tense]
The bell **rang,** and the classroom **emptied.** [past tense]

(2) When describing events that occur at different times, use verbs in different tenses to show the order of events.

EXAMPLES I **play** football now, but I **played** basketball in junior high. [Because I am playing football now, the present tense form *play* is correct. My playing basketball occurred in the past and did not continue into the present; therefore, the past tense is correct.]
Sabrena **mentioned** that she **had invited** some of her neighbors to the party. [Because Sabrena made the statement in the past, the past tense form *mentioned* is correct. She invited the neighbors before she made the statement; therefore, the past perfect form *had invited* is correct.]

The tense you use depends on the meaning you want to express.

EXAMPLES I **believe** they **own** the Flamingo Cafe. [Both verbs are in the present tense to indicate that both actions are occurring now.]
I **believe** they **owned** the Flamingo Cafe. [The change to the past tense in the second verb implies that they no longer own the Flamingo Cafe.]

Joan **said** that she **worked** at the textile mill. [Both verbs are in the past tense to indicate that both actions no longer occur.]
Joan **said** that she **will work** at the textile mill. [The change in the second verb implies that Joan did not work at the textile mill when she made the statement but that she planned to work there.]

USAGE

24g. Avoid the use of *would have* in "if clauses" that express the earlier of two past actions. Use the past perfect tense.

NONSTANDARD	If he would have taken more time, he would have won.
STANDARD	If he **had taken** more time, he would have won.
NONSTANDARD	I would not have been late if I would have had a watch.
STANDARD	I would not have been late if I **had had** a watch.
NONSTANDARD	If you would have stopped by, you could have met my cousin.
STANDARD	If you **had stopped** by, you could have met my cousin.

EXERCISE 11 Using Tenses Correctly

Each of the following sentences contains an error in the use of tenses. Identify the error, and then give the correct form of the verb.

1. Pam finally appreciated the old saying that every cloud had a silver lining.
2. By the time we graduate in June, Ms. Vargas will be teaching Spanish for twenty-four years.
3. Although Denny's skill was demonstrated during the season, he was not chosen to play in the All-Star game.
4. If they would have called sooner, we would have given them a ride.
5. When Jeremy finally got to the dentist, his tooth already stopped hurting.
6. The company hired Ms. Littmann because she lived for many years in Japan.
7. By the time I presented my report before the committee, the members have already studied several other reports on nuclear waste disposal.
8. Mr. Frey already complained to the neighbors many times before he called the police.
9. By then I will receive my first paycheck.
10. If she forgot the directions, we could have been lost.
11. Hiram R. Revels, the first African American senator, was a minister and teacher before he entered politics.

12. If they had enough money, they could have taken a taxi to the opening of that new musical.
13. As I thought about our argument, I was sure you lost your temper first.
14. Next Saturday is a very important anniversary for Mai's family; they will be living in the United States for exactly one year.
15. When we reviewed the videotapes of the game, we saw that the other team committed the foul.
16. The clerk remembered that the manager has ordered the new shipment last Tuesday.
17. How could I have forgotten that Great Britain included England, Wales, Scotland, and Northern Ireland?
18. We estimate that when we're in our forties, we will be working more than twenty years.
19. If Gary would have read the ad more carefully, he could have saved more than fifty dollars on his new camera.
20. J.D. would have done much better on the art history exam if he reviewed the chapter on Aztec stonework.

USAGE

The Present Infinitive and the Present Perfect Infinitive

PRESENT INFINITIVE	to be	to discover
PRESENT PERFECT INFINITIVE	to have been	to have discovered

24h. The ***present infinitive*** is used to express an action or a state of being that occurs after another action or state of being.

EXAMPLES **Charlotte had expected to go with us.** [The action expressed by *to go* follows the action expressed by *had expected*.]

Charlotte had planned to ask her boss for time off. [The action expressed by *to ask* follows the action expressed by *had planned*.]

24i. The ***present perfect infinitive*** is used to express an action or a state of being that occurs before another action or state of being.

EXAMPLES **My little brother pretended to have read my diary.** [The action expressed by *to have read* precedes the action expressed by *pretended.*]
I would like **to have gone** to the movie with you. [The action expressed by *to have gone* precedes the action expressed by *would like.*]

REFERENCE NOTE: For more information about infinitives and how they are used, see pages 663–664.

The Present Participle and the Present Perfect Participle

PRESENT PARTICIPLE	being	discovering
PRESENT PERFECT PARTICIPLE	having been	having discovered

24j. The ***present participle*** is used to express an action or a state of being that occurs at the same time as another action or state of being.

Receiving word of their freedom in June 1865, former slaves in Texas created the Juneteenth holiday. [The action expressed by *receiving* occurs at the same time as the action expressed by *created.*]
Celebrating Juneteenth this year, my family gathered at my grandmother's house on June 19. [The action expressed by *celebrating* occurs at the same time as the action expressed by *gathered.*]

24k. The ***present perfect participle*** is used to express an action or a state of being that comes before another action or state of being.

EXAMPLES **Having missed** the midterm exam, I took a makeup test. [The action expressed by *having missed* precedes the action expressed by *took.*]
Having been accepted by several colleges, Rosa chose one. [The action expressed by *having been accepted* precedes the action expressed by *chose.*]

REFERENCE NOTE: For more information about participles and how they are used, see pages 657–658.

EXERCISE 12 **Using Tenses Correctly**

Each of the following sentences contains an error in the use of verbs. Identify the error and then give the correct form of the verb.

1. Spending three hours on a review of chemistry, we then worked on irregular French verbs.
2. Tutankhamen, Helen of Troy, and Shakespeare are the three people I would have most liked to have met.
3. To have written about Pueblo ceremonies, I would have to do more research.
4. Flying from Missouri to California before, we remembered to set our watches back.
5. We wanted to have avoided any controversy.
6. Having attempted to travel across the African continent, the explorers encountered both vast deserts and dense swamp forests.
7. Native Arctic peoples learned to have survived in a harsh environment.
8. They were hoping to have had a multiple-choice test in history instead of an essay exam.
9. If you want to go shopping, I would have driven you to the mall.
10. Standing in line for more than two hours, Tamisha finally got tickets to the Hammer concert.

Active Voice and Passive Voice

24l. ***Voice*** **is the form a transitive verb takes to indicate whether the subject of the verb performs or receives the action.**

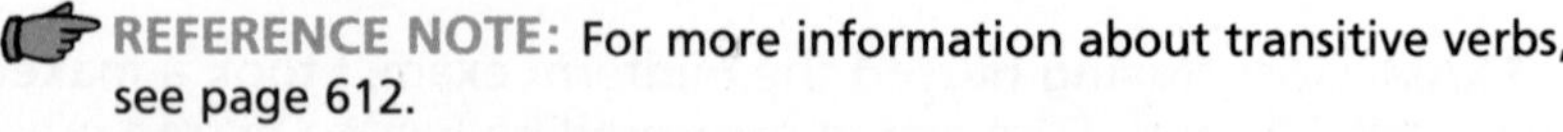

REFERENCE NOTE: For more information about transitive verbs, see page 612.

Transitive verbs may be in the *active voice* or the *passive voice.* When the subject of a verb performs the action, the verb is in the ***active voice.*** When the subject receives the action, the verb is in the ***passive voice.***

As the examples on the next page show, verbs in the active voice take objects, and verbs in the passive voice do not.

ACTIVE VOICE	Mark Riley **anchors** the local evening news. [*News* is the direct object.]
PASSIVE VOICE	The local evening news **is anchored** by Mark Riley.
ACTIVE VOICE	Han **took** many of the photos in the yearbook. [*Many* is the direct object.]
PASSIVE VOICE	Many of the photos in the yearbook **were taken** by Han.
ACTIVE VOICE	The firefighters **have extinguished** the blazing fire. [*Fire* is the direct object.]
PASSIVE VOICE	The blazing fire **has been extinguished** by the firefighters.
PASSIVE VOICE	The fire **has been extinguished.**

From these examples, you can see how an active construction can become a passive construction.

- The object of the verb in the active voice becomes the subject of the verb in the passive voice.
- The subject of the verb in the active voice becomes an object of the preposition *by*. (As the last example shows, this prepositional phrase is not always necessary.)

The Retained Object

A verb in the active voice often has an indirect object as well as a direct object. When such a verb is put into the passive voice, either object can become the subject. The other object then serves as a complement called a ***retained object.***

S V IO DO

ACTIVE	Mrs. Platero gives each new employee a tour of the plant.
PASSIVE	Each new employee is given a tour of the plant (by Mrs. Platero). [The indirect object *employee* becomes the subject, and the direct object *tour* becomes the retained object.]
PASSIVE	A tour of the plant is given each new employee (by Mrs. Platero). [The direct object *tour* becomes the subject, and the indirect object *employee* becomes the retained object.]

A verb in the passive voice always includes a form of *be* and the verb's past participle. The form of *be* and the helping verb, if any, indicate the tense of the verb phrase.

USAGE

CONJUGATION OF THE VERB *GIVE* IN THE PASSIVE VOICE	
PRESENT TENSE	
SINGULAR	*PLURAL*
I am given	we are given
you are given	you are given
he, she, it is given	they are given
Present Progressive: am, are, is being given	
PAST TENSE	
SINGULAR	*PLURAL*
I was given	we were given
you were given	you were given
he, she, it was given	they were given
Past Progressive: was, were being given	
FUTURE TENSE (*will* or *shall* + infinitive)	
SINGULAR	*PLURAL*
I will (shall) be given	we will (shall) be given
you will be given	you will be given
he, she, it will be given	they will be given
Future Progressive: will (shall) be being given	
PRESENT PERFECT TENSE (*have* or *has* + past participle)	
SINGULAR	*PLURAL*
I have been given	we have been given
you have been given	you have been given
he, she, it has been given	they have been given
PAST PERFECT TENSE (*had* + past participle)	
SINGULAR	*PLURAL*
I had been given	we had been given
you had been given	you had been given
he, she, it had been given	they had been given
FUTURE PERFECT TENSE (*will have* or *shall have* + past participle)	
SINGULAR	*PLURAL*
I will (shall) have been given	we will (shall) have been given
you will have been given	you will have been given
he, she, it will have been given	they will have been given

REFERENCE NOTE: The conjugation of *give* in the active voice is on pages 788–789.

The Uses of the Passive Voice

24m. Use the passive voice sparingly.

Choosing between the active voice and the passive voice is a matter of style, not correctness. In general, however, the passive voice is less direct, less forceful, and less concise than the active voice. In fact, the passive voice may produce an awkward effect.

AWKWARD PASSIVE The final event was completed when a triple somersault was done by Mario.

ACTIVE Mario **completed** the final event by doing a triple somersault.

AWKWARD PASSIVE Steady rains were hoped for by all of us, but a hurricane was wanted by none of us.

ACTIVE All of us **hoped** for steady rains, but none of us wanted a hurricane.

A string of passives is particularly awkward.

STRING OF PASSIVES I was invited by Ms. Long to visit her animal shelter. Rows of cages had been placed along two sides of a large storage shed. Dozens of cats, dogs, hamsters, and guinea pigs were held in the cages. A large parrot was even spotted by me. In one corner of the noisy building, a scrawny, brown puppy was being hand-fed by an assistant. Ms. Long said so many unwanted pets had been brought to her by people, homes could not be found for all of them. It was agreed by us that the responsibility of owning a pet should be understood by people before one is bought.

ACTIVE Ms. Long **invited** me to visit her animal shelter. She **had placed** rows of cages along two sides of a large storage shed. The cages **held** dozens of cats, dogs, hamsters, and guinea pigs. I even **spotted** a large parrot. In one corner of the noisy building, an assistant **was hand-feeding** a scrawny, brown puppy. Ms. Long said people **had brought** her so many unwanted pets that she **could** not **find** homes for all of them. We agreed that people **should understand** the responsibility of owning a pet before they **buy** one.

Passive voice constructions are not always awkward. In fact, the passive voice is useful in the following situations:

(1) when you do not know who performed the action

EXAMPLE All of the tickets **had been sold** weeks before the concert.

(2) when you do not want to reveal the performer

EXAMPLE Shoddy work **was done** on the building.

(3) when you want to emphasize the receiver of the action rather than the performer

EXAMPLES Lasers **are used** in industry, communications, and medicine.
Ivy Swan **has been emulated** by many young singers.

USAGE

 EXERCISE 13 **Revising Sentences in the Passive Voice**

Revise the following sentences by changing verbs in the passive voice to active voice wherever you think the change is desirable. If you think the passive is preferable, write *C*. For each sentence, be prepared to explain why you kept or changed the passive voice verb.

1. After the new computers had been installed by the service reps, a training session was given to us by them.
2. If the children had been enchanted by Mr. Wright's tales before, they would be even more enthralled by his new story of a fantasy kingdom.
3. A community meeting was held by the area homeowners to discuss the landfill project, which had been proposed by the City Council.
4. The value of storytelling is explained in an ancient Seneca myth.
5. While the decorations are being created by Clarence, the buffet will be prepared by Edna.
6. Potatoes had been cultivated by the Incas for more than twenty centuries before they were grown by Europeans.
7. The 1539 expedition of Francisco Vásquez de Coronado was guided by Estevanico, a well-known black explorer.
8. The chapters on constitutional amendments, which had been assigned to us last week by Mrs. Robinson, were reviewed by us before the test.

9. Shinae Chun is admired and respected by her colleagues.
10. If the practicality of home robots had been demonstrated by Mike Smith, his request for funding would not have been rejected by the committee.

Mood

Mood is the form that a verb takes to indicate the attitude of the person using the verb. Verbs may be in one of three moods: *indicative, imperative,* or *subjunctive.*

24n. The ***indicative mood*** is used to express a fact, an opinion, or a question.

EXAMPLES Heitor Villa-Lobos **was** a composer who **became** known for his use of Brazilian folk music.
Amy Tan **is** a gifted writer.
Can you **tell** me when the United States **entered** World War I?

REFERENCE NOTE: For examples of all of the tense forms in the indicative mood, see the conjugations on pages 788–789 and 790–791.

24o. The ***imperative mood*** is used to express a request or a command.

A verb in the imperative mood has only one form. That form is the same as the verb's infinitive form.

EXAMPLES **Tell** me when the United States entered World War I.
Please **pass** the salsa.

24p. The ***subjunctive mood*** is used to express a suggestion, a necessity, a condition contrary to fact, or a wish.

In the subjunctive mood, only the present tense and the past tense have distinctive forms. The other tense forms are the same as those in the indicative mood.

Notice in the following partial conjugation of *be* how the present tense and the past tense in the subjunctive mood differ from those in the indicative mood. [Note: The use of *that* and *if,* which are shown in parentheses, is explained on this page and on page 807.]

PRESENT INDICATIVE		PRESENT SUBJUNCTIVE	
SINGULAR	*PLURAL*	*SINGULAR*	*PLURAL*
I am	we are	(that) I be	(that) we be
you are	you are	(that) you be	(that) you be
he is	they are	(that) he be	(that) they be
PAST INDICATIVE		**PAST SUBJUNCTIVE**	
I was	we were	(if) I were	(if) we were
you were	you were	(if) you were	(if) you were
he was	they were	(if) he were	(if) they were

The present subjunctive form of a verb is the same as its infinitive form. *Be* is the only verb whose past subjunctive form is different from its past indicative form.

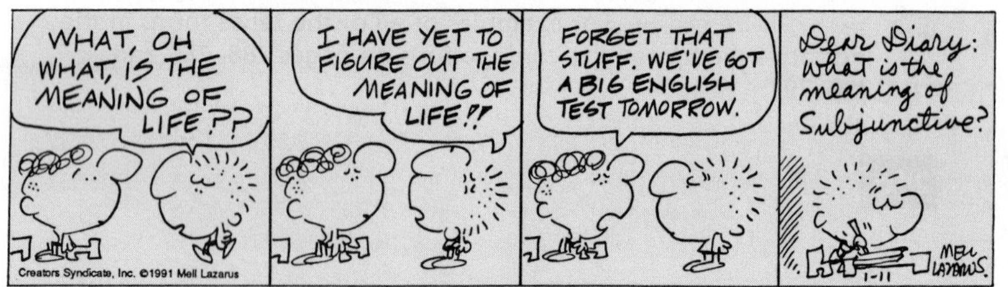

(1) The *present subjunctive* is used to express a suggestion or a necessity.

The verb in a subordinate clause beginning with *that* is usually in the subjunctive mood when a word in the independent clause indicates a suggestion (such as *ask, request, suggest,* or *recommend*) or a necessity (such as *necessary* or *essential*).

EXAMPLES We recommended that Marva Collins **be invited** to speak.

The students have urged that John **be reinstated.**

I move that the motion **be approved.**

It is essential that she **have** a chance to compete.

(2) The ***past subjunctive*** is used to express a condition contrary to fact or to express a wish.

A clause beginning with *if, as if,* or *as though* often expresses a condition contrary to fact—something that is not true. In such a clause, use the past subjunctive.

EXAMPLES If I **were** you, I'd be pleased.
If she **were** to apply, she would undoubtedly be admitted.
My friend Doris teases me as though she **were** my sister.

Similarly, use the past subjunctive to express a wish.

EXAMPLES I wish I **were** on a Caribbean island.
Jaime wishes that his mother **weren't** feeling ill.

USAGE

EXERCISE 14 **Using the Subjunctive Mood Correctly**

Some of the following sentences contain errors in the use of the subjunctive mood. If a sentence is incorrect, give the correct form of the verb. If a sentence is correct, write C.

1. Willis had insisted that every employee is invited to the company's Juneteenth picnic.
2. I'd be a lobster fisherman if I was living on Cape Cod.
3. Gloria was confused all day because it seemed as though it was Friday, but it was only Thursday.
4. Striking out again, Katie moaned, "I wish I was a better hitter!"
5. Vernon lost many of his friends when he began acting as if he were better than they.
6. If bowling was an elective at our school, Lisa and Joshua would be at the front of the line to sign up for it.
7. "I wish this book was a little shorter," sighed Sabrena as she turned to page 378.
8. We often complain about working too many hours; but if we were to work fewer, we would be complaining about smaller paychecks.
9. I wish I was able to go to the sneak preview of the new Spike Lee movie, but I have to work.
10. "I wish this was next year so that I would already be in college," Takala said.

REVIEW F Proofreading Sentences for Errors in the Form and Use of Verbs

For each of the following sentences, correct the error in the form or use of the verb.

1. If we would have checked, we'd have known the library was closed.
2. The movie was especially liked by Kira and her brother because of the beautiful nature photography.
3. If I was Luís, I would have argued with the umpire.
4. Cindy retraced her steps and found the cafe at which she left her credit card.
5. I never realized that hurricanes and typhoons were really the same thing.
6. As he slowly turned the key, the door suddenly swings wide open.
7. Last week, the school newspaper has printed Kim's story.
8. Winning the medal, she revised her practice schedule and gave herself more free time.
9. By the time the next presidential election comes up, I will be in the United States for six years.
10. Mr. Washington wanted to shown them his collection of African sculptures, but he was suddenly called away on business.

REVIEW G Proofreading a Paragraph for Errors in the Form and Use of Verbs

Most of the sentences in the following paragraph contain errors in the form and use of verbs. If a verb is incorrect, give the correct form. If a sentence is correct, write *C.*

[1] Have you ever seen a band of light shimmering over a hot road, as though a pool of water was lying just ahead? [2] Mirages have been just one of many types of illusions that will fool the average observer. [3] The simple illustration shown on the next page will allow you to have experienced another kind of illusion. [4] In a few minutes, the flying bird will be returned to its cage by you. [5] However, to do so, it is essential that you are calm and give the experiment your full attention. [6] Fix your stare on the bird for a minute or two, then focus on the white space in the center of the cage that stands next to the bird. [7] Having stared at the white space, you will, at the same

time, see the bird slowly appear. [8] However, when the bird appears, you will probably have noticed something strange—its feathers will be green and purple. [9] Although you have no longer been looking at the bird, its image (or, rather, its after-image) has remained on your retina. [10] The afterimage is composed of colors opposite to the bird's original red and yellow colors.

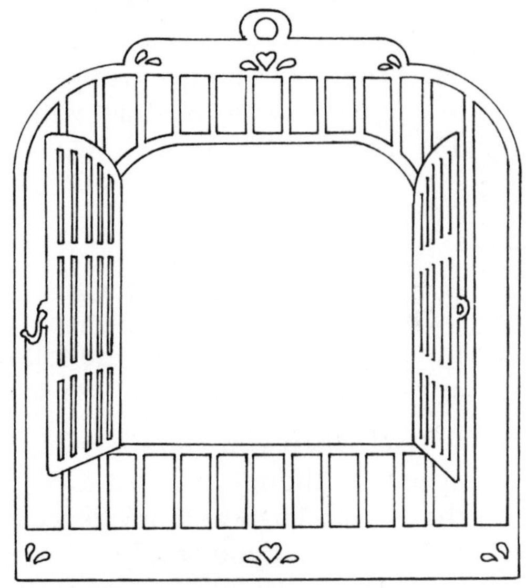

Review: Posttest

A. Proofreading Sentences for Correct Verb Usage

Some of the following sentences contain errors in the use of verbs. If a sentence is incorrect, revise it, using the correct verb. If a sentence is correct, write C.

1. They were setting on the bench and feeding the ducks.
2. She thought the runner had broke the world record.
3. We would have preferred to have eaten Chinese food.
4. Mrs. Ames was pleased that when the driver's test was taken by her son, he passed easily.
5. The shoppers laid down their purchases carefully.
6. We cheered when the movie finally begun.

7. If I was Anne, I would ask for a promotion and a raise.
8. They would have liked to interview the astronauts.
9. On vacation they plan to have gone deep-sea fishing.
10. Yesterday I swum in the Millers' new pool.
11. The rate of inflation has raised steadily.
12. When they returned to the scene, they discovered that the weapon was taken.
13. When I enter college, my parents will be married thirty years.
14. When we saw the group perform, Julia, the lead vocalist, just broke her contract with a big recording company.
15. If we had the chance, we would have stopped by your house.

B. Proofreading for Correct Verb Usage

Revise each sentence in the following paragraph by correcting any incorrect verb forms. If a sentence is correct, write *C.*

[16] When you were a child, you may have played with an abacus as though it was a toy. **[17]** Possibly, a teacher told you that the abacus was a device for counting—for adding and subtracting. **[18]** If you would have spent the time, you might have learned to calculate on this simple device. **[19]** An abacus consists of a series of wooden bars on which beads have slided. **[20]** Because the abacus has been widely used for hundreds of years, many forms have been taken by it. **[21]** For example, on a Chinese abacus, you move beads toward a crossbar to add a sum, while other types of abacuses did not even have a crossbar. **[22]** Mastering the appropriate technique, operators calculate quickly and accurately. **[23]** In fact, on any number of occasions, people using abacuses have beat people using calculators in speed trials. **[24]** Consequently, an abacus sits beside many tradespeople all over Asia, just as it has did for centuries. **[25]** A century from now, the abacus will probably have remained practical, rugged, portable, fast, accurate, and comparatively inexpensive.

25 CORRECT USE OF MODIFIERS

USAGE

Forms of Adjectives and Adverbs; Comparison

Diagnostic Test

A. Selecting Modifiers to Complete Sentences

For each of the following sentences, select the correct modifier from the pair given in parentheses.

EXAMPLE **1.** The hurricane hit the town very (*sudden, suddenly*).
1. *suddenly*

1. The music sounds (*strange, strangely*) on this old record player.
2. The rehearsals for *Porgy and Bess* are going as (*good, well*) as can be expected at this point.

3. Jeanne looked (*casual, casually*) in my direction.
4. My stepbrother Dylan is younger than (*anyone, anyone else*) in his class.
5. The coast road is more scenic, but Route 180 is usually (*quicker, quickest*).
6. "These aerobic exercises seem (*easier, more easier*) to do than the exercises I have been doing," Audrey said.
7. Have you seen a (*friendlier, more friendlier*) spaniel than mine?
8. "Olympia Dukakis was (*real, really*) outstanding in the movie *Moonstruck*," Chris said.
9. The close of the letter read, "With our (*most sincerest, sincerest*) thanks."
10. When you get to the stop sign, turn (*sharp, sharply*) to the left.

B. Proofreading a Paragraph for Correct Use of Modifiers

Most of the sentences in the following paragraph contain errors in the use of modifiers. If a sentence is incorrect, revise the sentence to correct the error. If a sentence is correct, write *C*.

[11] Making a pot on a potter's wheel, or "throwing" a pot, is more relaxing than any artistic activity I know of. **[12]** I feel peacefully as the wheel spins and I shape the ball of clay with my fingers. **[13]** Sometimes I plan what to make, but other times a pot takes shape slow, almost by itself. **[14]** To me, kneading the clay to get rid of air bubbles is the more difficult of the dozen or so steps in throwing a pot. **[15]** The real exciting part is pulling up on the clay to form a cone and then pressing a hole in the center. **[16]** To prevent the pot from becoming lopsided, I have to work steady and keep the wheel spinning. **[17]** I'm happiest while gently pressing the clay and forming the walls of a pot. **[18]** This stage is more pleasant than any other stage because I can daydream as my fingers seem to do the work almost automatically. **[19]** Most of the time, though, I have to concentrate careful to make a perfect pot. **[20]** I usually don't feel too badly if a pot doesn't turn out right the first time; part of the fun is starting over.

Forms of Modifiers

A ***modifier*** is a word that limits the meaning of another word. The two kinds of modifiers are the *adjective* and the *adverb.*

An ***adjective*** limits the meaning of a noun or a pronoun.

EXAMPLES a **perfect** score an **eager** participant
a **clear** night the **last** one

An ***adverb*** limits the meaning of a verb, an adjective, or another adverb.

EXAMPLES walks **briskly** **gradually** appeared
completely innocent working **remarkably** hard

Most modifiers with an *–ly* ending are used as adverbs. Many adverbs, in fact, are formed by adding *–ly* to an adjective.

ADJECTIVES	usual	calm	brief	absurd	appropriate
ADVERBS	usually	calmly	briefly	absurdly	appropriately

Some modifiers ending in *–ly* may be used as adjectives.

EXAMPLES **monthly** budget **early** indication **likely** outcome

A few modifiers have the same form whether they are used as adjectives or as adverbs.

ADJECTIVES	ADVERBS
a **fast** train	moves **fast**
a **little** speech	spoke **little**
an **early** start	starting **early**

Uses of Modifiers

25a. Use an adjective to modify the subject of a linking verb.

The most common linking verbs are the forms of *be: am, is, are, was, were, be, been,* and *being*. A linking verb is often followed by a *predicate adjective*—a word that modifies the subject.

EXAMPLES The company's training program is **rigorous.**
The baby soon became **tired** and **cranky.**

25b. Use an adverb to modify an action verb.

An action verb is often modified by an adverb—a word that explains *how, when, where,* or *to what extent* the action is performed.

EXAMPLES The world's population is increasing **rapidly.**
The astronaut spoke **enthusiastically** about her successful mission in space.

Some verbs may be used as linking verbs or action verbs.

EXAMPLES Carlos looked **happy.** [*Looked* is a linking verb. Notice that the modifier following it, *happy,* is an adjective.]
Carlos looked **happily** at his latest design. [*Looked* is an action verb. Notice that the modifier following it, *happily,* is an adverb.]

To determine whether to use an adjective or an adverb after a verb, replace the verb with the appropriate form of the linking verb *seem.* If *seem* makes sense in the sentence, the original verb is being used as a linking verb, which calls for an adjective. If *seem* is absurd in the sentence, the original verb is being used as an action verb, which calls for an adverb.

EXAMPLES Carlos looked happy. [Since *Carlos seemed happy* makes sense, *looked* is being used as a linking verb and calls for the adjective *happy.*]
Carlos looked happily at his latest design. [Since *Carlos seemed happily at his latest design* is absurd, *looked* is being used as an action verb and calls for the adverb *happily.*]

REFERENCE NOTE: See pages 612–613 for more information about linking verbs and action verbs. For more about predicate adjectives, see pages 642–643.

USAGE

EXERCISE 1 Selecting Modifiers to Complete Sentences

Select the correct modifier from the pair given in parentheses in each of the following sentences.

1. The sled's runners slid (*smooth, smoothly*) over the ice.
2. The weather outside looks (*miserable, miserably*).
3. Neka embroidered the rain-bird symbol (*perfect, perfectly*), checking each stitch as she worked.

4. Doesn't the official explanation of the budget cut sound (*incredible, incredibly*) to you?
5. Why was she looking at me (*suspicious, suspiciously*)?
6. This apple tastes (*peculiar, peculiarly*) to me.
7. Mike smiled (*proud, proudly*) when he told us about his West African heritage.
8. Dawn goes jogging (*regular, regularly*).
9. He disappeared (*silent, silently*) into the underbrush.
10. The conference room smelled (*stuffy, stuffily*).

EXERCISE 2 Selecting Modifiers to Complete Sentences

For each sentence in the following paragraph, select the correct modifier from the pair given in parentheses.

[1] In this picture, Debbie Allen dances (*energetic, energetically*) in a scene from the TV series *Fame.* [2] You might say that fame itself looks (*comfortable, comfortably*) on her. [3] Allen, who grew up in Houston, Texas, has danced (*continual, continually*) since the age of three. [4] She attended the Houston Ballet School, graduated from Howard University, and then headed (*confident, confidently*) to New York City. [5] On Broadway, she was (*triumphant, triumphantly*) in the revivals of the musicals *West Side Story* and *Sweet Charity.* [6] Later, she (*successful, successfully*) choreographed *Fame* and won two Emmy Awards for her work on that show. [7] Allen looks (*natural, naturally*) in a director's chair, too, and has directed episodes of such TV shows as *A Different World* and *Quantum Leap.* [8] Through the

years, she has worked (*diligent, diligently*) and has battled racism and sexism to succeed. [9] Never one to accept second best, Allen has risen (*steady, steadily*) to the top in her profession. [10] In interviews, Debbie Allen seems (*proud, proudly*) of her achievements but ready for new challenges, too.

Eight Troublesome Modifiers

Bad and *Badly*

USAGE

Bad is an adjective. *Badly* is an adverb. In standard English, only the adjective form should follow a sense verb, such as *feel, see, hear, taste,* or *smell,* or other linking verb.

NONSTANDARD This leftover chicken smells badly.
STANDARD This leftover chicken smells **bad.**

NOTE: The expression *feel badly* has become acceptable in informal situations, but use *feel bad* in formal speaking and writing.

Good and *Well*

Good is an adjective. *Well* may be used as an adjective or an adverb. Avoid using *good* to modify an action verb. Instead, use *well* as an adverb meaning "capably" or "satisfactorily."

NONSTANDARD The track team did good at the meet.
STANDARD The track team did **well** at the meet.

NONSTANDARD Bao performs good even under pressure.
STANDARD Bao performs **well** even under pressure.

As an adjective, *well* means "in good health" or "satisfactory in appearance or condition."

EXAMPLES Yes, I feel quite **well,** thank you.
You look **well** in your new outfit.
All is **well** with us.

Real and *Really*

Real is an adjective. *Really* is an adverb meaning "actually" or "truly." Although *real* is commonly used as an adverb meaning "very" in everyday situations, avoid its use in formal speaking and writing.

INFORMAL Your new car is real nice.
FORMAL Your new car is **really** nice.

INFORMAL He played real well in the tryouts.
FORMAL He played **really** well in the tryouts.

Slow and *Slowly*

Slow is an adjective. *Slowly* is an adverb. Although *slow* is also labeled as an adverb in many dictionaries, this usage applies only to informal situations and colloquial expressions, such as *drive slow* and *go slow.*

INFORMAL She eased slow out of the cockpit.
FORMAL She eased **slowly** out of the cockpit.

EXERCISE 3

Revising Sentences to Correct Errors in the Use of *Bad—Badly, Good—Well, Real—Really,* and *Slow—Slowly*

For each of the following sentences, if a modifier is incorrect, give the correct form. If the sentence is correct, write *C.*

EXAMPLE **1.** After a long rehearsal, the dance troupe performed good.
1. *well*

1. After she had lost the election, Bernadette felt very bad.
2. Charlotte seemed real happy about getting an A on her history test.
3. Ms. Stein is a good teacher who prepares her lessons well.
4. Some shades of blue and green go good together.

USAGE

5. Chen tried to teach me to use chopsticks, but the lesson didn't go very good.
6. "I'm positive I did good on that test," Anzu confidently remarked.
7. Since it is very sweet, the Turkish candy halvah should be served in small pieces and eaten slowly.
8. Everyone wondered whether the stone he found was a real diamond.
9. "Remember to speak slow when you give your speech," Mr. Schmidt advised the nervous candidate.
10. "Life can't be treating you all that bad," I told Walker.

REVIEW A **Determining the Correct Use of Modifiers**

Each of the following sentences contains an italicized modifier. If the modifier is incorrect, give the correct form. If the modifier is correct, write *C*. Then identify the word that each modifier describes.

EXAMPLE **1.** Something sounds *strangely* next door.
1. *strange*

1. The players did *good* in the fourth quarter.
2. The bread dough rose too *quick*.
3. We walked *slow* on the icy sidewalk.
4. Sam feels *bad* about forgetting your birthday.
5. She sounded very *angrily* on the phone.
6. These new jeans do not fit me *good* at all.
7. Rita answered the questions *precisely*.
8. Fortunately, no one was hurt *bad* in the accident.
9. Mr. Tate's company can do the job *efficiently*.
10. The judge rapped her gavel *sharp* to restore order.

REVIEW B **Proofreading for Correct Use of Modifiers**

Most of the sentences in the following paragraph contain errors in the use of modifiers. Identify each incorrect modifier and give the correct form. If a sentence is correct, write *C*.

[1] The popularity of country and western music (C & W) has grown tremendous in the last twenty-five years. [2] In fact, many radio stations all over the nation are playing C & W exclusive. [3] Nowadays, country music appeals to fans of near all ages and occupations. [4] For example, one recently American

president, George Bush, officially declared his fondness for country music when he attended the Country Music Awards ceremony. [5] Top country stars, such as Clint Black, Reba McEntire, and Garth Brooks, not only have best-selling albums but play to increasing large numbers of fans. [6] In the photo below, for example, Garth Brooks looks cheerfully as he acknowledges his fans' enthusiastic applause. [7] Many C & W performers, such as Brooks, are known for their wildly successful music videos. [8] Some country singers feel badly about the problems in America and have started taking musical stands on social issues. [9] Others do real well singing songs on the traditional country themes of love and heartache. [10] Veteran performer Loretta Lynn, country music's own "Coal Miner's Daughter," is shown here singing movingly before an admiring crowd.

Comparison of Modifiers

25c. ***Comparison*** refers to the change in the form of an adjective or an adverb to show increasing or decreasing degrees in the quality that the modifier expresses.

There are three degrees of comparison: *positive, comparative,* and *superlative.*

	POSITIVE	COMPARATIVE	SUPERLATIVE
Adjectives	big	bigger	biggest
	eager	more eager	most eager
	good	better	best
Adverbs	late	later	latest
	swiftly	more swiftly	most swiftly
	well	better	best

Regular Comparison

(1) Most one-syllable modifiers form the comparative and superlative degrees by adding *–er* and *–est.*

POSITIVE	COMPARATIVE	SUPERLATIVE
neat	neater	neatest
warm	warmer	warmest
fast	faster	fastest
straight	straighter	straightest

(2) Some two-syllable modifiers form the comparative and superlative degrees by adding *–er* or *–est.* Other two-syllable modifiers form the comparative and superlative degrees by using *more* and *most.*

POSITIVE	COMPARATIVE	SUPERLATIVE
gentle	gentler	gentlest
lively	livelier	liveliest
agile	more agile	most agile
clearly	more clearly	most clearly

If you are not sure how a two-syllable modifier is compared, check a dictionary.

REFERENCE NOTE: For guidelines on spelling modifiers with *–er* and *–est,* see pages 966–968.

(3) Modifiers of more than two syllables form the comparative and superlative degrees by using *more* and *most.*

POSITIVE	COMPARATIVE	SUPERLATIVE
expensive	more expensive	most expensive
delightful	more delightful	most delightful
quietly	more quietly	most quietly
poetically	more poetically	most poetically

(4) To show a decrease in the qualities they express, all modifiers form the comparative and superlative degrees by using *less* and *least.*

POSITIVE	COMPARATIVE	SUPERLATIVE
weak	less weak	least weak
useful	less useful	least useful
contentedly	less contentedly	least contentedly
urgently	less urgently	least urgently

Irregular Comparison

Some modifiers do not follow the regular methods of forming the comparative and superlative degrees.

POSITIVE	COMPARATIVE	SUPERLATIVE
bad	worse	worst
good	better	best
well	better	best
little	less	least
many	more	most
much	more	most

EXERCISE 4 **Writing the Comparative and Superlative Forms of Modifiers**

Give the comparative form and the superlative form of each of the following modifiers. Use a dictionary to check any words you are unsure of.

EXAMPLE **1.** flat
1. *flatter, flattest*

1. tiny **3.** wistful **5.** curious **7.** thin **9.** gently
2. ill **4.** modest **6.** proudly **8.** good **10.** abruptly

USAGE

Uses of Comparative Forms and Superlative Forms

25d. Use the comparative degree when comparing two things. Use the superlative degree when comparing more than two.

COMPARATIVE Although both Laura and Justin wrote about the development of the Swahili culture, Laura's paper was **longer.** [comparison of two papers]
After listening to both candidates, we concluded that Ms. García was the **more highly** qualified. [comparison of two candidates]

SUPERLATIVE Of the four major river-valley cultures that arose long ago in Africa and Asia, the Huang He was probably the **most fully** isolated from the others. [comparison of four civilizations]
I bought this model of car because it gets the **best** mileage. [comparison of many models]

NOTE: In informal situations, the superlative degree is sometimes used to emphasize the comparison of only two things. Avoid such use of the superlative degree in formal speaking and writing.

INFORMAL Which park did you enjoy most, Yellowstone or Hot Springs?
FORMAL Which park did you enjoy **more,** Yellowstone or Hot Springs?

The superlative degree is also used to compare two things in some idiomatic expressions.

EXAMPLE Put your best foot forward.

PICTURE THIS

Until now, you never imagined that chemistry could be so fascinating! Viewing this image through a microscope, you realize that science can, indeed, be stranger than fiction. This beautiful "landscape" is actually a magnified piece of agate (a semiprecious stone). Since your chemistry teacher expects your lab report to include careful, precise notes on what you see, write a clear, accurate description of this microscopic image. In your description, use at least three adjectives and two adverbs.

John I. Koivula/Courtesy of Nikon Small World Photo Competition

Subject: a piece of agate seen through a microscope
Audience: yourself and your chemistry teacher
Purpose: to record information; to inform

25e. Include the word *other* or *else* when comparing one member of a group with the rest of the members.

NONSTANDARD Diamond, a crystalline form of carbon, is harder than any mineral in the world. [The diamond is one of the minerals of the world. Logically, the diamond cannot be harder than itself.]

STANDARD Diamond, a crystalline form of carbon, is harder than any **other** mineral in the world.

NONSTANDARD	Pete has won more races than anyone in his club. [Pete is a member of the club. Logically, he cannot have won more races than himself.]
STANDARD	Pete has won more races than anyone **else** in his club.

25f. Avoid double comparisons.

A ***double comparison*** is the result of using two comparative forms (usually *–er* and *more*) or using two superlative forms (usually *–est* and *most*) to modify the same word.

NONSTANDARD	Alice is a more faster swimmer than you.
STANDARD	Alice is a **faster** swimmer than you.
NONSTANDARD	She is the most smartest girl in school.
STANDARD	She is the **smartest** girl in school.

USAGE

EXERCISE 5 Using the Comparative and Superlative Forms of Modifiers

Revise the following sentences by correcting the errors in the use of the comparative and the superlative forms of modifiers. If a sentence is correct, write *C*.

EXAMPLE **1.** That was the most highest grade Oscar ever earned on a Spanish test.
1. *highest*

1. Colleen thought nothing could be as bad as the snow; but when the ice storm hit, she said, "This is even worser!"
2. Both twins, Holly and Julie, have brown eyes, but Holly's are darkest.
3. In each graduating class, the valedictorian is the student whose academic average is higher than that of any senior.
4. Thomas Jefferson is generally regarded as one of the more important Americans in United States history.
5. To gain a more clear understanding of the problems in the Middle East, people need to learn more about the history of that region.
6. Suzanne made the mistake of buying less paint than she needed for the small room.
7. Performing better than all the gymnasts, Mary Lou Retton was the first American to win an Olympic gold medal in her sport.

8. Myles is taking more classes than I.
9. Dividing the pumpkin pie in two, Felicia gave me the largest portion.
10. According to my friend Juan, Houston, Texas, is more interesting and more exciting than any city in that state.

REVIEW C **Using Modifiers Correctly**

Some of the following sentences contain errors in the use of modifiers. Revise each incorrect sentence to correct the error. If a sentence is correct, write *C*.

1. I am least prepared to take the test than you.
2. Jim speaks Portuguese more fluently than anyone in our class.
3. You cheered more often than anyone at the concert.
4. Mr. Brown is many pounds more heavier than I.
5. The picture looks much more clearer on this television set than on that one.
6. We thought Patti was the most talented of all the actors in the community play.
7. I read the shorter of the three books for my report.
8. I have narrowed my choices to two colleges, and I want to visit them to see which I like best.
9. She was less determined to win than her sister was.
10. Modeling her mother's silk kimono, Toshi seemed even gracefuller than usual.

REVIEW D **Proofreading for Correct Use of Modifiers**

Most of the sentences in the following paragraph contain errors in the use of modifiers. If a sentence is incorrect, revise the sentence to correct the error. If a sentence is correct, write *C*.

[1] Of all the world's movie directors, Akira Kurosawa of Japan is considered one of the greater. [2] He is certainly better known in the United States than any Japanese director. [3] In addition to directing, the multitalented Kurosawa has edited and written many of his films. [4] Acclaimed by critics, his films not only look beautifully, but they also contain serious moral themes. [5] Among the more popular of his dozens of films is *Ran,* which blends Shakespeare's *King Lear* with a Japanese folk tale. [6] Kurosawa made the story more forcefuler for his

Japanese audience by having the conflict be between a father and three sons instead of three daughters. [7] That conflict is real apparent in this scene from *Ran*. [8] Moviegoers in the United States also enjoyed Kurosawa's film *Dersu Uzala*, which won an Academy Award for bestest foreign film. [9] The stark scenery in that film certainly shows how fiercely the Siberian wilderness can be. [10] If you have the chance to see these two films, you can decide which one you like best.

USAGE

WRITING APPLICATION

Using Comparisons in a Consumer's Guide

Each day, you make choices about how to spend your time and money. You decide which movies to see, which products to buy, which clubs and sports to participate in. Often, you arrive at a decision by comparing two or more alternatives. You express such comparisons by using adjectives and adverbs in comparative and superlative forms.

EXAMPLE I buy Pimple-Go acne medication because it works **more quickly** than No-Blemish. Pimple-Go also has the **strongest** formula available over the counter.

WRITING ACTIVITY

With so many products and services claiming to be the "best," how do you know which ones to choose? You and your classmates have decided to compile an informal consumer's guide to some everyday products and services available in your community. Choose a product, such as sandwiches or jeans, or a service, such as car washing or hair cutting. Write a paragraph or two comparing at least three different choices for the product or service and telling which, if any, you think is best. In your writing, use at least three comparative and two superlative forms of modifiers.

Prewriting You and your classmates may want to work together to compile a list of products and services. Then decide which type of product or service each person will write about. Jot down notes on at least three alternatives, judging the quality, effectiveness, and cost of each. Use your notes to help you compare the brands. Be sure to judge each by the same criteria. You may wish to look in some reliable consumer guides to see the kinds of criteria their evaluators use.

Writing Begin your draft by identifying the type of product or service you are evaluating and listing the brands you will focus on. Then give a detailed comparison of the brands. Rate the alternatives on quality, effectiveness, and value. Give specific, objective reasons for your opinions.

Evaluating and Revising Ask a classmate to read your draft. Have you evaluated each alternative thoroughly? Have you stated your opinion clearly? Are the reasons for your opinion clear? If not, add, cut, or revise information. Be sure that you've used at least three comparative and two superlative forms of modifiers.

Proofreading and Publishing Check your writing for errors in grammar, usage, punctuation, and spelling. Pay special attention to modifiers, and revise any double comparisons. You and your classmates may wish to publish a consumer's guide by compiling your evaluations in a booklet. You can then use the booklet as a handy reference for choosing local products or services.

USAGE

Review: Posttest

A. Using Modifiers Correctly

Most of the following sentences contain errors in the use of modifiers. If a sentence is incorrect, revise the sentence to correct the error. If a sentence is correct, write *C*.

EXAMPLE **1.** Among my three brothers and sisters, my sister Giselle has the better sense of humor.
1. *best*

1. Which is widest, the Mississippi River or the Colorado River?
2. When the temperature reached 103 degrees in August, the board of health warned people not to go outdoors unless they absolutely had to.
3. That is the most palest shade of blue I have ever seen.
4. Because the drummer played bad, the band's melody line was drowned out.
5. Pointing to the two glasses partially filled with water, the magician asked, "Which glass has the least water?"
6. When you dress for a job interview, you should wear the styles and colors of clothing that look attractively on you.
7. If Mark keeps pedaling his bike that slow, he'll never get home before dark.
8. Has Thomas been saving money regular for his trip to the Yucatán?
9. Philadelphia and Atlantic City are the largest cities near my home, but Philadelphia is the closest.
10. Even though they can't play their guitars too good, their albums sell well.
11. "Nurse López, I feel remarkably well today, better than I have ever felt before," said Mr. Parker.
12. "Sharon has been working harder than anyone here," I said.
13. My brother William became the strongest player on the wheelchair basketball team.
14. You can adjust the control on the television set to make the picture a little less brighter.
15. The cheese smells badly but tastes good.

B. Selecting Modifiers to Complete Sentences

For each sentence in the following paragraph, select the correct modifier from the pair given in parentheses.

[16] It's (*real, really*) amazing what house movers can accomplish! **[17]** One of the (*more, most*) interesting house-moving feats involved the Queen Anne Mansion in Eureka Springs, Arkansas. **[18]** Built in 1891, the three-story home, with a tower and wrap-around porch, was moved (*efficient, efficiently*) from Carthage, Missouri. **[19]** Beginning in May, 1984, crews worked (*quick, quickly*) to dismantle the mansion. **[20]** They used special tools and worked (*careful, carefully*) to cut and pry the building apart. **[21]** The contractor had planned (*good, well*), and the first pieces of the home arrived in Eureka Springs in October of that year. **[22]** The ninety-mile move, the (*larger, largest*) ever seen in that area, required thirty-seven long flatbed trucks and three storage vans. **[23]** The new owners looked on (*happy, happily*) as workers reassembled the mansion's more than two thousand exterior stones, its wooden walls and floors, its hand-beveled windows, and its central oak staircase. **[24]** The restored Victorian mansion, which opened for tours in 1985, has a more unusual history than (*any, any other*) house in the city. **[25]** It now looks (*impressive, impressively*), set atop a hill near downtown Eureka Springs.

USAGE

26 Placement of Modifiers

Misplaced and Dangling Modifiers

Diagnostic Test

A. Revising Sentences by Correcting Faulty Modifiers

The following sentences contain misplaced, dangling, and two-way modifiers. Revise each sentence so that its meaning will be clear on first reading.

1. The Kovaks gave a toy robot to one of their children with a square glass head and flashing red eyes.
2. Pounding the piano keys with all her might, the chords of the prelude resounded through the concert hall.
3. We saw a herd of sheep on the way to our hotel in Wales.
4. To succeed in college, a great deal of time must be spent studying.
5. Topped with yogurt, many people love fresh strawberries.

6. When only five years old, Dad took me camping on the Fort Apache Reservation in Arizona.
7. While trying to get ready for school, the doorbell rang suddenly.
8. Elaine told Joanne after the first act the drama gets more exciting.
9. By putting money aside regularly, a small savings account will grow steadily larger.
10. A tarantula bit one of the dock workers that had a hairy, huge body as big as a man's hand.

B. Revising Sentences by Correcting Faulty Modifiers

The following sentences contain misplaced, dangling, and two-way modifiers. Revise each sentence so that its meaning will be clear on first reading.

11. Jody said on Saturday Fred should go to the antique and classic car show.
12. Seeing a red 1928 Hispano-Suiza motorcar, his family's minivan seemed bulky and drab to Rick.
13. The Volkswagen "Beetle" remains one of the world's most popular cars first made in Germany in 1938.
14. Captivated by the Italian sports cars, the 1938 Alfa Romeo impressed Mark.
15. Mr. Reynolds showed a Model T Ford to his daughter that came off the assembly line in 1924.
16. Would you please tell Thelma after lunch Mary Beth plans to watch the documentary about the history of European and American motorcars?
17. To keep a classic car in excellent condition, much money and patience often are needed.
18. I got a chance to ride in a 1914 Rolls-Royce Continental that the Arnolds restored during the parade.
19. After writing a report about classic luxury motorcars, the 1940 Packard and 1938 Lagonda De Ville were of special interest to me.
20. Looking at the various exhibits, it is easy to see why very early cars were called horseless carriages.

Misplaced Modifiers

A modifying phrase or clause that is placed too far from the word it sensibly modifies is called a ***misplaced modifier.***

26a. Avoid using a misplaced modifier.

To correct a misplaced modifier, place the phrase or clause as close as possible to the word you intend it to modify.

MISPLACED I finished reading the book that Alice Walker wrote about Langston Hughes during spring break. [Did Alice Walker write the book about Langston Hughes during spring break?]

CLEAR **During spring break** I finished reading the book that Alice Walker wrote about Langston Hughes.

MISPLACED My uncle served us his prize-winning flan filled with a sense of pride. [Was the flan filled with a sense of pride?]

CLEAR **Filled with a sense of pride,** my uncle served us his prize-winning flan.

MISPLACED The thief tried to run away from the police officer abandoning the stolen car and dashing into the woods. [Was the police officer abandoning the stolen car and dashing into the woods?]

CLEAR **Abandoning the stolen car and dashing into the woods,** the thief tried to run away from the police officer.

MISPLACED I bought a small computer for the accounting staff, which gave everyone a great deal of trouble. [Did the staff give everyone a great deal of trouble?]

CLEAR I bought the accounting staff a small computer, **which gave everyone a great deal of trouble.**

Avoid placing a phrase or clause so that it seems to modify either of two words. Such a misplaced modifier is often called a ***two-way,*** or ***squinting, modifier.***

MISPLACED Mary said during rehearsal Lori acted nervous. [Did Mary say this about Lori during rehearsal, or did Lori act nervous during rehearsal?]

CLEAR **During rehearsal** Mary said Lori acted nervous.

CLEAR Mary said Lori acted nervous **during rehearsal.**

MISPLACED Tell Marco before he goes to his karate class I want to see him.

CLEAR **Before he goes to his karate class,** tell Marco I want to see him.

CLEAR Tell Marco I want to see him **before he goes to his karate class.**

REFERENCE NOTE: For information about using commas with modifying phrases and clauses, see pages 909–910.

EXERCISE 1 Revising Sentences by Correcting Misplaced Modifiers

The following sentences contain misplaced modifiers. Revise each sentence so that its meaning is clear and correct.

EXAMPLE **1.** Recently vetoed by the president, Congress is amending the tax bill.

1. *Congress is amending the tax bill recently vetoed by the president.*

1. Captain Andre Callioux was one of many heroic African American soldiers who fought during the Civil War in the Union Army.
2. Mrs. Rodríguez announced at the end of the period she would treat the students to a real Mexican fiesta.
3. One of our observers sighted a plane through binoculars that she could not identify.
4. The causeway has a drawbridge to permit the passage of large boats from which all fishing is prohibited.
5. Please tell Terry when he gets home from the mall Mom wants him to make dinner.
6. At Tuesday's meeting, the mayor discussed the enormous cost of draining Buskill Swamp with city council members.
7. Father bought a gadget from a fast-talking salesclerk that was guaranteed to reduce gas consumption in our car.
8. Li Hua inherited that antique fan from her great-aunt that has a mother-of-pearl handle.
9. Ms. Steinberg, the explorer, described her trips through the jungle in our social studies class.
10. Uncle Jim said after reading all the consumer guides and asking his friends for advice he would decide what kind of personal computer to buy.

PICTURE THIS

You are a writer for the magazine *Art Notes*, and you're reviewing a new exhibit of abstract paintings. At the exhibit, this painting, called *Untitled*, by Tony Da immediately catches your attention. Write a paragraph or two about the painting to include in your review of the exhibit. First describe the painting, and then give your opinion of it. If your readers visit the exhibit, should they make a special point of seeing this painting? Tell why or why not. In your review, use at least five modifying phrases and clauses.

Subject: an abstract painting
Audience: readers of an art magazine
Purpose: to evaluate a painting in an exhibit; to persuade

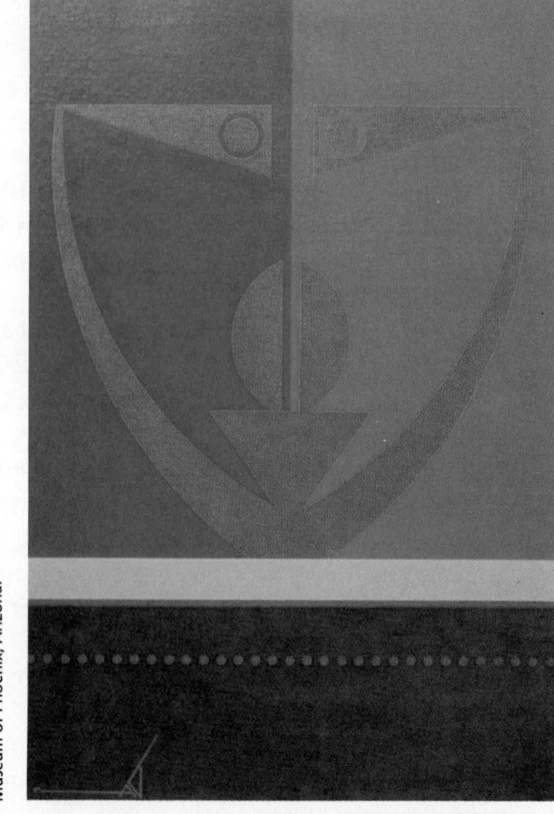

Dangling Modifiers

A modifying phrase or clause that does not sensibly modify any word or group of words in the sentence is called a ***dangling modifier.***

26b. Avoid using a dangling modifier.

You may correct a dangling modifier by adding a word that the phrase or clause can sensibly modify, by adding words to the phrase or clause so that its meaning is clear, or by rewording the sentence.

DANGLING After reading the article "Keeping America Beautiful," a recycling program was organized in their neighborhood. [Who read the article?]

CLEAR **After reading the article "Keeping America Beautiful," Luís and Olan** organized a recycling program in their neighborhood.

CLEAR **After Luís and Olan read the article "Keeping America Beautiful,"** they organized a recycling program in their neighborhood.

DANGLING To win the election, your support will be needed. [Is your support trying to win the election?]

CLEAR **To win the election, I** will need your support.

CLEAR **If I am to win the election,** I will need your support.

DANGLING Representing the conservative viewpoint, the liberals opposed her. [Were the liberals representing the conservative viewpoint?]

CLEAR **Representing the conservative viewpoint, she** was opposed by the liberals.

CLEAR **Since she represented the conservative viewpoint,** the liberals opposed her.

DANGLING Convicted of stealing a loaf of bread for his sister's seven starving children, Jean Valjean's sentence was five years in prison. [Was Jean Valjean's sentence convicted?]

CLEAR **Convicted of stealing a loaf of bread for his sister's seven starving children, Jean Valjean** was sentenced to five years in prison.

CLEAR **Jean Valjean was convicted of stealing a loaf of bread for his sister's seven starving children** and was sentenced to five years in prison.

NOTE: A few dangling modifiers have become standard idiomatic expressions.

EXAMPLES **Judging from the audience's response,** the band's new number will be a big hit.
Relatively speaking, the cost of living remained static for several years.
To be perfectly frank, the rate of inflation is still too high.

REFERENCE NOTE: For more information about idiomatic expressions, see page 534.

EXERCISE 2 Revising Sentences by Correcting Dangling Modifiers

The following sentences contain dangling modifiers. Revise each sentence so that its meaning is clear and correct.

EXAMPLE **1. Before moving to San Angelo, Miami had been their home.**
1. *Before they moved to San Angelo, Miami had been their home.*

1. Listening to his grandfather's stories, it was amazing to learn that several of their ancestors had worked with the Underground Railroad.
2. Architecturally striking, everyone is impressed by the new building's size and elegance.
3. When selecting a college, a number of factors should be considered.
4. While talking with some friends of mine, the topic of careers in dentistry came up.
5. After searching all over the bookstore, Amy Tan's novel was found in the "Best-seller" section.
6. To keep the guacamole dip from turning brown, its surface should be covered with a thin layer of lemon juice.
7. After working in the fields all day, little energy was left for social activities.
8. To understand many of the allusions in modern literature, a knowledge of Greek and Roman myths is essential.
9. Having promised to be home by midnight, Mom was still waiting up when the door opened at two o'clock.
10. Riding in the glass-bottomed boat, hundreds of beautiful tropical fish could be seen.

 REVIEW

Revising Sentences by Correcting Faulty Modifiers

The sentences in the following paragraph contain misplaced and dangling modifiers. Revise each sentence so that its meaning will be clear on first reading.

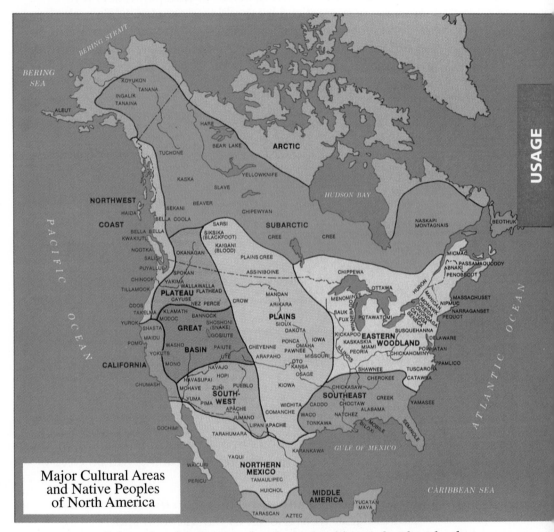

Major Cultural Areas and Native Peoples of North America

[1] I found a fascinating book at the library book sale that includes this map showing where Native Americans traditionally lived on the Plains. [2] You can see the homelands of the major Plains peoples, looking at the map. [3] The size of the Great Plains especially surprised me, extending farther north and south than I had thought. [4] While thumbing through the

book, this picture of a Sioux encampment caught my attention. [5] Living much of the year in villages, farming was the main activity of most of these peoples. [6] However, I read during the summer they hunted buffalo. [7] They followed the buffalo across the plains, which provided them with food and clothing. [8] Characterized by a strong sense of independence, a form of democracy was practiced by the Plains peoples. [9] To make key decisions, votes were cast at council meetings. [10] I'm going to find out more about such peoples as the Crow and Cheyenne, having read this fascinating book about the peoples of the Plains.

Review: Posttest

A. Revising Sentences by Correcting Faulty Modifiers

The following sentences contain misplaced and dangling modifiers. Revise each sentence so that its meaning will be clear on first reading.

1. Preferring the mountains rather than the seashore, the Adirondacks were chosen as our vacation spot.
2. After working in Washington for more than twenty years, the methods of lobbyists were familiar.
3. This bank approves car loans to qualified individuals of any size.
4. Because they were untamed, the signs warned that the animals were dangerous.

5. One can see more than a hundred lakes, flying at an altitude of several thousand feet.
6. Jack bought a book of shorthand lessons along with his new typewriter, which he read and studied diligently.
7. Living constantly under the watchful eyes of the police, her nervousness increased.
8. We followed several routes that early Spanish explorers took on vacation last year.
9. Salvador said after the game the referee explained his unpopular decision to the two team captains.
10. Rounding a sharp curve on El Camino del Rio on the way to Big Bend, a detour sign warned us of danger.

B. Revising Sentences by Correcting Faulty Modifiers

The following sentences contain misplaced and dangling modifiers. Revise each sentence so that its meaning will be clear on first reading.

11. Among popular mystery writers, the novels of Agatha Christie continue to lead sales.
12. Phoebe said in the summer Karl is planning to read all of Christie's novels about the Belgian detective Hercule Poirot.
13. Pat saw Christie's whodunit play *The Mousetrap* last year in London, which has been running since 1952.
14. Concluding the play, the audience is always told by the cast not to give away the surprise ending.
15. After reading all of Christie's novels, our library received many requests for books by another great mystery writer, Dorothy L. Sayers.
16. When in junior high school, Mom bought me my first Sayers mystery.
17. A British nobleman and amateur detective, there are few criminal investigators who rival Lord Peter Wimsey.
18. After reading a detective story by Ngaio (pronounced Ny-o) Marsh, New Zealand became an interest of mine.
19. One of my favorite mysteries, I have read Marsh's *Died in the Wool* three times.
20. Fond of mysteries, novels such as *Devices and Desires* by British author P. D. James keep Ben spellbound.

27 A Glossary of Usage

Common Usage Problems

Diagnostic Test

A. Identifying Correct Usage

For each of the following sentences, choose the correct word or words in parentheses.

EXAMPLE **1. We were (*kind of, rather*) disappointed with the results.**
1. *rather*

1. After Shirley had starred in our spring play, she acted (*like, as if*) she were a famous movie star.
2. When we need the tape, we never know where (*it's at, it is*).
3. At the restaurant where I work, all four of us divide the tips evenly (*between, among*) ourselves.
4. As I was about to pay for my new jeans, I discovered that I (*had, hadn't*) scarcely any money in my wallet.
5. (*Accept, Except*) for Carlos and Glenn, everyone went to the fair.

6. The reason we are moving is (*because, that*) our parents have always wanted to live in Oregon.
7. Although we do the same type of work, Hasina and I are (*affected, effected*) differently by it.
8. (*Bring, Take*) the dog with you when you go for a walk.
9. Looking at the crisp green beans, Rosa said, "(*This, Those*) kind of bean has always been my favorite."
10. Both of Emily's grandmothers (*immigrated, emigrated*) here from Poland.

B. Identifying Correct Usage

For each sentence in the following paragraph, choose the correct word or words in parentheses.

EXAMPLE **[1]** (*Don't, Doesn't*) a hot summer day make you long for an ice-cold drink?
1. *Doesn't*

[11] Even during ancient times, people (*which, who*) were sweltering in the heat found ways to cool off. **[12]** Around 3000 B.C., the Egyptians beat the heat when they (*discovered, invented*) the cooling effect of evaporation. **[13]** The Egyptians poured water into shallow trays made of clay; (*than, then*) they put the trays on a layer of straw. **[14]** As the temperature dropped during the night, the water quickly evaporated, forming a thin layer of ice, (*which, and which*) was eagerly gathered early the next morning. **[15]** Because more ice forms in very dry air, the (*amount, number*) of ice crystals depended on the dryness of the air. **[16]** A thousand years later, wealthy Babylonians would use the (*effects, affects*) of evaporation to cool their homes. **[17]** At twilight, they had the exterior walls and interior floors doused with water; as it evaporated from (*these, said, such, same*) surfaces, the houses cooled down dramatically. **[18]** In ancient India, the same (*type, kind of*) system was adapted for home cooling. **[19]** Wet grass mats hung in windward windows were (*liable, likely*) to create a considerable, as much as thirty-degree, drop in temperature inside the house. **[20]** To maintain cooling, either someone kept the mats wet during the night, or (*a, an*) reservoir over the windows slowly dripped water on the mats.

A ***glossary*** is an alphabetical list of special terms or expressions with definitions, explanations, and examples. You'll notice that some examples in this glossary are labeled *standard, nonstandard, formal,* or *informal.* The label ***standard*** or ***formal*** identifies usage that is appropriate in serious speaking and writing situations (such as in speeches and in compositions for school). The label ***informal*** indicates standard usage common in conversation and in everyday writing such as personal letters. The label ***nonstandard*** identifies usage that is suitable only in the most casual speaking situations and in writing that attempts to re-create casual speech. In doing the exercises in this chapter, be sure to use only formal standard English.

REFERENCE NOTE: See page 513 for more about standard English. Problems in spelling, such as the difference between *already* and *all ready,* are discussed on pages 977–985.

a, an These ***indefinite articles*** refer to one of the members of a general group. Use *a* before words beginning with a consonant sound. Use *an* before words beginning with a vowel sound.

EXAMPLE It was **an** honor and **a** surprise to receive **an** award for my work as **a** hospital volunteer. [Notice that *an* is used before *honor* because *honor* begins with a vowel sound even though the first letter is the consonant *h.* The article *a* is used before *hospital* because *hospital* begins with a consonant sound.]

accept, except *Accept* is a verb meaning "to receive." *Except* may be either a verb or a preposition. As a verb, *except* means "to leave out." As a preposition, *except* means "excluding."

EXAMPLES Did you **accept** the gift?
Did the new census **except** homeless people? [verb]
We were busy every evening this week **except** Tuesday. [preposition]

adapt, adopt *Adapt* means "to change or adjust something in order to make it fit or to make it suitable." *Adopt* means "to take something and make it one's own."

EXAMPLES The play was **adapted** from a popular book.
My aunt and uncle **adopted** a nine-year-old boy from Guatemala.

affect, effect *Affect* is a verb meaning "to influence." As a verb, *effect* means "to bring about" or "to accomplish." As a noun, *effect* means "the result [of an action]."

EXAMPLES Try not to let unkind remarks **affect** you.
The school board **effected** drastic changes in the budget. [verb]
The **effects** of the hurricane were evident the next day. [noun]

all the farther, all the faster These expressions are used informally in some parts of the United States. In formal situations, use *as far as* or *as fast as.*

INFORMAL Thirty miles per hour was all the faster the first airplane could travel.
FORMAL Thirty miles per hour was **as fast as** the first airplane could travel.

allusion, illusion An *allusion* is an indirect reference to something. An *illusion* is a mistaken idea or a misleading appearance.

EXAMPLES Amy Tan's writings include numerous **allusions** to Chinese mythology.
At one time, many people shared the **illusion** that the earth was flat.
The movie's special effects created the **illusion** of space travel.

alumni, alumnae *Alumni* (ə lum'nī) is the plural of *alumnus* (a male graduate). *Alumnae* (ə lum'nē) is the plural of *alumna* (a female graduate). As a group, the graduates of a coeducational school are usually called *alumni.*

EXAMPLES Both men are **alumni** of Harvard University.
All of my sisters are **alumnae** of Hollins College.
My parents went to their **alumni** reunion.

among See **between, among.**

amount, number Use *amount* to refer to a singular word. Use *number* to refer to a plural word. (See also **number,** page 858.)

EXAMPLES The **amount** of research on stress has increased. [*Amount* refers to the singular word *research.*]
A large **number** of studies have been conducted. [*Number* refers to the plural word *studies.*]

USAGE

said she had gone (*all the farther, as far as*) a black woman could in business. [4] Eventually, she invested in a sizable (*number, amount*) of oils, shampoos, and lotions and began experimenting with them in a washtub. [5] When she was done, Walker had a formula that softened coarse hair; later, she would patent (*an, a*) hair-straightening comb that gave users soft, manageable coiffures. [6] The public, however, was reluctant to (*accept, except*) Walker's new products, and she had to go door-to-door, selling her system of hair care. [7] The success of her dynamic personal demonstrations enabled Walker to purchase (*a, an*) additional office. [8] Before long, her offices, laboratory, manufacturing plant, (*and etc., etc.*), took up a whole city block, and thousands of Walker's sales representatives canvassed not only America but also Europe, where the performer Josephine Baker used the Walker method to obtain her sleek hairstyle.

[9] A pioneer in the development, sales, and marketing of cosmetics, Madame Walker insisted that her salespeople (*adopt, adapt*) a strict program of hygiene, a requirement that later became part of state cosmetology laws. [10] As a wealthy older woman, she did not forget her years of poverty and toil, and many (*alumnae, alumni*) of Tuskegee Institute and Palmer Memorial Institute were grateful for the scholarships that Walker funded for young women.

bad, badly See page 816.

because In formal situations, do not use the construction *reason . . . because*. Instead, use *reason . . . that*.

INFORMAL The reason I'm late is because my car had a flat tire.

FORMAL The reason I'm late is **that** my car had a flat tire. [This sentence can also be revised to make the statement more directly: *I'm late because my car had a flat tire.*]

being as, being that Avoid using either of these expressions for *since* or *because*.

EXAMPLE **Because** [not *Being as*] Elena lived in Mexico until she was almost eight years old, she can speak both Spanish and English quite fluently.

beside, besides *Beside* is a preposition meaning "by the side

USAGE

of" or "next to." *Besides* may be used as either a preposition or an adverb. As a preposition, *besides* means "in addition to" or "except." As an adverb, *besides* means "moreover."

EXAMPLES Who sits **beside** you in English class?
Besides my homework, I still have chores to do. [preposition]
It's too cold to go camping; **besides,** the forecast calls for rain. [adverb]

between, among Use *between* when referring to only two items or to more than two when each item is being compared individually to each of the others.

EXAMPLES The final chess match was **between** Anne and Lisa.
Don't you know the difference **between** mambo, salsa, and merengue? [*Between* is used because each dance is compared individually to each of the other dances; in other words, the dances are compared two at a time.]

Use *among* when you are referring to more than two items and are not considering each item in relation to each other item individually.

EXAMPLE College admissions offices must decide **among** thousands of qualified applicants.

bring, take *Bring* means "to come carrying something." *Take* means "to go carrying something."

EXAMPLES I'll **bring** my collection of Black Heritage postage stamps for the Black History Month display.
Please **take** the recycling bin out to the curb when you leave for school.

bust, busted Avoid using these words as verbs. Use a form of *break* or *burst,* depending on the meaning.

EXAMPLES How did your glasses get **broken** [not *busted*]?
My car's radiator hose **burst** [not *busted*].

but, only See **The Double Negative,** pages 864–865.

can't hardly, can't scarcely See **The Double Negative,** pages 864–865.

could of See **of.**

USAGE

credible, creditable, credulous *Credible* means "believable."

EXAMPLE The children gave a **credible** excuse for breaking the vase.

Creditable means "praiseworthy."

EXAMPLE Her quick thinking and competent action were **creditable.**

Credulous means "inclined to believe too readily."

EXAMPLE The **credulous** listeners thought that the Martians really had invaded Earth.

data *Data* is the plural form of the Latin *datum*. In standard informal English, *data* is frequently used, like a collective noun, with singular pronouns and verbs. In formal usage, *data* takes plural pronouns and verbs.

INFORMAL As soon as the census data was published, it was immediately challenged.
FORMAL As soon as the census **data were** published, **they** were immediately challenged.

discover, invent *Discover* means "to learn of the existence of [something]." *Invent* means "to bring something new into existence."

EXAMPLES Engineers **discovered** oil deposits in Michigan.
Sequoyah **invented** a written Cherokee language based on the spoken Cherokee language.

done *Done* is the past participle of *do*. When used as a main verb, *done* requires an auxiliary, or helping, verb. Avoid using *done* for *did,* which does not require an auxiliary verb. [Note: When used as a gerund or a participle, *done* does not always require an auxiliary verb.]

NONSTANDARD We done all our chores today.
STANDARD We **have done** all our chores today.
STANDARD We **did** all our chores today.

don't, doesn't *Don't* is the contraction of *do not*. *Doesn't* is the contraction of *does not*. Use *doesn't,* not *don't,* with singular subjects except *I* and *you*.

EXAMPLES Franklin **doesn't** [not *don't*] ever skip school.
Our local grocery store **doesn't** [not *don't*] carry mangoes.

PICTURE THIS

You are working in the physics lab after school. While doing some routine tests to learn about the properties of convex surfaces, you hold this crystal ball up to your face. You can scarcely believe your eyes! Instead of seeing your own reflection, you see this mysterious man peering out at you from an unfamiliar room. You quickly stifle your impulse to shout, and your scientific curiosity takes over. With your free hand, jot down a detailed description of the image that you see. Hypothesize about the source of the image. In your description, use correctly at least five of the following words. As you revise what you've written, consult the **Glossary of Usage** to check any usages you're not sure about.

affect	illusion	beside	among
effect	as if	besides	don't
allusion	like	between	doesn't

Subject: unexpected image in a crystal ball
Audience: yourself; your physics teacher
Purpose: to record information; to form a hypothesis

M.C. Escher (1898–1972); "Hand with Reflecting Globe", Lithograph

effect See **affect, effect.**

emigrate, immigrate *Emigrate* means "to leave a country or a region to settle elsewhere." *Immigrate* means "to come into a country or a region to settle there."

EXAMPLES The war forced people to **emigrate** from their homeland.
Marie's grandparents **immigrated** to the United States in 1960.

etc. See **and etc.**

everywheres See **anyways, anywheres.**

except See **accept, except.**

famous, notorious *Famous* means "widely known." *Notorious* means "widely but unfavorably known."

EXAMPLES Gloria Steinem is a **famous** leader of the women's movement in the United States.
In the 1920s, Al Capone was a **notorious** gangster.

farther See **all the farther, all the faster.**

fewer, less Use *fewer,* which tells "how many," to modify a plural noun. Use *less,* which tells "how much," to modify a singular noun.

EXAMPLES I worked **fewer** hours this week than last week.
I worked **less** time this week than last week.

good, well See page 816.

EXERCISE 3 **Identifying Correct Usage**

Choose the correct word or words in parentheses.

1. (*Being that, Because*) Eric is shy, he doesn't say much.
2. When the car broke down, they had only thirteen dollars (*between, among*) the six of them.
3. (*Beside, Besides*) our volunteer work, our club sponsors an annual ski trip.
4. Please (*bring, take*) your guitar when you come to my party.
5. Jon is so (*credulous, credible, creditable*) that he believed your crazy story.
6. They sold (*fewer, less*) new cars than used cars.
7. In what year was the transistor (*invented, discovered*)?

8. Their reason for being late to the rehearsal was (*because, that*) they missed their bus.
9. Did Carla (*bring, take*) her camera on her trip to Panama?
10. Basketball is his favorite sport (*beside, besides*) tennis.
11. All the critics praised Gene Wilder's (*creditable, credulous*) performance in his most recent movie.
12. They (*done, did*) well in the playoffs.
13. Angie forgot to (*bring, take*) her homework assignment when she went to school this morning.
14. (*Among, Between*) the four of us, we can paint the house.
15. The dog ate all of the leftovers (*accept, except*) the okra.
16. Lupe's family (*emigrated, immigrated*) from the Philippines when she was nine years old.
17. I had (*fewer, less*) cavities than my sister.
18. Alan Shepard, Jr., became (*famous, notorious*) as the first American in space.
19. Kristine decided to (*invent, discover*) a computer game of her own.
20. Cold weather (*don't, doesn't*) bother him very much.

EXERCISE 4 **Correcting Errors in Usage**

Most of the following sentences contain errors in usage. If a sentence contains any errors in usage, revise the sentence. If a sentence is correct, write *C*.

EXAMPLE **1. We excepted the telegram nervously.**
1. *We accepted the telegram nervously.*

1. Frank has less hobbies than his friend.
2. Being as Bernard Malamud is my favorite writer, I was excited to find one of his novels at the yard sale.
3. Would you please take this monstrosity out of here?
4. Sue Ellen plays and enjoys many sports: baseball, tennis, bowling, field hockey, volleyball, and etc.
5. One of the main reasons for the widespread concern for eagles is because many are dying from lead poisoning.
6. The manager divided the work between the four of us.
7. The Chinese ballet dancer immigrated from his homeland to find creative freedom.
8. Have any of you did your research for your report yet?
9. To prepare her report, Judy used current data that were published by the Department of the Treasury.
10. Roy said it don't matter, but I can see that he is angry.

REVIEW A **Proofreading for Correct Usage**

Most sentences in the following paragraphs contain usage errors. If a sentence is incorrect, correct each error in usage. If a sentence is correct, write *C*.

[1] One of the most powerful works of art anywheres, the bull shown below was painted some fifteen thousand years ago in Lascaux, France. [2] The painting remained hidden until 1940, when a dog named Robot darted down a hole and the four young men following him accidentally invented these marvelous cave paintings. [3] According to one of these adventurous boys, Marcel Ravidat, it was he who painstakingly enlarged the hole and wriggled down into the now-notorious caverns. [4] With only a weak light to guide him, he soon tripped and fell; luckily, his flashlight did not bust. [5] When Ravidat aimed the light at the walls, an herd of animal figures leapt into view. [6] As the other boys joined him, the sight of the giant bulls, cows, elk, stags, and etc., filled the young men with joy and wonder, prompting them to celebrate with a wild dance. [7] With difficulty, the boys got out of the cavern, promising to return and admonishing each other, "Don't tell anyone about this!"

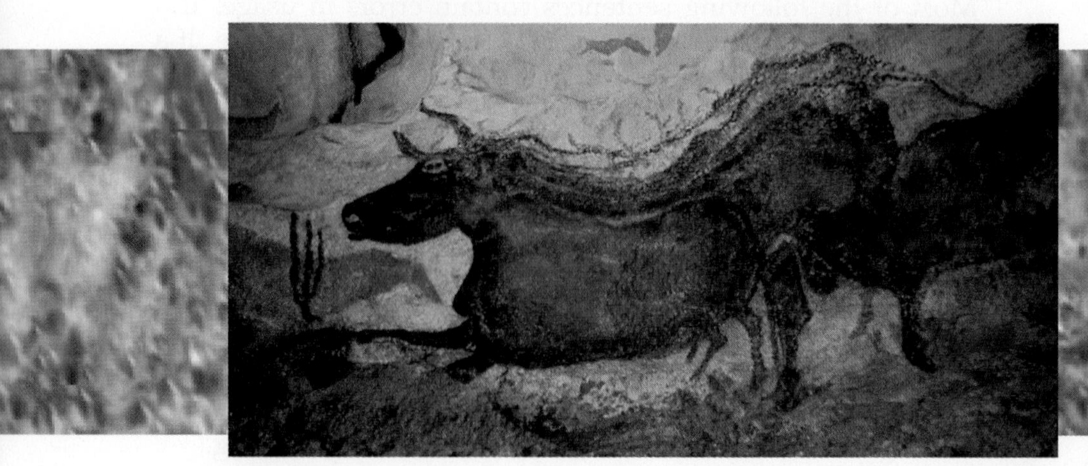

[8] When they left home the next day, the boys brought a stronger light with them. [9] Impatiently, they investigated the cave until they found a passage that was so deep and dark that no one accept Ravidat would enter it. [10] Using a rope, the boys lowered him down the dangerous vertical passage all the farther he could go. [11] At the bottom, Ravidat hardly knew

where he was at, but gradually he began to explore this new area. [12] Soon, a picture of a human body with a bird's head appeared, and though it spanned less feet than the great bulls, it was just as awesome. [13] One by one, each of the other boys came down to glimpse the image of the strange creature, and which is shown being knocked over by a bison. [14] This eerie figure effected the boys differently than the bull did; instead of feeling triumphant, they were left shaken and pale.

[15] For Ravidat and his friends, these days were joyous and exciting beside being sometimes frightening. [16] Quite possibly, the artists who done the paintings hoped to instill these very emotions in viewers long ago. [17] Despite all the datum that scientists have since collected about the age and meaning of the paintings, much about them remains uncertain. [18] Some scientists believe that the purpose of the paintings was to initiate young hunters; other theorists think that the paintings were meant to magically increase the amount of game animals; but most scientists agree that the paintings were considered sacred and were kept secret. [19] The reason they have survived for so long is because they were secreted away in dark caves, protected from light and kept at a constant humidity. [20] Being as modern-day tourists have introduced destructive microorganisms into the Lascaux caverns, the caves are now, unfortunately, closed to the public.

had of See **of.**

had ought, hadn't ought Do not use *had* or *hadn't* with *ought.*

NONSTANDARD You had ought to be more patient.
STANDARD You **ought** to be more patient.

NONSTANDARD I hadn't ought to spend any more money.
STANDARD I **ought not** to spend any more money.

hardly See **The Double Negative,** pages 864–865.

he, she, it, they Do not use an unnecessary pronoun after its antecedent when the antecedent is a subject. Such an error is called the ***double subject.***

NONSTANDARD Faith Ringgold, who was recently featured in a one-woman show, she designs remarkable story quilts.
STANDARD Faith Ringgold, who was recently featured in a one-woman show, designs remarkable story quilts.

USAGE

hisself, theirselves Avoid using these words for *himself* and *themselves.*

EXAMPLE Lou built the shed **himself** [not *hisself*].

illusion See **allusion, illusion.**

immigrate See **emigrate, immigrate.**

imply, infer *Imply* means "to suggest something indirectly." *Infer* means "to interpret" or "to get a certain meaning from a remark or an action."

EXAMPLES Mayor Hanson **implied** during yesterday's press conference that she would run for reelection.
I **inferred** from the mayor's comments that she would run for reelection.

in, into *In* means "within." *Into* means "from the outside to the inside." In formal situations, avoid using *in* for *into.*

INFORMAL Feeling nervous, Jim opened the door and walked in the personnel office.
FORMAL Feeling nervous, Jim opened the door and walked **into** the personnel office.

invent See **discover, invent.**

it See **he, she, it, they.**

kind(s), sort(s), type(s) With the singular form of each of these nouns, use *this* or *that.* With the plural form, use *these* or *those.*

EXAMPLES **This kind** of package is recyclable, but **those kinds** are not.
These types of examples are helpful.

kind of, sort of In formal situations, avoid using *kind of* for the adverb *somewhat* or *rather.*

INFORMAL You look kind of worried.
FORMAL You look **rather** [or **somewhat**] worried.

kind of a, sort of a In formal situations, omit the *a.*

INFORMAL What kind of a car is that?
FORMAL What **kind of** car is that?

lay, lie See pages 784–785.

learn, teach *Learn* means "to gain knowledge." *Teach* means "to provide with knowledge."

EXAMPLE If you will **teach** me how to play the guitar, I will **learn** some traditional Mexican folk songs.

leave, let *Leave* means "to go away." *Let* means "to permit" or "to allow." Avoid using *leave* for *let*.

EXAMPLES **Let** [not *leave*] us finish our dinner.
I knew I shouldn't have **let** [not *left*] them borrow my car.

less See **fewer, less.**

liable See **likely, liable.**

lie, lay See pages 784–785.

like, as *Like* is a preposition. In formal situations, do not use *like* for the conjunction *as* to introduce a subordinate clause.

INFORMAL The plan worked like they thought it would.
FORMAL The plan worked **as** they thought it would.

REFERENCE NOTE: See pages 675–683 for more information about subordinate clauses.

like, as if In formal situations, avoid using the preposition *like* for the conjunction *as if* or *as though* to introduce a subordinate clause.

INFORMAL I feel like I have the flu.
FORMAL I feel **as if** [or **as though**] I have the flu.

likely, liable In formal situations, use *likely* to express simple probability and *liable* to express probability with potential harm or misfortune.

EXAMPLES Ginny is **likely** to arrive any minute.
The children playing in the abandoned building are **liable** to get hurt.

Liable is also used to mean "responsible" or "answerable."

EXAMPLE The Smiths are **liable** for the damages that their dog caused.

might of, must of See **of.**

USAGE

myself, ourselves Avoid using pronouns ending in *–self* or *–selves* to replace personal pronouns as subjects or objects.

EXAMPLES Amy and **I** [not *myself*] appreciate your help.
Could you do a favor for Wanda and **us** [not *ourselves*]?

REFERENCE NOTE: For more information about the kinds of pronouns, see pages 602–605. For more about how personal pronouns are used as subjects and objects, see pages 728–735.

EXERCISE 5 Correcting Errors in Usage

For each of the following sentences, choose the correct word or words in parentheses.

1. In his address to Congress, the president (*implied, inferred*) that an economic reversal might occur soon.
2. When you have time, will you (*learn, teach*) me to sew?
3. He slipped on the wet deck and fell (*in, into*) the water.
4. We (*ought, had ought*) to have asked Allison to give us her chimichanga recipe.
5. You look (*like, as if*) you've just seen a ghost!
6. Doyle and (*I, myself*) worked together on this project.
7. If you (*had, had of*) asked me, I would have told you.
8. Have you been changing the oil and filter every 3,000–5,000 miles (*as, like*) you're supposed to?
9. (*Leave, Let*) them stay if they don't want to go with us.
10. Her recordings of West African folk tales are (*liable, likely*) to become classics.

REVIEW B Correcting Errors in Usage

Most of the following sentences contain errors in usage. If a sentence contains an error in usage, revise the sentence. If a sentence is correct, write *C*.

1. The magician dazzled us with flawless allusions.
2. Without any warning, the cat jumped from the chair and leaped in my arms.
3. The children helped theirselves to more vegetable curry.
4. Your room looks like it's been hit by a tornado.
5. What can you infer from the refrain in Paul Laurence Dunbar's poem?

6. You hadn't ought to complain so much.
7. Jane and myself are the editors of our yearbook.
8. What sort of a CD player does Margaret plan to buy with her Christmas bonus?
9. I asked my boss if he would let me have next Wednesday afternoon off.
10. Some people they're always making a fuss about nothing.

REVIEW C Proofreading for Correct Usage

Each sentence in the following paragraph contains an error in usage. Correct each error.

[1] Georges Seurat he spent his short career studying the mysteries of the human eye, light, and color. [2] One of the results of his study is this painting, which is composed of thousands, perhaps millions, of kind of small dots. [3] This sort of a technique is called pointillism, a name derived from the small

Georges Seurat, French, 1859–1891, "A Sunday on La Grande Jatte, 1884," oil on canvas, 1884–86, 207.6 × 308 cm, Helen Birch Bartlett Memorial Collection 1926.224/© 1992 The Art Institute of Chicago, All Rights Reserved.

points of color on the canvas. [4] Rather than mix paint theirselves, artists using this technique let the viewer's eyes blend the colors. [5] Seen from a certain distance, the small points of color flow together and become solid like the pixels on a computer screen or the dots of a printed photograph do. [6] In fact, some critics believe that observations of modern printed photographs learned Seurat all about pointillism. [7] However, these critics had ought to examine Seurat's painting more closely. [8] Unlike some of his contemporaries, Seurat was, indeed, interested in the new photographic technology; however, the dots that make up his paintings are rather large, and obviously these type of points are not meant to appear completely solid. [9] If you go to a museum to see one of these kind of paintings, estimate the diagonal length of the picture and then step back about three times that distance. [10] From this viewpoint, a pointillist painting is liable to flicker or shimmer with the very vibrancy of life itself.

nauseated, nauseous *Nauseated* means "sick." *Nauseous* means "disgusting" or "sickening."

EXAMPLES After riding the roller coaster, the child became **nauseated.**
The chemical reaction gave off a **nauseous** odor.

no, nobody, none, no one, not, nothing, nowhere See **The Double Negative,** pages 864–865.

nor See **or, nor.**

notorious See **famous, notorious.**

nowheres See **anyways, anywheres.**

number Use a singular verb after the expression *the number of.* Use a plural verb after the expression *a number of.*

EXAMPLES **The number of** candidates **was** surprising.
A number of candidates **were** nominated by the committee.

number See **amount, number.**

of *Of* is a preposition. Do not use *of* in place of *have* after verbs such as *could, should, would, might, must,* and *ought [to].* Also, do not use *had of* for had.

NONSTANDARD You could of told me that you were going to be late.
STANDARD You **could've** told me that you were going to be late.

NONSTANDARD You ought to of seen the look on his face.
STANDARD You **ought to have** seen the look on his face.

NONSTANDARD If I had of known that the party was casual, I wouldn't of worn this dressy outfit.
STANDARD If I **had** known that the party was casual, I **wouldn't have** worn this dressy outfit.

Avoid using *of* after other prepositions such as *inside, off,* and *outside.*

EXAMPLE Leslie turned **off** [not *off of*] the parkway.

off, off of Do not use *off* or *off of* for *from.*

NONSTANDARD I got some good advice off that mechanic.
STANDARD I got some good advice **from** that mechanic.

or, nor Use *or* with *either;* use *nor* with *neither.*

EXAMPLES **Either** Celia Cruz **or** Gloria Estefan will host the awards show.
Neither Gwen **nor** Lily has been absent this term.

ought See **had ought, hadn't ought.**

ought to of See **of.**

persecute, prosecute *Persecute* means "to attack or annoy someone constantly." *Prosecute* means "to bring legal action against someone for unlawful behavior."

EXAMPLES The dictator **persecuted** those who opposed him.
The district attorney **will prosecute** any person caught looting.

phenomena *Phenomena* is the plural form of the word *phenomenon.* Do not use *phenomena* as a singular noun.

PLURAL We studied **those phenomena** of nature, which **are** quite rare.
SINGULAR We studied **that phenomenon** of nature, which **is** quite rare.

reason . . . because See **because.**

Reverend, Honorable Do not use these titles before a person's last name alone. Do use the word *the* before the title.

NONSTANDARD Reverend King, the Reverend King, Honorable Inouye
STANDARD the Reverend Martin Luther King, Jr., the Reverend M. L. King, Jr., the Reverend Dr. King, the Honorable Daniel Inouye

rise, raise See pages 786–787.

same, said, such In business or legal writing, these words are sometimes used in the following kinds of constructions. Avoid such uses in general writing.

LEGAL The artist had worked hard on the sculptures and had same fully insured.
GENERAL The artist had worked hard on the sculptures and had **them** fully insured.

LEGAL The said sculptures were fully insured.
GENERAL **Those** [or **The artist's**] sculptures were fully insured.

LEGAL Someone suggested that the artist overstate the value of the sculptures; however, the artist didn't approve of such.
GENERAL Someone suggested that the artist overstate the value of the sculptures; however, the artist didn't approve of **such dishonesty.**

says Do not use *say* after a past-tense verb. *Said* is the past-tense form.

NONSTANDARD Then she glared at me and says, "Where have you been?"
STANDARD Then she glared at me and **said,** "Where have you been?"

scarcely See **The Double Negative,** pages 864–865.

she See **he, she, it, they.**

should of See **of.**

sit, set See pages 785–786.

slow, slowly See page 817.

some, somewhat In formal situations, avoid using *some* to mean "to some extent." Use *somewhat.*

INFORMAL Tensions between East and West began to ease some.
FORMAL Tensions between East and West began to ease **somewhat.**

somewheres See **anyways, anywheres.**

sort(s) See **kind(s), sort(s), type(s)** and **kind of a, sort of a.**

sort of See **kind of, sort of.**

USAGE

take See **bring, take.**

than, then *Than* is a conjunction used in comparisons. *Then* is an adverb telling *when.*

EXAMPLES Tyrone is more studious **than** I am.
Take your diploma in your left hand and shake hands with the principal; **then** leave the stage and return to your seat.

that See **who, which, that.**

them Do not use *them* as an adjective. Use *those.*

EXAMPLE Have you seen **those** [not *them*] murals by Judith Baca at the art museum?

they See **he, she, it, they.**

this here, that there Avoid using *here* or *there* after *this* or *that.*

EXAMPLE **This** [not *This here*] magazine has an article about Japanese koto player Kazue Sawai.

this, that, these, those See **kind(s), sort(s), type(s).**

type(s) See **kind(s), sort(s), type(s).**

type, type of Avoid using *type* as an adjective. Add *of* after *type.*

NONSTANDARD That's the type job I'd like to have.
STANDARD That's the **type of** job I'd like to have.

ways Use *way,* not *ways,* when referring to distance.

INFORMAL At dusk we were still a long ways from home.
FORMAL At dusk we were still a long **way** from home.

well, good See page 816.

when, where Do not use *when* or *where* to begin a definition.

NONSTANDARD A hurricane is when a tropical cyclone has winds greater than 75 miles per hour.
STANDARD A hurricane is **a tropical cyclone that has winds greater than 75 miles per hour.**

NONSTANDARD An implosion is where something bursts inward.
STANDARD An implosion is an **inward burst.**

USAGE

where Do not use *where* for *that.*

EXAMPLE I read **that** [not *where*] the Smithsonian Institution has preserved more than one thousand of William H. Johnson's paintings.

where . . . at See **at.**

who, which, that *Who* refers to persons only. *Which* refers to things only. *That* may refer to either persons or things.

EXAMPLES Shah Jahan was the Indian ruler **who** [or that] built the Taj Mahal.
The monument, **which** is the tomb of the ruler's wife, is adorned with verses from the Koran.
Have you seen any pictures of the building **that** symbolizes India for so many people in other lands?

who, whom See pages 744–745.

would of See **of.**

EXERCISE 6 Correcting Errors in Usage

Most of the following sentences contain errors in usage. If a sentence contains an error in usage, revise the sentence. If a sentence is correct, write C.

1. Backlighting is when the main source of light is placed in back of the subject being photographed.
2. I never saw that type camera before.
3. Why don't you borrow some change off of Rhoda?
4. A number of unusual themes has already been proposed for the senior prom.
5. Neither Chico or Robert has any albums by Tish Hinojosa.
6. Sharon turned to me and says, "Did you see the beautiful sari that woman was wearing?"
7. You should of seen *Young Soul Rebels,* which was directed by Isaac Julien.
8. The aurora borealis is a spectacular phenomena of nature in the northern sky.
9. We stayed up to watch the late-night horror movie, which wasn't worth the loss of sleep.
10. It's a long ways to Memphis, but we may reach northern Tennessee by morning.

REVIEW D **Proofreading for Correct Usage**

Most of the sentences in the following paragraphs contain errors in usage. If a sentence is incorrect, correct the error. If a sentence is correct, write *C*.

[1] Last July, I accompanied Reverend Kemp and his wife Angela on a sightseeing trip to Alaska. [2] On our flight to Fairbanks, we saw a double rainbow—a marvelous phenomena that we felt was a lucky sign. [3] At the hotel, we began to plan what we would do the next day, but the number of possibilities were huge, and we didn't know where to start. [4] Finally, we decided that we would neither stay in our rooms or eat dinner at the hotel; instead, we would go for a drive that evening. [5] As we headed for the car, I saw on a poster where the World Eskimo-Indian Olympics were being held that very day. [6] "Doesn't this sound like fun?" I asked, showing Mrs. Kemp the advertisement for the games.

[7] The Kemps agreed, and as soon as we arrived at the fairgrounds, we introduced ourselves to a Mrs. McBride. [8] She was a friendly woman which was happy to tell us about the games. [9] I was surprised some at the many different events that had been scheduled. [10] Said games included tests of skill, such as the Alaskan high kick, and tests of strength, such as drop-the-bomb.

[11] The Alaskan high kick is where a person sitting on the ground tries to kick a ball suspended in midair. [12] An event requiring exceptional balance, the Alaskan high kick is an example of the type skills that were traditionally needed by Native Alaskans. [13] The drop-the-bomb competition begins when three men lift another man off of the ground. [14] The man who is held by his wrists and ankles must remain perfectly horizontal while them three other men carry him. [15] The contestant who is carried the longest ways without sagging wins the event.

[16] As Mrs. McBride finished describing the games, she smiled and says, "This is the thirty-first year we've held the Eskimo Olympics." [17] Than she proudly pointed out Cecelia Chanerak, who was sailing through the air during the blanket toss. [18] This event is when a group of people stretch out a hide blanket and throw a man or a woman as high as possible; the winner must jump the highest and keep the best balance. [19] I must confess that I got a bit nauseous watching people fly

USAGE

up so far in the air, but I managed to snap a picture anyway. [20] That there day was one of the best of our trip, and when I got back home, I eagerly described the Eskimo-Indian Olympics to my family and friends.

USAGE

The Double Negative

A ***double negative*** is a construction in which two negative words are used where one is enough. Double negatives were acceptable during Shakespeare's time, but they are now considered nonstandard.

Common Negative Words

barely	never	not (n't)
but (meaning "only")	no	nothing
	nobody	nowhere
hardly	none	only
neither	no one	scarcely

NONSTANDARD	She has never missed none of Toni Morrison's books.
STANDARD	She has **never** missed **any** of Toni Morrison's books.
STANDARD	She has missed **none** of Toni Morrison's books.
NONSTANDARD	I have not said nothing about your plans.
STANDARD	I have **not** said **anything** about your plans.
STANDARD	I have said **nothing** about your plans.
NONSTANDARD	I hadn't never heard Estonian music before.
STANDARD	I **hadn't ever** heard Estonian music before.
STANDARD	I had **never** heard Estonian music before.

WINTHROP reprinted by permission of NEA, Inc.

USAGE

NOTE: Avoid the common error of using *n't,* the contraction of *not,* with another negative word, such as *barely, hardly,* or *scarcely.*

NONSTANDARD	I can't hardly see anything in this fog.
STANDARD	I can **hardly** see anything in this fog.
NONSTANDARD	Our lunch break was so short that we didn't scarcely have time to eat.
STANDARD	Our lunch break was so short that we **scarcely** had time to eat.

The words *but* and *only* are negative when they are used as adverbs meaning "no more than." In such cases, the use of another negative word with *but* or *only* is considered informal.

INFORMAL	I don't have but one pair of dress shoes.
FORMAL	I have **but** one pair of dress shoes.
FORMAL	I have **only** one pair of dress shoes.

EXERCISE 7 **Identifying Correct Usage**

Choose the correct word from the pair given in parentheses.

EXAMPLE **1. I don't have (*any, none*) left.**
1. *any*

1. Benjamin will never get (*nowhere, anywhere*) until he starts believing in himself.
2. Luís (*can, can't*) hardly keep from being proud of you.
3. I was so sleepy that I (*could, couldn't*) hardly keep my eyes open.
4. The detectives (*haven't, have*) no clues in the case.
5. There (*is, isn't*) no good reason for your being late.
6. We hadn't (*ever, never*) tasted papaya before.
7. Neither of them wants (*nothing, anything*) to do with the preparations for the dance.
8. We (*had, hadn't*) but one choice to make.
9. The candidates (*have, haven't*) only three minutes each to state their positions.
10. The manager insisted that there wasn't (*any, no*) reason for making the customers wait so long.

USAGE

REVIEW E **Correcting Errors in Usage**

Most of the following sentences contain errors in usage. If a sentence contains an error, revise the sentence. If a sentence is correct, write *C*.

1. We had to adapt the stage lighting for the rock concert.
2. The professor made an illusion to Ralph Ellison's novel *Invisible Man.*
3. The organization helped a large amount of Asian refugees find work.
4. Where did you stay at over Thanksgiving?
5. Everyone except Tim has excepted the invitation.
6. Among the two performers, I like Quincy Jones better.
7. The data on acid rain is not complete.
8. My parents immigrated from Cuba before I was born.
9. Have you ever read about the pirate Bluebeard, who was famous for his cruelty?
10. Were you credulous enough to believe the fortuneteller?
11. My sister she attends Iowa State University.
12. We implied from Rudy's comment that the movie was dull.
13. The Coopers grew all the vegetables theirselves.

14. I had ought to spend more time with my friends.
15. He has been the catcher for every game this year, and he is beginning to look kind of tired.
16. Ms. Robinson learned me all I know about public speaking.
17. What kind of a car is that?
18. At the school assembly yesterday, the Honorable Murphy encouraged students to register to vote as soon as they turn eighteen.
19. There were four freshmen which made the basketball team.
20. A number of suggestions have been submitted to the prom decorations committee.

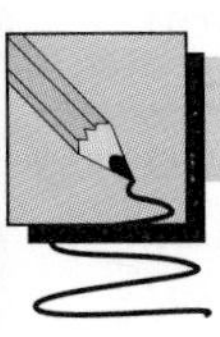

WRITING APPLICATION

Using Standard English in a Story

English usage varies from place to place and from group to group. However, standard English is familiar to almost all people who speak English, no matter what their background. Following the rules of standard usage in writing helps to ensure that the widest possible range of readers will understand what you have to say.

In literature, writers sometimes break the rules of standard English to achieve a particular effect. In writing a story, an author might use nonstandard English in dialogue to capture the sound of a speaker's language. In the rest of the story, however, the writer would probably use standard English to appeal to as diverse an audience as possible. As you read the excerpt below, notice how the writer uses both standard and nonstandard English in his short story.

> She still held him. But she bent down enough to permit him to stoop and pick up her purse. Then she said, "Now ain't you ashamed of yourself?"
>
> Firmly gripped by his shirt front, the boy said, "Yes'm."
>
> The woman said, "What did you want to do it for?"
>
> The boy said, "I didn't aim to."
>
> She said, "You a lie!"
>
> Langston Hughes, from "Thank You, M'am"

WRITING ACTIVITY

Some experiences are so strange, moving, or funny that they just beg to be told in a story. Recently you heard about or had such an experience and wrote about it in your journal. Now, you've decided to develop the journal entry into a short story. Write a fictional narrative based on your journal entry. Use both true and imaginary details to create an entertaining story. You may use nonstandard English in dialogue, but be sure to write the rest of the story in standard English. Use the **Glossary of Usage** to check any words or phrases you're not sure about.

Prewriting Think about something strange, inspiring, or funny that happened to you or to someone you know. If you keep a journal, you may want to skim through it for ideas. Think about how to develop one particular experience into a short story. Decide on the characters and the setting of the story, and determine your narrator's point of view. Finally, create a brief plot outline. Be sure to include a *conflict,* a problem that the main character or characters must solve. (For help with developing a short-story plot, see pages 171–172.)

Writing Using your prewriting notes, write a first draft of your story. As you write, you will want to expand on your original ideas. Add interest to your story by inventing vivid details. In writing dialogue, you may find it useful to include some colloquial or nonstandard expressions to make your characters' speech sound more natural. You may use as many or as few details from real life as you wish. However, do not use real names of people.

Evaluating and Revising Ask a friend or a relative to read your draft. Is the story interesting and believable? Can your reader picture the setting and characters? Jot down your reader's suggestions, and decide which, if any, to use in your story. Also, add any details that you think will improve the plot, setting, or characterization. Next, focus on your writing style. Revise your sentences to make them clearer and more concise. As you revise, be sure to use the **Glossary of Usage** to help you find and correct nonstandard usages.

Proofreading Read over your story to find any errors in grammar, usage, spelling, or punctuation. Be sure that you've placed quotation marks around dialogue. (See pages 935–939 for more about using quotation marks.) Check to be sure that any nonstandard usages are intentional, not accidental.

Review: Posttest

A. Correcting Errors in Usage

Most of the following sentences contain errors in usage. If a sentence contains an error, revise the sentence. If a sentence is correct, write *C*.

EXAMPLE **1. I was surprised to learn that Roberto's parents are wealthy, because he doesn't act like he's rich.**
1. ***I was surprised to learn that Roberto's parents are wealthy, because he doesn't act as if he's rich.***

1. Please enclose a copy of your birth certificate, and we will return said document at a later date.
2. You hadn't ought to be so careless with your new watch.
3. The Student Council's arguments had little affect on the faculty's vote on the new dress code for school dances.
4. Theo don't care what others think; he has the courage to say what he believes.
5. Tricia, Angelo, and myself have tickets to the White Sox game next Saturday.
6. Whenever I feel sad, I can't hardly wait to talk with my friend Marcus, who always cheers me up.
7. Arthur Fiedler he made the Boston Pops' concerts popular with millions of people all over America.
8. The reason we're so late is because our car battery was dead and we had to get a jump-start.
9. We didn't know whether the light was a phenomena of nature or a UFO.
10. I have never seen this kind of insect before.
11. Because Eula made a mistake when she put the film in the camera, none of her pictures could be developed.

12. We plan to visit Tim at Christmas being as we haven't seen him in three years.
13. She asked Tom if he was going to the dance, and he says, "Maybe I'll go and maybe I won't."
14. Where was Beth at last night when all of us went to the game?
15. Our teacher said we done a creditable job on our project.

B. Proofreading for Correct Usage

For each sentence in the following paragraph, correct the error in usage.

[16] There are hardly no tales in the world that are as popular as the story of Cinderella. **[17]** Almost everywheres, people tell some version of this folk tale. **[18]** The reason for the story's popularity is probably because its themes of love and wealth appeal universally. **[19]** However, each culture adopts the tale by changing the heroine's name and other details. **[20]** According to the datum collected by folklorists, almost seven hundred versions of the Cinderella story exist. **[21]** In the English version, Cinderella is granted a wish by her fairy godmother; in Scotland, Rashin Coatie wishes on a dead calf's bones; and in Italy, it is a magic date tree who grants Zezolla's wish. **[22]** In the Chinese version, perhaps the oldest Cinderella story, the main character is Yeh-hsien, who is prosecuted by her stepmother. **[23]** In this version, the stepmother, famous for her cruelty, gives Yeh-hsien the dangerous task of drawing water from very deep wells. **[24]** As in other Cinderella stories, a slipper drops off of Yeh-hsien's foot on her way back from a festival. **[25]** The ending of said stories is always the same—the mistreated heroine, no matter what her name is, finds love and happiness with the man who searches for the owner of the slipper.

28 CAPITALIZATION

Standard Uses of Capital Letters

Diagnostic Test

A. Identifying Standard Uses of Capital Letters

For each of the following pairs of items, select the letter of the item that is correctly capitalized according to standard usage.

EXAMPLE **1. a.** a Movie starring Lena Horne
b. a movie starring Lena Horne
1. *b*

1. **a.** in honor of Secretaries Day
   b. in honor of Secretaries day
2. **a.** one of the nations in the middle east
   b. one of the nations in the Middle East
3. **a.** took courses in English, Spanish, and chemistry
   b. took courses in English, Spanish, and Chemistry

4. **a.** the crew of the Space Shuttle *Columbia*
   b. the crew of the space shuttle *Columbia*
5. **a.** at the intersection of Sixth avenue and Market street
   b. at the intersection of Sixth Avenue and Market Street
6. **a.** a trip to Yosemite National Park
   b. a trip to Yosemite national park
7. **a.** fought the Battle of Saratoga during the Revolutionary war
   b. fought the Battle of Saratoga during the Revolutionary War
8. **a.** enjoyed Toni Morrison's *the Bluest Eye*
   b. enjoyed Toni Morrison's *The Bluest Eye*
9. **a.** a visit to the world Trade Center
   b. a visit to the World Trade Center
10. **a.** a biography of the American novelist James Baldwin
    b. a biography of the american novelist James Baldwin

MECHANICS

B. Proofreading a Paragraph for Correct Capitalization

Proofread the following paragraph, changing capital letters to small letters and small letters to capitals where necessary. If a sentence is correct, write *C*.

EXAMPLE **[1] The National Museum Of American History is a branch of the Smithsonian institution.**
1. *of, Institution*

[11] Popularly known as "the Nation's attic," the Museum grew out of the U.S. National Museum, which was built to house the collections of the U.S. Patent office. **[12]** Today, many Americans seem to consider the museum an extension of their own attics. **[13]** Each year hundreds of items arrive at the museum unsolicited, many of them addressed simply "Smithsonian, Washington, d.c." **[14]** According to Katherine Neill Ridgley, Manager of public-inquiry mail at the Smithsonian, the packages are often accompanied by wistful letters stating, "i want this to go to a place where it will be appreciated." **[15]** Staff historian Ellen Roney Hughes considers the offerings evidence that Americans have a strong sense of History. **[16]** "They realize the importance," she says, "of both ordinary things and extraordinary things." **[17]** "Extraordinary" is an apt description for one recent donation—a rubber chicken that had accompanied an Expedition to Antarctica. **[18]** Other packages contain less-startling objects; one would-be donor sent his Great-grandmother's wedding dress, and another submitted a polaroid snapshot of a stuffed alligator. **[19]** People from both the north and the South regularly contribute letters and other memorabilia dating from the Civil war. **[20]** Most of the items are returned to their owners, yet the contributions continue; perhaps the senders reason that since the museum welcomed Archie Bunker's armchair from the television series *All in The Family*, it will welcome their treasures, too.

In your reading, you may notice variations in the use of capital letters. Most writers, however, follow the rules presented in this chapter. In your own writing, following these rules will help you communicate clearly.

28a. Capitalize the first word of every sentence.

EXAMPLES **R**eading the article, I learned about the Blessingway and other traditional Navajo ceremonies.
What is the formula for converting degrees Celsius to degrees Fahrenheit?

(1) Capitalize the first word of a sentence following a colon.

EXAMPLE The committee issued the following statement: **I**n light of these statistics, we recommend that four-way stop signs be installed.

(2) Capitalize the first word of a resolution following the word *Resolved*.

EXAMPLE Resolved: **T**hat government support of the arts be increased.

(3) Capitalize the first word of a direct quotation.

EXAMPLE When he surrendered in 1877, Chief Joseph declared, "**F**rom where the sun now stands I will fight no more forever."

When quoting from another writer's work, do not capitalize the first word of the quotation unless the other writer has capitalized it.

EXAMPLE In his speech of surrender in 1877, Chief Joseph declared that he would "fight no more forever."

REFERENCE NOTE: For more information about using capital letters in quotations, see pages 935–936.

Traditionally, the first word in a line of poetry is capitalized.

EXAMPLE **H**e clasps the crag with crooked hands;
Close to the sun in lonely lands,
Ringed with the azure world, he stands.

The wrinkled sea beneath him crawls;
He watches from his mountain walls,
And like a thunderbolt he falls.

Alfred, Lord Tennyson, "The Eagle"

For reasons of style, however, some writers do not follow this rule.

EXAMPLE The art of losing isn't hard to master;
so many things seem filled with the intent
to be lost that their loss is no disaster.

Elizabeth Bishop, "One Art"

When quoting from another writer's work, always follow the style of the writer.

MECHANICS

(4) Capitalize the first word of a statement or question inserted in a sentence without quotation marks.

EXAMPLE My question is, **W**ill this action solve the problem?

28b. Capitalize the pronoun *I* and the interjection *O*.

The interjection *O* is usually used for invocations and is followed by the name of the person or thing being addressed. Don't confuse *O* with the common interjection *oh,* which is capitalized only when it appears at the beginning of a sentence and is usually followed by a mark of punctuation.

EXAMPLES Where could **I** have put my book report?
Rejoice in the Lord, **O** ye righteous!
He was driving, **oh,** about thirty-five miles an hour.

28c. Capitalize proper nouns and proper adjectives.

A ***common noun*** names any one of a group of persons, places, or things. A ***proper noun*** names a particular person, place, or thing. A ***proper adjective*** is formed from a proper noun.

COMMON NOUNS	PROPER NOUNS	PROPER ADJECTIVES
king	King Arthur	Arthurian legend
country	Thailand	Thai restaurant
city	Moscow	Muscovite voters
people	Algonquians	Algonquian customs
religion	Buddhism	Buddhist shrine

In proper nouns made up of two or more words, do not capitalize

- articles (*a, an, the*)
- short prepositions (those with fewer than five letters, such as *at, of, for, with*)
- coordinating conjunctions (*and, but, for, nor, or, so, yet*)

EXAMPLES Alfred the Great
Gulf of Oman
International Union for the Conservation of Nature and Natural Resources

Some proper nouns and proper adjectives have lost their capitals after long usage.

EXAMPLES a cardigan (sweater) china (dishes)
morocco leather creole sauce

Others may be written with or without capitals.

EXAMPLES Roman (roman) numerals Venetian (venetian) blinds
plaster of Paris (paris) Gothic (gothic) style

If you're not sure whether to capitalize a word, check an up-to-date dictionary.

REFERENCE NOTE: For more information about common and proper nouns, see page 600. For more about proper adjectives, see page 953.

(1) Capitalize the names of persons.

GIVEN NAMES	**J**amal	**C**hristina	**Y**oshi	**A**licia	**M**arco
SURNAMES	**T**seng	**Y**oungblood	**J**ohnson	**M**artínez	**C**ostner

NOTE: Some names may contain more than one capital letter. If you are not sure about the spelling of a name, check with the person or consult a reference source.

EXAMPLES		
	De **L**a **R**enta	de la **R**enta
	Von **R**yan	von **R**yan
	Morning **S**tar	**M**orningstar
	La **F**ontaine	**L**afontaine
	Dupont	du **P**ont
	Mac**K**enzie	**M**ackenzie

Capitalize the abbreviations *Jr.* and *Sr.* following a name.

EXAMPLES Martin Luther King, **J**r. John D. Rockefeller, **S**r.

REFERENCE NOTE: The abbreviations of other titles such as *Mr., Dr., Gen., RN,* and *Ph.D.* are also capitalized. For more about punctuating abbreviations, see pages 902–903.

(2) Capitalize geographical names.

TYPE OF NAME	EXAMPLES	
Towns and Cities	**C**ampbellsville **M**anila	**P**igeon **F**orge **S**an **J**uan
Counties and Townships	**M**aricopa **C**ounty **C**oncord **T**ownship	**O**rleans **P**arish **L**awrence **T**ownship
States	**A**laska	**S**outh **C**arolina
Regions	the **S**outh **G**reat **P**lains	**W**estern **H**emisphere **N**ew **E**ngland

NOTE: Words such as *north, eastern,* and *southwestern* are not capitalized when indicating direction.

EXAMPLES flying **s**outh for the winter
living in the **w**estern part of the state

REFERENCE NOTE: The abbreviations of names of states are always capitalized. For more about using and punctuating such abbreviations, see pages 902–903.

MECHANICS

TYPE OF NAME	EXAMPLES	
Countries	**Z**imbabwe	**S**audi **A**rabia
Continents	**A**ntarctica	**N**orth **A**merica
Islands	**I**sle of **W**ight	**S**olomon **I**slands
Mountains	**M**ount **S**t. **H**elens **P**obeda **P**eak	**S**ierra **M**adre **S**ugarloaf **M**ountain
Other Land Forms and Features	**P**ainted **D**esert **P**alo **D**uro **C**anyon **D**ismal **S**wamp	**K**eweenaw **P**eninsula **O**uachita **N**ational **F**orest
Bodies of Water	**I**ndian **O**cean **L**ake **H**uron **D**ead **S**ea	**A**mazon **R**iver **P**ersian **G**ulf **G**uanabara **B**ay
Parks	**L**ake **C**lark **N**ational **P**ark	**O**zark **N**ational **S**cenic **R**iverways
Roads, Streets, and Highways	**R**oute 66 **I**nterstate 10 **Q**uail **B**riar **D**rive **E**ast **T**hird **S**treet	**R**aintree **R**oad **B**luegrass **P**arkway **F**ifth **A**venue **G**ulf-to-**B**ay **B**oulevard

REFERENCE NOTE: In addresses, abbreviations such as *St., Blvd., Ave., Dr.,* and *Ln.* are capitalized. For more about abbreviations, see pages 902–903.

NOTE: The second word in a hyphenated number begins with a lowercase letter.

EXAMPLE Twenty-second Street

A word such as *city, lake, park,* or *street* is capitalized only when it is part of a proper noun.

PROPER NOUNS	COMMON NOUNS
in **S**ioux **C**ity	in the **c**ity
near **L**ake **O**keechobee	near the **l**ake
through **M**esa **V**erde **N**ational **P**ark	through the **p**ark
on **D**unbar **S**treet	on the next **s**treet

MECHANICS

EXERCISE 1 Identifying Standard Uses of Capitalization

For each of the following pairs of items, select the letter of the item that is correctly capitalized.

1. a. the Nile river
   b. the Nile River
2. a. She said, "Tell me, too."
   b. She said, "tell me, too."
3. a. Bering strait
   b. Bering Strait
4. a. Fifty-Second Street
   b. Fifty-second Street
5. a. Hoover Dam
   b. Hoover dam
6. a. Charles Adams, Jr.
   b. Charles Adams, jr.
7. a. New Jersey Turnpike
   b. New Jersey turnpike
8. a. austin, Texas
   b. Austin, Texas
9. a. an American Citizen
   b. an American citizen
10. a. Los Angeles County highways
    b. Los Angeles County Highways
11. a. east of the river
    b. East of the river
12. a. the Iberian peninsula
    b. the Iberian Peninsula
13. a. people of the Far East
    b. people of the far east
14. a. the Brooklyn Bridge
    b. the Brooklyn bridge
15. a. an Irish setter
    b. an Irish Setter
16. a. Billy The Kid
    b. Billy the Kid
17. a. We heard him say he was "pleased to be here."
    b. We heard him say he was "Pleased to be here."
18. a. Eastern seaports
    b. eastern seaports
19. a. Plum county
    b. Plum County
20. a. the grand Canyon
    b. the Grand Canyon

EXERCISE 2 Using Standard Capitalization

Write each of the following items, using capital letters where they are needed.

1. cook county
2. an african village on the atlantic coast
3. four miles south of route 10
4. ranching in the south
5. forty-ninth street
6. olympic national park
7. a city like new orleans, louisiana
8. a popular spanish singer
9. a beautiful gray arabian stallion
10. james o'toole, jr.

MECHANICS

PICTURE THIS

The year is 1925, and you are visiting a cousin in New York City. Earlier today, you and your cousin were walking down Center Street when you saw this surprising sight. You're still so amused by the scene that you've decided to write to your best friend back home. Write a letter describing the Center Street traffic jam. In your letter, use at least six proper nouns and four proper adjectives.

Subject: a cat holding up traffic
Audience: your best friend
Purpose: to inform; to entertain

(3) Capitalize the names of organizations, teams, business firms, institutions, buildings, and government bodies.

TYPE OF NAME	EXAMPLES
Organizations	**N**ational **C**ollegiate **A**thletic **A**ssociation **L**eague of **W**omen **V**oters **H**umane **S**ociety of **A**ustin **N**ational **F**orensic **L**eague
Teams	**D**etroit **R**ed **W**ings **S**an **A**ntonio **S**purs **S**eattle **S**eahawks **O**ak **R**idge **R**angers
Business Firms	**P**rocter and **G**amble **C**ompany **I**nternational **B**usiness **M**achines **P**an **A**merican **A**irlines **U**ptown **D**iscount **S**hoe **S**tore
Institutions	**B**everly **H**ills **H**igh **S**chool **C**atawba **V**alley **T**echnical **C**ollege **S**mithsonian **I**nstitution **M**assachusetts **G**eneral **H**ospital
Buildings	**S**hubert **T**heater **P**laza **H**otel **L**eaning **T**ower of **P**isa **G**rand **C**entral **S**tation
Government Bodies	**H**ouse of **R**epresentatives **F**ederal **A**viation **A**dministration **D**epartment of **C**ommerce **P**eace **C**orps

NOTE: The names of organizations, businesses, and government bodies are often abbreviated to a series of capital letters.

EXAMPLES		
	National **O**rganization for **W**omen	**NOW**
	American **T**elephone & **T**elegraph	**AT&T**
	National **S**cience **F**oundation	**NSF**

Usually the letters in such abbreviations are not followed by periods, but always check an up-to-date dictionary or other reliable source to be sure.

REFERENCE NOTE: For more information about abbreviations, see pages 902–903.

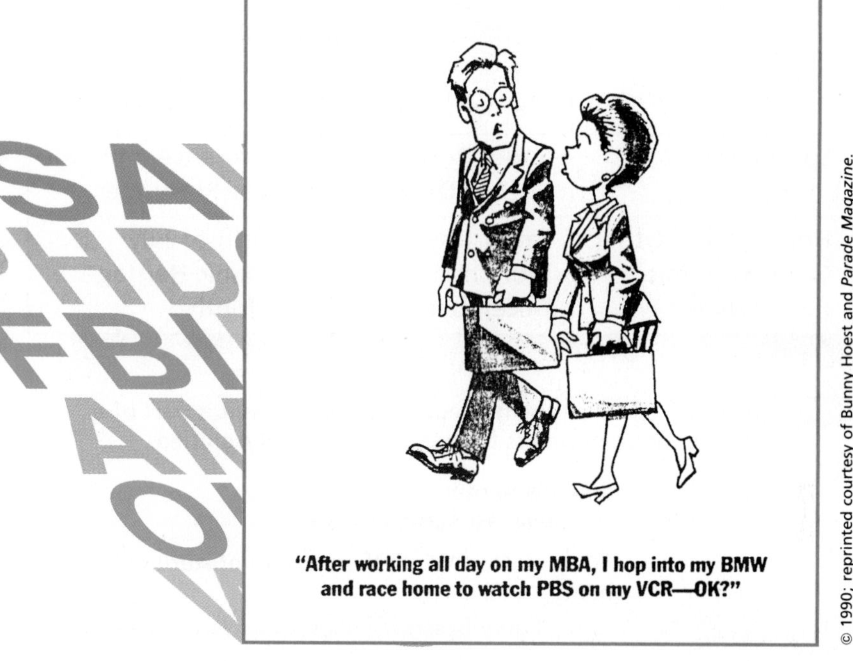

"After working all day on my MBA, I hop into my BMW and race home to watch PBS on my VCR—OK?"

Do not capitalize a word such as *hotel, theater, church,* or *school* unless it is part of a proper noun.

PROPER NOUNS	COMMON NOUNS
Chelsea **H**otel	at the **h**otel
Webster **H**igh **S**chool	a nearby **h**igh **s**chool
Fox **T**heater	a crowded **t**heater
First **B**aptist **C**hurch	in the **c**hurch

Do not capitalize words such as *democratic* and *republican* when they refer to principles or forms of government. Capitalize such words only when they refer to the political parties.

EXAMPLES a **d**emocratic policy the **D**emocratic **P**arty (or **p**arty)

Notice that the word *party* in the name of a political party may begin with a capital letter or a small letter.

(4) Capitalize the names of historical events and periods, special events, and holidays and other calendar items.

TYPE OF NAME	EXAMPLES	
Historical Events and Periods	**R**enaissance **V**ietnam **W**ar	**E**lizabethan **A**ge **A**merican **R**evolution
Special Events	**S**uper **B**owl **S**pecial **O**lympics	**C**onference on **W**orld **H**unger
Holidays and Other Calendar Items	**L**abor **D**ay **M**onday **D**ecember	**F**ourth of **J**uly **H**ispanic **H**eritage **M**onth

NOTE: Do not capitalize the name of a season unless it is part of a proper noun or unless the season is being personified.

EXAMPLES an early **w**inter
the **S**uncoast **S**ummer **F**estival

"O wild West Wind, thou breath of **A**utumn's being, . . ."

Percy Bysshe Shelley, "Ode to the West Wind"

MECHANICS

(5) Capitalize the names of nationalities, races, and peoples.

EXAMPLES **A**sian **C**aucasian **N**orse **O**jibwa
Zulu **H**ispanic **A**ztec **A**frican **A**merican

(6) Capitalize the names of religions and their followers, holy days and celebrations, holy writings, and specific deities.

TYPE OF NAME	EXAMPLES	
Religions and Followers	**C**hristianity **B**uddhist **H**induism	**J**udaism **M**ethodist **T**aoist
Holy Days and Celebrations	**C**hristmas **P**urim	**R**amadan **P**otlatch
Holy Writings	**T**almud **V**eda	**N**ew **T**estament **K**oran
Specific Deities	**A**llah **G**od	**J**ehovah **B**rahma

The words *god* and *goddess* are not capitalized when they refer to deities of ancient mythology. The names of specific mythological deities are capitalized, however.

EXAMPLE Cassandra could foretell the future but was condemned by the **g**od **A**pollo never to be believed.

NOTE: Some writers always capitalize pronouns that refer to the Deity. Other writers capitalize such pronouns only if necessary to prevent confusion.

EXAMPLE The priest asked God to bring peace to **H**is people.

(7) Capitalize the brand names of business products.

EXAMPLES **P**olaroid camera **X**erox copier
Nintendo video game **J**if peanut butter

Notice that the names of the types of products are not capitalized.

(8) Capitalize the names of ships, trains, aircraft, spacecraft, monuments, awards, planets, and any other particular things, places, or events.

TYPE OF NAME	EXAMPLES	
Ships	*Merrimac*	*Cunard Princess*
Trains	*Orient Express*	*North Coast Limited*
Aircraft	*Spirit of St. Louis*	*Air Force One*
Spacecraft	*Atlantis*	*Apollo 11*
Monuments	Lincoln Memorial	Statue of Liberty
Awards	Academy Award	Pulitzer Prize
Planets, Stars, Constellations	Neptune Sirius Big Dipper	Mercury Canis Major Cassiopeia

NOTE: The words *sun* and *moon* are rarely capitalized. Do not capitalize the word *earth* unless it is used along with the name of another heavenly body that is capitalized.

EXAMPLES gazing at the **s**un, **m**oon, and stars
below the surface of the **e**arth
the distance between **V**enus and **E**arth

MECHANICS

28d. Do not capitalize the names of school subjects, except for course names followed by a number and for the names of languages.

EXAMPLES	art	algebra	chemistry
	Art 102	Algebra I	Chemistry II
	English	Spanish	German

NOTE: As a rule, nouns identified by a number or letter are capitalized.

EXAMPLES **R**oom 31 **P**arlor B **S**chool **D**istrict 18 **C**hapter 4

Do not capitalize the class name *senior, junior, sophomore,* or *freshman* unless it is part of a proper noun.

EXAMPLES The **j**uniors and the **s**eniors will hold their talent show on May 4.
The **J**unior-**S**enior Revue will be held on May 4.

EXERCISE 3 Using Standard Capitalization

Rewrite each of the following items, using capital letters where they are needed. If an item is correct, write *C.*

1. itawamba junior college
2. a hotel across town
3. central high school
4. She is a junior.
5. medal of freedom
6. a royal typewriter
7. winter blizzard
8. the barclay hotel
9. trigonometry
10. physics I
11. labor day
12. history class
13. apple computer
14. the senior class picnic
15. bureau of the census
16. *zephyr* (train)
17. the crusades
18. the world series
19. newport athletic club
20. the rings of saturn

REVIEW A Proofreading a Paragraph for Correct Capitalization

Proofread the following paragraph, changing capital letters to small letters or small letters to capitals where necessary. If a sentence is correct, write *C.*

EXAMPLE [1] Only well-educated, highly skilled candidates are chosen as mission specialists with Today's National Aeronautics and Space administration (NASA).

1. *today's, Administration*

[1] A physician who speaks four languages and is trained in modern dance, dr. Mae Jemison (above) is one of NASA's most sought-after speakers. [2] Jemison, the first African american woman astronaut, grew up in Chicago and won a scholarship to Stanford university in northern California. [3] At Stanford she turned her attention to chemical engineering and African and Afro-american studies. [4] Later, while earning her Medical degree at Cornell University in Ithaca, new York, she worked at a refugee camp in Thailand. [5] After obtaining her m.d. degree, she served as a Peace corps medical officer in the west African nations of Sierra leone and Liberia. [6] Jemison joined NASA in 1987 while working as a general practitioner and attending graduate Engineering classes in Los angeles. [7] With her first space flight scheduled for the Fall of 1992, she relishes bringing people "A view of the space program they may not [otherwise] get." [8] As the United States gets closer to building a space station and sending crews to the Moon and Mars, the number of mission specialists is expected to increase dramatically. [9] As a result, more opportunities will be available to female and minority candidates who excel in research, science, and engineering. [10] "everyone has skills and talents," Jemison emphasizes, "and no one has a lock on scientific ability or physical ability."

28e. Capitalize titles.

(1) Capitalize a title belonging to a particular person when it comes before the person's name.

EXAMPLES **C**aptain Valdés **J**ustice O'Connor
Senator Inouye **P**resident White Feather

Generally, do not capitalize a title used alone or following a person's name.

EXAMPLES the **c**aptain of the ship
every **j**ustice of the U.S. Supreme Court
Daniel Inouye, a **s**enator from Hawaii
Uta White Feather, the class **p**resident

For clarity or special emphasis, you may capitalize a title used alone or following a person's name. In addition, a few titles are always capitalized. If you are unsure of whether to capitalize a title, check in a dictionary.

EXAMPLES Both the **P**resident and the **V**ice **P**resident met with Yitzhak Shamir, the **P**rime **M**inister of Israel.
The **S**urgeon **G**eneral explained HIV testing to us.

Generally, capitalize a title when using it alone in direct address.

EXAMPLES Goodbye, **P**rofessor.
Thank you, **S**ir [or sir].

NOTE: Do not capitalize *ex–*, *–elect, former,* and *late* when using them with titles.

EXAMPLES governor-**e**lect ex-President Reagan

(2) Capitalize a word showing a family relationship when the word is used with a person's name but *not* when it is preceded by a possessive.

EXAMPLES **U**ncle Juan **C**ousin Denisa **G**randfather Ewing
your **m**other my **a**unt Eunice Jay's **c**ousin Ramón

NOTE: A word showing a family relationship is capitalized when used in place of a person's name.

EXAMPLE I think that someone must have told **G**randma about the surprise party.

(3) Capitalize the first and last words and other important words in titles of books, periodicals, poems, stories, plays, historical documents, movies, radio and television programs, works of art, and musical compositions.

Unimportant words within titles are

- articles (*a, an, the*)
- short prepositions (those with fewer than five letters, such as *in, of, to, for, from, with*)
- coordinating conjunctions (*and, but, for, nor, or, so, yet*)

TYPE OF TITLE	EXAMPLES
Books	*A Portrait of the Artist as a Young Man* *The Death of the Moth and Other Essays*
Periodicals	*San Diego Tribune* *People Weekly*
Poems	"Ode on a Grecian Urn" *I Am Joaquín*
Stories	"The Old Man at the Bridge" "The Train from Rhodesia"
Plays	*The Merchant of Venice* *A Land Beyond the River*
Historical Documents	Declaration of Independence Magna Carta
Movies	*It's a Wonderful Life* *Dances with Wolves*
Radio and TV Programs	*Billboard's Top 40 Countdown* *The Tonight Show*
Works of Art	*Nike of Samothrace* [sculpture] *I and the Village* [painting]
Musical Compositions	*Ragtime Dance* "The Sky Is Crying"

NOTE: The article *the* is often written before a title but is not capitalized unless it is the first word of the title.

EXAMPLES the *Science Digest* the *St. Louis Dispatch*
The Count of Monte Cristo *The Spectator*

EXERCISE 4 Using Standard Capitalization

Write each of the following items, using capital letters where they are needed. If an item is correct, write *C*.

1. captain Ahab
2. *guernica* (painting)
3. a sergeant in an army
4. the club president
5. aunt Betty
6. senator Dole
7. mayor Fulton of Nashville
8. *down and out in paris and london* (book title)
9. the speaker of the House of Representatives
10. Rabbi Klein, a military chaplain
11. ex-president Reagan
12. the leader of a brass band
13. Ms. Solomon, the center director
14. the mayor-elect
15. the bill of rights
16. your aunt
17. the *Los Angeles times*
18. duties of a legislator
19. Mildred Zaharias, former national golf champion
20. "the world is too much with us" (poem)

REVIEW B Using Standard Capitalization

Write in order the words that should be capitalized in each of the following sentences, and capitalize the words correctly.

1. In their english classes this term, the juniors have read *o pioneers!*, a novel written by willa cather about swedish immigrants in nebraska.
2. A recent report from the secretary of labor included the following statement: most of the new jobs in the next decade will be in service fields.
3. According to professor De La Rey, the first of Tennyson's *idylls of the king* was published in 1859, the same year as the publication of Darwin's *the origin of species*, FitzGerald's translation of omar khayyám's *rubáiyát*, and Dickens's *a tale of two cities*.
4. In "canto I" the poet Ezra Pound describes an ominous sea voyage to the same mythical land of the dead visited by the hero Odysseus in the *Odyssey*, an epic by the greek poet Homer.
5. Speaking to a reporter from the *Tri-County Clarion*, coach Sheila Smith explained the drafting of a team resolution, which read, in part, "Resolved: that we will win all of our games next year."

MECHANICS

6. In ancient egypt the people worshiped many gods equally until the sun god Ra became the principal deity.
7. Dr. Bruce Jackson, jr., principal of the high school, formerly taught mathematics I classes and an introductory class in computer science offered to freshmen and sophomores.
8. From the St. Croix island national monument in Maine to the Huleia wildlife refuge in Hawaii, public lands managed by the federal government, including the military, equal a large percentage of the nation's total acreage.
9. Suzanne o'Rourke, president of the jogging club, has an exercise route that takes her three times a week through Myers park, down Carriage street, and then back west to Dean avenue.
10. The will of the swedish industrialist and inventor of dynamite, Alfred Nobel, established the Nobel prize to honor those who have benefited the world in the areas of literature, medicine, physics, chemistry, and peace; a prize in economics was added in 1969.

Proofreading a Paragraph for Correct Capitalization

MECHANICS

Proofread the following paragraph, changing capital letters to small letters and small letters to capitals where necessary. If a sentence is correct, write *C*.

EXAMPLE [1] An intriguing museum in Western Oklahoma celebrates the diversity and vitality of Native American Culture.

1. *western, culture*

[1] The Southern Plains Indian Museum on Highway 62 East of Anadarko, Oklahoma, was founded in 1947. [2] Administered by the Indian arts and crafts board, an agency of the U.S. department of the Interior, the museum showcases the creative achievements of the Kiowa, Comanche, Kiowa-Apache, Southern Cheyenne, Southern Arapaho, Wichita, Caddo, Delaware, and Ft. Sill Apache peoples. [3] The display of authentically detailed traditional costumes, shown on the next page, highlights the Museum's permanent collection. [4] Also on permanent display are four dioramas and a mural by nationally renowned Artist and sculptor Allen Houser, a Ft. Sill Apache; these exhibits illustrate the traditional social and ceremonial

customs of the region's peoples. [5] The museum also offers changing exhibits of contemporary arts and crafts, including painting, beadwork, metalwork, and featherwork. [6] These displays, as well as frequent one-person shows and demonstrations, are held in cooperation with the Oklahoma Indian Arts and Crafts cooperative, an independent business owned and operated by native American artists and craftworkers. [7] The Cooperative operates the museum's gift shop and certifies the authenticity of all products sold there. [8] One special attraction during the Summer is a display on the museum grounds of full-scale tepees, like these, painted by contemporary artists. [9] Another attraction is the week-long American Indian Expo held each August at the Caddo county Fairgrounds adjacent to the museum. [10] The largest gathering of native American peoples in the State of Oklahoma, the exposition features dance contests, a pageant, horse races, and parades.

Southern Plains Indian Museum, Anadarko, Oklahoma

Southern Plains Indian Museum, Anadarko, Oklahoma

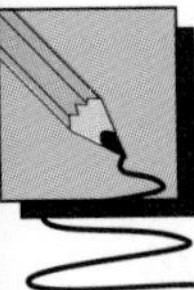

WRITING APPLICATION

Using Standard Capitalization in a Letter

Following the rules of capitalization is not just a matter of correctness. By choosing a capital letter or a small letter to begin a particular word, a writer indicates how the reader should interpret that word. How do the differences in the use of capitals and small letters affect the meaning of the following pair of sentences?

EXAMPLES From my informal survey, I found that the harpers, the bishops, the kings, and the knights feel that you should purchase a passage to India.

From my informal survey, I found that the Harpers, the Bishops, the Kings, and the Knights feel that you should purchase *A Passage to India.*

Notice in the examples above that italics also affect the meaning of a sentence. For more about how to punctuate titles, see pages 933–934 and 938–939.

WRITING ACTIVITY

Your school's library has received funding to expand its collection, and now students and teachers have been invited to make suggestions for new materials. Write a letter to the librarian naming five titles—books, periodicals, or videocassettes—that you think the library should acquire. Give a brief description of each title, and tell why you think each would be a worthwhile addition to the library. Be sure to use correct capitalization in your note.

Prewriting Jot down a list of novels, biographies, how-to manuals, reference books, newspapers, literary journals, educational videocassettes, and other materials that you think would be helpful additions to the library. Choose five titles from your list. Note whether each title is fiction or nonfiction; a book, a periodical, or a videocassette; one volume or several volumes. Briefly describe the subject matter of each title. You may want to visit the public library to collect or confirm information.

Writing Use your notes to help you write your first draft. Give clear, specific information about each book, periodical, or video. Convince the librarian that each would make a useful addition to the library. Explain why it's important for students to have easy access to these materials.

Evaluating and Revising Put your first draft aside for a few hours or overnight. Then read it critically. Is your letter persuasive? Does it follow the proper form for a business letter? (For more about business letters, see pages 1056–1064.) Be sure that all of your information is accurate and complete. Check your draft against your prewriting notes to see if you've left out any important details.

Proofreading and Publishing Use this checklist to help you proofread your letter. Have you

- spelled each title correctly?
- followed the rules of standard capitalization?
- underlined each title or enclosed it in quotation marks correctly?
- corrected any errors in grammar, usage, spelling, and punctuation?

You and your classmates may want to compile your information and write a group letter to the librarian suggesting needed additions to the library's collection.

Review: Posttest

A. Using Standard Capitalization

Many of the following sentences contain errors in standard capitalization. For each error, write the standard form of the word. If the sentence does not contain any errors, write *C*.

EXAMPLE **1.** Manolo Cruz will be attending Stanford university in the Fall.

1. *University, fall*

1. I am studying russian, English, and Art this Semester.
2. Go north for two Streets and then turn east on Central Avenue.
3. In the History of the United States, only one person, Gerald R. Ford, has held the nation's highest office without being elected president or Vice President.
4. Last summer I enjoyed reading *To Kill A Mockingbird* by Harper Lee, a southern writer.
5. HOMES is an acronym for the five great lakes: Huron, Ontario, Michigan, Erie, and Superior.
6. The first American woman in space, Sally Ride, was a member of the crew aboard the space shuttle *challenger* launched from cape Canaveral, Florida, on June 18, 1983.
7. The Mountain Ranges in the Western states offer a variety of hiking experiences for those who love the outdoors.
8. Despite their political differences, my mother, a Democrat, and my father, a Republican, worked together to increase voter registration.
9. Because Michael's letter was addressed to 730 Lexington Place instead of to 730 Lexington Court, it was delayed.
10. America's political and economic interests are closely tied to those of its northern neighbor, Canada, and to those of its southern neighbors, Mexico and the central American countries.

MECHANICS

B. Proofreading a Paragraph for Correct Capitalization

Proofread the following paragraph, changing capital letters to small letters and small letters to capitals where necessary. If a sentence is correct, write *C*.

EXAMPLE **[1] Chattanooga, Tennessee, is the seat of Hamilton county.**
1. *County*

[11] Chattanooga, on the Georgia border in Southeast Tennessee, is building its future by inviting visitors to explore its past. **[12]** The city has been welcoming tourists since at least 1866, when an ad in the *Chattanooga Times* invited northerners to visit with the assurance that the Ku Klux Klan had no power in Chattanooga. **[13]** Today a multimillion-dollar plaza on the banks of the Tennessee river marks the city's original site, a landing established about 1815 by a trader named john Ross. **[14]** exhibits throughout the plaza depict the city's history, including the forced removal of the Cherokee to Indian Territory (now Oklahoma) in 1838. **[15]** Ross, who was himself part Cherokee and who vehemently protested the removal, led that tragic journey, which became known as the trail of Tears. **[16]** The city of Chattanooga plans to build a trolley system to connect the plaza at Ross' landing to the restored Chattanooga Choo-Choo Terminal and Station on Market Street, where visitors can see a car and an engine from the first train that provided passenger service between the north and the South. **[17]** Chattanooga's status as a rail center made the City strategically important to both sides during the Civil War. **[18]** As the junction point for railroads to Atlanta, Georgia, and Memphis, Nashville, and Knoxville in Tennessee, Chattanooga provided a vital link for the movement of confederate troops and equipment. **[19]** In fact, the struggle for control of the railroads in the fall of 1863 led to a series of battles in and around the city that may have determined the outcome of the war. **[20]** For it was the Union general William Tecumseh Sherman's victory in the last of those confrontations, the Battle of Mission Ridge on November 24–25, that cleared the way for his devastating march through Georgia to the Sea.

SUMMARY STYLE REVIEW

Names of Persons	
Margot Fonteyn	a dancer
Mr. David G. DeLotto, Jr.	a teacher
William the Conqueror	an English king

Geographical Names	
Kansas City	a city in Kansas
Cuyahoga County	a county in Ohio
in the North, Southwest, Middle East	heading north, south, east, west
Argentina	a country in South America
Isle Royale	an island in Lake Superior
Mount Ararat	a mountain in Turkey
Mississippi River	a river flowing into the Gulf of Mexico
East Sixty-first Street	across the street

(continued)

SUMMARY STYLE REVIEW *(continued)*

Names of Organizations, Teams, Business Firms, Institutions, Buildings, Government Bodies	
the **T**oastmasters **C**lub	a public-speaking **c**lub
San **D**iego **P**adres	a **b**aseball **t**eam
Boeing **C**ompany	an aircraft **c**ompany
Lakeland **H**igh **S**chool	a large **h**igh **s**chool
Black **H**awk **C**ollege	four years in **c**ollege
the **C**hrysler **B**uilding	a tall **b**uilding
Department of **E**ducation	a **d**epartment of **g**overnment
Names of Historical Periods and Events, Special Events, Calendar Items	
the **B**ronze **A**ge	a prehistoric **a**ge
the **A**merican **C**ivil **W**ar	a **c**ivil **w**ar
the **W**orld **S**eries	a **s**eries of baseball **g**ames
Thanksgiving **D**ay	a national **h**oliday
March, **J**une, **S**eptember, **D**ecember	**s**pring, **s**ummer, **a**utumn, **w**inter
Names of Nationalities, Races, Peoples	
Egyptian	a **n**ative of **E**gypt
Caucasian	a **r**ace
Native **A**mericans	indigenous **p**eoples of the Western Hemisphere
Names of Religions, Their Followers, Holy Days, Celebrations, Holy Writings, Specific Deities	
Islam	the religious **f**aith of Muslims
Ash **W**ednesday	the first **d**ay of Lent
Hanukkah	a Jewish **f**estival
Holy **B**ible	a **h**oly **b**ook
God	Zeus, a Greek **g**od
Brand Names	
Levi's	**b**lue **j**eans
Kleenex	**f**acial **t**issues
Names of Languages, Specific Courses	
French, **S**panish, **L**atin	**l**anguages
Home **E**conomics **101**	my **h**ome **e**conomics **c**lass
American **H**istory **II**	a **c**ourse in American **h**istory

(continued)

MECHANICS

SUMMARY STYLE REVIEW *(continued)*

Names of Other Particular Things, Places, Events	
Santa Maria	a ship
Riverina XPT	a train
Concorde	an aircraft
Columbia	a spacecraft
Tomb of the Unknowns	a monument
George Peabody Award	an award
Little Dipper	a group of stars in the constellation Ursa Minor
Earth, Jupiter, Saturn	the surface of the earth
Room 212	the second room on the left
Oakdale Senior Prom	a group of seniors
Biosphere II	a scientific study of the biosphere

Titles	
Governor Richards	a governor
President Kennedy	the president of the club
Aunt Elena	Sonia's aunt
a message from Mother	a message from my mother
Portraits of the Valley and Other Works	a book
"Kubla Khan"	a poem
"The Secret Sharer"	a short story
Androcles and the Lion	a play
the *Wall Street Journal*	a newspaper
the Bill of Rights	a document
Robin Hood: Prince of Thieves	a movie
The Wonder Years	a television program
Mona Lisa	a work of art
"America the Beautiful"	a musical composition

MECHANICS

29 PUNCTUATION

End Marks and Commas

Diagnostic Test

A. Correcting Errors in the Use of End Marks and Commas in Sentences

Add, delete, or change end marks or commas to correct any of the following sentences that are incorrectly punctuated. If a sentence is correct, write *C*.

EXAMPLES
1. Well I think it's a good idea.
1. *Well, I think it's a good idea.*
2. We went to the mall, to the movies, and to our favorite restaurant, this afternoon
2. *We went to the mall, to the movies, and to our favorite restaurant this afternoon.*

1. Mr. Stanton will you please give me a reference.
2. Students who do well in academic subjects should in my opinion be commended by their school administrators.
3. No Sandy will not leave until the fifth of August.
4. Hoping to meet Arsenio Hall we got tickets to a taping of his show.

5. Look at the size of the fish I caught.
6. On Jan 1 2000 my niece will celebrate her twenty-first birthday.
7. Mom or Dad or Uncle Paul will cook dinner tonight.
8. On the last day of school the juniors will prepare juice, toast, and ham, and eggs for the seniors.
9. Please address all complaints to Dr Joseph Redwing Jr Department of Consumer Affairs 4749 Prospect Street Eugene OR 97401.
10. My grandmother a housekeeper all her life saved her money invested wisely and put both of her children through college.

B. Correcting Errors in the Use of End Marks and Commas in Paragraphs

Add, delete, or change end marks or commas in the following paragraphs to correct sentences that are incorrectly punctuated. If a sentence is correct, write *C*.

EXAMPLE [1] When I wrenched my back playing basketball I consulted a doctor, who specializes in sports medicine.

1. *When I wrenched my back playing basketball, I consulted a doctor who specializes in sports medicine.*

MECHANICS

[11] Sports medicine is a branch of medicine concerned with preventing and treating injuries, suffered during participation in sports. **[12]** Initially practiced by doctors working with professional sports teams, the practice of sports medicine has grown rapidly as interest in amateur sports and physical-fitness programs has increased.

[13] One ailment that doctors, who specialize in sports medicine, frequently encounter is tendinitis the inflammation of a tendon. **[14]** Tendons are the tough fibrous inelastic tissues that connect muscles to bones or other body parts. **[15]** "Tennis elbow," for example is a form of tendinitis caused by straining the tendons, that attach the muscles of the lower arm at the elbow.

[16] You don't have to be active in sports to benefit from advances in sports medicine for those advances are now being applied in the workplace. **[17]** Repetitive strain injury (RSI) caused by tendinitis can afflict anyone, whose job requires performing the same motion hundreds or even thousands of times a day. **[18]** In fact RSI strikes workers as varied as meat packers, word processors fruit pickers supermarket checkout clerks and musicians. **[19]** Because permanent disability can set in if RSI is left untreated physicians are teaming up with ergonomists scientists who adapt working conditions or the work itself to prevent injuries. **[20]** Employers, are finding that the preventive measures are a sound investment not a waste of money, paying for themselves many times over in increased productivity reduced turnover, and lower medical costs.

End Marks

Sentences

An ***end mark***—a *period,* a *question mark,* or an *exclamation point*—is used to indicate the purpose of a sentence. A period is also used at the end of many abbreviations.

29a. A statement (or declarative sentence) is followed by a period.

EXAMPLES Mexico City is the home of the Ballet Folklórico**.**

My words are like the stars that never change**.**

Chief Seattle, "Speech of Chief Seattle"

29b. A question (or interrogative sentence) is followed by a question mark.

EXAMPLES When will Terrell prepare the wild rice**?**

Have you read Lorraine Hansberry's *To Be Young, Gifted, and Black***?**

(1) Do not use a question mark after a declarative sentence containing an indirect question.

MECHANICS

INDIRECT QUESTION Mariana wants to know when Junko Tabei climbed Mount Everest.
QUESTION When did Junko Tabei climb Mount Everest?

(2) Polite requests in question form may be followed by either a question mark or a period.

EXAMPLE Would you please return these books to the library?
or
Would you please return these books to the library.

(3) A question mark should be placed inside the closing quotation marks when the quotation is a question. Otherwise, it should be placed outside the closing quotation marks.

EXAMPLES Cara asked, "Did Scott Joplin compose the opera *Treemonisha*?" [The quotation is a question.]
Do you agree with the Spanish proverb "Whoever gossips to you will gossip about you"? [The entire sentence, not the quotation, is a question.]

MECHANICS

29c. An exclamation is followed by an exclamation point.

EXAMPLES What a talented artist Frida Kahlo was!
I can't stand that noise!

(1) An interjection at the beginning of a sentence is usually followed by a comma but may be followed by an exclamation point.

CUSTOMARY Ah, there you are!
RARE Ah! There you are! [Notice that an exclamation point may be used after a single word as well as after a sentence.]

(2) An exclamation point should be placed inside the closing quotation marks when the quotation is an exclamation. Otherwise, it should be placed outside the closing quotation marks.

EXAMPLES "What a good movie!" exclaimed Natalie as she left the theater. [The quotation is an exclamation.]
How quickly she said, "You'll love it"! [The entire sentence, not the quotation, is an exclamation.]

29d. An imperative sentence may be followed by either a period or an exclamation point.

EXAMPLES Please write me a letter**.**
Hold that line**!**

HI AND LOIS, reprinted with special permission of King Features Syndicate, Inc.

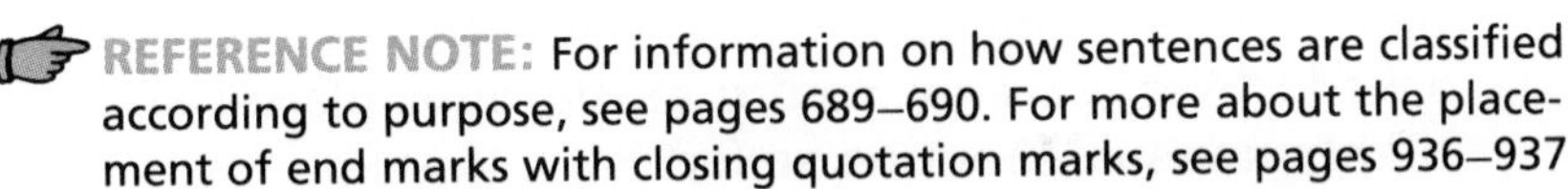
REFERENCE NOTE: For information on how sentences are classified according to purpose, see pages 689–690. For more about the placement of end marks with closing quotation marks, see pages 936–937.

EXERCISE 1 Correcting a Passage by Adding End Marks

Many periods and all exclamation points and question marks have been omitted from the following passage. Write each word that should be followed by an end mark, and add the appropriate end mark. If a new sentence begins after the end mark, capitalize the first word of the sentence. For any quotation requiring an end mark, include the closing quotation mark to show the proper placement of the end mark.

EXAMPLES [1] Dr. Lynn Block, director of research for the Hubert Larson Soap Company, looked at her appointment calendar
[2] "oh, no" she groaned

1. *calendar.*
2. *"Oh, no!"; groaned.*

[1] Today she must conduct interviews to hire a new secretary [2] "how nerve-racking it is when an applicant is unprepared" [3] nonetheless, she was ready for the 9:00 A.M. interview

[4] At 9:35 A.M., the receptionist ushered in the late arrival [5] "Oh, dear" thought Dr. Block as she surveyed the young man's torn jeans, unironed T-shirt, and shaggy hair [6] to questions about his qualifications, the young man answered only yes or no instead of mentioning specific details, and he did not apologize for his lateness [7] "Well," Dr. Block puzzled, "this person has good experience and typing skills, but he certainly doesn't seem to want the job"

[8] The next applicant, Ms. Smith, entered wearing a professional tool belt with well-cared-for carpentry tools around her waist [9] she said, "I'm so sorry to disturb you [10] I must have taken a wrong turn when I got off the elevator [11] I'm interested in the maintenance position being advertised"

[12] "I'll say" exclaimed Dr. Block [13] she directed the woman to the maintenance office on the other side of the building and wished her luck [14] To herself, she mused, "Whew at this rate, I may never get a secretary" [15] By then the next interviewee had arrived—on time [16] "Now what" wondered Dr. Block. [17] Looking up to see a neatly dressed young man, she asked, "Are *you* sure you're in the right place [18] it's been a highly unusual morning so far"

[19] he replied, "Oh, yes I'm applying for the secretarial position" [20] he gave brief, helpful explanations and asked appropriate questions about the job. [21] About his career plans, he said, "I would someday like to be an office manager [22] I like office work and believe good management is vital to a smooth operation"

[23] "You're right about that" exclaimed Dr. Block. [24] After the interview ended, Dr. Block pondered her choices [25] she thought, "Well, he doesn't have as much experience or quite as high a typing rate as the first interviewee, but I know whom I'm going to hire"

MECHANICS

Abbreviations

29e. An abbreviation is usually followed by a period.

Names of Persons	Ida B. Wells E. M. Forster
Titles Used with Names	Mr. Mrs. Ms. Dr. Jr. Sr.
Kinds of Organizations	Co. Inc. Corp. Assn. Ltd.

NOTE: Commonly known abbreviations for the names of organizations and services in areas such as government, education, and broadcasting media are written without periods. Each letter of the abbreviation is capitalized.

EXAMPLES FBI HUD ZIP ROTC PTA MTV BBC PBS

Parts of Addresses	Ave. St. Rd. Blvd. P.O. Box
Names of States	Ala. Del. Neb. Ky. S. Dak. Wisc. N.Y. Ariz. R.I. N. Car.

NOTE: A two-letter state abbreviation without periods is used when it is followed by a ZIP code. Each letter of the abbreviation is capitalized and no comma separates the abbreviation from the ZIP code.

EXAMPLE Tampa, **FL** 33624

Times	A.M. P.M. B.C. A.D.
Customary Units of Measure	oz. lb. in. ft. yd. mi. tsp. qt. doz. pt. cu. ft.

NOTE: Abbreviations for metric units of measure are usually written without periods.

EXAMPLES mm kg ml

When an abbreviation with a period is written at the end of a sentence, another period is not used as an end mark. However, a question mark or an exclamation point is used as needed.

EXAMPLES The Méndezes are moving to Broken Arrow, Okla.
Are the Méndezes moving to Broken Arrow, Okla.**?**

REFERENCE NOTE: For information on capitalizing abbreviations, see pages 876, 877, and 880.

PICTURE THIS

While reading the Sunday newspaper, you come upon this amazing photograph. The man in the picture is performing a bungee jump, a carefully supervised freefall from a height of several hundred feet. The special elastic cord will stop his fall before he can reach the ground. Seeing this photograph starts you thinking. Why do people set mental and physical challenges for themselves? What purpose do such challenges serve? What sorts of challenges do you set for yourself? Write a journal entry on the topic of personal challenges. In your entry, use each of the three types of end marks at least once, and include at least two abbreviations.

Subject: personal challenges
Audience: yourself
Purpose: to express your opinion; to record your thoughts

Brian Van Leeuwen, 28, a Sandia Labs engineer who is paraplegic, takes a daring plunge from a platform in Albuquerque, N.M., as part of a bungee-jumping experiment., Van Leeuwen said he made the jump strapped to his wheelchair because the chair is part of him.

Commas

Items in a Series

29f. Use commas to separate items in a series.

EXAMPLES She had been a correspondent for the wire service in London, Paris, Rome, and Madrid. [words]
I studied for the test on the way to school, during homeroom, and in study hall. [phrases]
The reporter wanted to know who I was, where I went to school, and how I felt about getting my driver's license. [clauses]

NOTE: Do not place a comma before the first item or after the final item in a series.

INCORRECT The students in auto mechanics class learned, to replace the spark plugs, check the fluid levels, and change the oil, in several makes of cars.

CORRECT The students in auto mechanics class learned to replace the spark plugs, check the fluid levels, and change the oil in several makes of cars.

(1) When *and, or,* or *nor* joins the last two items in a series, you may omit the comma before the conjunction. Never omit the final comma, however, if such an omission would make the sentence unclear.

EXAMPLES Soccer, basketball and lacrosse are my best sports. [The sentence is clear without the final comma.]
Joetta, Lucia and Ben are rehearsing a scene from the musical *Grease.* [The sentence is unclear without the comma. It appears that Joetta is being addressed.]
Joetta, Lucia, and Ben are rehearsing a scene from the musical *Grease.* [The sentence clearly states that all three people are rehearsing.]

Some writers prefer always to use the comma before the conjunction in a series. Follow your teacher's instructions on this point.

NOTE: Words customarily used in pairs are set off as one item in a series, such as *bag and baggage, law and order,* and *macaroni and cheese.*

EXAMPLE For supper they served a tossed salad, spaghetti and meatballs, garlic bread, milk, and fruit.

(2) If all the items in a series are joined by *and, or,* or *nor,* do not use commas to separate them.

EXAMPLE **Derrick and Han and Jina will represent the senior class.**

(3) Short independent clauses may be separated by commas.

EXAMPLE **Kelly plays the electric guitar, Diego plays the piano, and Chee sings.**

REFERENCE NOTE: Independent clauses in a series are usually separated by a semicolon. For more about this use of the semicolon, see pages 928–929.

29g. Use a comma to separate two or more adjectives preceding a noun.

EXAMPLES **Katherine Dunham is a creative, talented dancer and choreographer.**
Did you see that boring, silly, worthless movie?

Do not use a comma before the final adjective in a series if the adjective is thought of as part of the noun.

EXAMPLES **Lawanda hung colorful, delicate Chinese lanterns around the patio.** [*Chinese lanterns* is regarded as a single compound noun.]
It was a crisp, clear fall day. [*Fall day* is considered one item.]

You can use two tests to determine whether an adjective and a noun form a unit.

TEST 1: Insert the word *and* between the adjectives. If *and* fits sensibly between the adjectives, use a comma. In the first example above, *and* fits logically between the first two adjectives (*crisp* and *clear*) but not between *clear* and *fall.*

TEST 2: Change the order of the adjectives. If the order of the adjectives can be reversed sensibly, use a comma. *Clear, crisp fall day* makes sense, but *clear, fall, crisp day* does not.

NOTE: If one of the words in a series modifies another word in the series, do *not* separate them with a comma.

EXAMPLE Why did he wear a **bright red** cap?

MECHANICS

EXERCISE 2 Correcting Sentences by Adding Commas

For each of the following sentences, write each word that should be followed by a comma, and place a comma after it. If a sentence is correct, write *C.*

EXAMPLE **1.** The firefighters arrived promptly extinguished the blaze and returned to the station.
1. *promptly,; blaze,*

1. She is a bright charming young woman.
2. Albert Cunningham prepared a tossed green salad ham and cheese sandwiches and iced tea.
3. Armando sang danced and juggled in the talent show.
4. My parents always ask me where I'm going who'll be there and when I'll be home.
5. Should we go to the mall or to the park or to Yoko's house?

Independent Clauses

29h. Use a comma before *and, but, or, nor, for, so,* and *yet* when they join independent clauses.

EXAMPLES The sky looks clear, yet rain has been forecast.
I saw a performance of August Wilson's *Fences*, and now I am eager to read his other plays.

NOTE: Always use a comma before *for, so,* or *yet* joining independent clauses. You may omit the comma before *and, but, or,* or *nor* whenever the independent clauses are very short and the sentence will not be confusing or awkward without the comma.

EXAMPLES We didn't enjoy the film but you might. [clear without comma]
I will work with Emma and Josh will help Madison. [awkward without comma]
I will work with Emma, and Josh will help Madison. [clear with comma]

Don't confuse a compound sentence with a simple sentence that has a compound verb.

COMPOUND SENTENCE Ashley and I looked everywhere for the sheet music, but we couldn't find it. [two independent clauses]

SIMPLE SENTENCE Ashley and I looked everywhere for the sheet music but couldn't find it. [one independent clause with a compound verb]

MECHANICS

EXERCISE 3 Correcting Sentences by Adding Commas

For each of the following sentences, write the word that should be followed by a comma, and place a comma after it.

1. We're eating dinner now but I'll call you back as soon as we finish.
2. Are you busy Friday night or would you like to go to the movies with me?
3. Don't forget to take your history book home this weekend for the test is Monday.
4. The recipes in *Spirit of the Harvest: North American Indian Cooking* are adapted for modern cooks yet the ingredients listed are all traditional.
5. Quilting is a practical folk art and it is also a relaxing and enjoyable pastime.

REVIEW A Correcting Errors in the Use of End Marks and Commas in a Paragraph

Add, delete, or change end marks or commas in the following paragraph to correct sentences that are incorrectly punctuated. If a sentence is correct, write *C.*

EXAMPLE [1] Do you know what the second-largest city in Russia is.

1. *Do you know what the second-largest city in Russia is?*

[1] In 1697, Czar Peter I of Russia toured Western Europe, liked what he saw and determined to remodel his nation along Western lines. [2] Six years later he decreed that a whole, new city be built at the eastern end of the Gulf of Finland on land recently reconquered from Sweden. [3] Peter hired leading Russian French, and Italian architects to create a city with planned squares, wide avenues, and extensive parks, and gardens. [4] He named the city St Petersburg and in 1712 moved the capital there from Moscow. [5] The German name of the capital was kept for two centuries but in Aug 1914, was Russianized to *Petrograd* by Czar Nicholas II [6] Three years later the city witnessed both the abdication of Nicholas and the return from exile of the Russian, Marxist revolutionary V. I Lenin. [7] Petrograd served as the first capital of Soviet Russia after the Communist Revolution of Nov 1917 but lost that

status to Moscow early the following year. [8] Then in Jan. 1924 the Second Congress of the Soviets of the USSR. changed the city's name to Leningrad to honor the recently deceased Lenin. [9] Further, name changes seemed unlikely once the Communist system became firmly entrenched. [10] Yet in 1991 the Russian people went to the polls, repudiated the name Leningrad and reclaimed their beautiful historic city's original name—St Petersburg.

Nonessential Elements

29i. Use commas to set off nonessential clauses and nonessential participial phrases.

A ***nonessential*** (or ***nonrestrictive***) clause or participial phrase contains information that is not necessary to the meaning of the sentence.

NONESSENTIAL CLAUSES
Carla Harris**, who was offered scholarships to three colleges,** will go to Vassar in the fall.
The word *telethon***, which is a combination of the words *television* and *marathon*,** is an example of a portmanteau word.

NONESSENTIAL PHRASES
Antonio**, following his grandmother's recipe,** prepared *arroz con pollo* for his home economics class.
Both of the kittens**, frightened by the thunder,** jumped into my lap.

Each nonessential clause or phrase in the examples above can be omitted without changing the main idea expressed in the rest of the sentence.

EXAMPLES
Carla Harris will go to Vassar in the fall.
The word *telethon* is an example of a portmanteau word.
Antonio prepared *arroz con pollo* for his home economics class.
Both of the kittens jumped into my lap.

An ***essential*** (or ***restrictive***) clause or participial phrase is not set off by commas because it contains information that is necessary to the meaning of the sentence.

ESSENTIAL CLAUSES Carla Harris is the only senior **who was offered scholarships to three colleges.**

Mercury is the planet **that is closest to the Sun.**

ESSENTIAL PHRASES Any student **wanting to participate in the readathon** should sign up in the library by Friday.

The lines **cited at the beginning and the end of the speech** are from Omar Khayyám's *Rubáiyát.*

Notice how the omission of the essential clause or phrase affects the main idea of the sentence.

EXAMPLES Carla Harris is the only senior.
Mercury is the planet.
Any student should sign up in the library by Friday.
The lines are from Omar Khayyám's *Rubáiyát.*

NOTE: Adjective clauses beginning with *that* are usually essential.

Some clauses and participial phrases may be either essential or nonessential. The presence or absence of commas tells the reader how the clause or phrase relates to the main idea of the sentence.

ESSENTIAL Dave took his problem to the librarian **who is an authority on children's literature.** [The library has more than one librarian, but only one is an authority on children's literature.]

NONESSENTIAL Dave took his problem to the librarian**,** **who is an authority on children's literature.** [The library has only one librarian.]

REFERENCE NOTE: See pages 674–683 for more information on clauses and pages 657–658 for more information on participial phrases.

EXERCISE 4 Identifying Essential and Nonessential Clauses and Phrases

In the following sentences, identify each italicized phrase or clause as *essential* or *nonessential.* Add commas where they are needed.

1. Employees *who always have a ready smile* make the job seem easier.
2. She is wearing the shirt *that she received for her birthday.*

MECHANICS

3. A chile relleno *consisting of a stuffed, breaded green chile* is Eduardo's favorite appetizer.
4. People *who are overly nervous* may not make good drivers.
5. Adults *whose development has been studied and recorded as they grow older* continue to mature, usually in predictable stages, after the age of eighteen.
6. Cities *that seem alike* bear a closer look.
7. Lake Chad *covering an area of about six thousand square miles* is West Africa's largest body of water.
8. The Federal Reserve System *serving as the central bank of the United States* monitors money and credit growth.
9. That law *which may have met a real need one hundred years ago* should be repealed or rewritten to deal with today's situation.
10. The Suez Canal *extending more than a hundred miles* links the Mediterranean Sea and the Red Sea.

REVIEW B **Correcting Errors in the Use of Commas in a Paragraph**

MECHANICS

Add or delete commas in the following paragraph to correct sentences that are incorrectly punctuated. If a sentence is correct, write *C*.

EXAMPLE [1] **Rona asked me, when the Old Spanish Days fiesta is.**
1. *me*

[1] Each August visitors are welcomed to the Old Spanish Days fiesta sponsored by the city of Santa Barbara in California. [2] The festival, which lasts five days, attracts nearly half a million people. [3] It honors the Spaniards, who colonized the area, beginning in the early 1700s. [4] The festivities start on Wednesday with blessings and singing and dancing at *La Fiesta Pequeña* which is Spanish for "Little Festival," outside Mission Santa Barbara on E. Los Olivos and Laguna streets. [5] The mission founded in 1786 is one of the best preserved of the twenty-one missions, that the Spanish established in California between 1769 and 1823. [6] Costumed dancers and colorful floats enliven Thursday's *Desfile Histórico* ("Historic Parade"), which recounts how Spanish conquistador Sebastian Vizcaino sailed into the nearby bay in 1602 why he named the bay Santa Barbara and what drew settlers to the area. [7] A free, variety show that begins later in the day and continues nightly features Spanish flamenco dancers and Mexican folkloric dancers like those,

pictured here. [8] On the weekend artists and craftworkers set up booths along Cabrillo Blvd. and State St., and sell hand-made items. [9] Fiesta-goers needn't go hungry for authentic Latin foods such as tortas, tacos, enchiladas, *flautas* and tamales are sold in the two open-air markets. [10] What an eventful fun-filled five days Old Spanish Days provides!

MECHANICS

Introductory Elements

29j. Use a comma after certain introductory elements.

(1) Use a comma after *yes, no,* or any mild exclamation such as *well* or *why* at the beginning of a sentence.

EXAMPLES Yes, you are welcome to join us.
Well, what do you think?
Why, the whole story sounds suspicious!

(2) Use a comma after an introductory participial phrase.

EXAMPLES **Proofreading my report,** I saw that I had written *gorilla,* instead of *guerrilla, warfare.*
Almost hidden by the dense brush, the tiny, brown rabbit sat absolutely still.

NOTE: Do not confuse a gerund phrase used as the subject of a sentence with an introductory participial phrase.

GERUND PHRASE **Planting the Japanese quinces along the fence** took several hours.
PARTICIPIAL PHRASE **Planting the Japanese quinces along the fence,** I stepped on a mound of fire ants.

(3) Use a comma after two or more introductory prepositional phrases.

EXAMPLES **At the end of the block just beyond the new railroad station,** my grandparents own and operate a small restaurant.

Near the beginning of the trail alongside the lake, the scout leader found an overturned canoe.

NOTE: A single introductory prepositional phrase does not require a comma unless the phrase is parenthetical or unless the sentence is confusing or awkward without the comma.

EXAMPLES **During spring break** we're going camping in the mountains. [clear without comma]

By the way, you're late. [The comma is needed because the phrase is parenthetical. See pages 914–915.]

From Laura, Lee had borrowed a sleeping bag, a canteen, and a flashlight. [The comma is needed to avoid reading "Laura Lee."]

(4) Use a comma after an introductory adverb clause.

EXAMPLES **While the orchestra tuned their instruments,** the stagehands checked the curtain.

As soon as we finished eating, we cleared the table for a game of mah-jongg.

EXERCISE 5 **Correcting Sentences by Adding Commas**

For each of the following sentences, write each word that should be followed by a comma, and place a comma after it.

1. When they had finished playing the musicians moved their instruments offstage to make room for the dancers.
2. By the end of the second day of school nearly all of the students seemed to have found their assigned classrooms teachers and lockers.
3. Oh I meant to ask Gloria if she had watched the Chinese New Year parade.
4. In the second half of the third period Johnson caught a twenty-yard pass and raced into the end zone.
5. After a lengthy discussion of the options the committee voted to reject both of the themes proposed for the prom and to seek fresh ideas.

Interrupters

29k. Use commas to set off elements that interrupt a sentence.

(1) Appositives and appositive phrases are usually set off by commas.

An ***appositive*** is a noun or a pronoun placed beside another noun or pronoun to identify or explain it. An ***appositive phrase*** consists of an appositive and its modifiers.

EXAMPLES An interview with Florence Cohen, **the well-known landscape architect,** will appear in the *Herald.*
Sipa, **a game similar to volleyball,** is a popular sport in the Philippines.

Sometimes an appositive is so closely related to the word or words preceding it that it should not be set off by commas. Such an appositive is called a ***restrictive appositive.***

EXAMPLES the landscape artist **Fernando Amorsolo**
the novel ***Go Tell It on the Mountain***
the preposition ***with***

(2) Words used in direct address are set off by commas.

EXAMPLES Will you explain to the class, **Lena,** how you solved the last problem?
Dexter, please help your brother set the table.
You seem upset, **my friend.**

(3) Parenthetical expressions are set off by commas.

Parenthetical expressions are remarks that add incidental information or relate ideas to each other.

Commonly Used Parenthetical Expressions		
after all	I believe	naturally
at any rate	incidentally	nevertheless
by the way	in fact	of course
consequently	in general	on the contrary
for example	in the first place	on the other hand
for instance	meanwhile	that is
however	moreover	therefore

MECHANICS

EXAMPLES The train will**, I am sure,** be on time.
On the contrary, exercise is relaxing.
Jameson was the first to solve the puzzle**, naturally.**

Some of these expressions are not always parenthetical. When an expression is not used parenthetically, it is not set off by commas.

EXAMPLE My grandfather**, by the way,** created these colorful sand paintings. [parenthetical, meaning "incidentally"]
We could see **by the way** Melinda worked that she wanted to do her best. [not parenthetical, meaning "by the manner in which"]

Frequently, your intention determines the punctuation you use. If you want your reader to pause for a parenthetical expression, set it off with commas; if not, leave it unpunctuated. Sometimes, though, the placement of the expression in a sentence determines the punctuation.

EXAMPLES That is **indeed** startling news. [no pause]
That is**, indeed,** startling news. [pause]
Indeed, that is startling news. [comma required by placement of expression]

I hope this report will clarify the situation for you. [no comma because of placement]
This report will**, I hope,** clarify the situation for you. [commas required by placement of expression]

NOTE: A contrasting expression introduced by *not* is parenthetical and should be set off by commas.

EXAMPLE Frank Robinson**, not Jackie Robinson,** was the first African American to manage a major league baseball team.

REFERENCE NOTE: Parentheses and dashes are sometimes used to set off parenthetical expressions. See pages 955–956.

EXERCISE 6 Correcting Sentences by Adding Commas

For each of the following sentences, write each word that should be followed by a comma, and place a comma after it. If a sentence is correct, write *C*.

EXAMPLE **1.** My take-home pay at any rate is less than yours.
1. *pay, . . . rate,*

MECHANICS

1. The Red Sea not the Black Sea separates Northeast Africa and the Arabian Peninsula.
2. My father's youngest sister Aunt Pilar is an architect in New Orleans.
3. The future of course is largely in your hands.
4. Naturally well-nourished babies have a better chance of surviving infancy.
5. Call Felipe as soon as you can Hope.
6. A rose window by the way resembles an open rose.
7. In 1901 Chiricahua Apache leader Geronimo took part in President Theodore Roosevelt's inaugural procession.
8. In college however students arrange their own schedules.
9. Alex Haley the author of *Roots* attributed his interest in writing to stories his grandmother and great-aunts told.
10. The fairy tale "Cinderella" I believe originated in ninth-century China.

REVIEW C **Correcting Sentences by Adding Commas**

For each of the following sentences, write each word that should be followed by a comma, and place a comma after it. If a sentence is correct, write *C*.

1. The plot of that book a murder mystery is in my opinion far too complicated.
2. If you give us your application now our office will process it before the deadline which is this afternoon.
3. Ancient Mayan ruins tropical rain forests and beautiful mountains are just a few of the sights I saw in Guatemala where my cousins live.
4. Please understand friends that as much as I would like to I cannot be at the picnic the game and the track meet all at the same time.
5. The people riding in the front seat of the roller coaster were the ones who screamed the loudest.
6. Hiroshi whom you met last night is an exchange student from Kyoto a large city in Japan.
7. Looking for economical transportation Harry who had never bought a car before nervously investigated all of the possibilities at Country Motors.
8. Before you start putting that jigsaw puzzle together Rosa make sure that all of it will fit on the table.

9. When Jamie had finished the chicken and salad were all gone and the beans carrots and potatoes had been left untouched.
10. In my opinion *Coming to America* not *Beverly Hills Cop* is Eddie Murphy's best movie.

Conventional Uses

29l. Use a comma in certain conventional situations.

(1) Use a comma to separate items in dates and addresses.

EXAMPLES **Hawaii achieved statehood on August 21, 1959, becoming the fiftieth state.**
Write to me at 423 Twentieth Street, Salt Lake City, UT 84101, after the first of May.

Notice that a comma also separates the final item in a date (*1959*) and in an address (*84101*) from the words that follow it. Notice also that a comma does *not* separate the month from the day (*August 21*), the house number from the street name (*423 Twentieth Street*), or the state name from the ZIP code (*UT 84101*).

NOTE: Do not use a comma when writing

- the day before the month

EXAMPLE The Hubble Space Telescope was launched on **25 April** 1990.

- only the month and the day

EXAMPLE We began rehearsals on **June 20.**

- only the month and the year

EXAMPLE A severe storm hit Luzon in **October 1991.**

- a preposition between the items in a date or an address

EXAMPLE Joanna lives at **301 Green Street in San Diego.**

(2) Use a comma after the salutation of a friendly letter and after the closing of any letter.

EXAMPLES **Dear Angela,** **Sincerely yours,**

REFERENCE NOTE: For more on punctuating the salutation in a business letter, see page 1058.

(3) Use a comma after a name followed by an abbreviation such as *Jr.*, *Sr.*, or *Ph.D.*

EXAMPLES **Peter Grundel, Jr.** **Lorraine Henson, Ph.D.**

NOTE: Within a sentence, these abbreviations are followed by a comma as well.

EXAMPLE **Hazel Sellers, M.D., will be the guest speaker.**

Unnecessary Commas

29m. Do not use unnecessary commas.

Use a comma only when a rule requires one or when the meaning would be unclear without one.

INCORRECT **Amy, and I put a videocassette, and a fashion catalog in the time capsule.**

CORRECT **Amy and I put a videocassette and a fashion catalog in the time capsule.**

MECHANICS

REVIEW D **Correcting Sentences by Adding End Marks and Commas**

Write the following sentences, adding end marks and commas where needed.

1. Stalled in the traffic jam the motorcyclists Carl and Lou who were on their way home settled in to wait
2. In AD 1238 the Thai people created the first Thai nation named *Sukothai* which means "dawn of happiness"
3. Our new apartment at 310 Columbia Avenue Fort Wayne Indiana is comfortable but I wish we were still living at 2125 West Third Street in Omaha Nebraska
4. Jay Carson Jr a senior with excellent organizational skills arranged for the benefit concert setting the date and ticket sales hiring the musical talent and handling the publicity
5. In 1936 the library staff at the *Tribune* began recording the newspaper on microfilm and now the library contains microfilm copies of every issue from October 14 1858 up to the most recent one
6. Our company which we started as high school seniors provides home office and factory cleaning services

7. When the doctor informed me that on the one hand only a very small percentage of people suffer a bad reaction to the vaccine and that on the other hand the disease that it prevents is nearly always fatal what could I do but agree to have the shot
8. How good it was to see Aunt Marissa Uncle Bill and all of our cousins back in Tennessee
9. The island of Tierra del Fuego named the Land of Fire by Ferdinand Magellan because of the many bonfires he saw there lies off the southern tip of South America in a cold windy climate
10. Benjamin Banneker the noted inventor astronomer and mathematician served on the commission that surveyed and laid out Washington DC

REVIEW E Correcting Errors in the Use of End Marks and Commas in a Paragraph

Add, delete, or change any end marks or commas in the following paragraph to correct each sentence that is incorrectly punctuated. If a sentence is correct, write *C*.

EXAMPLE [1] The Japan America Theatre is the performing arts stage of the Japanese American Cultural and Community Center in Los Angeles Cal..

1. *The Japan America Theatre is the performing arts stage of the Japanese American Cultural and Community Center in Los Angeles, Cal.*

[1] Since it opened in 1984 the theater which you can see on the next page has won worldwide acclaim for the quality and scope of its productions. [2] Those productions range from all-male casts (such as the one shown) performing works in the sixteenth-century Grand Kabuki tradition to American premieres of contemporary works by leading Japanese choreographers. [3] The theater doesn't just book productions, but rather works closely with the artists, whom it presents. [4] In fact according to managing director for programs, Cora Mirikatani, between 60 and 70 percent of the theater's presentations are developed in partnership with the artists. [5] In 1988, for example the theater staged the first, Broadway-style Japanese musical, *Utamoro: The Musical* Tako Izumi's story of eighteenth-century wood-cut artist Utamoro. [6] To make the work more

accessible to American audiences, the Los Angeles production pared down the slang in the Tokyo version, emphasized movement and gesture more, and provided narration, and supertitles in English. [7] It also used more elaborate costumes, wigs, and masks, to convey the splendor of the Edo period. [8] Recognizing that outstanding art transcends national boundaries the theater features performing artists of all nationalities. [9] In recent years, for example, both New York City's Theater of the Open Eye and the Los Angeles Chamber Ballet have performed there. [10] In addition a few years ago Indian sitar player Ravi Shankar working with American musicians created an original composition incorporating classical Japanese instruments into an Indian musical form.

WRITING APPLICATION

Using Commas Correctly to Make Your Writing Clear

In many writing situations, you will find it helpful to express your ideas concisely. Often, you can combine short sentences by turning one sentence into an adverb clause and attaching it to the other sentence. The subordinating conjunction at the beginning of the clause shows the relationship between the two ideas. The relationship may be one of time, cause or reason, purpose or result, or condition. What relationship does the subordinating conjunction show in the following combined sentences?

ORIGINAL I read the instructions to the players. Mary and Jerome pass out the game pieces.

COMBINED Mary and Jerome pass out the game pieces while I read the instructions to the players.

or

While I read the instructions to the players, Mary and Jerome pass out the game pieces.

Notice in the combined sentences above that the adverb clause may be placed at either the beginning or the end of a sentence. The placement of the clause determines what punctuation you should use. Notice also that a comma is placed after the adverb clause used as an introductory element.

MECHANICS

WRITING ACTIVITY

You and some friends are planning to study together for an important final exam. To make the study sessions more interesting, you've decided to create a game using the information to be covered on the exam. Invent a game based on a subject you are studying in school—perhaps history, chemistry, or English. Then write a set of instructions for playing the game. In your instructions, use at least five adverb clauses. Be sure to use commas correctly.

Prewriting First, jot down several ideas for a game based on one of your school subjects. For example, you might have ideas for a geographical or historical trivia game or a word game using literary terms. If you wish, team up with a few classmates for a brainstorming session. Then, decide which idea you want to develop. What are the rules of the game? What, if any, game pieces are needed? Take notes for your instructions. Arrange the information in an easy-to-follow order.

Writing Begin your draft by giving a brief, general description of the game. Then give complete, step-by-step instructions for playing the game. Add rules and steps that occur to you as you write, keeping your audience in mind. Be sure to explain the game clearly so that a reader can play it from your instructions.

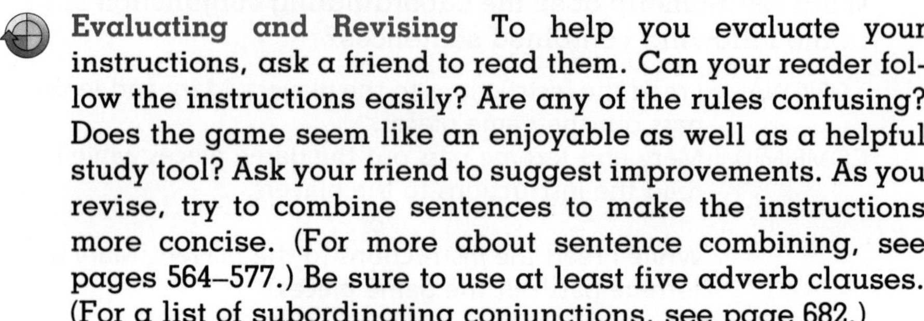

Evaluating and Revising To help you evaluate your instructions, ask a friend to read them. Can your reader follow the instructions easily? Are any of the rules confusing? Does the game seem like an enjoyable as well as a helpful study tool? Ask your friend to suggest improvements. As you revise, try to combine sentences to make the instructions more concise. (For more about sentence combining, see pages 564–577.) Be sure to use at least five adverb clauses. (For a list of subordinating conjunctions, see page 682.)

Proofreading and Publishing Read your instructions carefully to find any errors in grammar, usage, punctuation, or spelling. Pay special attention to punctuation. Be sure that you've used commas correctly with introductory elements, interrupters, and items in a series. You may want to publish your game by distributing the instructions to your classmates as a study tool.

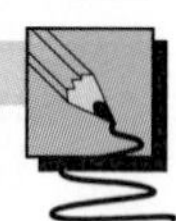

Review: Posttest

A. Correcting Errors in the Use of End Marks and Commas in Sentences

Write the following sentences, adding, deleting, or changing end marks and commas as necessary. If a sentence is correct, write *C*.

EXAMPLE **1.** My best friend has moved to 9782, Revere Avenue, New York NY 10465

1. *My best friend has moved to 9782 Revere Avenue, New York, NY 10465.*

1. Marilyn and Antonio who both work at a nearby child-care center greatly enjoy inventing, and playing games with the children.
2. Unfolding the solar panels placing satellites into orbit and conducting medical experiments had kept the space shuttle crew busy
3. Because we had to rekindle the fire twice our cookout was delayed
4. Well if you apply to all eight colleges Paul you will pay a sizable sum in application fees
5. "It is my pleasure to introduce Vernon K Foster Jr. who has recently returned from a visit to Nairobi Kenya," said Adele Peters president of our school's Student Foreign Exchange League
6. The diplomats both educated at American University in Washington DC were assigned posts in Athens Greece and Nicosia Cyprus.
7. "The house is on fire" shouted my father. "Everyone get out right now".
8. On the far wall to the right of the main entrance you will see a striking oil painting done in matte black, ash white, and neutral gray.
9. Studying *Beowulf* for the first time the class particularly enjoyed Grendel the grim gruesome monster
10. The treasurer's report did I believe make it clear that the senior class has been very successful in its fund-raising activities this year.
11. Interrupting his friends Philip asked, "Are you ready to leave".
12. We spent the morning cleaning the basement and sorting boxes but in the afternoon we rode our bikes along lovely country roads.
13. We have already decided to hold our first class reunion on July 4 2003 at the Bollingbroke Hotel in San Francisco California
14. Using hyperbole the store claimed in a colorful full-page newspaper ad that it will be having the "World's Most Spectacular Labor Day Sale."
15. When they went to the prom did Martha wear a lavender lace gown with blue satin ribbons and did George wear a light blue tuxedo

B. Correcting Errors in the Use of End Marks and Commas in a Paragraph

Add, delete, or change any end marks and commas in the following paragraph to correct sentences that are incorrectly punctuated. If a sentence is correct, write *C*.

EXAMPLE [1] In looking through a United States atlas have you ever been tempted to use it, as a menu to serve a meal of places named for foods.

1. *In looking through a United States atlas, have you ever been tempted to use it as a menu to serve a meal of places named for foods?*

[16] For an appetizer, that will take the edge off your family's hunger, without filling them up serve a relish tray assembled from Pickleville in Utah, Olive in Montana, and Pepperton in Georgia along with Rolls from Arizona and Indiana and Butters from North Carolina **[17]** You might follow that opener with a salad made with Tomato from Mississippi dressed with Mayo from Maryland, Thousand Island from New York, or French from New Mexico, or Wyoming. **[18]** Seafood-loving families won't be disappointed for you can find Whitefish in Washington, Salmon in Idaho, Haddock in Georgia and Trout in Louisiana. **[19]** Families that enjoy red meat can savor selections from Rib Lake in Wisconsin, Lambs Junction in South Carolina, Rabbithash in Kentucky, or indeed Beef Island in the Virgin Islands. **[20]** If your family prefers poultry on the other hand, consider Chicken from Alaska, or Duck or Turkey from North Carolina **[21]** You'll want to serve some vegetables too so choose your family's favorites from Corn in Oklahoma, Bean City in Florida, Greens in Kansas and Michigan, and Pea Patch Island in Delaware. **[22]** For a delicious nourishing side dish look no further than Noodle in Texas, Rice in Minnesota or Virginia, or Wild Rice in North Dakota. **[23]** Naturally Milk River in Montana, Goodwater in Alabama, and Tea in South Dakota will remind you to include a beverage or two. **[24]** Round out your satisfying meal with Oranges, which you'll find in among other places California and Vermont, and Almonds from Alabama and Wisconsin **[25]** And when your kid brother raves about the meal, but complains about having to do the dishes, simply suggest that he get out the atlas and see how far it is to Soap Lake, Washington.

SUMMARY OF USES OF END MARKS AND COMMAS

29a	Use a period at the end of a statement.
29b	Use a question mark at the end of a question.
29c	Use an exclamation point after an exclamation.
29d	Use either a period or an exclamation point at the end of an imperative sentence.
29e	Use a period after most abbreviations.
29f	Use commas to separate items in a series.
29g	Use a comma to separate two or more adjectives preceding a noun.
29h	Use a comma before *and, but, or, nor, for, so,* and *yet* when they join independent clauses.
29i	Use commas to set off nonessential clauses and nonessential participial phrases.
29j	Use a comma after certain introductory elements. (1) After a word such as *yes, no,* or any mild exclamation at the beginning of a sentence (2) After an introductory participial phrase (3) After two or more introductory prepositional phrases (4) After an introductory adverb clause
29k	Use commas to set off elements that interrupt a sentence. (1) Appositives and appositive phrases (2) Words in direct address (3) Parenthetical expressions
29l	Use a comma in certain conventional situations. (1) Between items in dates and addresses (2) After the salutation of a friendly letter and the closing of any letter (3) After a name followed by an abbreviation such as *Jr., Sr.,* or *Ph.D.*

MECHANICS

30 PUNCTUATION

Other Marks of Punctuation

MECHANICS

Diagnostic Test

A. Proofreading Sentences for Correct Punctuation

The following sentences contain errors in the uses of semicolons, colons, dashes, parentheses, brackets, italics (underlining), quotation marks, apostrophes, and hyphens. Rewrite each sentence, correcting each error.

EXAMPLE **1. I just saw Paulas picture's of Washington, D.C.**
1. ***I just saw Paula's pictures of Washington, D.C.***

1. Traffic was stopped for the citys Martin Luther King Day parade consequently, a massive traffic jam developed.
2. One of my favorite Biblical passages is the story of Jesus and the Samaritan woman in John 4, 5–42.
3. Since Bethany visited Europe last summer, she has been using foreign expressions such as bonjour and ciao.
4. "How long will it take for these three rolls of film to be developed"? I asked.
5. Our English class agrees that James Baldwin's short story The Rockpile is one of the best we have ever read.
6. Please turn down the radio I'm getting a headache.

7. The confusion occurred because I thought that the brief case was your's, not Dorothy's.
8. Very-successful people, whether they excel in politics, the arts, or sports, share a common trait: self motivation.
9. We might and according to the tour schedule should have a free afternoon in Rome the first city on the tour.
10. The newspaper quoted Mr. Busch as saying, "People who take it Auto Mechanics I usually are glad they did"

B. Proofreading Paragraphs for Correct Punctuation

Rewrite the following paragraphs, adding and deleting punctuation as needed.

[11] The National Museum of American History formerly the National Museum of History and Technology is a fascinating place its part of the Smithsonian Institution in Washington, D.C. **[12]** You may ask I know I did what makes the museum so fascinating. **[13]** The museum offers changing displays on vari ous themes represented by extremely-diverse artifacts of the United State's culture. **[14]** When we visited the three story building we saw the actual flag that inspired Francis Scott Key to write The Star Spangled Banner and a pair of ruby slippers that Judy Garland wore in the film The Wizard of Oz 1939. **[15]** Another crowd pleaser was the museums collection of First Ladies gowns. **[16]** Children shouldnt miss the Hands-On History Room they can explore our history and culture there in well planned, creative ways.

[17] We spent all day looking for such cultural keepsakes as the Fonzs jacket from the television show Happy Days however there were also many scientific and technological displays to see. **[18]** One of these displays the Foucault Pendulum was almost impossible to overlook upon entering the building. **[19]** Some of the other scientific treasures were: Henry Fords Model T car, our country's oldest working steam engine cotton gins, and Samuel Morse's telegraph. **[20]** We also allowed time for such interesting displays as the National Philatelic Collection, which was especially popular with stamp collectors like my dad, a country store post office, which came from a West Virginia town, and a variety of other wonderful exhibits.

Semicolons

30a. Use a semicolon between independent clauses that are closely related in thought and are not joined by *and, but, for, nor, or, so,* or *yet.*

EXAMPLES Three candidates have filed for the new commission seat**;** all of them have experience in public office.

No man is an island entire of itself**;** every man is a piece of the continent, a part of the main.

John Donne, from "Meditation 17"

Do not join independent clauses unless there is a close relationship between the main ideas of the clauses.

NONSTANDARD Madagascar is a small nation made up of several islands; for many years, scientists have studied this country because of its unusual wildlife.

STANDARD Madagascar is a small nation made up of several islands**.** For many years, scientists have studied this country because of its unusual wildlife.

30b. Use a semicolon between independent clauses joined by a conjunctive adverb or a transitional expression.

A ***conjunctive adverb*** or a ***transitional expression*** indicates the relationship between the independent clauses that it joins.

EXAMPLES The speech was long and repetitious**; consequently,** people in the audience began fidgeting in their seats and whispering among themselves.

To excel the past we must not allow ourselves to lose contact with it**; on the contrary,** we must feel it under our feet because we raised ourselves upon it.

José Ortega y Gasset, from "In Search of Goethe from Within, Letter to a German"

Commonly Used Conjunctive Adverbs

accordingly	however	moreover
besides	indeed	nevertheless
consequently	instead	otherwise
furthermore	meanwhile	therefore

Commonly Used Transitional Expressions

as a result	for instance	on the contrary
for example	in fact	that is

NOTE: When a conjunctive adverb or a transitional expression is used *between* independent clauses, it is preceded by a semicolon and followed by a comma.

EXAMPLE The leaders of the two nations saw no hope for a settlement**; however,** they were willing to meet again.

When used *within* a clause, the conjunctive adverb or transitional expression is set off by commas.

EXAMPLE The leaders of the two nations saw no hope for a settlement; they were willing**, however,** to meet again.

REFERENCE NOTE: For more information about conjunctive adverbs and transitional expressions, see pages 686–687.

30c. Use a semicolon (rather than a comma) before a coordinating conjunction to join independent clauses that contain commas.

EXAMPLE Stephen Foster wrote many songs, including "Oh, Susanna," "Camptown Races," and "Beautiful Dreamer"**;** but he is perhaps best remembered for "My Old Kentucky Home," which became the state song of Kentucky.

NOTE: When the independent clauses contain only one or two commas, the semicolon is not needed. However, a semicolon is required when there are so many commas that the sentence would be confusing without the semicolon.

30d. Use a semicolon between items in a series if the items contain commas.

EXAMPLES Winners in the competition were Alina Murphy**,** first place**;** Jeff Bates**,** second place**;** and Eduardo Davis**,** third place.

On our trip to South America**,** we visited Santiago**,** Chile**;** Bogotá**,** Colombia**;** and Lima**,** Peru.

Correcting Sentences by Adding Semicolons

Rewrite the following sentences, adding semicolons where they are needed.

1. Performers in the show were Tony Fleming, trumpet and trombone Donna Lee Bryant, clarinet and saxophone and Phyllis Ward, drums and steel guitar.
2. The first Alaskans most likely traveled to North America from Asia around twenty thousand years ago they may have been following caribou herds.
3. The new republic at once began increasing production and distribution of goods furthermore, it also appealed to other nations for financial assistance.
4. I bought my father several gifts, including a book, a shirt, and a battery charger, but I couldn't find the present for my sister, who wants a Harry Connick, Jr., tape.
5. Legislators were in a difficult position they had to finance more services without calling for increased taxes.

Colons

30e. Use a colon to mean "note what follows."

(1) Use a colon before a list of items, especially after expressions like *as follows* and *the following.*

EXAMPLES **Central America comprises seven countries: Belize, Costa Rica, El Salvador, Guatemala, Honduras, Nicaragua, and Panama.**

The volumes of poetry that form Edward Brathwaite's autobiographical trilogy are as follows: *Rights of Passage, Masks,* and *Islands.*

NOTE: Do not use a colon before a list that serves as a direct object or an object of a preposition.

EXAMPLES **We collected blankets, canned goods, medical supplies, and clothing for the flood victims.** [The list is the direct object of the verb *collected.*]

The concert included performances by Placido Domingo, Luciano Pavarotti, and José Carreras. [The list is the object of the preposition *by.*]

(2) Use a colon before a long, formal statement or quotation.

EXAMPLE The Gettysburg Address, delivered by President Lincoln during the American Civil War, begins with these words: "Four score and seven years ago our fathers brought forth on this continent a new nation, conceived in liberty, and dedicated to the proposition that all men are created equal."

REFERENCE NOTE: For more information about using long quotations, see page 938.

(3) Use a colon between independent clauses when the second clause explains or restates the idea of the first.

EXAMPLES Those hanging lamps are the most popular kind: They are inexpensive, come in many colors, and are easy to install.

A cutting word is worse than a bowstring: A cut may heal, but the cut of the tongue does not.

African proverb

30f. Use a colon in certain conventional situations.

(1) Use a colon between the hour and the minute.

EXAMPLES 8:00 A.M. 9:30 in the evening

(2) Use a colon between a chapter and verse in referring to passages from the Bible.

EXAMPLES Proverbs 3:3 Ecclesiastes 3:1–8

(3) Use a colon between a title and subtitle.

EXAMPLES "Ghosts and Voices: Writing from Obsession" [article]

Arrangement in Black and Gray No. 1: Portrait of the Artist's Mother [painting]

Billie Holiday: The Golden Years [recording]

(4) Use a colon after the salutation of a business letter.

EXAMPLES Dear Ms. Ayala: To Whom It May Concern:
Dear Sir or Madam: Dear Editor:

NOTE: Use a comma after the salutation of a friendly letter.

EXAMPLE Dear Grandma and Grandpa,

EXERCISE 2 Correcting Sentences by Adding Colons

Rewrite the following sentences, adding colons where they are needed.

1. Not surprisingly, my mom, who was a big fan of *Star Trek* during the '60s, now regularly watches *Star Trek The Next Generation*.
2. Two of my favorite stories from the Bible are the battle between David and Goliath in I Samuel 17 4–58 and the story of the good Samaritan in Luke 10 25–37.
3. Groups of art students, all going to see Egyptian, Greek, and Assyrian exhibits, boarded the buses at 8 30 A.M. and arrived at the museum at 10 00 A.M.
4. She revised her report three times she looked first at the content, then she considered organization, and then she read the report for style.
5. Our local paper is divided into the following five sections news, features, business, sports, and classified advertising.

REVIEW A Correcting Paragraphs by Adding Semicolons and Colons

Rewrite the following paragraphs, adding semicolons and colons where they are needed.

[1] Arthur Mitchell blazed new trails in the world of ballet he became the American Ballet Theater's first African American male principal dancer, and he founded the Dance Theater of Harlem. [2] As a young man, Mitchell studied tap dance, modern dance, and ballet at a special high school for the performing arts, the challenges of ballet especially appealed to him. [3] After graduation from high school in 1952, Mitchell enrolled in the School of American Ballet, part of the New York City Ballet however, he continued modern dancing in other companies.

[4] Mitchell's fine technique and commanding style, evident in the photograph on the next page, were impressive consequently, he was invited to join the New York City Ballet in 1955. [5] Director George Balanchine admired Mitchell as a result, Balanchine choreographed dances for Mitchell and cast him in many leading roles. [6] Among the New York City Ballet productions featuring Mitchell were these *Agon, Arcade, The Nutcracker*, and *Creation of the World*. [7] The company was often

criticized for showcasing an African American dancer nevertheless, Balanchine remained adamant in his support for Mitchell.

[8] During his years with the New York City Ballet, Mitchell broke racial barriers, received much praise on foreign tours, and helped organize ballet companies in many countries but in 1968 Mitchell decided to form his own ballet company and school, which became the Dance Theater of Harlem. [9] The all-black ballet company quickly established a name for itself in fact, it is acclaimed throughout the world. [10] Critics and audiences have responded enthusiastically to such productions as the following *Creole Giselle, Fancy Free,* and *Firebird.*

MECHANICS

Italics (Underlining)

Italics are printed characters that slant to the right. To indicate italics in handwritten or typewritten work, use underlining.

PRINTED ***The Once and Future King*** **was written by T. H. White.**

TYPED <u>The Once and Future King</u> was written by T. H. White.

NOTE: If you use a personal computer, you may be able to set words in italics. Most word-processing software and many printers are capable of producing italic type.

30g. Use italics (underlining) for titles of books, plays, long poems, periodicals, newspapers, works of art, films, television series, long musical compositions, trains, ships, aircraft, and spacecraft.

TYPE OF NAME	EXAMPLES	
Books	*Arctic Dreams*	*Wuthering Heights*
Plays	*The King and I*	*West Side Story*
Long Poems	*I Am Joaquín*	*The Song of Roland*
Periodicals	*National Geographic*	*Senior Scholastic*
Newspapers	*San Diego Tribune*	*Wall Street Journal*
Works of Art	*Three Dancers*	*The Thinker*
Films	*Out of Africa*	*Gone with the Wind*
TV Series	*World of Discovery*	*I Love Lucy*
Long Musical Compositions	*Appalachian Spring* *Don Giovanni*	*The Saint of Bleecker Street*
Trains, Ships, Aircraft, Spacecraft	*Orient Express* *Enola Gay* *Hindenburg*	*Queen Mary* *Atlantis* *Skylab 1*

MECHANICS

NOTE: The article *the* before the title of a newspaper is neither italicized nor capitalized when written within a sentence.

EXAMPLE I found some good ideas in several back issues of the *New York Times.*

REFERENCE NOTE: For information about titles that are not italicized but are enclosed in quotation marks, see page 939.

30h. Use italics (underlining) for words, letters, and figures referred to as such and for foreign words not yet adopted into English.

EXAMPLES The most common word in English is *the;* the letters used most frequently are *e* and *t;* and the numbers most often confused are *7* and *9.*

The Latin phrase *ad astra per aspera* means "to the stars through difficulties."

EXERCISE 3 **Correcting Sentences by Adding Underlining**

Rewrite the following sentences, underlining each word that should be italicized.

1. Is the Pietà the only work Michelangelo ever signed?
2. For my birthday I received a print of Rosseau's The Jungle and a tape of the soundtrack for the musical Cats.
3. Die dulci fruere means "Have a nice day" in Latin, according to the book Latin for All Occasions by Henry Beard.
4. Chris Burke, who was born with Down's syndrome, became a successful actor in the TV series Life Goes On.
5. Frank Capra, a Sicilian immigrant, made such film classics as It's a Wonderful Life and Mr. Smith Goes to Washington.

Quotation Marks

30i. Use quotation marks to enclose a ***direct quotation***—a person's exact words.

Be sure to place quotation marks both before and after a person's exact words.

EXAMPLES Eleanor Roosevelt said, **"**No one can make you feel inferior without your consent.**"**

"People are trapped in history and history is trapped in them,**"** wrote author James Baldwin in *Notes of a Native Son.*

Do not use quotation marks to enclose an ***indirect quotation***—a rewording of a direct quotation.

DIRECT QUOTATION Natalie said, "My favorite singer is Whitney Houston."

INDIRECT QUOTATION Natalie said that her favorite singer is Whitney Houston.

(1) A direct quotation begins with a capital letter.

EXAMPLE In *Up from Slavery,* Booker T. Washington said, "I have learned that success is to be measured not so much by the position that one has reached in life as by the obstacles which he has overcome while trying to succeed."

MECHANICS

When the quotation is only a part of a sentence, do not begin it with a capital letter.

EXAMPLE A film critic has called the movie "**a** futile attempt by the director to trade on his reputation as a creator of blockbusters."

(2) When an expression identifying the speaker interrupts a quoted sentence, the second part of the quotation begins with a small letter.

EXAMPLE "When we do the best that we can," explained Helen Keller, "**w**e never know what miracle is wrought in our life, or in the life of another." [Notice that each part of a divided quotation is enclosed in quotation marks.]

When the second part of a divided quotation is another sentence, it begins with a capital letter.

EXAMPLE "Please don't open the door," he shouted. "**W**e're developing film."

(3) A direct quotation is set off from the rest of the sentence by a comma, a question mark, or an exclamation point, but not by a period.

EXAMPLES "For tomorrow, please read the article about the Sherpas of Nepal**,**" requested Ms. Estevan.

"Who is the president of the Philippines**?**" asked Nathan.

"The Wildcats have upset the Rockets**!**" exclaimed the sportscaster.

NOTE: If the quotation is only a word or a phrase, do not set it off by commas.

EXAMPLE In his speech, Enrique said that "one for all and all for one" is the key to a successful club.

(4) When used with quotation marks, the other marks of punctuation are placed according to the following rules:

- Commas and periods are always placed inside the closing quotation marks.

EXAMPLE "Generosity**,**" said Nathaniel Hawthorne, "is the flower of justice**.**"

- Semicolons and colons are always placed outside the closing quotation marks.

EXAMPLES "Eva," my grandmother said, "you should keep up with your chores"; then she reminded me that it was my turn to vacuum.

Gail Sloan described the following as "deserted-island reading": *An Encyclopedia of World History,* the complete works of Shakespeare, and *Robinson Crusoe.*

- Question marks and exclamation points are placed inside the closing quotation marks if a quotation is a question or an exclamation. Otherwise, they are placed outside.

EXAMPLES The teacher asked me, "Where did you find this information about José Rizal?"

Someone behind me shouted, "Watch out!"

Did Franklin Roosevelt say, "The only thing we have to fear is fear itself"?

How proud and happy Colleen was when her supervisor told her, "You deserve a raise"!

NOTE: In a sentence that ends with a quotation, only one end mark is necessary.

INCORRECT Have you ever asked yourself, "Where will I be ten years from now?"?

CORRECT Have you ever asked yourself, "Where will I be ten years from now?"

MECHANICS

(5) When writing dialogue, begin a new paragraph every time the speaker changes, and enclose each speaker's words in quotation marks.

EXAMPLE "Don't stand chattering to yourself like that," Humpty Dumpty said, looking at her for the first time, "but tell me your name and business."

"My *name* is Alice, but—"

"It's a stupid name enough!" Humpty Dumpty interrupted impatiently. "What does it mean?"

"*Must* a name mean something?" Alice asked doubtfully.

"Of course it must," Humpty Dumpty said with a short laugh: "*my* name means the shape I am—and a good handsome shape it is, too. With a name like yours, you might be any shape, almost."

Lewis Carroll, from *Through the Looking-Glass*

(6) When quoting a passage that consists of more than one paragraph, place quotation marks at the beginning of each paragraph and at the end of only the last paragraph in the passage.

EXAMPLE **"The engine cuts again, and then catches, and each time it spurts to life I climb as high as I can get, and then it splutters and stops and I glide once more toward the water, to rise again and descend again, like a hunting sea bird.**

"I find the land. Visibility is perfect now and I see land forty or fifty miles ahead. If I am on my course, that will be Cape Breton. Minute after minute goes by. The minutes almost materialize; they pass before my eyes like links in a long slow-moving chain, and each time the engine cuts, I see a broken link in the chain and catch my breath until it passes."

Beryl Markham, from *West with the Night*

NOTE: A long passage quoted from a printed source is often set off from the rest of the text. The entire passage may be indented or set in smaller type. The passage is sometimes single-spaced instead of double-spaced. (Modern Language Association [MLA] guidelines, however, call for double-spacing.) When a quotation is set off in any of these ways, no quotation marks are necessary.

MECHANICS

(7) Use single quotation marks to enclose a quotation within a quotation.

EXAMPLES **Mrs. Winters said, "Cristina, please tell us what you think Alexander Pope meant when he said, 'To err is human, to forgive divine.' "** [Notice that the period is placed inside the single quotation mark.]

Mrs. Winters asked, "Do you think the moral of the story could be 'To err is human, to forgive divine'?" [The question mark is placed between the double quotation marks and the single quotation mark because only Mrs. Winters' words, not Pope's, are a question.]

30j. Use quotation marks to enclose titles of short works, such as short stories, short poems, essays, articles, songs, episodes of television series, and chapters and other parts of books.

TYPE OF TITLE	EXAMPLES
Short Stories	“Raymond’s Run” “Chee’s Daughter” “The Necklace” “A Worn Path”
Poems	“My Mother Pieced Quilts” “A Black Man Talks of Reaping”
Essays	“A Child’s Christmas in Wales” “Fenimore Cooper’s Literary Offenses”
Articles	“How to Choose a Career” “Water: Not as Cheap as You Think”
Songs	“We Are the World” “The Star-Spangled Banner”
TV Episodes	“The Trouble with Tribbles” “Secret of the Dead Sea Scrolls”
Chapters	“The War in the Persian Gulf” “Biology: The Study of Life”

REFERENCE NOTE: For examples of titles that are italicized, see page 934.

30k. Use quotation marks to enclose slang words, invented words, technical terms, dictionary definitions of words, and any expressions that are unusual in standard English.

EXAMPLES In the drama club’s latest production, Dylan plays the role of Lyndon, a “nerd.”

The running of the bulls through the streets (one might say “bullevards”) of Pamplona, Spain, is an annual event.

What do you mean by “looping” the computer instructions?

The name *Arkansas* is derived from the Sioux word for “downstream people.”

What do Southerners mean when they say they are “fixing to” do something?

NOTE: Avoid using slang words in formal speaking and writing whenever possible. When using technical terms, be sure to explain their meanings. If you are not sure whether a word is appropriate or its meaning is clear, consult an up-to-date dictionary.

EXERCISE 4 Correcting Sentences by Adding Quotation Marks, Other Punctuation Marks, and Capitalization

Revise the following sentences by adding quotation marks, other marks of punctuation, and capitalization.

EXAMPLE **1. Jim asked have you read James Alan McPherson's story Why I Like Country Music.**

1. Jim asked, "Have you read James Alan McPherson's story 'Why I Like Country Music'?"

1. How many of you Mrs. Martínez asked have studied a foreign language for more than two years.
2. Nice try Donna was what the coach said.
3. We should have started our homework earlier said Beth we have answered only three questions so far.
4. Where have you been she asked.
5. Someone once asked Bernard Shaw how old he was, and he answered I'm as old as my tongue and a few years older than my teeth.
6. Can you tell me asked Mrs. Ross how many syllables are in a haiku?
7. Was it Elizabeth Barrett Browning asked Lani who wrote the poem Shall I Compare Thee to a Summer's Day?
8. Cast off shouted the captain we're bound for Panama.
9. Would you let us hand in our research papers next week Ms. Lewis we asked none of the books we need are in the library.
10. Alice whispered thank you for lending me the article Is There Life on Other Planets?

MECHANICS

PICTURE THIS

Sometimes the most challenging part of writing a story is creating natural-sounding dialogue between characters. To practice your dialogue-writing skills, you've come to the restaurant shown on the next page to watch people having casual conversations and to write what you imagine they are saying. Taking your cues from their body language and facial expressions, write down an imaginary dialogue between two of the people in this picture. In your dialogue, try to capture the people's personalities and moods. Change speakers at least four times, being sure to use quotation marks and paragraph breaks correctly.

Subject: a conversation between two people
Audience: yourself
Purpose: to practice writing dialogue; to be creative

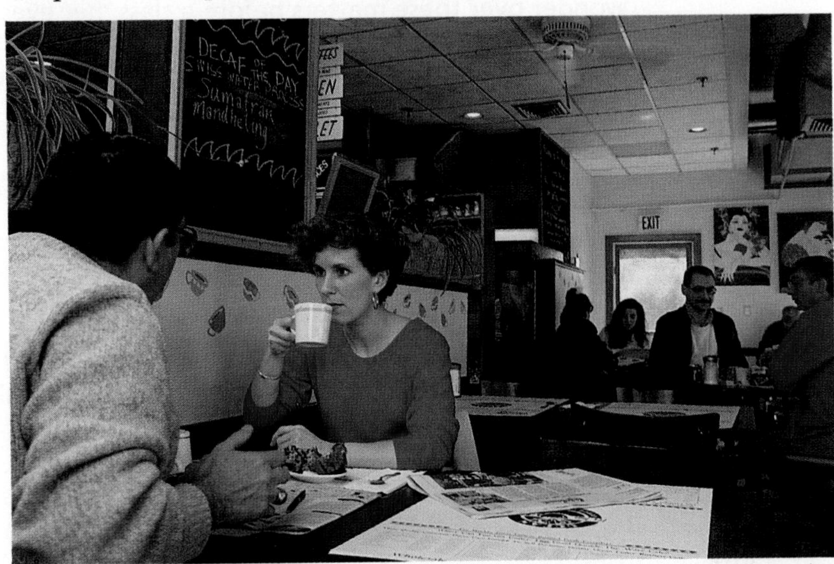

Ellipsis Points

30l. Use ellipsis points (. . .) to mark omissions from quoted material and pauses in a written passage.

ORIGINAL At Lincoln, making us into Americans did not mean scrubbing away what made us originally foreign. The teachers called us as our parents did or as close as they could pronounce our names in Spanish or Japanese. No one was ever scolded or punished for speaking in his native tongue on the playground. Matti told the class about his mother's down quilt, which she had made in Italy with the fine feathers of a thousand geese. Encarnación acted out how boys learned to fish in the Philippines. I astounded the third grade with the story of my travels on a stagecoach, which nobody else in the class had seen except in the museum at Sutter's Fort. After a visit to the Crocker Art Gallery and its collection of heroic paintings of the golden age of California, someone showed a silk scroll with a Chinese painting. Miss Hopley herself had a way of expressing wonder over these matters before a class, her eyes wide open until they popped slightly. It was easy for me to feel that becoming a proud American, as she said we should, did not mean feeling ashamed of being a Mexican.

Ernesto Galarza, from *Barrio Boy*

(1) If the quoted material that comes before the omission is not a complete sentence, use three ellipsis points with a space before the first point.

EXAMPLE In his autobiography, Galarza recalls, "It was easy for me to feel that becoming a proud American, **. . .** did not mean feeling ashamed of being a Mexican."

(2) If the quoted material that comes before the omission is a complete sentence, keep the end mark and add the ellipsis points.

EXAMPLE Galarza remembers that his teachers encouraged him and his classmates to share stories about their families and backgrounds: "Matti told the class about his mother's down quilt, which she had made in Italy**. . . .** Encarnación acted out how boys learned to fish in the Philippines. I astounded the third grade with the story of my travels on a stagecoach**. . . .**"

(3) If one or more than one sentence is omitted, the ellipsis points follow the end mark that precedes the omission.

EXAMPLE About Lincoln School, Galarza writes, "At Lincoln, making us into Americans did not mean scrubbing away what made us originally foreign**. . . .** It was easy for me to feel that becoming a proud American, as she [the principal] said we should, did not mean feeling ashamed of being a Mexican."

Notice in the last example that the words *the principal* are included to identify *she.* The words are enclosed in brackets to show that they have been inserted into the quotation and are not the exact words of the speaker.

REFERENCE NOTE: For more on using brackets, see page 957.

(4) To show that a full line or more of poetry has been omitted, use an entire line of spaced periods.

ORIGINAL

I dream of Hanoi:
Co-ngu Road
ten years of separation
the way back sliced by a frontier of hatred.
I want to bury the past
to burn the future
still I yearn
still I fear
those endless nights
waiting for dawn.

Nguyen Thi Vinh, from "Thoughts of Hanoi"

WITH OMISSION

I dream of Hanoi:
. . . .
ten years of separation
. . . .
still I yearn
still I fear
those endless nights
waiting for dawn.

Notice that the line of periods is as long as the line of poetry above it.

(5) To indicate a pause in a written passage, use three ellipsis points with a space before the first point.

EXAMPLE "Well, . . . I don't know what to say," Sarah answered.

EXERCISE 5 **Using Ellipsis Points Correctly**

Omit the italicized parts of the following passages. Use ellipsis points to correctly punctuate each omission.

1. It was nearly the time of full moon, *and on this account, though the sky was lined with a uniform sheet of dripping cloud,* ordinary objects out of doors were readily visible.

Thomas Hardy, "The Three Strangers"

MECHANICS

2. The old native stood, *breath blowing out the skin between his ribs, feet tense,* balanced in the sand, smiling and shaking his head.

Nadine Gordimer, from "The Train from Rhodesia"

3. In the world's broad field of battle,
In the bivouac of Life,
Be not like dumb, driven cattle!
Be a hero in the strife!

Henry Wadsworth Longfellow, from "A Psalm of Life"

4. Remember, I am not recording the vision of a madman. *The sun does not more certainly shine in the heavens, than that which I now affirm is true. Some miracle might have produced it, yet the stages of the discovery were distinct and probable.* After days and nights of incredible labor and fatigue, I succeeded in discovering the cause of generation and life; nay, more, I became myself capable of bestowing animation upon lifeless matter.

Mary Shelley, from *Frankenstein*

5. When the lights went on, little boys like a bevy of flies assembled around the lamppost for gossip and stories. *Elsewhere in a similar manner men gathered to throw dice or cut cards or simply to talk.* The spectacle repeated itself at each crossing where there was a street lamp ringed to a post.

George Lamming, from *In the Castle of My Skin*

Apostrophes

Possessive Case

The ***possessive case*** of a noun or a pronoun shows ownership or relationship.

OWNERSHIP	RELATIONSHIP
Alice Walker's poetry the **student's** suggestions **your** opinion	**Crowfoot's** family **five dollars'** worth **my** grandparents

30m. Use an apostrophe in forming the possessive of nouns and some pronouns.

(1) To form the possessive of a singular noun, add an apostrophe and an *s.*

EXAMPLES the senator**'s** comments Charles**'s** grades
tennis racquet**'s** size player**'s** turn

NOTE: When forming the possessive of a singular noun ending in an *s* sound, add only an apostrophe if the noun has two or more syllables and if the addition of *'s* will make the noun awkward to pronounce. Otherwise, add *'s.*

EXAMPLES the seamstress**'** work
for goodness**'** sake
Achilles**'** battles
Mr. Martinez**'** article

(2) To form the possessive of a plural noun ending in *s,* add only the apostrophe.

EXAMPLES the girls**'** team the Millses**'** back yard
the winners**'** trophy the governors**'** conference

The few plural nouns that do not end in *s* form the possessive by adding an apostrophe and an *s.*

EXAMPLES women**'s** tournament children**'s** playground

NOTE: Do not use an apostrophe to form the plural of a noun.

INCORRECT Two of the novel's that Jean Rhys wrote are *Wide Sargasso Sea* and *Voyage in the Dark.*
CORRECT Two of the **novels** that Jean Rhys wrote are *Wide Sargasso Sea* and *Voyage in the Dark.*

(3) Do not use an apostrophe with possessive personal pronouns or with the possessive pronoun *whose.*

INCORRECT We thought the top score was her's.
CORRECT We thought the top score was **hers.**

INCORRECT I have witnessed democracy at it's best.
CORRECT I have witnessed democracy at **its** best.

INCORRECT Who's notebook is this?
CORRECT **Whose** notebook is this?

Possessive Personal Pronouns

my, mine	our, ours
your, yours	their, theirs
his, her, hers, its	

REFERENCE NOTE: Do not confuse the possessive pronouns *your, their, theirs, its,* and *whose* with the contractions *you're, they're, there's, it's,* and *who's.* See pages 985, 984, 950, and 980.

(4) To form the possessive of an indefinite pronoun, add an apostrophe and an *s.*

EXAMPLES **Everyone's** vote counts equally.
She consented to **everybody's** request for a class meeting.

NOTE: In such forms as *anyone else* and *somebody else,* the correct possessives are *anyone else's* and *somebody else's.*

REFERENCE NOTE: For a list of indefinite pronouns, see page 605.

(5) Form the possessive of only the last word in a hyphenated word, in the name of an organization or a business firm, or in a word group showing joint possession.

EXAMPLES father-in-law**'s** hobby
the Economic and Social Council**'s** members
Lewis and Clark**'s** expedition

When a possessive pronoun is part of a word group showing joint possession, each noun in the word group is also possessive.

EXAMPLE **Lusita's, Joshua's,** and **my** report

(6) Form the possessive of each noun in a word group showing individual possession of similar items.

EXAMPLE **Maria Bethania's** and **Aster Aweke's** albums

(7) Use an apostrophe in possessive forms of words that indicate time, such as *minute, hour, day, week, month,* and *year,* and possessives indicating an amount in cents or dollars.

EXAMPLES a **minute’s** work five **minutes’** work
a **day’s** rest three **days’** rest
one **cent’s** worth five **cents’** worth

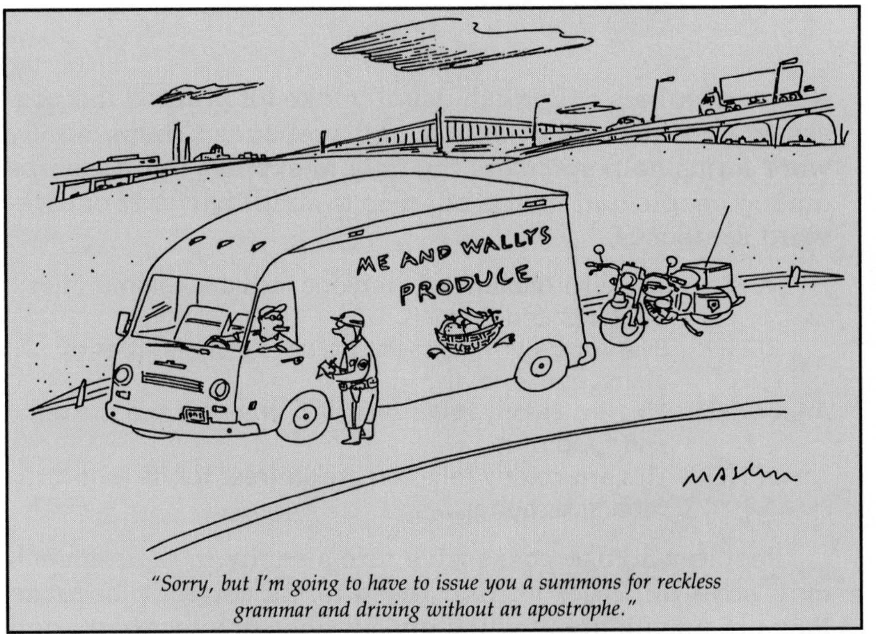

"Sorry, but I'm going to have to issue you a summons for reckless grammar and driving without an apostrophe."

 EXERCISE 6 **Forming Possessive Nouns and Pronouns**

Each of the following groups of words expresses a possessive relationship by means of a prepositional phrase. Revise each word group so that a possessive noun or pronoun will express the same relationship.

EXAMPLE **1.** a vacation of two weeks
1. *a two weeks' vacation*

1. hats of the firefighters
2. dressing room of the star
3. job of my sister-in-law
4. character of a person
5. business of Jorge and her
6. speech of the mayor-elect
7. a pause of a moment
8. owner of the Doberman pinscher
9. highlights of the film
10. kimonos of the women
11. costumes of the matadors
12. worth of four dollars
13. admission prices of adults and children
14. prize of Ralph Bunche
15. sides of it
16. remarks of the judges
17. trip of Maria and Cam
18. a wait of an hour
19. responsibility of everyone
20. CD of the group Genesis

WRITING APPLICATION

Using Apostrophes Correctly in Writing

Native speakers of English usually take for granted the possessive case forms of nouns and pronouns. These handy word forms help speakers not only to express relationships among people and things but also to simplify wordy or awkward sentences.

WORDY	The environment of everyone includes communities of plants and animals.
BETTER	**Everyone's** environment includes communities of plants and animals.
AWKWARD	This ant colony relies on acacia trees for the shelter and food of it.
BETTER	This ant colony relies on acacia trees for **its** [not *it's*] food and shelter.

People who use possessive forms easily in their speech may have difficulty writing these forms correctly because they are unsure about when apostrophes are necessary and where they should be placed. To determine whether a noun is in the possessive case, try converting it into a prepositional phrase. For example, *the **boy's** cap* becomes *the cap **of the boy.*** If the noun can't be converted into a prepositional phrase, the noun is not possessive.

MECHANICS

WRITING ACTIVITY

In biology class you have learned that a *community* is a group of living things that forms a system of production, consumption, and decomposition. Now your biology teacher wants each person in your class to observe a community and write a report on his or her findings. Your assignment:

- Identify a community of organisms and form a hypothesis about how the members of that community interact.
- Observe the interactions of plants and animals in the community for at least ten minutes a day for several days.
- Take notes on your observations.
- Decide whether the data you've collected support your hypothesis.

- Write up your hypothesis, observations, and conclusions in a brief report. (Be sure to use apostrophes correctly to form the possessive case of nouns and pronouns.)

Prewriting Almost any place can house a living community—a decaying log, an aquarium, a garden, a tree, a crack in the sidewalk, a compost heap, a pond, a window box of plants, even your own room. Choose a community that you can observe easily. Be sure to record the date and time of each observation. If possible, use a magnifying glass or microscope to discover organisms not visible to the naked eye. After you have completed your observations, review your notes carefully. How does the information you've gathered compare with your original hypothesis? What tentative conclusions can you draw about how the community functions?

Writing Write a draft of your report. Begin by describing the setting of the community and identifying the organisms that live there. State your hypothesis, and clearly present your observations. Then, state your conclusions. Explain how they differ from or support your original hypothesis. Finally, write your report in the formal English appropriate for scientific writing. (For more about formal English, see pages 519–523.)

Evaluating and Revising Check your draft against your notes. Be sure that you do not state your own opinions as if they are factual observations. (For more about the difference between facts and opinions, see pages 68 and 302–303.) Do your conclusions follow clearly from your observations? Have you left out any important information? Have you included any unnecessary information? Revise your report as necessary. Be sure that you've used only formal English. Use possessive case forms of nouns and pronouns to revise wordy or awkward sentences.

Proofreading Proofread your report for errors in grammar, usage, spelling, and punctuation. Take special care with possessive forms, using apostrophes only where they belong.

Contractions

30n. Use an apostrophe to show where letters, numbers, or words have been omitted in a contraction.

A ***contraction*** is a shortened form of a word, word group, or number in which an apostrophe takes the place of the letters, numbers, or words that are omitted.

EXAMPLES				
	I am	**I'm**	they had	**they'd**
	he has	**he's**	where is	**where's**
	let us	**let's**	we are	**we're**
	of the clock	**o'clock**	we have	**we've**
	1950s	**'50s**	you will	**you'll**

The word *not* can be shortened to *n't* and added to a verb, usually without any change in the spelling of the verb.

EXAMPLES				
	is not	**isn't**	has not	**hasn't**
	does not	**doesn't**	should not	**shouldn't**
	do not	**don't**	were not	**weren't**
EXCEPTIONS	will not	**won't**	cannot	**can't**

Do not confuse contractions with possessive pronouns.

CONTRACTIONS	POSSESSIVE PRONOUNS
It's [*It is*] time to go. **It's** [*It has*] been snowing since noon.	**Its** diameter is almost 2,290 kilometers.
Who's [*Who is*] the captain? **Who's** [*Who has*] been using the computer?	**Whose** umbrella is this?
You're [*You are*] late.	**Your** skates are in the attic.
They're [*They are*] in the gym. **There's** [*There is*] only one left.	We are learning about **their** customs. This equipment is **theirs.**

NOTE: Contractions are perfectly acceptable in most writing and speaking situations. However, in formal writing, such as in essays for school and in business letters, avoid using nearly all contractions of verb forms, years, and the word *not.*

Plurals

30o. Use an apostrophe and an *–s* to form the plurals of all lowercase letters, some uppercase letters, and some words referred to as words.

EXAMPLES ***Hawaii* ends with two *i*'s.** [Without the apostrophe, the plural of *i* would spell *is*.]
Not many names begin with *U*'s, but the names of my favorite bands do—U2 and UB40. [Without the apostrophe, the plural of *U* would spell *Us*.]
Jeremy's *No want to*'s are just a sign that he's a normal two-year-old.

You may add only an *–s* to form the plurals of such items—except lowercase letters—if the plural forms cannot be misread.

EXAMPLE **Most of his grades this term are Bs.**

Be sure to use apostrophes consistently.

EXAMPLE **The printed *T*'s look like *I*'s.** [Without the apostrophe, the plural of *I* would spell *Is*. The apostrophe in the plural of *T* is included for consistency.]

NOTE: To form the plurals of abbreviations that end with a period, add *'s*.

EXAMPLES **Ph.D.'s M.A.'s**

To form the plurals of abbreviations not followed by periods, add either *'s* or *–s*.

EXAMPLES **VCR's** *or* **VCRs**
CD's *or* **CDs**

EXERCISE 7 Proofreading for the Correct Uses of the Apostrophe

Proofread the following phrases and sentences, adding apostrophes where needed. If an item is correct, write *C*.

1. mens sports cars
2. statements of a mayor-elect
3. Its a pagoda, isn't it?
4. sand in its gears
5. Shes wearing a sari, Im sure.
6. If he lets us, well go too.
7. Her cousins choices were the same as hers.
8. Lets see whats going on.
9. I've found its no help.
10. office of the rabbi

11. Whats its title?
12. on a minutes notice
13. party of Frank and Carlos
14. Whos on Vickys bicycle?
15. this tacos ingredients
16. How many *is* are there in *Mississippi*?
17. mices nest
18. His grades in French are all As.
19. musicals of Rodgers and Hammerstein
20. practice of Olmos and Ramírez

Hyphens

30p. Use a hyphen to divide a word at the end of a line.

When dividing a word at the end of a line, remember the following rules:

- Do not divide a one-syllable word.

INCORRECT Alicia chose to write her report about the plight of the homeless.

CORRECT Alicia chose to write her report about the
plight of the homeless.

- Divide a word only between syllables.

INCORRECT Isn't Ethan running for student council president this year?

CORRECT Isn't Ethan running for student council president this year?

NOTE: When you are not sure about the syllabication of a word, look in a dictionary.

- Divide a hyphenated word at the hyphen.

INCORRECT Hirohito was the emperor of Japan for six-
ty-three years.

CORRECT Hirohito was the emperor of Japan for sixty-
three years.

- Do not divide a word so that one letter stands alone.

INCORRECT Proofreading my report, I saw that I had o-
mitted an important quotation.

CORRECT Proofreading my report, I saw that I had
omitted an important quotation.

30q. Use a hyphen with compound numbers from *twenty-one* to *ninety-nine* and with fractions used as modifiers.

EXAMPLES **forty-two** applicants
a **two-thirds** majority [*Two-thirds* is an adjective modifying *majority.*]
about **three-fourths** empty [*Three-fourths* is an adverb modifying *empty.*]
two thirds of the voters [*Two thirds* is not an adjective. *Thirds* is a noun modified by the adjective *two.*]

30r. Hyphenate a compound adjective when it precedes the word it modifies.

EXAMPLES		
	well-liked author	an author who is **well liked**
	world-renowned composer	a composer who is **world renowned**

NOTE: Some compound adjectives are always hyphenated.

EXAMPLE a **well-balanced** meal a meal that is **well-balanced**

If you are unsure about whether a compound adjective is hyphenated, look up the word in a dictionary.

Do not use a hyphen if one of the modifiers is an adverb ending in *–ly.*

EXAMPLE a **highly polished** surface

30s. Use a hyphen with the prefixes *ex–, self–,* and *all–,* with the suffix *–elect,* and with all prefixes before a proper noun or proper adjective.

EXAMPLES		
	ex-mayor	**non-**European
	self-control	**anti-**Fascist
	all-star	**pro-**Canadian
	president**-elect**	**Pan-**American

NOTE: Although you may see a variety of spellings for some words (*reelect, re-elect, reëlect*), the preferred style today is to close up most prefixes not listed in rule 30s.

EXAMPLES biannual reevaluate semiarid miniseries

MECHANICS

30t. Use a hyphen to prevent confusion or awkwardness.

EXAMPLES **re-collect** [prevents confusion with *recollect*]
anti-icer [avoids the awkwardness of *antiicer*]

EXERCISE 8 Using Hyphens

Revise the following groups of words by adding hyphens where they are needed. If a word group is correct, write *C*.

1. almost two thirds full
2. preColumbian artifact
3. well spoken individual
4. a highly motivated employee
5. antiimperialism

REVIEW B Correcting Paragraphs by Adding Italics (Underlining), Quotation Marks, Ellipsis Points, Apostrophes, and Hyphens

Rewrite the following paragraphs, adding italics (underlining), quotation marks, ellipsis points, apostrophes, and hyphens where they are needed.

[1] "This painting, Cow's Skull: Red, White, and Blue, really intrigues me; Im sure its extremely symbolic, Darla said. [2] What do you think of it"?

[3] Youve asked the right person, replied Anthony, because Georgia O'Keeffe is one of my favorite painters. [4] One biography of her, which is simply titled Georgia O'Keeffe, tells how shed collect horses and cows skulls in New Mexico and then paint pictures of them. [5] This well known work, which she painted in 1931, *is* symbolic; the paintings colors represent O'Keeffe's pro American feelings.

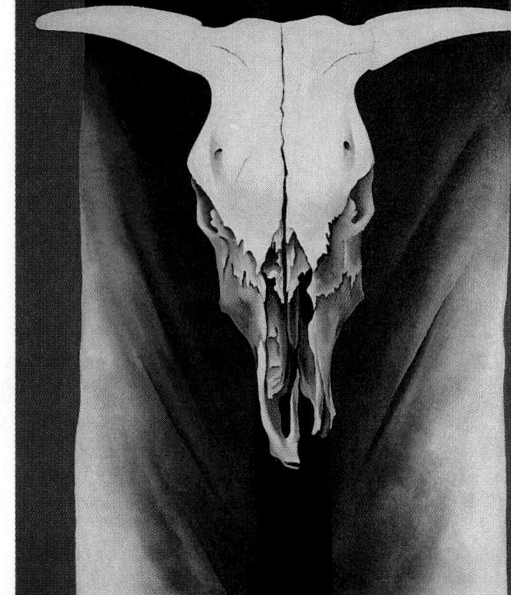

Georgia O'Keeffe (1887–1986). *Cow's Skull: Red, White and Blue.* Oil on Canvas, H. 39 7/8" W. 35 7/8" (101.3 × 91.1 cm). The Metropolitan Museum of Art, The Alfred Stieglitz Collection, 1952. (52.203)

MECHANICS

[6] "I like this photograph of O'Keeffe, too, Darla added. [7] Dont you think she looks extremely self reliant and self assured?"

[8] "Well, . . thats probably an understatement, chuckled Anthony. [9] "O'Keeffe, who was born in Wisconsin in 1887, developed her own independent style in art and life. [10] Shes best known for her abstract paintings, especially the ones of flowers and of New Mexico desert scenes, such as her painting Ranchos Church—Taos.

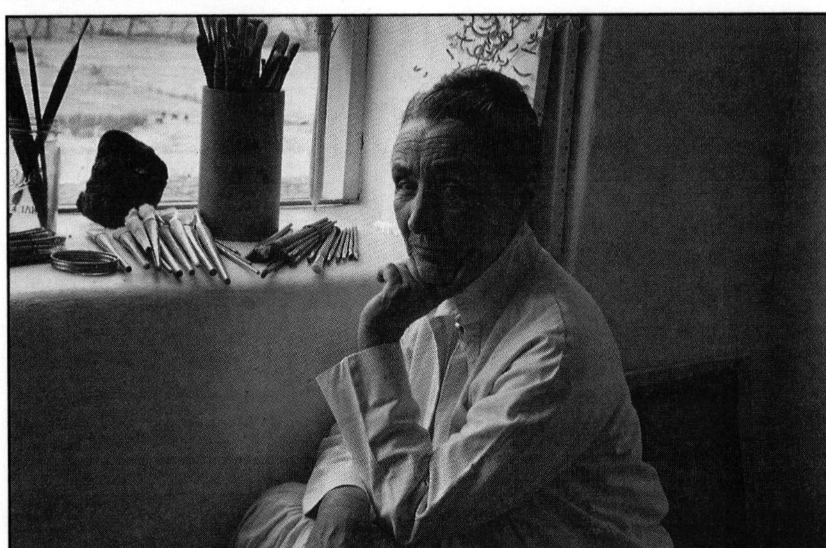

Georgia O'Keeffe, 3 1/4 × 4 1/4 saf. neg., January 15, 1953. Laura Gilpin, Photographer. Laura Gilpin Collection, Amon Carter Museum, Ft. Worth, TX.

Dashes

30u. Use a dash to indicate an abrupt break in thought.

EXAMPLES The director of the film—I can't recall his name—said that there would be a sequel.

The truth is—and you probably already know this—we can't finish the project on time.

30v. Use a dash to mean *namely, in other words,* or *that is* before an explanation.

EXAMPLES It was a close call—the sudden gust of wind pushed the helicopter to within inches of the power line.

The early Native American civilizations—the Mayan, the Incan, and the Aztec—depended mainly on farming for their livelihood.

Parentheses

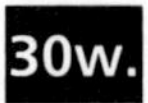

30w. Use parentheses to enclose informative or explanatory material of minor importance.

EXAMPLES **Former Representative Barbara Jordan (Texas) was on that committee.**
The length of the Mekong River is 4,186 kilometers (about 2,600 miles).

Be sure that the material within parentheses can be omitted without changing the basic meaning or structure of the sentence.

IMPROPER USE OF PARENTHESES **Tina had been shopping (in that store) most of her life.** [The idea in parentheses is important to the meaning of the sentence.]

A sentence enclosed in parentheses may fall within another sentence or may stand by itself.

(1) A parenthetical sentence that falls within another sentence
- should not begin with a capital letter unless it begins with a word that should always be capitalized
- should not end with a period but may end with a question mark or an exclamation point

EXAMPLES The largest island of the Solomon Islands **(see the map on page 453)** is Guadalcanal.
I hope I persuaded Alex **(is he a senior?)** to help us.

(2) A parenthetical sentence that stands by itself
- should begin with a capital letter
- should end with a period, a question mark, or an exclamation point

EXAMPLES The largest island of the Solomon Islands is Guadalcanal. **(See the map on page 453.)**
Alex asked me if he could help us. **(What do you think I said?)**

NOTE: When parenthetical material falls within a sentence, punctuation never comes before the opening parenthesis but may follow the closing parenthesis.

INCORRECT According to this article about Grandma Moses, (1860–1961) she began to paint in her seventies.
CORRECT According to this article about Grandma Moses (1860–1961)**,** she began to paint in her seventies.

Brackets

30x. Use brackets to enclose an explanation within quoted or parenthetical material.

EXAMPLES Ms. Grayson was quoted as saying in her acceptance speech: "I am honored by this [the award], and I would like to share the recognition with those who made my work possible."

By a vote of 5 to 4, the Supreme Court overturned the lower court's ruling. (See page 149 [Diagram A] for a chronology of the case.)

EXERCISE 9 Correcting Sentences by Adding Dashes, Parentheses, and Brackets

Add dashes, parentheses, and brackets where they are needed in each of the following sentences.

1. Dr. Percy Lavon Julian, who was born in Montgomery, Alabama, is noted for developing helpful drugs from this surprised me, too soybeans.
2. My cousin Matthew my father's brother's son plans to open an aerobics and yoga center on the north side of town.
3. Some offspring of famous performers Michael Douglas, Liza Minnelli, Jeff and Beau Bridges, and Jane Fonda, for example have established award-winning careers for themselves.
4. Christine was quoted as saying in her valedictory speech: "We seniors are not at an ending but a beginning, and it graduation marks an exciting time of change in our lives."
5. For the new course in government and society, students are required to analyze the nonfiction writings of Ayn Rand 1905–1982 and to read her novel *Anthem.*

REVIEW C Proofreading a Paragraph for Correct Punctuation

Rewrite the following paragraph, adding semicolons, colons, dashes, parentheses, brackets, italics (underlining), quotation marks, apostrophes, and hyphens where they are needed.

[1] As you can see in the pictures on the next page, Jim Thorpe his Native American name was Wa-tho-huck looked exactly like what he was a strong athlete. [2] No discussion of

Americas outstanding sports figures would be complete without reference to Thorpe, who in 1950 was voted the greatest athlete of the centurys first half. [3] His feats in football, track, and baseball remain unique and his strength and speed are legendary. [4] Born of Irish, French, and Native American heritage and reared in Prague, Oklahoma, Thorpe began earning honors early in his life. [5] He was an all American halfback for two years while playing for the local school and broke all previous records in winning the gold medals for the pentathlon and the decathlon at the 1912 Olympic Games, where he was hailed as the greatest athlete in the world. [6] Because hed already begun playing professional baseball, however, he was forced to return his medals a year later. [7] (They were restored posthumously in 1982) [8] Thorpe spent six outstanding years in professional baseball, but he became best known as a football player who could do everything well run, pass, catch, punt, and more. [9] He played professional football for more than ten years. [10] In 1969, sixteen years after his death and on the National Football Leagues fiftieth birthday, Thorpe was named to footballs all time all professional team.

REVIEW D **Proofreading a Dialogue for Correct Punctuation and Capitalization**

Rewrite the following dialogue, adding commas, semicolons, quotation marks, apostrophes, and capital letters where they are needed. If a sentence is correct, write *C*.

[1] Roger Morton sat back for a moment feeling proud of himself.

[2] Have you finished those sample business letters yet asked Ms. Zimsky, the typing teacher.

[3] Yes Roger replied. [4] I think Ive improved on the format, too. [5] Look how much space Ive saved on each page!

[6] Ms. Zimsky glanced down. [7] These arent done the way they are in the book. [8] Just do them that way for now. [9] You need to finish this chapter today, or youll be way behind. [10] Theres no time to talk about format.

[11] Embarrassed and tired, Roger later told his friend Annette about the incident.

[12] Your problem she explained isnt that you improved the letters its that you didn't get Ms. Zimskys permission first. [13] I learned that any time you want to change a procedure, no matter how great an improvement the change will make, you should first talk your idea over with the person who will need to approve it. [14] Try discussing your suggestions again when Ms. Zimsky has more time.

[15] Roger went back to the typing classroom after school, and Ms. Zimsky listened to his ideas.

[16] Oh, I see what youre doing she said. [17] Its really a very good idea in fact I think Ill share it with the whole class. [18] See you tomorrow, Roger.

[19] See you tomorrow said Roger and thanks for listening, Ms. Zimsky. [20] If I think of any other improvements, Ill be sure to discuss them with you first.

Review: Posttest

A. Proofreading Sentences for Correct Punctuation

Each of the following sentences contains at least one punctuation error in the use of semicolons, colons, dashes, parentheses, brackets, italics (underlining), quotation marks, apostrophes, or hyphens. Rewrite each sentence, punctuating it correctly.

EXAMPLE **1. Why did you wait until the last minute asked my friend Tanya when I told her my problem?**

1. ***"Why did you wait until the last minute?" asked my friend Tanya when I told her my problem.***

1. When I read The Hobbit, my favorite chapter was the one in which Bilbo meets Gollum.
2. Among the members of the Fine Arts Commission who met in New York City were some very talented people Diane Keaton, actress Paul McCartney, musician Paul Taylor, choreographer and Lee Krasner, artist.
3. My brothers and sisters and I have been encouraged to be self reliant since we were children.
4. The rapid spread of the bacterial infection see the time line and the map below posed a grave puzzle to the medical experts.
5. We're going to win this game! said the soccer coach to the newspaper sportswriter.
6. Paulette sent in my application before the deadline how ever she neglected to put a stamp on the envelope.
7. When a graduate of our high school recently appeared on television playing Scott Joplin's Maple Leaf Rag, a new interest in ragtime music blossomed at Franklin High School.
8. "The packages sitting over there are your's, arent they" asked Tamala.
9. Although the oil contract had not been renewed, the oil company had made a delivery the customers complained when they received the bill.
10. The mayor elect met for two hours yesterday afternoon with members of the Allentown Youth Council see the picture on page 17.
11. At Book Lore the bookstore where I work we sold twenty seven copies of that book in one day.
12. Ill never forget the first time I read Walt Whitmans poem When Lilacs Last in the Dooryard Bloom'd said Megan it made me feel the tragedy of Abraham Lincolns death.
13. Within the next three week's, new television stations will begin broadcasting from the following cities Kalamazoo, Michigan, Salinas, California and Fairbanks, Alaska.
14. Helena knew the day would be less than perfect when she heard herself saying Don't forget to dot your ts and cross your is.
15. The article I read in Travel Today began, "Come to the Galápagos Islands six hundred miles west of Ecuador, and see blue footed birds and green iguanas.

B. Proofreading a Paragraph for Correct Punctuation

Rewrite the following paragraph, punctuating each sentence correctly.

[16] When you hear the word *composer,* you probably think of the world renowned musical masters of long ago Mozart, Bach, Beethoven, and Chopin, among others. **[17]** However, you dont really have to think that far back the twentieth century also has produced some outstanding talents. **[18]** Youll probably recognize at least one of these modern composers George Gershwin, Benjamin Britten, Leonard Bernstein, Richard Rodgers, or Paul McCartney. **[19]** Yes, McCartney and other rock musicians have produced many memorable compositions for example, McCartney and his long time composing partner John Lennon gave us such popular ballads as Yesterday and Michelle. **[20]** Richard Rodgers worked with lyricist Oscar Hammerstein, II, on many projects including the following musical plays Oklahoma, South Pacific, The King and I, and The Sound of Music. **[21]** Leonard Bernstein, too, was involved in many musical productions, but perhaps his most famous is West Side Story. **[22]** Both Bernstein and Rodgers are known primarily for their Broadway musicals however, much of their music has become standard outside the theater. **[23]** Benjamin Britten, on the other hand, is often ranked as Englands greatest technical composer his difficult operas, such as Death in Venice, are performed only by highly-skilled musicians and vocalists. **[24]** George Gershwin 1898–1937 was one of Americas finest and best loved composers. **[25]** He wrote the opera Porgy and Bess, which contains the all time classic song Summertime.

EXERCISE 1 Spelling Words by Syllables

Divide each of the following words into syllables, inserting a hyphen between syllables. Be sure that the division of each word includes all of the letters of the word.

EXAMPLE **1. evacuate**
1. *e-vac-u-ate*

1. modern
2. similar
3. library
4. surprise
5. privilege
6. disastrous
7. quiet
8. embarrassing
9. perspiration
10. boundary
11. candidate
12. equipment
13. recognize
14. business
15. representative
16. entrance
17. accidentally
18. mischievous
19. government
20. unnecessary

Spelling Rules

ie and *ei*

31a. Write *ie* when the sound is long e, except after *c.*

EXAMPLES	**thief**	**believe**	**field**	**ceiling**	**receive**	**deceive**
EXCEPTIONS	**seize**	**either**	**weird**	**leisure**	**neither**	

31b. Write *ei* when the sound is not long e, especially when the sound is *a.*

EXAMPLES	**forfeit**	**neighbor**	**freight**	**height**	**weigh**
EXCEPTIONS	**ancient**	**conscience**	**mischief**	**friend**	**view**

EXERCISE 2 Spelling *ie* and *ei* Words

Spell each of the following words correctly by supplying *ie* or *ei.*

1. for. . .gn
2. br. . .f
3. rel. . .ve
4. s. . .ge
5. v. . .l
6. n. . .ce
7. sl. . .gh
8. gr. . .f
9. p. . .ce
10. retr. . .ve
11. counterf. . .t
12. ach. . .ve
13. handkerch. . .f
14. perc. . .ve
15. conc. . .ve
16. w. . .rd
17. rec. . .pt
18. bel. . .f
19. f. . .nd
20. ch. . .f

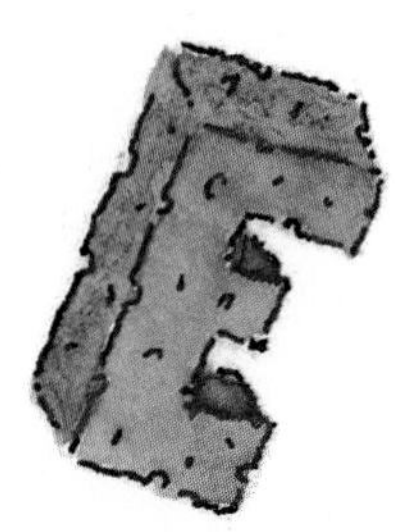

B.C., by permission of Johnny Hart and Creators Syndicate, Inc.

–*cede,* –*ceed,* and –*sede*

31c. The only English word that ends in –*sede* is *supersede.* The only words ending in –*ceed* are *exceed, proceed,* and *succeed.* All other words with this sound end in –*cede.*

EXAMPLES **accede concede intercede precede recede secede**

Adding Prefixes

A ***prefix*** is one or more than one letter or syllable added to the beginning of a word to create a new word that has a different meaning.

31d. When adding a prefix, do not change the spelling of the original word.

EXAMPLES
a + moral = **a**moral
mis + spell = **mis**spell
re + print = **re**print
over + run = **over**run
il + legal = **il**legal
in + elegant = **in**elegant
im + movable = **im**movable
un + necessary = **un**necessary

Adding Suffixes

A *suffix* is one or more than one letter or syllable added to the end of a word to create a new word with a different meaning.

31e. When adding the suffix *–ness* or *–ly,* do not change the spelling of the original word.

EXAMPLES mean + ness = mean**ness** final + ly = final**ly**
open + ness = open**ness** social + ly = social**ly**

EXCEPTIONS For most words ending in *y,* change the *y* to *i* before adding *–ness* or *–ly:*
heavy + ness = heavi**ness** ready + ly = readi**ly**
happy + ness = happi**ness** busy + ly = busi**ly**

NOTE: One-syllable adjectives ending in *y* generally follow rule 31e.

EXAMPLES dry + ness = dry**ness** shy + ly = shy**ly**

EXERCISE 3 Spelling Words with Prefixes and Suffixes

Spell correctly each of the following words as indicated.

1. over + rate
2. habitual + ly
3. green + ness
4. im + material
5. dis + appoint
6. mis + apprehend
7. practical + ly
8. un + abated
9. un + natural
10. silly + ness
11. il + legible
12. in + appropriate
13. dis + appear
14. mis + step
15. re + construct
16. in + animate
17. dis + similar
18. keen + ness
19. un + avoidable
20. merry + ly

31f. Drop the final silent e before a suffix beginning with a vowel.

EXAMPLES care + ing = car**ing** use + able = us**able**
active + ity = activ**ity** large + er = larg**er**

EXCEPTIONS Keep the final silent *e*
- in a word ending in *ce* or *ge* before a suffix beginning with *a* or *o: noticeable, courageous*
- in *dye* and in *singe* before *–ing: dyeing, singeing*
- in *mile* before *–age: mileage*

MECHANICS

31g. Keep the final silent e before a suffix beginning with a consonant.

EXAMPLES	use + less = use**less**	care + ful = care**ful**
	nine + ty = nine**ty**	amuse + ment = amuse**ment**
EXCEPTIONS	nine + th = nin**th**	argue + ment = argu**ment**
	true + ly = tru**ly**	judge + ment = judg**ment**
	awe + ful = aw**ful**	acknowledge + ment = acknowledg**ment** *or* acknowledge**ment**
	whole + ly = whol**ly**	

31h. For words ending in *y* preceded by a consonant, change the *y* to *i* before adding any suffix that does not begin with *i*.

EXAMPLES	funny + er = funn**ier**	twenty + eth = twent**ieth**
	reply + ed = repl**ied**	reply + ing = reply**ing**

NOTE: Some one-syllable words do not follow rule 31h.

EXAMPLES **dryness** **slyly**

31i. For words ending in *y* preceded by a vowel, keep the *y* when adding any suffix.

EXAMPLES	gray + est = gray**est**	convey + ing = convey**ing**
	pay + ment = pay**ment**	employ + ed = employ**ed**

EXCEPTIONS **lay—laid** **pay—paid** **say—said** **day—daily**

31j. Double the final consonant before adding a suffix that begins with a vowel if the word (1) has only one syllable or has the accent on the final syllable and (2) ends in a single consonant preceded by a single vowel.

EXAMPLES	slim + er = sli**mmer**	prefer + ing = prefe**rring**
	excel + ed = exce**lled**	forget + able = forge**ttable**

Do not double the final consonant unless the word satisfies both of the conditions.

EXAMPLES **benefit + ed = benefited** [*Benefit* ends in a single consonant preceded by a single vowel but does not have the accent on the final syllable.]
select + ing = selecting [*Select* has the accent on the final syllable but does not end in a single consonant.]

When a word satisfies both conditions but the addition of the suffix causes the accent to shift, do not double the final consonant.

EXAMPLES refer + ence = refer**ence**
prefer + able = prefer**able**

EXCEPTIONS excel—excel**lent**, excel**lence**, excel**lency**

NOTE: The final consonant of some words may or may not be doubled. Either spelling is acceptable.

EXAMPLES cancel + ed = cancel**ed** *or* cancel**led**
travel + ing = travel**ing** *or* travel**ling**
program + er = program**er** *or* program**mer**

If you are not sure whether you should double the final consonant, consult a dictionary.

EXERCISE 4 **Spelling Words with Suffixes**

Spell out each of the following words, as indicated.

1. defer + ed
2. defer + ence
3. hope + ing
4. approve + al
5. discover + er
6. safe + ty
7. prepare + ing
8. obey + ing
9. spicy + er
10. propel + ing
11. desire + ed
12. control + ed
13. hope + less
14. green + er
15. due + ly
16. run + ing
17. singe + ing
18. remote + est
19. name + less
20. red + est

MECHANICS

REVIEW A **Proofreading a Paragraph to Correct Misspelled Words**

Proofread the following paragraph, correcting any misspelled words. If all the words in a sentence are spelled correctly, write C.

EXAMPLE [1] Accordding to legend, Jean-Jacques Dessalines created the Haitian flag by removeing the white panel from the French flag.

1. *according; removing*

[1] When news of the French Revolution reached the colony of Saint Dominigue on the Caribbean island of Hispaniola, the African slaves and the freed islanders of mixxed ancestry rebeled against the French colonists. [2] Uniting the two rebel

groups, the man on the left below, General Pierre Dominique Toussaint L'Ouverture, conquerred the entire island and abolished slavery in 1802. [3] The next year, however, Toussaint was siezed by the French and deported to France, where he dyed a prisoner. [4] General Jean Jacques Dessalines, shown below in the center, then declared the island independent and renamed it Haiti. [5] Declaring himself emperor, Dessalines ordered that this fortress, the Citadelle, and a series of smaller fortresses be built to prevent the Europeans from restablishing power on the island. [6] Dessalines' breif reign lasted only until 1806, when he was assassinated in an uprising believed to have been ploted by his cheif rival, General Henri Christophe, shown below on the right. [7] Christophe, unable to control the legislature, in 1807 set up a separate state in northern Haiti and had himself crowned Henri I, King of Haiti. [8] Convinced that imposing structures such as the Citadelle would boost his nation's stature, Christophe launched an extensive building program carryed out by forced labor. [9] Hospitals and schools sprang up, and work on the Citadelle progressed steadyly, but eventualy the people rebeled. [10] In 1820, having suffered a series of strokes and unerved by an impending mutiny, Christophe, the last of the revolution's three great generals, committed suicide.

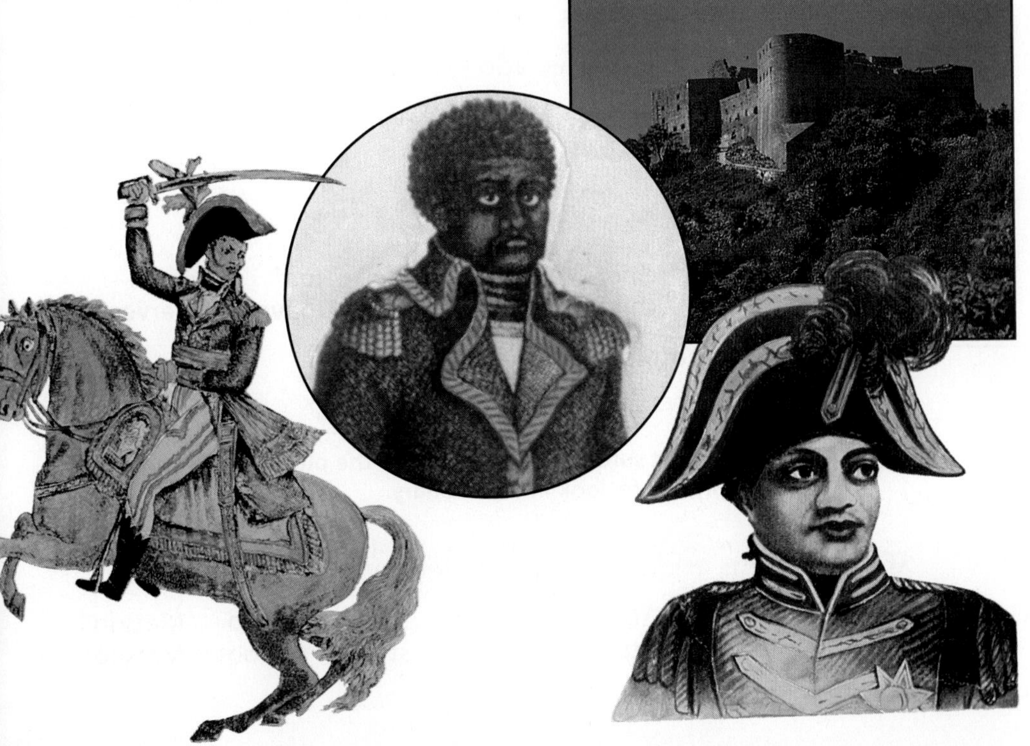

Forming the Plural of Nouns

31k. Remembering the following rules will help you spell the plural forms of nouns.

(1) For most nouns, add *–s.*

SINGULAR	artist	song	lake	flower	muscle	Wilson
PLURAL	**artists**	**songs**	**lakes**	**flowers**	**muscles**	**Wilsons**

(2) For nouns ending in *s, x, z, ch,* or *sh,* add *–es.*

SINGULAR	dress	box	waltz	birch	bush	Ruíz
PLURAL	**dresses**	**boxes**	**waltzes**	**birches**	**bushes**	**Ruízes**

(3) For nouns ending in *y* preceded by a vowel, add *–s.*

SINGULAR	monkey	journey	essay	decoy	alley	Friday
PLURAL	**monkeys**	**journeys**	**essays**	**decoys**	**alleys**	**Fridays**

(4) For nouns ending in *y* preceded by a consonant, change the *y* to *i* and add *–es.*

SINGULAR	fly	enemy	lady	trophy	ally	theory
PLURAL	**flies**	**enemies**	**ladies**	**trophies**	**allies**	**theories**

For most proper nouns, add *–s.*

EXAMPLES **Brady—Bradys** **Mallory—Mallorys**

(5) For some nouns ending in *f* or *fe,* add *–s.* For others, change the *f* or *fe* to *v* and add *–es.*

SINGULAR	roof	chief	carafe	knife	loaf	wharf
PLURAL	**roofs**	**chiefs**	**carafes**	**knives**	**loaves**	**wharves**

For proper nouns, add *–s.*

EXAMPLES **Cardiff—Cardiffs** **Wolfe—Wolfes**

NOTE: If you are not sure about how to spell the plural of a noun ending in *f* or *fe,* look in a dictionary.

(6) For nouns ending in *o* preceded by a vowel, add *–s.*

SINGULAR	radio	studio	cameo	stereo	igloo	Matsuo
PLURAL	**radios**	**studios**	**cameos**	**stereos**	**igloos**	**Matsuos**

MECHANICS

(7) For many nouns ending in *o* preceded by a consonant, add *–es*.

SINGULAR	tomato	potato	hero	veto	torpedo	echo
PLURAL	tomatoes	potatoes	heroes	vetoes	torpedoes	echoes

For some common nouns, especially those referring to music, and for proper nouns, add *–s*.

SINGULAR	burrito	silo	photo	piano	soprano	Navajo
PLURAL	burritos	silos	photos	pianos	sopranos	Navajos

NOTE: For some nouns ending in *o* preceded by a consonant, you may add either *–s* or *–es*.

SINGULAR	motto	tornado	mosquito	zero	banjo
PLURAL	mottos	tornados	mosquitos	zeros	banjos
	or	*or*	*or*	*or*	*or*
	mottoes	tornadoes	mosquitoes	zeroes	banjoes

If you are in doubt about the plural form of a noun ending in *o*, check the spelling in a dictionary.

(8) The plural of a few nouns is formed irregularly.

SINGULAR	mouse	woman	tooth	goose	foot	child
PLURAL	mice	women	teeth	geese	feet	children

(9) For most compound nouns, form the plural of only the last word of the compound.

SINGULAR	seatbelt	bookshelf	two-year-old	baby sitter
PLURAL	seatbelts	bookshelves	two-year-olds	baby sitters

(10) For compound nouns in which one of the words is modified by the other word or words, form the plural of the word modified.

SINGULAR	sister-in-law	runner-up	passer-by	senior citizen
PLURAL	sisters-in-law	runners-up	passers-by	senior citizens

NOTE: Some compound nouns have two acceptable plural forms.

SINGULAR	attorney general	court-martial	notary public
PLURAL	attorney generals	court-martials	notary publics
	or	*or*	*or*
	attorneys general	courts-martial	notaries public

Check an up-to-date dictionary whenever you are in doubt about the plural form of a compound noun.

(11) For a few nouns, the singular and the plural forms are the same.

SINGULAR AND PLURAL	**sheep**	**deer**	**species**	**trout**
	moose	**aircraft**	**Chinese**	**Sioux**

(12) For some nouns borrowed from other languages, the plural is formed as in the original language.

SINGULAR	**alumnus** [male]	**alumna** [female]	**phenomenon**
PLURAL	**alumni** [male]	**alumnae** [female]	**phenomena**

A few nouns borrowed from other languages have two acceptable plural forms. For each of the following nouns, the plural form preferred in English is given first.

SINGULAR	**index**	**appendix**	**formula**	**cactus**
PLURAL	**indexes**	**appendixes**	**formulas**	**cactuses**
	or	*or*	*or*	*or*
	indices	**appendices**	**formulae**	**cacti**

NOTE: Whenever you are in doubt about which spelling to use, remember that a dictionary lists the preferred spelling first.

(13) To form the plural of figures, of most uppercase letters, of signs, and of most words referred to as words, add an *–s* or both an apostrophe and an *–s*.

SINGULAR	***5***	**1990**	***B***	+	***and***
PLURAL	***5*s**	**1990s**	***B*s**	+**s**	***and*s**
	or	*or*	*or*	*or*	*or*
	***5*'s**	**1990's**	***B*'s**	+**'s**	***and*'s**

To prevent confusion, add both an apostrophe and an *–s* to form the plural of all lowercase letters, certain uppercase letters, and some words referred to as words.

EXAMPLES The word *Philippines* contains three ***p*'s** and three ***i*'s.** [Both letters are lowercase.]

Most of her grades are ***A*'s.** [Without an apostrophe the plural of *A* could be confused with the word *As.*]

In the last paragraph of your story, I can't tell which women the ***her*'s** refer to. [Without an apostrophe the plural of the word *her* could be confused with the word *hers.*]

REFERENCE NOTE: For more information about forming these kinds of plurals, see page 951.

EXERCISE 5 **Spelling the Plural Forms of Nouns**

Spell the plural form of each of the following nouns.

1. candy
2. sheep
3. hairdo
4. turkey
5. medium
6. video
7. torch
8. belief
9. embargo
10. gas
11. fly
12. alto
13. poncho
14. shelf
15. radish
16. editor in chief
17. spoonful
18. twelfth-grader
19. Gomez
20. goose

REVIEW B **Explaining the Spellings of Words**

By referring to the rules on the preceding pages, explain the spelling of each of the following words.

1. misstate
2. stubbornness
3. peaceable
4. ladies
5. alumnae
6. leisure
7. occurred
8. writing
9. roofs
10. weigh

Writing Numbers

31l. Spell out a ***cardinal number***—a number that states how many—that can be expressed in one or two words. Otherwise, use numerals.

EXAMPLES	**thirteen** seniors	**forty-four** days	**one thousand** books
	346 seniors	**365** days	**1,345** books

Do not spell out some numbers and use numerals for others in the same context. If numerals are required for any of the numbers, use numerals for all of the numbers.

INCONSISTENT The Congress of the United States is composed of one hundred senators and 435 representatives.

CONSISTENT The Congress of the United States is composed of **100** senators and **435** representatives.

However, to distinguish between numbers appearing beside each other, spell out one number and use numerals for the other.

EXAMPLE We bought **seven 15**-pound sacks.

31m. Spell out a number that begins a sentence.

EXAMPLE **Four hundred twenty-one** students participated in the contest.

If a number appears awkward when spelled out, revise the sentence so that it does not begin with the number.

AWKWARD Two hundred twenty-three thousand six hundred thirty-one votes were cast in the election.
IMPROVED In the election, **223,631** votes were cast.

31n. Spell out an *ordinal number*—a number that expresses order.

EXAMPLES Junko Tabei, the **first** [not *1st*] woman who climbed Mount Everest, was born in Japan in 1939.
Of the fifty states, Tennessee ranks **thirty-fourth** [not *34th*] in total land area.

31o. Use numerals to express numbers in conventional situations.

TYPE OF NUMBER	EXAMPLES		
Identification Numbers	Room 12 Channel 4	pages 246–315 State Road 541	Model 19-A lines 3–19
Measurements/ Statistics	72 degrees 14 percent	$6\frac{1}{2}$ yards 84 years old	32.7 ounces ratio of 6 to 1
Dates	July 4, 1776	1200 B.C.	A.D. 2000
Addresses	345 Lexington Drive Tampa, FL 33628-4533		
Times of Day	8:20 P.M. (*or* p.m.)		7:35 A.M. (*or* a.m.)

NOTE: Spell out a number used with *o'clock*.

EXAMPLE **ten** o'clock

EXERCISE 6 Using Numbers in Sentences

Each of the following sentences contains at least one error in the use of numbers. Revise each sentence.

1. When you go to Washington, D.C., visit the Frederick Douglass National Historic Site, which is located at One Thousand Four Hundred Eleven W Street, SE.
2. Since he was 15, my brother's 1st choice as a college major has been computer science, and his second choice has been mathematics.
3. 590 people attended the play on opening night, September fourth, setting an attendance record for the community theater.
4. Did you realize that ninety-seven percent of the earth's water supply is salt water?
5. According to the chart on page three, only fifty-one of the company's 360 products are sold in this region.

REVIEW C Proofreading a Paragraph to Correct Misspelled Words

Proofread the following paragraph, correcting any misspelled words. If all the words in a sentence are spelled correctly, write *C*.

EXAMPLE [1] **Did you see the Channel Seven report on the new system for assigning areas code?**
1. ***7; area codes***

[1] As the map on the next page shows, all area codes in the United States have either zeros or ones as the middle digit; the 2nd digit signals the computerized telephone switching equipment that the call is long distance. [2] When large citys such as Los Angeles use up the supply of potential numbers within a code, the city is simply divided into two parts, and each part is assigned a new code. [3] By August 1991, however, only three area codes were still unassigned, not nearly enough to meet the growing demand for numbers for cellular phones, fax machines, pocket pagers, and computer modems. [4] Yet those 3 codes will have to handle the load until July 1995, because it will take until then for all of the nation's telephone switchs to be reprogrammed for a new system devised by Bellcore, the

telephone industry research organization. [5] Already in effect in 23 area codes, the new system will add six hundred forty codes to the current supply of 152 and increase the number of potential phone numbers to approximately 6,000,000,000. [6] In many

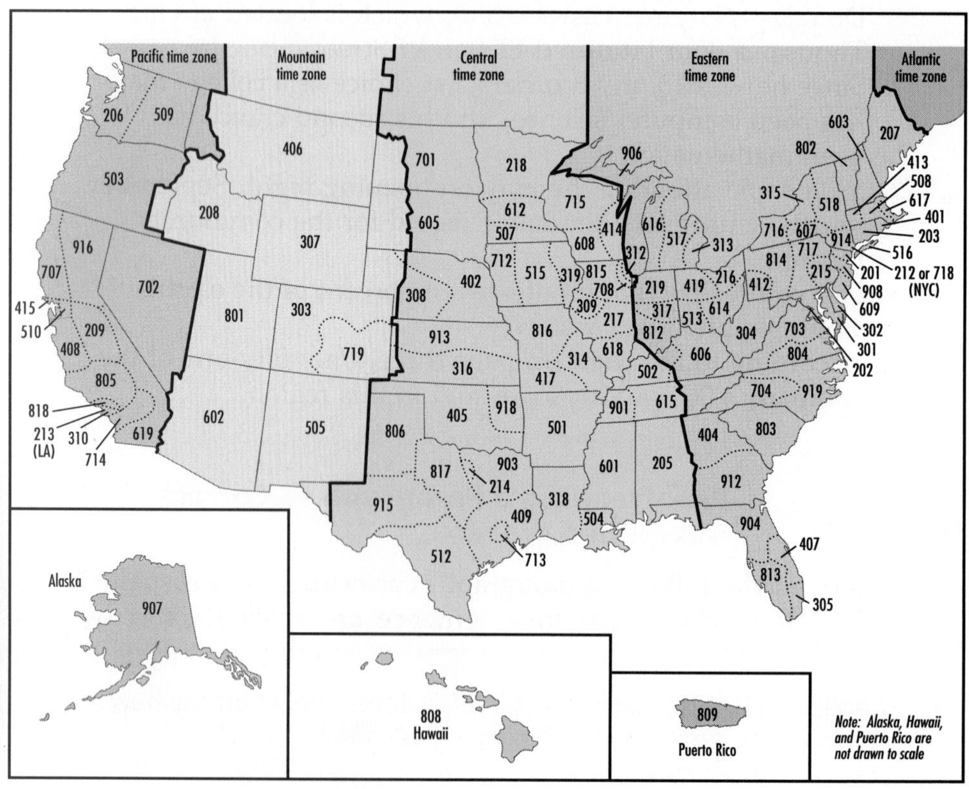

areas, however, the Bellcore system will require callers to dial the area code on all long-distance calls, even those to numbers within their own area code. [7] Some telephone company executivs object to the proposed system, saying that it will create problems not only for thier companys but also for other businesses. [8] The president of one telephone company even characterized Bellcore's plan as leadding telephone users "like lambs to the slaughter." [9] He has proposed a system of 4-digit area codes, which would increase the potential number of codes tenfold but would require assigning every telephone customer a new number. [10] In the end, the outcome will be determinned by the state agencies that regulate public utilitys, for Bellcore can only recommend changs, not enforce them.

Words Often Confused

all ready	*all prepared* Give the signal when you are *all ready.*
already	*previously* I had *already* read several articles about the customs of the Micmac people of Canada.
all right	[Although the spelling *alright* appears in some dictionaries, it has not become standard usage.]
all together	*everyone in the same place* We were *all together* for the holidays.
altogether	*entirely* Her reaction was *altogether* different from what I had expected.
altar	[noun] *a table or stand at which religious rites are performed* The priest was standing beside the *altar.*
alter	[verb] *to change* If we are late, we will *alter* our plans.
born	*given birth* Where was Zora Neale Hurston *born*?
borne	*carried; endured* The people there have *borne* their hardships bravely.
brake	[verb] *to slow down or stop;* [noun] *a device for slowing down or stopping* *Brake* cautiously on wet roads. A defective *brake* caused the accident.
break	[verb] *to cause to come apart; to shatter;* [noun] *a fracture* Try not to *break* any dishes. The X-ray shows a *break* in your left fibula.

capital	[spelling used in all cases except when referring to a building in which a legislature meets]
	Washington, D.C., is the *capital* of the United States. [*city*]
	Do they have enough *capital* to start their business? [*wealth*]
	In most states, murder is a *capital* offense. [*punishable by death*]
	That is a *capital* idea. [*of major importance*]
capitol	*a building in which a legislature meets* [capitalized when it refers to a building for a national legislature]
	The *capitol* faces a park.
	On our visit to Washington, D.C., we toured the *Capitol*.

clothes	*wearing apparel*
	Should these *clothes* be dry-cleaned?
cloths	*pieces of fabric*
	Use these *cloths* to dust the furniture.

MECHANICS

EXERCISE 7 Distinguishing Between Words Often Confused

From the choices in parentheses, select the correct word or words for each of the following sentences.

1. Mother was (*all together, altogether*) too surprised to protest.
2. We have (*born, borne*) more than our share of the burden.
3. What was the Supreme Court decision on (*capital, capitol*) punishment?
4. When you are (*already, all ready*), I will help you.
5. We polished the car with (*cloths, clothes*).
6. They will (*altar, alter*) the building to suit tenants.
7. The dome on the (*capital, capitol*) is illuminated at night.
8. The club members were (*all together, altogether*) only once.
9. If you (*brake, break*) a window, you will pay for it.
10. Are the sandwiches (*already, all ready*) prepared, or do we need to make them?

coarse	[adjective] *rough; crude* This fabric is as *coarse* as burlap.
course	[noun] *path of action; part of a meal; series of studies* [also used after *of* to mean *naturally* or *certainly*] What *course* should I follow to find a job overseas? Soup was the first *course.* I am taking a *course* in creative writing. Of *course* I'll help you set the table.
complement	[noun] *something that makes whole or complete;* [verb] *to make whole or complete* The *complement* of a 50° angle is a 40° angle. [The two angles complete a 90° angle.] Their part of this job *complements* mine. [Together the parts complete the job.]
compliment	[noun] *praise; a courteous act or expression;* [verb] *to express praise or respect* Thank you for the *compliment.* The tennis coach *complimented* me on my backhand.
consul	[noun] *a person appointed by a government to serve its citizens in a foreign country* The American *consul* in Quito helped us during our visit.
council, councilor	[noun] *a group called together to accomplish a job* [noun] *a member of a council* The *council* met to vote on the proposal. Did each *councilor* vote in favor of the proposal?
counsel, counselor	[noun] *advice;* [verb] *to advise* [noun] *one who gives advice* I accepted the wise *counsel* of Ms. Ariyoshi. Ms. Ariyoshi had *counseled* me to take Algebra II. Ms. Ariyoshi is my guidance *counselor.*

MECHANICS

des´ert	[noun] *a dry region* The Sahara is the world's largest *desert.*
desert´	[verb] *to leave or abandon* She would never *desert* her friends in their time of need.
dessert´	[noun] *the final course of a meal* For *dessert* we had strawberry yogurt.
formally	*in a proper or dignified manner, according to strict rules* The Nobel prizes are *formally* presented on December 10.
formerly	*previously; in the past* Katherine Dávalos Ortega was *formerly* the treasurer of the United States.
its	[possessive form of *it*] The community is proud of *its* school system.
it's	[contraction of *it is* or *it has*] *It's* a symbol of peace. *It's* been a long time since your last visit.
later	[adjective; adverb] *more late* We will send the package at a *later* time. I will help you *later.*
latter	[adjective] *the second of two* (as opposed to *former*) When given the choice of a volleyball or a tennis racket, I chose the *latter.*
lead	[verb, pronounced "leed"] *to go first; to guide* Who will *lead* the parade?
led	[verb, past tense of *lead*] She *led* the team to victory.
lead	[noun, pronounced "led"] *a heavy metal; graphite in a pencil* The magician truly believed that he could transform *lead* into gold. I bought new *leads* for my mechanical pencil.

MECHANICS

Distinguishing Between Words Often Confused

From the choices in parentheses, select the correct word for each of the following sentences.

1. These supplies will (*complement, compliment*) those that you already have.
2. What did you order for (*dessert, desert*)?
3. Why does he use such (*course, coarse*) language?
4. I do not enjoy parties conducted as (*formally, formerly*) as this one.
5. We are not sure which (*course, coarse*) to follow.
6. Are you sure (*its, it's*) not too late?
7. I worked last summer as a camp (*councilor, counselor*).
8. He spoke to both the mayor and the superintendent, and the (*later, latter*) was more helpful.
9. Last season, Albert (*lead, led*) the team to a championship.
10. Our (*consul, counsel*) in China has returned to Washington.

loose	[adjective, pronounced "loos"] *free; not close together; not firmly fastened* The *loose* chickens roamed the barnyard. They stumbled in the *loose* sand. Some of the shingles on the roof are *loose.*
lose	[verb, pronounced "looz"] *to suffer loss of* When did you *lose* your books?
miner	[noun] *a worker in a mine* Her father is a coal *miner.*
minor	[noun; adjective] *a person under legal age;* [adjective] *less important* A *minor* cannot marry without a parent's or guardian's consent. They raised only *minor* objections.
moral	[adjective] *good; virtuous;* [noun] *a lesson of conduct* His conduct showed him to be a *moral* person. The class understood the *moral* of the story.
morale	[noun] *spirit; mental condition* The victory boosted the team's *morale.*

passed	[verb, past tense of *pass*] *went beyond* The red car *passed* me at the finish line.
past	[noun] *time gone by;* [adjective] *of a former time;* [preposition] *beyond* To understand the present, you need to study the *past*. For some people, *past* events are much more interesting than present ones. After you drive *past* the shopping mall, turn right at the first traffic light.
peace	*calmness* (as opposed to *war* or *strife*) Doesn't everyone prefer *peace* to war?
piece	*a part of something* I fed the dog a boneless *piece* of turkey as a special treat.
personal	[adjective] *individual; private* The celebrity declined to answer any *personal* questions.
personnel	[noun] *a group of people employed in the same work or service* The *personnel* of the company ranged in age from sixteen to sixty-four.
plain	[adjective] *not fancy; clear;* [noun] *an area of flat land* The tourist cabin was small and *plain* but quite comfortable. Our problem is *plain* to see. The *plain* stretched before them for miles.
plane	[noun] *a flat surface; a tool; an airplane* Geometry is the study of imaginary flat surfaces, or *planes*. The carpenter used a *plane* to smooth the edge of the board. Waiting for the fog to lift, the *plane* circled the airport for an hour.

principal	[noun] *the head of a school;* [adjective] *main or most important*
	Jorge's mom, Mrs. Pacheco, is the assistant *principal* at our school.
	The *principal* cause of accidents is carelessness.
principle	[noun] *a rule of conduct; a fact or a general truth*
	The plaintiff accused the defendant of having no *principles.*
	We have been studying many of the *principles* of aerodynamics.

quiet	[adjective] *still; silent*
	The library is usually *quiet,* but it wasn't today.
quite	[adverb] *completely; rather; very*
	I had *quite* forgotten her advice.
	Angela's report on the lifestyle of the Amish was *quite* interesting.

MECHANICS

EXERCISE 9 Distinguishing Between Words Often Confused

From the choices in parentheses, select the correct word for each of the following sentences.

1. All three nations signed a (*peace, piece*) treaty.
2. Do these printed instructions seem (*plain, plane*) to you?
3. This store's sales (*personal, personnel*) are very helpful.
4. The (*principal, principle*) of solar energy is not too difficult to understand.
5. If you (*loose, lose*) your concentration, you might (*loose, lose*) the tennis match.
6. What are the four (*principal, principle*) parts of the verb "to shrink"?
7. Mrs. Wilson insists that students remain absolutely (*quiet, quite*) during study period.
8. Does every fable have a (*moral, morale*)?
9. On my way to school every day, I always walk (*passed, past*) the bakery.
10. Now that he is officially no longer a (*miner, minor*), he can vote in the upcoming election.

stationary	[adjective] *in a fixed position* The rabbit remained *stationary* as the hawk circled above.
stationery	[noun] *writing paper* I received a box of *stationery* at Christmas.
than	[conjunction, used for comparisons] Jupiter is larger *than* any other planet.
then	[adverb] *at that time; next* First, make an outline; *then* write the composition according to the outline.
their	[possessive form of *they*] The performers made *their* own costumes.
there	[adverb] *at that place;* [expletive, used to begin a sentence—see page 636] We were *there* at two o'clock. *There* were four of us in the final round of competition.
they're	[contraction of *they are*] *They're* going with us to the jazz festival.
to	[preposition; part of the infinitive form of a verb] Are you going *to* Puerto Rico this summer? My father showed me how *to* prepare sushi.
too	[adverb] *also; more than enough* Lamont is a senior, *too.* It is *too* late to go now.
two	[adjective] *totaling one plus one;* [noun] *the number between one and three* We had only *two* dollars. *Two* of my favorite singers are Linda Ronstadt and Tracy Chapman.
waist	[noun] *the midsection of the body* She wore a colorful obi around her *waist.*
waste	[noun] *unused material;* [verb] *to squander* Pollution can be caused by industrial *wastes.* Don't *waste* your time.

MECHANICS

who's	[contraction of *who is* or *who has*] *Who's* in charge of the recycling program? *Who's* been using my computer?
whose	[possessive form of *who*] *Whose* castanets are these?
your	[possessive form of *you*] Is this *your* car?
you're	[contraction of *you are*] *You're* a true friend.

EXERCISE 10 Distinguishing Between Words Often Confused

From the choices in parentheses, select the correct word for each of the following sentences.

1. They had neglected to close (*there, their*) lockers.
2. I wanted to go to camp, (*to, two, too*).
3. Tie the rope around your (*waist, waste*).
4. The platform, we discovered when we tried to move it, was (*stationary, stationery*).
5. No one could remember (*whose, who's*) name had been drawn first.
6. As soon as (*their, they're*) printed, we will ship the books.
7. Write your letters on business (*stationary, stationery*).
8. (*Your, You're*) lucky to have such a good job.
9. I cannot do any more (*then, than*) I have done.
10. I was surprised at (*you're, your*) taking that attitude.

REVIEW D Distinguishing Between Words Often Confused

From the choices in parentheses, select the correct word or words for each of the following sentences.

1. Columbia is the (*capital, capitol*) of South Carolina.
2. Have you discussed this problem with your guidance (*councilor, counselor*)?
3. The vegetation in the (*dessert, desert*) surprised us.
4. My companion (*lead, led*) me down a dark passage.

5. We were (*all ready, already*) to start before dawn.
6. Try not to (*lose, loose*) your keys.
7. Each success helps to build (*moral, morale*).
8. Members of the (*counsel, council*) are elected annually.
9. My red tie (*complements, compliments*) my blue suit.
10. The mission was accomplished without loss of (*personal, personnel*).

REVIEW E

Proofreading Paragraphs to Correct Misspelled Words

Proofread the following paragraphs, correcting any misspelled words. If all the words in a sentence are spelled correctly, write *C*.

EXAMPLE [1] **We spent this passed weekend in San Francisco.**
1. ***past***

[1] Many of the more than 100,000 Hispanics who live in San Francisco make they're homes in the Mission District. [2] They come from many different countries, of coarse, but altogether they've created one of San Francisco's most inviting areas. [3] Comprising twenty square blocks on the city's south side, the District takes it's name from the mission founded in 1771 by Franciscan missionary Junípero Serra.

[4] The whitewashed adobe mission is formerly named Mission San Francisco de Asís, but its popularly known as Mission Dolores after the name of a nearby stream. [5] One of the few structures that survived the devastating earthquake of 1906, it's beleived to be the oldest intact building in the city. [6] Its gilded alter was among the most ornate in the twenty-one Spanish missions Fray Junípero founded in what is now California. [7] The basilica, the grander church next door too the original mission, was demolished in the 1906 earthquake but was latter rebuilt. [8] Nestled between the to buildings, a small park invites visitors to spend a quite moment resting before exploring further.

[9] Even the most unobservant visitor can't fail to notice the striking outdoor murals, like the one on the left on the next page, which brighten walls throughout the neighborhood; all together, their are forty-five of these murals. [10] Its not surprising that quiet a few well-known Hispanic artists, including Amalia Mesa-Bains, Enrique Chagoya, and to many others to list here, launched they're careers there.

300 Spelling Words

The following list contains three hundred words that are commonly misspelled. The words are grouped so that you can study them ten at a time.

abundant	allegiance	biscuit
academically	alliance	blasphemy
accelerator	allotting	boulevard
accessible	annihilate	buffet
accidentally	anonymous	bureaucrat
acclimated	apologetically	burial
accommodation	apparatus	business
accompaniment	apparent	calculation
accomplishment	arrangement	camouflage
accuracy	atheistic	capable
acknowledge	atmosphere	capitalism
acquaintance	attendance	carburetor
adequately	awfully	caricature
admission	background	catastrophe
admittance	ballet	cellar
adolescence	bankruptcy	cemetery
advantageous	barbarian	changeable
advertisement	beggar	chassis
aerial	beneficial	Christianity
allege	bibliography	circumstantial

colossal
commercial
communist
competition
complexion
conceivable
connoisseur
conscientious
consciousness
consistency

controlling
controversy
courtesy
cruelty
curriculum
deceitful
decision
definitely
descendant
desirable

despair
desperately
detrimental
devastation
devise
dilemma
diligence
disagreement
disastrous
disciple

discrimination
dissatisfied
ecstasy
efficiency
embarrassment
emperor
emphasize
endeavor
enormous
entertainment

enthusiastically
entrance
environment
especially
espionage
exercise
exhaustion
exhibition
expensive
familiarize

fascination
fascism
feminine
financier
fission
forfeit
fulfill
fundamentally
galaxy
gauge

government
grammatically
guaranteed
guidance
harassment
hereditary
hindrance
horizontal
hygiene
hypocrisy

ideally
immediate
incidentally
independent
indispensable
inevitable
inexperienced
influential
ingenious
initiative

innocent
institution
intellectual
interference
irrelevant
irresistible
irritating
kerosene
laborious
larynx

license
liquor
livelihood
luxurious
magistrate
magnificence
maintenance
malicious
manageable
maneuver

marriageable
martyrdom
materialism
meadow
mediocre
melancholy
melodious
metaphor
miniature
mischievous

misspelled
mortgage
mosquito
municipal
mysterious
naive
necessary
neurotic
noticeable
nucleus

nuisance
nutritious
obedience
occasionally
occurrence
omitting
opportunity
orchestra
outrageous
pageant

pamphlet
paralysis
parliament
pastime
peasant
pedestal
penicillin
perceive
permanent
permissible

persistent
perspiration
petition
phenomenon
physician
picnicking
playwright
pneumonia
politician
precede

presence
prestige
presumption
prevalent
privilege
probably
procedure
propaganda
prophesy
psychoanalysis

pursue
quietly
rebellion
receive
recommendation
recruit
reference
referred
refrigerator
rehearsal

relieve
reminiscent
representative
responsibility
restaurant
safety
seize
separation
sergeant
siege

significance
souvenir
specimen
sponsor
statistics
straight
strategic
stubbornness
succeed
succession

summed
superintendent
supersede
suppress
surprise
surroundings
susceptible
symbolic
symmetrical
synonymous

tariff
temperament
temperature
tendency
theoretical
tolerance
tomorrow
tortoise
traffic
tragedy

transcend
transparent
tried
twelfth
tyranny
undoubtedly
universal
unmistakable
unnatural
unnecessary

unscrupulous
vaccine
vacuum
variation
vaudeville
vegetable
vehicle
vengeance
versatile
vigilance

villain
vinegar
visage
welcome
whisper
whistle
withhold
yacht
yawn
yield

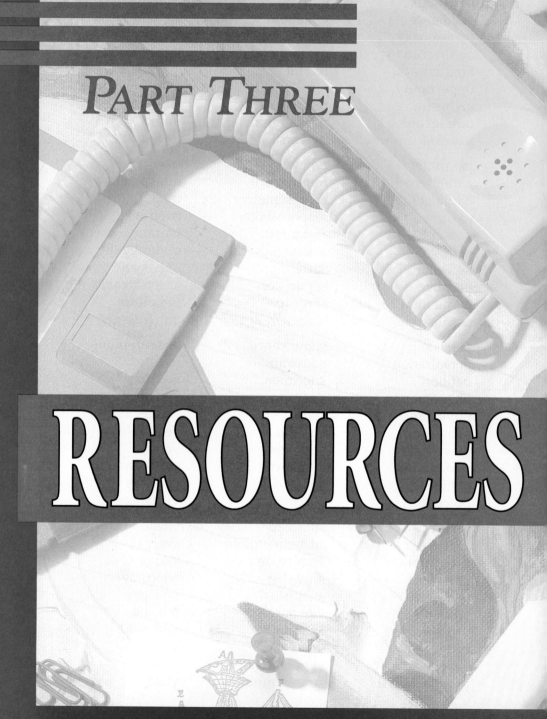

PART THREE

RESOURCES

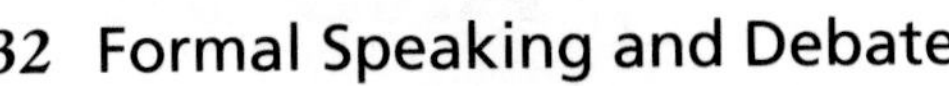

32 FORMAL SPEAKING AND DEBATE

Skills and Strategies

In most cases, a formal speech takes place at a predetermined time and location. There are many different settings and many occasions where you will find this type of public speaking. One factor that most formal speeches have in common is that the speaker can prepare in advance the particular message that he or she wants to convey to the audience at the prearranged time.

As you prepare for any type of formal speaking, you can use specific techniques and strategies to help you communicate your intended message to your audience. You can also learn techniques to help you evaluate a speech effectively when you are a member of an audience.

Becoming an Effective Speaker

If you plan, prepare, and practice your speech, you are more likely to be successful in accomplishing your purpose for speaking. There are several important factors that you should consider when you plan your speech, including

- your purpose for speaking
- the topic you are speaking about
- the occasion for your speech and the audience you will be speaking to

Preparing a Speech

Preparation is the key to a good speech. The first step is to consider your purpose for speaking. For example, some of the most common purposes are to inform, to persuade, or to entertain.

PURPOSE	DESCRIPTION OF SPEECH	EXAMPLES OF SPEECH TITLES
To inform	gives facts *or* explains how to do something	Job Opportunities for the Year 2000 How to Make a Silk-Screened Poster
To persuade	attempts to change an opinion *or* attempts to get listeners to act	Why Our Town Should Fine Polluters How Violence on Television Affects Children
To entertain	relates an amusing story or incident	My Most Awkward Moment

Selecting a Topic

Although your speech topic will sometimes be assigned to you, often you can choose your own topic. If you are able to choose your topic, be sure to select something you're interested in. If you aren't interested in your subject, you can't expect your audience to be very enthuasiastic either. To plan effectively, you will need to answer the following questions as you select your topic.

- *What is your overall purpose in speaking?* Do you want to inform, persuade, or entertain your listeners?
- *What is the occasion for the speech?* Will the topic you are considering fit the occasion?
- *How much time will you have?* Can your speech topic be limited to a length that you can cover effectively in the time allowed?

Analyzing Your Audience

As you plan your speech and limit your topic, you will also need to consider the needs and interests of your audience.

AUDIENCE CONSIDERATIONS		
QUESTIONS ABOUT AUDIENCE	EVALUATION	YOUR SPEECH WILL NEED TO
What does the audience already know about this subject?	very little	provide background or details to inform your listeners more completely
	a little	include some background details
	a lot	focus on interesting issues or aspects of the topic
How interested will the audience be in this subject?	very interested	maintain your listeners' interest
	somewhat interested	focus on aspects of the topic that most interest them
	uninterested	focus on persuading your listeners that this topic is very important

Organizing Speech Notes and Materials

After you have focused your speech topic so that it suits your overall purpose as well as your audience's needs and interests, gather and organize the information that you plan to present in your speech.

REFERENCE NOTE: For more information about researching information, see pages 435–493 and 1019–1035.

Most experienced public speakers prefer to use a method of speaking that allows them to speak comfortably to their audience. An ***extemporaneous speech*** is prepared but not memorized. For an extemporaneous speech, you usually write out a complete outline of your speech, and then you prepare note cards to guide you when you are presenting your speech. This method of speaking gives you an opportunity to use the most natural way of speaking and looking at your audience.

GUIDELINES FOR SPEECH NOTE CARDS

1. Write only one key idea, possibly accompanied by a brief example or detail, on each card.
2. Make a special note card for a quotation or a series of dates or statistics that you plan to read word for word.
3. Make a special note card to indicate when you should pause to show a visual, such as a chart, diagram, graph, or model.
4. Number your completed cards to keep them in order.

Practicing Your Speech

Once you have developed your outline and written your stack of note cards, you're ready to practice your speech. Failure to rehearse the presentation sufficiently is the most common reason for awkwardness and ineffectual delivery by inexperienced speakers. As experienced speakers know, you have to practice your speech thoroughly in order to make it sound spontaneous. Remember that there are only three aspects by which your audience can judge your speech, and that you can improve all of these with practice:

1. *Your ideas:* Your written speech outline that you have now transferred onto your speech notes contains your central message. Rehearse until you are comfortable and familiar with the entire speech that you plan to deliver. Try to use expressive words that help your listeners visualize clearly the ideas you want them to understand.
2. *Your body:* Your "body language" should reinforce the message you intend to convey to your audience. The way

you stand at the podium, the way you move as you talk, and the way you interact with the audience all make a definite impression on your listeners.

- *Stand confidently.* Look alert and interested in what you're saying.
- *Use natural gestures.* Use relaxed, normal gestures as you speak.
- *Make eye contact with your audience.* Looking directly at many different people in your audience makes it seem as though you are speaking conversationally with them.

3. *Your voice:* Speak loudly and clearly to ensure that everyone in your audience can hear you. Try to make sure your voice is interesting to listen to; use a normal variety of vocal patterns.
   - *Volume.* Be loud enough to be heard; however, you can raise and lower your volume for emphasis as you speak.
   - *Pitch.* Use the natural rise and fall of your voice to emphasize various ideas; avoid a monotone.
   - *Stress.* Give emphasis to important words or phrases.
   - *Rate.* Speak at a comfortable, relaxed pace; however, you can vary your rate, or you can pause briefly for emphasis where such a pause would be effective.

Delivering a Speech

Several different methods can be used to present your speech. The type of speaking occasion usually dictates the most suitable method.

METHODS OF DELIVERING A SPEECH		
TYPE OF SPEECH	ADVANTAGES	DISADVANTAGES
Manuscript speech (read to audience word for word from a prepared script)	provides exact words you wish to say; less chance of errors or omissions	doesn't permit audience feedback; tends to be dull

(continued)

METHODS OF DELIVERING A SPEECH *(continued)*		
TYPE OF SPEECH	ADVANTAGES	DISADVANTAGES
Memorized speech (memorized word for word from script and recited to audience)	gives speaker freedom to move around and look at audience	may not sound natural; requires much practice and memorization; risk of forgetting speech
Extemporaneous speech (outlined and carefully prepared, but not memorized; note cards often used)	sounds natural; allows speaker to respond to audience in a natural manner	requires practice and preparation
Impromptu speech (given on the spur of the moment, without notes or preparation)	sounds very natural	can sound disorganized; is not suitable for a formal speech

On radio or television, speakers often use manuscripts so they can stay within rigid time limits. For speech contests or for formal programs, speeches are often memorized. Whenever a speaker must give an unexpected short speech, it's usually impromptu.

However, for a formal speech that is delivered to a live audience, the extemporaneous method is usually preferred. Audiences respond more enthusiastically to extemporaneous speeches because they usually sound more natural and also provide the best opportunities for response and interaction between the speaker and the audience.

Speaking Effectively

Before you give your speech, you may feel nervous. This feeling is normal. However, it's important for you not to allow nervousness to distract you to the extent that it affects your speaking. Here are some suggestions that can help.

1. *Be prepared.* Avoid excessive nervousness by carefully organizing your speech and becoming familiar with your note cards and any visuals you plan to use.
2. *Practice your speech.* Rehearse as if you're giving the actual presentation.
3. *Focus on your purpose for speaking.* Concentrate on what you want your listeners to feel, believe, or do as a result of your speech.

Active Listening

Hearing and listening aren't the same. If you can detect sounds, hearing just happens; however, listening requires you to think about and analyze what you hear. There are a number of techniques that you can use, enabling you to listen well and to evaluate a speech effectively.

Listening Politely

If you are evaluating a speaker's message, you should be sure to give the speaker a chance to express his or her complete message. Speakers react to you as an audience member, depending on your responses as you listen.

Here's how to be a courteous listener.

1. *Respect the speaker.* Be tolerant of individual differences. Show respect for the speaker's cultural background, such as customs, race, or religion.
2. *Don't interrupt.* Wait until the speaker finishes.
3. *Pay attention.* Don't distract others.
4. *Keep an open mind.* Try to understand the speaker's point of view. Also, be aware of how your own point of view affects the way you evaluate the opinions and values of others.
5. *Don't judge too soon.* Wait until you hear the speaker's whole message before you begin to make your final judgments about the speech.

Using the LQ2R Method

The LQ2R study method is especially helpful when you are listening to a speaker who is giving information—for example, a teacher giving a lecture in class.

L *Listen* carefully to all of the material as it is being presented to you. Focus your attention on the speaker's words and the meaning of the speaker's message.

Q *Question* yourself as you listen. Make a list, either mentally or by taking notes, of the most important questions that occur to you as you listen to the speaker's presentation.

R *Recite* in your own mind the information as you hear it being presented. Mentally summarize the information or jot down notes as you listen.

R *Re-listen* as the speaker concludes the presentation. Major points may be reemphasized.

Listening Critically

Listening critically means evaluating and analyzing while you listen. Critical listening is particularly important whenever you are listening to information that is new to you or in any situation when you are listening to a speaker who is trying to persuade you to feel, believe, or do something.

Some persuasive speakers may use propaganda devices to influence their listeners. ***Propaganda devices*** are statements, sometimes based on invalid arguments, that are used to convince listeners to believe in something or to take some action. For example, the mass media—such as television, radio, and newspapers—carry many paid advertisements that try to influence you by using propaganda or persuasive devices. You will be better able to evaluate a speaker's message without being misled by unfair appeals if you learn to recognize some of the common propaganda devices. (See pages 291–343 for more about persuasive methods.)

You can't possibly remember every word a speaker says when you listen to a speech. However, if you listen critically, you'll be able to identify and analyze the most important parts of the speaker's message.

GUIDELINES FOR LISTENING CRITICALLY	
Find main ideas.	What are the most important points? Listen for clue words a speaker might use, such as *major, main, most important,* or similar words.
Identify significant details.	What dates, names, or facts does the speaker use to support the main points of the speech? What kinds of examples or explanations are used to support the main ideas?
Distinguish between facts and opinions.	A fact is a statement that can be proved to be true. An opinion is a belief or a judgment about something; it cannot be proved to be true.
Identify the order of organization.	What kind of order is the speaker using to arrange the details in his or her presentation—time sequence, spatial order, order of importance?
Note comparisons and contrasts.	Are some details compared or contrasted with others?
Understand cause and effect.	Do some of the events that the speaker mentions relate to or affect others?
Predict outcomes and draw conclusions.	What can you reasonably conclude from the facts and evidence that you have gathered from listening to the speech?

 **REFERENCE NOTE:** For more information about interpreting and analyzing information, see pages 1072–1075.

Debating

A debate is a special type of formal speaking. A formal debate involves two groups, or teams, who discuss a controversial topic publicly in a systematic manner. The topic under discussion is called the ***proposition.*** One team, the *affirmative team,* argues that the proposition should be accepted or adopted. The other side, the *negative team,* argues that the proposition should be rejected. To win the debate, the affirmative side must present enough proof to establish its case.

Stating a Debate Proposition

The central issue in a debate is a proposition that is stated as a resolution and limited to a specific idea. The proposition should be an issue that is actually debatable, and should offer each side an equal chance to build a reasonable case. The proposition should be clearly stated in language that is understandable to the debaters and to the audience.

DEBATE PROPOSITIONS		
TYPE	DEFINITION	EXAMPLE
Proposition of fact	determines what is true or false	*Resolved:* That pollution is endangering the world's oceans.
Proposition of value	states the value of a person, place, or thing	*Resolved:* That the American system of education offers learning opportunities to the majority of citizens.
Proposition of policy	determines what action should be taken	*Resolved:* That some form of compulsory public service should be required of all citizens.

Preparing a Debate Brief

A debate requires preparation. Each of the opposing teams must research the proposition; then each team plans a strategy for the debate.

1. *Research the proposition carefully.* Refer to books, newspapers, and other periodicals to glean useful information. Record on note cards all of the facts and evidence that you find.
2. *Identify specific issues.* The ***issues*** in a debate are the specific differences between the affirmative and the negative positions. Every debatable proposition rests on several issues. To prove your proposition, list the most significant arguments you have for supporting your side of the proposition. To refute your opposition, list the most important reasons you think your opponents will give for disagreeing with your views.
3. *Support your arguments.* Based on the information that you have gathered during your research, identify evidence that will support your arguments. You might use examples, quotations, statistics, expert opinions, analogies, or logic as support for your arguments. Also, identify any evidence that can be used to refute arguments your opponents are likely to use.
4. *Build a brief.* A ***brief*** is an outline for debate. It contains a logical arrangement of all the arguments needed to prove or disprove a proposition, as well as the evidence you have gathered to support your arguments. (See the model brief on page 1003.)

Refuting the Opposing Arguments

In addition to building a strong case for or against the proposition, each team must argue against, or refute, its opponents' case. To refute your opponents' arguments, you should

- state clearly the arguments you are going to refute
- tell the audience how you plan to refute each argument
- present proof to refute each argument by using facts, statistics, quotations, and so on
- explain how the proof you have presented effectively refutes your opponents' arguments

EXCERPT OF A BRIEF—OPPOSING ARGUMENTS

Resolved: That law enforcement agencies should be given greater freedom in investigation and prosecution of crime.

Affirmative

I. Restrictive Supreme Court rulings on law enforcement have resulted in continued increase of major crime.
   A. Violent crime has increased; it has shown an increase of 200% since 1961.
   B. The general crime rate has increased by 25% during the last 5 years, an increase that was considerably greater than the increase in population over the same period of time.

II. Removing the restrictions on law enforcement agencies would improve protection for all citizens.
   A. Law enforcement officials would be free to perform their work more effectively.
   B. Because they will be able to work with fewer restrictions, law enforcement officials will be able to collect more evidence and solve more crimes.
   C. The crime rate will decrease as people recognize that they do not have the legal loopholes to escape the law.

III. Giving law enforcement agencies greater freedom is the best solution to the problem of crime in the United States.
   A. Other solutions, like citizens' crime watches, are only partially effective. Law enforcement agencies still have to have the freedom to investigate and prosecute.
   B. It would reduce crime; and because fewer crimes would be committed, it would reduce the number of victims.

Negative

I. The current restrictions are not necessarily the cause of the increase in the crime rate.
   A. There is no evidence of a direct link between the rulings of the Supreme Court and an increase in crime.
   B. The rise in the crime rate is directly related to an increase in population.

II. Giving greater freedom to law enforcement agencies would not improve the protections for citizens.
   A. Removal of safeguards to citizens will lead to abuse of authority.
   B. Rather than decreasing, the crime rate would increase as more people are arrested for minor infractions.

III. Giving greater freedom to law enforcement agencies is not the best solution to the problem of the growing crime rate because it would create other problems.
   A. It would lead to a loss of civil liberties and threaten every citizen's right to freedom from harassment.
   B. The increase in arrests for minor crimes would increase the backlog in the court system.

Building a Rebuttal

A rebuttal is a restatement or a rebuilding of your case. (The word *rebuttal* is related to the word *buttress,* both meaning "something that supports or reinforces.") During this part of the debate, each side gets a chance to repair or rebuild the arguments that have been attacked by the opposing team. An effective rebuttal should

- restate your original arguments
- state your position on your opponents' attacks
- present proof that supports your arguments
- point out any weaknesses in your opponents' arguments
- summarize your original arguments and present any additional evidence you have gathered that supports your position

Debating Courteously

A debate should always be won or lost on the basis of reasoned argument and convincing delivery. Traditionally, debaters treat one another courteously. Even when debaters cross-examine or refute an opponent, ridicule, sarcasm, or personal attacks are not acceptable. In addition, debaters should never deliberately misquote their opponents or attempt to distract or disturb them.

As a courtesy, it is customary to refer to participants by terms such as "The first negative speaker," "My worthy opponent," "My colleague," or "My teammate."

Speaking Order for a Debate

Most debates are divided into two parts. During the first part, both teams make ***constructive speeches,*** attempting to "build" their cases by presenting their arguments for or against the proposition, and attempting to refute, or disprove, the points that they believe will be raised by the opposing team. After a brief intermission, the second part of the debate begins, and both teams make ***rebuttal speeches,*** replying in their closing speeches to damaging arguments that have been raised by the opposing team.

ORDER OF SPEAKING FOR A STANDARD DEBATE	
1. CONSTRUCTIVE SPEECHES	**2.** REBUTTAL SPEECHES
a. First affirmative	**a.** First negative
b. First negative	**b.** First affirmative
c. Second affirmative	**c.** Second negative
d. Second negative	**d.** Second affirmative

Cross-Examination Debate Format. The opposing teams in a cross-examination debate question their opponents' major points immediately after each constructive speech, requiring the debaters to think critically and respond quickly.

ORDER OF SPEAKING FOR A CROSS-EXAMINATION DEBATE

1. CONSTRUCTIVE SPEECHES
   a. First affirmative constructive
   b. Cross-examination by second negative
   c. First negative constructive
   d. Cross-examination by first affirmative
   e. Second affirmative constructive
   f. Cross-examination by first negative
   g. Second negative constructive
   h. Cross-examination by second affirmative
2. REBUTTAL SPEECHES
   a. First negative rebuttal
   b. First affirmative rebuttal
   c. Second negative rebuttal
   d. Second affirmative rebuttal

Lincoln-Douglas Debate Format. In a Lincoln-Douglas debate there is only one speaker on each team. Also, propositions in this type of debate are always propositions of value rather than propositions of fact or policy. This one-on-one format is often used when opposing political candidates debate each other. It is named for a series of debates between Abraham Lincoln and Stephen Douglas, rival candidates in a senatorial election in 1858.

ORDER OF SPEAKING FOR A LINCOLN-DOUGLAS DEBATE

1. CONSTRUCTIVE SPEECH
   a. Affirmative constructive
   b. Cross-examination by negative
   c. Negative constructive
   d. Cross-examination by affirmative
2. REBUTTAL SPEECHES
   a. Affirmative rebuttal
   b. Negative rebuttal
   c. Affirmative rebuttal

Conducting and Judging a Debate

A chairperson often presides during a debate. A speaker may appeal to the chairperson if any debating procedures or time limits have been violated by the opposing team.

The most common method of determining the winner of a debate is by decision of three appointed judges. The judges are expected to base their decision on the merits of the debate and not on their own views about the proposition. Occasionally, the audience may be invited to vote for the winning team.

Review

EXERCISE 1 Preparing and Giving a Speech

Choose a topic for a three- to five-minute speech to be presented to your English class. Consider the occasion, the interests of the listeners in your classroom audience, and your own interests when selecting a topic. Write down—in sentence form—your purpose for speaking. Do research to gather material, make an outline, and prepare note cards. Include at least one visual. Then deliver your speech, using effective speaking techniques as outlined on pages 995–998.

EXERCISE 2 Listening Critically

Listen to a short speech presented by a classmate, by your teacher, or on television or radio. Take brief notes. Then answer the following questions about the speech.

1. Identify the purpose of the speech: to inform, to persuade, or to entertain.
2. What are the main ideas expressed in the speech?
3. What details are used to support or explain the key ideas in the speech?
4. In what ways did the speaker's voice (and body language, if seen) contribute to the message of the speech?
5. Did the speaker achieve the purpose he or she intended? Explain why or why not.

EXERCISE 3 Preparing a Debate Brief

Working in groups of four or six, write a proposition for debate. Each group will then divide into affirmative and negative teams, research the topic, and prepare written debate briefs, using the example on page 1003 as a model. Select one of the following suggested topics, or select an alternate topic. Write the chosen topic in the correct debate-proposition style (see page 1001).

1. Minimum wage laws
2. Patents for genetic engineering
3. Unemployment benefits
4. Student input on curriculum for schools
5. Violence on television
6. Value-added tax for resale of artwork
7. National health insurance
8. Recycling programs
9. Prisoners' rights
10. Uniforms in public schools

EXERCISE 4 Conducting a Debate

Stage a debate, using the affirmative and negative teams, the debate proposition, and the briefs developed for Exercise 3. Select one of the debate formats discussed on pages 1004–1005, and assign specific time limits. Appoint a chairperson to preside over the debate. Select judges for the debate or create a ballot for use by the whole class when deciding the outcome.

33 COMMUNICATION SKILLS

Types and Techniques

To communicate effectively, you need to use skills for speaking as well as listening. Because people spend so much time speaking and listening, it seems that communication should happen automatically. However, true communication takes effort. Wherever or whenever it may occur, communication always has a purpose: to share information or ideas. Specific techniques you can learn and practice will help you improve your communication skills.

RESOURCES

The Communication Cycle

Communication occurs in a cycle. When a speaker expresses feelings or ideas, listeners respond to the speaker's message. This response is called ***feedback;*** it may be in the form of a verbal response (words) or a nonverbal response (such as gestures, facial expressions, body language, or nonword sounds like sighs or giggles).

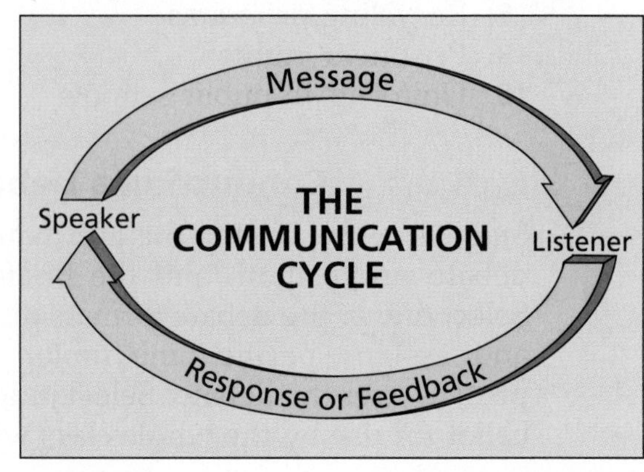

Giving and Receiving Information

The purpose of some of the simplest communication situations is to convey information. In these circumstances, the communication is successful when the speaker gives the information clearly and precisely and when the listener interprets and understands the information correctly. One common example of this type of communication is giving or receiving instructions or directions. Look at the following chart for suggestions to improve your effectiveness whether you are the speaker or the listener in a situation that involves instructions.

GIVING AND RECEIVING DIRECTIONS

Giving	Receiving
Divide the instructions into steps, making each step as simple and easy to understand as possible. Explain the steps in an order that makes sense.	Listen to each step. Look for words—such as *first, second, next, then,* and *last*—that tell you when each step ends and the next one begins.
Remember to include each step or all the necessary information for completing the process.	Listen for the number of steps and the order of steps. Picture yourself doing each step. Take notes if necessary.
Check to see if your listener understands the instructions. If necessary, repeat all directions or instructions so that the other person can remember them.	Make sure you have all the necessary information and understand the directions. Ask questions if you are unclear about any step.

On the following page are some suggestions for improving your communication when you are giving or receiving telephone messages.

GIVING AND RECEIVING TELEPHONE MESSAGES	
MAKING CALLS	**RECEIVING CALLS**
If you reach the wrong number, tell the person who answers that you are sorry for the disturbance.	Be understanding if someone dials your number by error. Everyone makes mistakes.
Avoid calling early in the morning, late at night, or at mealtimes.	If someone calls at an inconvenient time, ask if you may return the call later.
Say who you are as soon as the person answers. If the person you're calling is not there, leave your name and number and perhaps a short message.	Say hello when you answer. Take a message if the call is for someone who is out. Repeat the message to make sure you wrote it correctly.
Don't stay on the phone too long. If you place the call, it's your responsibility to end it.	If you need to end the call, say politely that you need to go. You might offer to call back at another time.

Interviews

The purpose of an interview is to communicate by exchanging ideas or information. You might take part in an interview when you gather information, apply for a job, or apply for admission to a college.

Conducting an Interview

You may need to interview certain people for firsthand information when you are preparing a research paper, a class report, a speech, or a newspaper article. Here are suggestions about how to be an effective interviewer.

Preparing for the Interview

- Make arrangements well in advance. Set up a time that is convenient for the other person to meet with you.
- Make a list of questions to ask. Make sure the questions are arranged in a logical order and require more than *yes* or *no* answers.

Participating in the Interview

- Arrive on time.
- Be polite and patient.
- With the other person's permission, take notes or use a tape recorder.
- Avoid argument. Be tactful and courteous. Remember, the interview was granted at your request.
- Listen carefully and ask follow-up questions if you do not understand an answer or if you feel that you need more information.
- Follow up the interview. Review your notes to refresh your memory, and summarize the material you have gathered. Send a note expressing your appreciation for the interview.

Interviewing for a Position

You can usually expect to be interviewed when you apply for a position. For example, a prospective employer will usually interview you before deciding whether to hire you. Other situations that call for interviews include entering college, joining a club or organization, and applying for a scholarship or grant.

HOW TO INTERVIEW FOR A JOB

1. *Arrange an appointment.* Write a business letter of application (see pages 1061–1063) in which you request an interview for the job. If you are granted an interview, be prompt for your appointment.
2. *Bring a résumé.* If you haven't already submitted it, take your résumé (see page 1063) to the interview and give it to the interviewer.

(continued)

HOW TO INTERVIEW FOR A JOB *(continued)*

3. *Be neat and well-groomed.* It's important to look your best when applying for any type of job.
4. *Answer questions clearly and honestly.* Answer the questions the interviewer asks, adding any additional information that might inform the employer that you are the right person for the job.
5. *Ask questions.* Job applicants often ask for information about work hours, salary, or chances for advancement. By your questions, show that you know something about the company or organization.
6. *Be prepared to be tested.* The employer may require you to take tests that demonstrate your skills or intelligence or reflect your personality.
7. *Follow up the interview.* After the interview, it's polite to write a short thank-you note (see page 1061). Tell the interviewer that you appreciated the opportunity for the interview and that you look forward to hearing from the organization in the near future.

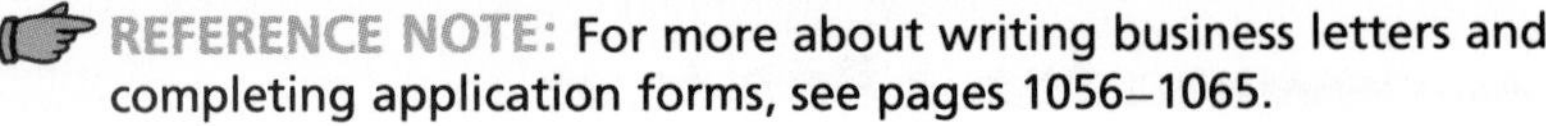
REFERENCE NOTE: For more about writing business letters and completing application forms, see pages 1056–1065.

Group Discussions

Group discussions are common in all types of gatherings, such as cooperative learning groups, school clubs, community organizations, labor unions, or legislative assemblies. An effective group discussion always has a specific purpose. Some of the most common purposes for group discussions are

- to share ideas
- to suggest solutions for solving a problem
- to make an evaluation, decision, or recommendation

Whenever a group is deciding on the purpose to be accomplished by its discussion, an important factor is the time available. If there's a specific time limit, the group will need to consider this when deciding on its goal.

Informal Group Discussions

An informal group discussion is one that takes place between members of a small group. This usually means that the group is small enough to allow everyone to take part without having to use formal rules and procedures.

In order to be effective, all participants must play a role in group discussions. Each participant's role is valuable and each has specific responsibilities in the discussion. For example, a chairperson may be elected or appointed for the group. The chairperson's role is to keep the discussion focused on the subject and moving smoothly. Another group member may serve as secretary or reporter, taking notes during the discussion and preparing a summary or report of the group's decisions.

Remember that every group discussion should have a clear purpose to be achieved. In some groups, participants may keep the discussion organized by following a prepared outline of topics in the order in which they will be discussed, called an ***agenda.*** The chairperson sets the agenda in some groups; in others, the agenda is established by a preliminary discussion and is agreed upon by the group or committee members.

Here are some of the responsibilities of members of a group discussion.

A Chairperson's Responsibilities

1. Announce the topic to be discussed, identify the goal, and explain the agenda.
2. Follow the agenda, keeping the discussion focused on the topics to be discussed.
3. Encourage active participation by each group member.
4. Avoid disagreements by being objective and settling conflicts or confusions fairly.

A Secretary's or Reporter's Responsibilities

1. Make notes of significant information, decisions, findings, or actions of the group.
2. Prepare a final report.

A Participant's Responsibilities

1. Take part in the discussion.
2. Cooperate with other members, being fair and considerate of others' opinions and suggestions.

Formal Group Discussions

Groups that meet on a regular basis often conduct their discussions of important issues following an established set of rules known as ***parliamentary procedure.*** The single most authoritative source is a book called *Robert's Rules of Order, Revised* by Henry Robert.

The basic principles of parliamentary procedure as found in *Robert's Rules of Order* protect the rights of individual members of the group while providing a systematic means for dealing with issues that come before the group for a decision.

Here are some of the basic principles of parliamentary procedure:

- The majority decides.
- The minority has the right to be heard.
- Decisions are made by voting.

The benefits of a system of parliamentary procedures are that it allows a group to deal in an orderly, organized way with issues that are raised and decisions that need to be made about those issues. This system provides the following advantages:

- Only one issue is decided at a time.
- Everyone is assured of the chance to be heard.
- All sides of an issue are debated in open discussion.

ORDER OF BUSINESS

A formal group meeting usually follows the standard order of business suggested in *Robert's Rules of Order.* The words spoken may vary slightly, but the general idea is shown in the examples below.

1. *Call to order:* The chairperson says, "The meeting will come to order."
2. *Reading and approval of the minutes:* The chairperson says, "The secretary (or recorder) will read the minutes from our last meeting." The secretary reads these minutes, and the chairperson inquires, "Are there additions or corrections to the minutes?" The minutes are then approved, or they are corrected and then approved.

(continued)

ORDER OF BUSINESS *(continued)*

3. *Officer's reports:* The chairperson calls for a report from other officers by saying, for example, "Will the treasurer please give us a report?"
4. *Committee reports:* The chairperson may ask the presiding officer of standing committees and then of special committees to make reports to the group.
5. *Old business:* Any issues that were not resolved at the last meeting may now be discussed. The chairperson may ask, "Is there any old business to be discussed?"
6. *New business:* Any new issues that have not previously been discussed may now be addressed.
7. *Announcements:* The chairperson may ask the members, "Are there any announcements?"
8. *Adjournment:* The chairperson ends the meeting, saying, "The meeting is now adjourned."

PROCEDURES FOR DISCUSSION OF BUSINESS

The meeting follows specific procedures for discussion of business.

1. Anyone who wishes to speak must be recognized by the chairperson.
2. A participant may introduce a motion, or proposal, for discussion, by beginning "I move that. . . ."
3. To support the motion, another member must second it, saying "I second the motion." A motion that is not seconded is dropped.
4. A motion that has been seconded may be discussed by the group.
5. Other motions made by members may amend the motion under consideration; may limit, extend, postpone, or set time limits on debate; or may refer the motion to a committee.
6. After discussion, the group votes on the motion. The chairperson usually votes only in the case of a tie.

Oral Interpretation

An ***oral interpretation*** is the presentation of a work of literature to a group of listeners in order to express the meaning contained in the literary work. Acting skills as well as speaking skills—vocal techniques, facial expression, body language, and gestures—are used to convey the overall meaning of the literary work.

Choosing and Adapting Material

It's easier to select material for an oral interpretation if you have a specific purpose and audience in mind. You will probably have different considerations for every occasion for which you prepare an oral interpretation. Factors you will need to consider include the length of time that will be allowed for your presentation and your audience's interests. Props or costumes are not usually used for oral interpretations; instead, the audience uses its imagination.

An abbreviated version, or *cutting,* of a work of fiction or nonfiction, a long poem, or a play is usually prepared for an oral interpretation. Here are some suggestions you can use for making a cutting.

1. In chronological order, follow the story line of the literary work.
2. Delete dialogue tags such as *he responded grumpily*. Instead, use these clues to tell you how to interpret the character's words as you express them.
3. Delete passages that don't contribute to the overall effect or general impression you intend to create with your oral interpretation.

Presenting an Oral Interpretation

When you prepare your oral interpretation, you may need to write an introduction that sets the scene, tells something about the author, or gives some necessary details about what has already taken place in the story.

When presenting an oral interpretation, you may want to prepare a *reading script*, which is usually typed (double-spaced) and can be marked to help you during your interpretive reading. For example, you might mark a slash (/) to indicate where you'd like a dramatic pause or underline words as a reminder that you want to emphasize those words.

When you have developed your reading script, rehearse several different interpretations. Be sure you're satisfied that you have chosen the best way to express the literary work's meaning.

Remember that your voice and body are important in conveying your meaning. Use your voice so that your pitch (high or low sounding), your rate of speaking, and your tone of voice suit your presentation. Pronounce words carefully. Use your body and your voice to portray various characters in distinctive ways. Use body language and gestures to emphasize the meaning of the selection or to reveal the character's personality traits as you narrate and act out what they say and do in the story.

Review

EXERCISE 1 **Preparing for an Informational Interview**

Select a topic that requires firsthand information from an individual. Design a checklist that includes setting up the interview, doing research, and preparing questions to ask the person being interviewed. Make sure that the questions you plan to ask the person you interview are organized and clear and that they require thoughtful responses.

EXERCISE 2 **Preparing for a Job Interview**

Check the classified section of a local newspaper and find a job that you might like and for which you are qualified. List the questions that you would expect an interviewer to ask you and the answers you would provide. Also, make a list of questions you would ask the interviewer about the job or position.

EXERCISE 3 Practicing a College Entrance Interview

Working with a partner, make a list of questions you would probably be asked by a college admissions officer. Then make a list of questions you might ask this representative. Have one person act as the interviewer and the other as the person being interviewed. Present the interview in class and respond to the feedback from your classmate.

EXERCISE 4 Presenting a Group Discussion

Your class is to select a discussion topic from the following list or find a topic of its own. Phrase the topic in the form of a specific, focused question. Then divide into groups small enough to allow thorough discussion of the topic. Select a reporter to report the group's findings to the class.

1. Training for a job
2. Ecology
3. Television violence
4. Choosing a college
5. Trade relations with other countries

EXERCISE 5 Presenting an Oral Interpretation

Select a portion of a literary work suitable for an oral presentation, and adapt the material for a short presentation to your class. First, prepare a reading script. Include an introduction that tells the author and title of the selection and that provides enough background information so that your audience can understand the meaning of the scene. Then, present your oral interpretation to your class.

34 The Library/Media Center

Finding and Using Information

Libraries contain information in many forms. Written materials include manuscripts, books, pamphlets, and newspapers. In recent years, information has also been stored in other forms, such as audio and video recordings and computer data files. The library is now often called a media center or media resource center because of the wide variety of information resources it contains.

RESOURCES

The Librarian

Don't overlook one of the most valuable resources found in a library—your librarian. A librarian is a trained professional who can be your guide in locating and using the library's stored information. Your librarian may even be able to help you find information available from other libraries or information services.

Finding Books in the Library

The Call Number

The contents of a library are classified and arranged using an organized system of ***call numbers,*** identification codes that are usually found printed on the book's spine. Call numbers are assigned according to one of two classification systems: the *Dewey decimal system* or the *Library of Congress system.*

The Dewey Decimal System

Nonfiction. The Dewey decimal system groups nonfiction books and some works of literature into ten broad categories, numbered according to their subject matter. Each of these broad subject areas covers a wide range of subdivisions.

DEWEY DECIMAL CLASSIFICATION SYSTEM		
NUMBERS	SUBJECT AREAS	EXAMPLES OF SUBDIVISIONS
000–099	General Works	encyclopedias, periodicals, bibliographies
100–199	Philosophy	psychology, ethics, personality
200–299	Religion	theology, bibles, mythology
300–399	Social Science	economics, education, government, law
400–499	Philology or Language	grammar, dictionaries, foreign languages
500–599	Science	biology, chemistry, geology, mathematics
600–699	Technology	agriculture, engineering, health, medical science, environment
700–799	The Arts	motion pictures, music, painting, photography, sports
800–899	Literature	criticism, drama, essays, poetry
900–999	History	archaeology, geography, travel, collective biographies

NOTE: Some libraries use the letter *R* before the call numbers of reference books in any of these categories.

Fiction. The Dewey decimal system arranges works of fiction alphabetically according to the authors' last names. Works by the same author are arranged alphabetically according to the first important word of the title (excluding *A, An,* and *The*).

Some libraries shelve short story collections separately and may assign them Dewey decimal numbers.

The Library of Congress System

Subject categories are identified by a letter code in the Library of Congress system. The first letter of a book's call number always shows the general category.

LIBRARY OF CONGRESS CLASSIFICATION SYSTEM			
GENERAL CATEGORIES			
A	General Works	M	Music
B	Philosophy, Psychology, Religion	N	Fine Arts
C–F	History	P	Language and Literature
G	Geography, Anthropology, Recreation	Q	Science
H	Social Science	R	Medicine
J	Political Science	S	Agriculture
K	Law	T	Technology
L	Education	U	Military Science
		V	Naval Science
		Z	Bibliography and Library Science

Your library's reference desk will have a complete list of letter codes for Library of Congress categories and subcategories.

The Card Catalog

The ***card catalog*** is a cabinet of drawers filled with alphabetically arranged cards: *title cards, author cards, subject cards* (for nonfiction), and sometimes cross-reference cards.

Catalog cards give the title, author, and call number of the book; they may also give publication facts, indicate the book's page count, and show that the book contains illustrations or diagrams.

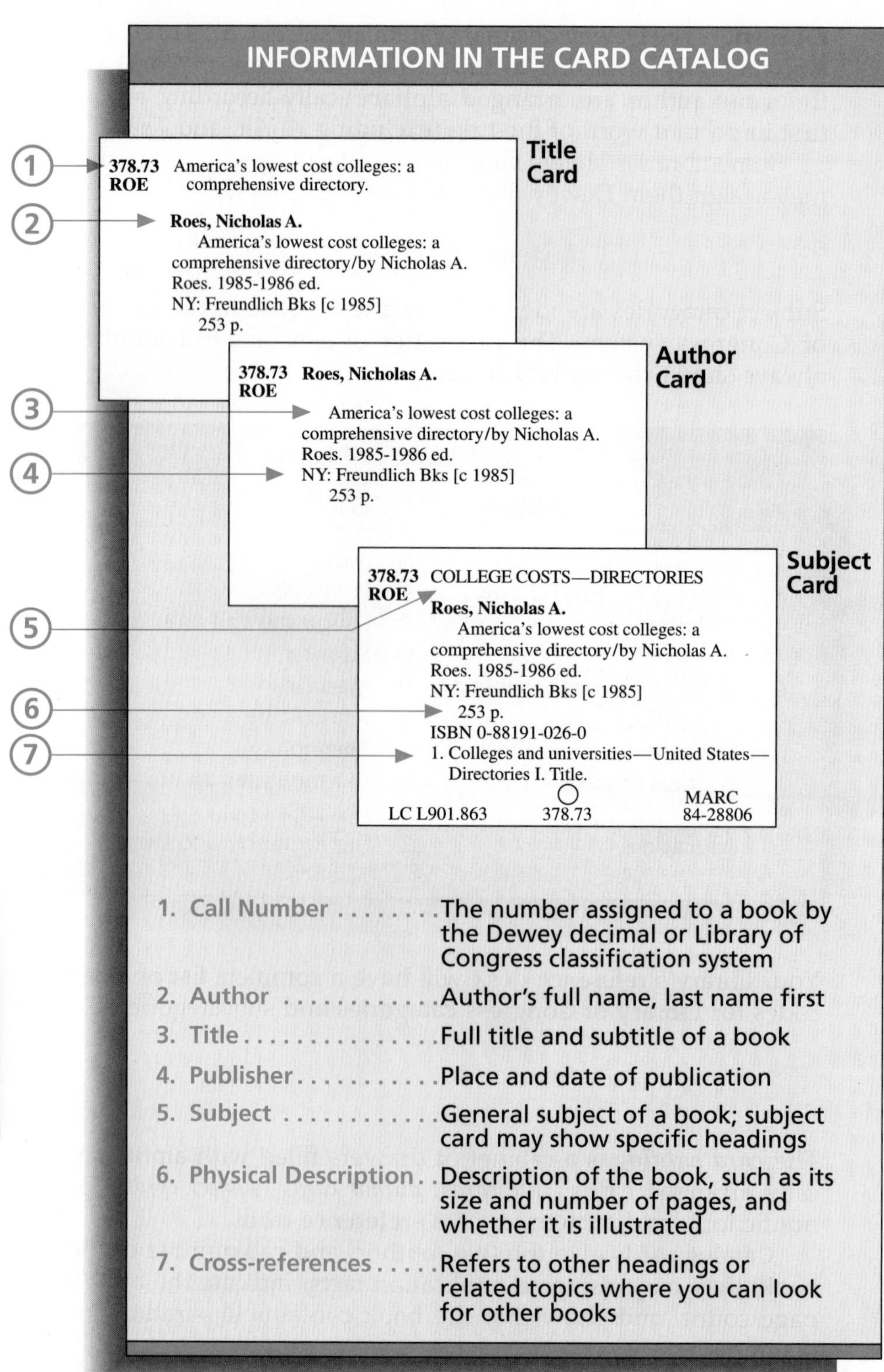
INFORMATION IN THE CARD CATALOG
Title Card
378.73 ROE America's lowest cost colleges: a comprehensive directory.
Roes, Nicholas A.
America's lowest cost colleges: a comprehensive directory/by Nicholas A. Roes. 1985-1986 ed.
NY: Freundlich Bks [c 1985]
253 p.
Author Card
378.73 ROE Roes, Nicholas A.
America's lowest cost colleges: a comprehensive directory/by Nicholas A. Roes. 1985-1986 ed.
NY: Freundlich Bks [c 1985]
253 p.
Subject Card
378.73 ROE COLLEGE COSTS—DIRECTORIES
Roes, Nicholas A.
America's lowest cost colleges: a comprehensive directory/by Nicholas A. Roes. 1985-1986 ed.
NY: Freundlich Bks [c 1985]
253 p.
ISBN 0-88191-026-0
1. Colleges and universities—United States—Directories I. Title.
LC L901.863
378.73
MARC 84-28806
1
2
3
4
5
6
7
1. Call Number . . . . The number assigned to a book by the Dewey decimal or Library of Congress classification system
2. Author . . . . Author's full name, last name first
3. Title . . . . Full title and subtitle of a book
4. Publisher . . . . Place and date of publication
5. Subject . . . . General subject of a book; subject card may show specific headings
6. Physical Description . . Description of the book, such as its size and number of pages, and whether it is illustrated
7. Cross-references . . . . . Refers to other headings or related topics where you can look for other books

The On-line Catalog

An ***on-line catalog*** is a card catalog on a computer. On the computer keyboard you type in an author's name, a title, or a subject. Then the computer displays on its screen information similar to what you'd find under this heading in the card catalog. Benefits of an on-line catalog are its speed and ability to give additional information, such as whether a book is checked out or if it is available at another library.

Using Reference Materials

The *Readers' Guide*

The *Readers' Guide to Periodical Literature* indexes articles, poems, and stories from more than one hundred magazines.

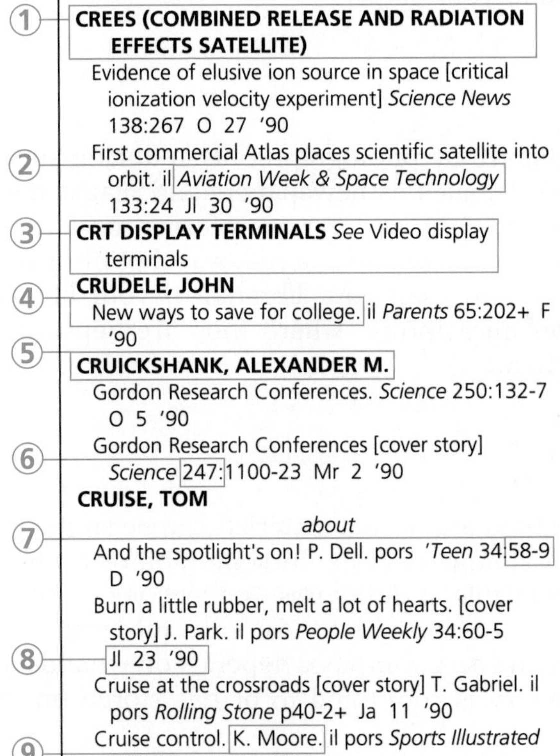

①
CREES (COMBINED RELEASE AND RADIATION EFFECTS SATELLITE)
Evidence of elusive ion source in space [critical ionization velocity experiment] *Science News* 138:267 O 27 '90
②
First commercial Atlas places scientific satellite into orbit. il *Aviation Week & Space Technology* 133:24 Jl 30 '90
③
CRT DISPLAY TERMINALS *See* Video display terminals
CRUDELE, JOHN
④
New ways to save for college. il *Parents* 65:202+ F '90
⑤
CRUICKSHANK, ALEXANDER M.
Gordon Research Conferences. *Science* 250:132-7 O 5 '90
⑥
Gordon Research Conferences [cover story] *Science* 247:1100-23 Mr 2 '90
CRUISE, TOM
about
⑦
And the spotlight's on! P. Dell. pors *'Teen* 34:58-9 D '90
Burn a little rubber, melt a lot of hearts. [cover story] J. Park. il pors *People Weekly* 34:60-5
⑧
Jl 23 '90
Cruise at the crossroads [cover story] T. Gabriel. il pors *Rolling Stone* p40-2+ Ja 11 '90
⑨
Cruise control. K. Moore. il pors *Sports Illustrated* 72:50-2+ Je 11 '90

Paperback editions of the *Readers' Guide* are published throughout the year, with each issue listing materials published in the previous two to four weeks. At the end of the year these paperback issues are then bound into a single, hardcover volume.

As the sample entries on page 1023 show, magazine articles are listed by subject and by author but not by title. The *Readers' Guide* also gives cross-references, indicated by the words "*see*" or "*see also.*" A key at the front of the *Readers' Guide* explains abbreviations used in the entries.

The Vertical File

Most libraries contain a collection of various up-to-date materials, such as pictures, pamphlets, newspaper clippings, government publications, and catalogs. These materials are usually organized by subject and stored in a special file cabinet called the ***vertical file.*** Your librarian will be able to tell you where the vertical file is located in your library.

Microforms

Many libraries save space by photographically reducing some categories of periodicals, such as newspapers and magazines, and storing them on ***microforms.*** The microforms most commonly found in a library are *microfilm* (a roll or reel of film) and *microfiche* (a sheet of film). Ask your librarian if your library stores periodicals on microforms, where they are kept, and how you can view them.

Computers

Large volumes of printed and visual materials can be stored by computer on optical storage devices. In some libraries, reference materials are available in ***databases***—collections of information that are stored on a computer for easy retrieval. The information you can find on a computer depends on what database systems the library is connected to or has stored on its computer.

Recorded Materials

Audiovisual materials are often available through your library. They can be a valuable source of research information. These may include videotapes—containing documentaries or other educational programs about specific topics—or audiocassettes of speeches or lectures by experts discussing topics related to their particular specialty.

Review

EXERCISE 1 **Using the Card Catalog**

For each of the following numbered descriptions, use the card catalog or the on-line catalog to find a specific book. Write each book's title, author or editor, and call number.

1. a collection of essays about ecology
2. a guide to career choices
3. a recent book on a specific sport
4. a book by each of the following authors: Sandra Cisneros, John Cheever, and James Baldwin
5. a biography of a particular scientist

EXERCISE 2 **Using the *Readers' Guide***

Find answers to the following questions in the *Readers' Guide.*

1. Where are the *Readers' Guide* volumes kept in your library?
2. What is the date of the most recent monthly issue?
3. In the *Readers' Guide,* find a subject heading for popular music. List any *"see"* or *"see also"* references that you find under this heading.
4. Check in the *Readers' Guide* under the subject heading of *health.* Write down the title, author, magazine, date, and page numbers for three articles listed.
5. Find an entry for a review of a book that interests you. Write down the information given in the entry, spelling out any abbreviations.

EXERCISE 3 Learning the Arrangement of Your Library

Draw a diagram of your school library, and label the areas where the following resources are found. [Note: Below your diagram, list any of these resources that your library does not have.]

1. the card catalog (or on-line catalog)
2. the fiction section
3. the reference section
4. the *Readers' Guide*
5. current issues of magazines
6. the librarian's desk
7. the vertical file
8. microforms
9. computers
10. the checkout and return desk

35 REFERENCE WORKS

Principal References and Their Uses

In the library you will find a special, separate section known as the *reference section*. Reference works contain facts and information organized in a way that makes it easier to find whatever details you need. If you are familiar with your library's reference books and other resources, you will have a wealth of information at your disposal.

The Reference Section of the Library

Through its many reference works, your library can give you answers to almost any question you can imagine. Become familiar with the location of the reference section in your library. Learn to be a more resourceful researcher, able to find information from a variety of sources.

Common Reference Works

BOOKS OF SYNONYMS	
EXAMPLES	DESCRIPTION
Funk & Wagnalls Standard Handbook of Synonyms, Antonyms, & Prepositions	lists entries alphabetically, as in a dictionary
The New Roget's Thesaurus in Dictionary Form	alphabetical listing of synonym entries
Roget's International Thesaurus	uses a categorized index system of synonyms; words grouped into categories and subcategories
Webster's New Dictionary of Synonyms	alphabetical listings; explains differences in meaning between variety of synonyms

ENCYCLOPEDIAS	
EXAMPLES	DESCRIPTION
Collier's Encyclopedia *The Encyclopedia Americana* *The Encyclopaedia Britannica* *The World Book Encyclopedia*	common multivolume works; articles arranged alphabetically by subject; may contain an index in a separate volume; may have an annual supplement of up-to-date information
Lincoln Library of Essential Information *The New Columbia Encyclopedia* *The Random House Encyclopedia*	single-volume works; articles are briefer and less comprehensive in coverage than in multivolume encyclopedias

GENERAL BIOGRAPHICAL REFERENCE BOOKS	
EXAMPLES	DESCRIPTION
Biography Index	tells where to find books and periodicals with biographical information about specific, prominent people
Current Biography Yearbook	monthly issues, bound at year end; often has photographs
The Dictionary of American Biography	profiles famous deceased Americans; multiple volumes
The Dictionary of National Biography	profiles famous deceased British people; multiple volumes
The International Who's Who *Webster's New Biographical Dictionary*	profile famous people of many nationalities; have details about their births, careers, and accomplishments
Who's Who in America	famous living Americans; same kind of information as *Who's Who;* one volume
Who's Who Among Black Americans	famous African Americans; one volume

LITERARY BIOGRAPHIES	
EXAMPLES	DESCRIPTION
American Authors 1600–1900 *American Women Writers* (series) *British Authors of the Nineteenth Century* Magill's *Cyclopedia of World Authors* *Dictionary of Literary Biography* *Twentieth Century Authors*	profiles of authors; usually have details about dates of authors' birth or death, titles of major works and dates when they were published, awards or honors won; some contain brief critiques of selected authors' works

SPECIAL FIELD BIOGRAPHIES	
EXAMPLES	DESCRIPTION
American Men and Women of Science *Biographical Dictionary of American Sports* (series) *Biographical Dictionary of Film* Vasari's *Lives of the Most Eminent Painters, Sculptors, and Architects*	profiles of individuals known in specific field or career

ATLASES	
EXAMPLES	DESCRIPTION
Goode's World Atlas *Hammond Medallion World Atlas* *National Geographic Atlas of the World* *The New York Times Atlas of the World*	maps; may also contain statistics about industries, raw materials, exports and imports, or climate
HISTORICAL ATLASES	
EXAMPLES	DESCRIPTION
The American Heritage Pictorial Atlas of United States History *Atlas of World Cultures* Heyden's *Atlas of the Classical World* *Rand McNally Atlas of World History* *Rand McNally World Facts & Maps* *Shepherd's Historical Atlas*	graphic representation of historical changes, such as the rise and fall of empires, movement of peoples, and spread of cultures

ALMANACS AND YEARBOOKS	
EXAMPLES	DESCRIPTION
The World Almanac and Book of Facts	summary of year's notable events; index usually found in front
Information Please Almanac, Atlas & Yearbook	less formal and complete than *World Almanac;* articles may be longer, more comprehensive
The International Year Book and Statesmen's Who's Who	facts about international organizations, nations of the world, and sketches of world leaders
Statistical Abstract of the United States	statistics on many topics, such as population, health and nutrition, education, and age distribution

INDEXES AND BIBLIOGRAPHIES	
EXAMPLES	DESCRIPTION
The New York Times Index *The National Geographic Magazine Cumulative Index* *Art Index* *Biography Index* *Social Sciences Index* *General Sciences Index*	provide information as a guide to articles in periodicals or other information sources
A Biographical Guide to the Study of Western American Literature *Three Centuries of English and American Plays: A Checklist* *World Historical Fiction Guide*	lists of books or articles; grouped by subject, author, or time period; annotated bibliographies include descriptions and notes

BOOKS OF QUOTATIONS	
EXAMPLES	DESCRIPTION
Bartlett's *Familiar Quotations* Flesch's *The New Book of Unusual Quotations* *A New Dictionary of Quotations on Historical Principles from Ancient and Modern Sources* *The Oxford Dictionary of Quotations*	famous quotations; usually indexed by subject; some are arranged by author or time period; often tell author, source, and date of quotation

REFERENCES TO LITERATURE	
EXAMPLES	DESCRIPTION
Granger's Index to Poetry	tells where to find specific poems; indexed by subject, title, and first line
Subject Index to Literature	tells where to find short stories and poems; entries are indexed by subject
Benét's Reader's Encyclopedia	contains information about works of literature, such as plots, main characters, summaries of poems, descriptions of artworks and music, etc.
Book Review Digest *Book Review Index* *Essay and General Literature Index* *An Index to One-Act Plays* *Play Index* *Short Story Index* *Subject Index to Poetry*	guides to book reviews, essays, short stories, plays, poems, and other literary works that may be found in periodicals or in collections or anthologies

LITERATURE AND AUTHOR DIRECTORIES	
EXAMPLES	DESCRIPTION
American Authors and Books *The Cambridge History of American Literature* *Harper's Dictionary of Classical Literature and Antiquities* *The Oxford Companion to American Literature* *The Oxford Companion to English Literature*	contain information about authors and their major works; may include brief critiques

SPECIAL REFERENCES FOR SPECIFIC SUBJECTS	
EXAMPLES	DESCRIPTION
The Encyclopedia of American Facts and Dates *The Encyclopedia of Religion* *The International Encyclopedia of the Social Sciences* *Facts on File* (series of books and yearbooks) *The New Grove Dictionary of Music and Musicians* (series) *McGraw-Hill Encyclopedia of Science & Technology* *The Sports Encyclopedia* *Webster's New Geographical Dictionary*	contain information related to specific topics or of interest to researchers in specific fields; may include short biographies of major figures or evaluations of major contributions to the special field

CURRENT EVENTS RESOURCE	
EXAMPLES	DESCRIPTION
Social Issues Resources Series (SIRS) (audiotapes, videotapes, reprints of newspaper and magazine articles, photographs, letters, and posters)	up-to-date information on many important subjects, such as crime, family issues, scientific discoveries, or data from the National Archives

COLLEGE REFERENCE BOOKS	
EXAMPLES	DESCRIPTION
Barron's Index of College Majors	arranged by state, highlights majors offered at each school
Barron's Profile of American Colleges *Peterson's Guide to Two-Year Colleges* *Peterson's Guide to Four-Year Colleges*	cover many accredited four-year colleges; include articles on choosing a college, preparing applications, taking entrance exams; contain information on student life, application deadlines, financial aid, computer facilities, etc.
College Admissions Data Handbook	four volumes; arranged by regions; covers mostly same information as *Barron's*
The Directory of Educational Institutions	covers business schools that offer programs in secretarial science, business administration, accounting, etc.
Technical, Trade, and Business School Data Handbook	divided into regional volumes; includes community and junior colleges; index of programs and index of schools

COLLEGE ENTRANCE EXAM GUIDES	
EXAMPLES	DESCRIPTION
Barron's Basic Tips on the SAT *Barron's How to Prepare for the American College Testing Program* *Official Guide to the ACT Assessment*	contain specific information relating to performing well on college entrance exams

COLLEGE FINANCIAL GUIDES	
EXAMPLES	DESCRIPTION
Peterson's College Money Handbook *Meeting College Costs* *The College Cost Book* *Directory of Financial Aids for Women* *Directory of Financial Aids for Minorities*	contain information about grants, scholarships, and loans that may be available through colleges and universities

CAREER GUIDES	
EXAMPLES	DESCRIPTION
The Encyclopedia of Careers and Vocational Guidance *The Dictionary of Occupational Titles* *Occupational Outlook Handbook* *Career Opportunities Series* *Guide to Federal Jobs*	contain information about various industries and occupations, such as job descriptions, projected figures for employment for specific occupations, and job-related education requirements

EXERCISE 1 **Finding Specific References**

Explain the principal uses of each of the following resource works.

1. *The International Who's Who*
2. *Shepherd's Historical Atlas*
3. *A Biographical Guide to the Study of Western American Literature*
4. *Subject Index to Literature*
5. *The Oxford Companion to English Literature*

EXERCISE 2 **Selecting Reference Books**

Name the reference book you would use to find each of the following items of information.

1. names of the U.S. senators from your state
2. facts about the Secretary General of the United Nations
3. the special power possessed by Clothe, a mythological character
4. titles and authors of biographies of the president of the United States
5. the second most important export of Pakistan

EXERCISE 3 **Finding Reference Books**

Find and list three books in your library from one of the following categories. For each book, give the call number and title, describe the contents and arrangement, and explain when students should use it.

biographical reference books
literature reference books
guides to colleges and universities
reference books on history or science
books about authors
books of quotations
almanacs
reference books on art or music

36 The Dictionary

Arrangement and Contents

A dictionary is a record of the ways in which words are used. In a dictionary, you can find the meaning and spelling of a word as well as the way the meaning changes in different contexts. Some dictionaries provide information about the history of a word and list its synonyms and antonyms. Most dictionaries tell how a word should be pronounced and how it changes its spelling or meaning as it is used for different parts of speech.

Types of Dictionaries

Many different versions of dictionaries are available for the English language. Each version contains different kinds and amounts of information. The two types of dictionaries used as references about word usage by most speakers of the English language are *unabridged dictionaries* and *abridged* (or *colleg* dictionaries. Unabridged dictionaries are large books tl are usually found in libraries. Abridged (or college) dictiona are more likely to be found in homes or in school classroc

Contents of a Dictionary Entry

emp|ty (emp′tē) ***adj.*** **-ti|er, -ti·est** ⟦ME *emti* & (with intrusive *-p-*) *empti* < OE *æmettig*, unoccupied, lit., at leisure < *æmetta*, leisure (< *æ-*, without + base of *motan*, to have to: see MUST[1]) + *-ig*, -Y[2]⟧ **1** containing nothing; having nothing in it **2** having no one in it; unoccupied; vacant *[an empty house]* **3** carrying or bearing nothing; bare **4** having no worth or purpose; useless or unsatisfying *[empty pleasure]* **5** without meaning or force; insincere; vain *[empty promises]* **6** [Colloq.] hungry —***vt.*** **-tied, -ty·ing 1** to make empty **2** *a)* to pour out or remove (the contents) of something *b)* to transfer (the contents) *into, onto,* or *on* something else **3** to unburden or discharge (oneself or itself) —***vi.*** **1** to become empty **2** to pour out; discharge *[the river empties into the sea]* —***n.**, pl.* **-ties** an empty freight car, truck, bottle, etc. —**empty of** lacking; without; devoid of —**emp′ti|ly** ***adv.*** —**emp′ti·ness** ***n.***

SYN.—**empty** means having nothing in it *[an empty box, street, stomach, etc.]*; **vacant** means lacking that which appropriately or customarily occupies or fills it *[a vacant apartment, position, etc.]*; **void**, as discriminated here, specifically stresses complete or vast emptiness *[void of judgment]*; **vacuous**, now rare in its physical sense, suggests the emptiness of a vacuum See also VAIN —***ANT.*** **full**

1. **Entry word.** The boldfaced entry shows how the word is spelled and its division into syllables. The entry word may also show the word's capitalization and alternate spellings.
2. **Pronunciation.** A word's pronunciation is shown by diacritical marks and phonetic respelling. A pronunciation key explains the sounds represented by these symbols. Accent marks show which syllables receive greater stress.
3. **Part-of-speech labels.** These labels (usually abbreviated) show how the entry word is to be used in a sentence. Because some words may be used as more than one part of speech, a part-of-speech label is given in front of each numbered (or lettered) series of definitions.
4. **Other forms.** Spellings may be shown for other forms of the word. These may include complete or partial spellings of the comparison forms of adjectives and adverbs, a variety of verb tenses, or plural forms of nouns.
5. **Etymology.** The origin and history of a word is its etymology. Many word entries tell how the word (or its parts) came into English, tracing it from its earliest known form and indicating the language it came from.
6. **Examples.** Context phrases or sentences may illustrate how the entry word is used.

7. **Definitions.** If there are multiple meanings, the definitions are numbered or lettered to differentiate them. Most dictionaries arrange definitions in order of the frequency of their current use; however, some list definitions in historical order, arranged according to the date of their entry into the English language. Consult your dictionary; its introduction will explain the system it uses in arranging definitions.
8. **Special usage labels.** A definition may be restricted to certain forms of speech (such as [colloquial] or [archaic]). Or, a definition may be used only in a certain field, such as *Physics, Bot.* (botany), or *Chess.* Your dictionary contains a key to explain abbreviations used.
9. **Related word forms.** These are various forms of the entry word, usually created by adding suffixes or prefixes.
10. **Synonyms and antonyms.** At the end of some word entries, synonyms or antonyms may be included.

Information in Dictionaries

Unabridged Dictionaries

An ***unabridged dictionary*** is a valuable source of information about most words in the English language. Unabridged dictionaries offer thousands of word entries, including words that are rarely used. They usually give more information about their entry words, such as fuller word histories or longer lists of synonyms or antonyms, than abridged dictionaries.

The largest unabridged dictionary is ***The Oxford English Dictionary,*** or the ***OED,*** as it is often called. Because the *OED* attempts to define every word used in the English language, it is the world's largest dictionary, consisting of many volumes. The *OED* identifies the approximate date of a word's first appearance in English and illustrates, in a quotation, the way the word was used at that time. The *OED*'s entries also show the changes in spelling or meaning that a word has had over the centuries. Because it features information about the history and changes of a word rather than a word's current meanings, the *OED* is not usually used for ordinary reference purposes.

Unabridged dictionaries other than the *OED* most often take the form of a single, large volume. *Webster's Third New International Dictionary,* for example, is one well-known, single-volume unabridged dictionary. It is called *international* because it includes words that vary in spelling or meaning as they are used in several English-speaking countries. Most of its entries, however, are in current use in the United States. Another well-known unabridged dictionary is the *Random House Dictionary of the English Language.*

Abridged Dictionaries

The most commonly used reference book in the United States is an *abridged* or *college dictionary.* ***Abridged dictionaries*** contain fewer word entries than unabridged dictionaries, and they do not give as much information about their words. However, abridged dictionaries are frequently updated, so they are the most valuable, portable reference for the current meanings and uses of words. In addition to word entries, most abridged dictionaries contain tables or appendixes with other types of reference information, such as lists of commonly used abbreviations, charts of weights and measures, or brief listings of the rules of grammar and punctuation.

Specialized Dictionaries

A ***specialized dictionary*** limits its entries to those that are related to a specific subject or field. For example, you can find specialized dictionaries for terms used in sports, art, science, medicine, literature, and many other subjects.

Some specialized dictionaries contain terms or phrases not included in a general dictionary, such as idiomatic expressions or slang words. Other specialized dictionaries contain ordinary words that have been grouped or arranged to suit a particular purpose. For example, dictionaries for crossword-puzzle fans group words according to alphabetical combinations. This arrangement would quickly allow you to find many five-letter words with *-ha-* as the second and third letters.

A foreign language dictionary is another type of specialized dictionary; it contains foreign words and phrases. It may also contain conjugations for a language's irregular verbs or a summary of its rules of grammar or punctuation.

Review

EXERCISE 1 Finding Information in the Dictionary

Using an abridged or college dictionary, find the following information.

1. What restrictive label, if any, is given for the word *cryptic*?
2. Which is the correct spelling? *penuchel, pennucckle, pinochle,* or *pinnoccle*?
3. What is *Bay State* the nickname for?
4. How do *canvas* and *canvass* differ in meaning?
5. What is the meaning of the Latin phrase *vide supra*?
6. How many different meanings are given in your dictionary for the word *shuffle*?
7. Give the slang meaning or meanings for the word *lug*.
8. Copy the correct pronunciation for *mucilaginous,* including diacritical marks. Be able to pronounce it correctly.
9. Write the plural of *analysis*.
10. What meaning does the word *passive* have in chemistry?

EXERCISE 2 Finding the Etymologies of Words

Using an abridged or college dictionary, find the etymologies of the following words. (Refer to the guide at the front of your dictionary for the meanings of abbreviations and symbols.)

EXAMPLE **1.** car
1. *comes from Middle English and Norman French* carre, *derived from the Latin word* carrum *or* carrus, *originally a name for a two-wheeled Celtic war chariot* (carros, *in Gallic); may be traced to the Indo-European base word* *kers–, *meaning "to run"*

1. churn
2. hedge
3. pedigree
4. fang
5. rigid
6. elope
7. maneuver
8. theorem
9. library
10. sauce

RESOURCES

37 Vocabulary

Learning and Using New Words

Your vocabulary is a valuable resource, giving you the tools with which you can express your ideas and feelings effectively. The larger and more developed your vocabulary, the more likely you are to find success in high school, in college, and in your future career. Because of this correlation, standardized tests such as college entrance examinations and job placement examinations contain sections that are devoted to testing vocabulary.

Develop a Word Bank

One way to improve your vocabulary is to collect a treasury of words. With each addition to your word bank, you will add to your knowledge and command of words. Every time you encounter new words in your reading or in conversations, write these words in your notebook along with their definitions. Then check your dictionary to ensure that you understand the meaning and the use of each word.

Using Context Clues

You can often perceive the meaning of new words that you hear in conversation or discover in reading passages by examining the way that these unfamiliar words are used. The words, phrases, or sentences that surround a word and contribute to an understanding of its meaning are called its *context*.

You can use ***context clues*** to decipher the meaning of many unfamiliar words. The following chart shows examples of some of the most common types of context clues.

TYPES OF CONTEXT CLUES	
TYPE OF CLUE	EXPLANATION
Definitions and Restatements	Look for words that define or restate the meaning of a word. ■ The tyrant resented the *derogation* of his authority as the elected representatives of the new democracy began to assume control.
Examples	A word may be accompanied by an example that illustrates its meaning. ■ By the end of the flight, the *garrulous* child had irritated all the passengers around her by her unceasing prattle.
Synonyms	Look for clues that indicate an unfamiliar word is similar in meaning to a familiar word. ■ As the *gonfalon* that welcomed the conventioneers to the arena wafted lazily over the speaker's lectern, the slow swing of the banner began to lull the bored audience to sleep.
Comparisons	Sometimes an unknown word may be compared to more familiar words. ■ Three soldiers *bivouacked* alongside the creek at twilight, making a campfire and staking out tents before darkness fell.

TYPES OF CONTEXT CLUES *(continued)*	
TYPE OF CLUE	EXPLANATION
Contrast	An unfamiliar word may sometimes be contrasted to more familiar words. ■ The Chihuahua is *minuscule* compared to a huge dog like the Great Dane.
Cause and Effect	Look for clues that indicate an unfamiliar word is related to the cause or is the result of an action, feeling, or idea. ■ Because of the *epeirogeny* that has gradually uplifted parts of the California coast, there are places where steep mountains border the sea.

Determining Meanings from the General Context

Context clues may not be obvious within the immediate surroundings of an unfamiliar word. Sometimes the meaning of a word may not become clear to you until you have read an entire passage. However, by analyzing the general context, you can infer the meaning of the unfamiliar word using general context clues, drawing on your own knowledge of the topic, and evaluating the relationship between the unfamiliar word and information in the reading passage.

Using Word Parts

English words are usually one of two types: words that can be divided into smaller parts (*inexplicable, misunderstanding*) and words that cannot (*house, teeth*). ***Base words*** are complete, independent words that can stand alone. Words that can be subdivided are made up of two or more word parts. These word parts include

- roots
- prefixes
- suffixes

Knowing the meanings of the most frequently occurring word parts can help you figure out the meanings of unfamiliar words.

Word Roots

The *root* of a word is the part that carries the word's core meaning. New words are formed when other word parts are added to a word root.

The English language borrowed many word roots from Greek and Latin. If you learn some of these roots and their meanings, you can use them to determine the meanings of the words that are formed from these word roots.

COMMON WORD ROOTS		
ROOT	MEANING	EXAMPLES
GREEK		
–astr(o)–	star	astronaut, astronomy
–bio–	life	biosphere, biometry
–chrom–	color	polychromatic, chromograph
–cycl(o)–	circle, wheel	cyclone, bicycle
–dem–	people	democracy, demographics
–graph–	write, writing	graphologist, lithograph
–hydr–	water	dehydrate, hydroplane
–log–, –logy–	study, word	ecology, epilogue
–phil–	like, love	photophilous, bibliophile
–phono–	sound	symphony, cacophony
–zo–	life, animal	zoological, zoophobia
LATIN		
–aud–, –audi–	hear	audition, audit
–ben–, –bene–	good	benefactor, benevolent
–cent–	hundred	percent, centenarian
–cogn–	know	incognito, cognate
–duc–, –duct–	draw, lead	introduce, induce

COMMON WORD ROOTS *(continued)*		
ROOT	MEANING	EXAMPLES
LATIN *(cont'd)*		
–loc–	place	local, circumlocution
–magn–	large, grand	magnificent, magnanimous
–man–	hand	maneuver, mandate
–mater–, –matr–	mother	maternity, matrilineal
–mor–, mort–	death	immortal, mortuary
–omni–	all	omnipotent, omnivorous
–pater–, –patr–	father	patriot, paternity
–prim–	early, first	primordial, primer
–solv–	loosen, accomplish	absolve, dissolve
–spir–	breath	spirit, conspire
–uni–	one	unison, unification
–vid–, –vis–	see	videotape, visualize

Prefixes

A ***prefix*** is a word part that is added onto the beginning of a word or in front of a word root to form a new word. The new word's meaning reflects the combined meanings of its parts.

COMMON PREFIXES		
PREFIX	MEANING	EXAMPLES
GREEK		
a–	lacking, without	amoral, atypical
anti–	against, opposing	antibody, antisocial
dia–	through, across	diagram, dialectic
hyper–	excessive	hyperactive, hyperbole
hypo–	under, below	hypoallergenic, hypodermic
mon–, mono–	one	monarchy, monochromatic

(continued)

COMMON PREFIXES *(continued)*		
PREFIX	MEANING	EXAMPLES
neo–	new	neonatal, neoclassic
para–	beside, beyond	parallel, paramilitary
peri–	around	periscope, peripheral
psych–, psycho–	mind	psychoanalysis, psyche
sym–	with, together	symbolic, symptom
LATIN AND FRENCH		
ab–	from, away	abduct, abhor
contra–	against	contrast, contraband
de–	away, from, off	depart, deflate
dif–, dis–	away, not, opposing	difficult, discomfort
e–, ef–, ex–	away, from, out	eject, efface, expiration
inter–	among, between	intersect, interval
intra–	within	intravenous, intramolecular
per–	through	permeate, periscope
post–	after, following	postoperative, postpone
pre–	before	predict, predisposition
pro–	forward, favoring	propel, progress
re–	back, backward, again	refrain, reverse, refit
retro–	back, backward	retroactive, retrospective
semi–	partly, half	semisweet, semiserious
ultra–	beyond, excessively	ultrasonic, ultramodern

COMMON PREFIXES *(continued)*		
PREFIX	MEANING	EXAMPLES
OLD ENGLISH		
be–	around, about	begrime, befriend
for–	away, off, from	forbid, forsake
mis–	badly, not, wrongly	misadventure, miscopy
over–	above, excessively	oversee, overbite
un–	not, reverse of	unquestionable, unsound

REFERENCE NOTE: For guidelines on spelling when adding prefixes, see page 965.

Suffixes

A *suffix* is a word part that is added onto the end of a word or after a word root to form a new word. There are two main kinds of suffixes: those that provide a grammatical signal of some kind but do not greatly change the basic meaning of the word (*–s, –ed, –ing*) and those that create new words. The following suffixes are primarily those that create new words.

COMMON SUFFIXES		
NOUN SUFFIXES	MEANING	EXAMPLES
GREEK, LATIN, AND FRENCH		
–ance, –ence	act, condition	radiance, excellence
–cy	state, condition	advocacy, redundancy
–er, –or	doer, action	banker, inheritor
–ism	act, doctrine, manner	criticism, ostracism
–tude	quality, state	attitude, fortitude
–ty, –y	quality, state, action	subtlety, reality
–ure	act, result, means	pleasure, measure

(continued)

COMMON SUFFIXES *(continued)*		
NOUN SUFFIXES	MEANING	EXAMPLES
OLD ENGLISH		
–dom	state, rank, condition	officialdom, martyrdom
–hood	state, condition	likelihood, childhood
–ness	quality, state	kindness, craziness
ADJECTIVE SUFFIXES	MEANING	EXAMPLES
GREEK, LATIN, AND FRENCH		
–able, –ible	able, likely	likable, legible
–ate	having, characteristic of	desperate, irate
–esque	in the style of, like	arabesque, statuesque
–fic	making, causing	horrific, scientific
–ous	marked by, given to	glorious, laborious
OLD ENGLISH		
–en	like, made of	golden, frozen
–ful	full of, marked by	restful, wonderful
–less	lacking, without	fearless, restless
–some	apt to, showing	irksome, handsome
–ward	in the direction of	upward, skyward
VERB SUFFIXES	MEANING	EXAMPLES
GREEK, LATIN, AND FRENCH		
–ate	become, cause to be	punctuate, alleviate
–esce	become, grow, continue	coalesce, effervesce
–fy	make, cause to have	magnify, falsify
–ize	make, cause to be	energize, agonize
OLD ENGLISH		
–en	cause to be, become	strengthen, lighten

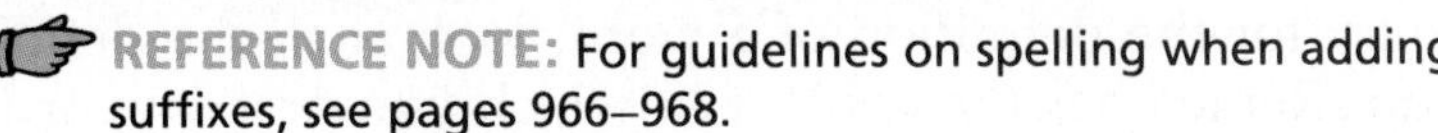
REFERENCE NOTE: For guidelines on spelling when adding suffixes, see pages 966–968.

RESOURCES

Other Ways to Form New Words

The English language continuously grows and changes, adding new words frequently. Most new words that are added to English are formed by combination when ***affixes,*** prefixes or suffixes, are added to a base word or to a word root to make a new word. However, in some cases two base words are combined or put together with a hyphen to make a new word. Here are some of the most common ways new words are made.

PROCESS	DESCRIPTION	EXAMPLES
combining	two base words combined to make a compound *or* a word combined with an affix	eggshell, bird's-eye unbend, masterful
shortening	omitting part of the original word to shorten it or to change it to another part of speech	cabriolet → cab burglar → burgle nuclear → nuke
blending	combining and shortening two words	breakfast + lunch = brunch smoke + fog = smog
shifting	changing the meaning or usage of a word	host (n.) → host (v.) farm (n.) → farm (v.)

Choosing the Appropriate Word

Using the Dictionary

Whenever you express your ideas or feelings by writing or speaking, the words you choose need to match your purpose. At times this can be tricky, since most words in the English language can have more than one meaning. If you consult a dictionary for the definition of a word, look at *all* the definitions given. Remember the context in which you first saw or heard the word. Then match the various definitions to this context until you find the one that is best suited.

Dictionaries often give sample contexts to help you pinpoint the appropriate definition. Compare the sample contexts in the dictionary with the context in which you first saw or heard the word to be sure you've identified the correct meaning.

Choosing the Right Synonym

Synonyms are words with the same or almost the same meaning. However, there are often subtle shades of difference in the meanings of synonyms. Consult a dictionary or thesaurus to be sure you understand exact meanings of words.

Many words have two kinds of meaning: *denotative* and *connotative.* The ***denotative*** meaning of a word is the meaning given by a dictionary. The ***connotative*** meaning of a word is the feeling or tone associated with it. For example, the words *snicker* and *chuckle* both mean "to laugh." However, the word *chuckle* has a more positive connotation than *snicker,* which suggests a sly, derisive laugh.

 REFERENCE NOTE: For more information about denotative and connotative meanings, see pages 526–527.

Analogies

Analogies provide a special type of context in which you are asked to analyze the relationship between one pair of words in order to identify or to supply a second pair of words that has the same relationship.

Analogy questions frequently appear on standardized tests because they measure your command of vocabulary as well as your ability to identify relationships and patterns between words. On standardized tests, analogies are frequently presented in multiple-choice form similar to the following example.

EXAMPLE: 1. THERMOMETER : TEMPERATURE : : ________
A speedometer : car
B snow : cold
C barrel : rain
(D) ruler : length

RESOURCES

HOW TO ANSWER ANALOGY QUESTIONS	
Analyze the first pair of words.	Identify the relationship between the first two items. In the example given, a *thermometer* is an instrument that is used to measure *temperature.*
Express the analogy in sentence or question form.	The example given above could be read as "A *thermometer* has the same relationship to *temperature* as . . . (what other pair of items among the choices given?)."
Find the best available choice to complete the analogy.	■ If you are given multiple choices, select the pair of words that has the same type of relationship between them as the first pair given in the question. (In this example, only choice *D* shows the same relationship, which is that of a tool for measuring to the thing it measures.) ■ If you are required to fill in the blank to complete the analogy, you are often given one word of the second pair of items. Then you are expected to supply the final word that fits the relationship.

Although there are many different relationships that can be represented in analogies, a smaller number of specific relationships are fairly common. Examples of these common types are shown in the following chart.

TYPES OF ANALOGY RELATIONSHIPS	
TYPE	EXAMPLE
Word to synonym	JUMP : LEAP :: slide : skid
Word to antonym	SERENE : AGITATED :: groggy : alert
Cause to effect	MATCH : HEAT :: water : wetness
Part to whole	TALON : HAWK :: tentacle : octopus
Whole to part	FOREST : TREES :: swarm : bees
Item to category	ZINC : MINERAL :: neon : gas
Time sequence	ACORN : OAK :: cocoon : butterfly
Object to function	JEWELRY : ADORNMENT :: umbrella : protection
Action to object	ADHERE : GLUE :: pry : crowbar
Action to performer	COOKING : CHEF :: shaving : barber

Review

EXERCISE 1 Using Context Clues

For the italicized word in each of the following sentences, write a short definition based on the clues you find in the context. Check your definitions with those in the dictionary.

1. The group *propagated* their ideas through television, billboards, and word of mouth.
2. The medicine was supposed to be *lenitive,* but instead it made the pain worse.
3. By his *oscitancy,* I see he didn't get enough sleep last night.
4. It would be a better world if people were always judged by inner beauty instead of *pulchritude.*
5. Since he had a talent for making hats, he became the town's *milliner.*

EXERCISE 2 Using the General Context to Determine Meaning

For each italicized word in the paragraph that follows, write your own definition or synonym. Then check the definitions of each word in a dictionary. If you guessed incorrectly, check the context in the passage again to look for clues you might have missed.

The greenhouse effect traps the sun's heat in the atmosphere, resulting in the [1] *calefaction* of the earth's surface. This process is [2] *analogous* to the heating of a greenhouse. When the sun's rays penetrate the glass exterior of a greenhouse, the interior heats up. Glass walls and roof allow the sun's energy to enter at the speed of light but they [3] *decelerate* the escape of the resulting heat. Similarly, sunlight [4] *permeates* and heats Earth's atmosphere. Much of the heat escapes, but some is [5] *detained* in the atmosphere, absorbed by gases such as carbon dioxide, ozone, and water vapor. These gases then release [6] *superfluous* heat, warming the earth's surface. Growing amounts of carbon dioxide in the atmosphere intensify the effect. The [7] *primary* reason for this increase is the [8] *incineration* of fossil fuels, which release carbon dioxide when they are burned. Also, the [9] *decimation* of forests, whose vegetation absorbs carbon dioxide, reduces the likelihood of a decrease in carbon dioxide levels. Some of the possible [10] *repercussions* of an intensified greenhouse effect are higher ocean levels, raised temperatures, and shifted rainfall patterns.

EXERCISE 3 Learning New Words with Latin and Greek Roots

Underline the root or roots in each of the following words. Using your dictionary, write a brief definition of the word.

EXAMPLE **1.** cognizant
1. *cognizant—being knowledgeable or aware; informed*

1. astrometry
2. chromatic
3. lithograph
4. hydrography
5. unilateral
6. visor
7. demography
8. logogram
9. primacy
10. ductile

EXERCISE 4 Understanding the Meanings of Prefixes

Give the meaning of each of the following words. Then identify the prefix in each word and its meaning. Be prepared to explain the link between the meaning of the prefix and the meaning of the whole word.

EXAMPLE **1.** antithesis
1. *meaning: direct contrast or opposition of ideas*
prefix: anti (against, opposing)

1. paramount
2. abscond
3. monocular
4. forgo
5. retrocede

EXERCISE 5 Identifying Suffixes and Defining Words

For each word, identify the suffix and guess what the whole word means. Use a dictionary to check your answers.

EXAMPLE **1.** novelty
1. *–ty; the state or condition of being novel (new or unusual)*

1. wisdom
2. innocence
3. Romanesque
4. liquefy
5. realize

EXERCISE 6 Completing Analogies

In the following items, choose the pair of words whose relationship is most similar to that of the pair in capital letters.

1. STAPLER : ATTACH :: **(a)** paper : tape **(b)** blowtorch : weld **(c)** needle : cloth **(d)** define : dictionary
2. MAST : BOAT :: **(a)** column : ceiling **(b)** mane : horse **(c)** sail : anchor **(d)** neck : body
3. TRAIN : TRANSPORTATION :: **(a)** wheel : car **(b)** steam : engine **(c)** rose : flower **(d)** boat : canoe
4. PERFECT : DEFECTIVE :: **(a)** pure : clean **(b)** cracked : molded **(c)** bleached : dyed **(d)** interested : intrigued
5. INTENTION : PURPOSE :: **(a)** end : means **(b)** dedication : goal **(c)** flavor : smell **(d)** dedication : devotion

38 Letters and Forms

Style and Contents

For a variety of purposes, well-written letters are the most effective means of communication. For example, you may want to ask for information, order products, make a complaint, express your appreciation, or apply for a job. Other types of letters you may need to write are certain kinds of social correspondence. You may also find it necessary to complete printed forms. The overall success of your letters and completed forms will be affected by their contents as well as by their appearance.

The Appearance of a Business Letter

There are certain standards of style and format that are generally followed for business letters.

- Use plain paper ($8\frac{1}{2}''$ x $11''$).
- Type your letter if possible (single-spaced, leaving an extra line between paragraphs). Otherwise, write legibly, using black or blue ink.
- Center your letter on the page with equal margins, usually one inch, on all sides.
- Use only one side of the paper. If you need a second page, leave a one-inch margin at the bottom of the first page and carry over at least two lines to the second.
- Avoid markouts, erasures, or other careless marks. Check for typing errors and misspellings.

Writing Business Letters

The Parts of a Business Letter

A business letter contains six parts:

(1) the heading
(2) the inside address
(3) the salutation
(4) the body
(5) the closing
(6) the signature

Two styles are commonly used for business letters. With the ***block form,*** every part of the letter begins at the left-hand margin, and paragraphs are not indented. In the ***modified block form,*** the heading, the closing, and the signature are aligned along an imaginary line just to the right of the center of the page. The other parts of the letter begin at the left-hand margin. All paragraphs are indented.

Block Style

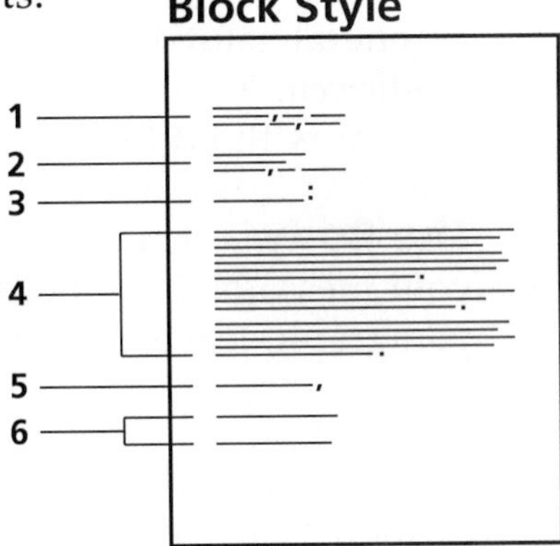

Modified Block Style

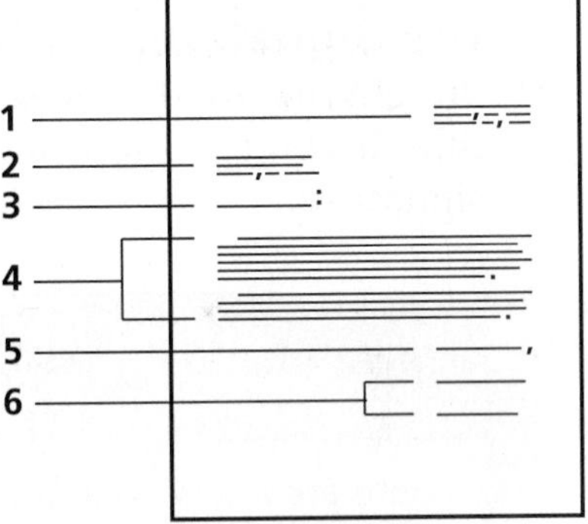

The Heading. The heading usually consists of three lines:

- your street address (or post office box number)
- your city, state, and ZIP code
- the date that you wrote the letter

The Inside Address. The inside address indicates the name and address of the person or organization you are writing. If you're writing to a specific person, use a courtesy title (such as *Mr.*, *Ms.*, *Mrs.*, or *Miss*) or a professional title (such as *Dr.* or *Professor*) in front of the person's name. After the person's name, include the person's business or job title (such as *Editor* or *Admissions Officer*), followed by the name and address of the company or institution.

The Salutation. The salutation is your greeting. If you are writing to a specific person, begin with *Dear,* followed by a courtesy title or a professional title and the person's name. End the salutation with a colon.

If you don't have the name of a specific person, you can use a general salutation, such as *Dear Sir or Madam* or *Ladies and Gentlemen.* You can also use a department or a position title, with or without the word *Dear.*

The Body. The body, or main part, of your letter contains your message. If the body of your letter contains more than one paragraph, leave a space between paragraphs.

The Closing. The closing should end your letter courteously. Several closings that are often used in business letters include *Yours truly, Sincerely,* and *Regards.* Capitalize only the first word of the closing.

The Signature. Your signature should be written in ink, directly below the closing. Sign your full name. Do not use a title. If you type your letter, type your name neatly below your signature.

GUIDELINES FOR THE CONTENTS OF A BUSINESS LETTER

Here are a few valuable suggestions for your business letters.

- *Use a courteous, positive, and professional tone.* Maintain a respectful, constructive tone—even if you're angry. Rude or insulting letters are nonproductive.
- *Use formal, standard English.* Avoid slang, dialect, contractions, or abbreviations. Business letters are usually formal in tone and use of language.
- *State your purpose clearly and quickly.* Assume that the person reading your letter is busy and tell why you are writing in the first or second sentence of the letter.
- *Include all necessary information.* Provide all the information your reader needs to understand and respond appropriately to your letter.

Types of Business Letters

Request or Order Letters

A ***request letter*** asks for something. For example, you might write a college to request a course catalog or a city's chamber of commerce for a brochure about business opportunities. An ***order letter*** is a special kind of request letter that is written to order merchandise by mail, especially when a printed order form is not available.

Here are the body and the closing of a sample request letter.

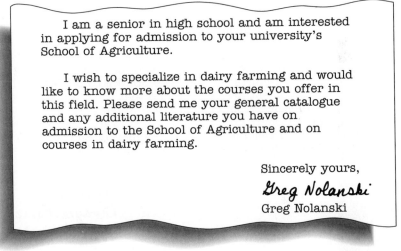

I am a senior in high school and am interested in applying for admission to your university's School of Agriculture.

I wish to specialize in dairy farming and would like to know more about the courses you offer in this field. Please send me your general catalogue and any additional literature you have on admission to the School of Agriculture and on courses in dairy farming.

Sincerely yours,

Greg Nolanski

Greg Nolanski

When you are writing a request or order letter, follow these guidelines.

1. State your request clearly.
2. If you're asking for something to be sent to you, enclose a self-addressed, stamped envelope.
3. For a special request, make sure your request is reasonable and that it's submitted well in advance.
4. If you're ordering something, include all important details, such as the size, style, and price. Include information about the magazine or paper in which you saw the item advertised. Compute correctly if there are costs involved, including any necessary sales tax or shipping charges.

Complaint or Adjustment Letters

A ***complaint*** or ***adjustment letter*** is written to point out errors that require attention and correction.

Here is a sample adjustment letter.

8511 Gallo Ct.
Evans, CO 80620
April 4, 1993

Customer Service Dept.
Haley Clothing Co.
535 7th Ave.
Orange, CA 92667

Dear Sir or Madam:

On May 25, I sent an order to you that included requests for several items of clothing, including two red T-shirts, No. 86, size 36, @ $10.00. When the shipment arrived, I found that these shirts were missing from the package.

I assume that this was merely an oversight and would appreciate your sending the two shirts as soon as possible.

Sincerely,
Dwayne Patterson
Dwayne Patterson

When you are writing a complaint or adjustment letter, follow these suggestions.

1. Register your complaint as soon as possible.
2. Explain exactly what is wrong. Necessary information might include
   - what product or service you ordered or expected
   - why you are not satisfied (damaged goods, incorrect merchandise, bad service)
   - how you were affected (lost time or money)
   - what you want the company to do about it
3. Keep the tone of your letter calm and courteous.

Appreciation or Commendation Letters

An ***appreciation*** or ***commendation letter*** compliments or expresses appreciation to a person, a group, or an organization. For example, you might write to a restaurant, telling how much you liked the food or the service and encouraging the management to keep up the good work.

Here is a sample appreciation letter.

725 Ironwood Tr.
Janesville, WI 53545
April 10, 1993

College-Bound Seniors
26 Riverside Court, Suite 112
Madison, WI 53701

Dear Dr. Powell:

I would like to thank you on behalf of the Senior class at Stokewell High School for the very informative and eye-opening college choices seminar that you conducted at our school yesterday.

Many of us did not realize how many decisions there are to make in college. I'm sure that we as a class are now better informed and more prepared to choose our classes, majors, and minors. We hope you continue your good work.

Thanks again,
Sandra Chin
Sandra Chin
Senior Class Secretary
Stokewell High School
Janesville, WI 53545

Letters of Application

The purpose of a letter of application is to provide a possible employer or a selection committee with information that will convince them that you are a good candidate for a position. The position you are applying for may be membership in an organization, a scholarship, a job, or a similar type of position.

Here is a sample of an application letter.

4693 Ketcham Drive
Pocatello, ID 83214
June 12, 1993

Personnel Director
Winslow Machine Tools
96 Harbison Street
Pocatello, ID 83201

Dear Personnel Director:

Please consider me an applicant for the mechanic position advertised in Sunday's Journal.

I am a recent graduate of Central High School. My course of study has included mechanics and shop classes. I have had experience with most types of modern mechanical equipment.

Last summer I worked for my uncle, Frank Castellano, at his machine shop, repairing all types of machinery from lawn mowers to stock car engines. I was personally responsible for one large project--rebuilding a vintage motorcycle--which required hand-tooling and fitting many ancient parts.

I will be glad to supply you with the names of references who can tell you about my qualifications for this position.

I am available for a personal interview at your convenience. My telephone number is 936-7845. I can be reached most evenings after 5:00 p.m.

Very truly yours,

Marty Castellano

Marty Castellano

RESOURCES

Remember the following points when you write a letter of application.

1. Identify the job or position you are applying for. Tell how you heard about it.
2. Depending on the position, you might include
   - your age, grade in school, or grade-point average
   - your experience; or your activities, awards, and honors
   - personal qualities or characteristics that make you a good choice for the position
   - the date or times you are available

3. Offer to provide references. Your references should include two or three responsible adults (usually not relatives) who have agreed to recommend you. Be prepared to supply their addresses and telephone numbers.

The Personal Résumé

A ***résumé*** is a summary of your background and experience often used as part of an application for a position. When you apply for a job, it is common to submit a résumé along with your letter of application. There are many different ways to arrange the information on a résumé. Whatever arrangement you select, be sure your résumé looks neat and businesslike.

A SAMPLE RÉSUMÉ

STEPHANIE J. HOSKIN

4974 Kenton Rd.
Brecksville, OH 44141
Telephone: (216) 491-9263

EDUCATION:	Tecumseh High School, graduated 1992 Major studies: College preparatory courses, business, and accounting Grade point average: 3.3 (B)	
WORK EXPERIENCE:	Summer 1991	Volunteer office worker Milltown Art Museum Brook Park, OH
	Summer 1990	Junior lifeguard YWCA Broadview Heights, OH
SKILLS:	Shorthand:	110 words a minute
	Typing:	60 words a minute
	Business Machines: dictating, calculating, and duplicating machines	
	Extracurricular activities: Secretary, Student Council of Tecumseh High; member, Junior Jaycees	
REFERENCES:	Dr. Mary Sue Wellston, Principal Tecumseh High School Brecksville, OH	(216) 491-1195
	Micah Goldfarb, Teacher Tecumseh High School Brecksville, OH	(216) 491-0643
	Ms. Glenda Ramirez, Director Milltown Art Museum Brecksville, OH	(216) 491-9543

Addressing an Envelope

You should send a business letter in a plain business envelope. Write or type your name and address in the upper left-hand corner of the envelope. Then write or type the name and address of the person or organization to whom you are writing (the addressee) just to the right of an imaginary line in the center of the envelope. The addressee's name and address should exactly match the inside address on the letter. Use the two-letter postal service abbreviations for state names, and be sure to include correct ZIP codes.

Completing Printed Forms and Applications

As you begin applying to colleges or applying for jobs, you'll be asked to fill out a variety of forms and applications. The information on your form or application can be processed by the person or organization if you fill the form out neatly, completely, and legibly.

GUIDELINES FOR COMPLETING FORMS

1. Always read the entire form to make sure you understand exactly what items of information you are being asked to supply.
2. Type neatly or print legibly, using a pen or pencil as directed.
3. Include all information requested. If a question does not apply to you, write *N.A.* or *not applicable* instead of leaving the space blank.
4. Keep the form neat and clean. Avoid crossouts.
5. When you have completed the form, proofread it carefully and correct any spelling, grammar, punctuation, or factual errors.
6. Submit the form to the correct person or mail it to the correct address.

APPLICATION FOR COLLEGE ADMISSION

PERSONAL INFORMATION

1. Last name *Yee* First *Elizabeth* Middle *Lillian* 2. Phone *(617) 995-6929*
3. Weight *110* 4. Height *5' 2"* 5. Birthdate *7/10/76*
6. Address *812 Ashland Drive, Bedford, Massachusetts, 01730*
7. Siblings:

Name	Age	Current Occupation
Robert Yee	*12*	*Student*

8. Father's occupation *Teacher (4th Grade)* 9. Mother's occupation *School Nurse*
10. Will you apply for financial aid? *Yes*

ACADEMIC INFORMATION

11. List schools attended (Grades 7–12)

Name	City, State, ZIP	Dates	Principal/Head
Bedford High School	*Bedford, MA 01730*	*9/83–Now*	*Dr. Albert Souza*
Altamonte Jr. High	*Boston, MA 02108*	*9/80–6/83*	*Mrs. Susan Yamoto*

12. Prizes, honors, awards *Science Fair prize, '91, '92*
13. Rank in high school graduating class *6th in class of 612*
14. If you have been out of high school for more than one year, describe your activities, employment, classes and colleges attended *N/A*
15. Possible major *Chemistry* 16. Career goal *Medical Research*

EXTRACURRICULAR ACTIVITIES

17. List school, community, and church activities

Activity	Achievements
Piano Accompanist for school	*Accompanied choir for 4 years; toured New England, Feb. '91*
Volunteer Coordinator at Elmwood Children's Home	*Coordinated student volunteers at placement home for children waiting for foster care*

18. Other activities, hobbies, interests *Reading; Music (piano lessons for 11 years); Computers and computer programming; Hiking ; Pets; Babysitting*
19. Which three books that you read during the past year most impressed you? List title and author. *Foundation by Isaac Asimov; Cosmos by Carl Sagan; In Search of Schrodinger's Cat by John Gribbin*

EMPLOYMENT EXPERIENCE

20. List jobs held, including part-time work

Employer	Type of Work	Hours Weekly	Dates
Newton Public Lib.	*Library Aide*	*10 (approx.)*	*Summers '91–'92*
Mrs. Carla Perez	*Babysitting*	*6*	*Every Saturday, '92*

RECOMMENDATIONS

21. List the names and addresses of three people (including one teacher and one employer)
Mr. Alonzo Hernandez, Head, Science Dept. Bedford H.S., Bedford, MA 01730
Mr. Robert Ryan, Supervisor, Children's Room, Newton Public Library, Newton, MA 02175
Mr. Sylvia Brown, 5960 Arlington St., Boston, MA 02116

THE INFORMATION ON THIS APPLICATION IS TRUE AND COMPLETE

Date *12/1/88* Signature *Elizabeth M. Yee*

RESOURCES

Writing Informal or Social Letters

Sometimes the most appropriate way to communicate with people you know personally is through the mail. When you want to thank someone formally, congratulate someone for an accomplishment, send an invitation, or respond to an invitation, you should write a personal letter.

Personal letters are much less formal in style than business letters. For example, social letters don't include an inside address and most use the modified block form.

Thank-you Letters. The purpose of a thank-you letter is to express appreciation for special effort or a gift. Try to include more than just "thank you." Say how the person's gift or efforts were particularly helpful or appreciated.

Invitations. An informal invitation should contain specific information about a planned event, such as the occasion, the time and place, and any other details your guests need to know.

Letters of Regret. If you have been invited to a party or a specific social function and will be unable to attend, it's polite to send a letter of regret. A written reply is especially appropriate if you were sent a written invitation with the letters *R.S.V.P.* (in French, these letters are an abbreviation for "please reply").

EXERCISE 1 **Writing Business Letters**

Write any two of the following business letters. Use either the block or the modified block form, and place the six parts of the business letter correctly on the page. Use your own return address and today's date, but make up any other information you need to write the letters.

1. Write a letter to any company you want, ordering at least three items advertised in a magazine or newspaper. Order more than one of some of these articles.
2. Write a letter of adjustment to a business firm, asking why you have received a bill for an order for which you have already paid. Give all important dates and details.
3. Write a letter to your favorite magazine, identifying a feature that you find particularly pleasing. State the reasons why you especially enjoy this feature.
4. Write a letter of complaint or appreciation to an elected official responding to this person's position on an issue. Explain why you agree or disagree. Request a response.
5. From your local newspaper, select a help-wanted advertisement and answer it with a letter of application.

EXERCISE 2 **Writing a Résumé**

Choose a job that interests you. Then write a personal résumé that shows you are qualified for such a position. Include a short cover letter that explains how you heard about the job and requests a personal interview. Proofread the final version.

EXERCISE 3 **Completing Forms**

Choose one of the following activities.

1. Complete an auto insurance application form, using information about your car or a car owned by a friend or relative.
2. Locate a mail-order catalog and select several items to order. Complete the mail-order form in the catalog, indicating the items you have chosen.
3. Complete an application form for employment with a company.

EXERCISE 4 **Writing Social Correspondence**

Write a personal letter for one of the following situations.

1. Write a letter of regret explaining that you will not be able to attend an event to which you have been invited.
2. Write a thank-you letter expressing appreciation for a gift or favor you have received.
3. Write an invitation letter for an event you are planning.

39 Studying and Test Taking

Using Skills and Strategies

Throughout your life, you will need strategies to help you analyze, evaluate, and apply information for a variety of purposes. The ability to handle information effectively is an important skill that you will need to use in many different situations, both within and beyond the classroom.

RESOURCES

Implementing a Study Plan

Productive study habits are crucial to success. To help you improve your study routine, here are a few methods that have proven to be effective.

- keep track of your assignments and due dates
- select a time and place to study that is free from distractions
- divide large assignments into manageable steps and then schedule time to complete each step
- allow a reasonable amount of study time to complete each of your assignments

Strengthening Study Skills

Reading and Understanding

You read many different types of materials, but how you read these materials depends on your purpose for reading them.

READING RATES ACCORDING TO PURPOSE		
READING RATE	PURPOSE	EXAMPLE
Scanning	Reading for specific details or points of reference	Hunting for the atomic number of einsteinium in the periodic table
Skimming	Reading for main points	The night before an economics test, studying your notes on how to calculate compound interest
Reading for mastery	Reading to understand and remember	Reading the manual for your printer to find out how to load the paper

RESOURCES

Writing to Learn

Writing is a part of learning; it helps you clarify thoughts, react to ideas, note observations, and evaluate plans. Writing also helps you analyze and recall information. Different types of writing help you in various learning situations.

TYPE OF WRITING	PURPOSE	EXAMPLE
Freewriting	To help you focus your thoughts and identify key ideas	Writing notes on the Industrial Revolution before writing an essay

(continued)

TYPE OF WRITING	PURPOSE	EXAMPLE
Autobiographical Dictionaries	To help you examine the meaning of important events in life	Recording your impressions of your visit to a prospective college
Diaries, Autobiographical Notes	To help you recall your impressions and express your feelings	Writing about an argument and reconciliation with your best friend
Journals and Learning Logs	To help you record your observations, descriptions, solutions, and questions	Writing down each step in the process of an experiment on wave motion
	To help you present a problem, analyze it, and propose a solution	Writing ideas for improving your school to discuss at a planning meeting

Using a Word Processor as a Writing Tool

Since it eliminates time-consuming tasks, the word processor makes it easier to produce a final document. In addition, word processing helps you throughout the writing process.

Prewriting. It's easy to freewrite and brainstorm ideas on the computer. Later you can fill in notes or outlines without having to retype them.

Writing First Drafts. With a little practice, you can compose your thoughts fluently and rapidly on the word processor.

Evaluating. The word processor is great for analyzing work in progress. If you save a copy of your document, you can insert and delete text freely. If you later decide that you don't like the changes, your original document is retrievable from its original file.

Revising. A word processor can be a great timesaver when you're revising. You can easily insert, move, or delete text wherever you wish. When you're finished, you can print out a clean copy.

Proofreading. Many word processors have a spell-checking function that can help you find spelling errors. You may also find a search-and-replace function that you can use to correct a specific type of error wherever it occurs throughout a document.

Writing the Final Version. When you have made all of your revisions and have proofread and made all of your corrections, you can quickly produce one or multiple final copies on your printer.

Using the SQ3R Method

Francis Robinson, an educational psychologist, developed a study method called *SQ3R*. This study method is made up of five simple steps.

S *Survey* the entire study assignment to get an overview of the material. Read all titles, headings, subheadings, and terms in boldface and italic type. Also, look over any charts, outlines, and summaries.

Q *Question* yourself. What should you know after completing your reading? Make a list of questions to be answered. Also, look at any questions provided at the end of a reading selection.

R *Read* the material carefully. Think of answers to your questions as you read.

R *Recite* in your own words the answers to each of the questions that you identified earlier.

R *Review* the material by rereading quickly, looking over the questions, and recalling the answers.

REFERENCE NOTE: For study techniques to help with listening skills, see pages 998–1000.

Interpreting and Analyzing Information

Finding the Main Idea

To get the meaning out of a passage you are reading, you will need to be able to identify how the information it contains fits together. An important first step is to determine the main idea of the selection.

Stated Main Idea. The main idea of a passage is often stated directly in one or two specific sentences that express the thesis of the passage.

Implied Main Idea. At times the main idea of a passage is not stated directly but is implied, or suggested, instead. In this case, you will need to find the main idea by analyzing all of the supporting details of the passage to decide what overall meaning these details express.

HOW TO FIND THE MAIN IDEA

- Identify the overall topic. (What subject is the passage, as a whole, about?)
- Identify what the passage reveals about the topic. (What is the real message of the passage, when it is taken as a whole?)
- Sum up the meaning of the passage in one clear sentence.
- Review the passage. (If you have correctly identified the main idea, all of the other details included in the passage will support it.)

REFERENCE NOTE: For additional information on finding the main idea, whether stated or implied, see pages 64–66.

Recognizing Relationships Among Details

After you have identified the main idea of a reading passage, the next step is to identify the supporting details and analyze how these items of information are related to each other and to the main idea.

FINDING RELATIONSHIPS AMONG DETAILS	
Identify specific details.	What details answer specific questions such as *Who? What? When? Where? Why?* and *How?* (*5W-How?* questions)?
Distinguish between fact and opinion.	What information can be proved true or false? (facts) What statements express a personal belief or attitude? (opinions)
Identify similarities and differences.	Are there any details that are shown to be similar to or different from one another?
Understand cause and effect.	Do prior events impact or affect later events?
Identify an order of organization.	In what kind of order are the details arranged—chronological order, spatial order, order of importance, or any other organizing pattern?

Reading Passage

During the sixteenth and seventeenth centuries, Europeans experienced a dramatic change in their ideas about the universe. Today, historians call this period the Scientific Revolution.

Although the new worldview in Europe during the 1500s and 1600s had its roots in the work of scientists and philosophers during the Middle Ages, the kind of science performed by Nicolaus Copernicus, Galileo Galilei, and Isaac Newton was strikingly new. Medieval science had relied on natural, individual observation and blind faith to authority, but the new science differed from the older science in three unique ways.

Sample Analysis

DETAIL: Where and when did the Scientific Revolution take place?

ANSWER: *It occurred in Europe during the sixteenth and seventeenth centuries.*

DETAIL: What were the central beliefs of medieval philosophers?

ANSWER: *Medieval philosophers relied on individual observation and blind faith in authority.*

First, this new science was very methodical. Exact observations were made about the universe through mathematical reasoning. Because mathematics is rigorously logical, there followed careful attention to what we now call the scientific method: stating an experimental aim, forming a hypothesis, conducting an experiment, gathering the results, and forming conclusions.

Second, the new science relied upon technology. The telescope, for example, let scientists see the cosmos in the kind of detail that, in turn, allowed mathematical descriptions to be made. The role played by the printing press is also very important. By 1500, there were over a thousand printers in Europe, who had published several million books. This spread of knowledge through books allowed scientists to explain their work and compare it with the work of others.

Third, the new science was conducted in communities dedicated to learning. By the end of the seventeenth century, universities had established centers for scientific study. Learned societies were also formed by governments. The government of England formed the Royal Society in 1660, and the French government set up the Academy of Sciences in 1666. Through the new technology of printing, these societies also established journals to circulate information on scientific discoveries. Both the French *Journal des Savants* and the English *Philosophical Transactions* began in 1665.

Nicolaus Copernicus (1473–1543) may be said to have begun the movement with publication of his book *On the Revolutions of the Heavenly Spheres.* This Pol-

FACT: Who were the leaders of the Scientific Revolution?
ANSWER: *They were Nicolaus Copernicus, Galileo Galilei, and Isaac Newton.*

OPINION: What is the author's opinion of the relationship of science during the Middle Ages to science during the 1500s and 1600s?
ANSWER: *While the author believes that the Scientific Revolution was influenced by medieval science, the author also believes that medieval science was limited by natural observation and blind faith in authority.*

SIMILARITY: What is the similarity between the telescope and the printing press?
ANSWER: *Both are technologies that influenced scientists.*

DIFFERENCE: What is a main difference between medieval science and science of the 1500s and 1600s?
ANSWER: *Medieval scientists worked individually; new scientists worked in communities.*

ish astronomer and mathematician challenged the widespread view that the sun revolved around the earth. Instead, he proposed that the sun was the center of the universe and that all the planets, including the earth, revolved around it. Because it was feared that Copernicus's ideas were controversial, the publication of his book was delayed until his death.

Galileo Galilei (1564–1642), an Italian mathematician, was the first scientist to make use of the telescope. He is best known for illustrating that the universe can be understood by mathematical reasoning. Many contemporaries of Galileo thought that his ideas were disturbing and too controversial; a number of his fellow scientists condemned his work.

Isaac Newton (1642–1727) is best known for his work *Mathematical Principles of Natural Philosophy* (1687). An English mathematician, Newton began investigations that led him to believe that the universe was a uniform machine that operated according to mechanistic, regular laws. His worldview greatly influenced scientific belief until the German scientist Albert Einstein (1879–1955) proposed the theory of relativity in the twentieth century.

CAUSE: Why was the publication of Copernicus's book delayed until his death?
ANSWER: *Because it was feared that Copernicus's ideas were too controversial.*

EFFECT: What was the effect of Newton's work?
ANSWER: *His view of the universe predominated until Einstein introduced his theory of relativity in the twentieth century.*

ORGANIZATION: Why are Copernicus, Galileo, and Newton profiled at the end of the passage?
ANSWER: *The tenets of the Scientific Revolution are discussed first, then the major contributors (logical order).*

RESOURCES

Applying Reasoning Skills

You draw conclusions and make inferences by evaluating, interpreting, and analyzing the facts and evidence presented in a reading passage. A ***valid conclusion*** is one firmly grounded in evidence or logic. Based on your analysis of the reading passage on pages 1073–1075, you might make the following conclusions or inferences about the Scientific Revolution.

Controversial ideas were not often published in Copernicus's time. (Evidence: Copernicus's book was not published until after his death because of its controversial ideas.)

Newton's view of the universe working as a machine was eventually proven to be limited. (Evidence: The passage states that Newton's views influenced science only until Einstein offered his theory of relativity, meaning that Einstein's ideas displaced Newton's because Einstein's theory was an improvement over Newton's.)

An ***invalid conclusion*** is one that is not consistent with the evidence presented. For example, it would be invalid to conclude that the Scientific Revolution meant that Europe led the world in scientific knowledge. The passage speaks only of Europe; it omits mention of technology achieved by civilizations such as those in the Middle East and China.

HOW TO DRAW CONCLUSIONS AND MAKE INFERENCES	
Gather all the evidence.	What facts or details have you learned about the subject?
Evaluate the evidence.	Do you know enough to make a few observations based on facts or reasonable assumptions?
Make appropriate connections.	What can you reasonably conclude or infer from the evidence you have gathered and evaluated?

Analyzing Graphics and Illustrations

Reading materials frequently include graphics, such as diagrams, maps and charts. Graphics visually organize bodies of information. For example, look at the following chart.

This chart quickly shows you a comparison of the various types of television programs viewed in several countries.

Suppose you were an advertiser for an international company selling a new soft drink and that your market researchers had determined that ads for this type of soft drink have the most favorable impact on viewers of entertainment programs. One look at the graph would show you that Canada and the United States are the countries whose viewers see the greatest percentage of entertainment programs.

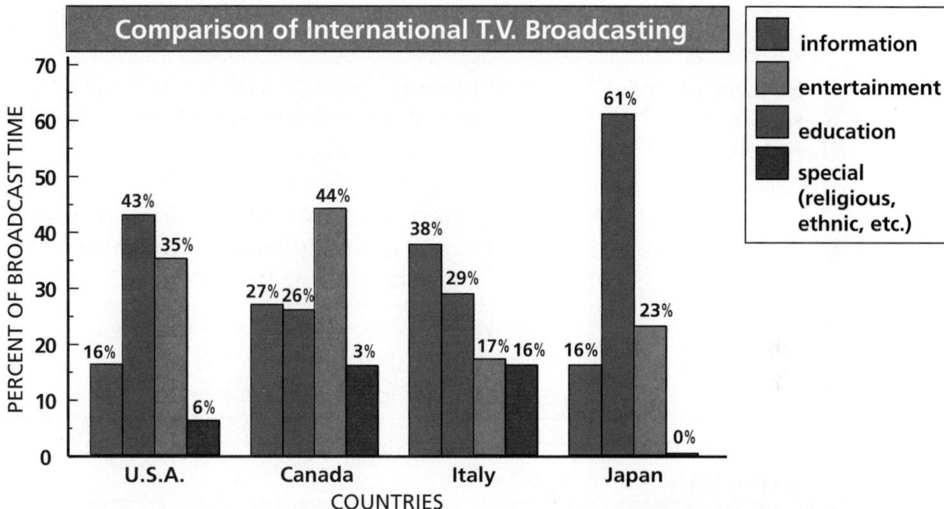

What if you had a product you wanted to sell to viewers of educational programs? As the graph shows, Japan's viewers see the greatest percentage of educational programs. Where should you try to sell ads that appeal to viewers of information programs? According to the graph, Italy should be your target market.

Graphs such as the one shown, therefore, help you make decisions more easily because you can quickly see complex relationships between items of data.

Applying Study Methods

There are several study skills and methods for organizing and processing information. Among the most common are

- taking notes
- classifying
- organizing information visually
- outlining
- paraphrasing
- summarizing
- writing a précis
- memorizing

Taking Notes

If you take careful notes, they can be a valuable tool for remembering what you hear or read. Notes also organize your information for studying, taking tests, and writing research papers.

HOW TO TAKE STUDY NOTES	
Recognize and record main points.	Set off main points as headings in your notes. ■ In a lecture, key words and phrases such as *major* or *most important* and similar clues may indicate key points. ■ In a textbook, chapter headings and subheadings are usually reliable indicators of main ideas.
Summarize.	Don't record every detail. Summarize or abbreviate, using single words or phrases to record key ideas and supporting details.
Note important examples.	A few vivid examples can help you recall the main ideas.

The following example shows study notes about the reading passage on pages 1073–1075. Notice that the main points in the passage are listed in groups. Then each of these groups of main points is given a heading that identifies the key idea.

Characteristics of Scientific Revolution

- *mathematical and methodical (scientific method)*
- *relied on technology—telescope (helped observation), printing press (spread knowledge)*
- *conducted in communities—ideas exchanged in universities, learned societies (English—Royal Society, French—Academy of Sciences); journals established—Journal des Savants (1665, France), Philosophical Transactions (1665, England)*

RESOURCES

Major Figures of the Scientific Revolution

- Nicolas Copernicus (1473-1543), Polish
  wrote On the Revolutions of the Heavenly Spheres; proposed sun as center of universe; ideas controversial (book not published until he died)
- Galileo Galilei (1564-1642), Italian
  first to use telescope; showed universe describable through mathematics
- Isaac Newton (1642-1727), English
  wrote Mathematic Principles of Natural Philosophy; theory: universe a machine with regular laws (eventually replaced by Einstein's theory of relativity)

Classifying

Classifying is a method of organizing items by arranging them into categories or groups. When you group these items, you are identifying the relationships or patterns among the various items.

EXAMPLE What characteristics do each of the following people have in common?

Robert Browning; Elizabeth Barrett Browning; Matthew Arnold; Alfred, Lord Tennyson; William Wordsworth; Samuel Taylor Coleridge

ANSWER All of these people were British poets who lived during the nineteenth century.

You also use classifying when you identify patterns. For example, look at the relationship between the following sequence of numbers.

What's the next number in the sequence below?

48 53 43 58 38 ____?____

ANSWER To the first number (48), *5* is added to produce 53. From this number, *10* is subtracted to produce 43. To this number, *15* is added to produce 58; then *20* is subtracted to produce 38. The pattern is to add, then subtract, by increments of five. Therefore, to produce the next number in the series, you should add *25* to produce *63.*

Organizing Information Visually

The techniques of visually organizing information are valuable as study methods; you can use them to make the information in some types of written passages easier to understand. These techniques include charting, mapping, or diagraming. For example, the passage that follows compares and contrasts the storytelling elements of film and fiction.

The storytelling elements of fiction are also found in film. Both fiction and film, for example, use plot to move a story along; in both media the action rises, builds to a climax, and is finally resolved. Characterization is another shared element; both fiction and film show characters who change over time or whose personalities and relationships to one another affect the action of the story. Theme is also used in film and fiction; the central idea of the story is expressed as clearly in a short story by Doris Lessing as it is in a film by Orson Welles. Setting, too, is a common element.

Film and fiction also share similarities in structure; in both media a completed work is made up of smaller, cohesive structural units. A shot, the basic unit of a film, can be compared to a sentence, the basic meaningful unit of writing. Just as paragraphs link groups of related sentences, so scenes link up various related shots. Sequences in a film may be compared to the chapters of a book. Taken as a whole, the completed book may therefore be compared to the final version of a film.

However, because film relies on moving, visual images, the techniques it uses are different from those of printed, verbal fiction. For instance, fiction often relies on the author's point of view, the relationship the author creates to his or her fictional world. In film, however, the relationship of author to idea is often conveyed by the way one moving image is joined to the next in editing: the fade, dissolve, wipe, and cut help the viewer understand the attitude the filmmaker has toward the subject. In addition, while atmosphere in a work of fiction must be conveyed through verbal description, filmmakers use technical devices such as lighting, camera angle, focus, and a variety of special lenses to give a motion picture its mood.

It would be difficult to read this passage and recall each detail. However, if you organize the information visually in a chart such as the one that follows, you will find the material easier to understand and remember.

FICTION	FILM
Storytelling Elements plot characterization theme setting	Storytelling Elements same same same same
Structural Parts sentence paragraph chapter book	Structural Parts shot scene sequence film
Techniques verbal point of view expressed through language atmosphere achieved by language	Techniques visual point of view achieved by editing: fade, dissolve, wipe, cut atmosphere achieved by technical devices: lighting, camera angle, focus, lenses

Outlining

An ***outline*** records only the most important information and ideas. In addition, an outline puts key ideas together, showing their relationship to one another and their order of importance.

However, if you are taking lecture notes, you may want to use an informal outline form. This method can help you to organize information quickly. (See the sample notes shown on pages 1078–1079.)

FORMAL OUTLINE FORM

1. Main Point
   A. Supporting Point
      1. Detail
         a. Information or detail

INFORMAL OUTLINE FORM

Main Idea
  Supporting detail
  Supporting detail
  Supporting detail

Paraphrasing

A ***paraphrase*** is a restatement of someone's ideas in your own words. A paraphrase can help you analyze the meaning of a poem or complex prose passage. Since a paraphrase is often approximately the same length as the original, this technique is not often used for long passages of writing.

Paraphrasing a Literary Selection. This type of paraphrase is intended to express in simpler terms the meaning of a work that is written in complex language, such as a poem. For example, you might be asked to paraphrase a poem like the following.

Sonnet 25
by William Shakespeare

Let those who are in favor with their stars
Of public honor and proud titles boast,
Whilst I, whom fortune of such triumph bars,
Unlooked for joy in that I honor most.
Great princes' favorites their fair leaves spread
But as the marigold at the sun's eye,
And in themselves their pride lies burièd,
For at a frown they in their glory die.

> The painful warrior famousèd for fight,
> After a thousand victories once foiled,
> Is from the book of honor razèd quite,
> And all the rest forgot for which he toiled.
>   Then happy I, that love and am beloved
>   Where I may not remove nor be removed.

As an example, here is a possible paraphrase of this poem.

> Although some people enjoy renown and recognition, the speaker has neither. Instead, the speaker hints at a quiet enjoyment of something valued highly. The speaker says that, after all, those popular at court enjoy only temporary regard; without noble favor, they close up like a flower without sunlight. Royal disfavor withers them. Even the hero of a thousand victories needs only one defeat to lose the prestige for which he fought so long. Therefore, the speaker finds fulfillment in love, which is a shared happiness that—once present—cannot be destroyed.

Paraphrasing Prose. Sometimes you may need to paraphrase a portion of an essay, an article, or another type of prose work. For instance, in writing an essay, you may need to paraphrase another person's ideas in order to support your opinion.

For example, here is an excerpt from "Self-Reliance," an essay by Ralph Waldo Emerson.

> What I must do is all that concerns me, not what the people think. This rule, equally arduous in actual and in intellectual life, may serve for the whole distinction between greatness and meanness. It is the harder, because you will always find those who think they know what is your duty better than you know it. It is easy in the world to live after the world's opinion; it is easy in solitude to live after our own; but the great man is he who in the midst of the crowd keeps with perfect sweetness the independence of solitude.

The following shows how you might paraphrase this passage and incorporate your paraphrase into a composition.

Nonconformists of all types have always attracted a certain approval in American culture. The heroes of American songs, legends, novels, and movies are typically the strong, independent types who persist in doing things their way despite all opposition. Ralph Waldo Emerson stated the credo of the rugged individualist in his essay "Self-Reliance." Emerson proclaimed his conviction that he alone was responsible for doing what he thought was right, not what everyone else believed was right. This obligation, he felt, was true both for real life and the life of the mind; he said this quality was the single most important means of differentiating between superior and inferior persons. Emerson admitted that it is difficult to hold to your own when you are surrounded by others who think they know better than you. He said that when you are among others, conformity is the simplest course of action; when you are alone, it is not difficult to do as you think best. However, only truly remarkable persons are able to live constantly surrounded by others and yet follow their own unique vision happily and pleasantly, as if they were alone.

HOW TO PARAPHRASE

1. Read the entire selection to get the overall meaning before you begin writing your paraphrase. Look up any unfamiliar words or phrases.
2. Identify the main idea of the selection. Keep it in mind while you write your paraphrase.
3. Identify the speaker in fictional material and poetry. (Is the poet or a narrator speaking?)
4. Write your paraphrase in your own words, using complete sentences and standard paragraph form.
5. Review the selection to be sure that your paraphrase expresses the essential ideas of the original.

Summarizing

Summarizing is restating the main ideas of written or spoken material in condensed form. A summary can help you record the basic meaning of a selection you are studying. It can also help you to think critically about what you have read, since writing a summary forces you to analyze material, identify the most important ideas, and then select ideas important enough to be included in the summary, eliminating less significant ideas.

HOW TO SUMMARIZE

1. Review the material carefully, identifying main ideas and supporting details.
2. Condense the material. Focus only on key ideas, deleting unnecessary details. Write a sentence in your own words about each main idea.
3. Use your list of main ideas to write your summary in paragraph form. Add transitional words as necessary to connect the ideas.
4. Revise your summary. Make sure that the information is expressed clearly and that you have remained faithful to the original ideas.

Here is a sample summary of the article on pages 436–439.

If you observe elephants, you sometimes see whole herds responding to something invisible and inaudible. The answer to this mystery may lie in an aerial throbbing often felt in the vicinity of elephants, a thrumming similar to one accompanying the lowest sound on a pipe organ. This throbbing may signal the presence of infrasound, sounds too low to be heard by humans. Infrasound can travel long distances unaffected by forests or grasslands. Infrasound communication could explain many previously unexplained actions of elephants.

Writing a Précis

When you write a ***précis,*** you shorten a piece of writing—an article, a chapter, a passage, a report—to its bare essentials. Summarizing skills are used in writing a précis. (See pages 1084–1085.) In addition, there are certain standard practices specifically related to précis writing.

GUIDELINES FOR WRITING A PRÉCIS

1. *Be brief.* A précis is seldom more than a third as long as the material being summarized, often less.
2. *Don't paraphrase.* A paraphrase is often the same length as the original.
3. *Stick to key points.* Cut details and descriptions.
4. *Use your own wording.* Don't just take phrases or sentences from the original.
5. *Be faithful to the author's points and views.* Don't add your own ideas or comments.

Here is a sample paragraph.

What is particularly strange about this new passivity regarding travel is that not so very long ago the reverse was considered to be the norm; once upon a time, flying was a highly participatory activity—as was automobile driving. As recently as sixty years ago, the driver of an ordinary car expected to be intimately involved with the event of driving by means of direct access to the steering wheel, brakes, transmission, and the outside environment. Since then, however, the automobile driver has given up any direct involvement with his or her vehicle in favor of power controls, automatic transmissions, on-board computerized readouts, and sealed-in passenger interiors. Nowadays, only the most adventurous people insist on direct participation in the act of driving by means of sports cars, the last vestige of the old ways. (134 words)

Here are major errors to be avoided in a précis.

COMMON ERRORS IN PRÉCIS-WRITING

TYPE OF ERROR	EXAMPLE
uses words taken directly from original	Until the 1950s, travel by air or auto was a <u>highly participatory activity</u>.

(continued)

COMMON ERRORS IN PRÉCIS-WRITING *(continued)*	
misses the point of the original; emphasizes unimportant points	Makers of modern vehicles have really improved many models by adding devices that make driving much less complicated.
writer of précis injected own ideas	Today, however, most cars insulate their drivers, and that detachment decreases the full enjoyment of travel.

As an example, here is a précis of the paragraph on page 1086 that is an acceptable length and is stated in the writer's own words.

> Detachment from the act of traveling is recent. Until mid-century, air or auto travelers interacted directly with the vehicles and surroundings. Today, however, most cars insulate drivers from direct contact with their machinery or the environment; only the boldest demand hands-on driving, still found in sports cars. (47 words)

Memorizing

When you memorize important information, you are more likely to remember what you need if you practice frequently in short sessions than if you try to cram at the last minute. Use the guidelines in the following chart.

HOW TO MEMORIZE

1. *Condense the information.* Information found in a textbook chapter, for example, can often be outlined, summarized, or condensed.
2. *Rehearse the material in several different ways.* Use several different senses as you commit the material to memory. Write or copy the material so you can see it and use touch and muscle movements. Recite the material aloud or walk back and forth while reciting the material to help "set" it in your mind.

(continued)

HOW TO MEMORIZE *(continued)*

3. *Use memory games.* Use the first letter of each word to form a new word. Make a rhyme or associate the information with some particularly vivid mental image.
4. *Repeat the material.* Recite the material frequently in short sessions.

Improving Test-Taking Skills

Preparing for Different Kinds of Tests

You can improve your performance on all types of tests if you learn various test-taking strategies and prepare carefully. For instance, your attitude is one of the most important factors that affect your performance on a test. If you believe you can do well and know that you have prepared as well as you can, you are more likely to concentrate your attention on doing well and focus on the test questions. It's common to feel somewhat anxious before a big test; however, you can learn to convert your nervous energy into concentrated attention and excellence in performance on the test.

Kinds of Tests

Classroom Tests. The typical classroom test is intended to measure your ability to use important academic skills or to show your knowledge of particular academic subjects. For example, in a Spanish class, your teacher might give you a test to see how well you have learned to conjugate the list of thirty irregular verbs that you were supposed to have covered in an assigned chapter of your textbook.

Frequently, there are a variety of types of test questions found on classroom tests. For example, your teacher might prepare a test made up of thirty true/false questions worth three points each and an essay question worth ten points. There are any number of combinations of test questions and scoring methods that may be used.

No matter the number or the type of questions, the purpose of classroom tests is always the same: to assess how much you know about a particular subject you have studied or to evaluate your ability to use a specific skill you have practiced. Thus, the best way to prepare for a typical classroom test is to be sure that you are familiar with the assigned material or that you have practiced the skill until you are proficient at it before it is time to take the test. If you review and use the study skills outlined earlier in this chapter, you can generally improve your performance on ordinary classroom tests.

Standardized Tests. On standardized tests, your score is evaluated according to a "standard" or "norm" which has been compiled from the scores of a great number of other students who have taken the same test. Some types of standardized tests may be developed by specific school districts or by your particular state. The best-known standardized tests are those that are given to numerous students across the United States:

- the *National Merit Scholars Qualifying Test (NMSQT)*
- the *Scholastic Aptitude Test (SAT-I Reasoning Test)*
- the *Scholastic Aptitude Test (SAT-II Subject Test)*
- the *American College Testing Program (ACT)*

Among these examples of the most common standardized tests, there are two basic types of tests administered: aptitude and achievement tests.

TYPES OF STANDARDIZED TESTS	
Aptitude (or Reasoning) Tests	▪ intended to evaluate basic skills or reasoning abilities that are needed in various general areas of higher-level study ▪ often cover material and skills you have learned during many years of study (such as verbal expression skills and critical thinking ability)
Achievement (or Academic Subject) Tests	▪ intended to measure knowledge of specific subjects (such as history, literature, sciences, mathematics, or foreign languages)

In general, the best strategies for preparing to take either one of these types of standardized tests include

- keeping up with your schoolwork during the year
- reading and writing often (in addition to regularly assigned material and classwork)
- steadily increasing your vocabulary

A specific suggestion for improving your performance is to become familiar with the types of test questions you will be expected to answer on the test you are scheduled to take. On pages 1091–1103 is information about the types of questions that the best-known standardized tests use when evaluating verbal expression and critical analysis. The following chart contains general suggestions about taking standardized tests.

HOW TO PREPARE FOR STANDARDIZED TESTS

1. *Learn what specific abilities will be tested.* Study any information booklets that are provided. Practice with these or with study guides found in bookstores or libraries.
2. *Know what materials you will need.* On the day of the test, you may need to bring specific materials, such as your official test registration card, number 2 pencils, or lined paper for writing an essay answer.
3. *Determine how the test is evaluated.* If there is no penalty for wrong answers, make your best guess on all questions possible. However, if wrong answers are penalized, make guesses only if you are fairly sure of the correct answer.

Taking Standardized Aptitude Tests

One key reason for standardized aptitude tests is to make a prediction of how likely you are to succeed in going on to a higher educational environment. College work requires large amounts of independent reading and writing, so one of the best indicators of how well you might perform at the college level is your ability to identify and correct problems with verbal expression as well as your ability to analyze and interpret the meaning, purpose, and organization of reading passages.

Kinds of Test Questions

Most test questions can be classified as either limited-response questions or open-response questions.

Limited-Response Questions. Limited-response questions give you a limited number of choices from which you must select the most appropriate answer. These include

- multiple-choice questions
- true/false questions
- matching questions

Open-Response Questions. Open-response questions ask you to provide a written response. These include

- fill-in-the-blank questions
- short answer questions
- essay questions

Tests of Verbal Expression

Standardized tests of verbal expression measure your ability to understand the meaning expressed in written passages and the grammatical correctness or clarity of written expression.

MATERIAL COVERED ON VERBAL EXPRESSION TESTS	
Grammar Questions	You identify the most correct answer, using standard grammar and usage rules. Test items often cover correct use of ■ subject-verb agreement (700–717) ■ principal parts of verbs (766–784) ■ pronouns (726–751)
Punctuation Questions	You identify use of correct punctuation. Test items often cover correct use of ■ end marks and commas (897–925) ■ semicolons and colons (928–933) ■ apostrophes, hyphens, dashes, and parentheses (944–956) ■ quotation marks (935–939)

(continued)

MATERIAL COVERED ON TESTS OF VERBAL EXPRESSION *(continued)*	
Sentence Structure Questions	You demonstrate knowledge of what is (and what is not) a complete sentence. Test items often cover correction of ■ fragments and run-on sentences (555–559) ■ combining sentences (564–580) ■ modifiers (811–829) ■ verb tense (788–799) ■ parallel structure (550–554) ■ transitional words (75–78)
Revision-in-Context Questions	You show appropriate revision of a part or a whole composition. Test items often cover correct use of ■ composition structure (95–123) ■ unity and coherence (71–78) ■ tone (32–34) ■ arranging ideas (35–39)
Rhetorical Strategies Questions	You show an understanding of strategies writers use to express ideas and opinions. Test items often cover ■ strategies of development (79–87) ■ sequence of ideas (35–39) ■ style and tone (31–34)

On the best-known standardized tests, these multiple-choice verbal expression test questions are not presented as isolated questions. Instead, they appear in the context of a reading passage. You are given a sample passage, usually a long paragraph, with several words and phrases underlined and numbered. Then you are given a series of test items related to the passage. You are expected to pick, from among the choices given, the answer that best expresses the meaning, is most grammatically correct, or is most consistent with the style and tone of the passage.

Following is a sample test passage with sample questions.

Sample Verbal Expression Test Passage

Everyone has fears. Young children are often terrified of being left alone in the dark, trembling in their beds at night. With a slightly queasy stomach—a passenger momentarily grips the seat arms as the huge jet lumbers up the runway for a takeoff. A high school student is faced with a three-minute speech in front of classmates. She feels weak-kneed and dry-mouthed as the moment approaches. These fears are normal; everyone has them, or is in danger of suffering such fears, at some time. For most people, however, the moment passes and so do the fear and its accompanying physical reactions. The child grows older and becomes less afraid of the dark; the traveler continues to fly; the student survives the speech.

SAMPLE VERBAL EXPRESSION QUESTIONS	
1. A. NO CHANGE (B.) stomach, a C. stomach. A D. stomach; a	[This is a question about punctuation; it requires you to know which mark of punctuation is appropriate here.]
2. Which of the following is the best revision of the portion of the passage indicated by the number 2? A. fears to be similar to them, B. everyone feels fears like these, (C.) fears that are similar to them, D. fears like them—	[This is a revision-in-context question; it requires you to use revision skills to best express the ideas in the passage.]
3. (A.) NO CHANGE B. did C. does D. would do	[This is a question about grammar; it requires you to know the correct subject-verb agreement.]

(continued)

SAMPLE VERBAL EXPRESSION QUESTIONS *(continued)*	
4. If the fourth and fifth sentences were combined into one sentence, how might it begin? A. A high school student has been faced with a three-minute speech, but. . . . B. A high school student in front of classmates feels. . . . (C.) When a high school student is faced with a three-minute speech in front of classmates, she feels. . . . D. When a high school student feels weak-kneed and dry-mouthed, then she. . . .	[This is a question about sentence structure; it requires you to know how to combine sentences effectively.]
5. This passage might go on to discuss (A.) how to avoid stage fright when giving a speech. B. ways of masking fear. C. the advantages of fears. D. fears that are hard to tame.	[This is a question about rhetorical strategies; you use writing knowledge and skills to make your predictions.]

There are only two basic types of questions used to test verbal expression on the best-known national tests.

MOST COMMON TYPES OF VERBAL EXPRESSION TEST ITEMS	
"NO CHANGE" items	■ give list of suggested revisions of underlined, numbered portions of passage ■ always contain one "NO CHANGE" choice (often printed in capital letters); means that indicated part is correct as is
critical thinking items	■ ask you to analyze and evaluate the passage as a whole ■ ask you to make inferences about portions of a passage as related to the whole

Tests of Critical Reading

Standardized tests may contain a number of limited-response questions that are intended to measure your ability to read and interpret a given piece of writing. Test questions of this type usually require you to look critically at a particular piece of writing to find the meaning, purpose, and organization of the selection. In addition, these questions usually require you to demonstrate your understanding of writing skills by evaluating the effectiveness of the passage in conveying the meaning that was apparently intended by the writer.

Questions used in tests of critical reading cover the following subject matter:

CRITICAL READING

- organization
- evaluation
- interpretation
- synthesis
- vocabulary in context
- style

MATERIAL COVERED ON CRITICAL READING TESTS	
Organization Questions	You identify organizational techniques that are used by the author of a reading passage. Test items often cover identification of ■ the author's use of particular writing strategies (79–87) ■ the main idea of a reading passage (1072–1075) ■ arrangement of specific details used to support the main idea of the passage (67–78) ■ transitional devices that are used to make the passage logical and coherent (74–78) ■ techniques used to conclude the passage (119–121)

(continued)

RESOURCES

MATERIAL COVERED ON CRITICAL READING TESTS *(continued)*	
Evaluation Questions	You analyze and evaluate the effectiveness of specific techniques used by the author of a reading passage. Test items often cover identification of ■ the author's opinion—directly or indirectly expressed—in the passage (1072–1076) ■ the author's intended audience (31–34) ■ the author's tone or point of view (31–34) ■ the author's purpose (31–34)
Interpretation Questions	You draw conclusions or make inferences about the meaning of information presented in a reading passage. Test items often cover identification of ■ ambiguities in information (540–563) ■ conclusions or inferences based on material given in a passage (1076) ■ specific conclusions or inferences that can be drawn about the author or the topic of in a passage (1072–1076)
Synthesis Questions	You show your understanding of how each part of a passage fits together into a whole. Test items often cover interpretation of ■ techniques used to unify deatils (71–73) ■ the cumulative meaning of details in a passage (1072–1076)
Vocabulary in-Context Questions	You infer the meaning of an unfamiliar word by an analysis of its context. Test items often cover determination of ■ the meaning of a passage to learn the definition of a word (523–529) ■ the meaning of an unfamiliar word, using context clues (1043–1044)

(continued)

MATERIAL COVERED ON CRITICAL READING TESTS *(continued)*	
Style Questions	You analyze a passage to evaluate the author's style. Test items often cover ■ the author's style (515–523) ■ the author's voice and tone (517–519) ■ the appropriateness of the author's style for the author's intended audience (31–34)

Here is a sample critical reading test passage with sample questions.

Sample Critical Reading Passage

During the period from 1660 through 1800, Great Britain became convinced of its place as the world's leader. Beginning with the restoration of Charles II to the throne, this period in England's history is best described as a period of authority.

Language itself became submitted to rules during this period. This need to "fix" the English language is best illustrated in the making of the *Dictionary of the English Language* by Samuel Johnson. Guides to the English language had been in existence before Johnson began his project in 1746. These, however, were often little more than lists of hard words. When definitions of common words were supplied, they were often unhelpful. For example, a "horse" was defined in an early dictionary as "a beast well known."

Johnson changed all that, but the task was not an easy one. Renting a house at 17 Gough Square, Johnson began working in the worst of conditions. Supported only by installments from his publisher, Johnson worked on the *Dictionary* with five assistants. Compared to the French Academy's dictionary, which took forty workers fifty-five years to complete (1639–1694), Johnson's dictionary was completed by very few people very quickly.

Balanced on a chair with only three legs, Johnson sat propped against a wall in a room scattered with books. Johnson would read widely from these books, mark quotations illustrating the use of a particular word, and give the book to his assistants so that they could copy the passage on slips of paper. These slips were then pasted in eighty large notebooks under the key words that Johnson had selected. "Fixing" the word by this method, Johnson could record a word's usage and its definition. To help the reader of the *Dictionary* gain a sense of the history of the word, Johnson also arranged the passages chronologically.

How many passages were used? According to Johnson's modern biographer Walter Jackson Bate, the original total number could have been over 240,000. How many words were defined by the lexicographer? Over 40,000 words appeared in two folio volumes in April of 1755. Did Johnson fully understand the enormous task he was undertaking when he began? As he told his contemporary biographer James Boswell, "I knew very well what I was undertaking—and very well how to do it—and have done it very well."

SAMPLE CRITICAL READING QUESTIONS

1. According to the passage, in which order (from earliest to latest) did the following events occur?

I. Johnson published his *Dictionary.*
II. The French Academy's dictionary was published.
III. Johnson rented a house at 17 Gough Square.
IV. Charles II was restored to the throne.

A. II, III, IV, I
(B.) IV, II, III, I
C. IV, I, II, III
D. IV, III, II, I

[This is an organization question; it requires you to identify the time sequence of each of these events and to arrange them in the correct historical time order.]

2. Shortly before the publication of the *Dictionary,* Johnson wrote a famous letter to the noble and wealthy Lord Chesterfield, who had been Johnson's sponsor during the project. The following lines are an excerpt from that letter.

> Seven years, my Lord, have past since I waited in your outward rooms, or was repulsed from your door; during which time I have been pushing on my work through difficulties, of which it is useless to complain, and have brought it, at last, to the verge of publication, without one act of assistance, one word of encouragement, or one smile of favor. Such treatment I did not expect, for I never had a Patron before. . . .

(continued)

RESOURCES

SAMPLE CRITICAL READING QUESTIONS *(continued)*

You could assume that Johnson is

(A.) critical of the lack of assistance from Chesterfield.
B. critical of the conditions under which he had to work.
C. critical of royalty.
D. critical of patrons.

[This is an evaluation question; it requires you to recognize the main point of the original passage and to analyze the second passage to identify which of these main points fits with Johnson's complaint.]

3. The word *fixing* in paragraph three is best taken to mean

A. repairing.
B. correcting.
(C.) standardizing.
D. augmenting.

[This is an interpretation question; you are asked to examine the context of the word noted in order to explain its meaning in the passage.]

4. It can be inferred from the description of Samuel Johnson that he was

(A.) a man who represented the eighteenth century.
B. a man who worked inconsistently.
C. a man who had never worked under impoverished conditions.
D. a man who was jealous and petty.

[This is a synthesis question; after reading in the passage about the details of the eighteenth-century preoccupation with standardization, you can conclude that Johnson's attempt to standardize English was symbolic of the times he lived in.]

5. The word *lexicographer* in paragraph five means

(A.) a maker of dictionaries.
B. a biographer.
C. a scholar.
D. a harmless fellow.

[This is a vocabulary-in-context question; it requires you to examine the context of the passage in which the word appears in order to determine the appropriate definition.]

(continued)

SAMPLE CRITICAL READING QUESTIONS *(continued)*
6. Readers of this passage are likely to describe it as A. informal. B. confessional. (C.) historical. D. biographical. [This is a question of style; you analyze the way the passage is written to determine the type of writing it represents.]

Tests of Critical Analysis

Standardized critical analysis tests measure your ability to use logic and reasoning to evaluate the context of a passage.

MATERIAL COVERED ON CRITICAL ANALYSIS TESTS	
Analogy Questions	■ You analyze the relationship between a pair of words and use reasoning skills to identify a second pair of words that have the same relationship (1051–1053). EXAMPLE: **1.** ANIMAL : CAT :: ________ A. speak : sneeze (B.) room : kitchen C. cold : ice cube D. match : flame
Logic Questions	You analyze the meaning of a sentence or a brief passage to fill in one or more blanks with the most appropriate words given. EXAMPLE: Since Johnson's huge task was so _____, he never did receive fair _____ for compiling the *Dictionary.* A. minimal . . . criticism (B.) herculean . . . remuneration C. banal . . . remuneration D. equivocal . . . compensation

RESOURCES

Essay Tests

An ***essay test*** is intended to measure your ability to express your understanding of selected material in an organized, written form. Writing an essay for a test calls for critical thinking and writing skills. A well-written essay answer must always be a complete response to the question asked and must always contain a sufficient amount of information to demonstrate thorough knowledge of the material.

Essay questions usually ask you to perform specific tasks, each of which is expressed with a verb. Each task requires a specific response that you can prepare for by becoming familiar with the key terms and the kinds of information called for.

ESSAY TEST QUESTIONS

KEY VERB	TASK	SAMPLE QUESTION
analyze	Take something apart to see how each part works.	Analyze the process of amending the U.S. Constitution.
argue	Take a viewpoint on an issue and give reasons to support this opinion.	Argue whether or not students who fail a class should repeat it.
compare	Point out likenesses.	Compare Mel Gibson and Laurence Olivier in *Hamlet.*
contrast	Point out differences.	Contrast the processes of fission and fusion.
define	Give specific details that make something unique.	Define the term *gouache* as an artistic medium.
demonstrate (also illustrate, present, show)	Provide examples to support a point.	Demonstrate the advantages of using a word processor.

(continued)

ESSAY TEST QUESTIONS *(continued)*		
KEY VERB	TASK	SAMPLE QUESTION
describe	Give a picture in words.	Describe the storm scene in *King Lear*.
discuss	Examine in detail.	Discuss the end of the Soviet Union.
explain	Give reasons.	Explain tidal waves.
identify	Point out specific persons, places, things, or characteristics.	Identify the major political figures in the Watergate scandal.
interpret	Give the meaning or significance of something.	Interpret the meaning of the Monroe Doctrine in terms of American foreign policy.
list (also outline, trace)	Give all steps in order or all details about a subject.	List events leading to the invasion of Kuwait by Iraq.
summarize	Give a brief overview of the main points.	Summarize the plot of Bernard Shaw's *Pygmalion.*

When you begin an essay test, scan the questions to see how many answers you are expected to write. If you have a choice between several items, pick those you can answer best. Plan how much time to spend on each answer; then stay on schedule.

Read the question carefully. There may be several parts to the answer.

Pay attention to important terms in the question. Pay attention to each key verb and identify the tasks that you need to accomplish in your essay.

Take a moment to use prewriting strategies. Make notes or a simple outline on scratch paper to help you plan your response.

Evaluate and revise as you write. You will not be able to redraft your whole essay, but you can edit to strengthen your essay.

QUALITIES OF A GOOD ESSAY ANSWER

- The essay is well organized.
- The main ideas and supporting points are clearly presented.
- The sentences are complete and well written.
- There are no distracting errors in spelling, punctuation, or grammar.

Review

EXERCISE 1 Using Study Skills

The following numbered items suggest ways for you to practice using the study skills discussed on pages 1068–1088.

1. In a brief paragraph, identify the circumstances in which you use each of the rates of reading noted on page 1069 to accomplish different purposes.
2. Choose a magazine article or a textbook chapter and use the SQ3R method outlined on page 1071 to list at least five questions. Write brief answers to each one.
3. Write a list of critical reading questions and answers about Isaac Asimov's "The Villain in the Atmosphere" (pages 363–369), using the sample analysis of the reading passage on pages 1073–1075 as a model.
4. Select a chapter from one of your textbooks that you have been assigned as homework and take study notes, using the strategies explained on pages 1078–1079.
5. Find a passage in a textbook, a magazine, or a newspaper that gives information that you can express in graphic form. Using the information and example on pages 1080–1081 as a model, make a visual representation of pertinent information from the passage.

EXERCISE 2 **Paraphrasing a Poem**

Write a paraphrase of "The Bear" by Nina Cassian (page 206), following the guidelines on pages 1082–1084.

EXERCISE 3 **Writing a Précis**

Write a précis of the excerpt by Judith Ortiz Cofer, from *Silent Dancing: A Partial Remembrance of a Puerto Rican Childhood* (pages 140–143), following the guidelines on pages 1085–1087.

EXERCISE 4 **Preparing for Tests of Verbal Expression**

Working in groups, find a passage in a nonfiction book or magazine article, and write a list of questions to test your classmates' verbal expression skills. Use the sample passage and sample questions on pages 1093–1094 as a model. Use the chart on pages 1091–1092 as a reference guide to sections in this textbook that you can consult for suggestions and as a resource to check your answers.

EXERCISE 5 **Preparing for Tests of Critical Reading**

Using the sample test passage on pages 1097–1098, answer the following questions.

1. Which of the following techniques does the author use in concluding the passage?
   A. restating the main idea.
   B. closing with a final, new thought.
   C. asking, then answering rhetorical questions.
   D. referring to the introduction.
2. The word *installments* in the third paragraph may be defined as
   A. ceremonial assignments of personnel.
   B. a series of payments.
   C. a number of permanent fixtures.
   D. a group of chapters of a book.
3. The author's predominant attitude about the subject seems to be
   A. approval of eighteenth-century political change.
   B. criticism of Johnson's writing and research methods.
   C. criticism of Johnson's ideas about language use.
   D. admiration of Johnson's achievements.

4. Which of the following interpretations is suggested by the last paragraph?
   A. Johnson was a self-confident, proud man.
   B. Johnson was a humble, self-effacing man.
   C. Johnson should never have tried his project.
   D. Johnson's health was ruined by the project.

5. This passage most probably has the purpose of
   A. classifying kinds of dictionaries.
   B. entertaining the reader.
   C. expressing the author's personality.
   D. informing the reader.

Glossary of Terms

A

Action verb Expresses physical or mental activity. (See page 612.)

Active voice The voice a verb is in when it expresses an action done *by* its subject. (See page 800.)

Adjective Modifies a noun or a pronoun. (See page 606.)

Adjective clause A subordinate clause that modifies a noun or a pronoun. (See page 676.)

Adjective phrase A prepositional phrase that modifies a noun or a pronoun. (See page 653.)

Adverb Modifies a verb, an adjective, or another adverb. (See page 616.)

Adverb clause A subordinate clause that modifies a verb, an adjective, or an adverb. (See page 681.)

Adverb phrase A prepositional phrase that modifies a verb, an adjective, or an adverb. (See page 654.)

Agreement The correspondence, or match, between grammatical forms. (See Chapter 21.)

Aim One of the four basic purposes, or reasons, for writing. (See pages 7 and 19.)

Ambiguous reference Occurs when a pronoun refers to either of two antecedents. (See page 755.)

Antecedent The word that a pronoun stands for. (See page 718.)

Appositive A noun or a pronoun placed beside another noun or pronoun to identify or explain it. (See page 666.)

Appositive phrase Consists of an appositive and its modifiers. (See page 666.)

Articles *A, an,* and *the,* the most frequently used adjectives. (See page 606.)

C

Case The form of a noun or pronoun that shows how it is used in a sentence. (See page 728.)

Cause-and-effect essay A form of writing in which a writer explains the causes and/or effects of a situation. (See Chapter 7.)

Chronological order A way of arranging ideas in a paragraph or composition according to when events happen. (See pages 35 and 74.)

Classification A strategy of development: looking at a subject as it relates to other subjects in a group. (See page 79.)

Clause A group of words that contains a subject and its predicate and is used as part of a sentence. (See page 674.)

Coherence A quality achieved when all the ideas in a paragraph or composition are clearly arranged and connected. (See pages 74 and 117.)

Comparison Refers to the change in the form of an adjective or an adverb to show increasing or decreasing degrees in the quality the modifier expresses. (See page 819.)

Comparison/Contrast essay A form of writing in which a writer discusses similarities or differences (or both) between two subjects. (See Chapter 6.)

Complement A word or group of words that completes the meaning of a verb. (See page 637.)

Complex sentence Has one independent clause and at least one subordinate clause. (See page 687.)

Compound-complex sentence Has two or more independent clauses and at least one subordinate clause. (See page 687.)

Compound sentence Has two or more independent clauses but no subordinate clauses. (See page 686.)

Conjunction Joins words or groups of words. (See page 621.)

Critical analysis A form of writing in which a writer examines and responds to a piece of literature critically. (See Chapter 10.)

D

Dangling modifier A modifying word, phrase, or clause that does not clearly and sensibly modify a word or a group of words in a sentence. (See page 835.)

Declarative sentence Makes a statement and is followed by a period. (See page 689.)

Description A strategy of development: using sensory details and spatial order to describe individual features of a specific subject. (See page 79.)

Direct object A word or word group that receives the action of the verb or shows the result of the action, telling *whom* or *what* after a transitive verb. (See page 639.)

Direct reference Connects ideas in a paragraph or composition by referring to a noun or pronoun used earlier. (See page 74.)

Double negative The use of two negative words when one is enough. (See page 864.)

E

Elliptical construction A clause or phrase from which words have been omitted. (See pages 683 and 741.)

Essential clause/Essential phrase Also called restrictive: is necessary to the meaning of a sentence; not set off by commas. (See page 909.)

Evaluating A stage in the writing process: making judgments about a composition's strengths and weaknesses in content, organization, and style. (See pages 6 and 20.)

Evaluation A strategy of development: making judgments about a subject in an attempt to determine its value. (See page 79.)

Exclamatory sentence Expresses strong feeling and is followed by an exclamation point. (See page 690.)

Expository writing Aims at being informative, explanatory, or exploratory. (See pages 7 and 19.)

G

General reference Occurs when a pronoun refers to a general idea rather than to a specific noun. (See page 756.)

Gerund A verb form ending in *–ing* that is used as a noun. (See page 660.)

Gerund phrase Consists of a gerund and its modifiers and complements. (See page 661.)

I

Imperative mood Used to express a direct command or request. (See page 805.)

Imperative sentence Gives a command or makes a request and is followed by either a period or an exclamation point. (See page 689.)

Indefinite reference Occurs when the pronoun *you, it,* or *they* refers to no particular person or thing. (See page 760.)

Independent clause Also called a main clause: expresses a complete thought and can stand by itself as a sentence. (See page 674.)

Indicative mood Used to express a fact, an opinion, or a question. (See page 805.)

Indirect object A word or word group that comes between a transitive verb and its direct object and tells *to whom* or *to what* or *for whom* or *for what* the action of the verb is done. (See page 639.)

Infinitive (1) One of the principal parts of a verb. (See page 766.) **(2)** A verb form, usually preceded by *to,* used as a noun, an adjective, or an adverb. (See page 663.)

Infinitive phrase Consists of an infinitive and its modifiers and complements. (See page 663.)

Interjection Expresses emotion and has no grammatical relation to the rest of the sentence. (See page 623.)

Interrogative sentence Asks a question and is followed by a question mark. (See page 689.)

Intransitive verb An action verb that does not take an object. (See page 612.)

L

Linking verb Connects the subject with a word that identifies or describes the subject. (See page 612.)

Literary writing Aims at creating imaginative works. (See pages 7 and 19.)

Logical order A way of arranging details in a paragraph or composition according to what makes sense. (See pages 35 and 74.)

M

Misplaced modifier A word, phrase, or clause that makes a sentence awkward by seeming to modify the wrong words. (See page 832.)

Modifier A word that limits the meaning of another word. (See page 813.)

Mood (1) The general feeling in a short story or other literary work. (See page 174.) **(2)** The form a verb takes to indicate the attitude of the person using the verb. (See page 805.)

N

Narration A strategy of development: relating events or actions over a period of time, usually using chronological order. (See page 79.)

Nonessential clause/Nonessential phrase Also called nonrestrictive: adds information not necessary to the main idea in the sentence and is set off by commas. (See page 909.)

Noun Names a person, place, thing, or idea. (See page 599.)

Noun clause A subordinate clause used as a noun. (See page 679.)

Number The form of a word that indicates whether the word is singular or plural. (See page 700.)

O

Objective complement A word or word group that helps complete the meaning of a transitive verb by identifying or modifying the direct object. (See page 640.)

Object of a preposition The noun or pronoun that ends a prepositional phrase. (See page 619.)

Order of importance A way of arranging details from least to most important or from most to least important. (See pages 35 and 74.)

P

Participial phrase Consists of a participle and its complements and modifiers. (See page 658.)

Participle A verb form used as an adjective. (See page 657.)

Passive voice The voice a verb is in when it expresses an action done *to* its subject. (See page 800.)

Persuasive essay A form of writing in which a writer supports an opinion and tries to persuade an audience. (See Chapter 8.)

Persuasive writing Aims at convincing people to accept an idea or to take action. (See pages 7 and 19.)

Phrase A group of related words that does not contain a verb and its subject and is used as a single part of speech. (See page 652.)

Point of view The vantage point, or position, from which a writer tells a story or describes a subject. (See page 174.)

Predicate The part of a sentence that says something about the subject. (See page 632.)

Predicate adjective An adjective that follows a linking verb and modifies the subject of the verb. (See page 642.)

Predicate nominative A noun or pronoun that follows a linking verb and refers to the same person or thing as the subject of the verb. (See page 642.)

Preposition Shows the relationship of a noun or a pronoun to some other word in a sentence. (See page 619.)

Prepositional phrase A group of words beginning with a preposition and ending with an object (a noun or a pronoun). (See page 652.)

Prewriting The first stage in the writing process: thinking and planning, deciding what to write about, collecting ideas and details, and making a plan for presenting ideas. (See pages 6 and 20.)

Problem-solution essay A form of exploratory writing in which a writer explains a problem and proposes an effective solution. (See Chapter 9.)

Pronoun Is used in place of a noun or more than one noun. (See page 602.)

Proofreading A stage of the writing process: carefully reading a revised draft to correct mistakes in grammar, usage, and mechanics. (See pages 6 and 20.)

Publishing The last stage of the writing process: making a final, clean copy of a paper and sharing it with an audience. (See pages 6 and 20.)

Purpose A reason for writing or speaking. (See pages 19 and 31.)

R

Reflective essay A form of writing in which an author explores and shares the meaning of an experience that was especially important to him or her. (See Chapter 4.)

Research paper A form of writing in which a writer presents factual information discovered through exploration and research. (See Chapter 11.)

Revising A stage of the writing process: making changes in a composition's content, organization, and style in order to improve it. (See pages 6 and 42.)

S

Self-Expressive writing Aims at expressing a writer's feelings and thoughts. (See pages 7 and 19.)

Sentence A group of words that contains a subject and a verb and expresses a complete thought. (See page 631.)

Simple sentence Has one independent clause and no subordinate clauses. (See page 686.)

Spatial order A way of arranging details in a paragraph or composition according to location. (See pages 35 and 74.)

Style A writer's unique way of adapting language to suit different occasions. (See Chapter 13.)

Subject Tells whom or what a sentence is about. (See page 632.)

Subject complement A word or word group that completes the meaning of a linking verb and identifies or modifies the subject. (See page 642.)

Subjunctive mood Used to express a suggestion, a necessity, a condition contrary to fact, or a wish. (See page 805.)

Subordinate clause Also called a dependent clause: does not express a complete thought and cannot stand alone as a sentence. (See page 675.)

Supporting sentences Give specific details or information to develop the main idea. (See page 67.)

T

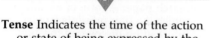

Tense Indicates the time of the action or state of being expressed by the verb. (See page 788.)

Theme The underlying meaning or message a writer wants to communicate to readers. (See page 404.)

Thesis statement Announces the limited topic of a composition and states the main, or unifying, idea about that topic. (See page 100.)

Tone The feeling or attitude a writer conveys about a topic. (See page 32.)

Topic sentence Expresses the main idea of a paragraph. (See page 64.)

Transitional expressions Words and phrases that indicate relationships between ideas in a paragraph or composition. (See page 75.)

Transitive verb An action verb that takes an object. (See page 612.)

Unity A quality achieved when all the sentences or paragraphs in a composition work together as a unit to express or support one main idea. (See pages 71 and 117.)

V

Verb Expresses an action or a state of being. (See page 612.)

Verbal A form of a verb used as a noun, an adjective, or an adverb. (See page 656.)

Verbal phrase Consists of a verbal and its modifiers and complements. (See page 656.)

Verb phrase Consists of a main verb preceded by at least one helping verb. (See page 614.)

Voice (1) The unique sound and rhythm of a writer's language. (See page 517.) **(2)** The form a transitive verb takes to indicate whether the subject of the verb performs or receives the action. (See page 800.)

W

Weak reference Occurs when a pronoun refers to an antecedent that has not been expressed. (See page 758.)

Writing A stage in the writing process: putting ideas into words, following a plan that organizes the ideas. (See pages 6 and 20.)

Writing process The series of stages, or steps, that a writer goes through to develop ideas and to communicate them clearly in a piece of writing. (See pages 6 and 20.)

Glossary

This glossary is a short dictionary of words found in the professional writing models in this textbook. The words are defined according to their meanings in the context of the writing models.

Pronunciation Key

Symbol	Key Words	Symbol	Key Words
a	asp, fat, parrot	b	bed, fable, dub, ebb
ā	ape, date, play, break, fail	d	dip, beadle, had, dodder
ä	ah, car, father, cot	f	fall, after, off, phone
e	elf, ten, berry	g	get, haggle, dog
ē	even, meet, money, flea, grieve	h	he, ahead, hotel
i	is, hit, mirror	j	joy, agile, badge
ī	ice, bite, high, sky	k	kill, tackle, bake, coat, quick
ō	open, tone, go, boat	l	let, yellow, ball
ô	all, horn, law, oar	m	met, camel, trim, summer
oo	look, pull, moor, wolf	n	not, flannel, ton
o͞o	ooze, tool, crew, rule	p	put, apple, tap
yo͞o	use, cute, few	r	red, port, dear, purr
yoo	cure, globule	s	sell, castle, pass, nice
oi	oil, point, toy	t	top, cattle, hat
ou	out, crowd, plow	v	vat, hovel, have
u	up, cut, color, flood	w	will, always, swear, quick
ʉr	urn, fur, deter, irk	y	yet, onion, yard
ə	a in ago	z	zebra, dazzle, haze, rise
	e in agent	ch	chin, catcher, arch, nature
	i in sanity	sh	she, cushion, dash, machine
	o in comply	th	thin, nothing, truth
	u in focus	*th*	then, father, lathe
ər	perhaps, murder	zh	azure, leisure, beige
		ŋ	ring, anger, drink

Abbreviation Key

adj.	adjective	*vi.*	intransitive verb
adv.	adverb	*vt.*	transitive verb
n.	noun		

A

ab • solve [ab zälv'] ***vt.*** To free.

a • but [ə but'] ***vt.*** To border on.

a • do • be [ə dō'bē] ***n.*** Sun-dried clay brick.

am • bro • sia [am brō'zhə] ***n.*** The legendary food of Greek and Roman gods; anything deliciously satisfying.

an • neal • ment [ə nēl'mənt] ***n.*** A strengthening.

an • ni • hi • la • tion [ə nī' ə lā'shən] ***n.*** Complete destruction.

ap • er • ture [ap'ər chər] ***n.*** A hole.

B

bar • ri • o [bär'ē ō] ***n.*** A Spanish-speaking city district or neighborhood.

be • grudge [bē gruj'] ***vt.*** To resent; to be reluctant to give.

bel • ly [bel'ē] ***vi.*** To swell out.

break • wa • ter [brāk'wôt' ər] ***n.*** A barrier to protect the shore from strong waves.

C

ca • fé con le • che [kä fe' côn le'che] ***n.*** Coffee with milk.

caf • tan [kaf'tən] ***n.*** A long, loose dress or robe with wide sleeves.

ca • price [kə prēs'] ***n.*** Whim; a decision made without reason, on impulse alone.

car • i • ca • ture [kar'i kə chər] ***vt.*** To imitate in an exaggerated or distorted manner.

ca • thar • sis [kə thär'sis] ***n.*** Lessening one's fears by indirectly feeling them through drama.

cir • cum • lo • cu • tion [sʉr' kəm lō kyo͞o'shən] ***n.*** A roundabout way of saying something.

crone [krōn] ***n.*** An old, wrinkled, ugly woman.

cum lau • de [ko͝om lou'dā] ***adj.*** Indicating above-average grades in college.

D

dim • i • nu • tion [dim'ə no͞o'shən] ***n.*** A decreasing.

dis • cord [dis'kôrd'] ***n.*** Conflict; also, lack of musical harmony.

E

ebb [eb] ***n.*** Low tide, when water flows back to the sea.

e • dict [ē'dikt'] ***n.*** An official order.

ef • faced [ə fāst'] ***adj.*** Erased.

ep • och [ep'ək] ***n.*** A period of time marked by change or related events.

F

feign [fān] ***vt.*** To pretend.

fil • i • al [fil'ē əl] ***adj.*** Of or like a son or daughter.

fore • fend [fôr fend'] ***vt.*** To forbid.

H

ham • let [ham'lit] ***n.*** A tiny village.

He • gi • ra [hi jī'rə] ***n.*** Mohammed's flight from Mecca; a journey or escape.

hel • ter-skel • ter [hel'tər skel'tər] ***adj.*** Confused; hurried and hectic.

in • cre • du • li • ty [in'krə do͞o'lə tē] ***n.*** Doubt; inability or unwillingness to believe.

in • ex • o • ra • bly [in eks′ə rə blē] ***adv.*** Continuously, with no chance of being stopped.

in • ex • pli • ca • ble [in eks′pli kə bəl] ***adj.*** Unexplainable.

in • teg • ri • ty [in teg′rə tē] ***n.*** Completeness; state of perfection.

in • tern • ment [in tʉrn′mənt] ***n.*** Confinement.

in • tone [in tōn′] ***vt.*** To speak in a dull manner.

in • tu • it [in to͞o′it] ***vt.*** To know without conscious reasoning.

jan • gling [jaŋ′gliŋ] ***adj.*** Sounding harsh and out of tune; also, quarreling noisily.

lean-to [lēn′to͞o′] ***n.*** A shelter whose roof rests on some object.

le • thar • gic [li thär′jik] ***adj.*** Sluggish and dull.

loathe [lōth] ***vt.*** To hate.

lu • gu • bri • ous [lə go͞o′brē əs] ***adj.*** Ridiculously sad.

man • date [man′dāt′] ***vt.*** To command with authority.

mat • ri • cide [mat′rə sīd′] ***n.*** Murder of one's mother.

min • is • ter [min′is tər] ***vi.*** To give help to or take care of.

mo • nad [mō′nad′] ***n.*** A separate, complete unit.

nar • cis • sis • tic [när′sə sis′tik] ***adj.*** Flattering.

O

o • paque [ō pāk′] ***adj.*** Not letting light, heat, electricity, etc., pass through.

P

pal • pa • ble [pal′pə bəl] ***adj.*** Capable of being felt, as air movement or pressure.

par • ry [par′ē] ***vt.*** To reply evasively.

pa • tri • cian [pə trish′ən] ***adj.*** Proud; noble.

pe • ter • ing [pēt′ər iŋ] ***adj.*** Gradually becoming weaker, then stopping.

phil • is • tine [fi lis′tin] ***adj.*** Narrow-minded; unable to appreciate the beauty or finer qualities of.

pla • cat • ed [plā′kāt′id] ***adj.*** Pacified.

plum • met [plum′it] ***vi.*** To decrease rapidly.

pro • di • gious [prō dij′əs] ***adj.*** Of great size or number.

R

ram • i • fi • ca • tion [ram′ə fi kā′shən] ***n.*** Far-reaching results.

rep • ro • ba • tion [rep′rə bā′shən] ***n.*** Disapproval.

S

she • nan • i • gan [shi nan′i gən] ***n.*** Nonsensical behavior.

short shrift [shôrt shrift] ***n.*** Very little attention.

smarm • y [smärm′ē] ***adj.*** Flattering but insincere.

spec • ter [spek′tər] ***n.*** A ghost or anything causing fear.

spec • trum [spek′trəm] ***n.*** The entire extent of a subject, category, etc.

straits [strāts] ***n.*** Condition or situation of distress.

T

tan · gi · ble [tan′jə bəl] ***adj.*** Having physical form; that can be touched.

tiered [tird] ***adj.*** Layered.

un · can · ny [un kan′ē] ***adj.*** Weird.

un · ob · tru · sive [un əb tro͞o′siv] ***adj.*** Not noticeable.

V

ve · he · ment [vē′ə mənt] ***adj.*** Violent; passionate.

ve · neer [və nir′] ***n.*** An attractive but shallow appearance.

vis · age [viz′ij] ***n.*** A face, with emphasis on the facial expressions.

Index

A

INDEX

INDEX

B

C

INDEX

D

INDEX

E

INDEX

H

M

N

INDEX

O

P

INDEX

INDEX

INDEX

INDEX

S

Y

Acknowledgments

For permission to reprint copyrighted material, grateful acknowledgment is made to the following sources:

American Association for the Advancement of Science: "Dinosaurs and Friends Snuffed Out?" by Richard A. Kerr from *Science*, vol. 901, p. 251, January 11, 1991. Copyright © 1991 by the AAAS.

The American Museum of Natural History: From "Clothes Make the Eskimo" by Vilhjalmur Stefansson from *Natural History*, vol. 64, no. 1. Copyright 1954 by The American Museum of Natural History.

Arte Público Press: From: "Primary Lessons" from *Silent Dancing: A Partial Remembrance of a Puerto Rican Childhood* by Judith Ortiz Cofer. Copyright © 1990 by Judith Ortiz Cofer.

The Asia Society: "Thoughts of Hanoi" by Nguyen Thi Vinh, translated by Nguyen Ngoc Bich. Copyright © 1975 by The Asia Society.

Isaac Asimov: "The Villain in the Atmosphere" by Isaac Asimov from *Past, Present, and Future.* Copyright © 1968 by Isaac Asimov.

aunt lute books, (415)558-8116: From "The Lion Sleeps Tonight" by Egyirba High from *Tight Spaces* by Kesho Scott, Cherry Muhanji, and Egyirba High. Copyright © 1987 by Kesho Scott, Cherry Muhanji, and Egyirba High.

Ballantine Books, Inc., a division of Random House, Inc.: From "Life Is Not A Television Show" from *My Teacher Is Driving Me Crazy* by Joyce L. Vedral, Ph.D. Copyright © 1991 by Joyce L. Vedral, Ph.D.

Barron's Educational Series, Inc.: From *How To Teach Your Old Dog New Tricks* by Ted Baer. Copyright © 1991 by Barron's Educational Series, Inc. From "Angela C" from *Composing a Successful Application Essay: Write Your Way Into College* by George Ehrenhaft. Copyright © 1987 by Barron's Educational Series, Inc.

Beacon Press: From "Stranger in the Village" from *Notes of a Native Son* by James Baldwin. Copyright © 1955 by James Baldwin.

The Boston Globe: "Out, out, telltale spot!" by Susan Trausch from *The Boston Globe*, October 3, 1990, p. 19. Copyright © 1990 by The Boston Globe.

Carol Publishing Group: From "Valedictorial speech to Rutgers University, graduating class, 1919" by Paul Robeson from *The Whole World In His Hands* by Susan Robeson. Copyright © 1981 by Susan Robeson. A Citadel Press Book.

Rosanne Coggeshall: From "Peter the Rock" by Rosanne Coggeshall from *The Southern Review.* Copyright © 1986 by Rosanne Coggeshall.

Darhansoff & Verrill Literary Agents: From "The World In Its Extreme" by William Langewiesche from *The Atlantic*, vol. 268, no. 5, November 1991. Copyright © 1991 by William Langewiesche.

Joan Daves Agency: From "I Have a Dream" by Martin Luther King, Jr. Copyright © 1963 by Martin Luther King, Jr.

Annie Dillard: From "To Fashion A Text" from *Inventing the Truth* by Annie Dillard. Copyright © 1987 by Annie Dillard.

Discover: From "Clever Kanzi" by Frederic Golden from *Discover*, vol. 12, no. 3, p. 20, March 1991. Copyright © 1991 by Discover Magazine. From "Bicycle in Dataspace" by Carl Zimmer from *Discover*, vol. 12, no. 7, pp. 36 & 40, July 1991. Copyright © 1991 by Discover Magazine. From "Large Pizza, Hold the Microchips" by Carl Zimmer from *Discover*, vol. 12, no. 4, p. 12, April 1991. Copyright © 1991 by Discover Magazine.

Doubleday, a division of Bantam Doubleday Dell Publishing Group, Inc.: From "The Rockpile" from *Going to Meet the Man* by James Baldwin. Copyright 1948, 1951, © 1957, 1958, 1960, 1965 by James Baldwin.

Dutton, an imprint of New American Library, a division of Penguin Books USA Inc.: From *China Boy* by Gus Lee. Copyright © 1991 by Augustus S.M.S. Lee.

Farrar, Straus & Giroux, Inc.: From "One Art" from *The Complete Poems: 1927–1979* by Elizabeth Bishop. Copyright © 1979, 1983 by Alice Helen Methfessel. From "Revelation" from *The Complete Stories* by Flannery O'Connor. Copyright © 1964, 1965 by the Estate of Mary Flannery O'Connor. From "West With the Night" from *West With the Night* by Beryl Markham. Copyright © 1942, 1983 by Beryl Markham. Published by North Point Press.

Harcourt Brace Jovanovich, Inc.: From *Problem-Solving Strategies for Writing* by Linda Flower. Copyright © 1981 by Harcourt Brace Jovanovich, Inc. From "Then He Goes Free" from *Cress Delahanty* by Jessamyn West. Copyright 1948 and renewed © 1976 by Jessamyn West.

HarperCollins Publishers Inc.: From *To Fashion a Text* by Annie Dillard. Copyright © 1987 by Annie Dillard. From "Letter from Birmingham Jail" from *Why We Can't Wait* by Martin Luther King, Jr. Copyright © 1963, 1964 by Martin Luther King, Jr. From "Memphis" from *Love Life* by Bobbie Ann Mason. Copyright © 1989 by Bobbie Ann Mason. First appeared in *The New Yorker.* From *House Made of Dawn* by N. Scott Momaday. Copyright © 1966, 1967, 1968 by N. Scott Momaday. From "Dog Training" from *One Man's Meat* by E. B. White. Copyright 1941 by E. B. White.

The Harvard Common Press: From *Forgotten Founder* by Bruce E. Johansen. Copyright © 1982 by Bruce E. Johansen.

August Heckscher: "Doing Chores" by August Heckscher.

Higher Education Research Institute, UCLA: From "Percentage of College Freshmen Planning to Major In," "Percentage Who Rate Themselves Above Average," and "Probable Career Choice" from *The American Freshman: National Norms for Fall 1990,* Astin et al. Copyright © 1990 by Higher Education Research Institute, UCLA.

Henry Holt and Company, Inc.: From *Silk Road* by Jeanne Larson. Copyright © 1989 by Jeanne Larson. From *Escalante: The Best Teacher in America* by Jay Mathews. Copyright © 1988 by Jay Mathews. Review of "Back to the Future" from *The Complete Guide to Videocassette Movies,* edited by Steven H. Scheuer. Copyright © 1987 by Steven H. Scheuer.

Houghton Mifflin Company: From *Silent Spring* by Rachel Carson. Copyright © 1962 by Rachel L. Carson. From "Almost a Family" from *Farewell to Manzanar* by Jeanne Wakatsuki Houston and James D. Houston. Copyright © 1973 by James D. Houston. All rights reserved. From *The Heart is a Lonely Hunter* by Carson McCullers. Copyright 1940 by Carson Smith McCullers, copyright renewed © 1967 by Carson McCullers. From "Dengue Fever" from *The Consul's File* by Paul Theroux. Copyright © 1972, 1974, 1975, 1976, 1977 by Paul Theroux. All rights reserved.

Johnson Publishing Company, Inc.: From "Marigolds" by Eugenia Collier from *Negro Digest,* November 1969. Copyright © 1969 by Johnson Publishing Company, Inc.

Alvin M. Josephy, Jr.: From *The Indian Heritage of America* by Alvin M. Josephy, Jr. Copyright © 1968 by Alvin M. Josephy, Jr.

Stephen King and TV Guide® Magazine: From "Now You Take 'Bambi' and 'Snow White' - That's Scary" by Stephen King from *TV Guide® Magazine,* June 13, 1981. Copyright © 1981 by News America Publications Inc.

Kitchen Table: Women of Color Press, Inc.: From "Reading and Writing" from *Seventeen Syllables and other stories* by Hisaye Yamamoto. Copyright © 1988 by Hisaye Yamamoto DeSoto. Originally appeared in *Hokubei Mainichi,* January 1988.

Alfred A. Knopf, Inc.: From "The Demon Lover" from *The Collected Stories of Elizabeth Bowen.* Copyright 1946 and renewed © 1974 by Elizabeth Bowen.

George Lamming: From *In the Castle of My Skin* by George Lamming. Copyright © 1970 by Longman Group Limited. Published by Schocken Books Inc.

Little, Brown and Company: From *Blue Highways: A Journey Into America* by William Least Heat Moon. Copyright © 1982 by William Least Heat Moon.

N. Scott Momaday: From "It Will Not Be Seen Again" from *The Names* by N. Scott Momaday. Copyright © 1976 by N. Scott Momaday.

William Morris Agency, Inc.: From "The Wonder Years" by Hugh Gallagher from *Literary Cavalcade,* May 1990. Copyright © 1990 by Hugh Gallagher.

William Morrow & Company, Inc.: From "Primitive Blues and Primitive Jazz" from *Blues People: Negro Music in White America* by LeRoi Jones. Copyright © 1963 by LeRoi Jones.

National Geographic Society: From "Scourge of the South May Be Heading North" from *National Geographic,* vol. 178, no. 1, July 1990. Copyright © 1990 by National Geographic Society. From "Elephant Talk" by Katharine Payne from *National Geographic,* vol. 176, no. 2, August 1989. Copyright © 1989 by National Geographic Society.

The Native Land Foundation: From *Native Land: Sagas of the Indian Americas* by Jamake Highwater. Copyright © 1986 by The Native Land Foundation.

New Directions Publishing Corporation: From *Martín and Meditations on the South Valley* by Jimmy Santiago Baca. Copyright © 1986, 1987 by Jimmy Santiago Baca. From *A Child's Christmas in Wales* by Dylan Thomas. Copyright 1952 by Dylan Thomas. From "Do Not Go Gentle Into That Good Night" from *Poems of Dylan Thomas.* Copyright 1952 by Dylan Thomas.

The New Republic, Inc.: From "American Indian History" by Bruce E. Johansen from "Correspondence" from *The New Republic,* vol. 199, no. 25, Issue 3,857, December 19, 1988. Copyright © 1988 by The New Republic, Inc. From "Founding Feathers" by Michael Newman from *The New Republic,* vol. 199, no. 19, Issue 3,851, November 7, 1988. Copyright © 1988 by The New Republic.

The New York Times Company: "The Colorization of Films Insults Artists and Society" by Woody Allen from *The New York Times,* June 12, 1987. Copyright © 1987 by The New York Times Company. From "A Giant Step" by Henry Louis Gates, Jr. from "About Men" section of *The New York Times,* December 9, 1990. Copyright © 1990 by The New York Times Company. From "Darkness at Noon" by Harold Krents from *The New York Times,* May 26, 1976. Copyright © 1976 by The New York Times Company. Quotation by Stephen L. Schechter from "Iroquois Constitution: A Forerunner To Colonists Democratic Principles" from *The New York Times,* June 28, 1987. Copyright © 1987 by The New York Times Company. Statistics from "CD's Rising" graph from *The New York Times,* August 25, 1991. Copyright © 1991 by The New York Times Company.

Newsweek, Inc.: From "The Lost Worlds of Ancient America" by Melinda Beck and from "I Won't Be Celebrating Columbus Day" by Suzan Shown Harjo from *Newsweek*, Columbus Special Issue, Fall/Winter 1991. Copyright © 1991 by Newsweek, Inc. From "Classrooms of Babel" by Connie Leslie with Daniel Glick and Jeanne Gordon from *Newsweek*, vol. CXVII, no. 6, February 11, 1991. Copyright © 1991 by Newsweek, Inc.

Harold Ober Associates, Incorporated: From "Thank You, M'am" from *The Langston Hughes Reader* by Langston Hughes. Copyright © 1958 by Langston Hughes. Copyright renewed © 1986 by George Houston Bass.

Omni Publications International Ltd.: From "Road Show" by Steve Nadis from *Omni*, vol. 12, no. 6, p. 40, March 1990. Copyright © 1990 by Omni Publications International Ltd.

Oxford University Press, Inc.: From *The Sea Around Us*, Revised Edition, by Rachel L. Carson. Copyright 1950, 1951, © 1961 by Rachel Carson; renewed 1979 by Roger Christie.

Pantheon Books, a division of Random House, Inc.: From "Why the Owl Has Big Eyes" from *American Indian Myths and Legends* by Richard Erdoes and Alfonso Ortiz. Copyright © 1984 by Richard Erdoes and Alfonso Ortiz.

Partisan Review: "In Search of Goethe from Within, Letter to a German" by José Ortega y Gasset from *Partisan Review*, December 1949, translated by Willard R. Trask. Copyright © 1949 by Partisan Review.

Jack Pate: From "I'd Rather Be a Cowboy than Anything" by Jack Pate from *Old Timer*. Copyright © 1976 by Old Timer.

Peter Pauper Press, Inc.: From a Mauritanian proverb from *African Proverbs*, compiled by Charlotte and Wolf Leslau. Copyright © 1962, 1985 by Peter Pauper Press, Inc.

Public Affairs Television, Inc.: From *Oren Lyons: The Faithkeeper* from transcript # BMSP-16, airdate July 3, 1991, written by Bill Moyers. Copyright © 1991 by Public Affairs Television, Inc.

Publishers Weekly: Quotation by George Steiner from *Publishers Weekly*, May 24, 1985. Copyright © 1985 by Publishers Weekly.

The Putnam Publishing Group: "The Killers" from *I Think I Don't Remember* by Art Buchwald. Copyright © 1985, 1986, 1987 by Art Buchwald. Copyright © 1987 by Los Angeles Times Syndicate. From *Riding the Iron Rooster* by Paul Theroux. Copyright © 1988 by Paul Theroux.

Quadrangle/New York Times Book Co., a division of Random House, Inc.: From "Heat Disorders: When the Body Gets Too Hot" from *Jane Brody's The New York Times Guide to Personal Health* by Jane E. Brody. Copyright © 1976, 1977, 1978, 1979, 1980, 1981, 1982 by The New York Times Company.

Random House, Inc.: From *Singin' and swingin' and gettin' merry like Christmas* by Maya Angelou. Copyright © 1976 by Maya Angelou. From "A Christmas Memory" from *Breakfast at Tiffany's* by Truman Capote. Copyright © 1956 by Truman Capote. Originally published in *Mademoiselle* magazine. From "Song: As I Walked Out One Evening" from *W. H. Auden: Collected Poems*, edited by Edward Mendelson. Copyright 1940 and renewed © 1968 by W. H. Auden. From "An Extravagance of Laughter" from *Going to the Territory* by Ralph Ellison. Copyright © 1986 by Ralph Ellison. From "Spotted Horses" from *Uncollected Stories of William Faulkner*. Copyright 1931 and renewed © 1959 by William Faulkner; copyright 1940 and renewed © 1968 by Estelle Faulkner and Jill Faulkner Summers. From *The Woman Warrior* by Maxine Hong Kingston. Copyright © 1975, 1976 by Maxine Hong Kingston. From *India: A Wounded Civilization* by V. S. Naipaul. Copyright © 1976, 1977 by V. S. Naipaul.

Reiman Publications, 5400 S. 60th Street, Greendale, WI 53129: From "Dog Tales" from *Country,* vol. 5, no. 5, October 1991. Copyright © 1991 by Reiman Publications, L.P.

Marian Reiner, Literary Agent, on behalf of Manuela Williams Crosno: "The Precious Stones of Axolotyl" by Manuela Williams Crosno, edited by Burton Goodman. Copyright © 1987 by Manuela Williams Crosno.

David Roberts: From "The Decipherment of Ancient Maya" by David Roberts from *The Atlantic,* vol. 268, no. 3, September 1991. Copyright © 1991 by David Roberts.

Lois Rosenthal: Quotation by Nikki Giovanni from an interview titled "Nikki Giovanni" by Lois Rosenthal from *On Being A Writer,* edited by Bill Strickland. Copyright © 1989 by Lois Rosenthal.

Skip Rozin: From "People of the Ruined Hills" by Skip Rozin. Copyright © 1972 by Skip Rozin.

Russell & Volkening, Inc.: "The Soft Voice of the Serpent" from *Selected Stories* by Nadine Gordimer. Copyright © 1952 and renewed © 1980 by Nadine Gordimer.

Carl Sagan and Scott Meredith Literary Agency, Inc.: From "Nuclear War and Climate Catastrophe: A Nuclear Winter" by Carl Sagan. Copyright © 1983 by Carl Sagan.

Laura Schiff: "The Bear" from *Lady of Miracles, Poems by Nina Cassian,* selected and translated by Laura Schiff. Copyright © 1982 by Laura Schiff.

Scholastic, Inc.: From *A Young Painter* by Zheng Zhensun and Alice Low. Copyright © 1991 by New China Pictures Company.

Scientific American, Inc.: From "The Spider and the Wasp" by Alexander Petrunkevitch from *Scientific American,* August 1952. Copyright © 1952 by Scientific American, Inc. All rights reserved.

Charles Scribner's Sons, an imprint of Macmillan Publishing Company: From *The Great Gatsby* by F. Scott Fitzgerald. Copyright 1925 by Charles Scribner's Sons; renewed copyright © 1953 by Frances Scott Fitzgerald Lanahan. From *Arctic Dreams* by Barry Lopez. Copyright © 1986 by Barry Holstun Lopez. From *Cry, the Beloved Country* by Alan Paton. Copyright 1948 and copyright renewed © 1976 by Alan Paton.

Simon & Schuster, Inc.: From "Days of Valor" from *Pioneer Women: Voices from the Kansas Frontier* by Joanna L. Stratton. Copyright © 1981 by Joanna L. Stratton.

Sports Illustrated: From "Focus" section titled "Skiing a Formidable Course" by Meg Lukens from *Sports Illustrated,* vol. 73, no. 27, December 31, 1990-January 7, 1991. Copyright © 1990–1991 by The Time Inc. Magazine Company. All Rights Reserved.

Stoddart Publishing Co. Limited: From "An End to Audience?" from *Second Words* by Margaret Atwood. Copyright © 1982 by The House of Anansi Press.

Sun Coast Media Group, Inc.: From "Our Fascinating Past" by Lindsey Williams from *Charlotte Sun Herald.*

Amy Taubin and The Village Voice: "He Did It" by Amy Taubin from *The Village Voice,* vol. XXXV, no. 1, January 1, 1991. Copyright © 1991 by The Village Voice.

Texas Folklore Society: From "The Mail Carrier" by Jovita González from *Tone The Bell Easy,* edited by Frank Dobie from *Publications of the Texas Folklore Society,* no. x, 1932. Copyright © 1932 by Texas Folklore Society. Published by Southern Methodist University Press, 1965.

The Time Inc., Magazine Company: From "A Bumper Crop of Biotech" by J. Madeleine Nash from *Time,* vol. 136, no. 14, October 1, 1990. Copyright © 1990 by The Time, Inc. Magazine Company.

Universal Press Syndicate: From "Dear Abby," November 20, 1991, by Abigail Van Buren. Copyright © 1991 by Abigail Van Buren.

University of Notre Dame Press: From *Barrio Boy* by Ernesto Galarza. Copyright © 1971 by University of Notre Dame Press.

Viking Penguin, a division of Penguin Books USA Inc.: From "The Train from Rhodesia" from *Selected Stories* by Nadine Gordimer. Copyright 1952 by Nadine Gordimer.

Vintage Books, a division of Random House, Inc.: From *The Woman Warrior* by Maxine Hong Kingston. Copyright © 1975, 1976 by Maxine Hong Kingston.

Maurice Walsh, Jr. as Executor of the Estate of Maurice Walsh: From *The Quiet Man* by Maurice Walsh. Copyright 1933 by Curtis Publishing Company; copyright renewed © 1960 by Maurice Walsh.

Webster's New World Dictionaries, a Division of Simon & Schuster, New York: The entry "empty" from *Webster's New World Dictionary,* Third College Edition. Copyright © 1988 by Simon & Schuster, Inc.

Wildness: Excerpt from "Yukon-Charley: The Shape of Wilderness" from *Crossing Open Ground* by Barry Lopez. Originally appeared under a different title and in a different form in *Wilderness,* Fall 1982. Copyright © 1982 by Wilderness.

PHOTO CREDITS

Abbreviations used: (t) top, (c) center, (b) bottom, (l) left, (r) right.

COVER: Ralph J. Brunke Photography

TABLE OF CONTENTS: Page vi(t), Archive Photos; vi(c), vi(b), Culver Pictures, Inc.; vii(t), V. Englebert/Leo de Wys, Inc.; vii(b), © Dr. Tom Hester, Texas Archeological Research Laboratory. The University of Texas, Austin; viii, © Nathan Bilow Photography; ix, Don King/ Lightwave/The Image Bank; xi, Everett Collection, Inc.; xiii, David R. Frazier Photolibrary; xiv, Nawrocki Stock Photo; xv, Skjold/Nawrocki Stock Photo; xvi, Jonathan Blair/Woodfin Camp Associates Inc.; xvii(t), © Rhoda Sidney/PhotoEdit; xviii, HRW Photo by Michelle Bridwell. Courtesy of the Texas Memorial Museum; xix, © Roger Werth 1985/Woodfin Camp & Associates, Inc.; xx, Paul J. Sutton/ Duomo; xxi, AP/ Wide World Photos; xxii, African American Cultural Center, Los Angeles, CA; xxiii(l), xxiii(r), © Bruno Barbey/Magnum; xxiv, © 1988 Kevin Schaffer/Allstock; xxvii, Culver Pictures, Inc.; xxviii, Fred Hirschmann; xxix(l), William Campbell/Time; xxix(r), Camera 5; xxx, © Sylvian Julienne 1983/Woodfin Camp & Associates, Inc.; xxxi, © Mike Yamishita 1986; xxxii(t), © Gale Gaona/South Coast Enterprises; xxxiii(t), AP/Wide World Photos; xxxiii(b), © Karen R. Pruess 1978; xxxiv, © Crandall/The Image Works; xxxv, Tony Freeman/PhotoEdit; xxxvi, George Disario/The Stock Market; xxxvii, Todd Powell/ProFiles West; xxxviii, T. Rosenthal/ SuperStock; xxxix, Bob Daemmrich/The Image Works; xli(l), Everett Press Collection/CSU; xli(r), Washington Bureau/Archive Photos.

CHAPTER 0: Page 2, Dr. Suess/Photograph by Nancy Crampton © 1987; 4, © Hanson Carroll/ Peter Arnold, Inc.; 5, © Daemmrich/Stock Boston; 6, P.R. Production/SuperStock; 7, © HMS Images/The Image Bank; 12(l), © 1983 Luis Villota/The Stock Market; 12(c), © 1993 Christopher Arnesen/Allstock; 12(r), Fridmar Damm/Leo de Wys Inc.; 13(r), © Luis Villota/The Stock Market.

CHAPTER 1: Page 16, Everett Press Collection/ CSU; 29(l), © Dick Luria 1992/FPG International; 29(c), FPG International; 29(r), Photoworld/FPG International; 32(tl), The Image Works; 32(tr), The Image Works; 32(bl), Debra Herskhowitz/ Bruce Coleman Inc.; 32(br), Stephen Kline/Bruce Coleman Inc.; 33, Wendell Metzen/Bruce Coleman Inc.; 36, (c) S. Gazin/The Image Works; 37(tl), Culver Pictures, Inc.; 37(c), HRW Photo Research Library; 37(r), Archive Photos; 37(bl), Culver Pictures, Inc.; 39, D. DeSteinheil/SuperStock; 41(l), City of Laredo, Texas/HRW Photo by Michelle Bridwell; 41(r), © Crews/The Image Works; 46, Courtesy of Dr. Phyllis Stearner; 48, Tony Freeman/PhotoEdit; 51, © Rhoda Sidney/ PhotoEdit; 53, R. Llewellyn/SuperStock; 54, Shooting Star International Agency, Inc.

CHAPTER 2: Page 58(t&b), 59(t&b), 60(t&b), The Schomburg Center for Research in Black Culture. The New York Public Library. Astor, Lennox & Tilden Foundations. The Estate of Carl Van Vechten, Joseph Solomon, Executor; 62, Subilbe Farm, Bill & Helen Gerdes; 65, Washington Bureau/Archive Photos; 66, © Tim Brown/ProFiles West; 68(a-f), HRW Photo By Michelle Bridwell; 70(r), J. Steenmans/Leo de Wys Inc.; 70(l), Mia & Klaus/SuperStock; 72, Jonathan Wright/Bruce Coleman Inc.; 75, Culver Pictures, Inc.; 77(t), 77(b), Texas School for the Deaf, Austin, TX/HRW Photo by Michelle Bridwell; 84(l), © Dr. Tom Hester, Texas Archeological Research Laboratory.
The University of Texas at Austin; 84(r), V. Englebert/Leo de Wys Inc.; 85(l), David R. Frazier Photolibrary; 85(r), Bobbi Carrey/The Picture Cube; 87(l), 87(r), Universal/Shooting Star International; 90(l), © Phil Savoir/Bruce Coleman Inc.; 90(r), David R. Frazier; 91(l), © Henley & Savage/The StockMarket; 91(r), Bob Daemmrich/ The Image Works.

CHAPTER 3: Page 96, AutoVision/Jay Schiffman; 101, Del Valle High School, Del Valle, Texas/HRW Photo by Michelle Bridwell; 102(l), Everett Collection, Inc.; 102(c), © William Taufic/ The Image Bank; 102(b), © Homer Skyes, 1981/ Woodfin Camp & Associates, Inc.; 103, Bruce Coleman Inc.; 104, McCallum High School, Austin, Texas/HRW Photo by Michelle Bridwell; 107, John Kelly/The Image Bank; 109, Murchison Middle School, Austin, Texas/HRW Photo by Michelle Bridwell; 110, Gabe Palmer/The Stock Market; 111, © Enrico Ferorelli; 113, Schuster/ SuperStock; 114, Steve Hurwitz/Bruce Coleman, Inc.; 118, © Nathan Bilow Photography; 120, © Crandall/The Image Works.

CHAPTER 4: Page 127(t), Archive Photos; 127(b), Washington Bureau/Archive Photos; 128, American Stock/Archive Photos; 130(t), HRW Photo by Michelle Bridwell; 130(b), © Roy Morsch/ The Stock Market; 131, Don King/Lightwaves/ The Image Bank; 133(l), Stephen Wilkes/The Image Bank; 133(r), The Image Bank; 135, R. Llewellyn/SuperStock; 138, Nick Pavloff/The Image Bank; 140, Courtesy of Arte Publico Press; 142, David R. Frazier Photolibrary; 145(l), Harvey Lloyd/The Stock Market; 145(r), David W. Hamilton/The Image Bank; 148(tl), Myrleen Ferguson/PhotoEdit; 148(tr), © Michael Yada/Zephyr Pictures; 148(bl), © Jim Pickerell 1989/West Light; 148(br), Richard Hutchings/InfoEdit.

CHAPTER 5: Page 169(tl), Everett Collection Inc.; 169(tr), MGM Studios/SuperStock; 169(b), Shooting Star; 176, C. Simms/SuperStock; 178, Albano Guatti/The Stock Market; 180, C. Orrico/ SuperStock; 201, Archive Photos.

CHAPTER 6: Page 212, 213, 219(l), Everett Collection, Inc.; 219(r), FPG International; 220(l), Culver Pictures, Inc.; 220(r), Archive Photos;

221(l), A. Kerstitch/Bruce Coleman, Inc.; 221(r), © Ken Lucas/Biological Photo Service; 222(l), FPG International, Inc.; 222(r), J. Barnell/SuperStock; 223, Bettmann; 226, 227, Visual Communications Archives/Asian American Studies Central, Inc.; 228, Everett Press Collection /CSU; 232(l), The Image Works; 232(r), George Disario/ The Stock Market; 233(l), W. Woodworth/SuperStock; 233(r), 234, FPG International; 235, HRW Photo Research Library; 239, Todd Powell/ProFiles West; 241, Tony Freeman/PhotoEdit; 247, G.D. Dodge/Bruce Coleman Inc., New York; 248, Jose Luis G. Grande/Bruce Coleman Inc., New York.

CHAPTER 7: Page 258(l), Shooting Star International Photo Agency, Inc.; 258(c), P. Cantor/ SuperStock; 258(r), © Brian Lovell/Nawrocki Stock Photo; 260, James D. Wilson/Woodfin Camp & Associates, Inc.; 264, SuperStock; 267, Jim Zuckerman/Westlight; 269, © Nathan Benn 1985/Woodfin Camp & Associates; 271, © Alon Reininger/Unicorn Stock Photos; 273, Alan Oddie/PhotoEdit; 274, Mary Kate Denny/PhotoEdit; 276, Tony Freeman/PhotoEdit; 278, W. Strode/SuperStock; 280(tl), Michal Heron/ Woodfin Camp & Associates, Inc.; 280(tr), The Image Bank; 280(b), Elizabeth Zuckerman/PhotoEdit; 282, Craig Aurness/Westlight; 285, © Manfred Kage/Peter Arnold, Inc.; 286, G. Glod/SuperStock.

CHAPTER 8: Page 293, © Thomas Kristich/ Retna Pictures; 298, A. Koropp/SuperStock; 299, Everett Press Collection/CSU; 302, Gary Braasch/ Woodfin Camp & Associates, Inc.; 303, Photograph by Erich Hartmann, Magnum Photos/ HRW Photo Research Library; 304, Nawrocki Stock Photo; 310, PhotoEdit; 311(l), R. King/ SuperStock; 311(c), David R. Frazier Photolibrary; 311(r), Joe Sohm/Nawrocki Stock Photo; 313, A. Gescheiot/The Image Bank West; 314(l), 314(r), 315(l), 315(r), 316(l), 316(r), 317(l), 317(r), Shooting Star International Photo Agency, Inc.; 320, 321(l), 321(c), 321(r), Bob Daemmrich Photography; 322, © Tom Stoddart 1990/Woodfin Camp & Associates, Inc.; 326, © Paul Conklin/Uniphoto Picture Agency; 327, © Alan Oddie/PhotoEdit; 336, Wally McNamee/ Woodfin Camp & Associates, Inc.; 339(l), Shooting Star; 339(r), Photofest; 341(b), Robert Brenner/ PhotoEdit; 341(t), HRW Photo Research Library.

CHAPTER 9: Page 347, Nawrocki Stock Photo; 350, 352, 353, Del Valle Schools, Del Valle, TX/ HRW Photo by Michelle Bridwell; 355, Photo Courtesy of Teach for America, New York, New York; 358, David Young-Wolff/PhotoEdit; 360, Catherine Karnow/Woodfin Camp & Associates, Inc.; 361, Paul Conklin/PhotoEdit; 364, Bill Ross/ Woodfin Camp & Associates, Inc.; 365, C.M. Fitch/SuperStock; 366, © Billy E. Barnes/Stock Boston; 367, Mike Kirkpatrick/ProFiles West; 369, David Falconer/© David R. Frazier Photolibrary ; 371, W. Rosseau/SuperStock; 373(l), P.R. Production/SuperStock; 373(r), © Tony Freeman/ PhotoEdit; 374, Popham Elementary School, Del Valle, Texas/HRW Photo by Michelle Bridwell; 382, Bob Adelman/Magnum; 383, FPG International; 387(l), Everett Collection; 387(r), Shooting Star International Photo Agency, Inc.

CHAPTER 10: Page 390, Shooting Star International Photo Agency; 391(t), Everett Collection; 391(b), Everett Collection; 392, Shooting Star International Picture Agency; 395, Svenskt Pressfoto/Archive Photos; 408, Skjold/Nawrocki Stock Photo; 413(l), David R. Frazier Photolibrary; 413(r), © Mark Antman/The Image Works; 421, T. Rosenthal/SuperStock; 427, HRW Photo Research Library/New York State Museum Albany, New York; 430(l), Everett Collection, Inc.; 430(r), © Larry Busacca/Retna Ltd.; 433, Laredo Independent School District's Instructional Television Studio/HRW Photo by Michelle Bridwell.

CHAPTER 11: Page 436, Robert Semeniok/The Stock Market; 437, David Woods/The Stock Market; 438, Niki Mareschal/The Image Bank; 441(t), Peter Beney/The Image Bank; 441(c), K. Gibson/ SuperStock; 441(b), Art Kane/The Image Bank; 444, Cameramann Int'l., Ltd.; 449, Gabe Palmer/ The Stock Market; 451, Jeffrey W. Myers/Nawrocki Stock Photo; 455, Johathan Blair/Woodfin Camp & Associates, Inc.; 460(t), Archive Photos; 460(b), Culver Pictures, Inc.; 472, John Curtis/ The Stock Market; 489(l), R. Llewellyn/SuperStock; 489(r), FPG International; 492, United High School & Laredo High School/HRW Photo by Michelle Bridwell.

CHAPTER 12: Page 498(l), Charlene Smith/ProFiles West; 498(r), "The Book of Durrow". The Beginning of the Gospel of Saint Mark/The Board of Trinity College, Dublin/Photo by The Green Studio Limited, Dublin.; 514(t), Lewis Portnoy/The Stock Market; 514(bl), © Richard Price/ Westlight; 514(br), W. Morgan/Westlight.

CHAPTER 13: Page 529, J. W. Nixon High School, Laredo, Texas/HRW Photo by Michelle Bridwell.

CHAPTER 14: Page 543, Culver Pictures; 547(l), Australia Picture Library/L&B Hemmings/Westlight ; 547(r), Janeart Ltd/The Image Bank; 548, Bridgeman Collection/SuperStock; 549, Panoramic Stock Images/Nawrocki Stock Photo; 553(l), Culver Pictures, Inc.; 553(r), Everett Press Collection/CSU; 554(t), 554(bl), 554(br), HRW Photo by Michelle Bridwell. Courtesy of the Texas Memorial Museum; 559, McCallum High School, Austin, Texas/HRW Photo By Michelle Bridwell; 561, Photofest.

CHAPTER 15: Page 567(t), © David H. Ellis/ Visuals Unlimited; 567(b), © David H. Ellis/ Visuals Unlimited; 570, UPI/Bettmann; 572(t), NASA/Peter Arnold, Inc.; 572(b), NASA/Peter Arnold, Inc.; 575, © Richard C. Reed/Unicorn Stock Photos; 577, © Roger Werth 1985/Woodfin Camp & Associates; 578, Everett Collection.

CHAPTER 16: Page 585, Paul J. Sutton/Duomo; 586, The Stock Market; 593, McCallum High School, Austin, Texas/HRW Photo By Michelle Bridwell.

CHAPTER 17: Page 602, AP/Wide World Photos; 609, FPG International; 615(l), Norman Owen Tonalin/Bruce Coleman, Inc.; 615(r), The Image Works; 623, © Kevin Schafer/Peter Arnold, Inc.; 625, African American Cultural Center, Los Angeles, CA.

CHAPTER 18: Page 640(l), 640(r), McCallum High School in Austin, Texas/HRW Photo by Michelle Bridwell; 641, Sygma; 644(l), © Bruno Barbey/Magnum; 644(r), © Bruno Barbey/ Magnum.

CHAPTER 19: Page 654(c), © David Austen 1981/Woodfin Camp & Associates. 654(r), © Frank Perkins/ProFiles West; 656, Everett Press Collection, CSU; 660, HRW Photo By Joe Jaworski; 662(tl), © Chip Porter 1980/Allstock; 662(tc), © Tom Bean 1989/Allstock; 662(tr), Alaska Division of Tourism; 662(bl), Alaska Division of Tourism; 666, Everett Collection; 669, © 1988 Kevin Schaffer/AllStock.

CHAPTER 20: Page 681(t), 681(b), Courtesy of Dr. Athelstan Spilhaus.; 691(l), 691(c), 691(r), Insect Farming & Trading Agency. Unitech Development & Consultancy PTY LTD, Morobe Province. Papua, New Guinea.

CHAPTER 21: Page 705, Culver Pictures, Inc.; 707, SuperStock; 715, © Roddey E. Mims/ Uniphoto Picture Agency; 722, Everett Collection, Inc.; 723, L. Berger/SuperStock.

CHAPTER 22: Page 734, Regan/Camera 5; 736, From the Collections of Henry Ford Museum & Greenfield Village.; 747(l), 747(r), © Mavournea Hay/Michelle Bridwell Photography.

CHAPTER 23: Page 757, Culver Pictures, Inc.; 759, NASA/Broadcast Images; 761, Miramax/ Shooting Star.

CHAPTER 24: Page 777, Fred Hirschmann; 795, J.R. Eyerman/Life Magazine © 1952 Time Inc.

CHAPTER 25: Page 815, Everett Collection, Inc.; 819(l), William Campbell/Time; 819(r), Camera 5; 826, Everett Collection.

CHAPTER 26: Page 837, Courtesy of Harcourt, Brace, Jovanovich, Inc.; 838, The Bettmann Archive.

CHAPTER 27: Page 845, Schomburg Center for Research in Black Culture. The New York Public Library. The Astor, Lennox and Tilden Foundations.; 852, © Sylvian Julienne 1983/Woodfin Camp & Associates, Inc.; 864, Lawrence Migdale.

CHAPTER 28: Page 879, From the book "Great News Photos & The Stories Behind Them" by John Faber, Historian. National Press Photographers Association; 885, NASA/HRW PhotoLibrary; 890(t), © Stan Byers.

CHAPTER 29: Page 904, Wide World Photos, Inc.; 912(t), 912(b), © Gale Gaona/South Coast Enterprises; 920(t), Japanese American Cultural & Community Center; 920(bl), 920(br), © Mike Yamashita 1986.

CHAPTER 30: Page 933, AP/Wide World Photos; 941, © Gale Zucker/Stock Boston; 958(l), 958(r), UPI/Bettmann.

CHAPTER 31: Page 969(tr), © Richard Steedman 1984/The Stock Market; 969(c), 969(bl), 969(br), Schomburg Center for Research in Black Culture. The New York Public Library. Astor, Lennox & Tilden Foundations; 987(l), 987(r), Karen R. Preuss © 1978.

ILLUSTRATION CREDITS

Linda Blackwell—156, 159, 268, 385

Rondi Collette—xxv, 208, 555, 556, 656, 675, 676, 965, 809

Mary Jones—64, 295, 587

Linda Kelen—81, 505, 506, 508, 527, 537, 569

Susan Kenmitz—xviii, 34, 80, 184, 186, 187, 190, 192, 397, 398, 401, 417, 517

Rich Lo—419, 623, 885

Pamela Paulsrud—173, 379, 425

Precision Graphics—655, 702, 779, 976

Doug Schneider—ix, xxiv, 131, 433, 669

Jack Scott—546

Steve Shock—x, 2, 60, 97, 163, 164, 166, 212–213, 426

Troy Thomas—xii, 254, 255, 256

Nancy Tucker—206